A *Brief* HISTORY OF MUSIC

❧ IN WESTERN CULTURE ❧

Mark Evan Bonds
Department of Music
University of North Carolina at Chapel Hill

PEARSON

Prentice
Hall

Upper Saddle River, New Jersey 07458

Library of Congress Cataloging-in-Publication Data
Bonds, Mark Evan.
A history of music in Western culture / Mark Evan Bonds.
    p. cm.
   Includes bibliographical references and index.
   ISBN 0-13-014320-0
   1. Music—History and criticism. I. Title.
  ML160.B75 2003
780'.9—dc21   2002042493

Vice President/Editorial Director: Charlyce Jones Owen
Senior Acquisitions Editor: Christopher T. Johnson
Editorial Assistant: Evette Dickerson
Editor-in-Chief of Development: Rochelle Diogenes
Development Editor: Teresa Nemeth
Marketing Manager: Chris Ruel
Marketing Assistant: Kimberly Daum
AVP, Director of Production and Manufacturing: Barbara Kittle
Managing Editor: Joanne Riker
Production Editor: Joseph Scordato
Production Assistant: Marlene Gassler
Permissions Supervisor: Ron Fox
Manufacturing Manager: Nick Sklitsis
Manufacturing Buyer: Benjamin Smith
Creative Design Director: Leslie Osher
Senior Art Director: Anne Bonanno Nieglos
Interior Design: Anne Bonanno Nieglos, Laura Gardner, Carmen DiBartolomeo, C2K, Inc.
Cover Design: Carmen DiBartolomeo, C2K, Inc.
Cover Illustration: John Singer Sargent (1856–1925), American,
    Rehearsal of the Pasdeloup Orchestra, oil on canvas, SuperStock
Photo Researcher: Francelle Carapetyan
Image Permission Coordinator: Fran Toepfer
Composition: Interactive Composition Corporation
Printer/Binder: The Courier Companies
Cover Printer: Phoenix Color Corporation

Credits and acknowledgements borrowed from other sources and reproduced, with permission, in this textbook appear on appropriate page within text, and in the Source Notes beginning on page 482.

Pearson Education Ltd.
Pearson Education Singapore, Pte. Ltd.
Pearson Education Canada, Ltd.
Pearson Education–Japan

Pearson Education Australia Pty. Ltd.
Pearson Education North Asia Ltd.
Pearson Educación de Mexico, S.A. de C.V.
Pearson Education Malaysia, Pte. Ltd.

10 9 8 7 6 5 4 3 2 1
ISBN 0-13-183860-1

To Dorothea, Peter, Andrew

Overview of Contents

Contents

Composer Profiles

Primary Evidence

Focus Boxes

Preface

This book is an abridged and slightly altered edition of *A History of Music in Western Culture* (Prentice Hall, 2003). Like the original text, *A Brief History of Music in Western Culture* rests on the premise that the history of music is best conveyed by focusing on a carefully selected repertory of musical works. Once familiar with a representative body of music, students can better grasp the requisite names, dates, and concepts of music history, including an understanding of the evolution of musical styles and music's changing uses within the Western tradition. Even more importantly, students will gain a sound basis from which to explore other musical works and repertories.

A *Brief History of Music in Western Culture* builds its narrative around the core repertory represented in the accompanying two-volume *Anthology of Scores* and corresponding set of twelve compact disks. This text is not an encyclopedia. My goal, rather, has been to help students gain a broad understanding of the nature of music, its role in society, and the ways in which these have changed over time.

Finally, *A Brief History of Music in Western Culture* seeks to challenge students to think critically about its subject. The history of music is too often presented (and learned) as one long series of indisputable facts. I have tried to integrate into this text enough documents—primary sources—to demonstrate that the raw materials of history are often open to conflicting interpretations. Indeed, the most interesting historical issues tend to be precisely those about which experts disagree.

FEATURES OF THE TEXT

The narrative of *A Brief History of Music in Western Culture* is closely integrated with the accompanying *Anthology of Scores*. Every work in the anthology gets a discussion in the text, called out with a note in the margin, and the anthology is ordered to follow the sequence in which those discussions occur within the text.

Following a Prologue on the music of classical Antiquity, the text is divided into six parts, each corresponding to a major era in music history: Medieval, Renaissance, Baroque, Classical, 19th century, and 20th century. The text concludes with a brief epilogue on music today.

Each part begins with a **prelude** that summarizes the historical and social background of each era. The first chapter in each part provides an overview of the major stylistic characteristics and theoretical concerns of the music of the era. Parts 4 (Classical period), 5 (19th century), and 6 (20th century) conclude with a brief survey of all the major composers of their respective eras.

The text also offers a variety of features and pedagogical tools:

♦ The opening pages of each prelude include a **comparative timeline** that lists major musical events side by side with other significant historical events.

♦ An **outline** at the beginning of each chapter gives students an overview of the content of the chapter.

♦ **Key terms** are highlighted in each chapter and defined in a **glossary** at the end of the book.

♦ Significant composers are featured in **composer profiles** that include key biographical information and a survey of principal works.

- ◆ **Primary evidence** boxes contain excerpts from relevant contemporary documents, exposing students to some of the raw materials of music history.
- ◆ **Focus** boxes highlight important information that expands on aspects of the core narrative.
- ◆ Numerous **examples, tables, and diagrams** help students grasp key points and visualize musical structures.
- ◆ The last chapter in each part concludes with a set of **discussion questions** designed to stimulate reflection on broad issues in music history.

Finally, the detailed captions to the illustrations in *A Brief History of Music in Western Culture* reveal the wealth of information—about music, composers, and their role in society—embedded in these images. Four inserts with more than 20 color illustrations are distributed throughout the book.

ABOUT THIS BRIEF EDITION

This book is aimed at instructors and students who must cover the entire history of Western music in one or two semesters. I have retained the basic narrative of the original text: no composer or work has been eliminated from the discussion, though contexts have necessarily been reduced here for reasons of space and time. This *Brief History* highlights fewer documents and presents a more limited number of diagrams, focus boxes, and illustrations than does the original text. Students will nevertheless find here the essentials of music history presented in such a way as to be grasped within a limited amount of time.

SUPPLEMENTARY INSTRUCTIONAL MATERIALS

The supplementary print and multimedia materials available for the original text are also applicable to *A Brief History of Music in Western Culture*.

Anthology of Scores in Two Volumes

The more than 250 works in the *Anthology of Scores to A History of Music in Western Culture* have been carefully selected to represent the developments in music history elucidated in the text. Every work in the *Anthology of Scores* is discussed in the text. Volume I covers Antiquity through the Baroque Era; Volume II covers music of the Classical Era through the 20th Century.

Recordings

Two sets of six compact disks complement the text and *Anthology of Scores*. Produced by Naxos of America in close coordination with Prentice Hall, the two compilations are arranged chronologically and mirror the content of the *Anthology*.

Instructor's Resource Manual

The *Instructor's Resource Manual with Tests* provides a summary, bibliography, a bank of test questions, and suggested discussion topics and activities for each chapter of the text. These are carefully organized to ease class preparation, instruction, and testing.

Companion Website™ (www.prenhall.com/bonds)

The *Companion Website*™ for *A History of Music in Western Culture* provides students an opportunity to delve more deeply into the ideas and personalities discussed in this briefer edition. Students can evaluate their progress with study and essay questions and report the results to the instructor. The site also includes an array of historical documents to complement those in the text. Many of the documents that appear in abbreviated form in the text appear complete on the site. Essay questions accompany each of these documents.

ACKNOWLEDGMENTS

I would like to begin by thanking Teresa Nemeth for her substantial and invaluable help in identifying the elements to be retained for this brief edition. For their thoughtful and often detailed comments, I am also grateful to the scholars who reviewed the manuscript of the original full text at various points in its development: Walter Bailey (Rice University), Michael J. Budds (University of Missouri), Anna Celenza (Michigan State University), Cynthia Cyrus (Vanderbilt University), Patricia Debly (Brock University), Andrew Dell'Antonio (University of Texas, Austin), Matthew Dirst (University of Houston), Lawrence Earp (University of Wisconsin), Sean Gallagher (Harvard University), Elizabeth Keathley (University of Tennessee), Kenneth Kreitner (University of Memphis), Susan Lewis (University of Victoria), Harry Lincoln (Binghamton University), Stan Link (Vanderbilt University), Massimo Ossi (Indiana University), Stephen Meyer (Syracuse University), Tom Owens (George Mason University), Georgia Peeples (University of Akron), Roberta F. Schwartz (University of Kansas), and Susan Forscher Weiss (John Hopkins University).

I am also grateful to many colleagues and students at the University of North Carolina at Chapel Hill for their help in writing this book. Fellow faculty members Tim Carter, John Covach, Annegret Fauser, Jon Finson, Sean Gallagher, Anne MacNeil, Jocelyn Neal, Severine Neff, and Tom Warburton all offered helpful advice (and an ear) at various stages of the project. Thanks, too, to the following students who helped in preparing the manuscript: Christina Tuskey, Jennifer Germann, Michelle Oswell, Seth Coluzzi, Ethan Lechner, and above all Peter Lamothe. The staff of the Music Library—particularly Dan Zager, Phil Vandermeer, Diane Steinhaus, and Eva Boyce—were unfailingly helpful and efficient.

Special thanks go to Suzanne Cusick (New York University) for her help in matters pertaining to Francesca Caccini, and to J. Samuel Hammond (Duke University Libraries), who provided help and advice at many points along the way. Jeremy Yudkin, my former colleague at Boston University, provided inspiration from the very start.

My editors at Prentice Hall have been a delight to work with from beginning to end. Chris Johnson has been the prime mover in this enterprise. I am particularly grateful to David Chodoff, my development editor, who helped turn a text into a textbook, and to Joe Scordato, Production Editor for Humanities and Social Sciences at Prentice Hall, who oversaw every detail of production. Elsa Peterson helped with the development of the 20th century chapters and coordinated the compilation of the anthology manuscript. Francelle Carapetyan was unflagging in her effort to track down the needed illustrations.

Finally, my deepest thanks go to my family. My parents were not directly involved in producing this book, but they made it possible in ways that go well beyond the obvious. My brother, Bob, gave invaluable advice at an early stage of the process. And it is to Dorothea, Peter, and Andrew that I dedicate this book, with love.

About the Author

Mark Evan Bonds teaches music history at the University of North Carolina at Chapel Hill. He holds degrees from Duke University (B.A.), Christian-Albrechts-Universität Kiel (M.A.), and Harvard University (Ph.D.). His publications include *Wordless Rhetoric: Musical Form and the Metaphor of the Oration* (1991) and *After Beethoven: Imperatives of Symphonic Originality* (1996). He has also edited *Beethoven Forum* and written numerous essays on the music of Haydn and Mozart.

Why Study Music History?

Why study music history? This is a fair question, one you have likely asked yourself, particularly if you happen to be using this book as part of a required course. The answer is that the study of music history provides many benefits. Among these are:

- **A greater understanding of music's emotional power and its role in society.** Music is one of the most powerful yet least understood of all the arts. It has played a significant role in every known culture in human history. In the Western world, people have used it in widely varying contexts. It has provided entertainment and has played a central role in many forms of religious worship. It has long been considered important to a well-rounded education. It has been admired for its therapeutic benefits since ancient times and it is tapped in shopping malls today for its ability to put people in the mood to buy. Political candidates identify themselves with theme songs and patriotic music helps promote feelings of national unity. Music has even been used for torture. Entire generations have defined themselves according to the music they have enjoyed. And today, music drives a multibillion-dollar industry.

- **A richer understanding of music's basic elements.** Composers and musicians have combined these elements—rhythm, melody, harmony, form, texture, and timbre—in a remarkable variety of ways since ancient times. The polyphony of the 13th century sounds quite different from early 20th-century ragtime, but both are composed from the same building blocks. Studying music history helps us understand how these elements have been manipulated over time to create such a diversity of effects. And in the process, it can make us better listeners.

- **A sense of changing musical styles across time.** Why, within the space of less than a hundred years, did Bach write in one style, Mozart in another, and Chopin in yet another? Why is so much of the music written after 1900 difficult to grasp on first listening? Why do musical styles change at all? Although we do not have to be able to answer these kinds of questions to enjoy the music of any composer or period, our attempts to do so can increase our understanding of it and deepen the pleasure it brings us.

- **A basis for exploring new works and repertories.** Familiarity with a wide range of representative works from different historical periods enhances our ability to understand works and repertories of different kinds, including those of non-Western cultures.

- **A greater ability to talk and write about music.** Music, the most abstract of all the arts, is notoriously difficult to describe in words. If we can say what a work of music is "about" or translate its meaning into words, why bother with the music at all? Still, the fact that we can never capture in prose the essence of music does not mean that we should remain silent on the subject. The very process of trying to write about music can help us appreciate what distinguishes it from fiction, poetry, painting, architecture, or any other form of human endeavor.

Prologue

Antiquity

Every known civilization has had music of some kind. The human voice is as old as the species itself, and a recorder-like object crafted from the thigh bone of a bear may have been made as long as 50,000 years ago by Neanderthals living in what is now Slovenia, in eastern Europe. The earliest indisputable musical instrument—a kind of flute made from the wing bone of a vulture—dates from about 34,000 B.C.E and was found in what is now southwestern France. The ancient civilizations of Egypt and Sumeria, which emerged between 4000 and 3000 B.C.E, left behind many images of people singing and playing instruments, particularly in connection with religious rituals.

TIMELINE

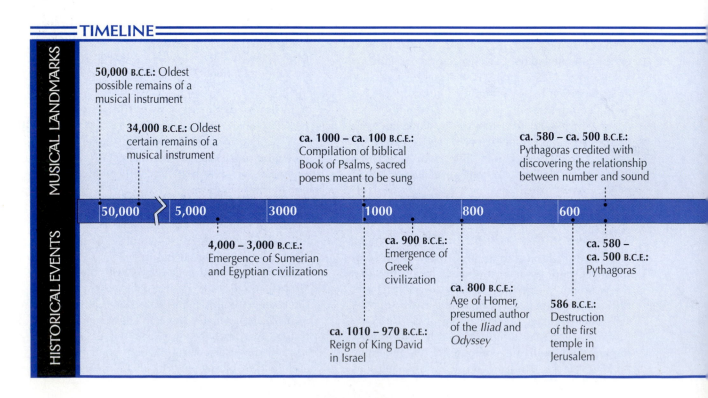

MUSICAL LANDMARKS

50,000 B.C.E.: Oldest possible remains of a musical instrument

34,000 B.C.E.: Oldest certain remains of a musical instrument

ca. 1000 – ca. 100 B.C.E.: Compilation of biblical Book of Psalms, sacred poems meant to be sung

ca. 580 – ca. 500 B.C.E.: Pythagoras credited with discovering the relationship between number and sound

50,000 | 5,000 | 3000 | 1000 | 800 | 600

HISTORICAL EVENTS

4,000 – 3,000 B.C.E.: Emergence of Sumerian and Egyptian civilizations

ca. 900 B.C.E.: Emergence of Greek civilization

ca. 1010 – 970 B.C.E.: Reign of King David in Israel

ca. 800 B.C.E.: Age of Homer, presumed author of the *Iliad* and *Odyssey*

ca. 580 – ca. 500 B.C.E.: Pythagoras

586 B.C.E.: Destruction of the first temple in Jerusalem

MUSIC IN THE BIBLICAL WORLD

The Old Testament has many references to music. Immediately after crossing the Red Sea in the exodus from Egypt, Miriam the prophetess, the sister of Moses and Aaron, used her tambourine to lead the Israelite women in song and dance to praise God for delivering her people (Exodus 15: 20–21). The young David cured Saul's melancholy by playing the harp (1 Samuel 16:14-23), one of the earliest recorded instances of music therapy. David went on to write many of the Psalms, and as king of Israel (about 1055–1015 B.C.E), he played a key role in establishing the order of worship, including the singing of psalms and hymns. The temple he envisioned in Jerusalem—completed by his son Solomon but destroyed by the Babylonians in 586 B.C.E—is reported to have been attended by 4,000 instrumentalists (1 Chronicles 23:5) and a cadre of 288 singers (1 Chronicles 25:7).

The precise nature of the music the Old Testament describes remains largely a matter of speculation, for no form of notation preserves it. From written accounts, we know that psalms and hymns were sung in unison, either antiphonally (two choirs alternating) or responsorially (soloist alternating with one choir). The words were chanted primarily to simple melodic formulas in a way that helped project the text across large spaces. Traditions of Jewish psalmody and hymnody played a vital role in the emergence of plainchant in the Christian church (see Chapter 1). More important still is the enduring association they created between music and feelings of intense spirituality.

ANCIENT GREECE

The direct source of many of the concepts that form the roots of the Western musical tradition are found in the works of the ancient Greeks. Some time around the 8th century B.C.E., the people of ancient Greece began to develop patterns of thought and social organization that differed in fundamental ways from those of other civilizations. Mythic explanations of the cosmos gave way to rational, more scientific modes of thought.

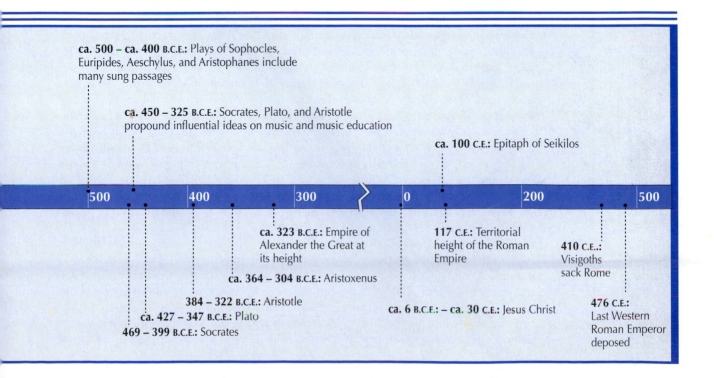

ca. 500 – ca. 400 B.C.E.: Plays of Sophocles, Euripides, Aeschylus, and Aristophanes include many sung passages

ca. 450 – 325 B.C.E.: Socrates, Plato, and Aristotle propound influential ideas on music and music education

ca. 100 C.E.: Epitaph of Seikilos

ca. 323 B.C.E.: Empire of Alexander the Great at its height

117 C.E.: Territorial height of the Roman Empire

410 C.E.: Visigoths sack Rome

ca. 364 – 304 B.C.E.: Aristoxenus

384 – 322 B.C.E.: Aristotle

ca. 427 – 347 B.C.E.: Plato

469 – 399 B.C.E.: Socrates

ca. 6 B.C.E. – ca. 30 C.E.: Jesus Christ

476 C.E.: Last Western Roman Emperor deposed

Philosophy emerged as a means of reconciling abstract reason with empirical reality. Personal self-knowledge became the central goal in the life of the individual, a goal reflected in the famous dictum of the 5th-century B.C.E. philosopher Socrates: "The unexamined life is not worth living."

The characteristic social and political unit of the ancient Greeks, the city-state, or *polis,* was a forge for many fundamental concepts about civic duty, social justice, and individual liberty that have had an enduring legacy on Western society. The democracy that emerged in the ancient Athens, however limited, was an approach to government no society had yet attempted.

Athens attained its political, commercial, and cultural height—its Golden Age—under the leadership of the statesman Pericles in the 5th century B.C.E. This was an era whose accomplishments included the construction of the Parthenon, the plays of Sophocles, Euripides, Aeschylus, and Aristophanes, and the philosophy of Socrates as transmitted by his student Plato. Toward the end of the 4th century B.C.E., the Greek city-states, weakened by incessant warfare, succumbed to the armies of Philip of Macedon and his son Alexander (whose tutor was the philosopher Aristotle). Alexander went on to conquer vast territories from the eastern Mediterranean to the Ganges in present-day India. This empire did not survive Alexander's death intact. Its successor states, however, spread Greek, or Hellenistic, culture widely in the eastern Mediterranean and in western Asia.

Music in Ancient Greek Society

Relatively little notated music has survived from ancient Greece, and most of the surviving 45 pieces are fragments. The musical culture of this era relied heavily on memory and improvisation. Yet we know from written accounts, archaeological evidence, and the surviving notated fragments that music played a central role in Greek culture.

The most important public venue for music in ancient Greece was the theater. Greek drama accorded a significant role to the chorus, which provided a running commentary and response to the actions unfolding on the stage, and we know from written accounts and internal evidence within the plays themselves that these choruses were sung. Ensembles could consist of men or women, or occasionally both. Choruses gave voice to the feelings of the community through a combination of word, music, and dance—all of which were considered inseparable in the ancient Greek view of music.

Music also played a central role in religious and civic rituals. Homer's *Iliad* describes how the Greeks propitiated the god Apollo by singing a "splendid hymn" in his honor for an entire day. The *Iliad* and *Odyssey* themselves are believed to have been sung to formulaic melodies. And the odes written by the 5th-century B.C.E. poet Pindar to commemorate the victors in the Olympic games were clearly intended to be sung: "Ode" and "song" were virtually synonymous in the Greek world. Singing was itself one of the competitive events in the Pythian games, held every four years at Delphi in honor of Apollo, a god closely associated with music.

The ancient Greeks also developed repertories of songs and instrumental music for specific social functions: weddings, banquets, funerals, working, and marching, for example. Writers of the time repeatedly warned against mixing genres of song and had a strong sense of which pieces were appropriate in certain settings and which were not.

Greek music, as best we can tell, was largely **monophonic**—consisting of a single melodic line—with the possibility of an accompanimental line that either doubled or modestly embellished the principal voice. The Greeks apparently did not cultivate

polyphony of any kind, at least not in the conventional sense of the term—the simultaneous sounding of independent parts of equal importance. Their vocal music emphasized instead the fusion of word, rhythm, and melody, which is precisely how Plato defined song (*melos*).

Greek Musical Theory

The musical system used in ancient Greece was based on a series of interlocking **tetrachords,** descending successions of four notes spanning the interval of a fourth. The inner notes within a tetrachord could be distributed according to one of three *genera* (the plural of *genus,* a class or category): diatonic, chromatic, or enharmonic. A series of four interlocking tetrachords plus one additional note combined to create the Greater Perfect System, a span of two octaves that encompassed the notes used in actual music. Melodies were organized according to the characteristics of one of several

Example A-1 The Greek *genera:* diatonic (a), chromatic (b), and enharmonic (c).

Greek musical notation. *The inscription on this 1st-century C.E. gravestone includes a song that was apparently an epitaph for the deceased. It begins with the words "I am a tombstone, an image. Seikilos placed me here as an everlasting sign of deathless remembrance." The song begins in the sixth line of text. The signs between the lines indicate rhythm—notated with an unusual degree of clarity—and pitch. Between 1883 and 1922, the owner of this stone removed the bottom line of music and text in the process of making the column even. Fortunately, an earlier scholar had made a rubbing of the full inscription, thus preserving the song in its entirety.*

Source: National Museum of Denmark, Copenhagen—Dept. of Classical and Near Eastern Antiquities/inv. no. 14897

Instruments of Ancient Greece

F O C U S

From written accounts and from the archaeological record—especially illustrations on pottery—scholars have been able to identify a wide range of musical instruments cultivated in ancient Greece.

The most important stringed instruments were the many types of lyres, each with its own characteristic sound and symbolic significance. A lyre consisted of a sound box from which curved arms extended, joined by a crossbar. Strings, attached between the crossbar and the sound box, were often played with a plectrum (a "pick"). Lyres were used either as solo instruments or to accompany voices.

The most prominent wind instrument was the aulos, a pair of pipes, one held in each hand, with a single or double reed. Like the instruments of the lyre family, the aulos could be used either as a solo instrument or to accompany a singer. Other wind instruments include the syrinx, a single reed pipe or panpipe, and various kinds of horns, made either from animal horns or from metal.

Percussion instruments included drums of many kinds, as well as the krotala (hollowed-out blocks of wood played in the manner of castanets) and kumbala (finger cymbals).

Music education in ancient Greece. *These images, from an Athenian vase made about 480 B.C.E., depict a variety of ancient Greek instruments and reflect the important place of music in the education of Athenian youth. In the top panel, the larger, older figures teach youths how to read and play the lyre. The bottom panel shows a figure playing an aulos (on the left) and another writing on a tablet (center). Plato, who recognized music's power but was deeply suspicious of its hold on the mind and spirit, recommended that youths learn just enough music to use it in society and to appreciate it as an art, but not to cultivate it as a profession. Although young women received education in music as well, schooling of all kinds separated the sexes entirely.*

Source: Staatliche Museen zu Berlin, Antikensammlung; Foto Marburg/Art Resource, N.Y.

tonoi (singular *tonos*). Writers of the time disagreed on the precise nature and number of *tonoi*, but their names refer to Greek ethnic groups and regions, indicating that at some distant time they were associated with the musical practices of those groups and regions: the Dorian *tonos* with southern Greece, for example, the Ionian with southwestern Greece, the Phrygian and Lydian with Asia Minor, and the Aeolian with the Greek islands. (The names used to classify modes in the Middle Ages were taken from these names, but the pitches and structures of the medieval modes were different from those of the original Greek *tonoi*. See Chapter 1.)

Epitaph of Seikilos

One of the works to have survived in ancient Greek notation is the *Epitaph of Seikilos*, so called because it appears on a tombstone inscription. This brief piece, dating from the 1st century C.E., is in the Ionian *tonos*, occupying an octave on E that includes C♯ and F♯, with special prominence given to the pitch A. This last pitch, the middle note of the octave on E, constitutes the *mese* ("mean") of the range. "In all good music," comments the author of the *Problems* (possibly Aristotle), "*mese* occurs frequently, and all good composers have frequent recourse to *mese*, and, if they leave it, they soon return to it, as they do to no other note."[1] Songs like this are known to have been accompanied on the lyre or some similar instrument, but the accompaniment itself was never notated and remains a matter of considerable speculation.

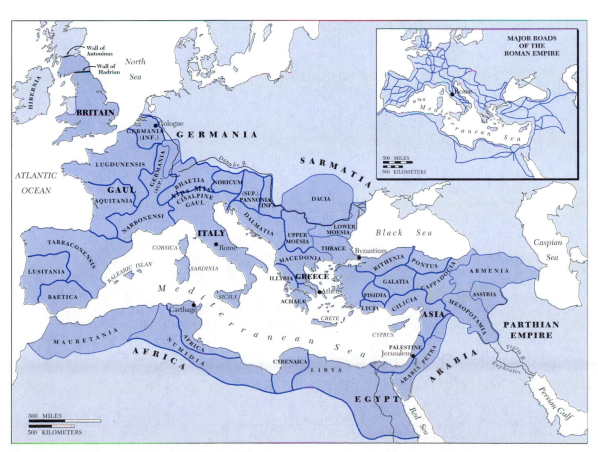

The Roman Empire at Its Greatest Extent, 117 C.E.

MUSIC IN THE ROMAN EMPIRE

Between the 2nd century B.C.E. and the early 1st century C.E., the Greek homeland and the Hellenistic kingdoms of the eastern Mediterranean succumbed to the armies of Rome. By 117 C.E., when it reached its greatest extent, the Roman Empire controlled the entire Mediterranean world and western Europe into Britain. For some 200 years, beginning with the reign of Augustus (27 B.C.E.–14 C.E.), Roman dominion brought stability and prosperity to this region.

Even before they conquered Greece, the Romans had absorbed many aspects of Greek culture, including its music. No Roman music has survived in notated form, yet we know from written accounts that music played an important role in many aspects of Roman life, including the theater and civic ritual.

THE MUSICAL LEGACIES OF ANTIQUITY

Beginning in the late 3rd century C.E., the Roman Empire entered a long period of decline. Pressured by Germanic invaders on its borders and stagnating economically, it fragmented into two major regions, eastern and western. During this time, Christianity rose to dominance within the empire, ultimately displacing the Greek and Roman pantheon to become the state religion. In 410, the Visigoths sacked Rome, and in 476, with the overthrow of its last emperor, the Western Roman Empire all but vanished. The Greek-speaking Eastern, or Byzantine, Empire would endure until the fall of its capital, Constantinople (modern Istanbul), to the Turks in 1453.

By the 5th century C.E., the music of antiquity and the oral tradition that accompanied it had also all but vanished. The theoretical writings of antiquity about music, however, continued to be transmitted through the works of such writers as Ptolemy (2nd century C.E.), Aristides Quintilianus (3rd century C.E.), and Alypius (4th century C.E.). These authors were known to such later figures as Boethius (ca. 480–524 C.E.; see Chapter 1) and Cassiodorus (ca. 490–ca. 583 C.E.), who transmitted the basic elements and terminology of Greek and Roman music theory to the medieval era.

Thus, although the music of antiquity was essentially lost to the medieval era, the attitudes of the ancient Greeks and Romans toward music have exerted an unbroken influence on Western thinking about the art down to the present day. Many of these attitudes and beliefs found their expression in myth. Other aspects of ancient perspectives toward music can be gleaned from philosophy, drama, poetry, and through writings concerned directly with music itself.

Music and the Cosmos

Pythagoras (6th century B.C.E.) is credited with having discovered the relationship between musical sound and number. According to legend, Pythagoras was passing by a blacksmith's forge one day and noticed that hammers of different weights were creating sounds in the intervals of an octave, a fifth, and a fourth. When he weighed the hammers, he discovered that their weight fell into the ratio 2:1 (octave), 3:2 (fifth), and 4:3 (fourth). Because of their mathematical simplicity, these intervals were considered "perfect" consonances. Pythagoras considered the mathematical basis of sound a fundamental law governing the relationship of all physical bodies in the universe.

Music and the Soul

The same forces perceived to govern the cosmos, including music, were also understood by the ancients to govern the human soul. Music thus had the power to alter behavior in the most fundamental way, creating either harmony or discord within the spirit of the individual.

The myth of Orpheus and Euridice gives powerful expression to this belief. Orpheus was a celebrated musician capable of calming wild beasts with his playing. When his wife, Euridice, died on their wedding day, he attempted to retrieve her from the underworld, Hades. To do so, he had to persuade the guardians of Hades to allow him—a mortal—to cross into the realm of the dead and then return to life. Charon, the boatman who ferries dead souls across the River Styx, refused this absurd request, but Orpheus's skill on the lyre was so powerful that Charon was overwhelmed and fell into a deep sleep. Orpheus similarly used music to persuade Pluto, god of the underworld, to release Euridice. The story thus suggests that through music, humans can bridge the otherwise unbridgeable divide between life and death.

Like the god Pluto, even the most powerful mortals are helpless to resist the spell of music. Not even the great Odysseus could resist the Sirens, whose seductive song lured sailors to dash their boats to pieces on their rock. The goddess Circe warned Odysseus that he could safely pass the Sirens only by plugging the ears of his crew with thick wax. Odysseus permitted himself to hear the Sirens's song after commanding his men to bind him to the mast of his ship.

The belief that music has the power to elevate or debase the soul, to enlighten or degrade the mind, was widespread in antiquity and is still current today. The **doctrine of ethos** held that music was capable of arousing listeners to certain kinds of emotions and behaviors. Plato, in the late 4th century B.C.E., recommended that youths learn to make music in the Dorian and Phrygian modes: the former because it imparted courage, the latter because it imparted thoughtfulness. Aristotle observed that some modes "make men noticeably mournful and restrained in mood, like the so-called Mixolydian," whereas other modes "soften the temper of the active intelligence. . . . It is the same with rhythms: some have a remarkably stable ethos, others an ethos which stirs the emotions; and of this latter class some are notably vulgar in their emotional effects while others better suit freeborn persons."[2]

Music and the State

The same powers that affect the individual also affect the state—which is, after all, a collection of individuals. Music education was thus an element of good citizenship in ancient Greece, for youth of both sexes. "Music has the power of producing a certain effect on the moral character of the soul," Aristotle declared, "and if it has the power to do this, it is clear that the young must be directed to music and must be educated in it." His teacher Plato had taken a far more restrictive approach to music education, even while acknowledging its importance:

> The overseers of our state must . . . be watchful against innovations in music and gymnastics counter to the established order, and to the best of their power guard against them. . . . For a change to a new type of music is something to beware of as a hazard of all our fortunes. For the modes of music are never disturbed without unsettling of the most fundamental political and social conventions.[3]

This fear of the subversive power of unfamiliar music (or any music) has cropped up countless times over the centuries. In the 20th century alone, older generations have condemned ragtime (in the 1910s), jazz (1920s), rock and roll (1950s and 1960s), heavy metal (1980s), and rap (1990s) as threats to the morals of American youth. The danger was seen to reside not only in the lyrics but also in the music itself, either because of its rhythm (ragtime, jazz, rock and roll) or volume and timbre (heavy metal). In one way or another, all of these repertories created anxiety about the disruption of the established order.

Vocal versus Instrumental Music

In Greek, the word *mousike* was understood to encompass not only elements of melody and rhythm, but also the words being sung and even the dance that might accompany them. Poetry and song, in Greek culture, were virtually indistinguishable. Instrumental music was thus seen as an inherently lesser art than vocal music. It was welcomed in its place but held in lower esteem. Aristotle, for example, argued that vocal music was superior to instrumental music because voices, whether human or animal, are found only in creatures that have a soul.

At the same time, instrumental music was regarded with a certain mixture of awe and suspicion, precisely because it was able to move listeners without recourse to words. Instrumental music is so elemental that it works at a level not fully susceptible to rational explanation. This helps explain the uneasy mix of attitudes toward instrumental music—condescension mixed with an acute awareness of its powers—that would characterize Western attitudes for the next 2,000 years.

Theory versus Practice

One of the most enduring legacies of classical antiquity was its division of music into two distinct categories: theory and practice. This dichotomy still pervades Western attitudes toward music. Pythagoras and his followers represent the earliest, most extreme, and most influential form of an essentially theoretical approach to the discipline. They were concerned not with the creation or performance of music, but with the discovery of music's essence, its mathematical basis in sound. The liberal arts were divided into two categories: the language arts of the *trivium* (grammar, rhetoric, and dialectic) and the mathematical *quadrivium* (arithmetic, geometry, astronomy, and music). The *trivium* comprised the arts of expression and persuasion, but as part of the *quadrivium,* music was considered an art of measurement. Practicing musicians, although widely admired for their performances, were not considered among the intellectual elite: they could entertain, but they could not edify their audiences.

Not all ancient philosophers were as convinced as Pythagoras and his followers that music should be conceived only as a sounding manifestation of abstract number. Aristoxenus (ca. 364 B.C.E.–304 B.C.E.) preferred to base his theories on a mixture of abstract reason and empirical perception. Aristoxenus, a pupil of Aristotle, judged the size of musical intervals by relying to a large extent on his ears, rejecting the exclusively abstract calculations of the Pythagoreans. But Aristoxenus was in the decided minority in his time, and the Pythagorean approach to theory would dominate for many centuries.

CONCLUSION

Although the musical repertories of classical antiquity were largely lost to subsequent eras, Greek attitudes toward music established basic patterns of thought that still hold. The Greeks perceived music as both an art and a science, a means of providing pleasure as well as insight into the nature of the universe. They recognized music's ethical and spiritual power and its ability to transcend reason, yet they also recognized its scientific basis in the principles of mathematical proportions. The legacy of classical antiquity would provide a strong foundation for the development of musical thought and practice in the medieval era.

DISCUSSION QUESTIONS

1. What did the ancient Greeks consider to be the essential elements of music? Would we use the same criteria today to describe the art?

2. What was the melodic basis of ancient Greek music, and how were ancient Greek melodies organized?

3. How do we know about the importance of music in ancient Greek and Roman culture? What might future societies conclude about the importance of music in ours?

4. In ancient Greece, music was considered essential to the education of the individual and the building of the state. What is the relationship between music and the modern state? (Consider, for example, such contexts as education, propaganda or advertising, religion, nationalism or patriotism, and cultivation of the arts.)

5. What are the most important musical legacies of antiquity?

Part One
The Medieval Era

Prelude

What we now call the medieval era spans almost an entire millennium, from the fall of the Western Roman Empire in 476 C.E. until the beginnings of the Renaissance in the early 15th century. *Medieval* means literally "between the ages," and the term was coined by later historians who looked back on these "Middle Ages" as an era of darkness between two periods of light, classical antiquity and the Renaissance.

Those who lived in the medieval era did not see themselves as living "between" anything, of course, and this period was scarcely one of unbroken darkness. The legacies of the Roman Empire were far too deep and widespread to have disappeared entirely. Western Europe continued to benefit from the institutions of Rome (and through it, indirectly, Greece), particularly the vast networks of roads, the common language of Latin, and, increasingly, the common religion of Christianity.

TIMELINE

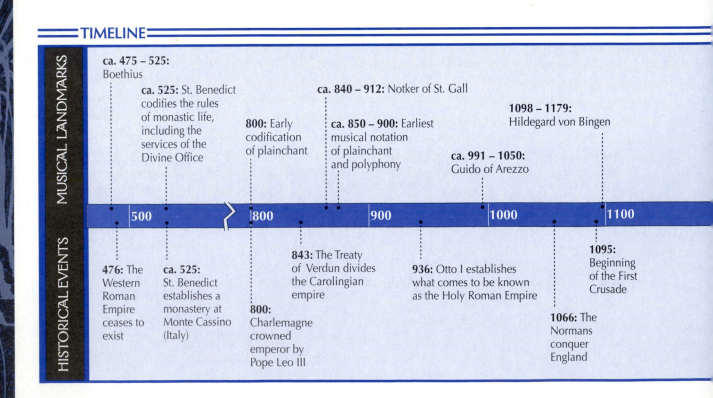

MUSICAL LANDMARKS

ca. 475 – 525: Boethius

ca. 525: St. Benedict codifies the rules of monastic life, including the services of the Divine Office

800: Early codification of plainchant

ca. 840 – 912: Notker of St. Gall

ca. 850 – 900: Earliest musical notation of plainchant and polyphony

1098 – 1179: Hildegard von Bingen

ca. 991 – 1050: Guido of Arezzo

500 | 800 | 900 | 1000 | 1100

HISTORICAL EVENTS

476: The Western Roman Empire ceases to exist

ca. 525: St. Benedict establishes a monastery at Monte Cassino (Italy)

800: Charlemagne crowned emperor by Pope Leo III

843: The Treaty of Verdun divides the Carolingian empire

936: Otto I establishes what comes to be known as the Holy Roman Empire

1066: The Normans conquer England

1095: Beginning of the First Crusade

With the fall of Rome, western Europe experienced a marked decline in political stability. Commerce withered as Arabic armies conquered North Africa and most of Spain in the 7th and 8th centuries, reducing contact between western Europe and the rest of the Mediterranean world. Population fell, infrastructure decayed, and learning of all kinds was lost. Basic engineering skills known in antiquity would not be recovered for almost 1,000 years. Entire libraries disappeared through fire or pillage. The collection of the great library at Alexandria, Egypt, with perhaps as many as 400,000 manuscripts during its glory years, would not be rivaled again for almost 2,000 years. For most of the medieval era, almost no one in western Europe could read ancient Greek; as a result, even those manuscripts by such philosophers as Plato and Aristotle that survived in the West could not be deciphered and were for all practical purposes lost until the later centuries of the era, when Latin translations began to appear. Although scholars in the Greek-speaking Byzantine Empire and in the Islamic world continued to cultivate Greek, contact between Eastern and Western scholars was extremely limited until the late medieval era.

The medieval world was also a dangerous place. Infant mortality was high, and most of those who survived childhood died before age 30. Diseases like dysentery, typhus, and smallpox posed a constant threat, and plagues were a recurring feature of life. Travelers moved in large groups whenever they could to protect themselves against vagabonds and brigands. The rule of law was little more than an abstract idea in many corners of the continent.

Many men and women withdrew from the secular world altogether and devoted themselves to the church. Self-sufficient monastic communities dotted the European countryside. In England alone there were some 500 monasteries by the beginning of the 14th century. The Benedictines, Carmelites, Dominicans, Franciscans, and other orders varied in their forms of worship and routines, but all were devoted to the principle of monasticism, a way of life based on a vow of poverty, chastity, and obedience. Monastic communities served as the primary repositories of learning in the medieval world.

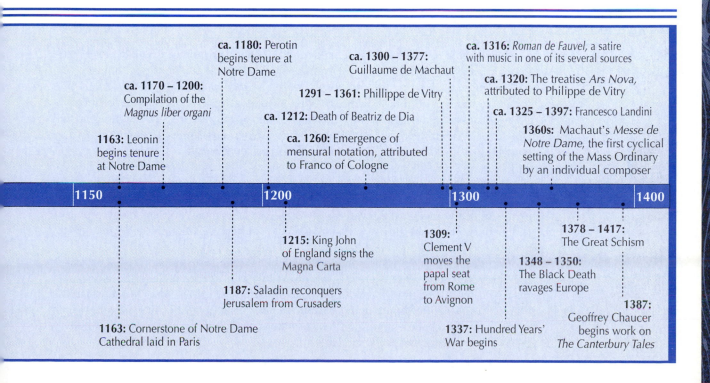

ca. 1180: Perotin begins tenure at Notre Dame

ca. 1300 – 1377: Guillaume de Machaut

ca. 1316: *Roman de Fauvel,* a satire with music in one of its several sources

ca. 1170 – 1200: Compilation of the *Magnus liber organi*

1291 – 1361: Phillippe de Vitry

ca. 1320: The treatise *Ars Nova,* attributed to Philippe de Vitry

ca. 1212: Death of Beatriz de Dia

ca. 1325 – 1397: Francesco Landini

1163: Leonin begins tenure at Notre Dame

ca. 1260: Emergence of mensural notation, attributed to Franco of Cologne

1360s: Machaut's *Messe de Notre Dame,* the first cyclical setting of the Mass Ordinary by an individual composer

| 1150 | 1200 | 1300 | 1400 |

1215: King John of England signs the Magna Carta

1309: Clement V moves the papal seat from Rome to Avignon

1378 – 1417: The Great Schism

1348 – 1350: The Black Death ravages Europe

1187: Saladin reconquers Jerusalem from Crusaders

1387: Geoffrey Chaucer begins work on *The Canterbury Tales*

1163: Cornerstone of Notre Dame Cathedral laid in Paris

1337: Hundred Years' War begins

Devoting themselves to lives of prayer and labor, monks and nuns prepared, collected, and preserved manuscripts of all kinds, including treatises on philosophy, medicine, law, astronomy, and mathematics—topics having little or nothing to do with religion or theology.

New political entities arose to fill the vacuum left by the collapse of Rome. The most powerful of these was that of Charlemagne, the ruler of the Franks. His realm extended across what is now France, western and central Germany, Austria, Switzerland, and northern Italy. Charlemagne consolidated his powers through a strategic alliance with the papacy and, on Christmas Day in 800, he was crowned in Rome by Pope Leo III as "Sovereign of the Roman Empire."

But Charlemagne's empire did not survive him. By the end of the 9th century his domain had been divided in three, with the Kingdom of France to the west, the Kingdom of Italy to the south, and the East Frankish Kingdom to the east. The last of these emerged as the center of the Holy Roman Empire, a loose confederation of states that, as the 18th-century French philosopher Voltaire famously quipped, was "neither holy, nor Roman, nor an Empire."

The looseness of this confederation was a political liability, but it proved an enormous boon to the arts, including music. Every one of the hundreds of duchies, principalities, and kingdoms across central and southern Europe employed its share of painters, poets, and musicians. By the end of the medieval era, the courts rivaled and in some respects even surpassed the church in the composition and consumption of new music.

While Germany fragmented, France and England began to emerge as centralized nation-states under the leadership of increasingly powerful monarchies. Here too, the arts flourished under the courts of kings and powerful nobles.

Medieval society was shaped by the system of feudalism, whose economic foundation was the self-sufficient estate, or manor. The peasants who worked the lands of the manor swore allegiance and service to the lord of the manor, who might in turn be the vassal of a more powerful noble. The steady growth of population and prosperity in the centuries after 1000 would ultimately spell the demise of the feudal system. As agricultural productivity increased and trade began to expand, towns and cities replaced the castle as the central marketplace for goods and services.

Courtly life revolved around a highly stylized code of conduct. In public, love could be expressed passionately but only from a distance: the ideal knight paid homage to a lady of noble birth by dedicating himself to her service and offering lavish poetry and song in her praise—but never directly. The idea of courtly love in its purest form always involved self-contained torment. The object of desire was either a maiden or a married woman, but in either case unattainable by the strictures of social convention. In this context, love took on a kind of abstract, almost religious quality. Indeed, many poems and songs in praise of "my lady" can be understood as being directed toward either the Virgin Mary or an earthly noblewoman.

The year 1000 marked the beginning of a wave of energy and optimism. The later centuries of the medieval era witnessed notable advancements in technology, architecture, education, and the arts. Paper, already common in Arabic lands for several centuries, was being produced in quantity in Europe by the 13th century.

Increasing prosperity and confidence combined with an upsurge in religious zeal in the late 11th century to inspire a series of military ventures to reclaim the Holy Land from Muslim rule. Although a failure from a military point of view, the Crusades had the unintended benefit of bringing the West into closer contact with Islamic culture, which for centuries had been cultivating such disciplines as philosophy, astronomy, mathematics (particularly algebra), and medicine.

In the 14th century, however, Europe entered a period of crisis. Population growth combined with crop failure to produce a devastating famine early in the century. A debilitating conflict between France and England known as the Hundred Years' War broke out in 1337. In the middle of the century the bubonic plague swept across Europe, killing as much as a third of its population. And beginning in 1378, conflicting claimants to the papacy created a schism in the church. These crises, however, helped provoke an intellectual and political ferment that would contribute to the Renaissance and Reformation as Europe recovered in the 15th and 16th centuries.

Perhaps the most remarkable of all technological and artistic achievements of the medieval era was Gothic architecture. With its emphasis on height, this style of building supplanted the earlier Romanesque style. Squat, compact structures gave way to buildings of unprecedented size, grace, and light. The Gothic cathedrals of Notre Dame in Paris and in Chartres were both begun in the middle of the 12th century.

Toward the end of the 13th century, a series of artists and writers emerged whose works seem remarkably forward looking—so much so, in fact, that they are often seen as heralds of the Renaissance. Painters like Giotto (ca. 1267–1337) and sculptors like Giovanni Pisano (ca. 1250–ca. 1314), both Italians, began to depict the human form in a new and fundamentally different way. The faces are more individualized, more fully differentiated, and far more realistic—in short, more like the art of classical antiquity. Similar insights into human nature emerge from the work of poets like Dante Alighieri (1265–1321), Giovanni Boccaccio (1313–1375), and Geoffrey Chaucer (1342–1400), who produced works of striking originality not in the international language of Latin, but in the vernacular languages of Italian and English.

The pace of learning as a whole gradually accelerated from the 12th century onward. The chief centers of scholarship began to shift from the church to the newly emerging universities, many of which grew out of cathedral schools. The dominant mode of thought in the new universities was known as scholasticism. Its proponents maintained that truth could be reached by a combination of reason and faith. The scholastic curriculum was based on the study of established authorities like Aristotle and St. Augustine. Empirical observation was not to be trusted, for the medieval mind was deeply suspicious of worldly appearances. Life on earth, after all, was considered transitory and decidedly inferior to the higher truths of divine eternity. Music was an important object of study in the new universities, but not musical performance. In the tradition of Pythagoras and the quadrivium, music was understood as a mathematical discipline—related more to geometry and astronomy than poetry or drama—that provided a source of insight into the relationship between number and the cosmos.

This preoccupation with theory at the expense of performance undermined the unwritten traditions of performance that might otherwise have survived between the musical practices of ancient and medieval worlds. The phenomenon of the sung drama was gone by the 5th century, as was the ability to read ancient musical notation. A new system of notation would not begin to emerge until the 9th century, and although elements of ancient musical theory endured through the writings of a few authors, their works were known to only a few and understood by fewer. The writings of the single most important theorist of the early medieval period, Manlius Severinus Boethius (480–524), for example, remained in obscurity until the 9th century.

The musical practices of the medieval era are thus difficult to reconstruct. Not until the late 9th century do we have notated sources of any kind, and even these are rare. Few manuscripts have survived the ravages of time. Much of medieval music was never written down at all. From all that we know about the music of the minstrels, it seems clear

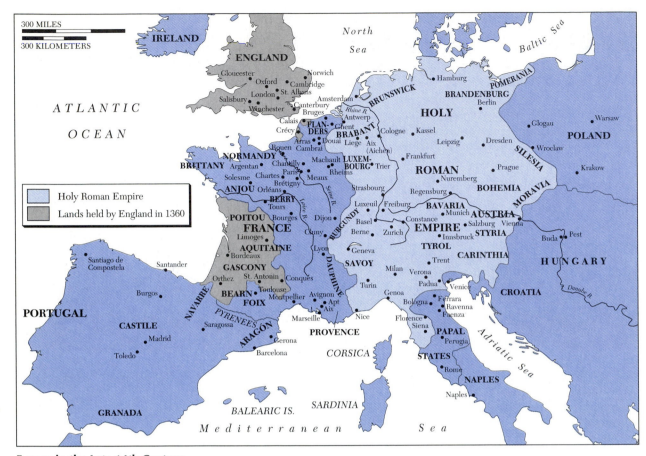

300 MILES
300 KILOMETERS

ATLANTIC OCEAN

IRELAND

ENGLAND
Gloucester · Oxford · Norwich
· St. Albans · Cambridge
Salisbury · London
Winchester · Canterbury

North Sea

Baltic Sea

Hamburg
POMERANIA
BRUNSWICK
BRANDENBURG
Berlin
HOLY
Amsterdam
Bruges
Antwerp
Rhine R.
FLAN-DERS
Ghent
BRABANT
Cologne · Kassel
Leipzig
Dresden
Glogau
Warsaw
POLAND
Wroclaw
Krakow
SILESIA
MORAVIA
ROMAN
Calais
Crécy
Arras · Douai
Cambrai
Liege · Aix (Aichen)
Frankfurt
Nuremberg
Prague
BOHEMIA
NORMANDY
BRITTANY
Argentan · Chantilly
Machault
LUXEM-BOURG
Trier
Regensburg
BAVARIA
Munich
AUSTRIA
ANJOU
Solesme
Paris
Chartes
Meaux
Rheims
Strasbourg
Luxeuil · Freiburg
Constance
EMPIRE
Salzburg
Innsbruck
Vienna
STYRIA
BERRY
Tours
Brétigny
Orléans
Bourges
Cluny
Dijon
Basel
Berne
Zurich
TYROL
Trent
Milan
Verona
Padua
Venice
CARINTHIA
HUNGARY
Buda · Pest
POITOU
FRANCE
Limoges
AQUITAINE
Bordeaux
Lyon
Geneva
SAVOY
Turin
Genoa
Bologna
Ferrara
Ravenna
Faenza
Florence
Siena
CROATIA
Danube R.
GASCONY
Orthez · St. Antonin
Conques
Toulouse
Montpellier
Avignon
Apt
Aix
Marseille
Nice
DAUPHINE
PAPAL STATES
Perugia
Rome
Adriatic Sea
BEARN
FOIX
PROVENCE
PORTUGAL
Santiago de Compostela
Santander
Burgos
CASTILE
Madrid
Toledo
NAVARRE
PYRENEES
ARAGON
Saragossa
Gerona
Barcelona
CORSICA
NAPLES
Naples
GRANADA
BALEARIC IS.
SARDINIA
Mediterranean Sea

Holy Roman Empire
Lands held by England in 1360

Europe in the Late 14th Century

The two sides of music. *This miniature from an early-12th-century manuscript shows two contrasting approaches to the art of music. King David (top) represents musicians who understand their art. The figure at the top left plays chime bells of varying sizes, suggesting Pythagorean proportions; with his right hand he plucks a monochord, a device with a single string used to measure the ratios of sound according to the mathematical divisions of the string. The singers to the right read from notated music. In the image at bottom, a beast makes music, beating on a simple drum. No written music is in sight, and the acrobats in the lower left do somersaults. The two scenes reflect the medieval belief in the superiority of theory over practice. They conjure up Guido of Arezzo's derisive distinction between a musicus and a cantor: "There is a great distance between a musician and singer / The latter says, the former understands what constitutes music. / For whoever does things without understanding them, is by definition a beast."*

Source: Reprinted by permission of the Master and Fellows of St. John's College, Cambridge

PRIMARY EVIDENCE

Three Categories of Musicians

In his *De institutione musica* ("Fundamentals of Music"), written in the early 6th century and widely read from the 9th century onward, Boethius answers the question "What is a musician?" by dividing those who deal with music into three classes. His distinction between theory and practice is a legacy of antiquity that would continue to influence the subsequent history of music.

• • • • •

Thus, there are three classes of those who are engaged in the musical art. The first class consists of those who perform on instruments, the second of those who compose songs, and the third of those who judge instrumental performance and song.

But those of the class which is dependent upon instruments and who spend their entire effort there—such as kitharists and those who prove their skill on the organ and other musical instruments—are excluded from comprehension of musical knowledge, since, as was said, they act as slaves. None of them makes use of reason; rather, they are totally lacking in thought.

The second class of those practicing music is that of the poets, a class led to song not so much by thought and reason as by a certain natural instinct. For this reason this class, too, is separated from music.

The third class is that which acquires an ability for judging, so that it can carefully weigh rhythms and melodies and the composition as whole. This class, since it is totally grounded in reason and thought, will rightly be esteemed as musical. That person is a musician who exhibits the faculty of forming judgments according to speculation or reason relative and appropriate to music concerning modes and rhythms, the genera of songs, consonances, and all the things which are to be explained subsequently, as well as concerning the songs of the poets.

Source: Ancius Manlius Severinus Boethius, *Fundamentals of Music,* trans. Calvin M. Bower, ed. Claude V. Palisca (New Haven: Yale University Press, 1989), p. 51.

that most of this repertory was improvised, produced on the spot for the lords and ladies of a particular court as the occasion demanded.

The medieval era covers almost 1,000 years. Not surprisingly, the music of this period is extremely diverse, ranging from monophonic plainchant, first consolidated sometime around the 6th or 7th century, to the intricate polyphony of the 13th and early 14th centuries. And the range of music that has survived is amply sufficient to reveal a richly varied musical culture that established basic concepts and techniques we take for granted today: notation, polyphony, and an elaborate theory by which to rationalize both the art and science of music.

Chapter 1

Plainchant and Secular Monophony

The earliest notated repertories of medieval music are monophonic. The oldest sources of **plainchant**—the monophonic sacred music of the Christian church—date from the last quarter of the 9th century; the first notated secular monophonic songs are found in manuscripts written about a century later. Both repertories flourished long before the emergence of notation, however, which makes it difficult to reconstruct their early history.

THE EMERGENCE OF PLAINCHANT

Although it is often called **Gregorian chant,** after its supposed creator, Pope Gregory I, plainchant existed well before his reign (590–604), and its development continued long afterward.

The origins and evolution of plainchant are inextricably linked to the development of the Christian liturgy—that is, the body of texts and actions prescribed for Christian worship services. Christianity originated as a sect of Judaism, and the earliest Christians preserved many of the traditions and practices of Jewish worship: the offering of prayers, the singing of hymns, and the systematic recitation or singing of psalms and other passages from Holy Scripture. The Eucharistic **Mass,** or celebration of Holy Communion, although a distinctively Christian practice, also has Jewish roots. It is a ritualistic reenactment of the Last Supper, Christ's celebration of the Jewish feast of Passover with his disciples the day before his crucifixion.

The patriarchs of the early church recognized the power of music to project the words of psalms and hymns with heightened intensity. At the same time, church leaders had qualms about mixing words and music in worship. The music, they worried, could distract listeners from the message of the text. Such ambivalence toward music in the liturgy would emerge repeatedly throughout the history of Christianity. Saint Basil (ca. 330–379), addressing this concern, rationalized the singing of psalms in this manner:

> . . . [the Holy Spirit] contrived for us these harmonious psalm tunes, so that those who are children in actual age as well as those who are young in behavior, while appearing only to sing would in reality be training their souls. For not one of these many indifferent people ever leaves church easily retaining in memory some maxim of either the Apostles or the Prophets, but they do sing the texts of the Psalms at home and circulate them in the marketplace.[1]

Surviving accounts document a wide diversity of liturgical and musical practices during Christianity's first 600 years. The church lacked a strong central authority, and liturgical and musical practices varied considerably from place to place. By the 7th century, several distinct rites had established themselves in the West. The most important of these were the Roman, the Ambrosian (used in northern Italy and named after St. Ambrose, who died in 397), the Gallican (in Frankish lands of what is now France and western Germany), and the Mozarabic or Visigothic (on the Iberian peninsula). Each of these rites maintained its own liturgy and repertory of chants.

How, then, did a comprehensive and unified repertory of plainchant come into existence? The answer is inextricably linked to the establishment of the Roman rite as the primary liturgy of the church. From the early 7th century onward, successive popes—the bishops of Rome—asserted their primacy within the Western church, and in so doing vigorously promoted the export of the Roman liturgy and with it a standardized body of chant. In the absence of musical notation, the popes relied on specially trained singer-clerics to carry this repertory of chant to distant realms. By the late 9th century, the legend had emerged that Pope Gregory I (Saint Gregory the Great), who reigned from 590 to 604, had been responsible not only for promoting the diffusion of the Roman liturgy, but for composing the chants himself, inspired by the Holy Spirit. Like all myths, this

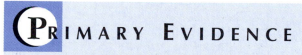

PRIMARY EVIDENCE

The Seductive Power of Music

Saint Augustine (354–430) was the bishop of the North African city of Hippo from 391 until his death. A prolific writer and influential thinker, he is considered a founder of Christian theology. In this passage from his autobiographical *Confessions*, he struggles with the role of music in worship.

• • • • •

I realize that when they are sung these sacred words stir my mind to greater religious fervor and kindle in me a more ardent flame of piety than they would if they were not sung; and I also know that there are particular modes in song and in the voice, corresponding to my various emotions and able to stimulate them because of some mysterious relationship between the two. But I ought not to allow my mind to be paralyzed by the gratification of my senses, which often leads it astray. For the senses are not content to take second place. Simply because I allow them their due, as adjuncts to reason, they attempt to take precedence and forge ahead of it, with the result that I sometimes sin in this way but am not aware of it until later.

Without committing myself to an irrevocable opinion, I am inclined to approve of the custom of singing in church, in order that by indulging the ears weaker spirits may be inspired with feelings of devotion. Yet when I find the singing itself more moving than the truth which it conveys, I confess that this is a grievous sin, and at those times I would prefer not to hear the singer.

Source: Saint Augustine, *Confessions*, Book X, 33, trans. and ed. R. S. Pine-Coffin (London: Penguin Books, 1961), pp. 238–239. Copyright 1961 by R. S. Pine-Coffin. Reproduced by permission of Penguin Books Ltd.

Pope Gregory and the Holy Spirit.
Pope Gregory I, according to legend, received the corpus of plainchant through the agency of the Holy Spirit, who visited him in the form of a dove and whispered the chant melodies into his ear. To the medieval mind, the legend was a reality and a cornerstone of the belief that the repertory of plainchant was a sacred gift. The image here is anachronistic insofar as no system of musical notation existed during the time of Pope Gregory I's reign (590–604). The earliest surviving notated sources date from about 300 years later. The curtain represents the distance between the simple scribe and the pope who would later become a saint. According to the legend, the scribe, puzzled by the pope's long intervals of silence while dictating the chant, peeked behind the screen and saw Gregory receiving the chant from the Holy Spirit.

Source: AKG London Ltd.

one had a basis in reality, for unquestionably an earlier pope had brought a substantial degree of order to what must have been a widely diverse body of melodies and texts. But it may have been another Gregory, Pope Gregory II, also a strong promoter of Roman primacy, who reigned from 715 to 731. Without notated sources, and in the absence of further documentation, we will probably never know with certainty exactly who played what role in the early dissemination of a unified plainchant repertory.

We do know, however, that this early consolidation of the chant was not universally accepted, at least not immediately. The Gallican, Ambrosian, and Mozarabic rites and their associated plainchant repertories continued to flourish alongside the Roman liturgy and its chants. It was ultimately not a pope, but a secular ruler, Charlemagne, who realized the papal goal of a primarily Roman liturgy in the West.

The emperor devoted considerable energy to the administration of his far-flung territories. He recognized that a unified liturgy—along with a unified body of music—would go a long way toward solidifying both the idea and practice of central authority. With the aid of the papacy, Charlemagne eventually succeeded in imposing a single, more or less standard liturgy—the Roman liturgy—throughout his empire. He established several singing schools to teach the chant to choirmasters, who in turn took these melodies (either memorized or notated) back to their home churches. The most important of these singing schools were in Metz (in what is now eastern France) and St. Gall (in what is now

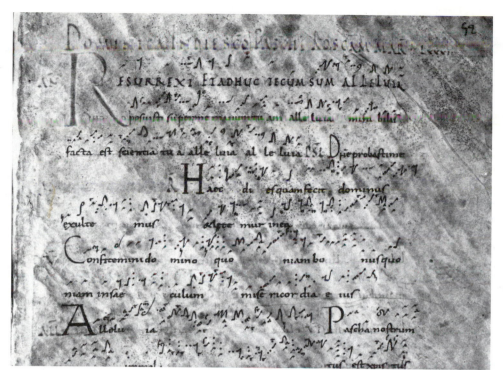

neumes

Non-diastematic chant notation. *The neumes of the earliest notated sources indicate the general contours but not the actual pitches of the chants. Shown here are the opening chants of the Mass Proper for Easter Sunday from one of the earliest notated chant manuscripts that has survived in its entirety—Laon 239—believed to have been copied in eastern France some time around 930.*

Source: Bibliotheque Municipale de Laon, France/MS. 239, folio 52

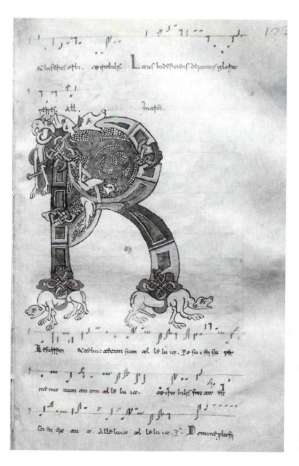

Partially diastematic chant notation. *During the 11th century, some scribes began to add a single line or pair of lines to indicate a fixed pitch or pitches. The opening of the Easter Sunday Introit* Resurrexi *in this chant manuscript copied in southern Italy in the 11th or 12th century illustrates the emerging technique of diastematic chant notation. The scribe has used a straight line labeld with an F-clef to indicate a fixed pitch and has meticulously arranged the Beneventan neumes to reflect their relative position in relation to this pitch. The notation is still somewhat ambiguous, however; only in the 13th and 14th centuries do we begin to see sources with pitches clearly notated on a full set of staff lines. The spectacularly elaborate initial "R" (for "Resurrexi") reflects the special importance of the feast day of Easter.*

Source: Biblioteca Capitolare, Benevento, Italy, Codex VI-34, fol. 123 recto/photo © 2002 Antonio Citrigno

eastern Switzerland). The Mozarabic and Ambrosian liturgies never disappeared entirely, but their use declined significantly.

To judge from the earliest preserved notated chant sources, which date from the beginning of the 10th century, Charlemagne succeeded admirably in his attempt to unify the corpus of liturgical music used throughout his realm. Notation emerged gradually in different forms in different places—an Aquitanian manuscript from southern France, for example, uses a set of note shapes unlike those found in Beneventan manuscripts of southern Italy—yet the repertory transcribed by these apparently independent sources is remarkably consistent from place to place.

If these chants were indeed disseminated by word of mouth, as most scholars believe, their preservation represents a remarkable feat of collective memory. The ability of singers to learn and memorize the chant repertory without musical notation helps explain why notation itself was so slow to develop. In this sense, the real puzzle is why notation ever emerged at all. Perhaps it resulted from the desire to set down in writing an object—the chant—considered to be divinely inspired. It seems not to have been connected with the rise of polyphony, whose earliest forms were apparently also performed without the aid of notation. Whatever the reason, the emergence of notation changed the way in which music was both created and transmitted.

THE ELEMENTS OF PLAINCHANT

Plainchant is pure melody, with no harmony, accompaniment, or added voices. Analyzing it requires a different set of criteria than that used for most other kinds of music. Five elements in particular are key to understanding plainchant: liturgical function, the relationship of words and music, mode, melodic structure, and rhythm.

Liturgical Function

The single most important factor defining the nature of any given chant melody is its function within the liturgy. A basic understanding of the Christian liturgy is therefore essential to understanding the musical styles of chant. The two main forms of worship were the Divine Office, a series of services held at specified times throughout the day, and the Mass, a ritual reenactment of Christ's Last Supper with his disciples.

In its broadest outlines, the liturgy of Western Christianity remained essentially consistent throughout western Europe from the time of Charlemagne's imposition of the Roman liturgy early in the 9th century until the Reformation in the 16th century. Even the language—Latin—was universal.

The Divine Office.   The **Divine Office** (also known as simply the **Office;** the term derives from the Latin *officium,* meaning "duty") owes much to the traditions of Jewish worship, which featured a fixed daily schedule of prayer and the singing of psalms. The Rule of Saint Benedict—the regulations governing monastic life promulgated by Saint Benedict (ca. 480–ca. 547)—codified the basic structure and content of the eight services that comprise the Office. The Office was observed primarily by cloistered monks and nuns rather than the laity. Local practices varied considerably and changed over time, but here is the general outline: Matins (2 or 3 A.M.), Lauds (dawn), Prime (6 A.M.), Terce (9 A.M.), Sext (noon), None (3 P.M.), Vespers (sunset), and Compline (before bedtime).

While these services varied considerably in length, every service centered on the recitation of psalms and included the singing of at least one **strophic** hymn (a hymn with each stanza set to the same melody) as well as readings from the scripture, which in turn were followed by a sung response. Some Offices included canticles, biblical passages not from the Psalms but recited or sung as such. Under the Rule of Saint Benedict, the entire Book of Psalms—all 150 of them—was recited once each week over the course of the Divine Office.

The Mass.   Mass was celebrated in monasteries and convents every day between Prime and Terce and in all churches every day in the early morning. It was open to any baptized member of the community in good standing with the church. The Mass consisted of a mixture of spoken, recited, and sung elements, some of which took place in every celebration of Mass (the Ordinary), some of which were specific to particular Sundays or feast days (the Propers).

The table here outlines the structure of the Mass as a whole.

THE STRUCTURE OF THE MASS			
Sung		**Recited or spoken**	
Ordinary	Proper	Ordinary	Proper
	1. Introit		
2. Kyrie			
3. Gloria			
			4. Collect
			5. Epistle
	6. Gradual		
	7. Alleluia (or Tract)		
			8. Gospel
9. Credo			
	10. Offertory		
		11. Offertory Prayers	
			12. Secret
			13. Preface
14. Sanctus			
		15. Canon	
		16. Lord's Prayer	
17. Agnus dei			
	18. Communion		
			19. Post-Communion
20. Ite missa est			

The Liturgical Year.   The church year revolves around two major feasts: Christmas, which celebrates Christ's birth, and Easter, which celebrates Christ's resurrection. Each of these feasts is preceded by a season of penitence—Advent before Christmas and Lent before Easter—and each is followed by a season of variable length—Epiphany after Christmas, Pentecost after Easter.

Relationship of Words and Music

Plainchant is a wonderfully effective way of projecting a text. From a purely practical point of view, the sung chant resonates longer, carries much farther, and is more readily audible in a large space like a church than a text that is merely read. Syllabic recitations of chant, with one note per syllable on a single pitch, are especially effective in this regard. Yet the urge to embellish such recitations musically—to deviate from the standard formulas of recitation on a fixed pitch—ultimately led to the creation of new chants that went well beyond merely practical needs. Simple and elaborate chants thus exist side by side in the liturgy, depending on the nature and function of the texts to be sung. From a musical perspective, chants fall into three broad stylistic categories: syllabic, neumatic, and melismatic (Example 1-1). In **syllabic** passages, each syllable of text has its own note. In the more embellished **neumatic** passages, each syllable is sung to two or three notes. And in the most florid **melismatic** passages, a single syllable is sung to many notes.

Syllabic Chant in the Mass.   Certain elements of the Mass, such as the Epistle or the Gospel, must convey relatively long texts, and for this reason they do not afford time for embellishment. The Epistle and Gospel for Easter Sunday, for example, both follow prescribed formulas and feature little melodic motion. The priest intoning these texts need only adjust the number of notes on a basic **recitation tone** to the number of syllables, deviating in a formulaic way from this central pitch at points corresponding to the grammatical middle and end of each sentence. These slight deviations allow the listener to hear the text as a series of distinct syntactic units. Closure at the end of the text is indicated by a distinctive drop in pitch, a **cadence** (a term derived from the Latin word *cadere,* meaning "to fall"). Similar patterns of recitation are evident in the Collect (a prayer; the word is pronounced with the accent on the first syllable), the Preface (so called because it leads into the Sanctus), and the Post-Communion (a prayer of thanks). The Secret is a prayer said silently by the priest at the high altar with a concluding Amen sung aloud to a reciting tone.

Epistle and Gospel from the Mass for Easter Sunday

Example 1-1 Syllabic (a), neumatic (b), and melismatic (c) chant.

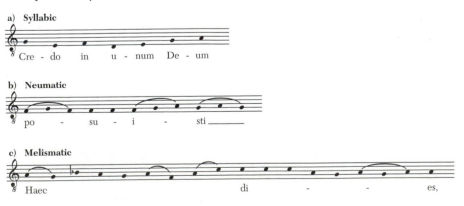

a) **Syllabic**

Cre - do   in   u - num   De - um

b) **Neumatic**

po -   su - i -   sti _____

c) **Melismatic**

Haec   di -   -   es,

Other chants with relatively long texts are syllabic without centering on a recitation tone. These include the various forms of the Gloria and Credo, as well as the Lord's Prayer (*Pater noster*) and the Sequence, a kind of hymn that appears after the Alleluia on special feast days. Like most Sequences, *Victimae paschali laudes* ("Praises to the paschal victim") follows a musical pattern in which repeated phrases of music are framed by individual phrases (a bb cc d). Although each phrase of music is different, the cadences are consistently similar and occasionally identical.

Sequence *Victimae paschali laudes* from the Mass for Easter Sunday

Neumatic Chant in the Mass.   Whereas syllabic chants tend to be functional but not of great interest from a musical point of view, other portions of the liturgy—those that do not incorporate so much text—receive more elaborate music. The Introit, Offertory, and Communion are sometimes called action chants because they accompany actions of the priest and his attendants who are celebrating Mass. The Introit is sung during the procession into the church, the Offertory during the presentation of the bread and wine, and the Communion during the distribution of the bread and wine.

These chants are typically built around a psalm verse. *Resurrexi*, the Introit for the Mass on Easter Sunday, for example, incorporates a psalm verse in its interior (*Domine, probasti me . . .*) and ends with the formulaic Doxology at the end (*Gloria Patri et Filio . . .*—"Glory be to the Father, and to the Son, and to the Holy Spirit . . ."). These sections of the chant are essentially recitational. But the introduction to the psalm verse is freely composed in terms of both its text and its music. The setting is neumatic, with melismas of four and five notes distributed liberally throughout. The Offertory and Communion for Easter are even more elaborate, with long melismas on the repeated word "alleluia" in both. The remaining items of the Ordinary—the Kyrie, Sanctus, Agnus Dei, and Ite missa est, all of which feature relatively brief texts—are also predominantly neumatic with a mixture of syllabic and mildly melismatic passages.

Introit *Resurrexi* from the Mass for Easter Sunday

Melismatic Chant in the Mass.   The most elaborate chants in the Mass are the Gradual and Alleluia, along with the Tract, which replaces the Alleluia during the penitential seasons of Advent and Lent. These chants feature relatively brief texts: the Alleluia for Easter Sunday, for example, consists of only six words. To recite such a short text in the same manner as the Epistle or Gospel would create an exceptionally brief unit of music. This kind of text demands a more elaborate presentation, and the Alleluia repertory in particular is known for its florid, exuberant melodies, especially on the final syllable of the word *alleluia,* a passage known as the ***jubilus*** (derived from the same root as "jubilation").

The Gradual, Alleluia, and Tract are called **responsorial chants** because the chorus alternates with ("responds to") the soloist. In the Gradual for Easter Sunday, *Haec dies*, the soloist intones the opening two words (up to the asterisk marked in the score), at which point the chorus enters (*quam fecit Dominus . . .*). This entire unit is known as the **respond.** The subsequent psalm verse, taken from Psalm 118:1 (*Confitemini Domino . . .*), is then sung by the soloist. In earlier times, the chorus's part of the respond would be repeated, but this practice had disappeared by the 13th century.

Gradual and Alleluia from the Mass for Easter Sunday

Example 1-2 The Eighth Psalm Tone.

Word and Music in the Chants of the Divine Office. The chants for the Divine Office reflect the nature of their texts in a similar fashion. Psalms, with their lengthy texts, are recited syllabically to one of the eight melodic formulas known as **psalm tones** (Example 1-2). Each psalm tone corresponds to one of the eight musical modes (discussed in the next section). The ninth psalm tone, the *Tonus peregrinus* ("wandering tone"), has two recitation tones but is limited largely to the singing of a single text, Psalm 113.

Textually, psalm verses consistently fall into two more or less equal halves, and the music of the psalm tones reflects this structure. Every psalm tone features a mediant cadence between the two halves of each verse and a terminal cadence sung at the end of each verse.

Psalm recitations in the Divine Office were preceded and followed by a more musically varied **antiphon.** At Vespers on Easter Sunday, for example, Psalm 109, *Dixit Dominus,* is recited to the eighth psalm tone and is both preceded and followed by the antiphon *Angelus autem Domini.* Antiphons tend to be relatively brief. Although syllabic, they are more melodically varied than the psalm recitations they frame. Most of the thousands of antiphons are performed in conjunction with the psalms, but a few dozen are used in processions on certain important feast days. A group of four antiphons in honor of the Blessed Virgin Mary—*Alma Redemptoris Mater, Ave Regina caelorum, Regina caeli laetare,* and *Salve Regina*—also function as independent chants and are sung at the end of Compline, one for each season of the liturgical year.

Hymns—whose texts are not scriptural—tend to be syllabic in style. They typically feature multiple strophes, as in the hymn for the Feast of Corpus Christi, *Pange lingua gloriosi corporis mysterium.*

Mode

Modes are scale types characterized by a specific pattern of whole steps and half steps. Melodies in any of the eight medieval modes end on a characteristic pitch (the **finalis** or final) and move up and down within a particular range (**ambitus**). Thus a melody in the first mode will end on the finalis D and be built from the pattern of pitches D-E-F-G-A-B-C-D, or to put it in terms of intervals (W = whole step, H = half step): W-H-W-W-W-W-H-W. A melody in the second mode will be built on the same pitches but range a fifth above to a fourth below the finalis, D.

The eight modes used in the classification of plainchant (Example 1-3) are based on the pitches D, E, F, and G, with each pitch supporting two modes, one called **authentic** (with an ambitus running an octave above the finalis), the other **plagal** (with an ambitus running a fifth above and a fourth below the finalis). In practice, the question of ambitus was fairly flexible. An authentic-mode chant, for example, might easily dip down a note or two below its final. Each of the modes featured its own particular recitation tone (also called a *repercussio*) used to recite long passages of text on a single note. Recitation tones play a particularly important role in the psalm tone associated with each of the eight modes.

The names later associated with these modes—Dorian, Phrygian, Lydian, Mixolydian—derive from Greek place names thought to be associated with each of the modes, rather in the same manner as the Greek *tonoi.* The Greek prefix "hypo-" means "under" and was applied to those modes with an ambitus that ranged under (and over) the finalis. But the original Greek meanings of these modal designations were poorly understood in medieval times and applied inconsistently. It seems preferable nowadays to use simple numerical designations (Mode 1, Mode 2, etc.).

Antiphon *Angelus autem Domini* and Psalm 109 *Dixit Dominus*

Hymn *Pange lingua gloriosi corporis mysterium*

Example 1-3 The medieval plainchant modes.

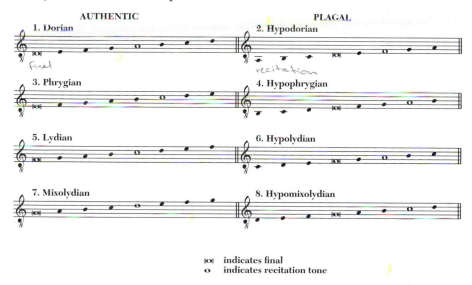

|ol| indicates final
o   indicates recitation tone

Although early chant manuscripts give evidence of at least some organization of their contents by mode, it was not until the 11th century that we find a systematic and consistent application of the eight-mode system, thanks in large part to the work of the Italian monk Guido of Arezzo (991–after 1033) and the German monk Hermannus Contractus (1013–1054). Most later chant manuscripts—from about the middle of the 11th century onward—assign every chant to a particular mode.

Melodic Structure

Plainchant melodies generally follow a limited number of intervallic patterns. In keeping with the function of projecting the text at hand, most chants feature a high percentage of stepwise intervals, punctuated by thirds and an occasional fourth or fifth (the fifths almost always ascending, not descending). Intervals greater than a fifth are quite rare, especially in the oldest layers of the chant repertory. Octave leaps might occasionally occur between two separate phrases of a chant but almost never within a musical or linguistic phrase.

The melody of the Introit for the Mass on Easter Sunday, *Resurrexi,* is fairly typical. The intervals are mostly conjunct with an occasional third up or down. The range of the opening section is limited to a fifth above D, with a brief descent to the C below. The middle section (the psalm verse, beginning with *Domine, probasti me*) explores a slightly higher range and centers on the Mode 4 recitation tone of A, as does the Doxology at the end (*Gloria Patri et Filio . . .*).

The Easter Gradual *Haec dies* ranges somewhat farther afield, as might be expected of the more musically elaborate genre of the Gradual. The Alleluia *Pascha nostrum* (Anthology) is even more elaborate, beginning with a tentative ascent from G to E followed by a gradual return to the starting pitch. The next unit begins high and moves downward, again ending on the finalis of Mode 7. The verse ("Pascha nostrum") begins in a relatively high range but does not at first stray very far from the recitation tone of D. With the word "immolatus," however, the music darts up into a very high range and stays there for quite some time before making a slow descent back to the finalis, G.

In theoretical terms, the pitches used in plainchant melodies do not derive from a system of successive diatonic octaves, but rather from a series of interlocking hexachords. In medieval theory, a **hexachord** is a group of six notes, all separated by whole steps except the third and fourth notes, which are separated by a half step. The individual notes of the hexachord are known by their **solmization syllables**—*ut, re, mi, fa, sol, la*—derived from the syllables and corresponding notes of the first six lines in the plainchant hymn *Ut queant laxis* (Example 1-4).

We must not think of these solmization syllables as the equivalent of our fixed pitches (such as "middle C" or "G below middle C"). Instead, the system of hexachords provided singers with a framework of pitch relationships: from *mi* to *fa* is always a half step, and it can always be found between the third and fourth pitches above *ut*, which itself was a movable pitch. Only much later did the solmization syllables come to be associated with fixed pitches in certain languages such as French, in which *ut, re, mi, fa, sol, la* are used today to indicate the pitches C, D, E, F, G, and A.

The entire range of available pitches—the **gamut**—was conceived of as a series of seven interlocking hexachords beginning on C, F, or G (Example 1-5). To help students remember this system, medieval theorists developed a mnemonic device known as the **Guidonian hand** (see the illustration on p. 29), so called because it was believed to have been developed by Guido of Arezzo, although it in fact appears in none of his surviving writings.

For a chant like *Ut queant laxis* (Example 1-4) or *Resurrexi* (the Introit for Easter Sunday, Anthology), solmization was simple, because these melodies stay within a single hexachord. But for a more elaborate chant like the Alleluia *Pascha nostrum* for Easter Sunday (Anthology), singers were required to apply a technique known as mutation,

Example 1-4 The opening of the hymn *Ut queant laxis:* the source of the solmization syllables.

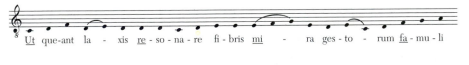

Ut que-ant la - xis re̲-so-na-re fi-bris mi - ra ges-to - rum fa̲-mu-li

tu-o - rum so̲l - ve po-pu-li la̲-bi-i re - a-tum San - cte Jo-han-nes.

That your servants may sing with deeper notes of your wondrous deeds, St. John, cleanse the guilt of unclean lips.

Example 1-5 The gamut.

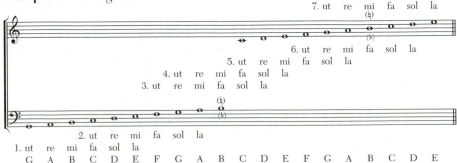

whereby a particular note within the course of a chant would function as a new syllable within an adjacent hexachord.

Rhythm

Rhythm is the most controversial issue in reconstructing medieval performance practices of plainchant. The official Vatican editions prepared by the monks of Solesmes advocate (and transmit) a style of chant in which all notes are of essentially equal value,

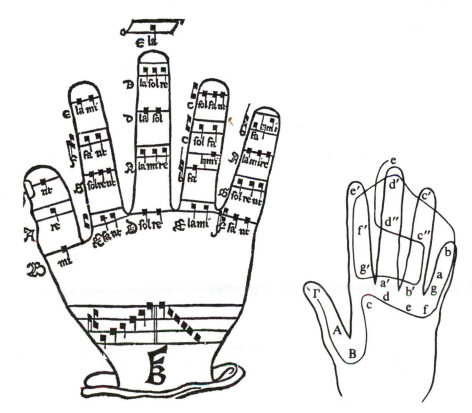

The Guidonian hand. *Attributed to Guido of Arezzo, the Guidonian hand was a mnemonic device for students learning solmization syllables and the structure of the gamut, which begins at the tip of the thumb and circles around the hand, each joint representing a particular pitch.*

Source: (Left) Colorado College Music Press. (Right). Reproduced by permission of the publisher from THE NEW HARVARD DICTIONARY OF MUSIC, edited by Don Michael Randel, p. 356, Cambridge, Mass.: The Belknap Press of Harvard University Press, © 1986 by the President and Fellows of Harvard College

The medieval monastery.
The Benedictine Abbey of Mont St. Michel, built on the coast of Normandy in northern France, reflects both the harshness and beauty of medieval monastic life. Protected from the outside world by rock, sand, and tides, it grew by accretion over many centuries. The monastery itself was founded in 708, and the oldest surviving buildings date from the period around 1000. Further construction continued off and on for another 500 years. The abbey at the very top represents both the physical and spiritual center of the monastery's daily life, the place where plainchant was recited in the eight daily services of Divine Office and the daily celebration of the Mass.

Source: Evans/Getty Images, Inc.—Hulton Archive Photos

with only slight degrees of variation—longer notes at the end of phrases, for example. But strong evidence in at least some of the earliest manuscripts and in the theoretical writings of the medieval era suggests that not all notes were performed evenly. Some scholars interpret certain markings, such as a short horizontal line over a note, to indicate a doubling of the note value. The precise meaning of such indications, however, is unknown, so the "equalist" approach has predominated in modern plainchant performances and recordings. Singers seek to project the rhythms of the words of the chants, but flexibly rather than in any systematic way.

THE EXPANSION OF PLAINCHANT

By the end of the 9th century, a core repertory of plainchant had been established for the entire liturgical year. Yet the monks and clerics of this time continued to add to the plainchant repertory by writing new music for the liturgies of newly established feast days to honor recently canonized saints. The chants of the Mass Ordinary also continued to expand after the 9th century. Because of their simplicity and everyday use, and because they had not been committed to writing, these melodies were not perceived as part of the legacy of Saint Gregory. Thus later monks and clerics felt a greater sense of freedom to add to this repertory.

But by far the most important source of new repertory after the 9th century resulted from a process known as **troping.** A **trope** is a musical or textual addition to an existing chant. The term comes from the Latin *tropus,* meaning "a turn of phrase," and is used here in the sense of embellishing or elaborating an otherwise plain statement. Tropes could be added to the beginning or end of a chant, or they could be interpolated into the chant itself.

One category of tropes added words to an existing melisma. These interpolated texts, known as *prosulae* (singular, *prosula,* from the same root as the English word "prose"), served as a kind of commentary on the original text. They also served as memory aids. In one of the earliest accounts of such a trope, Notker of St. Gall (ca. 840–912, also known as Notker Balbulus, "The Stammerer") explains that the practice arose from a need to make the chants easier to memorize. Textual troping was especially prevalent in the extended melismas of the Gradual, the Alleluia, and the Offertory, as well as those sections of the Mass Ordinary with brief texts, such as the Kyrie. The Sequence, authorized for special feast days, began life as a texted trope on the jubilus, the extended melisma at the end of the Alleluia. It eventually became a separate element of the liturgy in its own right and was cultivated with special intensity in the 10th century.

The Kyrie *Cunctipotens Genitor Deus* (Example 1-6) is a later (post-9th-century) chant that, during the 12th century, was troped with a new text. Between the two original words—the simple plea for mercy, *Kyrie eleison*—are interpolated the words *Cunctipotens Genitor Deus omni creator* ("All-powerful Father, God, creator of all things"). The troping process (with added words indicated in italics) thus leads to this:

Kyrie *Cunctipotens Genitor Deus omni creator* eleison

Lord, *All-powerful Father, God, creator of all things,* have mercy

Another kind of trope adds both words and new music to an existing chant. In one manuscript from the late 10th or 11th century, the Introit for the Mass on Easter Sunday, *Resurrexi* (Anthology), is preceded by an extended trope consisting of both words and music, with a series of similar tropes interpolated into the course of the Introit itself (Anthology). The troped text (indicated in italics here) comments on the words of the

Example 1-6 Kyrie *Cunctipotens Genitor Deus.*

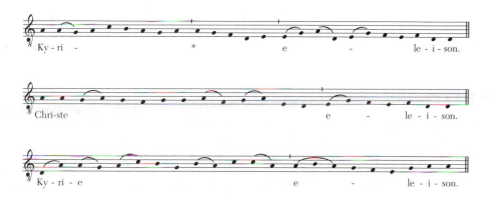

original Introit. The introductory trope sets the mood ("Rejoice and be glad . . ."), and subsequent interpolations comment on the original Introit text (in roman type), Christ's pronouncement to the visitors to his tomb on the morning of Easter Sunday ("I have risen . . .").

Gaudete et letamini quia surrexit dominus alleluia	*Rejoice and be glad, for the Lord has risen, alleluia.*
Iocundemur cum illo dicentes eia	*Let us delight in that, saying "Eia."*
Resurrexi	I have risen
Dum resurgeret in iudicio deus	*Until in judgment God would rise*
Et adhuc tecum sum alleluia.	And I am still with you, alleluia.
Contremuit terra xpisto surgente a mortuis . . .	*The earth trembled when Christ rose from the dead . . .*

This kind of troping reflects a much broader medieval phenomenon that permeated virtually every field, from theology to philosophy to astronomy to law: the desire to comment, to embellish, to gloss. Providing new commentary on an existing text was considered one of the most basic ways to advance knowledge. If enough viewpoints and arguments were taken into account, medieval thinkers reasoned, the truth of any given matter would surely come out in the end. Thus we have countless medieval manuscripts in which an original text is glossed and in which the glosses themselves become an object of still further commentary.

Certain passages in the liturgy became special favorites for troping because of their inherently dramatic nature. These passages were occasionally staged as **liturgical dramas**—dramas because the parts were represented by individuals, liturgical because the presentation was part of the service of worship.

Dramatized performances varied widely by time and location, as well as by their place in the liturgy. They are sometimes presented as tropes of the Introit at Mass, sometimes as additions to Matins. Hildegard von Bingen's *Ordo virtutum* is an example of a freely composed drama not connected with any existing chant or ritual but rather composed to texts and melodies entirely of Hildegard's own creation. The plot of this morality play—a dramatized allegory of good versus evil—centers on a series of disputes between the devil and 16 Virtues, each of which is represented by a different singer. Significantly, the devil has no music: he shouts all his lines. It would seem that hell, for Hildegard, was a world without music (see Composer Profile: Hildegard von Bingen).

Hildegard von Bingen
Ordo virtutum

By the middle of the 16th century, accretions to the repertory of liturgical plainchant—troped portions of the Ordinary, Introits, Offertories, and the like—had come to be viewed as unauthorized and corrupt. The reform-minded Council of Trent (1545–1563), reacting to the challenge of the Protestant Reformation, eliminated all troped texts and all but four Sequences from the liturgy (*Victimae paschali laudes* was one of the few to survive). For this reason, these textual tropes and most Sequences are not included in modern editions of the church's liturgical books. At least some of the melodies associated with these tropes have remained, however, like the Kyrie *Cunctipotens Genitor Deus*, whose music (without the troped words) can still be found in the *Liber usualis*.

Hymns offered yet another outlet for the creative impulses of composers working within the medieval church, who produced more than 1,000 melodies to these freely composed strophic texts. The melody of *Pange lingua gloriosi corporis mysterium*, to a text written by St. Thomas Aquinas in the 13th century for the Feast of Corpus Christi, exemplifies this repertory. It bears the melodic hallmarks of a later chant style, with a strong sense of melodic symmetry and direction.

Composers continued to write chants well into the Renaissance. No less a figure than Guillaume du Fay (see Chapter 4) composed a plainchant office in honor of the Virgin Mary as late as the 1450s. Other, less prominent composers were still writing chants in the 16th century. Chant continued to be performed in services regularly for more than 1,000 years, often in heavily modified form, including harmonized versions in the 18th and 19th centuries. Only with the Second Vatican Council of 1963–1965 did the tradition of plainchant as a vital element of the Roman Catholic liturgy come to an end.

SECULAR MONOPHONY

Plainchant had secular parallels in every European culture of the medieval era. As with plainchant, word and music were considered inseparable. Poet, composer, and singer were often one in the same person, and most of this repertory was transmitted orally long before any of it was ever committed to writing. Although the surviving sources preserve only a single line of music for any given work, images and written accounts suggest that these songs could also be accompanied by one or more instruments.

Songs in Latin

Songs in Latin passed easily across linguistic boundaries. The most famous collection of this kind is the *Carmina Burana*—"Songs of Benediktbeuern"—a name given in the 19th century in honor of the Benedictine monastery in Bavaria where the manuscript containing these songs was housed for many years. (Carl Orff's 1937 oratorio *Carmina Burana* is a more recent setting of 25 of the more than 200 texts in the collection.) The original manuscript, compiled in the late 13th century, is notorious for its songs about gambling, drinking, and erotic love. It also includes songs that satirize the moral teachings of the church and point out the shortcomings of priests and monks.

Such texts would have had great appeal to the wandering minstrels who went from town to town and court to court providing entertainment to any and all who would pay for it. One such group called itself the Order of the Goliards, after a nonexistent patron Golias (Goliath). They owed their allegiance to no particular court but earned their living by performing on the road. Other minstrels did more than sing: they juggled, danced, and performed acrobatic feats and magic tricks.

France

In contrast to plainchant, those who created and performed secular song put a premium on novelty. The **troubadours** (in southern France) and **trouvères** (in northern France) derive their names from the same root as the modern French *trouver* ("to find"). These poet-composer-performers "found"—or as we would say today, created—new texts and melodies alike. The trouvères wrote in medieval French, the troubadours in Occitan (also known as Provençal), a different Romance language related to both French and Spanish.

The troubadours and trouvères were at their most active in the 12th and 13th centuries. Their repertories included love songs, laments, pastorals, and dialogues. The

Composer Profile

Hildegard von Bingen
(1098–1179)

We can securely attribute more compositions to Hildegard von Bingen than to any other musician, male or female, who worked before the early 14th century. In spite of her impressive output, Hildegard did not consider herself a professional composer or musician. Born into a noble family in what is now western Germany, she entered a Benedictine convent at the age of 7 and took vows when she was 16. In her early 30s she began to experience visions and revelations, which she recorded in a series of books. Hildegard was the first woman to receive explicit permission from a pope to write on theology. She also wrote on such diverse subjects as medicine, plants, and lives of the saints, all while directing the life of a thriving convent as its abbess.

In a letter of protest to the prelates of Mainz, who as punishment for an offense forbade her nuns from celebrating the Divine Office with music, Hildegard writes an eloquent defense:

> In obedience to you we have until now given up the singing of the Divine Office, celebrating it only by quiet reading—and I heard a voice coming from the living light, telling of those various kinds of praise concerning which David speaks in the Psalms: "Praise him with the sound of the trumpet, praise him with the psaltery and the cithara, praise him with the tympanum and the chorus, praise him with strings and the organ, praise him with the well-sounding cymbals, praise him with the cymbals of jubilation. Let every spirit praise the Lord" [Psalm 150: 3–6]. In these words we are taught about inward concerns by external objects, how according to the makeup of material things (the properties of musical instruments) we ought best to convert and to refashion the workings of our interior man to the praise of the Creator . . .
>
> Thus it is just that God be praised in everything. And since man sighs and moans with considerable frequency upon hearing some song, as he recalls in his soul the quality of celestial harmony, the prophet David, considering with understanding the nature of what is spiritual (because the soul is harmonious) exhorts us in the psalm, "Let us confess the Lord on the cithara, let us play to him on the psaltery of ten strings" [Psalm 32:1], intending that the cithara, which sounds from below, pertains to the discipline of the body; that the psaltery, which sounds from above, pertains to the striving of the spirit; and that the ten strings refer to the contemplation of the Law. Thus they who without the weight of sure reason impose silence upon a church in the matter of songs in praise of God, and thereby unjustly deprive God of the honor of his praise on earth, will be deprived themselves of the participation in the angelic praises heard in Heaven, unless they make amends by true regret and humble penitence.[2]

Church officials eventually relented.

Principal Works

Hildegard herself organized her compositions into two large collections: the *Symphonia armonie celestium revelationum* ("Symphony of the Harmony of Celestial Revelations") and the *Ordo virtutum* ("Play of the Virtues"). The *Symphonia armonie* is a cycle of

relationship between noblemen and noblewomen in the texts of these songs is consistently governed by the elaborate etiquette of courtly love, which called for the woman to be idolized and praised from afar. Most of these works, regardless of subject matter, are strophic, both musically and textually. The longest form is the *chanson de geste* (literally, a "song of deed"), an epic account of chivalrous accomplishments. The popular *Chanson de Roland,* from the second half of the 11th century, for example, recounts the heroic adventures of one of Charlemagne's knights. This lengthy poem of more than 4,000 lines could be recited by a singer according to a formulaic pattern not unlike that of the psalm tones. Performers were expected to embellish and improvise on this basic pattern; as a result, individual songs transmitted in more than one source often show significant variants. Unlike plainchant, secular songs were not considered gifts of the Holy Spirit and were not regarded as objects of veneration. Stylistically, though, this repertory is not

liturgical works partly for the Mass (an Alleluia, a Kyrie, and seven Sequences) but mostly for the Office (43 antiphons, 18 responsory chants, 3 hymns, and 4 devotional songs). The *Ordo virtutum* is a morality play consisting of 82 monophonic songs that depict a struggle between the devil and the 16 Virtues (Charity, Obedience, Humility, Chastity, and so on). The settings of the poetry are predominantly syllabic; the cycle may have been performed in connection with the services of the Office.

KEY DATES IN THE LIFE OF HILDEGARD VON BINGEN

1098 Born in Bermersheim near Worms (now western Germany)

1106 Enters a Benedictine convent

1136 Becomes prioress of the abbey of St. Disibod in Diessenberg

1147 Establishes a new convent on the Rupertsberg, within the bishopric of Mainz

1152 Finishes her decade-long work on *Scivias* ("Know the Ways"), a manuscript that records and interprets her visions

1179 Dies on 17 September at her convent in Rupertsberg near Bingen (western Germany)

Hildegard von Bingen. *This image comes from a 12th-century manuscript copy of Hildegard's* Book of Divine Works, *a series of ten visions describing in mystical terms the relationship of humankind to the natural order of the universe. Looking toward heaven, Hildegard receives divine inspiration and writes on a tablet. The similarity to images of Saint Gregory receiving the plainchant from the Holy Spirit is striking (see p. 20).*

Source: Oggetto: Hildegard von Bingen (Codex Lucca 1942). MS. 1942 (c. 1v port). Lucca, Biblioteca Statale, su concessione del Ministero per i Beni e le Attività Culturali

unlike plainchant in its melodic structure: text settings are primarily syllabic and only occasionally melismatic. The rhythmic interpretation of the notated songs remains a particular matter of debate among modern-day scholars. As in the case of chant, most performers today prefer a flexible approach that allows the words to be declaimed in a fluid, natural manner.

Although some troubadours and trouvères were of noble birth, most were not, and these tended to be an itinerant lot. One of the most famous and prolific of all troubadours, Bernart de Ventadorn (ca. 1140–ca. 1190), was banished from two different courts for becoming too emotionally attached to the ladies of those courts; he spent the last years of his life in a monastery. Forbidden love also seems to have shaped the life of the Countess Beatriz de Dia (d. ca. 1212), whose *A chantar m'er de so*, in Occitan, may well be autobiographical. It is a moving lament written from a woman's perspective.

Beatriz de Dia
A chantar

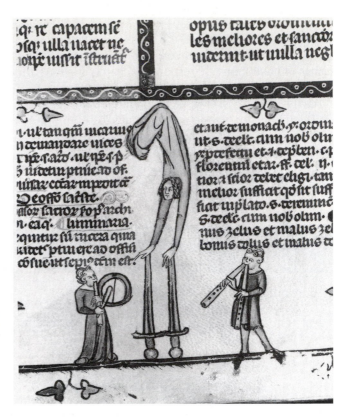

Music and social status.   *For many centuries, wind and per-cussion instruments were more closely associated with outdoor activities and the lower classes than were stringed instruments. The musicians shown here belong to the social class of acro-bats, actors, and* jongleurs *whose skills were widely enjoyed in the medieval era but whose personal status in society was quite low. The double flute on the right is an indirect descendant of the ancient Greek aulos; the pipe and tabor were typically played by a single instrumentalist who fingered the pipe with one hand and beat the drum with the other.*

Source: By permission of The British Library/Royal MS. 10. E. IV. fol. 58

According to an account written about a century after Beatriz's death, she was married to Guillaume, Count of Poitiers, but fell in love with a certain Raimbaut d'Orange, who was also a troubadour. She "made about him many good and beautiful songs," according to this source. Only one of Beatriz's poems—*A chantar*—has survived with music, but she almost certainly wrote music to other of her poems as well. The music moves within a relatively narrow ambitus, but its steady rise and fall, culminating in a climb to the melody's highest pitch in the penultimate line, imparts a sense of intense emotion to the words.

The Iberian Peninsula

Cantigas de Santa Maria, no. 140:
A Santa Maria dadas

The preserved repertory of *cantigas* ("songs") from the Iberian peninsula—present-day Spain and Portugal—is quite small. Only two sources transmit the poetry with melodies. One is a set of six songs by Martin Codax, an otherwise obscure composer working around 1230 in what is now northwestern Spain. The other source is a large and sump-tuously illustrated manuscript containing more than 400 *Cantigas de Santa Maria*, songs in honor of the Virgin Mary, prepared for (and possibly composed in part by) Alfonso el Sabio ("The Wise"), king of Castille and Leon from 1252 until 1284. Although sacred in subject matter, these songs were not liturgical. Their poetic and musical style, moreover, is consistent with what we know of the secular songs that were written in this place and time. The texts of the *cantigas* are written in Gallo-Portuguese, and most are set syllabi-cally in strophic form with a refrain.

Scholars have debated the extent of Arabic influence on the music of this repertory. Large portions of the Iberian peninsula had been under Muslim rule since the 8th century, and the impact of this culture on Spain and Portugal extended to virtually every aspect of life.

Germany

In German-speaking lands, the ***Minnesinger*** (literally, a singer of *Minne,* or courtly love) developed their own repertory of songs. The most famous of these poet-composer-performers were Tannhäuser (ca. 1230–1280), the central character in Wagner's 19th-century opera of the same name; Walther von der Vogelweide (ca. 1170–1230); and Wolfram von Eschenbach (1170–1220), author of the epic *Parzifal.* Chivalry, the praise of God, and the praise of noblewomen are recurrent themes in their songs. Many *Minnelieder* (*Lieder* means "songs") are written in **bar form** (AAB).

Walther von der Vogelweide's *Palästinalied* provides a good example of this repertory. In bar form and largely syllabic, it tells of a crusader knight's thrill at standing on the same ground as Christ had during his lifetime. (The First Crusade had captured Jerusalem, permitting Christians to make pilgrimages to the holy city.) Like the songs of the troubadours and trouvères, the Minnelieder were almost certainly performed to the accompaniment of instruments, but no notated source of this accompaniment has been preserved.

Walther von der Vogelweide *Palästinalied*

CONCLUSION

By the time the repertories of secular monophony reached their peak in the 11th and 12th century, polyphony had already established itself in the realms of both the sacred and secular. The repertory of liturgical plainchant would continue as an integral element of the Christian liturgy for many centuries, supplemented by newer works for multiple voices. Secular monophony, however, would gradually be supplanted by polyphonic genres by the end of the 14th century.

Polyphony to 1300

The gradual emergence of polyphony sometime around the 8th or 9th century is one of the most important stylistic developments in the history of music. The simultaneous juxtaposition of contrasting voices opened entirely new dimensions for composers, allowing them to move beyond the single line of plainchant to explore sonorities of two or more voices. Counterpoint, harmony, and texture became standard elements of Western music.

No one knows exactly when polyphony first began to be cultivated. The earliest notated sources date from the latter part of the 9th century, although it seems almost certain that this kind of texture was already in use in at least some areas before this time. As in the case of plainchant, practice preceded notation. But clearly the same drives that led to the monophonic troping of plainchants helped foster polyphony as well.

ORGANUM

The earliest known polyphonic compositions were based on existing plainchants and thus we can think of them, in effect, as vertical tropes. The original "text"—the combined words and melody of the chant—remained intact but was now elaborated and amplified through the addition of a new voice or voices layered on top of the chant.

The first preserved reference to polyphony in medieval times appears in a manuscript treatise known as the *Musica enchiriadis* ("Musical Handbook"), written during the middle or second half of the 9th century by an unknown author or authors, possibly in what is now eastern France. This instructional manual includes examples of what we now call **organum** (plural, **organa**), a polyphonic work consisting of an original plainchant melody in one voice along with at least one additional voice above or below. (The exact origin of the term *organum* is unclear: the word means "instrument" in Latin and could be applied to any instrument, although it later came to be associated specifically with the organ.) The *Musica enchiriadis* offers several examples of **parallel organum,** in which an additional voice runs parallel to an established plainchant melody at

Example 2-1 Parallel organum.
The solid notes indicate the principal voice; the hollow notes indicate the organal voice.

Tu   Pa - tris   sem - pi - ter - nus   es   fi - li - us.

You are the eternal son of the Father.

Source: *Te Deum*, phrase in parallel fifths, from *Musica Enchiriadis*. Text edition by Hans Schmid, *Musica et Scolica Enchiriadis*, Veröffentlichungen der Musikhistorisches Kommission, vol. 3 (Munich: Bayerische Akademie der Wissenschaften, 1981). Used by permission of the publisher.

Example 2-2 Four-part parallel organum.
The solid notes indicate the principal voice; the hollow notes indicate the organal voice.

Sit   glo - ri - a   Do - mi - ni   in   sae - cu - la;

May the glory of the Lord last forever.

Source: Four-part parallel polyphony from *Musica Enchiriadis*. Text edition by Hans Schmid, *Musica et Scolica Enchiriadis*, Veröffentlichungen der Musikhistorisches Kommission, vol. 3 (Munich: Bayerische Akademie der Wissenschaften, 1981). Used by permission of the publisher.

a constant interval. The plainchant melody is called the *vox principalis* (principal voice); the additional voice is called the *vox organalis* (the organal, or added, voice). In the simplest parallel organum, a single organal voice runs a fourth or fifth below the principal voice (Example 2-1). Other examples include four voices, with the principal voice doubled an octave down and the organal voice doubled an octave up (Example 2-2).

Not all organum in the *Musica enchiriadis* is so mechanical. In some cases (Example 2-3), the *vox organalis* begins on the same pitch as the *vox principalis* but remains fixed until the plainchant melody has climbed to the interval of a fourth above, returning to a unison at the ends of phrases. The second phrase of Example 2-3 is particularly interesting because it has more intervallic variety than the first, with two thirds and one fifth alongside the fourths.

Innovations in Organum

In later sources, more elaborate organum like that in the second phrase of Example 2-3 becomes increasingly common, a trend that coincides with the growing prominence of organum within the liturgy for certain feast days in some regions. This more intricate style characterizes many Alleluias, Sequences, Tracts, and responsary chants from the Divine Office in the Winchester Troper, compiled at Winchester Cathedral, England, sometime around 1000.

Another important stylistic innovation in organum appears in *Ad organum faciendum* ("On the Making of Organum"), a treatise written around 1100. Here, the *vox organalis* is placed above the *vox principalis*. This relationship—plainchant below, added voice above—would soon become standard. Around this same time, contrary

Example 2-3 Two-part organum.
The solid notes indicate the principal voice; the hollow notes indicate the organal voice.

| | | | | | | | | | | | | | |
Rex   cae - li,   Do - mi - ne,   ma - ris   un - di - so - ni,
Ti - ta - nis   ni - ti - di   squa - li - di - que   so - li.

O Lord, King of Heaven, and of the sounding sea,
Of the shining sun and the dark earth.

Te   hu - mi - les   fa - mu - li,   mo - du - lis   ve - ne - ran - do   pi - is,
Su   iu - be - as   fla - gi - tant   va - ri - is   li - be - ra - re   ma - lis.

Your humble servants worship you in sacred songs,
And urge you to agree to free them from all their evils.

Source: *Rex Caeli,* two-part polyphony, from *Musica Enchiriadis.* Text edition by Hans Schmid, *Musica et Scolica Enchiriadis,* Veröffentlichungen der Musikhistorisches Kommission, vol. 3 (Munich: Bayerische Akademie der Wissenschaften, 1981). Used by permission of the publisher.

Example 2-4 Organum in contrary motion.

[vox organalis]

Lau - da - te   Do - mi - ne   de _____ coe - lis.

[vox principalis]

Praise God in Heaven.

Source: *Laudate Domine de coelis,* two-part polyphony [with contrary motion] by John, from *Hucbald, Guido, and John on Music; Three Medieval Treatises,* transl. Warren Babb, ed. Claude Palisca (New Haven: Yale University Press, 1978), p. 161. Copyright Yale University Press, 1978. Used by permission of the publisher.

motion between voices begins to be preferred over parallel motion. One 12th-century writer (formerly known as John Cotton, now simply as John) recommended that "whenever there is an ascent in the original melody"—that is, in the chant—there should be "at that point a descent in the organal part and vice versa."[1] He illustrates this principle with the brief but striking passage shown in Example 2-4.

This innovation transformed the organal voice from a derivative of the original—running parallel to it at the interval of a fourth, a fifth, or an octave—into a distinctive and independent line of its own. Organum thus includes the earliest known instances of *counterpoint,* the simultaneous combination of independent musical lines. Contrapuntal texture allowed for the vertical expansion of sound through multiple voices of essentially equal weight. It also prompted medieval theorists to reevaluate what intervals might or might not be considered consonant. Octaves, fifths, and fourths had long been considered "perfect" intervals within the Pythagorean system because they could be expressed as mathematically simple ratios: octave = 2:1; fifth = 3:2; fourth = 4:3. Thirds and sixths

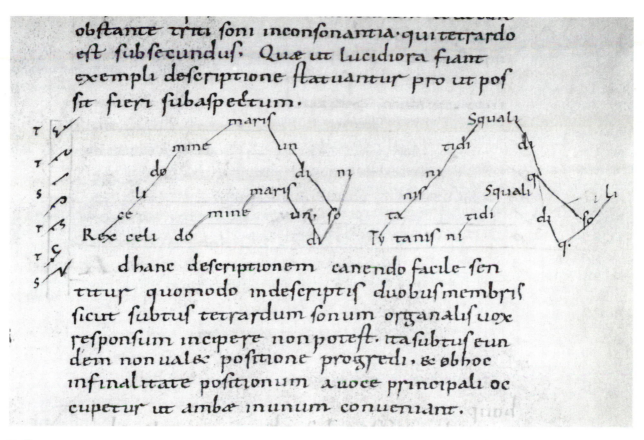

Early organum.   *It is no coincidence that one of the earliest sources of polyphony, the treatise entitled* Musica enchiriadis, *should also be one of the first to indicate fixed, unambiguously identifiable pitches. At this early stage of notation, the scribe of the* Musica enchiriadis *has not attempted to give any rhythmic signs beyond the words of the chant being sung, but the pitches are indicated quite precisely through the daseian signs in the margin at the left. Adapted from grammatical accent marks in ancient Greek, each of these corresponds to a specific pitch; the passage shown here is transcribed in Example 2-3.*

Source: Staatsbibliothek Bamberg/Msc. Var 1. fol. 57r

F O C U S

St. Martial

One of the most important centers for the production and collection of medieval chant and early polyphony was the Abbey of St. Martial de Limoges, in the region in south-central France known as Aquitaine. Like every abbey of any size, it had its own *scriptorium,* a scribal workshop in which monks with special calligraphic skills would copy old manuscripts and prepare new ones. The repertory of chant manuscripts using Aquitanian neumes is considerable. The librarians of St. Martial, moreover, seem to have gone out of their way to acquire manuscripts from smaller institutions, amassing one of the most impressive libraries of chant manuscripts in late medieval Europe. St. Martial was for the most part spared the ravages of war that damaged or destroyed so many of the monasteries in northern France. But like many French monasteries, it was closed in the wake of the French Revolution and demolished shortly afterward, in 1792. Fortunately, its manuscripts had been sold to the French royal library in 1730, and scholars today can consult this remarkable collection in the National Library of France, in Paris.

were deemed "imperfect consonances," although some writers were reluctant to accept various forms of these intervals, particularly the major and minor sixth. Important cadences always resolved to fifths, octaves, or unisons.

Yet another step in the development of organum was the introduction of multiple notes in the *vox organalis* over a single note in the chant. The resulting **melismatic organum** allowed for a much wider use of dissonance between the organal voice and the chant. This type of organum is particularly prevalent in manuscripts from northern Spain and from southwestern France, particularly the abbey of St. Martial (see Focus: St. Martial). The two-part organum on the plainchant Kyrie *Cunctipotens genitor deus* illustrates this new style of melismatic organum (for the original plainchant version, see Anthology). This particular organum comes from the Codex Calixtinus, a text written around 1120 to 1130 as a guide and songbook for pilgrims on their way to Santiago da Compostela in northwestern Spain, the site of the shrine of Saint James the Apostle.

An important effect of melismatic organum was to force performers to slow the pace of the chant melody in the lower voice to allow time for those singing the organal line to get in all their notes. As a result, the lower voice came to be designated the **tenor,** from the Latin *tenere,* meaning "to hold." For several more centuries at least, the term *tenor* would refer to the voice of a polyphonic work that "held" the chant; until the middle of the 15th century, this was usually the lowest voice. Only later did it become associated with a particular range. The added second voice in organum and later forms of polyphony came to be known as the **duplum.**

Kyrie
Cunctipotens
genitor deus

Notre Dame Organum

The most elaborate forms of organum appeared from a circle of largely anonymous composers working in and around the Cathedral of Notre Dame in Paris in the 12th century. Although a church had existed on this site for some time before, builders laid the cornerstone of the magnificent structure we now know as Notre Dame in 1163, and it was at just about this same time that a composer identified only as Léonin (or Leoninus, in the Latinized form) began to write large quantities of organa for the chants of the liturgical year. Although other contemporary composers were undoubtedly involved in this process, we may take Léonin as the prototypical composer of what is now called Notre Dame organum.

Léonin and his colleagues turned their attention primarily to the responsorial chants—that is, those plainchants performed in part by a soloist (or small group of soloists singing in unison), to which a chorus responds. Léonin left unchanged the choral portions of these chants, which continued to be performed monophonically by the chorus, but he wrote lengthy two-voice organa for those portions of the chants performed by the soloists. His organum setting of the Easter plainchant Gradual *Haec dies* (Anthology) may be diagrammed as follows:

	Respond		**Verse**	
Soloists	**Chorus**		**Soloists**	**Chorus**
Two-part organum	Plainchant		Two-part organum	Plainchant
Haec dies	*quam fecit Dominus . . .*		*Confitemini Domino . . .*	*misericordia ejus.*

Léonin's organal sections are either in **free organum** (also known as **unmeasured organum**) or in **measured organum** (also known as **discant organum**). In free organum, the duplum voice moves rapidly against the slower moving notes of the original chant. It was used in passages that in the original chant are neumatic, as on the opening words *Haec dies*. In measured organum, the two voices move at about the same speed in what is essentially a note-against-note style. This type of organum was used in passages that are melismatic in the original chant, such as on the word *Domino*, and, toward the end, on the words *in saeculum*.

Measured organum required a new kind of notation, one that could show the temporal relationship of the various voices. This new system of **rhythmic modes** allowed composers to distinguish between long and short notes in various combinations. Each of the six medieval rhythmic modes corresponds to a poetic meter, as follows:

Léonin (?)
Organum *Haec dies*

Mode	Poetic meter	Modern notation	Mode	Poetic meter	Modern notation
1	Trochaic	♩ ♪	4	Anapestic	♪♪ ♩.
2	Iambic	♪ ♩	5	Spondaic	♩. ♩.
3	Dactylic	♩. ♪♩	6	Tribrachic	♩ ♩ ♩

To notate these modes, composers used a system of **ligatures** adopted from traditional chant notation. Ligatures are neumes or notes combined in groupings of two, three, or four. But what had formerly been used merely to indicate pitch now took on rhythmic significance as well. Any given voice tended to stay within a single rhythmic mode for a fairly long period of time; composers rarely switched from one rhythmic mode to another in quick succession. It was standard practice, however, to set different voices in contrasting rhythmic modes at the same time. Tenors, for example, frequently adhere to the fifth rhythmic mode under an upper voice or voices moving in the first, second, or third modes.

Once these basic principles of composition and notation had been established, composers were able to add still further layers of musical commentary to their original glosses on a given chant. The composer known only as Perotin (Perotinus), a younger contemporary of Léonin, is credited with having added a third voice (**triplum**) and on rare occasions even a fourth voice (**quadruplum**) to organa for feasts of special significance. These are works of astonishing length. Even in a fairly lively performance, Perotin's four-voice organum for the Gradual *Sederunt* (for the Feast of St. Stephen, the day after Christmas) runs to almost 20 minutes.

Within a fairly short span of time over the course of the late 12th century, the composers working in and around the Cathedral of Notre Dame in Paris had assembled a sizable collection of polyphony for use throughout the liturgical year. This collection—a polyphonic counterpart to the chantbooks that had been in use for so long—came to be known as the *Magnus liber organi* ("The Great Book of Organum"). Although the earliest version (or perhaps versions) of this compilation have been lost, large portions of it were widely distributed throughout Europe, and those that have survived transmit a sizable repertory of two-, three-, and four-part organa.

CLAUSULA

The drive to gloss did not end with the composition of organum, not even for three and four voices. Composers like Perotin also composed many **clausulae**—brief polyphonic sections of discant organum—that could be substituted at will into the appropriate section of a larger existing work of organum. The **clausula** (to use its singular form) is thus not an independent composition that can be performed on its own. The tenor voice of a typical clausula in fact often consists of only a single word or even just a syllable or two of a longer word.

A single source typically provides clausulae for several different passages within the same organum, and even multiple clausulae for the same passage. The Florence manuscript of the *Magnus liber organi*, for example, contains no fewer than ten different clausulae for the passage on the words *in saeculum* (or *seculum*) within the Gradual *Haec* (or *Hec*) *dies*. In performing organum, singers were free to substitute whichever clausula or clausulae they desired in any combination. Alternatively, they could use no clausulae at all. From a liturgical point of view, what is important here is that regardless of the combination of clausulae chosen, all the notes and words of the original chant would be present in one form or another. The impetus for these works, it would seem, lay in the desire to write new music and to provide a layer of commentary above the plainchant. And stylistically, clausulae are no different from the music they were written to replace.

Clausula
In saeculum

MOTET

Although clausulae may have been fragmentary from a liturgical point of view, consisting of only a few syllables or words, the longer ones constituted a musical whole that began and ended in the same mode; the very word *clausula* itself comes from a Latin root meaning "to cadence" or "conclude." The only thing clausulae lacked to be performed separately was a text.

In the venerable medieval tradition of troping, some unknown individual or group of individuals working in the late 12th or early 13th century had the idea of underlaying a new text to the duplum of an existing clausula and performing the new work outside the liturgy of the church. Thus was born the genre of the **motet** (from the French word *mot*, meaning "word"). The term was fitting because the text for the duplum in many of the earliest motets was in the vernacular, not Latin. It is the presence of a contrasting text in the upper voice or voices that distinguishes the motet from its immediate ancestor, the clausula. The texted duplum was known as the **motetus** because it had words.

Musically, there are only minor differences between the clausula on *In seculum* just discussed and the motet *Lonc tens ai mon cuer / In seculum* found in a mid-13th-century manuscript. (By convention, the titles of 13th-century motets consist of the first word or words of each voice in order from top to bottom.) The text for the motetus—a love song—is decidedly secular. The introduction of secular words into what had previously been a sacred work is something found repeatedly in the repertory of medieval motets.

Motet
Lonc tens ai mon cuer / In seculum

Separated from its liturgical context, the tenor of a motet was no longer a sacred object—a portion of a larger plainchant—and composers were quick to take advantage of this fact. They began to manipulate the musical content of the tenor in various ways. In one version of the opening of the motet *Huic main / Hec dies*, for example, the anonymous composer uses the first eight notes of the chant in a conventional fashion but then breaks off, repeating these eight notes not once but twice. (The score in the anthology shows both this version and an alternate version from a different source.) The notes of the chant resume with the words *De fine amour . . .* but the opening eight notes come back one more time at the very end, to the words *moi n'a toucherés*. Although derived from a chant,

Motet
Huic main / Hec dies

this tenor has clearly lost not only its liturgical function but also its original musical shape, serving instead as the point of departure for an essentially new composition.

Other 13th-century motets bear no relationship at all to any preexistent work. The anonymous *A Paris / On parole / Frese nouvele* is based on a newly composed tenor with its own self-contained (if very brief) text in French. The tenor states its eight-measure unit of text and music a total of four times. At least one of the two upper voices, in turn, overlaps the cadential points of the tenor, thus creating a sense of forward momentum even while articulating points of rest within the three-voice texture. The text of the tenor—*Frese nouvele, muere france* ("Fresh strawberries! Nice blackberries!")—is a street vendor's call, the 13th-century equivalent of a peanut vendor's cry in a baseball stadium. As such, it justifies both the musical and textual repetition it receives here. The multiple repetition of rhythmic and melodic ideas would in fact become a central feature of *isorhythm*, a structural device found in many motets in the 14th century (see Chapter 3).

Motet
A Paris / On parole / Frese nouvele

The motetus and triplum of this same motet present two texts different from each other and different yet again from the tenor. The resulting **polytextual motet** is typical of the genre in the second half of the 13th century. The three texts of *A Paris / On parole / Frese nouvele* are all related in content. Above the street vendor's cry in the tenor, the triplum and duplum extol the virtues of Paris: good bread, good wine, good friends, even good prices to "to suit a poor man's purse." The texts of many other 13th-century motets are more diverse; some are even polyglot, with a motetus in Latin and a triplum in French, or vice versa. Subject matter is often equally unrelated.

By about 1230, motets had become so popular that no one seems to have been particularly interested in writing clausulae anymore. We are not altogether sure just who performed motets and under what circumstances. Given the nature of the sources and their notational sophistication, it seems most likely that they were sung by the same clerics who cultivated plainchant and organum. Johannes de Grocheo, a theorist writing around 1300, observed that a motet "ought not to be performed in the presence of common people, for they would not perceive its subtlety, nor take pleasure in its sound." Instead, motets should be performed only "in the presence of learned persons and those who seek after subtleties in art."

We also lack firm evidence on how these works were performed. The absence of any substantial quantity of text in most of the tenors has led some scholars to speculate that the tenor line may have been performed on instruments. But it seems equally plausible that this part could have been **vocalized**—that is, sung to a vowel sound, without a text. Another possibility of performance would have been to have instruments double the tenor line.

CONDUCTUS

The **conductus** (plural, **conductus** or **conducti**) offered yet another outlet for composers wishing to write either monophonic or polyphonic music in the late 12th and early 13th centuries. These works, for one, two, three, or occasionally four voices, are not based on borrowed material of any kind. The texts consist of freely composed poems written in metered verse that lend themselves to syllabic and strongly metrical musical settings. In the polyphonic conductus, unlike other medieval polyphonic forms, all voices move in roughly the same rhythm. The note-against-note part writing in this genre is so distinctive in fact that this manner of composition in medieval music has since come to be called *conductus style*.

Rhythmically, the notation of these pieces is ambiguous. They do not follow the system of modal rhythm evident in the measured sections of organum, clausula, and motet, but probably adhere to the modal rhythm of the texts themselves. Most sources align the

Conductus
Flos ut rosa floruit

voices with some care, using vertical lines to clarify the relationship of the different parts. The long melisma at the end of the last strophe of *Flos ut rosa floruit* is a characteristic feature of the genre known as a **cauda,** a term derived from the Latin word for "tail," the same root word from which *coda* would eventually evolve.

Conducti derive their name from the Latin word *conducere,* meaning "to escort," and these pieces were probably first used as processionals—that is, as music to be performed while a priest and his attendants entered and left the church. The conductus repertory is sizable: about 200 polyphonic works of this kind are found side by side with the organa and clausulae in the various manuscripts associated with the *Magnus liber organi.* Another, separate repertory of conducti survives in manuscripts from southwestern France and the Iberian peninsula. The writing of conductus continued in Germany and England into the second half of the 13th century but had largely ceased by the beginning of the 14th.

Gothic heights. *The interior of the Cathedral at Amiens, in northern France, is three times as high (43 meters, or about 142 feet) as it is wide. Begun in 1220, this masterpiece of Gothic architecture reflects certain parallels to the rhythmic strata of motets in this era: a wide base (comparable to a slow-moving tenor), with a smaller series of arches in the middle (the faster moving duplum), and a series of still smaller arches at the top, just below the vaulted ceiling (the triplum). Although such parallels are in one sense superficial, they correspond in a deeper way to the medieval penchant for variety and contrast within layered structures.*

Source: Art Resource, N.Y.

MENSURAL NOTATION

By the middle of the 13th century, the notational system using ligature groupings to indicate rhythmic modes could no longer accommodate the increasing rhythmic variety of the latest motets. In response, a new, more precise system emerged. The writer most widely credited with setting down the principles of this system—known as **mensural notation** (from the Latin *mensurata*, meaning "measured," in the sense of a division into units)—was Franco of Cologne. In his *Ars cantus mensurabilis* ("The Art of Measurable Song"), written sometime around 1280, Franco codified a system that retained the note shapes and many of the conventions of the rhythmic modes but that introduced one important modification in particular: Franco's system assigned specific rhythmic meanings to each of the various note shapes. The significance of this innovation can scarcely be underestimated, for it provided composers with a system capable of vastly greater flexibility, one that is essentially still in place today in spite of many subsequent modifications.

In the earliest variety of mensural notation, now known as **Franconian notation,** the main note values were the **long,** the **breve,** and the **semibreve.** The breve took its name from the Latin word for "brief," for this described its relationship to the long. In modern editions, the long is usually transcribed as a dotted half note or half note, depending on the context, and the breve as a quarter note.

Each of these notes could be divided into smaller units of two or three. Triple divisions, which Franco associated with the perfection of the Holy Trinity (God the Father, God the Son, God the Holy Spirit), were considered perfect. Duple divisions, in turn, were considered imperfect. The basic unit of measurement was the *tempus* ("time"; plural, *tempora*) and was associated with the duration of the breve. Perfect division of the long resulted in three breves of equal duration—three tempora, that is—but imperfect division resulted in two notes of unequal value, the first of which was known as an "altered" breve and consisted of a duration of two tempora. The breve, in turn, could be divided into three equal semibreves (perfect) or two unequal breves (imperfect), transcribed in modern notation as a half note followed by a quarter note. Seemingly complicated, the system was in fact perfectly suited to the music it represents, for it provided a smooth and supple sense of rhythm and syncopation that avoids the accented downbeat implicit in the concept of the bar line.

Franco's system did not gain immediate acceptance, but by the end of the 13th century his principles were in widespread use. Around 1280, Petrus de Cruce (Pierre de la Croix), a French composer and theorist, refined the Franconian system to allow for greater subdivision of the breve. **Petronian notation** allowed for as many as nine semibreves within the duration of a single breve, accommodating the increasingly rapid movement of motet tripla. (Motets notated in this new fashion, which typically feature a very rapidly moving triplum, are sometimes called Petronian motets.) The basic pulse of the music, in turn, shifted from the breve to the shorter semibreve. Petrus also introduced the **minim** and **semiminim,** so named because of their very short—minimal—duration. A minim could be either a third or half the duration of semibreve, but a semiminim was always equal to half a minim, never a third.

CONCLUSION

By the end of the 13th century, polyphony and a comprehensive system of notation were well established. A considerable repertory of organum, motets, and conductus enjoyed wide distribution throughout Europe. Within a few decades, however, this music would soon be regarded as an *ars antiqua*—an "old" art—that would give way to the *ars nova*—the "new art" of the 14th century.

Music in the 14th Century

Until the middle or end of the 13th century, the prevailing musical style of western Europe was essentially international. No distinctively regional styles of composition existed. Indeed, the organa, motets, and conductus emanating from Paris, as we have seen, were copied and distributed throughout the continent and even across the English Channel.

In the 14th century, by contrast, important regional differences began to emerge. Vernacular poetry—that is, poetry written in the native language of the poet, be it English, French, Spanish, or Italian—replaced Latin poetry in importance, and composers responded in kind, setting to music more and more texts written in their own tongue. Composers themselves became more prominent and less anonymous, actively connecting their names with their works with far greater frequency than in previous centuries.

FRANCE: THE *ARS NOVA*

In France, there was a growing sense that music had entered a new era in the early decades of the 14th century. Composers self-consciously called what they were doing the ***ars nova,*** or "new art." This term, which has become a label for much of 14th-century French music in general, is the title of a treatise written around 1320 and attributed to the theorist-composer Philippe de Vitry (1291–1361). At about the same time, Johannes de Muris (ca. 1300–1350) wrote his *Ars novae musicae* ("The New Art of Music"). Pope John XXII, unhappily acknowledging the influence of the *ars nova,* condemned it as decadent and dangerous in a papal bull in 1324–1325 (see Primary Evidence: The Pope Condemns the *Ars nova* on page 52). The theorist Jacques de Liège (ca. 1260–after 1330), in his *Speculum musicae* ("The Mirror of Music," 1330), also criticized the new practices.

What was this new art? Its chief characteristic was enhanced rhythmic flexibility. Much of Philippe de Vitry's treatise *Ars nova* is in fact devoted to issues of rhythmic notation, including the increased use of the minim and semiminim, the legitimization of duple meter as fully equal to triple, imperfection by notes of more remote values instead of by notes of the next shorter value, and the use of red ink to make otherwise perfect rhythmic values imperfect.

Vitry also played an important role in codifying the use of **mensuration signs.** These signs indicated whether the subdivision of breves and semibreves should be understood as perfect or imperfect. Two temporal relationships are relevant here: the *tempus* and the *prolatio*.

♦ The *tempus* is the relationship of the breve to the semibreve. When perfect, there are three semibreves to each breve; when imperfect there are two.

♦ The *prolatio* is the relationship of the semibreve to the minim. When perfect ("major"), there are three minims to each semibreve; when imperfect ("minor") there are two.

There are thus four possible combinations of perfect and imperfect *tempus* and *prolatio*. Each of the four basic mensuration signs indicates one of these four combinations, as Example 3-1 summarizes.

Example 3-1 Mensuration signs.

The system codified by Philippe de Vitry increased the clarity and flexibility of mensural notation. With only minor modifications, this system would stay in effect throughout the Renaissance and gradually develop into the modern system of notation in the 17th century. The modern-day time signature known as *alla breve*—a semicircle often corrupted into a stylized "C" with a line down the middle—is a vestige of early-14th-century mensural notation; even though we no longer use breves, we understand the sign to mean a beat of two half notes in each measure, the half note being the descendant of the medieval breve.

Le Roman de Fauvel

The *ars nova* style is amply evident in a number of works composed in or around 1316 for the satirical allegory *Le Roman de Fauvel* ("The Story of Fauvel"). The author of this allegory, Gervais de Bus, was a clerk who worked at the French court from 1313 until 1338. A commentary on the dangers of corrupt and incompetent government ministers, it tells the story of a donkey named Fauvel who, through the intercession of the goddess Fortuna, ascends to the throne of France. He marries Vainglory, and together they produce new Fauvels, bringing ruin to France and the world. The name *Fauvel* derives from the first letter of the following vices: **F**laterie (Flattery), **A**varice (Avarice, greed), **U**ialanie (Villainy), **V**ariété (Fickleness), **E**nvie (Envy), and **L**acheté (Cowardice).

Fauve, moreover, was the name of a color—a dark yellow—that was widely associated with evil, deceit, and vanity.

One of the 12 surviving manuscripts of *Le Roman de Fauvel* includes a number of interpolated musical compositions, ranging from short monophonic pieces to large-scale polyphonic motets. The polyglot motet *Garrit gallus / In nova fert / Neuma* may be by Philippe de Vitry himself, who refers to it in his treatise *Ars nova* to illustrate certain features of the new art.

The untexted tenor of *Garrit gallus / In nova fert / Neuma* is freely composed and bears the simple indication *Neuma*, a kind of generic designation for a melisma. The tenor is structured according to the principle of **isorhythm,** a term coined in the 20th century to describe a technique common to many motets and Mass movements written between roughly 1300 and 1450. An isorhythmic tenor is one based on a fixed rhythmic and melodic pattern that is repeated at least once (and usually more often) over the course of an entire work. Although the tenors of many clausulae of the 12th and 13th century featured repeating rhythmic patterns, the isorhythmic units of the 14th century are far longer and not so closely tied to the basic units of the rhythmic modes. Isorhythm became the preferred structure of the motet in the 14th century: most

Philippe de Vitry (?)
Garrit gallus / In nova fert / Neuma

Le Roman de Fauvel. *In the 14th-century* Roman de Fauvel, *the donkey Fauvel (top) marries Vainglory, and on their wedding night they are visited by noisy (and masked) music makers, as part of the tradition of charivari, in which revelers strive to disrupt the newlyweds. The instruments are mostly "high" (loud) ones: bells, cymbals, and many varieties of drums, along with a lone vielle.*

Source: Bibliotheque Nationale, Paris, France, MS FR. 146, Fol. 34

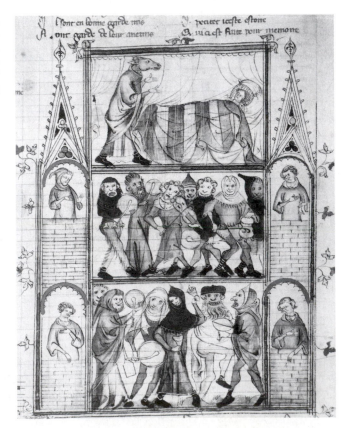

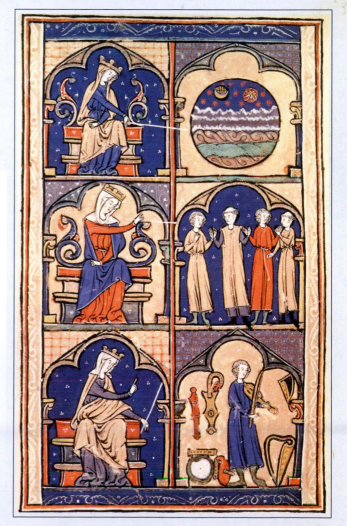

PLATE 2   The three varieties of music.

The manuscript of the *Magnus liber organi* now known as F (because it is housed in Florence, Italy) includes a frontispiece representing what medieval thinkers believed to be the three varieties of music. The figure on the left in each of the three panels is Musica, an allegorical representation of music. In the top panel she points with her fully-extended wand to an illustration of the four elements—earth, water, air, and fire (the stars)—representing music in its highest form: *musica mundana*, the "harmony of the spheres," created by the mathematical ratios of movement and distance among the heavenly bodies. The belief in this kind of music, inaudible to the human ear, dates back to the ancient Greeks. In the middle panel, Musica points with her partially-extended wand to four figures with their hands intertwined. These represent *musica humana* ("human music"), a harmonizing force that unites reason with the body, spirit with matter. The 5th-century theorist Boethius pointed out that "What human music is, anyone may under-stand by examining his own nature." *Musica humana* is also inaudible to human ears. In the bottom panel Musica, with her wand retracted, gestures admonishingly to a man surrounded by musical instruments and playing a vielle. This image represents *musica instrumentalis* ("sounding music"), music in its lowest form, but also the only one of the three that can be heard by mortals.

[Courtesy of Firenze, Biblioteca Medicea Laurenziana/Ministry for Cultural Affairs/Ms. Laur. Plut. 29.1, c. 1v]

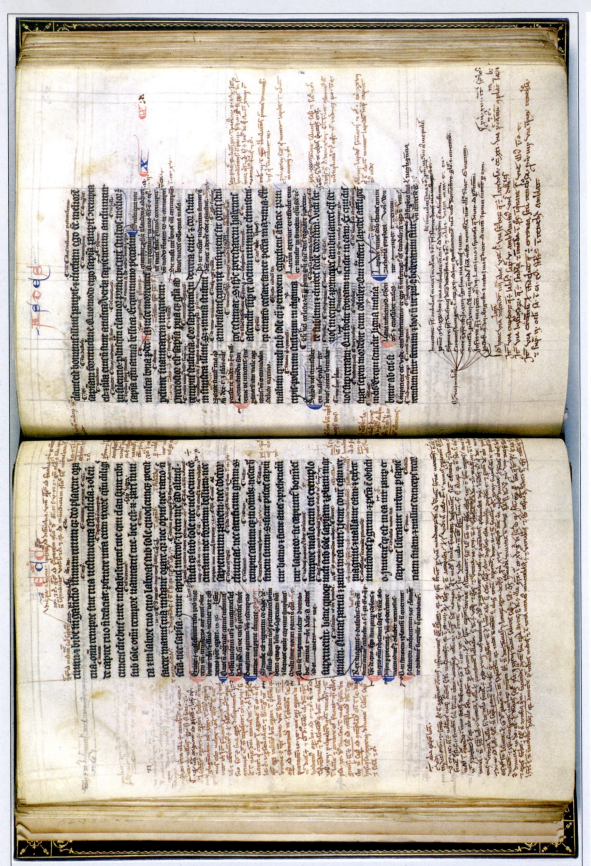

PLATE 3 The Art of Glossing. In the Medieval era, anything worth reading was worth glossing. The original text shown here—a 13th-century manuscript copy of the Old Testament's Book of Ecclesiastes, in Latin—was prepared from the very start with a gloss of its own in the lower left corner of the main text. The ample margins and wide spacing between lines have allowed at least three subsequent readers to enter still further commentaries, offering interpretations of particular words or extended passages, and even pro-viding glosses to earlier glosses. The practice of adding successive layers of commentary to an original source lies behind the medieval impetus to create textual and musical tropes for existing chants, and eventually to add new voices to an established plainchant melody.

[Private collection. Photo courtesy Bridwell Library, Perkins School of Theology, Southern Methodist University, Dallas, TX.]

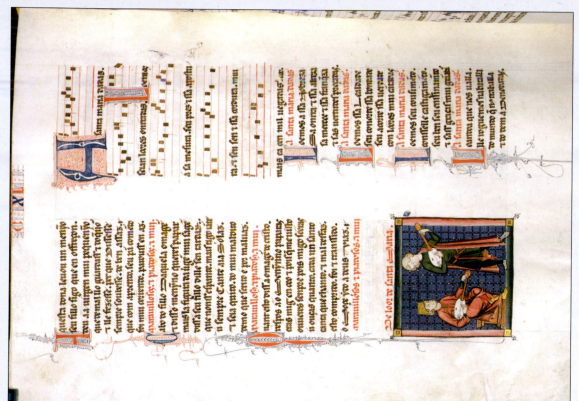

PLATE 5   The Cantigas de Santa Maria. The repertory of *cantigas* in honor of the Virgin Mary is preserved in two major manuscripts prepared in Spain during the second half of the 13th century. One of these sources includes many illuminations—small color illustrations—showing images of musicians and their instruments. Cantiga 140 (Anthology) is accompanied by an image of two lutenists, each of whom is using a plectrum to pluck the strings of his instrument. [Cantigas de Santa Maria, folio 140v. b. 1.2, Biblioteca del Monasterio del Escorial. ©Patrimonio Nacional]

PLATE 4   Francesco Landini. In the lavishly illustrated Squarcialupi Codex, the blind composer (see Chapter 2) is shown playing a portative organ at the head of one of his own compositions. Quite aside from its physical beauty, this manuscript also happens to be the largest and most important source of music from 14th-century Italy. It includes ballate, cacce, and madrigals by Landini, Jacopo da Bologna, and others. [Courtesy of Firenze, Biblioteca Medicea Laurenziana/Ministry for Cultural Affairs/Med. Palat. 87, c. 121v.]

PLATE 6 Ockeghem's *Missa prolationum*. The Chigi Codex is remarkable not only for its opulence, its illuminations, and its often bizarre marginal illustrations, but also for preserving so many works by a single composer, Johannes Ockeghem. Scholars have recently suggested that it may have been compiled as a memorial volume shortly after the composer's death in 1497. The manuscript is known by the name of one of its early owners, Favio Chigi, who later became Pope Alexander VII. These pages, from the opening of the Kyrie of Ockeghem's *Missa prolationum* (discussed in Chapter 5), show music for only two voices, but each voice generates the other, creating a double mensuration canon for four voices. At the beginning of the superius on the left-hand side are two different signs of mensuration: the circle (perfect *tempus*, imperfect *prolatio*) and a half circle (imperfect *tempus*, imperfect *prolatio*). This is the only indication to singers that each of the two voices is to sing the same notes in a different mensuration. The same holds true for the two voices on the right-hand side of the opening: the dot in the middle of the full circle indicates perfect *tempus* and perfect *prolatio*; while the dot in the middle of the half circle indicates imperfect *tempus* and perfect *prolatio*. The blackened notes on the page show that the notes lose one-third of their normal value; thus a blackened breve is the equivalent of two-thirds of a standard breve. Blackened notes are always imperfect.

Example 3-2 The *talea* of the tenor in *Garrit gallus / In nova fert / Neuma*.

of the 34 motets in the *Roman de Fauvel* are isorhythmic, as are most of Guillaume de Machaut's 23 motets.

The rhythmic pattern of an isorhythmic tenor is called its **talea** (meaning "cutting" or "segment"); the melodic pattern is called its **color** (a term borrowed from rhetoric and used to describe certain techniques of repetition). Although *talea* and *color* are sometimes of the same length within a given tenor, more often they are not. The *talea* of the tenor of *Garrit gallus / In nova fert / Neuma* (Example 3-2) is stated six times in succession, beginning at measures 1, 11, 21, 31, 41, and 51. The *color*, in contrast, is three times as long and stated in its entirety only twice, beginning at measures 1 and 31.

The tenor of this motet also illustrates the legitimization of duple meter in the *ars nova*. The *talea* is rhythmically symmetrical, and its central notes (marked in Example 3-2 in small brackets) are written in red in the original manuscript, signifying they are to be imperfected, that is, lose one-third of their normal value. The resulting alternation between triple and duple meters is one of the rhythmic novelties that so agitated Pope John XXII, who condemned the mixture of perfect and imperfect mensurations (see Primary Evidence: The Pope Condemns the *Ars nova*).

Polyphonic Settings of the Mass Ordinary

Composers of the 14th century devoted relatively little energy to polyphonic settings of the complete Mass Ordinary, limiting themselves largely to individual movements or pairs of movements (the Gloria and Credo, for example, or the Sanctus and Agnus dei). The idea of composing a polyphonic setting of the entire Mass Ordinary would become important in the 15th century but remained largely unexplored in the 14th.

One possible exception to this pattern is Guillaume de Machaut's *Messe de Nostre Dame* ("Mass of Our Lady"). Composed sometime during the early 1360s, the work is the only 14th-century polyphonic setting of the complete Mass Ordinary known to have been written by a specific composer. Yet even here, the musical connections among the various movements are subtle and do not revolve around shared musical material or a particular technique. The Gloria and Credo are clearly linked through extended passages that are closely similar, as are the Sanctus and Agnus dei, but the brief melodic gestures that have been interpreted by some critics as a kind of thread running through the entire cycle seem fairly inconsequential by comparison.

This lack of thematic unity, however, in no way detracts from the remarkable force of the music. Machaut differentiates between movements with large quantities of text and those with relatively little text. The former are set in a predominantly syllabic, conductus-like fashion (note against note), whereas the latter are set in the style of an isorhythmic motet.

Whatever their differences in style, all the movements are based on a plainchant version of the appropriate element of the Ordinary. Thus the tenor of the Kyrie derives from the plainchant Kyrie *Cunctipotens Genitor Deus* (see Example 1-6). The *talea* of the tenor in the first Kyrie is extremely brief (only four measures in modern transcription) and the only rest comes at the very end, which helps articulate each successive

Guillaume de Machaut
Messe de Nostre Dame

PRIMARY EVIDENCE

The Pope Condemns the *Ars nova*

The papal bull *Docta sanctorum patrum* of 1324–1325 gives eloquent witness to the church's ongoing ambivalence about the role of music in worship. The rhythmic flexibility of the *Ars nova*, according to Pope John XXII, promoted wantonness at the expense of devotion.

•••••

Certain disciples of the new school, much occupying themselves with the measured dividing of the *tempora,* display their prolation in notes that are new to us, preferring to devise new methods of their own rather than to continue singing in the old way. Therefore the music of the Divine Office is disturbed with notes of these small values. Moreover, they hinder the melody with hockets, they deprave them with descants, and sometimes they pad them out with upper parts made out of secular songs. The result is that they often seem to be losing sight of the fundamental sources of our melodies in the Antiphoner and Gradual, and forget what it is that they are burying under their superstructures. They may become entirely ignorant of the ecclesiastical modes, which they have already ceased to distinguish and the limits of which they abuse in the prolixity of their notes. The modest rise and temperate descents of plainsong, by which the modes themselves are recognized, are entirely obscured. The voices move incessantly to and fro, intoxicating rather than soothing the ear, while the singers themselves try to convey the emotion of the music by their gestures. The consequence of all this is that devotion, the true aim of all worship, is neglected, and wantonness, which ought to be eschewed, increases.

This state of things, which has become the common one, we and our brethren have come to regard as needing correction. Therefore we hasten to forbid these methods, or rather to drive them more effectively out of the house of God than has been done in the past. For this reason, having taken counsel with our brethren, we strictly command that no one shall henceforth consider himself at liberty to use these methods, or methods like them, in the singing of the canonical Office or in solemn celebrations of the Mass. . . .

Nevertheless, it is not our wish to forbid the occasional use—especially on feast days or in solemn celebration of the Mass and the Divine Office—of some consonances, for example, the octave, the fifth, and the fourth, which heighten the beauty of the melody. Such intervals, therefore, may be sung above the ecclesiastical chant, but in such a way that the integrity of the chant remains intact and that nothing in the prescribed music be changed. Used thus, the consonances would, more than any other music is able to do, both soothe the hearer and inspire his devotion without destroying religious feeling in the minds of the singers.

Source: Henry Raynor, *A Social History of Music from the Middle Ages to Beethoven* (London: Barrie & Jenkins, 1972), pp. 36–37.

return of the *talea.* The *color,* adhering to the pitches of the chant exactly, is stated only once. In a practice that became common around the middle of the 14th century, Machaut includes a voice known as the **contratenor** (meaning "against the tenor") that occupies the same range as the tenor. The contratenor, like the tenor, is isorhythmic, but its *talea* in the first Kyrie is longer. It is fully stated twice—in measures 1–12 and 13–25—then restated partially in the last two measures. By virtue of its length and internal rests, it keeps the motion of the lower voices moving forward. The *color* of the contratenor, unrelated to any preexisting melody, is stated only once. The motetus (duplum) and triplum move freely in more rapid rhythms. In the Christe and the final Kyrie, the *talea* of the tenor and contratenor voices coincide.

The addition of the contratenor provided composers with a greatly expanded range of options for **voice leading**—that is, the manner in which two or more voices move in relationship to one another. By the middle of the 14th century, only the third, fifth, sixth,

Example 3-3 Possible sonorities with three voices.

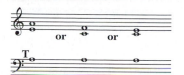

Example 3-4 Possible additional sonorities with four voices.

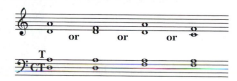

Example 3-5 Cadential patterns in the Kyrie of Machaut's *Messe de Nostre Dame,* including double leading-tone cadence at the end of Kyrie I (c).

and octave were considered acceptable intervals above the lowest sounding note. Given these restrictions, a fourth voice moving in the same range as the tenor—at times above it, at times below it—greatly increases the number of possible simultaneously sounding pitch combinations.

The melodic character of Machaut's Kyrie is typical of mid-14th-century polyphony: somewhat angular, with large leaps (an upward seventh in the contratenor of Kyrie I in measure 17, an upward major sixth in measure 21–22), **hockets** (from the Latin word for "hiccough") in measures 10 and 22, and a good deal of syncopation throughout.

The principal cadences follow the standard formulas of the day, with the two structural voices—the highest sounding voice and the tenor, which together provide the basic harmonic intervals—moving from a sixth to an octave (Example 3-5a) or from a third to a fifth (Example 3-5b).

Under certain circumstances, performers were expected to sharpen leading tones that were not notated as such (for a fuller discussion of this convention, part of what is known as *musica ficta,* see Focus: *Musica ficta* in Chapter 5). In the cadence at measure 27 of the Kyrie (and in Example 3-5c), we can be certain that performers would have sharpened the G in the triplum that precedes the closing A. Otherwise they would be singing a tritone—a forbidden interval—against the C♯ that Machaut explicitly specified in the duplum. The combination of G♯ and C♯ here is part of a **double leading-tone cadence,** a favorite device of 14th-century composers in which a sharped seventh leads to the octave and a sharped fourth leads to the fifth.

Double leading-tone cadences are also found at the end of the Kyrie II and III. All of these cadences include parallel octaves and fifths. The theorist Johannes de Garlandia had recommended against the use of such parallel movement as early as 1300, but it would continue to be used well into the 15th century, especially at cadences.

Secular Song

By the middle of the 14th century, three *formes fixes*—literally "fixed forms," or structural patterns—had established themselves as the most important varieties of secular song in France: the ballade, virelai, and rondeau. These were at once both poetic and musical forms, each with its own characteristic pattern of rhyme and musical repetition, with at least one line of refrain—that is, the same words sung to the same music in every

Composer Profile

Guillaume de Machaut
(ca. 1300–1377)

In the tradition of the 12th-century trouvères, Guillaume de Machaut was a poet as well as a musician. His texts abound with puns, extended imagery, and possibly encryptions. The formal structures can be complex at times, using rhyme and meter in ways that are far from ordinary. His *Livre du voir dit* ("Book of the True Poem") is a sprawling, quasi-autobiographical collection of letters, lyrics, and song settings written in praise of a young woman, Péronne d'Armentières, with whom Machaut was deeply infatuated late in his life.

Machaut's accomplishments in the realm of music are even more significant. He elevated the *formes fixes* of virelai, rondeau, and ballade to new heights and inspired subsequent generations of poets and composers to cultivate these genres. He also wrote what is apparently the first polyphonic setting of the Mass Ordinary as a coherent cycle.

Machaut always moved in elite circles, working at the courts of the Duke of Berry, the king of

KEY DATES IN THE LIFE OF GUILLAUME DE MACHAUT
ca. 1300 Born in northern France, possibly in Rheims
ca. 1323 Becomes royal secretary to King John of Luxembourg, king of Bohemia; travels with him as far east as Russia before the king's death in 1346
1335 Appointed a canon of the cathedral at Rheims but travels widely over the next 40 years, serving a variety of rulers
1377 Dies at Rheims

Navarre, and the king of Cyprus, as well as the French royal court. He kept tight control over the copying and distribution of his music: only 22 of his 143 musical works are preserved in sources known

strophe (or verse). Musically, each of these forms consists of two parts, conventionally labeled A and B. The first ending of a repeated part (A, B, or both) is known as its *ouvert* ("open") and the second ending as its *clos* ("close").

The text of the **ballade** usually consists of three strophes of seven or eight lines, the last of which is a refrain. The rhyme pattern varies. That of Machaut's *Je puis trop bien ma dame comparer* ("I may well compare my lady") is ababccdD. (Lowercase letters indicate lines of text that are different in each strophe; uppercase letters indicate the refrain, which is identical throughout, both textually and musically.) Other typical rhyme patterns for the ballade include ababbcbC, ababcdE, and ababcdeF.

Musically, the ballade falls into two distinct sections, the first of which is always repeated and the second of which is sometimes repeated. The music thus unfolds in the pattern AAB or AABB.

Ballades tend to be the most melismatic of all the *formes fixes* used in 14th-century France, with a rhythmically active uppermost voice. Machaut's *Je puis trop* is highly florid, yet the cadences are carefully aligned to the structure of the poetry. As in Machaut's four-part setting of the Mass, the tenor and contratenor lines weave in and out of one another.

The **virelai** follows the pattern AbbaA. The refrain, in other words, is sung at the beginning and end of each strophe. Virelais are typically set in a syllabic fashion, as in Machaut's *Douce dame jolie* ("Sweet pretty lady"). About three-fourths of Machaut's

Guillaume de Machaut
Je puis trop bien ma dame comparer

Guillaume de Machaut
Douce dame jolie

to have originated outside his immediate circle. The six "Machaut Manuscripts," consisting of some 2,100 leaves, were prepared under his supervision and transmit almost all his music in multiple copies, each with the inevitable variant versions associated with the process of copying by hand. The differences in the readings are sometimes slight, sometimes not.

Principal Works

Aside from his polyphonic setting of the Mass Ordinary, Machaut devoted himself exclusively to secular music, cultivating all the *formes fixes* of his day. His output includes some 42 ballades, 22 rondeaux, and 33 virelais. He also wrote 19 *lais,* lengthy monophonic works of 12 strophes but through-composed rather than strophic, reflecting the variety of different poetic forms from strophe to strophe. Almost all of Machaut's 24 motets are isorhythmic; 19 of them are for three voices, the remainder for four.

Guillaume de Machaut. *Love introduces his three children,* Doux Penser *(Sweet Thoughts),* Plaisance *(Pleasure), and* Espérance *(Hope) to the elderly composer at work in his study. This image is from one of the six "Machaut manuscripts" containing the composer's musical and poetic works and prepared directly under his supervision.*

Source: Bibliotheque Nationale, Paris, France, MS FR. 1584, Fol D

upper case = melody   lower case = text

33 virelais have come down to us as monophonic works, although this does not preclude the possibility that other voices were added, either as accompaniment or in the form of improvised counterpoint. Virelais, like all songs of this period, could also be performed instrumentally, without any text at all.

The **rondeau** (plural, **rondeaux**) consists of eight lines of text set to music following the scheme ABaAabAB. Machaut's rondeau *Ma fin est mon commencement* ("My End Is My Beginning") is a particularly ingenious application of the form. The cantus (the highest voice) and the contratenor—in a direct musical representation of the text—are exact **retrogrades** of each other. The cantus line, sung backward from end to the beginning, is exactly the same as what the tenor sings from beginning to end. The second half of the cantus line (measures 21–40, after the cadence in measure 20), in turn, is a retrograde version of the tenor line in measures 1–20. The idea that beginnings and endings are one and the same is deeply rooted in Christian theology, which connects death to physical and spiritual rebirth.

The *Ars subtilior* at the End of the 14th Century

The kind of ingenuity evident in Machaut's *Ma fin est mon commencement* was part of a broader fascination with musical puzzles that occupied many composers in the last quarter of the 14th century, particularly in France. Much of this repertory has been called

Guillaume de Machaut
Ma fin est mon commencement

mannered or mannerist because it is self-conscious, complex, and sometimes downright obscure. But the term *mannered* has negative connotations that are unfair to this fascinating repertory, and most scholars working in this field today prefer the newly coined designation of *ars subtilior* (Latin for "the more subtle art") to acknowledge the central roles that subtlety, understatement, and misdirection play in this music. Composers writing in this style viewed music not only as an art of sound but also as an object of contemplation that could engage and challenge the intellect as well as the soul.

Notational tricks make deciphering these works a delightful intellectual challenge, rather like doing an extremely difficult crossword puzzle. The manuscript originals can

Baude Cordier, *Tout par compas.* *In the Chantilly Codex, Baude Cordier's rondeau* Tout par compas *(Anthology) assumes the visual form of its text ("In a Circle I Am Composed"). The visual pun goes even farther:* compas *also means the drafting instrument of the compass, which is clearly the tool used to prepare the staves of this manuscript. The single line that generates the two canonic upper voices is notated in the outer circle; the tenor part is notated on the inner circle. The texts of the additional strophes are written in the circles at the four corners.*

Source: Ms 564/1047 fol. 12, "Tout Par Compas Suy Composee . . .", illuminated composition by Baude Cordier, from a collection of Medieval ballads, motets, and songs, 13th–14th century/Musée Condé, Chantilly, France/Giraudon/Bridgeman Art Library

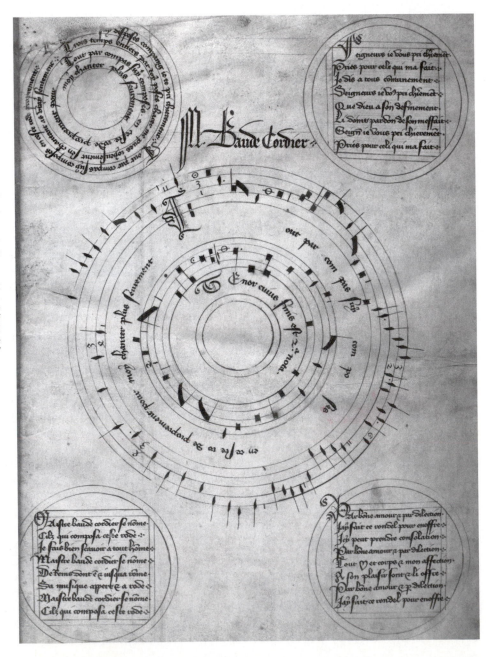

also be quite visually arresting. Jacob de Senleches's virelai *La harpe de mélodie* ("The Harp of Melody") is notated on staff lines embedded in the frame of a harp; Baude Cordier's *Belle, bonne, sage,* a love song, is notated in the shape of a stylized heart. In this same tradition, Cordier's rondeau *Tout par compas* ("In a Circle I Am Composed") is notated in a circle (see illustration). The two upper voices constitute a **canon,** in which one voice follows the other in strict imitation. The notational difficulties of these works, however, should not obscure their emotional intensity. Listening to them without the benefit (or burden) of the score, we can perhaps better appreciate them as music and not mere technical artifice.

    Cordier, like many composers of the *ars subtilior,* worked for a time at the papal court in Avignon, in southern France, at the time of the Great Schism. This was the period from 1378 to 1417 when rival popes claimed power over the church, one in Rome, the other in Avignon. (There was even a third pope for a brief time in Pisa.) As if to legitimize itself and increase its prestige, the court at Avignon spared no expense to attract the best available talent in many fields. The Italian poet Petrarch worked there for a time, as did a number of gifted (if now slightly obscure) composers such as Cordier, Jacob de Senleches, Anthonello de Caserta, a certain Grimace, and one Trebor ("Robert" spelled backward?).

    The early 15th century in France witnessed a turn away from the rhythmic complexities of the *ars subtilior* and toward a more straightforward style. This shift is generally associated with the beginning of the Renaissance era in music.

Cordier
Tout par compas

ITALY: THE TRECENTO

Many of the developments in French music during the 14th century have their counterparts in Italian music—so many, in fact, that some scholars speak of an Italian *ars nova.* The more common designation for Italian music of this period, however, is **trecento.** (The term means, literally, the 1300s, or the 14th century. **Quattrocento** is similarly used to designate Italian music of the 15th century.)

    The principal secular vocal genres of the trecento are the ballata, the caccia, and the madrigal. As with the *formes fixes* in France, each of these had its own particular textual and musical characteristics.

    The **ballata** (plural, **ballate**) is formally similar to the French virelai of the same period (not, as we might expect, to the ballade). The poetic form of the ballata is AbbaA, with a refrain framing the internal lines of each strophe. Most ballate have three strophes, but some have only one; most are polyphonic (usually for two or three voices), but a few monophonic ones exist as well.

    Francesco Landini's *Ecco la primavera* ("Behold, Spring"), for two voices, exemplifies the ballata genre. It features smooth melodic lines that project the text syllabically. Not all ballate are quite this syllabic, however. The openings of the first and second section of the music are said to rhyme, in that they share certain features of rhythm and melody, as do the corresponding cadential measures of the two sections. This kind of musical rhyme can be found in many ballate.

Landini
Ecco la primavera

    The 14th-century Italian **madrigal** began as a literary form that by the 1340s had crystallized into a series of two or three strophes, each consisting of three lines, with a two-line **ritornello** (refrain) at the very end. Musical settings of this poetry clearly reflect its textual structure. The ritornello is almost invariably set in a contrasting meter, as in Jacopo da Bologna's *Non al suo amante* ("Never to Her Lover"), with a triple-meter ritornello at the end of each duple-meter strophe. Almost all the trecento madrigal repertory is for two voices, with the upper voice the more florid of the two.

Jacopo da Bologna
Non al suo amante

**F
O
C
U
S**

Composers of the Trecento

Francesco Landini (ca. 1325–1397), blinded by smallpox as a child, served as organist at various churches in his native Florence. His works feature prominently in the Squarcialupi Codex, where he is portrayed with a portative organ on his knee (see color plate 4). The bulk of his surviving music consists of 140 ballate, of which about two-thirds are for two voices, the remainder for three. He also wrote nine madrigals, one caccia, and one virelai.

Jacopo da Bologna (flourished 1340–1360) wrote mostly madrigals, 25 of them for two voices, seven for three voices. He was active at the courts of Milan and Verona and wrote a treatise on mensuration, but little else is known about him.

Lorenzo da Firenze (d.1372 or 1373) was active at the church of San Lorenzo in Florence, where he may have studied with Landini. His surviving works include seven monophonic ballate, ten madrigals, a three-voice caccia (Anthology), and two Mass movements.

Johannes Ciconia (ca. 1370–1412), as scholars have recently discovered, is a name shared by two individuals who were both born in Liège (now Belgium) and were active as singers and composers in northern Italy. The younger of the two is now generally accepted as the composer of motets, Mass movements, and a variety of songs in both French (virelais) and Italian (ballate and madrigals).

By the end of the 14th century, the madrigal was in decline. The new vocal genre of the same name that arose in the 1520s (see Chapter 6) had no direct connection to it.

The **caccia** (plural, **cacce**) takes its name from the same root word as the English word "chase." Caccia texts often deal, aptly, with hunting, although they can also depict such lively scenes as fires, street vendors' cries, and the bustle of the marketplace. The music, usually for three voices, features two canonic upper parts and an independent tenor. Many (but not all) cacce conclude with a ritornello that can be monophonic, polyphonic, or canonic. Although written monophonically, the ritornello in Lorenzo da Firenze's *A poste messe* ("In Their Positions") can also be realized canonically.

Johannes Ciconia (ca. 1370–1412) is the leading composer of early-15th-century Italy. His *Doctorum principem / Melodia suavissima / Vir mitis* is an example of a new kind of work, the civic motet, written in praise of a particular person or place—in this case Francesco Zabarella, an official at the court of Padua in northern Italy and Ciconia's protector and patron. The *color* of the isorhythmic tenor is stated three times, each time in a different mensuration; thus, although the pitches of the tenor line repeat, the rhythmic pattern changes with each statement. The optional contratenor is constructed in the same way. The voice leading—with many hockets, a relatively free treatment of dissonance (especially in the contratenor), and cadential parallel fifths—is typical of the 14th century.

Lorenzo da Firenze
A poste messe

Ciconia
Doctorum principem / Melodia suavissima / Vir mitis

ENGLAND

A small but impressive repertory of English song has been preserved from the 13th and 14th centuries. These works are roughly contemporary with the great English poet Geoffrey Chaucer (1342–1400), whose *Canterbury Tales* are full of musical imagery and references to music making.

Stylistically, English composers and theorists were on the whole more inclined to use the interval of a third in practice than composers on the continent. As the early-14th-century commentator Walter Odington noted, although thirds could not be considered consonant "in number"—that is, on the basis of their numerical ratios—"the voices of men" with their "subtlety" could use thirds to create a "smooth mixture and full consonance." The oldest known canon in Western music, a setting of the poem *Sumer is icumen in,* testifies to this English predilection for thirds. Believed to have been written around 1250, it consists of a *rota*—or round for two voices—that unfolds over a two-part **rondellus,** in which the two voices exchange phrases (A and B) continuously, following this scheme:

Anonymous
Sumer is icumen in

A	B	A	B
B	A	B	A

The work is preserved in a manuscript that includes both Latin and English texts; which is the older version of the text is debatable, but they seem in any event to be separate—this is not, in other words, a polylingual motet.

The anonymous song *Edi be thu, heven-queene* ("Blessed Be Thou, Heaven-Queen") also makes liberal use of thirds and sixths as consonant intervals. The rhythmic interpretation of this and similar songs of the 14th century is open to debate. Although the original source for this song carefully aligns the two parts, it leaves ambiguous the duration of the notes. The version in the anthology follows the regular meters of the text, although this is only one of several possibilities. Either or both parts could be performed vocally or instrumentally.

Anonymous
Edi be thu, heven-queene

INSTRUMENTAL MUSIC

From written accounts and visual images—paintings and statues—we know that instruments played an important role in medieval music. They were routinely used to accompany or double vocal lines, and they were often used on their own, independently of voices. Purely instrumental music entertained guests at banquets, accompanied dancers, and signaled troops in battle. The basic instrument families that had been established in antiquity—strings, winds, percussion, and keyboard—continued to evolve in the medieval era. Returning crusaders introduced many instruments from the Islamic world to the West, including the lute, guitar, rebec, and shawm.

Despite ambivalence on the part of church patriarchs, visual evidence confirms that instruments—either alone or as accompaniment to singing—played an important role in medieval worship. Many medieval churches are adorned with carved images of musicians playing such diverse instruments as the vielle and rebec (bowed stringed instruments), lute, bells, trumpet, and organistrum (hurdy-gurdy). And at least some medieval manuscripts include illustrations that show singers and instrumentalists performing together.

Unfortunately, very little medieval instrumental music was ever written down. It operated instead within an unwritten tradition, one that relied on memory and improvisation. Composers rarely wrote music to be performed on specific instruments or by specific combinations of voices and instruments. Indeed, it would be difficult (and pointless) to draw a sharp distinction between vocal and instrumental music in medieval times. With the exception of plainchant and liturgical polyphony—elements of a sacred ritual whose words were of central importance—vocal and instrumental lines were essentially interchangeable. Musicians made ready use of whatever instruments happened to be available at any given moment.

The notated dance music we do have from the medieval era is characterized by short repeated sections called *puncta* ("points"). These modular units could be repeated, varied, and embellished at will according to the needs of the dance. The *Quinte estampie real*

Anonymous
La quinte estampie real

King David and his musicians. *From an early-12th-century psalter, this image shows King David playing a vielle, surrounded by musicians playing tabors (drums) and trumpets (top), harps (middle), and bells (bottom). From the 14th century onward, writers often distinguished between two main categories of instruments, "high" and "low," referring not to their register but to their volume. High instruments included trumpets and horns, shawms, bagpipes, and drums. Low instruments included portative organs, organistrums, recorders, transverse flutes, and stringed instruments like the lute, vielle, psaltery, and rebec, of which only the former would survive into the Renaissance.*

Source: The Warburg Institute

("Fifth Royal *Estampie*"), preserved in a French manuscript copied in the second half of the 13th century, illustrates the structural principles of medieval dance music in general. Each *punctum* ("point"), is repeated immediately, with a first and then a second ending comparable to the *ouvert* and *clos* of contemporary vocal forms. Here, the same pair of endings serves for all four *puncta*. Dances of this era were highly stylized, with elaborate steps executed at times by individual couples, at times by large groups dancing as a unit.

By all accounts, the medieval ear relished contrasting timbres. This penchant for a mixture of sound colors matches well the layered counterpoint of 12th- and 13th-century vocal polyphony, with its clear delineation between a slow-moving tenor in the lowest register and faster-moving voices in the higher ranges. This tendency toward differentiation continued in the polyphony of the 14th century. Not until the second half of the 15th century did a shift toward timbral homogeneity begin to emerge.

CONCLUSION

No single historical or musical event marks the end of the medieval era. But the second quarter of the 15th century witnessed a growing tendency toward simplified and homogeneous textures and a more carefully controlled use of dissonance.

Isorhythm, although still cultivated, declined in importance as a structural device, and polytextual motets gradually became the exception rather than the norm. All these stylistic developments would eventually come to be associated with the era of music history we now think of as the Renaissance.

DISCUSSION QUESTIONS

1. Why was musical notation so slow to develop in the medieval era?

2. Early leaders of the church, such as St. Augustine and St. Basil, recognized music's power to ennoble but also feared its power to seduce. How did they resolve this conflict? What forms has this conflict taken in our own time?

3. Who was responsible for unifying the chant repertory? What factors were involved in the process of unification?

4. What opportunities were available for creating new music for the liturgy after about 900 C.E.?

5. What techniques of composition in the medieval era can be related to the widespread practice of glossing written texts such as the Bible or commentaries on the Bible?

6. Why did rhythmic notation first appear when it did, and why did it develop in the way it did?

7. According to Church authorities the ideal function of plainchant was to heighten the text of the liturgy. In what respects did sacred polyphony reinforce or conflict with this ideal?

8. According to the theorist Johannes de Grocheo, the subtleties of the medieval motet were accessible only to learned listeners and beyond the grasp of common people. What parallels can be found to this situation in music today?

9. What innovations characterize the music of the *ars nova*, and why did Pope John XXII object to these innovations?

10. What attitude did church authorities take toward purely instrumental music?

Part Two
The Renaissance

Prelude

The Renaissance was both a cultural movement and a historical period. Its chronological range and defining characteristics are matters of ongoing debate, but in music the term is conventionally applied to the period from about 1420 to 1600.

The term *Renaissance*—"rebirth" in French—was coined by later historians to designate what they saw as an era marked by the revival, or rebirth, of attitudes and ideals rooted in classical antiquity. Many of the philosophical, technological, and artistic innovations of the Renaissance were inspired by the recovery of ancient works, particularly from Greece, that had for all practical purposes been lost to western Europe for almost a thousand years.

When Constantinople fell to the Turks in 1453, a new wave of manuscripts arrived in the luggage of scholars seeking refuge in the West. This influx of ancient works—and the ideas they contained—coincided with significant transformations in European society and its economy. By the early 15th century, the population was rising again after the devastations of the Black Death. Increased trade and prosperity challenged feudal

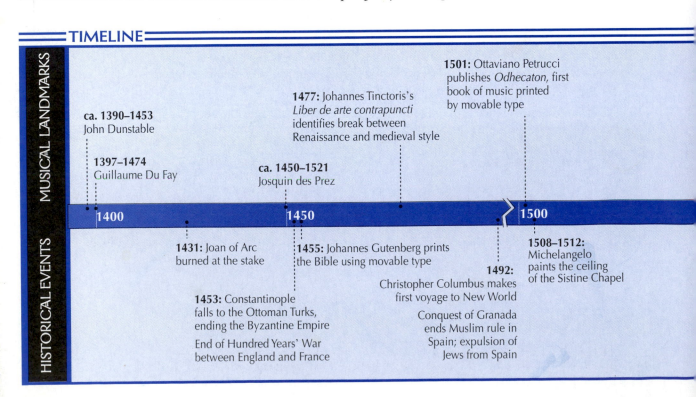

TIMELINE

MUSICAL LANDMARKS

ca. 1390–1453
John Dunstable

1397–1474
Guillaume Du Fay

ca. 1450–1521
Josquin des Prez

1477: Johannes Tinctoris's *Liber de arte contrapuncti* identifies break between Renaissance and medieval style

1501: Ottaviano Petrucci publishes *Odhecaton*, first book of music printed by movable type

1400   **1450**   **1500**

HISTORICAL EVENTS

1431: Joan of Arc burned at the stake

1453: Constantinople falls to the Ottoman Turks, ending the Byzantine Empire

End of Hundred Years' War between England and France

1455: Johannes Gutenberg prints the Bible using movable type

1492: Christopher Columbus makes first voyage to New World

Conquest of Granada ends Muslim rule in Spain; expulsion of Jews from Spain

1508–1512: Michelangelo paints the ceiling of the Sistine Chapel

structures and promoted the growth of cities and city-states, regions ruled from a single urban center.

The Italian peninsula proved particularly hospitable to the growth of cities and city-states based on industry, commerce, and banking.

North of the Alps, cities of the region known as the Low Countries—roughly equivalent to modern-day Belgium and the Netherlands—also emerged as powerful centers of trade, finance, and culture in the 15th century. As in Italy, growing affluence in such cities as Antwerp, Ghent, Tournai, and Liège provided a source of patronage for the production of great masterpieces of painting, architecture, and music. In France, the Hundred Years' War between England and France finally came to an end in 1453 with the expulsion of the English from all but a small corner of what is now northern France. Joan of Arc, burned at the stake in 1431, had rallied the French army and populace and in so doing helped create a sense of French nationality. In England, the War of the Roses (a decades-long struggle for the throne between the houses of York and Lancaster) was finally decided at the Battle of Bosworth Field in 1485, in which Henry Tudor (later Henry VII) defeated Richard III. The Tudors would rule England until the death of Elizabeth I in 1603.

The Holy Roman Empire—a loose confederation of principalities, duchies, and kingdoms across north-central Europe in the area of what is now Germany, Austria, and portions of northern Italy—expanded greatly in the late 15th and 16th centuries under the rule of the Habsburg dynasty. Thanks to a series of strategic marriages, the family's influence extended to the Burgundian lands, Spain, Portugal, and the Low Countries.

Spain itself was united in the late 15th century following the marriage of the rulers of its two most powerful kingdoms, Ferdinand of Aragon and Isabella of Castille. In 1492, they conquered Granada, the last center of Muslim rule in Spain. That same year, under the influence of the notorious Spanish Inquisition, Spain expelled all Jews who refused to convert to Christianity, and, after 1502, required Muslims to convert.

Through voyages of discovery and conquest, Spain acquired an immense empire that extended from what is now the southern and southwestern United States to Tierra del Fuego in South America. Flush with gold and silver from these lands, Spain enjoyed

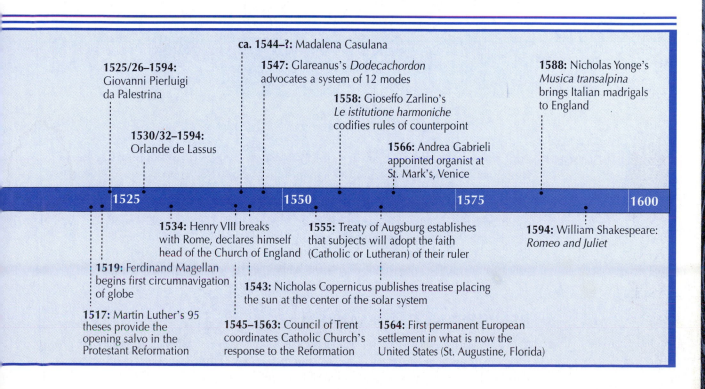

ca. 1544–?: Madalena Casulana

1525/26–1594: Giovanni Pierluigi da Palestrina

1547: Glareanus's *Dodecachordon* advocates a system of 12 modes

1588: Nicholas Yonge's *Musica transalpina* brings Italian madrigals to England

1558: Gioseffo Zarlino's *Le istitutione harmoniche* codifies rules of counterpoint

1530/32–1594: Orlande de Lassus

1566: Andrea Gabrieli appointed organist at St. Mark's, Venice

1525 — 1550 — 1575 — 1600

1534: Henry VIII breaks with Rome, declares himself head of the Church of England

1555: Treaty of Augsburg establishes that subjects will adopt the faith (Catholic or Lutheran) of their ruler

1594: William Shakespeare: *Romeo and Juliet*

1519: Ferdinand Magellan begins first circumnavigation of globe

1543: Nicholas Copernicus publishes treatise placing the sun at the center of the solar system

1517: Martin Luther's 95 theses provide the opening salvo in the Protestant Reformation

1545–1563: Council of Trent coordinates Catholic Church's response to the Reformation

1564: First permanent European settlement in what is now the United States (St. Augustine, Florida)

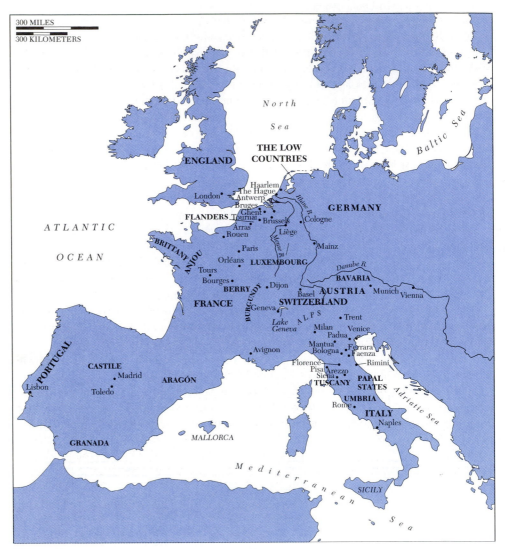

Renaissance Europe

unprecedented wealth and power in the 16th century. Philip II (son of the Holy Roman Emperor Charles V), who ruled Spain from 1556 to 1598, presided over a court of remarkable accomplishments in literature, architecture, painting, and music.

Other countries were quick to follow Spain's lead in colonizing the Americas and exploiting its rich natural resources. Portugal established extensive settlements in what is now Brazil; the English set up their first (unsuccessful) colony in North Carolina in 1587, and their first permanent colony in Jamestown, Virginia, in 1607. The Pilgrims, seeking relief from religious persecution, settled farther to the north in Massachusetts in 1620.

RENAISSANCE HUMANISM

The discovery of what was for Europeans a New World in 1492 opened up not only new territories but also new ways of thinking about the universe, prompting fundamental changes in the very perception of humanity's place in the world. The discovery of previously unknown but advanced civilizations like those of the Aztecs and Incas would help inspire emerging scientific theories that the earth was not the center of the universe.

The sudden abundance of pre-Christian sources from classical antiquity introduced Western minds to yet another new—or rather, very old—way of looking at the world. The ancient Greeks had measured the universe in terms of human values and reason, and many scholars of the early 15th century, adopting this "new" outlook for themselves, created a philosophical movement known as **humanism.** Renaissance humanists were committed to independent reasoning, careful study of the ancient classics in their original languages (particularly Greek), and a reliance on original sources rather than secondhand commentary about those sources. They also believed in the basic dignity of humankind. Humanists did not reject religion—indeed, many of them were among the most eloquent advocates of the church—but they sought understanding through a process guided as much by reason as faith.

Humanism was a sharp departure from the scholasticism that had dominated late medieval intellectual life. Scholasticism relied almost entirely on abstract thought and the accumulation of wisdom through disputation. Commentaries—and commentaries on commentaries—were an important venue of scholastic thought, provided they came from the pens of acknowledged authorities. Scholasticism harbored deep suspicions about the reliability of the human senses and therefore had little place for empirical evidence or observation. Humanism, in contrast, combined reason with empirical evidence with results that often challenged the received wisdom of even the greatest authorities.

The impact of humanists such as Desiderius Erasmus (1466–1536) and Lorenzo Valla (ca. 1407–1457) extended well beyond the fields of philosophy, theology, and science. Renaissance writers as a whole were deeply influenced by humanism and its efforts to explore the human mind. Following the lead of such late medieval figures as Dante Alighieri (1265–1321), Giovanni Boccaccio (1313–1375), and Geoffrey Chaucer (1342–1400), writers such as William Shakespeare (1564–1616) and François Rabelais (1483–1553) began to produce works in the vernacular—Italian, French, English, Spanish—which in turn contributed to an ever-growing sense of national identity in the various regions of Europe.

The speed with which ideas could be disseminated in Renaissance Europe accelerated exponentially with the invention of movable type and the printing press in the mid–15th century. After Johannes Gutenberg produced the first printed Bible in Mainz (Germany) around 1455, it became possible to generate multiple and essentially identical copies of the same work in a relatively short period of time at only a fraction of the cost of a comparable number of manuscripts. The first music printed with movable type appeared in Venice in 1501.

THE PROTESTANT REFORMATION

The Protestant Reformation arose as an expression of protest against corrupt church practices and a desire to reform them. Martin Luther (1483–1546) and his followers emphasized the individual's personal relationship to God and preached a doctrine of salvation based on faith rather than on works. Protestants also encouraged worship in the vernacular, although Luther himself upheld the importance of Latin both in the liturgy and in the education of youth. The political ramifications of Luther's stand were far reaching. The German people eventually split along Protestant and Catholic lines according to the professed faith of their local ruler. Luther himself was challenged on matters of doctrine by other Protestants as early as 1521, and a host of Protestant sects emerged over the ensuing decades. Henry VIII, chafing at the authority of the pope in Rome, declared himself head of the Church of England.

Renaissance Painting and Sculpture

The contrast between medieval and Renaissance perceptions of the world is particularly evident in the realm of painting and sculpture. Linear perspective, a method for creating the illusion of three-dimensional depth on a two-dimensional surface, had been familiar in an intuitive way to the ancient Greeks but was almost entirely lost over subsequent centuries. The Florentine artist Filippo Brunelleschi (1377–1446) was one of the first to reestablish the importance of linear perspective and articulate its geometric basis. Medieval artists had, for the most part, used nudity for depicting lasciviousness on earth or the torments of the damned in hell. In contrast, Renaissance artists, like the artists of antiquity, became interested in the human body as an object of admiration. They also display an unprecedented interest in the scientific details of human anatomy. This interest in human anatomy accompanied one of the most distinctive characteristics of Renaissance art, a desire to capture individual character in portraiture.

Renaissance artists began to think of themselves—and came to be regarded—as figures of study in their own right. Among the most prominent are Donatello (1386–1466; born Donato di Betto Bardi), Jan van Eyck (ca. 1390–1441), Leonardo da Vinci (1452–1519), Albrecht Dürer (1471–1528), Michelangelo Buonarotti (1475–1564), and Raphael (1483–1520; born Raffaello Sanzio).

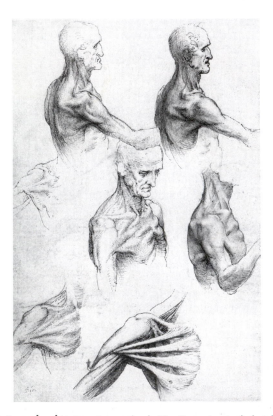

Arts and sciences. *Leonardo da Vinci's anatomical sketches could not possibly have been made during the medieval era. They attend too closely to anatomical accuracy and detail and betray a connection between draftsmanship and science—in terms of both anatomy and the geometry of perspective—that had been unknown since the time of the ancient Greeks.*

Source: Leonardo da Vinci (1452–1519), "Myology of the Shoulder Region." Pen and ink, some gray washes, 7-¾ × 9-¾ in. The Royal Collection © 2003 Her Majesty Queen Elizabeth II

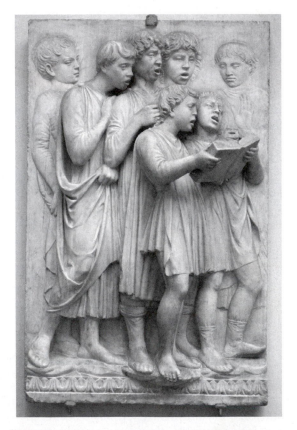

Humanist sculpture. *Each of the seven choir boys in Luca della Robbia's 1431 sculpture for the choir gallery of the Florence Cathedral has a distinctive appearance and personality. This contrasts sharply with the 12th-century depiction of King David and his musicians in the St. Alban's Psalter (p. 60), in which all seven figures have essentially the same visage.*

Source: Ted Spiegel/CORBIS BETTMANN

The Roman Catholic Church, as it gradually came to be known—prior to the Reformation, there had been only one church—did not sit idly by in the face of this religious revolution. It responded first by subjecting suspected heretics to trial, excommunication, and sometimes imprisonment or even death. The Counter-Reformation of the mid-16th century was a more systematic and positive attempt to retain or win back believers to the Roman Catholic Church, in part through a modification of doctrine and practices, in part through music.

MUSIC IN RENAISSANCE SOCIETY

As secular courts increased in size, number, and importance during the Renaissance, so too did their influence on the arts. Rulers now measured their greatness not only according to their territory, treasury, and military might, but also by what might be called their cultural capital. The arts as a whole benefited enormously from this newfound concern for cultural prestige. The Medicis in Florence, the Este dynasty in Ferrara, the Sforza dynasty in Milan, the collective leadership of the Republic of Venice, the Vatican in Rome, the royal court of Naples—all these and other principalities, duchies, and kingdoms throughout Italy, and eventually throughout Europe, placed great value on having talented poets, painters, sculptors, architects, and musicians active at their courts.

Any court with pretensions to cultural importance maintained its own roster of musicians to perform during services in the court chapel as well as for banquets, dances, and other festivities of a more secular nature. The size and quality of these musical organizations varied greatly; a well-funded *cappella,* as such an ensemble was called, typically consisted of between 12 and 20 musicians but could be larger or smaller according to the resources of the court treasury at any given time. Affluent courts actively recruited the best musical talent they could afford.

Composers and musicians were considerably more mobile in the Renaissance than before. The English composer John Dunstable spent a good portion of his career in France. Guillaume Du Fay, Josquin des Prez, and Orlande de Lassus, all born in the Low Countries, were drawn to the active cultural life of courts on the Italian peninsula. Du Fay spent time in the courts of Florence, Rome, and Milan; Josquin in Milan, Rome, and Ferrara; and Lassus in Mantua and Rome. All three returned north of the Alps later in their careers.

The church remained an important source of patronage as well. The surviving repertory indicates that the demand for new polyphonic liturgical music—from settings of the Mass Ordinary to hymns to motets—was enormous. Many affluent churches maintained resident composers, providing them with housing and a fixed income in exchange for music on demand.

The invention of the printing press provided yet another source of income for composers of all varieties of music, from secular songs to settings of the Mass Ordinary. Music that had once circulated in relatively scarce manuscripts could now be sold in quantity to the general public.

As during the medieval era, only a fraction of the music of the Renaissance was the work of professional composers and musicians. Most music was performed in the context of an unwritten tradition that operated outside any system of notation. For those who pretended to gentility, however, the ability to read music, sing, and play at least one if not more instruments was considered an essential grace. Royals themselves set the standard. The English king Henry VIII took great pride in his abilities both as a composer and singer. His daughter, Elizabeth I, was renowned as a lutenist and keyboard player (see p. 113).

The Emergence of Renaissance Style

In their quest to revive ancient practices, most Renaissance scholars and artists had actual models to study and imitate. Ancient buildings and sculpture were close at hand in Italy, for painters, sculptors, and architects. Writers had a growing body of ancient texts to emulate. But the sounds of ancient music had not been preserved, so for musicians, the imitation of models from classical antiquity was effectively impossible.

Not until the closing decades of the 16th century did scholars and musicians begin trying to recreate the musical practices of ancient Greece. Most Renaissance musicians were nevertheless firmly convinced that the music of their own time was inferior to that of the distant past. They reached this conclusion from the many references in ancient literature to music's miraculous power. In the words of the Spanish composer and theorist Bartolomé Ramos de Pareja (ca. 1440–ca. 1491):

> Without a doubt, music has immense effect upon and mighty power over the human soul, whether to calm or to rouse it. If in our time music does not work so many miracles, it is to be attributed not to the art, whose perfection exceeds that of nature, but to those who use the art badly. If those excellent [Greek] musicians . . . were called back to life they would deny that our music was invented by them—so inept, unharmonious, and dissipated has it been rendered through the corruption of certain singers.[1]

CONSONANCE AND DISSONANCE: TRUSTING THE EAR

Although they may have felt inferior to their ancient counterparts, Renaissance musicians felt confidently superior to their immediate predecessors. Influenced by humanism, new ways of thinking about the arts in general, and by the still broader sense that they were part of a cultural rebirth, commentators of the 15th century drew a clear distinction between what we now think of as medieval music and the music of their own time. Johannes Tinctoris (1435–1511), a renowned composer and the most prominent theorist of his generation, expressed this view bluntly. "[A]lthough it seems beyond belief," he declared in 1477, "there does not exist a single piece of music, not composed within the last forty years, that is regarded by the learned as worth hearing." Significantly, Tinctoris based his historical evaluation on actual composers and on works he knew. He did not rely on or even refer to the commentaries of past authorities. In short, he trusted "the judgment of my ears" over tradition.

Central to the difference between medieval and Renaissance music was the question of consonance and dissonance. Medieval theorists, drawing on the authority of Boethius and through him Pythagoras, gave priority to number and reason over sound in defining a consonant interval. They thus considered as consonant only those intervals that could be expressed as mathematically simple ratios: the octave (2:1), the fifth (3:2), and the fourth (4:3). Tinctoris and other Renaissance theorists rejected this antiempirical tradition, speaking instead of the "sweetness" of the third. Bartolomé Ramos de Pareja maintained that the ear could not in fact distinguish between the intervals of 81:64 (the major third) and 80:64 (reducible to 5:4). He therefore argued that the major third of 5:4 should be considered consonant, along with the interval of the minor third as 30:25 (6:5).

This empirical and practical challenge to traditional music theory manifested itself in other ways as well. The 11th-century theorist Guido of Arezzo, following Boethius, had drawn a sharp distinction between a *musicus,* one who understands the essential, mathematical nature of music, and a *cantor* ("singer"), a mere performer, little better than a beast, "for whoever does things without understanding them, is by definition a beast"[2] (see illustration "The Two Sides of Music," p. 16). Tinctoris endorsed the distinction, but with a practical twist. In his *Dictionary of Music* (published in 1473, the first work of its kind), he defines a *musicus* as someone who "after careful rational investigation" of music "through benefit of thought, assumes the office of singer."[3] Ramos de Pareja, in a treatise pointedly entitled *Musica practica* ("Practical Music"), dismissed the authority of Guido altogether on the grounds that he was "perhaps a better monk than a musician."[4] This dig at Guido roused the clergy, who denounced Ramos de Pareja as a virtual heretic.

More was at stake here than a difference of opinion about consonance and dissonance. Indeed, the Renaissance challenge to medieval scholasticism—in all areas of study, not just music—frightened many as a threat to the authority of the church and its teachings. The struggle between the acceptance of tradition and the new methods of critical thought would play itself out on many fronts over the course of succeeding centuries in the realms of astronomy, geography, theology, as well as music. The new attitude, exemplified by the willingness to question or even dismiss a large body of music and musical thought of the past, marks a significant shift in outlook and one that more than any single stylistic element characterizes the musical Renaissance.[5]

SONORITY: THE *CONTENANCE ANGLOISE*

According to Tinctoris, the "fountain and origin" of what he and his contemporaries perceived to be a distinctly new musical style "lies with the English, whose leading master was [John] Dunstable." From Dunstable (ca. 1390–1453), he traces it to the French composers Gilles Binchois (1400–1460) and Guillaume Du Fay (1397–1474), and from them to the leading composers of his own day, most notably Johannes

Ockeghem (ca. 1420–1496), Johannes Regis (ca. 1430–ca. 1485), and Antoine Busnois (ca. 1430–1492). Little is known about Dunstable's life, but it is likely he spent time in France in the service of the Duke of Bedford, who was fighting the French in the Hundred Years' War. If so, he would have been well situated to influence French composers. And, indeed, almost all of his music is preserved in continental rather than English manuscripts.

Tinctoris was not the first to perceive something new in the music of Dunstable, Binchois, and Du Fay. As early as 1442, the French poet Martin le Franc had singled out these composers as exemplars of what he called the **contenance angloise,** the "English guise," which he characterized as a "new way of composing with lively consonances." Although le Franc does not describe this style in any detail, he seems to have been responding to a new kind of sonority, in which the music is dominated by thirds, fifths, and sixths. The English predilection for thirds had already been evident in music of the late medieval era (see Chapter 3). Dunstable and his followers used these intervals in a manner that has since been described as one of **panconsonance,** a harmonic idiom that makes ample use of **triads** (vertical alignments of three notes whose basic pitches are separated by major or minor thirds) and limits the use of dissonance considerably.

Dunstable
Quam pulchra es

Dunstable's *Quam pulchra es* ("How Fair You Are"), a motet written sometime before 1430 on a text from the Song of Solomon, illustrates these characteristics. Its three voices are of more or less equal weight; none of them derives from preexistent material. They all have the same rhythmic profile, and they combine repeatedly to form triads that move in blocks, almost like a chorale or hymn. The intervals resulting from the interrelationship of the three voices are overwhelmingly consonant: dissonances, such as the "E" in the uppermost voice in measure 2, are few and rhythmically brief. The texture here is similar to that of the polyphonic conductus (see Chapter 2), yet the vertical alignment of sonorities clearly distinguishes it from that earlier form.

Du Fay
Flos florum

The influence of the *contenance angloise* on Du Fay is apparent in his *Flos florum,* believed to have been written ca. 1425–1430. This brief work is an example of a **cantilena motet,** which features a florid, lyrical top voice over a pair of slower moving lower voices. In spite of the rhythmic contrast, the intervals resulting from the interaction of these voices are strongly oriented toward thirds and triads, with triadic cadences at measures 7, 11, 40, and 59. The fifth nevertheless retains its traditional pride of place as the final cadential interval, as in Dunstable's *Quam pulchra es.*

Fauxbourdon and Faburden

Du Fay was an important figure in the development of **fauxbourdon,** another compositional technique that favored triadic sonorities and that emerged around 1430. A fauxbourdon is an unnotated line that runs parallel to the uppermost of two notated lines, usually at the interval of a fourth below, creating a harmonic texture rich in thirds

Du Fay
Conditor alme siderum

and sixths. The Advent hymn *Conditor alme siderum* ("Bountiful Creator of the Stars") alternates between plainchant (in the odd-numbered strophes) and three-voiced polyphony. In the polyphonic sections, the two higher voices sing a slightly embellished version of the original plainchant. Interestingly, the earliest preserved version of this work transmits the plainchant melody in mensural notation, bringing it into alignment with the rhythm of the alternating polyphony. This source also transcribes only one of the two upper voices in the polyphonic sections. The third voice is indicated simply by the word *fauxbourdon* written in the margin.

In the related contemporary English technique of **faburden,** musicians would interpolate lines both above and below a preexisting melody. The upper line would parallel the notated melody a fourth above, and the lower line would vary between thirds and fifths below it. This resulted in what we might today think of as sixth chords (that is, first-inversion chords, with the sixth scale degree in the root), although theorists of the time would not have perceived them as such. The net effect, however, as with fauxbourdon, was to reinforce the idea of thirds and sixths as consonant intervals.

New Sonority, Old Structure: Du Fay's *Nuper rosarum flores*

The new sonority characteristic of Renaissance style was not at first accompanied by new approaches to musical structure. Indeed, some of Du Fay's most significant early works are organized according to the medieval technique of isorhythm even as they explore new sonorities. The motet *Nuper rosarum flores* ("The Rose Blossoms"), written for the consecration of the newly completed dome of the cathedral in Florence on March 25, 1436, provides a revealing example of this mixing of old and new.

> **Du Fay**
> *Nuper rosarum flores*

The dome—designed by Filippo Brunelleschi (1377–1446), who also oversaw its construction—is a triumph of Renaissance engineering. The consecration of the dome was an event in honor of an architectural masterpiece, so it is no coincidence that the structure of the cathedral is reflected in Du Fay's motet. The **cantus firmus**—the term composers of the time were now using for the "fixed melody" that served as the basis of a composition—derives from the opening of the Introit *Terribilis est locus iste* ("Awesome Is This Place"), a chant employed (appropriately enough) in ceremonies for the dedication of a new church (see Example 4-1). Du Fay applies the cantus firmus in an unusual way here, stating it canonically in two voices, beginning in measure 29. The melody in the Tenor II line is stated a fifth above the melody in the Tenor, and each voice is based on a different isorhythm, so the two voices move at different speeds. It has been suggested that this two-voiced canonic cantus firmus structure may relate to the novel structure of Brunelleschi's dome, which consists of an inner frame supporting a separate outer skin.

Example 4-1 Opening of the Introit *Terribilis est locus iste.*

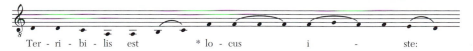

Ter - ri - bi - lis   est   * lo - cus   i - ste:

Less speculative is the relationship of the work's general proportions to Solomon's Temple in Jerusalem, which theologians had long viewed as the prototypical church. As described in I Kings, the Temple was laid out in the proportions 6:4:2:3, with 6 the total length of the building, 4 the length of the nave, 2 the width of the building and the length of the sanctuary, and 3 the height of the building. The Cathedral of Florence followed these same proportions, and Du Fay mirrors them precisely in the temporal presentation of the cantus firmus, which is stated four times in the proportions of 6:4:2:3.

The number symbolism in Du Fay's motet goes further still. The numbers 4 and 7 dominate throughout. The text consists of four strophes of seven lines, and the music is divided into four sections, one for each strophe, corresponding to the changes in the rhythm of the cantus firmus just outlined. Finally, each of these sections has a duration of 28 breves; the length of each section varies according to the mensuration sign used. The number 28, the product of 4×7, is also a perfect number, that is, a number that is the sum of all its factors, excluding itself ($1 + 2 + 4 + 7 + 14 = 28$).

In spite of its archaic isometric structure, the sonorities of *Nuper rosarum flores* are decidedly progressive. The music is full of what would now be called **root position triads.**

Composer Profile

Guillaume Du Fay
(1397–1474)

Guillaume Du Fay (or Dufay) was widely acknowledged during his lifetime as the leading composer of his day. Admired for both the quantity and quality of his compositions, he traveled widely throughout Europe. He served at the Papal Chapels in Rome, Florence, and Bologna, and was music director at the court of Savoy in northwestern Italy. His musical output embodies the transition from medieval to Renaissance style. He was also among the first of the so-called northern composers to spend a good portion of his career in Italy. At his death the noted composer Loysète Compère called Du Fay "the moon of all music, and the light of all singers."

Principal Works

MASSES AND MASS MOVEMENTS Most of Du Fay's half-dozen complete settings of the Ordinary are based on a single cantus firmus. Du Fay also wrote more than two dozen settings of individual Mass movements, pairs of movements (such as Gloria and

KEY DATES IN THE LIFE OF GUILLAUME DU FAY
1397 Born at Hainault (now in Belgium)
1419–1424 In Rimini and Pesaro (Italy); returns north to Cambrai (northern France)
1426–1428 In Bologna (Italy)
1428 Joins the Papal Chapel in Rome as a singer
1434–1435 Maestro di cappella (music director) at the court of Savoy (northwestern Italy)
1435–1437 Serves in Papal Chapel again, this time in Florence and Bologna
1439 Returns to Cambrai as canon of the cathedral; travels widely in subsequent decades
1474 Dies in Cambrai on November 27

Credo), or groups of three movements (Kyrie, Gloria, Credo). Most of these derive at least some portion of their melodic material from plainchant.

PRIMARY EVIDENCE

Music at the Consecration of the Dome of the Florence Cathedral

Giovanni Manetti, an eyewitness to the consecration of the Florence Cathedral's dome in 1436, described the music in almost mystical terms. We do not know if Du Fay's *Nuper rosarum flores* was the work played at the elevation, but Manetti's account is certainly consistent with the nature of the music.

• • • • •

[A]t the elevation of the Most Sacred Host, the whole space of the temple was filled with such choruses of harmony and such a concert of diverse instruments that it seemed (not without reason) as though the symphonies and songs of the angels and of divine paradise had been set forth from Heaven to whisper in our ears an unbelievable celestial sweetness. Therefore, in that moment, I was so possessed by ecstasy that I seemed to enjoy the life of the blessed here on earth; whether it happened so to others present I know not, but concerning myself I can bear witness.

Source: Guillaume Du Fay, *Opera omnia*, ed. G. De Van, Corpus mensurabilis musicae 1 (Rome, 1447–1449), II, p. xxvii.

MOTETS Du Fay wrote a wide range of polyphonic vocal music that falls under the designation of motet, including isorhythmic motets, cantilena

Guillaume Du Fay and Gilles Binchois. *This double portrait, from a manuscript version of Martin le Franc's* Le champion des dames *("The Champion of Women," 1440–1442), is directly connected to the text beneath it, which praises the two composers for having developed "a new way of composing / with lively consonances," presumably a reference to their frequent use of thirds and sixths. The dieresis over Du Fay's name suggests it is correctly pronounced as three syllables (Du Fa-ee). In other sources, the composer's name is given in three parts, with a "fa" in musical notation between the syllables "Du" and "y."*

Source: Giraudon/Art Resource, N.Y.

motets, and simple fauxbourdon antiphons. He also wrote four different settings of the Magnificat.

PLAINCHANT Du Fay was the last prominent composer to contribute to the plainchant repertory. He was commissioned in 1457 to write the music for both the Mass and Office for an entire feast day dedicated to the Virgin Mary. The monophonic music for this service, lost for centuries, came to light only in 1988 when a scholar working in a Belgian archive discovered it.

CHANSONS Other than a handful of Italian-language songs, all of Du Fay's secular music is in French. It includes 8 ballades, more than 60 rondeaux (not all of which have survived in their entirety), and 4 virelais.

The lowest line of Du Fay's motet is not always the basis—or root—of the harmony, but the lowest sounding voice usually is, whether it occurs in the Tenor, Tenor II, or motetus part. Thus the lowest sounding voice consistently provides the root of the triad sounding above it.

Although it would be anachronistic to speak in terms of a harmonic progression—like their medieval counterparts, Renaissance composers thought of harmony as a by-product of polyphonic voice leading—the patterned sonorities would certainly have struck contemporary listeners as quite different from the motets of the previous generation. And even in the two-voice sections, the most common intervals are thirds, sixths, and tenths.

JOSQUIN'S *AVE MARIA . . . VIRGO SERENA* AND THE STYLE OF THE RENAISSANCE

Judging from the many printed and manuscript sources in which it circulated, *Ave Maria . . . virgo serena* was one of Josquin's best known and most widely admired works during his lifetime. When the Venetian music printer Ottaviano Petrucci published his

Composer Profile

Josquin des Prez
(ca. 1450–1521)

IOSQVINVS PRATENSIS.

Josquin des Prez. *Although first published in 1611, some 90 years after the composer's death, this woodcut was based on an earlier portrait destroyed by fire in the 16th century. No other even remotely authentic image of the composer has survived.*

Source: AKG London Ltd.

J osquin, hailed by his contemporaries as one of the greatest composers of his time, was also one of the first composers whose reputation endured well past his death. "Josquin," wrote Martin Luther, "is master of the notes, which must express what he desires."[6] Thirty years after his death, theorists and pedagogues were still recommending his works as models for aspiring young composers. So great was Josquin's reputation, in fact, that some publishers sought to profit from it fraudulently. Several dozen works attributed to him in 16th-century prints are now known to have been written by others.

Indeed, it seems the more we learn about Josquin's life, the less we know with certainty. Only within the last five years have scholars discovered his true family name was Lebloitte and that "des Prez" was a nickname of sorts. Archival research has further revealed that two "Josquins" were working at the cathedral of Milan in the 1470s: the composer we know as Josquin des Prez, and another Josquin

TEXTURAL STRUCTURE OF JOSQUIN'S *AVE MARIA . . . VIRGO SERENA*		
Text section	**Measure number**	**Texture**
Salutation	1	Pervading imitation; four voices together only at the very end
Strophe 1	31	High vs. low, followed by full chordal texture
Strophe 2	55	High vs. low, followed by full imitative texture
Strophe 3	78	High. vs. low, nonimitative
Strophe 4	94	Fully voiced, note-against-note counterpoint
Strophe 5	111	Four voices, pervading imitation
Petition	143	Four voices, note against note, long rhythmic values

who served in the ducal chapel for some 40 years and was also a singer and composer.

We nevertheless have enough to know that Josquin was a highly self-confident individual, well aware of his talents. In 1502, a member of the court of Duke Ercole d'Este of Ferrara wrote to his master about two potential employees, Josquin and Heinrich Isaac:

> To me [Isaac] seems well suited to serve Your Lordship, more so than Josquin, because he is of a better disposition among his companions, and he will compose new works more often. It is true that Josquin composes better, but he composes when he wants to, and not when one wants him to, and he is asking 200 ducats in salary while Isaac will come for 120—but Your Lordship will decide.[7]

His Lordship eventually decided in favor of the more difficult—and expensive—Josquin.

Principal Works

Josquin wrote in virtually every vocal genre of his time. He composed some 18 Masses and 6 individual Mass movements, almost 100 motets, and about 70 chansons, most of which are in French, some in Italian, and others with no text at all. These numbers are approximate because of the uncertain status of some of the works attributed to him.

KEY DATES IN THE LIFE OF JOSQUIN DES PREZ

ca. 1450 Born in what is now northern France or Belgium, possibly in Saint-Quentin

1475–ca. 1480 Member of the chapel of King René of Anjou in Aix-en-Provence (southern France)

1484–1485 In the service of Cardinal Ascanio Sforza in Milan and Rome

1489–ca. 1495 Serves in the ducal chapel in Milan, then in the papal chapel in Rome

1503–1504 Serves in the chapel of Ercole d'Este in Ferrara

1504–1521 Provost of the collegiate church of Notre-Dame in Condé-sur-Escaut, in what is now northern France

1521 Dies in Condé-sur-Escaut

---

first collection of motets in 1502, he gave this work pride of place at the head of the volume. Like the Mona Lisa for Renaissance painting, Josquin's motet can serve as an exemplar for many of the characteristic features of Renaissance musical style.

Texture: Pervading Imitation

Predominantly triadic sonorities and carefully controlled dissonance are not the only features characteristic of Renaissance music. By the 1470s, many composers were making greater and greater use of a technique known as **pervading imitation,** in which a series of musical ideas are stated imitatively in all voices throughout an entire work or section of a work. By its very nature, pervading imitation requires all voices to sing (more or less) the same musical ideas, making them more or less equal in their melodic and rhythmic profiles. The resulting homogeneity of texture is a feature of much Renaissance music written from the late 15th century onward.

Ave Maria . . . virgo serena illustrates this new approach. Probably written during the 1470s or early 1480s, the work opens with a series of imitative entries that move systematically from the highest to the lowest voice. Each of these distinctive thematic units is

Josquin des Prez
Ave Maria . . . virgo serena

known as a **point of imitation.** Successive points of imitation and cadences of varying weight help articulate the individual sections even while moving the whole work forward.

Yet the work does not consist entirely of points of imitation using all four voices. Like most Renaissance composers, Josquin is careful to provide textural variety. He differentiates each unit of the text—an opening salutation to the Virgin, five strophes in praise of the Virgin, and a closing petition, a brief prayer invoking the protection of the Virgin— through a series of contrasting textures that are sometimes imitative and sometimes not. He also uses only two voices at certain junctures, at times playing off high against low registers.

Treatment of Text

By the middle of the 15th century, composers had generally abandoned polyglot texts in favor of a single text and an increasingly direct connection between words and music. The text of Josquin's motet extolls the Virgin Mary. Although its five internal strophes allude to five major feasts in honor of Mary, the text itself is not liturgical.

Josquin organizes *Ave Maria . . . virgo serena* around the structure of this text. Each strophe has its own thematic material, and each varies from the others in terms of texture, cadences, and the number of voices.

Cadential Structure

As in a great many musical works of the Renaissance, cadences play an important role in articulating the form of this motet. Each of its sections is more or less self-contained, depending on the strength of its closing cadence. Josquin calibrated the sequence of cadences with great care (see table "Cadential Structure of Josquin's *Ave Maria . . . virgo serena*"), moving from the weakest at the very beginning (two voices on the interval of a third, with rhythmic overlap into the next section) to the strongest at the end (four voices on the interval of a fifth, sustained for a duration of four full breves).

This kind of structure, based on discrete units that are more or less independent from one another, is known as **paratactic form.** Musically, no unifying themes or

CADENTIAL STRUCTURE OF JOSQUIN'S *AVE MARIA . . . VIRGO SERENA*				
Section	Measure number	Number of voices	Intervals in cadence	Rhythmic features
Salutation	30–1	4 → 2	Third	Overlaps into strophe 1
Strophe 1	53–4	4 → 3	Third	Overlaps into strophe 2
Strophe 2	77	3	Unison	No overlap
Strophe 3	93	2	Unison	No overlap
Strophe 4	110	3	Unison	No overlap
Strophe 5	141	3	Fifth	Followed by one breve rest
Petition	154–5	4	Fifth	Sustained over four breves

rhythmic patterns run throughout the work as a whole; instead, the structure consists of a succession of essentially closed and unrelated units (A, B, C, D, E, etc.). Paratactic form is characteristic of a great deal of Renaissance music, vocal as well as instrumental.

Mode

Like other composers of the Renaissance, Josquin worked within the framework of the eight-mode system that had been in use since medieval times (see Chapter 1). Individual voices would generally move within the confines of a particular mode. Identifying the mode of a work consisting of many voices was sometimes a challenge. Most theorists agreed, however, that the mode of any given polyphonic composition could be determined primarily by the range and final of the tenor voice. According to this system, *Ave Maria . . . virgo serena* is written in transposed hypolydian (on C).

Melody

Melody in Renaissance music is generally characterized by **conjunct motion**—that is, stepwise progressions, with only occasional leaps of more than a fifth, and even then rarely anything other than a sixth or an octave. As in plainchant, large leaps are generally followed by a move in the opposite direction, further contributing to the broader sense of balance between upward and downward movement. The opening motive of *Ave Maria . . . virgo serena* in fact derives from the plainchant melody associated with the Sequence "Ave Maria" (see Example 4-2) used in the Feast of the Annunciation.

Example 4-2 Sequence *Ave Maria.*

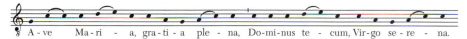

A - ve   Ma - ri - a, gra - ti - a   ple - na, Do-mi-nus te - cum, Vir-go se - re - na.

Source: Sequence *Ave Maria.* From Edward E. Lowinsky, *Josquin des Prez* (New York and Oxford: Oxford University Press, 1976), p. 538. Reprinted by permission of Oxford University Press.

Rhythm

Most Renaissance music lacks a sense of stressed downbeats and is organized rhythmically around a steady pulse called the ***tactus*** (Latin for "touch"). *Ave Maria . . . virgo serena* is thus typical of its time, for it avoids any strong sense of meter or consistently patterned rhythm. Each section of the work establishes its own characteristic rhythmic profile. Also typical of Renaissance music is the manner in which each section becomes somewhat more animated as it progresses, then slows down again toward its close. This same rhythmic pattern holds for the composition as a whole, with the final strophe the rhythmically fastest of all, and the petition at the very end the slowest, emphasizing its function of closure.

Harmony

Harmony in the Renaissance continued to be perceived as a by-product of voice leading, not as an end in its own right. It is therefore anachronistic to speak of Renaissance compositions in terms of later concepts of tonal harmony—to analyze them, say, in terms of the effects of a progression from a V chord to an I chord, as in the closing measures of Josquin's *Ave Maria . . . virgo serena.* Yet composers and listeners of the time were certainly aware of the effects of successive vertical sonorities. Consonance tables began to appear regularly in compositional treatises during the 1490s, an important indication that composers were thinking about their art—and teaching it—more and more in terms of what we today call harmony. In a treatise published in 1516, Pietro Aron explicitly discussed the means of moving from one chord to another.[8] Privately, the theorist Giovanni Spataro complained as early as 1529 that "even without studying the precepts of counterpoint everyone is a master of composing harmony."[9]

Conceptions of the compositional process changed fundamentally over the course of the Renaissance. In the medieval era, composers were often able to layer voices one on top of the other, as in organum, clausulae, and isorhythmic motets. Cantus firmus compositions continued this tradition of successive composition to some extent. But the more homogeneous texture evident in a work like Josquin's *Ave Maria . . . virgo serena* suggests a different approach to writing. This kind of texture, based on interlocking points of imitation, required composers to work out the implications of any given idea for all the voices more or less at once.

CONCLUSION

The characteristic style of Renaissance music emerged gradually over the course of the 15th century and continued to evolve throughout the 16th. None of its features appeared overnight: each asserted itself only incrementally, often against resistance. As is so often the case in the history of any art, these stylistic transformations were often generational. At any given time, older musicians might be maintaining traditional practices while their younger colleagues were embracing new attitudes and new approaches.

SUMMARY OF STYLE DIFFERENCES BETWEEN MEDIEVAL AND RENAISSANCE MUSIC

	MEDIEVAL	RENAISSANCE
TEXTURE	Layered, with voices moving at different speeds in most genres.	More homogeneous textures, with all voices of essentially equal importance; pervading imitation dominates from the latter decades of the 15th century onward.
RHYTHM	Sharp differentiation among various voices in certain genres (motet, chanson). Dominance of the rhythmic modes.	Generally balanced and evenly flowing. A steady pulse (the *tactus*) governs performance, and although this may change within the course of a work, it remains steady for long stretches at a time.
MELODY	Often angular, without a strong sense of a larger-scale shape.	Generally lyrical ("vocal"). Relatively less use of melodic material from preexistent sources.
HARMONY	Octaves, fifths, and fourths are consonant; thirds begin to emerge only gradually as consonant.	Thirds and sixths now considered consonant, fourths less so, particularly in practice. Relatively limited and carefully controlled use of dissonance.
FORM	Cantus firmus structures, isorhythm, *formes fixes* predominate.	Cantus firmus, isorhythm, *formes fixes* all continue until ca. 1490; afterward, chansons and motets are more likely to be paratactic (A, B, C, D, etc.), with individual subunits of a work more or less sharply demarcated from one another.
INSTRUMENTATION	Extremely limited repertory for instruments alone; great flexibility in doubling or replacing voices in vocal music.	Vocal works adhere to the a cappella (voice only) ideal, with the option of instruments doubling voices. Vocal and instrumental idioms are essentially interchangeable, with only a limited number of works written specifically and exclusively for instruments.

The Genres of Renaissance Music, 1420–1520

The development of musical style during the first 100 years of the Renaissance—roughly 1420 to 1520—can best be traced in greater detail by considering those genres of central importance to composers of this period. In the realm of sacred vocal music, these genres were the Mass and motet; in secular vocal music, the chanson and frottola. Instrumental music, although committed to writing only infrequently, preserves the keyboard and dance repertories of the time.

SACRED VOCAL MUSIC

The principal genres of sacred music in the Renaissance were the Mass and the motet. Composers of the 15th century and early 16th centuries cultivated both these genres with unprecedented intensity. From a stylistic perspective, both the Mass and the motet reflect all of the most important developments that occurred over the course of roughly three generations, from Dunstable (in the early 15th century) through Du Fay and Ockeghem (in the middle of the 15th century) to Josquin des Prez and his contemporaries (in the late 15th and early 16th centuries). Within the span of a generation—roughly the middle decades of the 15th century—cantus firmus technique supplanted isorhythm as the chief structural device in the composition of large-scale vocal works, including both Mass and motet. Although isorhythmic technique persisted for some time into the second half of the 15th century, it had largely disappeared by 1500. Pervading imitation, in turn, had become an important structural device by the beginning of the 16th century.

The Mass: Du Fay and Ockeghem

Composers of the late medieval era were not particularly interested in polyphonic settings of the complete Mass Ordinary. Guillaume de Machaut's *Messe de Nostre Dame* (Anthology; see Chapter 3), written in the late 1360s, remained the only work of its kind for almost a century.

The emergence of the **cyclic Mass**—a cycle of all movements of the Mass Ordinary integrated by a common cantus firmus or other musical device—signals an important shift in musical aesthetics. Composers now began to place issues of musical coherence above questions of liturgical propriety or the projection of the text. Machaut had based each movement of his Mass—Kyrie, Gloria, and so forth—on a different but liturgically appropriate plainchant. The result, in true medieval fashion, subordinated the polyphony to the chant. Renaissance composers were far more inclined to create Mass cycles connected by a common musical thread that may or may not have been liturgically appropriate.

Guillaume Du Fay is credited with six complete settings of the Mass. What is believed to be the first of these, the *Missa Se la face ay pale*, was written around 1450. The Mass takes its name from the ballade *Se la face ay pale* ("If My Face Is Pale"), which Du Fay himself had composed sometime during the 1430s. Two features of this Mass are significant: it is the first by any composer based on a cantus firmus from a secular source, and it is one of the first in which the tenor—the line carrying the cantus firmus—is no longer the lowest voice. This second feature is of particular importance, for with the lowest voice no longer bound to the cantus firmus, composers were free to exercise a wider range of vertical sonorities—what we now think of as harmony.

Du Fay
Missa Se la face ay pale

Du Fay
Se la face ay pale

The cantus firmus, derived from the tenor of Du Fay's ballade (Example 5-1), appears repeatedly throughout the Mass. It is absent only in internal sections in some movements, such as the Christe section within the Kyrie, for example, and the section beginning *Pleni sunt caeli* in the Sanctus.

The composer wrote a verbal canon (meaning "rule" or "law") at the beginning of each movement of the Mass to indicate the rhythmic value of the cantus firmus in that movement. At the opening of the Kyrie, for example, we find the notation *Canon: Tenor crescit in duplo*, which means the rhythmic value of the notes of the tenor as set down in the original notation of the chanson are to be doubled. Other canons are not quite so straightforward. At the head of both the Gloria and Credo we read (in translation from the original Latin): "The tenor is stated three times. The first time it grows by three, the second by two, the third as set down." In other words, the tenor is sung three times in succession, the first time at three times the value of the notated original, the second at twice the value, the third at the original of the notated value. The table on page 82 shows how Du Fay structured the Mass around the cantus firmus.

Although the cantus firmus is the most obvious and important of the devices unifying the various movements of this Mass, other elements also contribute to a sense of musical coherence. The thematic idea found in the opening measures of the top line in the Kyrie, for example, reappears at many points in subsequent movements, such as the beginning of the Christe and the beginning of the Gloria. Every movement except the opening Kyrie begins with a duet essentially identical to that found in the opening four measures of the Gloria. This **head motif**—a thematic idea in multiple voices placed prominently at the beginning of a movement or section of a movement—provides yet another element of coherence to the work as a whole.

Du Fay's Masses appear to have inspired an entire generation of composers to construct artful ways of unifying the movements of a Mass cycle. Many pursued the idea of

Example 5-1 The structure of the cantus firmus for Dufay's *Missa se la face ay pale.*

Source: *Dufay, Se la face ay pale:* structure of cantus firmus, from Howard Mayer Brown, *Music in the Renaissance* 2/e (Prentice-Hall, 1976, 1999), p. 45. © 1999. Reprinted by permission of Pearson Education, Inc., Upper Saddle River, NJ.

Ockeghem
Missa prolationum

manipulating a cantus firmus; others focused on the device of the unifying head motif. Still others used the musical canon as a unifying device. Easily the most remarkable of all works in this last category is Johannes Ockeghem's *Missa prolationum* ("Mass of the Prolations"), preserved in the sumptuous Chigi Codex. In this, the oldest surviving source of the work, only two of the four voices are actually notated: the other two can be

FORMAL LAYOUT OF DU FAY, *MISSA SE LA FACE AY PALE*, KYRIE AND GLORIA		
	Section of cantus firmus used	**Speed of cantus firmus**
Kyrie		
Kyrie I	AB	2 × original value
Christe	Cantus firmus omitted	
Kyrie II	C	2 × original value
Gloria		
Et in terra pax	Complete	3 × original value
Qui tollis	Complete	2 × original value
Cum sancto spiritu	Complete	Original value

Source: From H. M. Brown, *Music in the Renaissance* 2/e (Prentice-Hall, 1976, 1999), p. 46. © 1999. Reprinted by permission of Pearson Education, Inc., Upper Saddle River, NJ.

White Notation

The most important development in notation during the Renaissance occurred around the middle of the 15th century with the emergence of what we today call white mensural notation. In *white mensural notation*, standard longs and breves, instead of being filled in, or black, are left unfilled, or white. The change was largely practical: it eliminated the time required to fill in the note heads and it caused less wear and tear on paper, which was rapidly replacing parchment as the standard medium for books and manuscripts. (A well-developed paper industry had established itself in France, southern Germany, and Switzerland by the end of the 14th century.) The essential elements of mensural notation remained otherwise unchanged (see Chapters 2 and 3).

derived from them, for every movement is a double canon in which each pair of voices presents the same material moving in different prolations, which are transcribed in modern editions as different meters (see Example 3-1 and the accompanying discussion of mensuration signs in Chapter 3). In almost every movement, each voice has its own unique mensuration. When all four voices are present, so too are all four of the basic

Johannes Ockeghem. *Johannes Ockeghem (ca. 1410–1497), wearing eyeglasses (not new but still fairly rare at the time), leads his choristers in singing from a large choir book. The practice of singing from a single source reflects the expense of preparing manuscripts by hand.*

Source: Illustration from "Chants Royaux sur la Conception Cournee du Puy de Rouan" 1519–28 Ms Add 1537 f. 58v: "Motet exquis chef d'oeuvre de nature" The choir sings the Gloria/Bibliotheque Nationale, Paris, France/ Bridgeman Art Library

mensurations ("prolations")—hence the name of the Mass. Throughout, the upper voices are in imperfect prolation, the lower voices in perfect prolation.

As if this were not complex enough, Ockeghem varies the intervallic as well as the rhythmic relationship of the canonic lines across the Mass as a whole, creating an elaborate series of canons at successively higher intervals. Ockeghem's fascination with canon and other elaborate structural devices is typical of the Franco-Flemish composers who flourished in the late 15th and early 16th centuries. Composers clearly enjoyed demonstrating the variety of ways in which they could treat a single cantus firmus. Between the middle of the 15th century and the 17th century, more than two dozen composers based works on a tune known as *L'homme armé* ("The Armed Man"; Example 5-2), including Busnois, Ockeghem, Tinctoris, Obrecht, and Josquin. Part of the melody's appeal is doubtless to be found in its upward trajectory, straightforward rhythm, and strong sense of a tonal center. Yet many settings by different composers are so directly connected as to suggest that artists were consciously imitating one another—in homage, competition, or some combination of the two.

Strong evidence also suggests that at least some settings of *L'homme armé* were connected to political events and understood to convey a particular message. One current theory maintains that the cycle of six anonymous settings preserved in a manuscript in Naples originated from the Burgundian circle of Philip the Good's Order of the Golden Fleece in connection with a planned crusade against the Turks shortly after the fall of Constantinople in 1453—hence the appeal of a tune entitled "The Armed Man." Other scholars associate "The Armed Man" with the mythical hero Hercules, and by extension Hercules d'Este, who ruled Ferrara from 1471 until 1505. Whatever their validity, these theories suggest how musical symbolism extended beyond purely musical issues.

Example 5-2 The *L'homme armé* melody.

The armed man, the armed man...One should fear the armed man.
The warning has been shouted everywhere that everyone should be armed with a suit of mail.

Source: The *l'homme armé* melody reprinted by permission of the publisher from THE NEW HARVARD DICTIONARY OF MUSIC, ed. Don Michal Randel (Harvard University Press, 1986), p. 380. Cambridge, MA: The Belknap Press of Harvard University Press, Copyright © 1986 by the President and Fellows of Harvard College.

The Mass: Josquin des Prez and His Contemporaries

Written over a span of some five decades, from the 1470s through the 1510s, the Masses of Josquin des Prez provide a compendium of the structural options available to composers in this genre in the late 15th and early 16th centuries. Josquin's Masses fall into one of four categories defined by the structural techniques that characterize them: cantus firmus, canon, imitation (or parody), and paraphrase.

The cantus firmus masses derive their structuring melodies from a variety of sources and apply them in many different ways. Josquin's cantus firmus sources include plainchant, secular song, an arbitrary arrangement of solmization syllables (as in the *Missa La sol fa re mi*), and *soggetto cavato,* in which the cantus firmus "subject" (*soggetto*) is "carved" (*cavato*) out of a given word or name. The *Missa Hercules Dux Ferrariae,* for example, derives its cantus firmus from solmization syllables corresponding to the Duke of Ferrara's name.

The techniques by which Josquin applies a cantus firmus include strict, ostinato, and free:

◆   In strict technique, the cantus firmus remains consistently in the tenor, in keeping with earlier practice, although it may sometimes appear in additional voices as well. Examples of this technique include *Missa L'homme armé super voces musicales, Missa L'ami Baudichon,* and *Missa Hercules Dux Ferrariae.*

◆   In **ostinato** technique, the cantus firmus is repeated so consistently that it appears in at least one voice at all times. An ostinato is a thematic idea repeated without interruption many times within the course of a section or entire work. Examples of an ostinato cantus firmus in Josquin's Masses may be found in the *Missa La sol fa re mi* and in the opening Kyrie of the *Missa Hercules Dux Ferrariae* (see Example 5-3).

◆   In free technique the cantus firmus migrates from voice to voice or may drop out altogether from time to time, as in the *Missa Faisant regretz.*

Canonic Masses are structured according to the principle of strict canon, in which at least one of the notated voices generates a second. In Josquin's *Missa ad fugam,* for example, the superius and tenor voices are canonic throughout the entire Mass, and the other two voices are freely composed. The *Missa sine nomine* ("The Nameless Mass," so called because it bears no relationship to any earlier musical source) is Josquin's other canonic Mass.

Imitation Masses (also known as parody Masses) incorporate all the voices of an existing work—not just a single voice—into the fabric of the new work, or at the very least into the opening sections of key movements. Examples by Josquin include the *Missa Fortuna desperata* and the *Missa Malheur me bat,* both of which are based on popular chansons. The opening of the *Missa Fortuna desperata,* for example, is derived from all three voices of a chanson attributed to Antoine Busnois (died 1492). The opening measures of the superius and bassus parts of the Kyrie of Josquin's Mass are little more than lightly embellished versions of the original chanson. Yet Josquin also makes important modifications to the existing work. He shifts the music from duple to triple meter and reworks the rhythm of the tenor voice to make it move at a slower speed—that is, to function more like a strict cantus firmus. The added fourth voice in Josquin's work—the altus—also takes the tenor of the original as its point of departure.

Josquin carries the idea of reworking multiple voices a step further in subsequent movements of the *Missa Fortuna desperata.* In the Agnus Dei I, for example, he moves the **inversion** (melodic mirror image) of the superius of the chanson to the bass line

Busnois (?)
Fortuna desperata

Josquin
Missa Fortuna desperata

Example 5-3 Josquin, *Missa Hercules Dux Ferrariae,* Kyrie (opening).

Source: Josquin, *Missa Hercules Dux Ferrariae,* Kyrie (mm. 1-17). From *Josquin, Werke,* ed. A. Smijers (Leipzig: C.F.W. Siegel, 1935), p. 19. Used by permission of KVNM [Koninklijke Vereniging voor Nederlandse Muziekgeschiedenis], Utrecht.

and **augments** it (increases the length of the note values) fourfold. This bizarre twist is almost certainly a musical commentary on the fickleness of the goddess Fortuna, who is forever turning her wheel, bringing down the mighty and raising the lowly in a never-ending cycle. In keeping with this symbolism, the tenor melody returns in its original form in the bass line of the final Agnus Dei.

By the middle of the 16th century, imitation—also known as *parody,* but without any suggestion of the comedy we now associate with the term—would become the predominant structural principle for Mass settings. Giovanni Pierluigi da Palestrina (1525 or 1526–1594) would use this device in about half of his 104 Masses, and Orlande de Lassus (1532–1594) would use it in more than two-thirds of his 74 Mass settings (see Chapter 6). Sacred motets and secular songs both provided musical material for such works. Cantus firmus settings, in turn, would become increasingly rare over the course of the 16th century.

Paraphrase, in contrast to imitation, involves borrowing an existing melodic idea from a different work but elaborating it freely in all voices of a new work. In the *Missa Pange lingua,* Josquin's last Mass, written sometime after 1513, all four voices use melodic material derived from the plainchant hymn of the same name (Anthology) but often in highly embellished form, with substantial interpolations between pitches.

Josquin's contemporaries were no less ingenious in their settings of the Mass Ordinary. A few examples will serve to convey some sense of the variety of solutions they devised to the challenge of setting the same text to music over and over again.

Josquin
Missa Pange lingua

The original wheel of fortune.   *The goddess Fortuna (left) spins her wheel, on which kings (top) fall, then rise again according to the cycle of fate. This 15th century image is roughly contemporary with the anonymous chanson* Fortuna desperata *and Josquin's Mass setting based on this chanson.*

Source: The Ancient Art & Architecture Collection Ltd.

PRIMARY EVIDENCE

Josquin the Exemplary

In his massive *Dodecachordon* of 1547, Henricus Glareanus refers repeatedly to Josquin as the composer most worthy of emulation by younger artists. Here, he summarizes the reasons for his admiration.

• • • • •

No one has more effectively expressed the passions of the soul in music than this symphonist, no one has more felicitously begun, no one has been able to compete in grace and facility on an equal footing with him, just as there is no Latin poet superior in the epic to Maro [i.e., the Roman poet Virgil, author of the *Aeneid*]. For just as Maro, with his natural facility, was accustomed to adapt his poem to his subject so as to set weighty matters before the eyes of his readers with close-packed spondees, fleeting ones with unmixed dactyls, to use words suited to his every subject, in short, to undertake nothing inappropriately . . . so our Josquin, where his matter requires it, now advances with impetuous and precipitate notes, now intones his subject in long-drawn tones, and, to sum up, has brought forth nothing that was not delightful to the ear and approved as ingenious by the learned, nothing, in short, that was not acceptable and pleasing, even when it seemed less erudite, to those who listened to it with judgment. In most of his works he is the magnificent virtuoso, as in the *Missa [L'homme armé] super voces musicales* and the *Missa ad fugam;* in some he is the mocker, as in the *Missa La sol fa re mi;* in some he extends himself in rivalry, as in the *Missa de Beata Virgine* [written on the same cantus firmus as Antoine Brumel's Mass of the same name]; although others have also frequently attempted all these things, they have not with the same felicity met with a corresponding success in their undertakings.

Source: *Source Readings in Music History,* ed. Oliver Strunk, rev. ed. Leo Treitler (New York: Norton, 1998), pp. 430–1. Copyright 1998 W. W. Norton & Company, Inc. used by permission of the publisher.

In his *Missa Sub tuum praesidium,* Jacob Obrecht (ca. 1450–1515) uses the same cantus firmus throughout but adds a new voice in each successive movement, starting with a Kyrie for three voices and then moving to a Gloria for four voices, a Credo for five, a Sanctus for six, and concluding with a seven-voice Agnus Dei. An increasing number of chants, all of them associated with the Virgin Mary, are also worked into each successive movement. And in his *Missa carminum* ("Mass of Songs"), Heinrich Isaac (ca. 1450–1517) incorporated a whole series of German popular songs.

The Motet

For all their work in the realm of the Mass, composers of Josquin's generation devoted even more of their energies toward the genre of the motet, a prayer set to music. These works were written to fulfill one of three principal functions:

◆ **Liturgical.** Motets continued to function within the liturgy of the Mass Proper, but were limited largely to Offertory texts. Motets were rarely connected with the Office, which typically used less elaborate music, either plainchant or simple hymns.

◆ **Devotional.** Religious gatherings outside the liturgy became increasingly common during the 15th and 16th centuries. Groups called confraternities met on a regular basis for devotional (that is, nonliturgical) services to pray, sing hymns, and engage in contemplation. Some of these confraternities are known to have commissioned polyphonic settings of such texts as the sequence *Salve Regina.* Josquin's *Ave*

F
O
C
U
S

Tinctoris's Eight Rules for Good Counterpoint

Tinctoris concludes his *Liber de arte contrapuncti* ("Treatise on the Art of Counterpoint," 1477) with "Eight Rules to Be Observed in All Counterpoint." These can be summarized as follows:

1. All counterpoint ought to begin and end with a perfect consonance (i.e., a fifth or octave).
2. Avoid parallel fifths and octaves.
3. Successive consonances of the same kind are permitted if the tenor remains on the same note.

4. Individual lines must be as conjunct as possible, with leaps used in moderation.
5. Cadences should never fall outside of the mode of the work at hand.
6. Individual lines should not repeat the same notes over and over unless for special effect, as in imitating the sound of bells or trumpets.
7. Avoid successive cadences on the same pitches.
8. Variety must be sought in all counterpoint.

Maria . . . virgo serena, based largely on nonliturgical poetry, is another example of this kind of motet (see Chapter 4). Memorial services for the deceased were another important venue for the motet during the Renaissance.

◆ **Occasional.** Motets were often commissioned for specific occasions, such as Du Fay's *Nuper rosarum flores*, written for the dedication of the Cathedral of Florence (see Chapter 4). Other texts seem to have been written in response to specific events in the lives of monarchs, such as *Absalon, fili mi* (discussed later, possibly by Josquin, possibly by Pierre de la Rue), apparently written as a consolation to a monarch on the death of his son.

As in the case of the Mass, Josquin's motets demonstrate virtually the entire range of options open to motet composers of the late 15th and early 16th centuries. He always used a plainchant in some way—either as a cantus firmus or as the basis of a melodic paraphrase—whenever he set a text associated with a chant.

Josquin's motets abound in complex devices; even the texts are cunningly crafted at times. The first letter of the first word of the first seven lines of text in *Illibata Dei virgo nutrix* ("Incomparable Virgin, Nurse of God") together spell out "IOSQVIN"; the eighth line begins with the word "Des"; and the final four lines begin with the letters "PREZ." The composer thus embeds his name into the text of one of his Marian motets as an acrostic.

Ut phoebi radiis ("As Through the Rays [of the moon, sister of] Phoebus") is even more extraordinary. Its anonymous Latin text combines images from pagan sources as well as Christian poetry in praise of the Virgin Mary. Each line of text adds one more solmization syllable to its opening. Thus the first line begins with the word "Ut" ("As"), the second with "Ut re," the third with "Ut remi," and so on, through a complete hexachord ("Ut remi fas sola Petri currere prora"). Remarkably, the poetry makes sense, even if the syntax and imagery are a bit forced at times. The last line of the text's first part translates roughly: "As it is the destiny of the oar of Peter to navigate by means of one ship," referring to the disciple Peter, who was also a fisherman. The second half of the poem reverses the entire process, working backward from "La" to "La sol fa me re ut"—again, with each line of the text making linguistic sense. Josquin responds to these musical cues with melodic material corresponding to each line's implied musical pitches.

The motet *Absalon, fili mi* ("Absalom, My Son"), ascribed to Josquin but possibly by Pierre de la Rue (ca. 1452–1518), illustrates the expressive power of the motet and at the same time reminds us of just how many questions remain to be answered about much of

Josquin (?)
Absalon, fili mi

Musica ficta

Unquestionably the most controversial issue in Renaissance notation is **musica ficta,** a term applied to the practice of sharpening or flattening certain notes even though they are not notated as such. *Ficta* ("imagined") comes from the same root word as our "fictive" or "fiction" and refers to the "feigned" notes that lie outside the Guidonian hand, or gamut (see Chapter 1). Rules for the application of musica ficta can be divided into two categories: melodic and harmonic.

◆ Melodic rules were intended to avoid certain linear tritones. A singsong rhyme ("Una nota sopra *la* semper est canendum *fa*") helped students of the time remember that "the note above *la*"—that is, the sixth scale degree in the hexachord being used at any given moment—"is always to be sung as *fa*." In other words, an excursion of one note above the top note of the hexachord, the *la,* should always be a half step. In a hexachord on C, for example (C-D-E-F-G-A), the notated B above A (*la*) would be sung as if it were a *fa,* that is, as a half step above *la*—in short, as a B♭. In a hexachord on F (F-G-A-B-C-D), a notated E would be sung as an E♭.

◆ Harmonic rules were intended to avoid vertical tritones, semitones, and **cross-relations.** To make the required adjustments, singers had to listen carefully to the lines of others, a practice that was a basic part of musical training in the Renaissance. The student's rhyme here was "Mi contra fa est diabolus in musica"—that is, the interval of a half step ("*mi* against *fa*") sounding simultaneously was considered "the devil in music."

According to Renaissance theorists, the conventions of musica ficta were driven in some cases by necessity (*causa necessitatis*), in some cases by beauty (*causa pulchritudinis*). Necessity required the avoidance of tritones and cross-relations. Beauty required that certain cadences be approached by half steps.

Thus performers approaching a perfect consonance (an octave or fifth) by means of an imperfect consonance (a third or a sixth) were expected to use musica ficta to create a half step—what we today would call a leading tone. A notated minor sixth moving to an octave, for example, would be performed as in Example 5-4a, and a notated minor third moving to a fifth would be performed as in Example 5-4b.

In modern editions, an accidental above the note indicates it has been placed there by the editor; an accidental in its normal place, on the staff, indicates it was notated as such in the original source.

But it is not always clear how musicians actually applied these core conventions. Making a change in one voice could sometimes set in motion a cascading series of subsequent changes in the same and other voices. It is also unclear just how much dissonance the Renaissance ear could tolerate. Thus editors and performers who apply the rules of musica ficta mechanically run the risk of interpretations that are more bland than Renaissance composers or performers would have expected. Even Renaissance musicians and theorists did not always agree about the practice of musica ficta.

With the gradual decline of the hexachordal system and the growing dissemination of printed music, composers and publishers became increasingly specific about their instructions to performers in all aspects of music, from text underlay to tempo to the addition and cancellation of accidentals, no matter how conventional. By 1600, musica ficta had largely disappeared.

Example 5-4 Musica ficta for leading tones to octaves and fifths.

Renaissance music. The text is pieced together from three separate biblical passages, each of which deals with a father's lament on the death of his son. The motivation behind this patchwork text is uncertain. Some scholars believe it was written in response to the murder of Juan Borja, Duke of Gandía and eldest son of Pope Alexander VI, in June 1497. Other scholars have pointed to the death of Emperor Maximilian I's son Philip the Fair in 1506. Still other candidates include the English princes Arthur (son of Henry VII) and Henry (son of Henry VIII), both of whom died in infancy in the early years of the

16th century. In an early instance of **word-painting**—the use of musical elements to imitate the meaning of a specific passage of a text—the pain and depths of hell are represented by unusually low pitches.

SECULAR VOCAL MUSIC

A good deal of the secular vocal music of the 15th century was never committed to writing. Many of the songs current during this period were performed through a combination of memory, embellishment, and improvisation. The surviving sources nevertheless document the approximately parallel stylistic developments in the sacred and secular repertories of this time.

Chanson

Stylistic developments in the chanson during the period ca. 1420 to 1520 parallel those in the Mass and motet. These include the move from a layered to a more homogeneous texture, the rhythmic equalization of parts, and the increasing use of pervading imitation as the principal structural device. Of the *formes fixes* so prevalent in the 14th and early 15th centuries (see Chapter 3), only the rondeau survived through the end of the 15th. More than survive, however, it flourished, accounting for about three-fourths of the chanson repertory from the period 1450 to 1500.

To trace the evolution of the chanson in the 15th century, we will look at three representative works, each written by a different composer at a different time within the century: Du Fay's *Adieu ces bons vins de Lannoys* (1426), Hayne van Ghizeghem's *De tous biens pleine* (ca. 1470), and Heinrich Isaac's *Hélas, que devera mon coeur* (late 1480s).

Du Fay's rondeau *Adieu ces bons vins de Lannoys* ("Farewell These Good Wines of Lannoys") illustrates the composer's early style and is typical of many chansons written between around 1425 and 1450. It opens and closes with brief untexted passages that were likely performed instrumentally. Only the uppermost line, the superius, is texted in the sources, and the tenor and contratenor were probably performed on instruments. Indeed, many Renaissance sources transmit chansons with no text at all, suggesting this repertory might well have been performed at times entirely on instruments. The three voices in this particular chanson move in more or less the same rhythms throughout, with little syncopation. The tenor and the superius are the structural voices, providing all necessary consonances at openings and cadences. The contratenor is a filler voice: it cannot substitute for either the superius or the tenor to provide needed points of consonance. And in contrast to the other two voices, characterized by conjunct motion, the contratenor features several octave leaps.

Du Fay
Adieu ces bons vins de Lannoys

Hayne van Ghizeghem's *De tous biens plaine* ("Of All Good Things"), which first appears in sources compiled around the year 1470, represents the chanson style of the generation that came after Du Fay. Again, the options for performance range from three texted voices to entirely instrumental. And as before, the tenor and superius provide the essential pitches for all cadences, with the contratenor acting as a "filler" voice. But in contrast to Du Fay's rondeau, the melodic lines in Hayne's work are longer and more fluid, and there is a greater sense of rhythmic interplay among the various voices.

Judging from the number of sources in which it has been preserved and the remarkable number of arrangements and reworkings it inspired, Hayne's *De tous biens plaine* was one of the most popular chansons of its time.

Hayne van Ghizeghem
De tous biens plaine

Heinrich Isaac's *Hélas, que devera mon coeur*, composed in the late 1480s, reflects the growing importance of pervading imitation in Renaissance music of the late

Isaac
Hélas, que devera mon coeur

15th century. This three-voiced rondeau consists of four clearly articulated sections, each of which begins with a point of imitation and ends with a cadence:

FORMAL STRUCTURE OF ISAAC'S *HÉLAS, QUE DEVERA MON COEUR*				
Section	I	II	III	IV
Starting measure	1	18	30	44
Initial order of entry	CT, T, S	S, CT	CT, S, T	CT, S, T
Cadence on	C (unison)	F, C (fifth)	A (unison, S and T)	F (unison)

S = Superius, T = Tenor, CT = Contratenor.

The paratactic structure used here—successive points of imitation, with each section presenting new thematic material—would become the predominant form of all chansons for the next 100 years or more. Within each section, all voices share the same ideas and participate equally in the polyphonic fabric.

Frottola

For most of the 15th century, the song repertory in Italy was dominated by the French chanson. Only in the 1480s did native composers begin setting texts in their own language once again, in a genre broadly known as the **frottola** (plural **frottole**). The texts for these songs include freely structured poems as well as poems in a variety of established Italian literary forms. In contrast to the preoccupation with courtly love that

The frottola. *Lorenzo Costa (1460–1535) was at one time the chief painter at the court of Mantua, which, along with Ferrara, was one of the main centers of frottola composition. This particular painting, dating from ca. 1485–1495, captures the spirit of this popular genre. The two singers on the outside seem to be beating time with their hands, or perhaps even adding a percussive element to the music. The lutenist, who is also singing, keeps his eye on the open music book before him. The pocket fiddle and recorder stand at the ready, perhaps to be played in place of the voices at various points in the performance to provide variety.*

Source: Lorenzo Costa, (1459–1535) Italian, "A Concert", oil on panel 95.3 × 75.6 cm/National Gallery, London, UK/Bridgeman Art Library

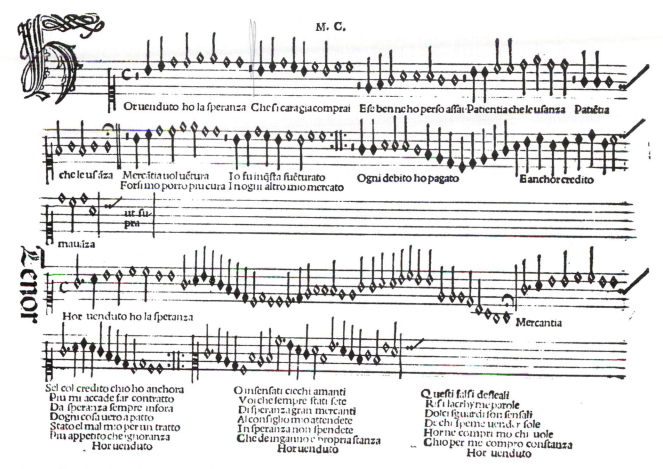

Petrucci's printed music. *Ottaviano Petrucci (1466–1539) was the first to print music by movable metal type. He recognized the commercial market for collections of both sacred and secular music and fulfilled an ongoing demand for chansons, frottole, motets, and Masses. Shown above is a portion of Marchetto Cara's frottola* Hor venduto ho la speranza *in its original four-voice version, as it appeared in Petrucci's* Frottole, Book 1 (1504). *Only two of the four voices are shown here, the cantus and the tenor. Petrucci's editions are beautifully printed. The music rarely seems cramped on the page, and the type is consistently crisp and elegant.*

Source: Bayerische Staatsbibliothek Munich, Musikabteilung, Rar. 878–1

predominates in chanson texts, frottola poetry tends to be lighthearted and often sarcastic or ironic. Musically, frottole tend to avoid imitation and contrapuntal artifice, again in contrast to contemporary chansons. Frottole are characterized instead by chordal textures and lively, dancelike rhythms with frequent use of syncopation and **hemiola** (a brief passage of duple-meter rhythms within an otherwise triple-meter context). Many frottole use formulaic rhythmic units like the one in Example 5-5.

Harmonic progressions in the frottola are often simple. In modern terminology, the genre makes frequent use of patterns like I-IV-V-I. The music could be performed entirely vocally, entirely by instruments, or by any of various combinations of voices and

Example 5-5 A typical frottola rhythmic pattern.

instruments. Many frottole were arranged for solo voice and lute, or for keyboard alone, for frottole were in high demand. The Venetian publisher Petrucci produced no fewer than 11 books of them between 1504 and 1514—a rate of roughly one a year.

The frottola was cultivated with greatest intensity by Italian-born composers, most notably Bartolomeo Tromboncino (ca. 1470–ca. 1535) and Marchetto Cara (ca. 1470–1525). Both were active in the northern Italian city of Mantua. Cara's *Hor venduto ho la speranza* appeared in the first book of frottole published by Petrucci in 1504 in a four-voice version and then later in a version for solo voice and lute in 1509, also published by Petrucci. The lute part of this later version, which is the one that appears in the anthology, is essentially polyphonic, in two voices.

Cara
Hor venduto ho la speranza

F O C U S

Major Composers of the 15th and Early 16th Centuries

ENGLAND

The tombstone of **John Dunstable** (ca. 1390–1453) describes him as a mathematician, astronomer, and musician. He traveled for many years in the service of the Duke of Bedford throughout northern France in the 1420s and 1430s and may well have met Du Fay, Binchois, and other French composers. His output consists largely of motets and Mass movements, along with a few songs.

Less is known about **Leonel (Lionel) Power,** who died in 1445 and seems to have been slightly older than Dunstable. He served in the Household Chapel of Thomas, Duke of Clarence, who was the brother of Henry V. In the last decade of his life, Power was master of the Lady Chapel Choir in Canterbury. Many of his works are included in the Old Hall Manuscript, and his settings of the Mass are among the earliest to use a single cantus firmus in all movements.

FRANCE AND THE LOW COUNTRIES

Gilles Binchois (ca. 1400–1460) was a contemporary of **Guillaume Du Fay** (ca. 1400–1474; see Composer Profile: "Guillaume Du Fay" in Chapter 4); the two composers cultivated many of the same genres. Binchois worked mostly in southern Belgium and northern France and did not travel nearly so widely as Du Fay. **Antoine Busnois** (ca. 1430–1492) composed Masses, motets, and chansons, and like Binchois spent most of his career in Burgundian lands.

Johannes Ockeghem (ca. 1420–1496) was the eldest of a remarkable series of composers to come from an area known as the Low Countries, now consisting of the Netherlands, Belgium, and the northernmost part of France. (These composers as a group are sometimes referred to as "Franco-Flemish" or "Franco-Netherlandish.") Ockeghem is remembered today in large part for his remarkably complex polyphony, and contemporaries praised his music for its subtlety. The composer and theorist **Johannes Tinctoris** (ca. 1435–?1511) dedicated his treatise on counterpoint to Ockeghem and hailed his works for their sweetness and beauty. Tinctoris's *Terminorum musicae diffinitorium* ("Dictionary of Musical Terms," Naples, 1473) was the first separately published book of its kind. He served for a time at the court of the king of Naples but traveled widely throughout his life.

Josquin des Prez (ca. 1450–1521; see Composer Profile: "Josquin des Prez," in Chapter 4) was the most illustrious member of the next generation from this region. **Jacob Obrecht** (1450–1505) and **Heinrich Isaac** (ca. 1450–1517) also spent considerable portions of their careers in Italy. Obrecht was music director at the Cathedral of Antwerp for a time but also worked at the court of Ferrara, where he died of the plague. He was a prolific composer of masses and motets, many of extraordinary complexity and artifice. Isaac served as organist and maestro di cappella at the court of Lorenzo de Medici in Florence, then later at the court of Emperor Maximilian I in Vienna. He wrote some 36 Masses as well as 15 individual Mass movements and more than 40 motets. His *Choralis Constantinus*, written for the cathedral of Konstanz in southern Germany, contains polyphonic settings for all the Mass Propers of the entire church year. A truly international composer, Isaac also wrote French chansons, German Lieder, and Italian frottole.

Italians may have been the principal composers of frottola, but others also contributed to the genre, including, possibly, Josquin. The very title of *El grillo* ("The Cricket"), attributed to Josquin, tells us we are far from the realm of courtly love in which the poetry of the chanson usually dwells. The musical style of this brief piece also contrasts sharply with that of contemporary chansons. *El grillo* is predominantly chordal in texture, occasionally **antiphonal** (in the back-and-forth between high and low voices in measures 11–14), and not at all imitative. Recent research suggests the composer may have been the "other" Josquin in the service of Cardinal Ascanio Sforza of Milan from 1459 to 1498. Whoever wrote the piece had a wonderful ear for translating animal sounds into music.

Josquin
El grillo

INSTRUMENTAL MUSIC

We know from paintings and written accounts that instrumental music in the Renaissance, as in the medieval era, was cultivated far more than notated sources would indicate. Performers routinely played from memory and often improvised. Notated vocal works, in turn, lent themselves to easy adaptation on any of a variety of instruments, and ample evidence suggests that chansons were routinely performed either in whole or in part on instruments.

Still, it is fair to say that composers of the 15th century rarely wrote music intended to be performed exclusively on instruments. The process of transforming vocal models into instrumental arrangements was left to performing musicians. A distinctly instrumental idiom would not begin to emerge until well into the 16th century.

Renaissance Instruments

The Renaissance inherited and expanded on the rich variety of instruments used during the medieval era. Indeed, it is fair to say that a greater variety of sound was probably available to musicians in the Renaissance than at any other time in the history of music before the 20th century. Many instruments have disappeared since then, such as the *lira da braccio* (a large viol-like instrument held on the shoulder), the crumhorn (literally, a "bent horn," a kind of J-shaped double-reed instrument), the bladder pipe (a type of bagpipe), and the racket (see illustration "Renaissance Forerunners of the Bassoon" on page 98), affectionately known in colloquial German of the time as the *Wurstfagott*—"sausage bassoon." Although these and other instruments of the time may seem exotic to us today, they were integral in creating a rich fabric of sound in a culture that reveled in timbral variety and contrast.

Keyboard.   The organ expanded steadily in size, range of pitches, number of pipes, and variety of timbres over the course of the Renaissance. By the early 16th century, most church organs of any size had multiple registers (sets of pipes). In addition to the main register (*Hauptwerk*, to use the German term by which it is often known), the most common additional register was the *Rückpositiv*, or Chair, a separate set of pipes situated underneath or behind the player.

The smaller portative (portable) organ was popular for use in the home. The smallest of these, which had a range of only about two octaves and required the performer to pump the bellows with one hand while playing with the other, were strictly for melodies. Larger instruments, known as positive organs, rested on the floor or on a table. A second person worked the bellows on these instruments, leaving the performer free to play with both hands.

The clavichord evolved out of the monochord in the early 15th century, although the earliest surviving examples date from almost 150 years later. It was an ideal domestic instrument: portable, quiet, and capable of being played by a single individual, without the aid of a bellows operator. The clavichord also offered the advantage of allowing the player to control the struck note from beginning to end, because the metal tangent hitting the string was directly connected to the key pressed down by the player.

The harpsichord also emerged in the late 14th century, although again, the earliest surviving instruments date from a good bit later, in the late 15th century. Early accounts refer to the instrument as a *clavicymbalum*, a key psaltery, with a mechanism that plucks the string rather than striking it. The typical Renaissance harpsichord is a single-manual (single-keyboard) instrument of four octaves with double stringing.

The Renaissance organ. *Like almost all surviving Renaissance organs, this instrument is the product of many additions and alterations over an extended period of time. The original instrument, by Peter Gerritz, was built in 1479–1480 for the Nicholaikerk in Utrecht (now in the Netherlands). The back positive, which obscures the bench where the player sits, was added in 1590, the pedals around 1600. The entire organ was later moved to the Koorkerk in Middelberg (also in the present-day Netherlands).*

Source: Courtesy of Tiroler Volkskunstmuseum, Innsbruck, Austria

Smaller varieties of the harpsichord emerged during the 15th century. The strings of the virginal run at right angles to the keys; the strings of the spinet run at an oblique angle. These smaller instruments were generally limited to a single set of strings and jacks and a single keyboard.

Stringed Instruments.   The lute, with its pear-shaped body and backward-angled peg box, was the most common plucked stringed instrument in the Renaissance. Most early lutes featured four or five courses, but by the early 16th century, six courses had become standard. Tuning was usually by fourths, with the interval of a third between the middle courses. Related instruments—without the backward-sloping peg box—included the vihuela and guitar, both of which originated in Spain, and the cittern, bandore (pandora), and orpharion, which differed in the shape of the body and the material used for the courses. The mandora and mandolin (similar to today's instrument) were also quite popular for domestic music making.

The viol and violin families both emerged at roughly the same time, in the late 15th century. Viols came in many shapes and sizes. Any viol meant to be played while being held in the arm was called a *viola da braccio* ("viol of the arm"); one held upright on the lap or between the legs was called a *viola da gamba* ("viol of the leg"). Whatever their size or manner of performance, viols are distinguishable from violins by virtue of their sloped shoulders, flat backs, fretted fingerboards, and six strings tuned in fourths, except for a major third between the two middle strings.

The violin family was somewhat slower to develop. The earliest account of four matched instruments with the same tuning dates from the middle of the 16th century. By 1564, Andrea Amati had opened his workshop in Cremona and within less than a hundred years the violin family had become the standard bowed stringed instrument across the continent.

Winds and Percussion.   The earliest known recorder dates from the late 14th century. By the end of the 15th century, this family of instruments had developed into four standard varieties, each corresponding to a human voice range: soprano, alto, tenor, and bass. The sopranino recorder, pitched an octave higher than the soprano, was also available.

The shawm and crumhorn remained the principal double-reed instruments throughout the Renaissance. These, too, developed in a variety of ranges from high to low. Shawms, often played in groups of three, were popular for dances and processions.

Another double-reed instrument was the curtal, which in spite of its various shapes and sizes always corresponded to the range of the tenor or bass voice (see illustration "Renaissance Forerunners of the Bassoon"). The racket, a related instrument with a deep, reedy sound, achieved its effect through a system of tightly wound cylindrical tubing that bent back on itself up to nine times in a space of only 11 inches or so.

Most Renaissance brass instruments, like those of the medieval era, were limited to the natural harmonics of a single key. The first instrument intended to negotiate notes outside the overtone series was the slide trumpet. The mouthpiece of this instrument was attached to a piece of movable tubing; the player held the mouthpiece firmly in one hand while pushing and pulling the rest of the instrument according to the desired pitch. The principle of sliding was applied with greater success on the trombone, also known as the sackbut, in which only a portion of the instrument, the slide, moved in and out.

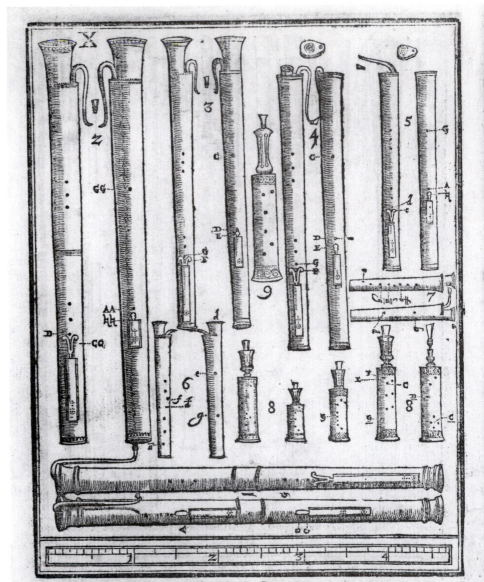

Renaissance forerunners of the bassoon. *Our knowledge of late-16th-century instruments depends heavily on a treatise by the German composer Michael Praetorius (1571–1621). The second volume of his* Syntagma musicum *(1619) is devoted entirely to instruments and contains detailed illustrations and measurements. Plate 10, shown here, includes examples of the sordun (lengthwise across the bottom), various varieties of the curtal (numbered 2–7), and rackets of different shapes and sizes (8–9). The only remaining modern descendants of these various instruments are the bassoon and double bassoon. Praetorius's treatise and others like it remind us of the remarkable variety of instruments from which Renaissance musicians could choose.*

Source: Bodleian Library, University of Oxford/Plate 10 "musical instruments" from volume 2 of Syntagma Musicum by Michael Praetorius, 1614. Reference Douce P. 709–711

"High" versus "low" instruments. *Renaissance writers on music consistently distinguish between "high" and "low" instruments based not on their range but on their volume. This image contrasts the loud "high" instruments on the right (crumhorn, trumpet, bagpipe, sackbut, cornetto) with the soft "low" ones on the left (viols, harpsichord, lute, cittern). Taken from a collection of music arranged for keyboard—Elias Nikolaus Ammerbach's* Ein New künstlich Tabulaturbuch *(Nuremberg, 1575)—this image puts a portative organ between the two groups, suggesting it is appropriate for music of all kinds.*

Source: Bayerische Staatsbibliothek Munich, Musikabteilung, 2 Mus. pr. 106/4

It was during the Renaissance that the straight trumpet—a single long instrument—began to be doubled back on itself, making it less awkward to hold. Although straight trumpets continued to be used for heraldic functions, the folded form of the instrument had become fairly common by the end of the 15th century. Crooks were eventually added as well to allow the instrument to negotiate at least some of the notes outside its overtone series.

Percussion instruments of the Renaissance included a wide range of drums, cymbals of many shapes and sizes, tambourines, triangles, and even wooden xylophones. Judging from paintings and accounts of this period, these were used far more frequently than the surviving musical notation would suggest. The psaltery (hammered dulcimer) was also a favorite domestic instrument.

Dance Music

Dance music, by its very nature, was rarely committed to writing in the early Renaissance. Performers instead typically worked from memory, embellishing new lines above standard bass patterns in much the same way as jazz ensembles do today. Notated manuscripts with the melodies for one type of dance—the **basse danse**—have come

A basse danse manuscript (1471).   *This page comes from one of the most unusual musical manuscripts of the Renaissance. It was written on black paper with white ink. There are two dances on this page. The one on the bottom is entitled* La basse danse du roy d'Espaigne *("The Basse Danse of the King of Spain").*

Source: Ms. 9.085 from a facsimile edition, Le manuscrit dit les Basses danses de la Bibliotheque de Bourgogne, ed. Ernest Closson (Brussels: Societe des Bibliophiles at Iconophiles de Belgique, 1912; Reprint edition: Geneva, Minkoff, 1976); reproduced with permission of the Royal Library of Belgium

down to us, but these convey little more than an outline of the improvised polyphony they supported, rather like a cheat book or fake book in modern-day jazz. The basse danse of the 15th century was a slow, stately dance for couples, executed with smooth, gliding steps. Melodies were typically notated in even note values (usually breves), with letters underneath that identify the sequence of associated dance steps.

CONCLUSION

The first 100 years of the Renaissance witnessed important changes in musical style. The standard sonority moved from a layered to a homogeneous texture. Cantus firmus technique replaced isorhythm as the predominant structural principle in large-scale works in the second half of the 15th century; and by the beginning of the 16th century, pervading imitation had become a standard feature in almost all genres of music.

The rise of music printing in the early 16th century, in turn, fundamentally altered the way in which music could be distributed and consumed. Compositions that once circulated either through oral transmission or through a mere handful of manuscripts (or even just a single source) could now be reproduced and distributed by the hundreds. By 1520, the music printing industry was poised to play a central role in both sacred and secular music. The rapid rise of new genres of secular song in the 1530s—the Parisian chanson in France and the madrigal in Italy—owes much to the ready availability of this repertory through print. In the realm of sacred music, printing played an equally significant role in both the Reformation and Counter-Reformation of the 16th century.

Music in the 16th Century

The years between 1520 and 1600 witnessed remarkable changes in Europe's musical landscape. Distinct secular repertories flourished in France, Italy, Spain, Germany, and England. Sacred music became an important weapon in the ongoing struggle between Protestants and Catholics. Composers began writing specifically for instruments for the first time. And in the closing decades of the century, an artistic phenomenon known as mannerism began to make itself felt in music, leading composers to explore new extremes in the setting of texts.

Rapid advances in music printing in the early decades of the 16th century played a key role in these changes, helping expand the range of consumers for music beyond the court and those few who had the resources to copy out large quantities of music. Less rhythmically intricate genres like the frottola (Chapter 5) and Parisian chanson supplanted the more complex chanson of the late 15th century. Arrangements of vocal music for lute and keyboard began to appear in large numbers. A growing movement to write poetry in the vernacular, especially in Italy, led to the emergence of a new genre, the madrigal. The Reformation and Counter-Reformation, in turn, inspired Protestants and Roman Catholics alike to rethink the relationship between words and music within their respective liturgies.

SECULAR VOCAL MUSIC

By the early 16th century, the rondeau, the last of the surviving *formes fixes* from the medieval era, had largely disappeared, replaced by more freely structured chansons based on the principle of pervading imitation. What emerged during the 1520s and 1530s were new approaches to setting vernacular texts: the Parisian chanson in France and the madrigal in Italy.

The Parisian Chanson

During the 1520s, a new genre of song now known as the **Parisian chanson** emerged in the French capital. Among its most notable composers were Claudin de Sermisy (ca. 1490–1562) and Clément Janequin (ca. 1485–ca. 1560), whose works were widely disseminated by the Parisian music publisher Pierre Attaingnant. Reflecting the influence of the Italian frottola, the Parisian chanson is lighter and more chordally oriented than earlier chansons. Like the frottola, it is generally homorhythmic and dominated by vertical sonorities that we would now think of as tonic, subdominant, and dominant chords. Although the works are notated polyphonically, their melodies, in the manner of songs for solo voice with lute accompaniment, are generally confined to the uppermost line.

Sermisy's *Tant que vivray* ("As Long As I Live") is a typical Parisian chanson. First published in 1528, it provided fodder for dozens of subsequent arrangements and reworkings (some with new texts) and was still being printed in anthologies more than a hundred years later. *Tant que vivray* is modest in dimension, with a lyrical melody that lies squarely in the uppermost voice. The text is conventional and unpretentious, a love song in praise first of love itself and then of the beloved. The rhythms and cadences of the music largely mirror those of the text, with one syllable per note except for a few discreet melismas toward the very ends of phrases, as in measure 10. Except for a hint of imitation on the words *Son coeur est mien. Le mien est sien* ("Her heart is mine, mine is hers") in measures 14–16, the text is declaimed in a predominantly chordal fashion.

Not all Parisian chansons were as simple as *Tant que vivray*. Janequin's *La guerre* ("The War") is a much longer work with greater independence among the voices and an extraordinary amount of onomatopoeia, in which the singers are asked to mimic the sounds of war: the sound of cannon, the clash of swords. *La guerre* is only one of several onomatopoeic songs by Janequin. The others are *Le chant des oiseaux* ("The Song of the Birds"), *La chasse* ("The Hunt"), *Les cris de Paris* ("The Cries of Paris"), and *Le caquet des femmes* ("The Women's Gossip").

Sermisy
Tant que vivray

The Italian Madrigal

By the 1530s, a new genre of vocal music was emerging in Italy with the **madrigal,** a secular vocal composition for three or more voices. The 16th-century madrigal has no direct musical connection to the 14th-century genre also known as the madrigal (see Chapter 3). The term was revived in the 1530s for a new type of polyphonic song, similar in some respects to the frottola but more ambitious in tone, both textually and musically. Early madrigals (from the 1530s and 1540s) often share with the frottola a characteristically chordal texture, but with time, true contrapuntal writing became increasingly prevalent in the genre. And whereas the frottola is almost invariably strophic, with different words sung to the same music, the madrigal is **through-composed,** setting each line of text to essentially new music. This approach allowed for the kind of explicit word-painting that became increasingly popular in the 16th century.

The impetus for the rise of the 16th-century madrigal began with the revival of interest in the 14th-century poetry of Francesco Petrarca (Petrarch, 1304–1374). Pietro Bembo (1470–1547), a poet in his own right, championed Petrarch's work and urged his contemporaries to emulate Petrarch's combination of *piacevolezza* ("pleasingness") and *gravità* ("seriousness" or "weight") along with his attention to the rhymes, rhythms, and sonorities of the Italian language. Among the most notable to respond to Bembo's call—and to provide, together with Petrarch himself, a rich source of texts for madrigal composers—were Jacopo Sannazaro (1457–1530), Ludovico Ariosto (1474–1533), Torquato Tasso (1544–1595), and Giovanni Battista Guarini (1538–1612). Madrigal texts of the 16th century follow no fixed form, but they tend to consist of a single stanza, with a free rhyme scheme. One of the more widespread poetic forms of the madrigal consists of lines that alternate between seven and eleven syllables. Many madrigals incorporate some kind of conceit—a striking image—that reveals itself only at the very end of the poem.

Performance practice.
A four-voice chanson being performed by three musicians reminds us that musicians of earlier times did not think in terms of "right" and "wrong" ways of performing a given repertory, but instead made creative use of whatever musical resources they had at their disposal. The anonymous artist of this painting from the second quarter of the 16th century took great pains to depict the actual music being played here—the notation of Claudin de Sermisy's chanson Joyssance vous donneray is so precise it can be easily read against modern editions of the work. The flute player is reading from the superius part book while the singer is performing the tenor part from what appears to be a separate sheet. The lutenist is probably filling in the other two voices.

Source: Master of Female Half Lengths (c. 1490–c. 1540) "The Concert"/Bridgeman Art Library

Madrigals were performed in many settings, from banquets to private homes. For most of the 16th century, the style of the music is relatively undemanding, accessible to the well-trained amateur. And judging by the number of published madrigal collections that have survived, the appeal of this music was enormous. Some 2,000 collections—most consisting of at least a dozen madrigals—were published between 1530 and 1600.

With its clear declamation, modest dimensions, limited use of word-painting, and predominantly chordal texture, Jacob Arcadelt's *Il bianco e dolce cigno* ("The White and Gentle Swan," first published in 1539) exemplifies the early madrigal. The text plays on two poetic conceits. One is the legend that swans, otherwise mute, sing just before they die. The other is a pun on the word *death,* used in one sense literally and in another as a euphemism (popular among Renaissance poets) for sexual climax. The poem's narrator contrasts the literal death of the swan, who sings yet is disconsolate, with his own desire for a euphemistic death "a thousand times a day." "Death," he explains, "fills me wholly with joy and desire."

Arcadelt's setting of this poem is at once tasteful and graphic. His music is more rhythmically supple than that of the typical frottola and he attends to the projection of individual words—the unexpected inflection on *piagendo* ("weeping") in measures 6–7, for example—without diverting the flow of the music as a whole. Toward the very end, however, on the words *di mille mort' il dì,* ("a thousand deaths a day"), he introduces a suggestively rapid-fire imitative counterpoint that resolves chordally on the words *sarei contento* ("would make me happy").

Cipriano de Rore's *Da le belle contrade d'oriente* ("From the Fair Regions of the East"), first published in 1566, exemplifies the stylistic changes that distinguish the mid-century madrigal from early manifestations of the genre. The part writing is more imitative and less chordal, and with five voices, the texture is fuller. By the 1560s, five voices had become the norm for madrigals, although works for four and even three voices continued to appear through the end of the century.

The text of Rore's madrigal, by an unknown poet, draws on the age-old image of two lovers parting at dawn. The young man describes himself as musing contentedly in the arms of his beloved when she cries out in anguish over his impending departure. She then embraces him even more tightly, so they become entwined like ivy and acanthus vines. Rore creates a distinctive musical profile for each line or pair of lines of this text, using melodic material with more internal contrasts than did Arcadelt. Rore also devotes more attention to individual words and phrases. He articulates the anxiety in the beloved's words *sola me lasci* ("you are leaving me alone")—and mimics their meaning— by setting them in a passage that the cantus (superius) voice sings entirely alone for a full measure (33). He conveys the meaning of the phrase *iterando gl'amplessi* ("repeating her embraces") with many repetitions (measure 62 onward). And he captures the image of acanthus entwining itself around ivy by setting the word *edra* ("ivy") to relatively slow notes and *acanto* ("acanthus") to a sinuously rapid melisma (measures 72–81).

It is easy to see why almost forty years later Claudio Monteverdi (see Chapter 8) would point specifically to this composition (among others) in defending an aesthetic in which the "harmony obeys [the] words exactly." Monteverdi considered Rore one of the true founders of what he called "modern music" precisely because of the way he had shaped his compositions around the text at hand.

Madalena Casulana's *Morir non può il mio cuore* ("My Heart Cannot Die,"), first published in 1566, is another representative mid-century madrigal that also happens to be among the earliest printed vocal works by a professional woman composer (see Composer Profile: "Madalena Casulana"). The poetic text plays on the age-old image of a lover "owning" the heart of his or her beloved. But the relationship here has obviously

Arcadelt
Il bianco e dolce cigno

Rore
Da le belle contrade d'oriente

1ˢᵗ woman composer to have / work printed to sale

Casulana
Morir non può il mio cuore

(a)

(b)

The cut-throat business of music publishing. *Music publishing was a highly competitive business in the 16th century. In 1538, Antonio Gardano opened in Venice what would eventually become one of the leading music publishing houses in all of Europe. Gardano's first anthology of motets was issued under the title* Mottetti del frutto. *The title page (a), appropriately enough, depicts a still life of fruit. Shortly afterward, the rival publishing firm of Buglhat, Campis, and Hucher of Ferrara issued a set of motets entitled* Moteti de la Simia *("Motets of the Monkey"). The fruit-eating monkey on the title page of the cantus part (b) symbolically refers to Gardano, whose shop in Venice was located in the Calle de la scimia ("Monkey Alley"). Another installment in Gardano's* Mottetti del frutto *series, published in 1539, features on its title page (c) a lion and a bear (the two chief elements of what we would now call Gardano's logo) who are in the process of eating a monkey, who is himself surrounded by half-eaten pieces of fruit. It seems that Buglhat, Campis, and Hucher had preempted Gardano in the publication of some motets that it had been Gardano's intention to publish first.*

Source: (a) Dover Publications, Inc. (b) Bayerische Staatsbibliothek Munich, Musikabteilung, 4 Mus. pr. 194/8 (c) Dover Publications, Inc.

(c)

Composer Profile

Madalena Casulana
(ca. 1544–?)

Madalena Casulana was the first professional woman composer to see her vocal music into print. Four of her madrigals (including *Morir non può il mio cuore*) appeared in an anthology of 1566 entitled *Il Desiderio* ("The Desire"), published by Girolamo Scotto of Venice. Two years later Casulana published these four madrigals and a fifth new one in her own *First Book of Madrigals for Four Voices*. The collection was successful enough to warrant a second edition in 1583, and she later issued two more books of madrigals, one for four voices, the other for five. Orlande de Lassus performed one of her pieces at the festivities for the marriage of Archduke Wilhelm of Bavaria in Munich in 1568. And in 1582, the music publisher Antonio Gardano dedicated to her Philippe de Monte's first book of madrigals for three voices—Gardano was trying to revive this earlier medium—and hailed Casulana as "the Muse and Siren of our age."

Casulana was well aware of her pioneering role. She dedicated her first book of madrigals to Isabella de' Medici Orsina, a patron of music who may also have been a composer in her own right. The self-deprecatory tone with which Casulana begins her letter of dedication is typical for this form—artists did not want to appear immodest when seeking the attention of potential patrons. But her subsequent outburst is anything but conventional, and it testifies to the frustration she surely felt in a profession overwhelmingly dominated by men:

> I know truly, Most Illustrious and Excellent Signora, that these my first fruits, because of their weakness, cannot produce the effect that I would like, which would be not only to give you some testimony of my devotion but also to show the world (to the extent of my knowledge in the art of music) the vain error of men, who so much believe themselves to be the masters of the highest gifts of the intellect, that they think those gifts cannot be shared equally by women.[1]

The documentary evidence on Casulana's life is lamentably scant. She was composing, singing, and

---

KEY DATES IN THE LIFE OF MADALENA CASULANA

ca. 1544 Born in northern Italy, possibly near Siena

1560s Sings, composes, and teaches composition in Venice

1566 Publishes her first madrigals in an anthology of works by several composers

1568 Publishes her first book of madrigals for four voices, followed by a second book two years later

1583 Publishes her first book of madrigals for five voices

After 1583 Date and place of death unknown

---

teaching both music and composition in Venice in the late 1560s, but we know little of her whereabouts in the 1570s or 1580s, and it is not known exactly when or where she died. She is believed to have married sometime after 1570 and moved away from Venice. No known image of her has survived.

No evidence suggests Casulana ever held an official position at any church, court, or other institution. Still, her example paved the way for subsequent madrigal publications by other women, including Paola Massarenghi of Parma (1585), Vittoria Aleotti of Ferrara (1591 and 1593), and Cesarina Ricci di Tingoli (1597). By the 17th century, as the careers of Francesca Caccini, Barbara Strozzi, and Elisabeth Jacquet de la Guerre attest (see Chapters 8 and 10), the publication of music by women would no longer be quite so unusual.

Principal Works

Casulana's known works consist exclusively of madrigals—67 altogether—all but one of which were issued in her three published books of madrigals (1566, 1568, 1583).

gone sour, and the imagery is quite violent. The narrator would like to drive a stake through his (or her) own heart, because it causes so much pain, "but it cannot be dragged out from your breast where it has lain for so long." The narrator also recognizes that to commit suicide would also kill the beloved. Whether this is a good thing or not remains wonderfully ambiguous.

Casulana's music projects the despairing tone of this poem in measured but effective terms. The music is sometimes contrapuntal (as in measures 1–3), sometimes chordal (as in measures 4–5). The rising chromatic progression at the end of the text on the line *so che morreste voi* ("I know that you would die"), beginning at measure 15 and repeated at measure 21, is particularly effective. The major third of the final cadence conveys the idea of death as a means of achieving peace.

Marenzio
Solo e pensoso

In the later decades of the 16th century, madrigal composers took word-painting to still greater extremes than before. Luca Marenzio's *Solo e pensoso* ("Alone and Pondering"), published in 1599 to a text by none other than Petrarch himself, illustrates the lengths to which composers were willing to go to capture the meaning and emotion of a text. The opening measure is harmonically extraordinary, moving from the outline of a G major triad to one on E major, with a spectacularly exposed octave leap in the alto that reverses the motion of the previously steady downward skips. The piece proceeds to unfold in an even more bizarre fashion. The whole notes in the uppermost line that progress from G to G♯ in measure 1 turn out to be the beginning of a long chromatic ascent that will span a ninth (to A in measure 15) and then descend chromatically back down a fifth by measure 22. Paratactic in form like almost every other madrigal of its time, Marenzio's *Solo e pensoso* uses musical means to emphasize key points in each line of the text.

Luzzaschi
T'amo mia vita

T'amo mia vita ("I Love You, My Life"), by Luzzasco Luzzaschi (1545–1607), illustrates another growing trend in the madrigal toward the end of the 16th century: the increasing importance of virtuosity. The florid embellishments in each of the three voices seem for the most part unconnected to the text at hand. They cannot be considered word-painting, for a similar figure serves for a wide variety of individual words. The same cadential gesture, for example, appears on *parola* ("word"), *amore* ("love"), *mia* ("mine"), *core* ("heart"), and *signore* ("lady").

Although not published until 1601, the work almost certainly dates from the 1590s if not earlier. It is part of a larger collection of "Madrigals for One, Two, or Three Sopranos" written expressly for the celebrated "Three Ladies of Ferrara," a group of extraordinarily talented singers whose performances were something of a legend throughout musical Europe (see Primary Evidence: "The Three Ladies of Ferrara"). Luzzaschi's published score includes a fully written-out harpsichord accompaniment that doubles the structural pitches of the vocal parts but also adds independent pitches of its own. By the end of the Renaissance, composers were exploring the possibilities of integrating voices and instruments to an unprecedented degree.

The Italian madrigal had its lighter side as well. Alongside the serious texts, polyphonic textures, and through-composed settings, composers also cultivated a number of subgenres that were decidedly less literary and less musically elaborate. These works often feature bawdy texts full of suggestive imagery and double entendres, and were frequently written in a local dialect. The works, often for only three voices, are strophic and mostly syllabic in their declamation. One common term for these subgenres as a whole was **villanella,** which originally meant a "country girl" but ultimately derives from the same root word as our "vile," suggesting something commonplace or vulgar. Other terms are *villanesca, villotta, canzonetta,* and *balletto.* Some of the most prominent madrigal composers of the 16th century, including Willaert, Lassus, and Marenzio, wrote works in

WORD-PAINTING IN MARENZIO'S *SOLO E PENSOSO*, PART I

Italian text	English translation	Starting measure	Textual emphasis and musical effect
Solo e pensoso i più deserti campi	Alone and pensive through the most deserted fields	1	Solitude and contemplation, conveyed by the isolation and extraordinary chromaticism of the uppermost voice
vo misurando a passi tardi e lenti,	I go with measured steps, dragging and slow	9	Slow steps, conveyed by long note values
e gl'occhi porto per fuggir intenti	And my eyes intently watch in order to flee	25	Running, conveyed by points of temporally close imitation
dove vestiggio human l'arena stampi.	From any spot where the trace of a man the sand imprints.	33	A fixed spot, conveyed by relatively static melody and rhythm
Altro schermo non trovo che me scampi	No other defense do I find to escape	44	Escape, conveyed by the rapid imitative figure on *scampi* ("escape")
dal manifesto accorger de le genti,	From the plain knowledge of people,	56	Commonplace people and knowledge, conveyed by a relatively undistinctive passage, stated only once
perché ne gl'atti d'allegrezza spenti	Because in my actions, of joy devoid	63	The absence of joy, conveyed by a thinner texture of mostly three voices
di fuor si legge com'io dentr'avampi.	From without one may read how I blaze within.	66	The contrast between external calm and inward agitation, conveyed by the juxtaposition of slow and rapid rhythms

CD 3
track 18

these lighter subgenres. And the leading music publishers of the day were not shy about printing them, for they sold well.

Lassus's *Matona mia cara* ("My Dear Lady"), published in 1581, offers a witty example of this repertory. It is a *todesca*, a German soldier's song that like others of its kind pokes fun at the heavy accent of a German mercenary, who in this particular instance is serenading a young woman in broken Italian.

Lassus
Matona mia cara

Secular Song in Germany, Spain, and England

Germany, Spain, and England all developed their own repertories of secular song over the course of the 16th century.

Germany.   The most prominent varieties of song in 16th-century Germany were the **Lied** ("Song") and **Tenorlied** ("Tenor Song"). The Tenorlied was so called because it

PRIMARY EVIDENCE

The Three Ladies of Ferrara

Luzzaschi's *T'amo mia vita* is one of many works written by various composers for the resident *Concerto delle donne* ("Ensemble of the Ladies") at the court of Ferrara, in northern Italy. The ensemble's most famous members were Laura Peverara (d. 1601), Livia d'Arco (d. 1611), and Anna Guarini (d. 1598). This group and others like it, especially in Mantua, attracted considerable attention and comment from visiting dignitaries. The account here, by the nobleman Vicenzo Giustiniani, was written sometime around 1628 and thus describes events that had occurred about thirty years before.

• • • • •

The ladies of Mantua and Ferrara were highly competent, and vied with each other not only in regard to the timbre and training of their voices but also, in the design of exquisite passages delivered at opportune points, but not in excess. . . . Furthermore, they moderated or increased their voices, loud or soft, heavy or light, according to the demands of the piece they were singing; now slow, breaking off with sometimes a gentle sigh, now singing long passages legato or detached, now groups, now leaps, now with long trills, now with short, and again with sweet running passages sung softly, to which sometimes one heard an echo answer unexpectedly. They accompanied the music and the sentiment with appropriate facial expressions, glances and gestures, with no awkward movements of the mouth or hands or body which might not express the feeling of the song. They made the words clear in such a way that one could hear even the last syllable of every word, which was never interrupted or suppressed by passages and other embellishments. They used many other particular devices which will be known to persons more experienced than I. And under these favorable circumstances the above-mentioned musicians made every effort to win fame and the favor of the Princes their patrons, who were their principal support.

Source: Vicenzo Giustiniani, *Discorso sopra la musica* (ca. 1628), trans. Carol MacClintock (s.l.: American Institute of Musicology, 1962), pp. 69–70.

Isaac
Innsbruck, ich muss dich lassen

Senfl
Zwischen Berg und tiefem Tal

typically incorporated a well-known tune in the tenor or other voice, making it, in effect, a secular cantus firmus genre. Heinrich Isaac put the melody for his *Innsbruck, ich muss dich lassen* ("Innsbruck, I Must Leave You") in the uppermost voice, whereas Ludwig Senfl put it in the slower moving tenor in his *Zwischen Berg und tiefem Tal* ("Between the Mountain and the Deep Valley").

Another type of German song was cultivated by members of what were called *Meistersinger* ("Master Singer") guilds. These were not professional musicians but rather tradesmen and craftsmen who formed societies and schools throughout Germany to foster the cultivation of music, poetry, and singing. (The 19th-century composer Richard Wagner made the most famous of all meistersingers, the cobbler Hans Sachs [1494–1576], the central figure in his 1868 opera *Die Meistersinger von Nürnberg*.) The guilds were governed by an elaborate system of rules and ranks and held regular competitions. Judges kept constant vigil against the violation of established norms. The songs were often written in bar form (AAB) in emulation of the medieval *Minnelieder* (see Chapter 1) and were performed by voice alone, with no accompaniment. Despite the rigid rules that governed them, many of the melodies from this repertory are memorable. Among them is Hans Sachs's *Silberweise* ("Silver Melody"), set to the words *Salve, ich grus dich* ("Hail, I greet you"). Some scholars have speculated that this melody was the model for the roughly contemporary melody of Martin Luther's most famous chorale, *Ein feste Burg ist unser Gott*. More likely, however, the two works emerged from a common fund of German folk and popular songs.

Sachs
Silberweise

F O C U S

Italian Madrigalists in the 16th Century

Composers of Italian madrigals in the 16th century span roughly four generations. The early and middle decades of the century were dominated by northerners, mostly from the Low Countries, such as Arcadelt, Willaert, Rore, and Lassus. By the end of the century, however, an impressive group of native-born Italians—the Gabrielis, Luzzaschi, Marenzio, Monteverdi—had established leadership in the genre.

1520s–1530s

Jacob Arcadelt (ca. 1505–1568) and **Philippe Verdelot** (?–ca. 1552), both from the Low Countries, were among the earliest composers to cultivate the Italian madrigal. Arcadelt spent most of his career in Rome and in France; Verdelot worked primarily in Venice and Florence. **Costanzo Festa** (ca. 1480–1545), the most important native Italian of the first generation of madrigalists, was a member of the Papal Chapel in Rome.

1540s–1550s

Adrian Willaert (ca. 1490–1562), born in what is now Belgium, studied with Jean Mouton in Paris and then moved to Ferrara, where he served at the court of the Este dynasty. He was appointed maestro di cappella at San Marco in Venice in 1527, and he held this prestigious post for the rest of his career. His pupils include Gioseffo Zarlino, Cipriano de Rore, and Andrea Gabrieli. **Cipriano de Rore** (1516–1565), also born in the region of present-day Belgium, succeeded Willaert at San Marco in Venice in 1562. He published eight books of madrigals in his lifetime.

1560s–1570s

Philippe de Monte (1521–1603), born in the Low Countries, was the most prolific of all madrigalists, issuing some 34 books of madrigals duirng his career. He traveled widely early in life, holding positions in Naples, Antwerp, and London. In 1567, he was appointed maestro di cappella to Emperor Maximilian II in Vienna.

Giovanni Pierluigi da Palestrina (1525 or 1526–1594; see the Composer Profile on page 119), although best known for his sacred music, composed more than 140 madrigals, many of which are based on spiritual texts. Two of his secular madrigals, *Io son ferito* and *Vestiva i colli,* however, were among the most popular works of their kind. **Orlande de Lassus** wrote a Mass based on the former, Palestrina himself one on the latter. Lassus (1532–1594; see the Composer Profile on page 127) published his first book of madrigals (for five voices) in 1555, his last in 1587. Altogether he wrote some 300 Italian madrigals, about 150 French chansons, and 150 German Lieder.

Andrea Gabrieli (1532 or 1533–1585), a native of Venice, studied with Willaert at San Marco. After an extended period in Germany, he returned to Venice in 1566 and eventually became first organist at San Marco. Gabrieli published madrigals for five voices (three books), six voices (two books), three voices (one book), as well as many other madrigals in various anthologies. His nephew and pupil **Giovanni Gabrieli** (ca. 1553/56–1612) composed madrigals as well. **Giaches de Wert** (1535–1596), also from the Flemish-speaking region of what is now Belgium, was a student of Cipriano de Rore in Ferrara but spent most of his career in Mantua, where he served as maestro di cappella. He was a prolific composer, publishing 13 books of madrigals, 11 of them for five voices.

1580s–1590s

Luzzasco Luzzaschi (?1545–1607), a native of Ferrara, studied with Cipriano de Rore and was himself a teacher of Girolamo Frescobaldi (see Chapter 10). Renowned as both an organist and composer, Luzzaschi published seven books of madrigals for five voices, along with many individual pieces that appeared in anthologies. **Luca Marenzio** (1553 or 1554–1599) worked at various times in both Rome and Ferrara. He published books of madrigals for three to six voices, including nine books of madrigals for five voices and six books for six voices. He also published five books of villanelle. **Claudio Monteverdi** (1567–1643), although associated primarily with the music of the Baroque era (see Chapter 8), published one book of canzonette for three voices and four books of madrigals prior to 1605 that stand squarely in the Renaissance tradition.

Milán
Al amor quiero vencer

Spain.   The principal genre of Spanish song in the Renaissance was the **villancico.** The term was first used in the late 15th century to identify a poetic form equivalent to the French virelai (AbbaA). The Spanish composer Luis Milán (ca. 1500–after 1561) published 12 villancicos in his *El Maestro* (Valencia, 1536), a large collection of works for solo vihuela—a guitarlike instrument with five to seven courses of gut strings tuned in the same manner as a lute—and for voice and vihuela.

The texture of *Al amor quiero vencer* ("I Want to Conquer Love") and other villancicos in Milán's collection is similar to that of the frottola: the uppermost voice dominates while the lower voices fill out the polyphonic framework.

El Maestro is important not only as the first collection of printed music for the vihuela, but also as the first publication of any kind to indicate performance tempos. Milán uses markings in Italian that range from molto lento to molto allegro.

England.   The Italian madrigal was transplanted to England first through manuscripts in the 1560s and then in a series of publications. The first of these, *Musica Transalpina* ("Music from Across the Alps"), published in 1588, was an anthology of 57 late-16th-century Italian madrigals with texts translated into English. The most notable among the composers represented were Ferrabosco, Marenzio, Palestrina, and de Monte. The English, at the time, were in the midst of an infatuation with things Italian. Shakespeare, for example, wrote a number of plays in the 1590s that are set in Italy, including *The Taming of the Shrew, The Two Gentlemen of Verona, Romeo and Juliet,* and *The Merchant of Venice.*

In 1597, the English composer Thomas Morley (1557–1602) complained the Italian fad was preventing his compatriots from appreciating the work of English composers. He expressed disgust with "the new-fangled opinions of our countrymen who will highly esteem whatsoever cometh from beyond the seas (and specially from Italy) be it never so simple, condemning that which is done at home though it be never so excellent."[2]

Morley
Now Is the Month of Maying

Morley, though, had an axe to grind—or more precisely, music to sell. He had already established himself as a composer of English madrigals and was eager to see the public taste move away from Italian music. He also conveniently avoided mentioning that he had based a number of his madrigals on Italian models. What's more, he adopted anglicized versions of the Italian terms canzonetti and balletti for his own lighter, dance-inspired madrigals. His early publications include *Canzonets, or Little Short Songs to Three Voyces* (1593) and a *First Book of Balletts to Five Voyces* (1595). The madrigal *Now Is the Month of Maying* from the collection of 1595 is almost entirely chordal in texture, very much in the style of Lassus's *Matona mia cara.* And perhaps almost as bawdy: the "barley break" in the last line refers to an old English game of mixed-sex tag in which the "losing" couple often wound up kissing.

Not all English madrigals are of this light, "fa la la" variety, however. Like the Italian madrigal, the English manifestation of the genre featured both a lighter and more serious side. Morley's own output includes works of a serious mood, some of which incorporate a chromaticism worthy of Lassus or Marenzio.

Dowland
Come, Heavy Sleep

Another English song type, closely related to the madrigal, is the **lute song,** whose chief proponent was the composer John Dowland (1563–1626). Lute songs are essentially strophic madrigals notated for lute and any combination of one or more voices. Dowland's setting of *Come, Heavy Sleep* plays on the perennial image of sleep as "the image of true death" both in its poetry and music. The long, languid arch of the cantus line captures an almost palpable sense of fatigue in its measured rhythms and repeated downward progressions.

Elizabeth I, lutenist. *England's Queen Elizabeth I put great store on her abilities as a lutenist and keyboard player but chose not to play in public, or at least before men. "The same day after dinner," recalled the diplomat Sir James Melville (1535–1617) of a day at court, "my Lord of Hunsdean drew me up to a quiet gallery . . . where I might hear the Queen play upon the virginals. After I had hearkened a while, I took by the tapestry that hung before the door of the chamber, and seeing her back was toward the door, I entered within the chamber, and stood a pretty space hearing her play excellently well. But she left off immediately, so soon as she turned her about and saw me. She appeared to be surprised to see me, and came forward, seeming to strike me with her hand; alleging she used not to play before men, but when she was solitary, to shun melancholy. She asked how I came there. I answered, As I was walking with my Lord of Hunsdean, as we passed by the chamber-door, I heard such melody as ravished me, whereby I was drawn in ere I knew how; excusing my fault of homeliness, as being brought up in the Court of France, where such freedom was allowed. . . . She enquired whether my Queen or she played best. In that I found myself obliged to give her the praise."*

Source: Nicholas Hilliard (1547–1619) Queen Elizabeth I Playing the Lute/Berkeley Castle, Gloucestershire, UK/ Bridgeman Art Library

English Madrigalists

The English madrigal enjoyed a brief but intense flowering during the last decade of the 16th century and the first decade of the 17th—roughly the same period in which Shakespeare was writing many of his greatest works. The genre's popularity was due in part to the advocacy of English song by Queen Elizabeth I, who was herself an accomplished musician.

Thomas Morley (1557–1602) was organist at Saint Paul's Cathedral and later a Gentleman of the Chapel Royal. He was one of the first native-born English composers to adopt the style of the Italian madrigal and author of an important treatise, *A Plaine and Easie Introduction to Practicall Musicke* (1597). He was also responsible for commissioning and publishing *The Triumphs of Oriana* (1601), an anthology of madrigals honoring Elizabeth I (identified metaphorically with the mythological shepherd queen Oriana).

Thomas Weelkes (ca. 1574–1623) was organist at Chichester Cathedral. His madrigal *As Vesta Was from Latmos Hill Descending* (published in Morley's *The Triumphs of Oriana*) is celebrated for its word-painting. But Weelkes stopped composing madrigals and devoted himself to sacred music at some point around 1600.

John Wilbye (1574–1638) served as a musician to Sir Thomas Kytson most of his life. He issued two books of madrigals, each for three to six voices, one in 1598 and the other in 1609.

John Dowland (1563–1626) was a self-described melancholic whose motto was *Semper Dowland, semper dolens* ("Always doleful, always Dowland")—he even pronounced the "o" in his last name in the same way as the "o" in "doleful." Many of his songs explore the theme of melancholy, including several sets of variations on the tune known as *Lachrimae* ("Tears").

SACRED VOCAL MUSIC

Until the early 16th century, western Europe had only one church, one central liturgy, and one liturgical language. No matter how great the local variations in practice, all parishes ultimately bowed to the authority of Rome and followed its Latin liturgy. The Reformation brought an abrupt end to this unity and created demands for a new kind of music. The Counter-Reformation, in turn, produced its own musical responses to the Protestant revolution.

Music of the Reformation

From the very beginning, Martin Luther recognized the power of music to spread the Protestant faith. He was himself a skilled lutenist, flutist, singer, and composer, and he deeply admired the works of Josquin des Prez. Luther never objected to polyphonic music or even works with Latin texts. Indeed, the new Protestant liturgy, although it increasingly emphasized worship in the vernacular, was closely patterned after the traditional Roman liturgy. Protestant composers still had cause to write motets that could serve as Introits, Graduals, and the like, and they could still set the Ordinary of the Mass, although no longer exclusively in Latin. Luther placed special emphasis on communal participation in worship and to that end encouraged the congregational singing of hymns—known in the German repertory as **chorales**—which in turn spawned a vast new repertory of melodies and texts.

Many of the earliest chorales were derived from existing melodies, both liturgical and secular. Luther's *Nun komm, der Heiden Heiland* ("Now Come, Savior of the

Heathen"), for example, adapts both the text and music of the plainchant Advent hymn *Veni, Redemptor gentium* ("Come, Savior of the People") (Example 6-1a and b). In the late 16th century, the melody of Heinrich Isaac's Tenorlied, *Innsbruck, ich muss dich lassen* ("Innsbruck, I Must Leave You"), became the basis for the chorale *O Welt, Ich muss dich lassen* ("O World, I Must Leave You"). Johann Sebastian Bach would later use the same melody twice (for different texts) in his *St. Matthew Passion* of 1728. Still other chorales were newly composed to new texts, including the chorale that became the unofficial anthem of the Reformation, *Ein feste Burg ist unser Gott* ("A Mighty Fortress Is Our God"). Luther himself wrote the melody and adapted the text from Psalm 46 ("God is our refuge and our strength . . . ").

Example 6-1 (a) The Latin hymn *Veni Redemptor gentium* and (b) Luther's chorale *Nun komm, der Heiden Heiland.*

Come, redeemer of the peoples, show through the birth by the Virgin
Let every age marvel that such a birth is worthy of God.

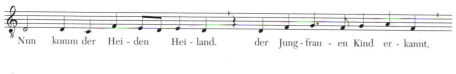

Now come, ye savior of the heathen, child born of a virgin,
that all the world might marvel, that God should give him such a birth.

Originally intended to be sung in unison by a congregation, chorale melodies soon began to be harmonized in increasingly sophisticated polyphonic settings. Johann Walter's setting of *Ein feste Burg ist unser Gott*, published in 1551, looks very much like a contemporary Tenorlied, with the principal melody in the tenor, surrounded by three other voices that move at a somewhat faster speed. The setting is well within reach of a moderately proficient choir. Walter (1496–1570) was the most prominent of the first generation of composers who wrote specifically for the Protestant liturgy.

    Luther embraced this polyphonic elaboration of chorale melodies. "We marvel when we hear music in which one voice sings a simple melody, while three, four, or five other voices play and trip heartily around it and adorn the tune wonderfully with artistic

Walter
Ein feste Burg ist unser Gott

PRIMARY EVIDENCE

Luther on Music

Like the church fathers of the 4th and 5th centuries, Luther felt compelled to justify the use of music in worship, for there were those who maintained the art was too frivolous for such a serious matter. The passage here is from Luther's preface to Georg Rhau's *Symphoniae iucundae* ("Delightful Symphonies," 1538), a collection of 52 motets, one for each Sunday of the liturgical year.

• • • • •

Here it must suffice to discuss the benefit of this great art [i.e., music]. But even that transcends the greatest eloquence of the most eloquent, because of the infinite variety of its forms and benefits. We can mention only one point (which experience confirms), namely, that next to the Word of God, music deserves the highest praise. She is a mistress and governess of those human emotions—to pass over the animals—which as masters govern men or more often overwhelm them. No greater commendation than this can be found—at least not by us. For whether you wish to comfort the sad, to terrify the happy, to encourage the despairing, to humble the proud, to calm the passionate, or to appease those full of hate—and who could number all these masters of the human heart, namely, the emotions, inclinations, and affections that impel men to evil or good?—what more effective means than music could you find? The Holy Ghost himself honors her as an instrument for his proper work when in his Holy Scriptures he asserts that through her his gifts were instilled in the prophets, namely, the inclination to all virtues, as can be seen in Elisha [II Kings 3:15]. On the other hand, she serves to cast out Satan, the instigator of all sins, as is shown in Saul, the king of Israel [I Samuel 16:23].

Source: Martin Luther, *Liturgy and Hymns*, ed. Ulrich S. Leupold (*Luther's Works*, vol. 53) (Philadelphia: Fortress Press, 1965), pp. 323–4. Used with approval of Augsbury Fortress Press, Minneapolis.

musical effect, thus reminding us of a heavenly dance where all meet in a spirit of friendliness, caress, and embrace."[3] Other Protestant leaders were not so receptive to polyphony. The Calvinists, under Jean Calvin, banned instrumental music of any kind from church and limited sacred music to the unaccompanied unison singing of the Psalms. Ulrich Zwingli (1484–1531) and his followers were even more extreme. They considered music too seductive and irrational a force to be permitted within the liturgy. Zwingli even ordered organs in many northern European churches to be destroyed. Luther deplored these extremes. "I am not satisfied with him who despises music, as all fanatics do," Luther declared. "Music is . . . a gift of God, not a gift of men."[4]

In England, the Reformation was driven by the monarchy. Henry VIII (1491–1547; reigned 1509–1547) wanted to have his marriage to Catherine of Aragon annulled because she had produced no male heir, but the pope refused to accommodate him. In response, Henry declared the Church of England, with himself at its head, to be independent of Rome. Liturgical reforms were slow to follow this rupture of 1527. With the publication of the first *Book of Common Prayer* in 1549, English began to replace Latin as the language of the liturgy, but the liturgy itself, now known as Communion Service, continued to follow the basic outline of the Mass Ordinary. This permitted musicians to maintain their existing repertory by converting the texts of existing Mass settings and motets into English.

Not surprisingly, composers soon took up the challenge and opportunity to write motets in the English language. These works, which eventually came to be known as **anthems,** took two forms: full and verse. The full anthem is for chorus throughout. The verse anthem alternates choral passages with passages for solo voice and instrumental accompaniment.

The most outstanding composers of anthems during the 16th century were Christopher Tye (1500–1573), Thomas Tallis (1505–1585), and William Byrd (1542–1623). Tallis's *Verily, verily I Say Unto You* exemplifies the noble simplicity of many of the earliest full anthems. The declamation is almost entirely chordal except for a few cadences (measures 11, 17–18) and a bit of word-painting on the rising figure that sets the phrase "and I will raise him up" (measures 19–20).

Tallis
Verily, Verily I Say Unto You

As the 16th century progressed, anthems became more elaborate. The composer William Byrd was a devout Catholic and as such had to be careful in his dealings with royal patrons. He wrote several settings of the Latin Mass as well as many widely admired settings of English texts that were used in Anglican services—that is, services of the Church of England. His full anthem *Sing Joyfully Unto God* features the six-voice texture so characteristic of late-16th-century vocal music. In many respects, the work resembles a sacred madrigal for chorus. It is paratactic in form and through-composed with discreet but unmistakable instances of word-painting. Note the rising figure on "Sing joyfully" in measure 1, for example, the long note values and upward leaps on "Sing loud" at measure 10, and the triadic, fanfarelike figure to the words "Blow the trumpet" at measure 30.

Byrd
Sing Joyfully Unto God

Music of the Counter-Reformation

After excommunicating Luther for heresy in 1521, the Roman Catholic Church began to reassess its stance toward the Protestant Reformation. The pope could not afford to alienate all of his German allies, and as a result Rome grew cautious and ambivalent in its response to changes north of the Alps in the 1520s and 1530s. By the 1540s, when it had become clear that Protestantism was firmly entrenched, Pope Paul III convened a special council to formulate a coordinated counter offensive to the challenges of the Reformation.

The Council of Trent met in three sessions (1545–1547, 1551–1552, 1562–1563) in Trento (Trent), Italy, to formulate doctrines of faith, revise the liturgy, and generally purge the Roman Catholic Church of various practices that had accrued over many centuries—including the sale of indulgences. In the realm of music, the council eliminated a number of plainchants that had been added to the liturgy since medieval times (such as the Sequence on which Josquin had based the opening of his *Ave Maria . . . virgo serena;* see Chapter 4). The council further declared that the function of sacred music was to serve the text and the text should be clear and intelligible to listeners. "The whole plan of singing," according to a report issued by the council in 1562,

> [S]hould be constituted not to give empty pleasure to the ear, but in such a way that the words be clearly understood by all, and thus the hearts of the listeners be drawn to the desire of heavenly harmonies, in the contemplation of the joys of the blessed. . . . They shall also banish from church all music that contains, whether in the singing or in the organ playing, things that are lascivious or impure.[5]

In pursuit of the ideal of textual intelligibility, some council members advocated a return to exclusively monophonic music—plainchant—in place of polyphony. The council rejected this radical move, and legend has it that it did so because of a work by the composer Pierluigi da Palestrina—his *Missa Papae Marcelli* ("Mass for Pope Marcellus," published in 1567). Although appealing, this story is not true. However, participants at the Council might very well have pointed to the straightforward and nonvirtuosic text setting in at least some of Palestrina's Masses in their defense of polyphony. The Credo of the *Missa Papae Marcelli,* for example, presents a lot of text in a relatively short time

Palestrina
Missa Papae Marcelli

in a way that allows the words to stand out clearly, particularly at the beginnings of phrases. Palestrina introduces musical variety and relieves the mostly chordal declamation of the text with discreet melismas from time to time.

Palestrina's Missa *Papae Marcelli* also reflects the routine acceptance of thirds and sixths as fully consonant intervals in practice by the middle of the 16th century. Although the Spanish theorist Bartolomé Ramos de Pareja had argued in the 1480s that these intervals should be considered consonant (see Chapter 4), it was not until the second half of the 16th century that this view became widely accepted.

Although it did not condemn polyphony, the Council of Trent did discourage the use of secular music as a model for sacred compositions. In so doing, it drew a distinction between sacred and secular musical sources that had not been apparent before. Du Fay and Josquin had routinely used secular music as a basis for at least some of their Masses, and even Palestrina in his earlier years composed half a dozen imitation Masses on secular madrigals or chansons. By the middle of the 16th century, however, attitudes toward this practice were beginning to change. As one writer of the day put it, whenever Masses based on secular songs or even on battle pieces were performed in church, "they impel everyone to laughter, so that it appears almost as if the temple of God had become a place for the recitation of lascivious and ridiculous things."[6]

INSTRUMENTAL MUSIC

The tradition of performing vocal music on instruments continued unabated throughout the 16th century, but for the first time in the history of music, composers also began to write substantial quantities of specifically instrumental music. The genres of 16th-century instrumental music fall into four broad categories:

◆ Intabulations

◆ Variations

◆ Abstract works, freely composed and adhering to no established scheme or vocal model

◆ Dance music

Intabulations

Vocal and instrumental genres were in many respects interchangeable. As in the 15th century, chansons were often performed either wholly by instruments or by a combination of voices and instruments. Almost half of all the pieces published during this time for plucked stringed instruments—lute, guitar, vihuela, cittern, pandora—are **intabulations,** a term used to cover any arrangement of an existing vocal work for a plucked string instrument or keyboard. The first publication ever devoted entirely to keyboard music—*Frottole intabulate da sonare organi,* published in Rome by Andrea Antico in 1517—consists entirely of intabulations of frottole. This was a repertory that sold well. The pieces themselves were already known to a wide public, and solo arrangements reduced the forces needed to perform them to a single musician.

Variations

Orators of the Renaissance, following the ancient models of Cicero and Quintilian, placed great value on the ability of public speakers to embellish the expression of an idea

Composer Profile

Giovanni Pierluigi da Palestrina
(1525 or 1526–1594)

From his time to ours, Palestrina's music—with its equal voices, seamless rhythmic flow, carefully controlled use of dissonance, and flawless part writing—has been hailed as quintessentially representative of Renaissance polyphonic style. This well-earned reputation was enhanced still further by the legend, not true but believed by music lovers for centuries, that his *Missa Papae Marcelli* convinced the Council of Trent not to ban

polyphonic music from the Roman Catholic liturgy. Not surprisingly, given his renown, Palestrina was the first 16th-century composer to have his complete works published. The release of this collection began in 1862.

KEY DATES IN THE LIFE OF PIERLUIGI DA PALESTRINA
ca. 1525 Born in Palestrina, near Rome
1537 Serves as choirboy at Santa Maria Maggiore, Rome
1544 Becomes organist at San Agapito, in Palestrina
1551 Appointed maestro di cappella of the Cappella Giulia in Rome
1555–1566 Serves as maestro di cappella first at St. John Lateran, then at Santa Maria Maggiore
1571 Returns to the Cappella Giulia as maestro di cappella
1594 Dies in Rome on February 2

Giovanni Pierluigi da Palestrina. *The title page of Palestrina's* Missarum liber primus *("First Book of Masses") published in Rome in 1554 shows the composer presenting his music to Pope Julius III. Palestrina's publication was the first of its kind by an Italian composer and as such marks the beginning of a gradual shift away from the predominance of northern composers and toward native-born artists in Italy in the second half of the 16th century.*

Source: CORBIS BETTMANN

Palestrina was musically more conservative than his near-contemporary Orlande de Lassus, and he worked within a narrower range of genres, but his output was equally impressive.

Principal Works

Palestrina wrote 104 settings of the Mass Ordinary (for from four to eight voices), about 375 motets, 35 Magnificats, 68 offertories, 11 litanies, about 80 hymns, 49 sacred madrigals (for five voices), and more than 90 secular madrigals (for three to six voices).

in different guises, varied in such a way as to both please and move an audience. Composers went about their task with much the same goal, shaping each restatement of a given theme in such a way as to delight and move listeners.

Cabezón
Diferencias sobre el canto de la Dama le demanda

Antonio de Cabezón's *Diferencias sobre el canto de la Dama le demanda* ("Variations on the Song 'The Lady Demands It'") takes as its theme the popular melody known in France as *Belle, qui tient ma vie* ("Beautiful One, Who Holds My Life"). Cabezón (1510–1566) first presents the melody in the uppermost voice and then takes it through a series of five variations. Typically for keyboard music of the mid–16th century, the register remains fairly narrow throughout, the melody is never far from the surface, and the technical demands on the player are relatively modest.

Freely Composed Works

Freely composed instrumental works adhere to no established scheme or vocal model. The most important genres of the 16th century include the ricercar, fantasia, toccata, canzona, and prelude.

Spinacino
Ricercar

In Italian, *ricercare* means "to research, to seek out," and the **ricercar** of the early 16th century is a freely composed work that "seeks out" a particular mode or thematic idea. The typical ricercar of this era is full of runs and passagework. Francesco Spinacino's ricercar, from the first book of his *Intabolatura de lauto* ("Lute Intabulations"), published by Petrucci in 1507, has all the hallmarks of improvisation: the dramatic pause after the opening stroke, the gradual accumulation of speed, and the eventual move from passagework to more tangible thematic ideas (beginning at measure 20) all create a sense of generative energy, a trajectory that moves from obscurity to focus, from generalities to specifics. At least some ricercars of this era appear to have been preludial in function, serving to establish the mode of a subsequent work. Each of the ricercars in Marc' Antonio Cavazzoni's keyboard collection of 1523, *Recerchari motetti canzoni* ("Ricercars, Motets, Canzonas"), for example, is followed by an intabulation of a preexistent motet in the same mode.

A generation later, however, the essence of the ricercar had changed fundamentally. By the middle of the 16th century, the genre had become primarily imitative; the sense of "seeking out" was now being applied to the exploration of the contrapuntal possibilities inherent in a series of themes. The ricercars in the *Intavolatura cioè Ricercari, Canzoni, Hinni, Magnificati* (Venice, 1542) by Girolamo Cavazzoni (ca. 1525–after 1577), Marc' Antonio's son, are structurally identical to the motets of their day and are based on the principle of pervading imitation.

Gabrieli
Ricercar del duodecimo tuono

The *Ricercar del duodecimo tuono* by Andrea Gabrieli (1532 or 1533–1585), published in 1589, stands squarely in the tradition of the polyphonic ricercar. The "duodecimo tuono" ("twelfth tone") of the title corresponds to the Ionian mode on C, which happens to be the equivalent of the modern-day major scale. The work can be performed by any combination of appropriate instruments with the needed ranges—strings, winds, brass. The writing here is not idiomatic to any particular instrument or for that matter to instruments at all; with an appropriately underlaid text, the parts could just as easily be sung. The practice of writing in a manner unique to a specific instrument is something that would not emerge until the 17th century, and even then only gradually.

Like the early ricercar, the **toccata** (from the Italian *toccare*, "to touch") is a sectional, freely constructed work unrelated to any preexistent material. The toccatas of Claudio Merulo (1533–1604) are typical of the genre in the second half of the 16th century. They abound in rapid passages that "touch" lightly on the keys and move

Interior of the Basilica of San Marco, Venice.   *From about the 1520s onward, the directorship of music at San Marco was one of the most prestigious positions in all of Italy if not all of Europe. The position was held at various times by such prominent composers as Adrian Willaert, Cipriano de Rore, Gioseffo Zarlino, and in the 17th century Claudio Monteverdi, Francesco Cavalli, and Giovanni Legrenzi. Venice had strong commercial and cultural ties to the east, and the architecture of San Marco reflects the influence of the Byzantine style. Many of the composers associated with San Marco, particularly Andrea Gabrieli (ca. 1510–1586) and his nephew Giovanni Gabrieli (1532 or 1533–1585), cultivated a style of performances involving antiphonal choirs (cori spezzati). These groups—choral, instrumental, or a mixture of the two—were in all likelihood not placed at opposite ends of the basilica's transept, as is often thought, but closer together at ground level.*

Source: Canaletto, "Venice: The Interior of S. Marco by Day," The Royal Collection © 2002, Her Majesty Queen Elizabeth II

freely between nonimitative and imitative sections. The **fantasia** of this era is structured according to the same principles. As its name implies, it allows for free flights of the composer's imaginative fantasy—what the English called "fancy." Thomas Morley, writing in 1597, characterized the genre in these terms:

> The most principal and chiefest kind of music which is made without a ditty [i.e., without words to be sung] is the Fantasy, that is when a musician taketh a point [i.e., theme] at his pleasure and wresteth and turneth it as he list, making either much or little of it according as shall seem best in his own conceit. In this may more art be shown than in any other music because the composer is tied to nothing, but that he may add, diminish, and alter at his pleasure. And this kind will bear any allowances whatsoever tolerable in other music except changing the air [i.e., the mode] and leaving the key, which in Fantasie may never be suffered. Other things you may use at your pleasure, bindings with discords, quick motions, slow motions, proportions, and what you list. Likewise this kind of music is, with them who practise instruments of parts [i.e., play in an ensemble], in greatest use, but for voices it is but seldom used.[7]

Sweelinck
Fantasia chromatica

Morley's definition captures an important technical element that characterizes many (but by no means all) instrumental compositions of the 16th century: the technique of intense thematic manipulation, what Morley calls the "wresting" and "turning" of the musical idea. These tendencies are amply evident in Jan Pieterszoon Sweelinck's *Fantasia chromatica*. Although transmitted in sources dating from the 1620s onward, the work may well have been written as early as the 1590s. It explores the musical implications of a single idea, a descending chromatic fourth, through augmentation (a lengthening of the original note values of the subject; measure 120), **diminution** (a speeding up of note values; measure 171), transposition, contrasting countersubjects (measure 95), sequencing, and a variety of textures.

Dance Music

The quantity of sources that preserve dance music increases dramatically in the 16th century. The skeletal, single-line notation of the 15th-century basse danse (see Chapter 5) gave way to a notation that fills in other voices as well. Published intabulations of dance music for lute and keyboard in the early 16th century help give us a much better picture of the kinds of dance music in the later part of the Renaissance.

Susato
Dances from *Het derde musyck boexken*

Praetorius
Dances from *Terpsichore*

Tielman Susato's *Het derde musyck boexken* (1551, "The Third Little Book of Music") and Michael Praetorius's *Terpsichore* (published 1612, named after the ancient Greek muse of dancing) contain many kinds of dances popular during the second half of the 16th century and the early decades of the 17th century. Each of these dances has its own distinctive steps, meter, tempo, and musical character. These are the most common dance types:

- **pavane:** slow, courtly dance in duple meter

- **passamezzo:** similar to the pavane, but with a lighter step

- **bourrée:** lively dance in duple meter with a prominent upbeat at the beginning of each section

- **saltarello:** lively dance that often follows a slower one

- **galliarde:** like a saltarello but even more vigorous, with larger leaps by the dancers

Composers of Keyboard Music in the 16th Century

Marc' Antonio Cavazzoni (ca. 1490–ca. 1570) was active in both Venice and Rome. His *Recerchari, motetti, canzoni, Libro I* (Venice, 1523) is the first set of independently composed keyboard music ever published. His son **Girolamo Cavazzoni** (ca. 1525–after 1577) wrote the first polyphonic ricercars in a collection published in Venice in 1542.

Antonio de Cabezón (1510–1566) was organist at the court of the Spanish king and Holy Roman emperor Charles V and later in the service of Prince Philip (who became Philip II of Spain). He traveled widely throughout Europe but returned to Spain for the final ten years of his life. His works were published posthumously under the editorship of his son Hernando (1541–1602), who succeeded his father as organist at the court of Philip II. Antonio de Cabezón's organ music includes *tientos* (predominantly contrapuntal works), arrangements of motets by various composers of his era, and a number of variations.

Claudio Merulo (1533–1604) served as organist at San Marco in Venice and then moved to Mantua and later to Parma, where he became court organist. Most of his music circulated in manuscript during his lifetime and was published only after his death. He is particularly renowned for his toccatas and ricercars.

Jan Pieterszoon Sweelinck (1562–1621) was born in Amsterdam and remained there as organist of the Oude Kerk (the "Old Church") for most of his life. He nevertheless exerted a tremendous influence throughout Europe both as a composer and teacher. Sweelinck greatly expanded the use of the pedal as an independent part and was one of the first to write extended fugues on a single subject.

William Byrd (1543–1623), arguably the greatest of the many keyboard composers active in England in the late 16th and early 17th centuries, was organist at the cathedral of Lincoln, then later at the Chapel Royal in London. He won fame for his choral music as well as his keyboard works, which are preserved in two major manuscripts, *My Ladye Nevells Booke* and the *Fitzwilliam Virginal Book*. His music also appears in the *Parthenia* of 1611, the first keyboard music to be published in England.

Music for the virginal. *As its title page proudly proclaims, Parthenia (London, 1613) was the first keyboard music to be printed—at least in England. It contains music by three of the greatest English composers of its time: William Byrd (1543–1623), John Bull (ca. 1562–1628), and Orlando Gibbons (1583–1625). Like the contemporaneous plays of William Shakespeare (1564–1616), the title page is full of puns. "Parthenia" are the dances of Greek maidens from classical antiquity, and the demure young woman shown here exudes the modesty that befits a maiden or virgin. She is playing a virginal, a small harpsichord with a single keyboard and a single set of strings running at right angles to the keys. And the subtitle—"The Maydenhead of the First Musicke"—refers to the novelty of this publication in England. The collection was presented to Princess Elizabeth and Prince Frederick on the occasion of their marriage in 1613.*

Source: This item is reproduced by permission of The Huntington Library, San Marino, California./Title page: Parthenia or The Maydenhead (London 1613) by William Byrd et al/RB 14176

- ◆ **volta:** vigorous "turning" dance (*voltare* means "to turn" in Italian), often in compound duple meter

- ◆ **branle:** "line dance," sometimes in duple meter (*branle simple*), sometimes triple (*branle gay*)

- ◆ **moresca:** "Moorish" dance, supposedly influenced by the Arabic cultures of northern Africa and Spain

- ◆ **rondo:** "round dance" performed by a large group moving in a circle at a lively tempo

Whatever their differences, all of these dances are built on the principle of **periodic phrase structure**—that is, they consist of many modular units of equal length. This structure derives from the basic function of social dance, which by its very nature consists of a prescribed pattern of steps that are repeated over and over again.

In Susato's *La Morisque*, for example, the phrasing falls very clearly into a 4 + 4 pattern that corresponds harmonically to what we would today think of as tonic moving to dominant (measures 1–4), followed by four measures that remain in the tonic. These smaller units of periodic phrase structure are based on a combination of melodic, harmonic, and rhythmic elements. Phrases that move from tonic to dominant (I–V) are called **antecedent** phrases (antecedent meaning "to come before"); phrases that move from the dominant back to the tonic (V–I) are called **consequent** phrases (consequent meaning "to follow as a result of something that has come before"). In the simplest kind of periodic phrase structure, a four-measure antecedent phrase is followed by a four-measure consequent phrase. This larger eight-measure unit, in turn, can be juxtaposed with another unit of eight measures (4 + 4), as in Susato's *La Morisque*.

⒫RIMARY EVIDENCE

Men, Women, and Dancing

From the Renaissance onward, dancing was an essential social skill in polite European society. Books on dance method were popular, and the dancing master was as much (or more) sought after for instruction as the music master. One of the most comprehensive and popular dance manuals of the Renaissance was Thoinot Arbeau's *Orchésographie* of 1589. In this dialogue from *Orchésographie,* Arbeau explains the social necessity of dance to his student Capriol.

• • • • •

CAPRIOL: I much enjoyed fencing and tennis, and this placed me upon friendly terms with young men. But, without knowledge of dancing. I could not please the damsels, upon whom, it seems to me, the entire reputation of an eligible young man depends.

ARBEAU: You are quite right, as naturally the male and female seek one another, and nothing does more to stimulate a man to acts of courtesy, honor, and generosity than love. And if you desire to marry you must realize that a mistress is won by the good temper and grace displayed while dancing, because ladies do not like to be present at fencing or tennis, lest a splintered sword or a blow from a tennis ball cause them injury. . . . And there is more to it than this, for dancing is practiced to reveal whether lovers are in good health and sound of limb, after which they are permitted to kiss their mistresses in order that they may touch and savor one another thus to ascertain if they are shapely or emit an unpleasant odor as of bad meat. Therefore, from this standpoint, quite apart from the many other advantages to be derived from dancing, it becomes an essential to a well-ordered society.

Source: Thoinot Arbeau, *Orchésography* (1589), trans. Mary Stewart Evans (New York: Dover, 1967), p. 12.

Dance music abounds in repetition, and in performance, the individual **reprises**—the larger sections to be repeated—can be played as often as desired. Two reprises together constitute a **binary form.** Binary form represents one of the earliest instances of **syntactic form,** in which a central idea is presented and varied over the course of an entire movement, in contrast to paratactic form, in which each new section presents an essentially new idea. Binary form takes its name from the fact that it always consists of two reprises, that is, sections to be repeated ("reprised"). Binary form provides the basis for a great many dance types and would eventually be incorporated into instrumental music not written expressly for dancing. During the course of the 18th century, in fact, binary form would provide the structural basis for sonata form (see Chapter 11).

Susato promised his audiences that these dances "could be played quite delightfully and easily on all musical instruments," and his claim goes beyond mere salesmanship. The lines are so straightforward that they could in fact just as easily be sung. But as in the case of Giovanni Gabrieli's ricercar, no distinctively instrumental idiom is evident here, or even some sixty years later in the instrumental dances of Michael Praetorius.

MANNERISM

Mannerism is a term from art history that designates a style of painting and sculpture characterized by the use of distortion, exaggeration, and unsettling juxtaposition for dramatic effect. Mannerist painters include Parmigianino (1503–1540; see illustration),

Visual mannerism. The Virgin of the Long Neck, *by the Italian painter Parmigianino (Francesco Mazzola, 1503–1540), illustrates many elements of mannerism. The basic proportions of the central figures are wildly distorted: the Madonna's neck, hands, and fingers are all extraordinarily elongated, as is the Christ child. To confuse matters even further, the angels to the left seem perfectly proportioned while the figure of Saint Jerome in the background seems almost comically tiny in relation to his positioning. The columns supporting nothing at all add to the enigmatic quality of this curious—mannerist—image.*

Source: Francesco Mazzola Parmigianino (1503–1540), Italian, "Madonna with the Long Neck," panel, 215.9 x 13 cm/Galleria degli Uffizi, Florence, Italy/Bridgeman Art Library

The Singer as Orator

Renaissance writers, in imitation of classical antiquity, liked to compare musicians to orators, implicitly giving primacy to the text being sung. Here, Nicola Vicentino advocates performing from memory and with a certain flexibility in rhythm and tempo, techniques commonly recommended to orators as well.

• • • • •

So one sings music *alla mente* [literally "from the mind," that is, as if improvised] to imitate the accents and effects of the parts of the oration—for what effect would the orator make if he recited a fine speech without arranging his accents and pronunciation, with fast and slow movements, and speaking softly and loudly? That would not move his hearers. The same should occur in music; for if the orator moves his auditors with the aforesaid manners, how much more would music, recited in the same manner, accompanied by harmony and well united, make a greater effect.

And music sung *alla mente* will be more welcome than that sung *sopra le carte* ["from the page"]. Let them take the example of the preachers and the orators. If they recited a sermon or oration from the written page it would not have any grace, nor be well received by the audience, for the [expressive] glances together with the embellishments greatly move an audience when they are used together . . . .

Source: Nicola Vicentino, *L'antica musica* (Rome, 1555), Book 4, Chapter 42; trans. by Carol MacClintock, *Readings in the History of Music in Performance* (Bloomington: Indiana University Press, 1979), pp. 76–7, 78–9. Reprinted by permission of Indiana University Press.

Tintoretto (1518–1594), and El Greco (1541–1614). In music it applies to a small but important repertory of works (both sacred and secular) written in the second half of the 16th century and characterized by a comparable process of distortion, including extreme dissonance, unusual harmonic progressions, and exaggerated word-painting.

Lassus
Prophetiae sibyllarum

The Prologue to Orlande de Lassus's *Prophetiae sibyllarum*, composed ca. 1550–1552, is a good example of musical mannerism. The Sibylline Prophecies of the title are the work of 2nd-century authors apocryphally attributed to the legendary Sibyls, ancient Greek prophetesses. The texts, which purport to foretell the birth of Christ, were accepted as genuine by Saint Augustine and other early Christian thinkers, giving the Sibyls a status equal to that of Old Testament prophets. Michelangelo painted five of the Sibyls onto the ceiling of the Sistine Chapel in the Vatican in 1508–1512. The Prologue, whose text may have been written by Lassus himself, reads (in translation): "Polyphonic songs which you hear with a chromatic tenor / these are they, in which our twice-six sibyls once sang with fearless mouth the secrets of salvation."[8] Lassus responds immediately to the idea of "chromaticism" with a series of jarring progressions. Within the opening nine measures, he uses all twelve chromatic pitches and builds triads on nine different roots.

Lassus presented the *Prophetiae sibyllarum* to his patron in a carefully prepared manuscript but never published it. These works are demanding for performers and listeners alike and were in all likelihood never intended for wide distribution. They belong to a category of music known at the time as **musica reservata**—that is, music "reserved" for a select audience of elite noble-born or aristocratic listeners.

The intense chromaticism of Lasso's *Prophetiae sibyllarum* reflects a broader effort by theorists and composers in the mid–16th century to recapture what they believed to be an important element of Greek music. A whole series of pieces from the mid and late

Composer Profile

Orlande de Lassus
(1530 or 1532–1594)

O ne of the most cosmopolitan composers who ever lived, Lassus—also known by the Italianized form of his name, Orlando di Lasso—moved easily between north and south, holding important positions at churches and courts in both Italy and Bavaria. His letters are sometimes written in a mixture of different languages—Italian, French, German, and Latin—and at times full of puns and wordplay. His music ranges from the deeply serious and even mystic (the *Prophetiae sibyllarum,* for example) to the ribald (*Matona mia cara*). The kinds of honors he received in the 1570s—he was ennobled by the Holy Roman Emperor and made a Knight of the Golden Spur by the pope—were rarely conferred on musicians.

Principal Works

Lassus was one of the most prolific composers in the history of music, writing more than 2,000 works in virtually every genre of his era, both sacred and secular. Most of his approximately 70 Masses are "imitation" Masses based on polyphonic models. He also composed more than 500 motets for 2 to 12 voices, about 100 settings of the Magnificat for 4 to 10 voices, and various psalms and hymns for the church. He wrote songs in three languages: about 200 Italian madrigals and *villanelle,* some 150 French chansons, and about 90 German Lieder.

POVR REPOS TRAVAIL

Hic ille Orlandus qui Lassum recreat orbem Discordemq; sua copulat harmonia.

NOBILI & EXIMIO VIRO DÑO ORLANDO DE LASSVS, SERNISS.mi V TRIVSQ; BAVARIAE DVCIS GVILIEL.mi MVSICI CHORI PREFECTO. *Johan. Sadeler eiusdē Principis chalcograph? obseruat. ergo scalpsit et dedicauit. Monachij. cum priuilegio Sac. Ces. M.*

Orlande de Lassus. *This copperplate engraving, made in 1593, shows the composer at the height of his career as music director to the Duke of Bavaria in Munich. The chain around his neck holds the medallion of the Knight of the Golden Spur, an honor conferred on him by Pope Gregory XIII in 1574.*

Source: Copyright Bibliotheque Royale Albert Ier, Bruxelles (Cabinet des Estampes/J. Saedler, Orlando de Lassus H603–B1.152

KEY DATES IN THE LIFE OF ORLANDE DE LASSUS

1530 or 1532 Born in Mons (now Belgium)

ca. 1544 Enters the service of the Gonzagas in Mantua; holds various positions throughout Italy over the subsequent decade

1553 Appointed maestro di cappella of St. John Lateran, Rome

1556 Joins the court chapel of Duke Albrecht V of Bavaria in Munich

1563 Becomes Kapellmeister to Duke Albrecht V of Bavaria and serves in this position for the remainder of his life while traveling frequently all the while

1570 Receives a patent of nobility from Emperor Maximilian II

1574 Made Knight of the Golden Spur by Pope Gregory XIII in 1574

1594 Dies in Munich on June 14

Lassus
Cum essem parvulus

16th century delve into chromatic possibilities, including Marenzio's madrigal *Solo e pensoso*, discussed earlier in the chapter. In Adrian Willaert's *Quid non ebrietas* (known as the "Chromatic Duo"), the tenor descends through a circle of fifths and ends on a notated seventh, presumably to be changed by musica ficta to an octave. Cipriano de Rore's madrigal *Calami sonum ferentes* is also extremely chromatic. Less extreme than his *Prophetiae sibyllarum* but no less mannerist is Lassus's six-voice motet *Cum essem parvulus* ("When I Was a Child"), published in 1579.

CONCLUSION

The year 1600 provides a conveniently round starting point for the end of the Renaissance and the beginning of the Baroque, although in reality many characteristics of Renaissance style maintained themselves well into the 17th century, just as many Baroque elements can be found in music from the closing decades of the 16th century. The interest of certain composers in mannerism was driven, after all, by the desire to enrich the poetic content of any given text through any musical means available, no matter how usual or radical. As such, mannerism embodies many of the ideals that would find an ever-growing acceptance in the music of the Baroque.

DISCUSSION QUESTIONS

1. What stylistic traits distinguish Renaissance from medieval music? How did Renaissance attitudes toward music differ from those of the medieval era?

2. In what ways did composers working around 1500 have a greater variety of musical textures at their disposal than did their counterparts fifty years before?

3. Many of the complex contrapuntal and structural devices found in the Masses and motets of such composers as Du Fay and Ockeghem are scarecely audible, even to the listener aware of their presence. What motivations might have driven these composers to create such elaborate but arguably inaudible devices?

4. In what ways do the Masses of Josquin des Prez offer a cross-section of compositional techniques in that genre for the period between roughly 1490 and 1520?

5. What textual and musical features remained consistent within the Italian madrigal throughout the 16th century? In what respects did the genre change between 1530 and 1600?

6. In what ways did the music of the Protestant Reformation build on established traditions, and in what ways did it break new ground?

7. What musical changes arose from the Counter-Reformation?

8. Only a fraction of the music performed during the Renaissance was written down. What kind of music was transmitted outside the written tradition? Are there similar divisions in music today?

9. How does dance music of the Renaissance differ stylistically from the typical vocal genres of the era, such as Mass, motet, or chanson?

10. In what ways was the musical mannerism of the second half of the 16th century an outgrowth of the musical traditions that preceded it?

Part Three
The Baroque Era

Prelude

The Baroque era in music—the period between roughly 1600 and 1750—coincides with what is often called the Age of Absolutism, during which many of Europe's monarchs laid claim to complete and sole authority over their dominions. Louis XIV, king of France from 1643 until his death in 1715, set the standard. He vigorously advocated the divine right of kings—the doctrine that rulers derive their authority not only through their ancestors but ultimately from God—and quashed the claims of the aristocracy to a share of power. "I am the state," he once famously declared. Along with military force, the French king used outward displays of material and cultural wealth to maintain his hold on power. He built a magnificent new palace on the site of a royal hunting lodge in Versailles, west of Paris, and made it the site of lavish entertainments, including fireworks, tournaments, dramas, ballets, and operas.

Louis XIV's extravagance and military adventures had depleted the French treasury by the time of his death. Yet whatever its consequences as a political system, absolutism proved a boon to the arts. The French king patronized the greatest French composer of the 17th century, Jean-Baptiste Lully (1632–1687; see Chapter 9), as well as the equally celebrated playwrights Molière (1622–1673) and Jean Racine (1639–1699). Dozens of

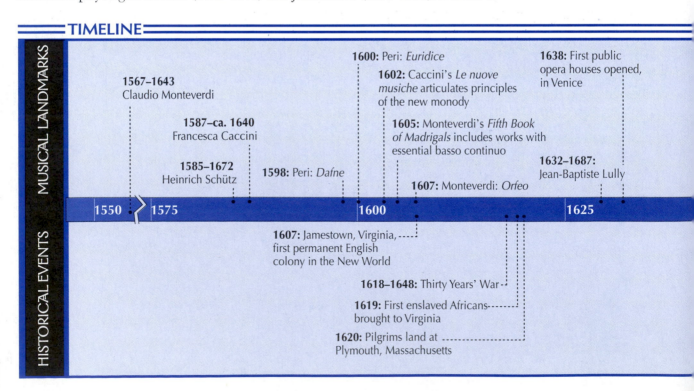

TIMELINE

MUSICAL LANDMARKS

1567–1643
Claudio Monteverdi

1587–ca. 1640
Francesca Caccini

1585–1672
Heinrich Schütz

1598: Peri: *Dafne*

1600: Peri: *Euridice*

1602: Caccini's *Le nuove musiche* articulates principles of the new monody

1605: Monteverdi's *Fifth Book of Madrigals* includes works with essential basso continuo

1607: Monteverdi: *Orfeo*

1638: First public opera houses opened, in Venice

1632–1687: Jean-Baptiste Lully

1550   1575   1600   1625

HISTORICAL EVENTS

1607: Jamestown, Virginia, first permanent English colony in the New World

1618–1648: Thirty Years' War

1619: First enslaved Africans brought to Virginia

1620: Pilgrims land at Plymouth, Massachusetts

smaller palaces modeled after Versailles sprang up across Europe as other rulers—even those of the most modest duchies and principalities—vied with one another to follow the lead of France and cultivate a comparably brilliant cultural life at their own courts. As far away as Russia, Peter I (1672–1725; known as "The Great") almost single-handedly transformed his nation into a European power, in part through military conquest, in part through cultural means. He established his capital in St. Petersburg in 1703 and built another palace nearby, the Peterhof, which soon became known as the "Russian Versailles." Poets, playwrights, composers, musicians, and dancers soon followed.

WAR, REVOLUTION, AND COLONIAL EXPANSION

Against this backdrop of splendor, Europe was engulfed in religious strife and a series of seemingly endless wars. The last, longest, and bloodiest of these, the Thirty Years' War (1618–1648), was fought largely on German territory but involved at different times France, Spain, Sweden, Denmark, and Holland, as well as the various central European entities that together constituted the Holy Roman Empire.

In England, the struggle between Parliament and the crown came to a head in the English Civil War (1642–1649), which ended in the death of King Charles I (reigned 1625–1649). From 1649 to 1660, England, nominally a republic, was in effect a military dictatorship dominated by Oliver Cromwell (1599–1658). In 1660, the monarchy was restored with the coronation of Charles II (reigned 1660–1685). The reign of William and Mary (1689–1702) marked the formal establishment of England as a constitutional monarchy in which the power of the throne depended on the consent of Parliament.

The puritanical Cromwell had been no friend to the arts, but with the restoration of the monarchy, they began to thrive again. Under the constitutional monarchy of the 18th century, the arts developed in significantly different ways than under the absolutist regimes that dominated much of the rest of Europe. Public support emerged as an important alternative to the patronage of church and court. Theaters and opera houses flourished in London to an extent rivaled only in Hamburg and Venice, both of which, significantly, were governed by essentially republican governments. All three cities were

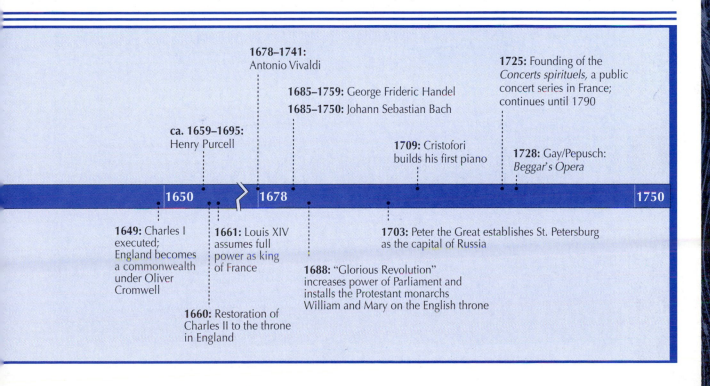

1678–1741: Antonio Vivaldi

1685–1759: George Frideric Handel

1685–1750: Johann Sebastian Bach

1725: Founding of the *Concerts spirituels,* a public concert series in France; continues until 1790

ca. 1659–1695: Henry Purcell

1709: Cristofori builds his first piano

1728: Gay/Pepusch: *Beggar's Opera*

1650 1678 1750

1649: Charles I executed; England becomes a commonwealth under Oliver Cromwell

1661: Louis XIV assumes full power as king of France

1703: Peter the Great establishes St. Petersburg as the capital of Russia

1688: "Glorious Revolution" increases power of Parliament and installs the Protestant monarchs William and Mary on the English throne

1660: Restoration of Charles II to the throne in England

Louis XIV as The Sun King. *Louis XIV styled himself* le roi soleil *("The Sun King"), and here, dressed in gold from head to toe, he plays the part of the center of the solar system, the monarch around whom all subjects revolved. Louis XIV was an accomplished dancer in his own right, and the costume he wears here is from the intermezzo* Ballet de la Nuit *("Ballet of the Night"), with vocal music by Jean de Cambefort (ca. 1605–1661), first performed in 1653. Louis XIV was passionate about the arts, particularly music and dance, and he commanded the financial resources to mount lavish productions of ballet and opera. Like many monarchs, he saw music and theater as a means of projecting his nation's cultural power.*

Source: French School (17th Century), King Louis XIV of France in the costume of the Sun King in the ballet La Nuit, 1653/Bibliotheque Nationale, Paris, France/Giraudon/Bridgeman Art Library

The French royal palace at Versailles. *All roads that didn't lead to Paris led to Versailles, about 6 miles west of the French capital, where Louis XIV built his magnificent palace in the mid–17th century. In the foreground is the enormous courtyard; behind the palace are the extensive gardens. French gardens at the time were laid out in a strict geometrical fashion; English gardens, in contrast, tried to recreate a sense of wildness and haphazardness, no matter how carefully they were planned. The palace of Versailles was a model for many lesser monarchs across Europe.*

Source: French Government Tourist Office

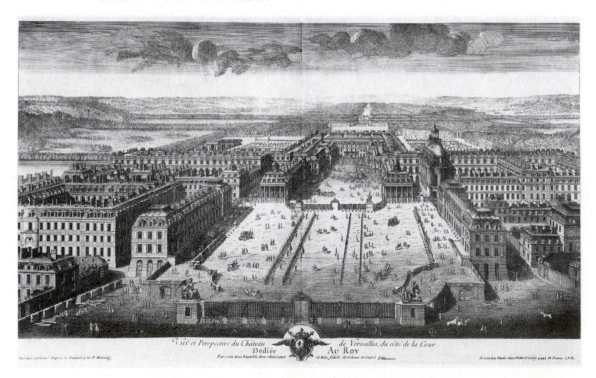

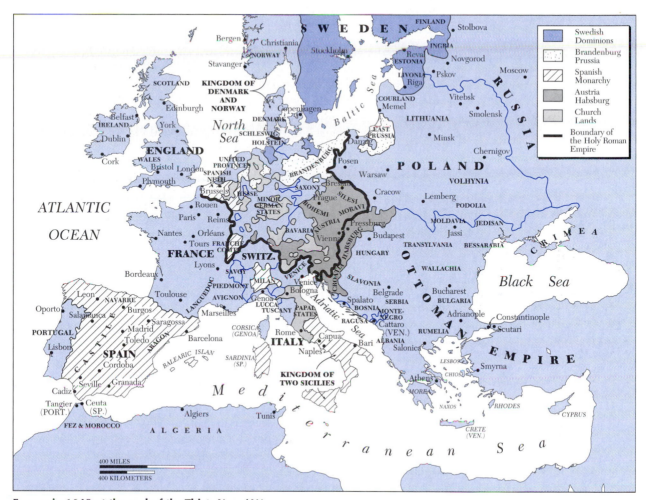

Europe in 1648 at the end of the Thirty Years' War

also centers of trade and commerce with a spirit of enterprise that extended to the arts as well. The result was the emergence of forms of entertainment calculated to appeal to a paying public as opposed to a private ruler.

In their ongoing quest for wealth and territory, many European powers colonized new territories abroad. Raw materials from throughout the world provided new capital for what was slowly becoming a global economy. But the wealth that flowed to Europe as a consequence of this expansion came at an enormous cost. The native peoples of the Americas, displaced from their lands and exploited in gold and silver mines, declined precipitously in population. And European planters, desperate for laborers to work their plantations, began a brutal trade in human beings, enslaving millions of Africans over the course of several centuries.

The expansion of commerce during the 17th and early 18th centuries was aided by the remarkable scientific advances of the age, particularly in the realm of astronomy and navigation. New findings challenged fundamental beliefs, enshrined in religious doctrine, about the relationships among the heavenly bodies. A new combination of empiricism and mathematical analysis is characteristic of the scientific approach to knowledge and the natural world that rose to dominance in the 17th century. The nation-states of 17th- and 18th-century Europe followed the advances in science with great interest and eventually began to sponsor their own national academies of science.

THE MUSICAL BAROQUE

The term *Baroque* derives from the Portuguese *barroco,* originally used to describe a misshapen pearl. The adjective *Baroque* was at first almost always used in a negative sense to convey the idea of the distorted or grotesque.

The application of the term *Baroque* to the era encompassing the 17th and early 18th centuries dates to the 19th century, when art historians used it to identify what they considered an age of decadence between the Renaissance and the Classical era. By the early 20th century, when music historians adopted it to designate the same era, the term had shed its negative connotations.

Stylistically, the music of the early Baroque era owes much to the late-Renaissance phenomenon of mannerism, in which composers set individual words of a text with exuberant and at times extreme gestures (see Chapter 6). As we will see, however, it is difficult to distill the essence of Baroque style into a single set of characteristics. The music of the era as a whole encompasses a wide range of harmonic practices and textures: individual composers often wrote in both old and new styles according to the circumstances at hand. Still, one common trait comes through: the premise that every work or movement of music can and should convey a single predominant emotion, known at the time as its **affect** (with the accent on the first syllable). Baroque musicians and performers were committed to representing the passions through music. These passions are not to be understood as personal self-expression, but rather as a means for creating in the mind and spirt of listeners a corresponding emotional state. Like good actors, Baroque musicians tried to move their audience by the artful imitation of emotion.

From a social perspective, the music of the Baroque era is as diverse as the society that nurtured it. Opera, which began and flourished under political absolutism, reinvented itself as a genre in the more public theaters that opened in Venice, Hamburg, and London over the course of the 17th century. What had originally been used to impress a small audience of elite listeners was recalculated to appeal to a broad public. Novelty was a key element of this appeal. To be financially successful, opera houses had to present new works every season. Catholic and Protestant churches vied to outdo one another in the opulence of their music, constantly demanding new music for their services.

This demand for the new was characteristic of the era as a whole and would persist well after 1750. Performers rarely played music by composers of a previous generation. As a result, composers who lived to a ripe age had the questionable privilege of seeing their own earlier works go out of fashion.

The church and the court remained the primary musical institutions of the Baroque era. These were, after all, two institutions with the financial resources to hire the best talent of the day.

Europe's expanding economy and the growing middle class it supported contributed to the increasing demand for new music. Publishers recognized a lucrative market for printed music aimed at amateurs. London, Paris, and Amsterdam emerged as the three most important centers for the music-publishing industry. In London, John Walsh established an important firm that would remain in his family from 1695 until 1766 and would publish works by Arcangelo Corelli (1653–1713), Henry Purcell (ca. 1659–1695), and above all George Frideric Handel (1685–1759). In Amsterdam, Estienne Roger was publishing Italian instrumental music of the day, including works by Giuseppe Torelli (1658–1709) and Corelli. The chief Parisian music publisher was the Ballard family firm, which held a royal monopoly until the French Revolution in 1789.

Developments in metallurgy made possible a new and more efficient music printing technology—engraving—that replaced music typesetting by the early 18th century. Unlike typeset forms, engraved plates could be stored for long periods, and publishers could pull them out of storage to run off new copies as demand warranted. Engraved music, without the broken lines characteristic of the earlier technology, was almost always superior to typeset music in quality.

Still, most music making in the Baroque era, as in previous eras, took place within an unwritten tradition in streets and fields, coffeehouses and taverns, private homes and barracks rather than in church, court, or opera house. This repertory—songs, dance tunes, variations, and simple melodies—is difficult to reconstruct, for musicians performed it from memory or improvised it on the spot (see "The Blind Hurdy-Gurdy Player", Plate 10 in Color Insert II). We have no payment records to these kinds of musicians, for if they were paid at all, it was unlikely to be with money. As in the case of previous eras, however, we can glean some idea of this repertory through passing written descriptions of this music and through artists' renditions of street scenes. The number of tunes transmitted aurally in the era before recordings was legion. Many of them were preserved in writing only when they caught the ear of a composer who incorporated them into a notated work (variations on a folk tune, for example). This repertory was, in effect, the popular music of its day.

Popular versus elite music: Hogarth's "The Enraged Musician."   *In this engraving of 1741, the English satirist William Hogarth (1697–1764) pits the written repertory against the unwritten one and raises the question of where music stops and noise begins. The angry violinist, indoors and above street level, dressed in a wig and fancy clothes, represents the written tradition of the upper classes. Note the printed music on his stand. On the wall to the far left is a poster for a revival of* The Beggar's Opera *(see Chapter 9), a work that notoriously lambastes the upper classes. The lower-class crowd below the window generates a welter of sounds that the spiked iron fence cannot keep at bay: the baby cries, the boy urinates, the astonished girl holds a rattle. The itinerant oboist (playing without notes) seems to be angling for a donation from the violinist. The woman holding the baby on the far left is singing and selling a ballad entitled "The Ladies' Fall," a commentary on her own state; anyone buying her wares will soon be adding his or her own voice to the fray. The knife sharpener, traveling up and down the street with his equipment, makes a living (and a sound) scraping, just like the violinist. The post horn, the merchants with bells, the street sweeper, the drummer boy: music (or is it noise?) is everywhere, and the professional musician cannot eliminate it.*

Source: William Hogarth, (1697–1764), "The Enraged Musician", c. 1741, etching and engraving on paper/Victoria & Albert Museum, London/Art Resource, NY

The New Practice

Many of the innovations we associate with Baroque music were driven by the continuing desire, evident already in the Renaissance, to recover the music of classical antiquity. The ancient Greeks had written repeatedly of music's miraculous powers. Their legendary hero Orpheus so charmed the gods of the underworld with song and lyre that he won the release of his beloved Euridice from death. How could it be that the effect of modern music seemed so tame in comparison?

SEARCHING FOR THE SECRETS OF ANCIENT GREEK MUSIC

Beginning around the middle of the 16th century, composers and theorists began to seek in earnest for an answer to this question. Recovering the music of classical antiquity was no easy task, however. The few sources of ancient Greek musical notation known at the time were poorly understood, leaving commentators ample room for speculation.

Most concurred that the dramas of Euripides, Aristophanes, and others had been sung, either in whole or in part, and that the words had taken priority over melody. Plato himself, after all, had described music as a form of heightened speech in which rhythm and pitch embellish a text.

Following this line of thought, a number of influential 16th-century writers and musicians began to reassess the balance between words and music. Composers increasingly embraced the idea that music should be driven by the word and the affect of a text—its predominant emotion—should be heightened by expressive musical devices. As early as 1555, the composer and theorist Nicola Vicentino declared in his treatise *Ancient Music Adapted to Modern Practice* that "the composer's sole obligation is to animate the words, and, with harmony, to represent their passions—now harsh, now sweet, now cheerful, now sad—in accordance with their subject matter." To this end, Vicentino advocated any musical means that might help produce the desired effect. "This is why every bad leap and every poor consonance, depending on their effects, may be used to set the words. As a consequence, on such words you may write any sort of step or harmony, abandon the mode, and govern yourself by the subject matter of the . . . words."[1]

A view of the musical cosmos, 1650. *Athanasius Kircher (1601–1680), a German Jesuit who lived in Rome the last 45 years of his life, was the author of an influential and encyclopedic treatise on music, published in Rome in 1650. The work's frontispiece, by the artist Johann Paul Schor, is an allegorical representation of the way music manifests itself throughout the cosmos, from the heavens on high to the earth below. The allegory draws on symbols from both Christianity and classical antiquity. At the top is the Trinity, symbolized by a triangle surrounding the all-seeing eye. Angels sing a canon on the word "Sanctus" ("Holy") for 36 voices divided among nine choruses of four voices each. In the center Apollo, the god of music and poetry, straddles the globe, which is ringed by the symbols of the zodiac. To the right, the winged horse Pegasus stands atop the steps leading to Mount Parnassus, home of the muses and gods in Greek mythology. In the left foreground, Pythagoras, leaning against a board that demonstrates his geometric theorem, points to blacksmiths pounding away at anvils. Pythagoras was credited with establishing some of the fundamental relationships between music and mathematics based on observations of smiths at work. The hammers, he is said to have demonstrated, created pitches whose intervals were proportional to their weight (2:1 for an octave, 3:2 for a perfect fifth, and so on). In the right foreground Musica, identifiable by the nightingale perched on top of her head, sits at the foot of Parnassus with a variety of modern 17th-century musical instruments.*

Source: Georg Olms Verlag AG

In his highly esteemed *Le istitutioni armoniche* ("The Foundations of Music"), Gioseffo Zarlino acknowledged that contrapuntal intricacies often made the words of vocal music hard to understand. And the composer Pierluigi Palestrina, as we have seen, was particularly concerned not to obscure sacred texts in his motets and settings of the Mass. Yet Zarlino, Palestrina, and most of their contemporaries stopped short of advocating anything less than a fully polyphonic texture.

A few musicians took a more radical view, however, and maintained that polyphony itself was responsible for the failure of contemporary music to match the power of the music of the ancients. The composer and lutenist Vincenzo Galilei (ca. 1520–1591), father of the celebrated astronomer Galileo Galilei, acknowledged in his *Dialogue on Ancient and Modern Music* of 1581 that Zarlino's rules of counterpoint were "excellent and necessary for the simple delight of hearing harmonies in all their variety . . . ; but for the expression of ideas they are pestilent."[2]

THE FLORENTINE CAMERATA

The real question was how to allow a single voice to predominate in a texture that was not essentially polyphonic. Between roughly 1573 and 1587, a group of poets, musicians, and noblemen gathered informally at the house of Count Giovanni de' Bardi (1534–1612) in Florence to discuss this and other issues relating to the arts. This group, which later came to be known as the **Florentine Camerata** (*camerata* means "club" or "society"), debated ways to recreate the style of singing used by the ancient Greeks in their dramas. In addition to Bardi and Vincenzo Galilei, the group included the composer Giulio Caccini (1545–1618) and the poet Ottavio Rinuccini (1562–1621).

Although the members of the Camerata did not keep a record of their proceedings, we can glean some idea of the conclusions they reached from the musical and theatrical entertainments Bardi was asked to organize for the 1589 Florentine wedding of Ferdinando de' Medici, grand duke of Tuscany, to Christine de Lorraine, princess of France. The centerpiece of these entertainments was a spoken comedy entitled

Giacopo Peri as Arion. *Giacopo Peri sings the title role of his* Il Canto d'Arione *("The Song of Arion"), the fifth intermedio of* La pellegrina, *presented at the wedding festivities of the Medici court in Florence in 1589. Peri's work includes an extended aria for solo baritone, two echoing voices, and accompanying strings. The singer's posture here is significant: he is shown in a relaxed, almost informal stance, emphasizing the quality of naturalness that was so dear to the proponents of the* seconda prattica.

Source: Foto Marburg/Art Resource, N.Y.

La Pellegrina ("The Pilgrim Woman"). Between the acts of this play the audience was treated to a series of six intermedi (what we today might call "entr'actes" or "intermezzos"), each featuring the miraculous powers of music in classical mythology.

Each of the intermedi consists of four or five movements (at least one of them instrumental) and features a mixture of traditional polyphony and newer styles of composition. The poetry was by Ottavio Rinuccini, Giovambattisto Strozzi, and Bardi himself, the music by Emilio de' Cavalieri, Giacopo Peri, Giulio Caccini, and Luca Marenzio. The lavish production spared no expense on stage design, machinery, and costumes.

In the fifth intermedio, *Il Canto d'Arione* ("The Song of Arion"), the composer Jacopo Peri sang the title role himself. His aria *Dunque fra torbide onde* ("Thus over Troubled Waters") recreates Arion's farewell to the world before being thrown overboard. The work is scored for four stringed instruments and three solo voice parts. Arion's line is labeled *parte principale* because it is clearly more important than the other two voices, which echo in response ("riposta") to Arion's melody and words. Except for some brief moments of overlap, however, the echoing voices do not sing simultaneously either with Arion or with each other. All three voices stand out from the instrumental accompaniment by virtue of their rhythmic freedom and melodic virtuosity. In this respect, we can see Peri moving toward a texture that is **homophonic**—consisting, that is, of a principal melodic line with subordinate accompanying voices. Homophony is particularly well suited to the clear projection of a text in the principal melodic voice. Yet the instrumental accompaniment here consists of four-part counterpoint, and on closer inspection, it turns out that the tenor, the principal singing voice, adheres in its outline to the tenor voice of the instrumental ensemble. Even though the tenor's line is elaborately embellished, it functions structurally within the framework of traditional four-part polyphony.

Peri
Dunque fra torbide onde

THE *SECONDA PRATTICA*

Peri and others continued to search for a means of more nearly matching the ancient Greek ideal of music as "naught but speech, with rhythm and tone coming after; not vice versa," to use the formulation of Giulio Caccini. The rhythms of music, according to this approach, should be modeled on the rhythms of speech—at times flowing, at times halting, full of various points of punctuation articulated through cadences of varying degrees of strength. This emphasis on the projection of the text lies at the heart of a new musical style that its advocates later called the **seconda prattica** (the "second," or later practice), to distinguish it from the **prima prattica** ("first," or earlier practice), the traditional style of Renaissance polyphony.

The *seconda prattica* emerged gradually over the course of the 1580s and 1590s as Peri, Caccini, and Cavalieri began to write works that placed a solo vocal line above an instrumental line that was conceived less as a polyphonic equal to the solo line than as a subordinate accompaniment to it. This supporting instrumental line was known as the **basso continuo**, a "continuous bass" that provided the harmonic framework for the solo voice above it. In notation, the basso continuo consists of a single bass line; in practice, the performer or performers playing it add upper voices as needed to fill out the harmonies implied by the bass. Through a series of numbers ("figures"), composers could indicate deviations from root-position harmonies—hence the term **figured bass**, often used synonymously with basso continuo.

The composition of the basso continuo ensemble was flexible and rarely specified by composers. Musicians were expected to use whatever instruments happened to be

Dancing with the gods.
Presented between the acts of a play, intermedi often brought spectators and actors together in performance. At the end of the intermedi in Florence in 1589, audience members could dance with the gods, who descended from the stage to mingle with the mortals. The scene shown here is from the Florentine intermedi of 1617 as performed in the Uffizi theater, but the principle of actors and audience mingling remains the same. Note the stairs descending from either side of the stage into the audience.

Source: Jacques Callot (1592–1635), The Medici Theater "Primo intermedio of La Liberazione di Terreno e d'Arnea", engraving/ Gabinetto dei Disegni e delle Stampe, Uffizi, Florence, Italy/ © Scala/Art Resource, NY

available and suitable to the size and character of the performance venue. At a minimum the basso continuo could consist of a single instrument capable of playing chords, such as a harpsichord, organ, or lute. Ideally it would combine a sustaining bass instrument, such as a viol or bassoon, with one or more chordal instruments, thereby providing both contrapuntal (horizontal) and chordal (vertical) support to the solo voice. The basso continuo created, in effect, a polarized texture between a melodic upper voice and a harmony-driven bass line, with the inner lines substantially reduced in significance and volume. Performers often doubled the bass line with multiple instruments but left the inner voices to the improvisatory skills of only one member of the ensemble, usually the lutenist or keyboard player. This doubling of the bass line created an enhanced sense of polarity between the lowermost and uppermost voices.

The range of stylistic possibilities opened up by the use of basso continuo was enormous. Functionally, the device provided a harmonic framework for a solo voice above it, thereby freeing composers from the obligation of writing in a consistently polyphonic manner. More important still, it allowed composers to project a sung text through a single voice, thereby bringing the music closer to what was perceived to be the ancient Greek manner of using melody and rhythm to sustain the word. Solo singing, in turn, allowed for the emergence of the new genre of **opera**—sung drama—in which individual singers assume the role of individual characters. Opera, too, was believed to be a part of the long-sought realization of ancient Greek musical practices.

By the 1630s, a new term—**monody**—had emerged to designate this combination of solo voice and basso continuo. Calling on singers to declaim text in a style that is at once measured and free, lyrical yet rhythmically fluid, monody lies partway between song and speech.

Monody opened up important new possibilities of performance. The soloist was now free to embellish at will, without rhythmic or motivic regard for any other melodic line. Ornamentation and pure flights of fancy unthinkable in polyphonic textures were now suddenly a very real option. All of this could help give the music an air of spontaneity in performance—what Caccini called *sprezzatura*, a certain freedom in the pace and manner of delivery, a kind of noble disregard for the meter and rhythm.

Caccini's monody *Sfogava con le stelle* from *Le nuove musiche* of 1602 illustrates the new practice vividly. The music, following the text, divides into two parts: the first (measures 1–11) is presented from the perspective of a narrator, who sets the scene of a lover venting his grief to the stars. The second (measures 12–57) presents the words of the lover himself, calling on the stars to convince his beloved to return his affections. The rhythms of the opening are slow and measured, and its pitches are confined to a limited range. But once the lover himself begins to declaim *O immagini belle Dell'dol mio ch'adoro* ("Oh, beautiful images of the one I adore . . . "), the music rises in pitch, velocity, and intensity. Caccini emphasizes key words either by long notes (*adoro*—"adore"—measures 15–16) or by rapid passagework (*ardori*—"passions"—measures 29–30). The vocal line throughout the second half gives the impression of spontaneity, as if the singer is thinking up the words on the spot: the pace of delivery is never predictable. The underlay follows the rhythms of a person speaking, at times slow or even hesitant, at other times rushing forward in a torrent.

Caccini's *Sfogava con le stelle* also illustrates another novelty of the *seconda prattica*, the unprecedented degree of virtuosity it sometimes required of performers. There is, of course, a paradox in the kind of virtuosic flourishes like those on the word *ardori* ("passions," measures 29–31). This gesture certainly provides, following Plato's definition of music, a sense of heightened speech by emphasizing perhaps the single most important word in the entire text. But it also makes the word itself less readily intelligible. Adherents of the new style argued that expressive, passionate texts called for expressive, passionate music. Detractors replied that overly flamboyant music undermined the very premise of the new practice, to free vocal music from anything that might obscure the clear projection of the words.

Giulio Caccini
Sfogava con le stelle

PRIMARY EVIDENCE

Giulio Caccini on the Principles of Monody

Monody was practiced for perhaps as long as two decades before it was first notated, or published, in Giulio Caccini's *Le nuove musiche* ("New Works of Music") of 1602. When Caccini finally published his collection, he realized its buyers would need some kind of guidance, some word of explanation about these novel works, and his account provides valuable details about the ways in which early monody was performed.

• • • • •

Seeing, as I am saying, that these kinds of music and musicians were offering no pleasure other than what harmony grants to the ear alone (since the mind cannot be moved by such music without understanding the words), it occurred to me to introduce a kind of music by which anyone could almost speak in music, using (as I have said elsewhere) a certain noble *sprezzatura* in the melody, passing sometimes over some discords while sustaining the pitch of the bass note (except when I wanted to use it in a regular way) and with the middle lines played by the instrument to express some *affetto* as those lines are not of much other use.

In madrigals as in arias I have always achieved the imitation of the ideas of the words, seeking out those notes that are more or less expressive, according to the sentiments of the words. So that they would have especial grace, I concealed as much of the art of counterpoint as I could. I have placed chords on the long syllables and passed over the short ones and also observed this same rule in making *passaggi*. For particular embellishments, however, I have sometimes used a few eighth notes (*crome*) up to the duration of a fourth of a *tactus* or up to a half [of the *tactus*] at the most, largely on short syllables. These can be allowed, because these go by quickly and are not *passaggi* but just an extra graceful touch, and also because good judgment suffers some exception to every rule. But because earlier I have stated that those long turns of the voice are badly used, I must point out that singers do not make *passaggi* because they are necessary to a good singing style, but because, I believe, they titillate the ears of those who understand less well what it means to sing *con affetto*. Because if they knew, then *passaggi* would be abhorred, since nothing is more contrary than they are to expressive singing (which is the reason I have been saying that those long runs are badly used). Therefore, I have introduced them in the kind of music that is less expressive, and used them on long, not short, syllables and in closing cadences.

Source: Giulio Caccini, Preface to *Le nuove musiche* (1602), in *Source Readings in Music History*, ed. Oliver Strunk; rev. edition ed. Leo Treitler (New York: Norton, 1998), pp. 608–9. Copyright 1998 W. W. Norton & Company, Inc. used by permission of the publisher.

The monodies of the early 17th century mark a clear break with earlier practices of the Renaissance. Fixed units with strong and weak beats replaced the Renaissance principle of the *tactus,* in which all beats receive essentially equal emphasis. Most music from the 17th century can be readily notated with bar lines in modern transcriptions, whereas Renaissance music rarely lends itself to such notation.

The increasing prominence of metrical units—fixed patterns of strong and weak beats—also manifested itself in the dance rhythms that permeate a good deal of 17th-century vocal music. Poetic texts that were themselves metrically regular lent themselves to a correspondingly regular musical setting. Thus, alongside free declamation in early monody, we also find an abundance of music—vocal as well as instrumental—that adheres to the principle of periodic phrase structure.

Giulio Caccini
Al fonte, al prato

Caccini's *Al fonte, al prato,* a monody from 1614, follows a rhythmic pattern identical to that of a great many dances of the time. Its spirit is similar to that of many frottole from the 16th century. The opening eight measures are constructed as an antecedent-consequent statement, with both the antecedent (measures 1–4) and consequent (measures 5–8) breaking down into two units of two measures each. Measures 8–16 follow a similar pattern, with a root-position tonic cadence in measure 16. The concluding four-measure vocal phrase (measures 17–20) confirms the cadence in the tonic, and an additional four-measure instrumental phrase (measure 21–24, the last measure held out an additional full measure) concludes the whole. The piece thus consists of three eight-measure units, each of which subdivides into patterns of 4 + 4.

Musically, monodies of the early 17th century strike at least some listeners today as less rich and less varied than their polyphonic counterparts. In the constant struggle to balance lyrical interest and textual intelligibility, monody consistently favored the latter. Peri, Caccini, and other early composers of monodies used chromaticism only sparingly. Their melodic lines are typically more straightforward than what may be found in contemporary polyphonic compositions, and frequent cadences often seem to interrupt the rhythmic flow of the music. But it was precisely these qualities—simplicity and directness, combined with a close adherence to the text—that appealed to contemporary audiences.

At the same time, the emergence of monody did not mean the death of polyphony. On the contrary, the *prima prattica* of Renaissance counterpoint—particularly the sacred music of Palestrina and his many imitators—continued to flourish well into the 17th century and beyond. Indeed, many more polyphonic a cappella madrigals than monodies were published in the first two decades of the 17th century, and the polyphonic style remained a touchstone of compositional prowess for composers throughout the Baroque era.

In the end, none of the monodists claimed to have truly recreated the music of Greek antiquity. But they firmly believed they had realized its modern equivalent, and the proof of this lay in the reaction of contemporary audiences. In describing a performance of Claudio Monteverdi's opera *Ariadne* in 1608, the composer Marco da Gagliano (1582–1643) declared that Monteverdi had written "the airs so exquisitely that one may truthfully aver that the virtues of ancient music were reborn, for all the audience was visibly moved to tears."[3]

ELEMENTS OF BAROQUE STYLE

The rise of the *seconda prattica* and monody marked the beginning of a series of stylistic changes that together define the music of the Baroque. The shift toward homophonic texture and the use of the basso continuo, as we have seen, permitted a far greater range of rhythmic freedom and virtuosity in the solo voice than had been seen in the equal-voiced textures of the *prima prattica*. The new virtuosity impelled composers to write differently for voices and instruments, and, when writing for instruments, to take into account their specific capabilities. The voice, after all, cannot sing a scale as fast as a violinist or oboist can play one, nor can a singer negotiate the same large melodic leaps an instrument can. Whereas the parts of a Renaissance chanson or madrigal might be performed interchangeably by voices and any of a variety of instruments, this kind of flexibility declined gradually over the course of the Baroque. In many instances, lines could be performed only on instruments, and often only on specific instruments. No other 150-year span in the history of music witnessed the development of so many new instruments and the transformation of so many existing instruments. And for the first time in the history of music, instrumental virtuosos began to rival vocalists in popularity and financial rewards.

An outgrowth of instrumental music's increasing importance is the rise of **program music** in the years around 1700. This is purely instrumental music that is in some way connected with a story or idea. For example, one of Johann Kuhnau's *Biblical Sonatas* of 1700 (Anthology; see Chapter 10), according to its score, depicts the battle between David and Goliath, the fall of the giant, and the flight of the Philistines.

Accompanying the changes in texture and performance forces was the cultivation of contrasting timbres. The ideal timbre in late Renaissance music was a blend of essentially uniform sounds, such as a chorus of voices or a set of matched instruments covering different ranges. Baroque musicians and audiences valued contrasts, for example of melody to accompaniment, voices to instruments, high to low, solo to tutti, loud to soft, or winds to strings.

It was during the 17th century that musicians began to think of harmony more and more in terms of chordal progressions, although counterpoint never lost its prestige in the heirarchy of musical theory or pedagogy. A mid-16th-century work like Palestrina's *Missa Papae Marcelli* (Anthology) can be readily analyzed in terms of modern-day harmonic theory (using concepts like tonic, dominant, and subdominant), but it would be anachronistic to do so, for Renaissance theorists and composers conceived of harmony as a by-product of counterpoint—that is, as a by-product of the relationship among the given voices or a work. For music written in the 18th century, however, such an analysis would be entirely appropriate. Similarly, there was a shift from modal to tonal writing. By 1700, the traditional modes—Dorian, Lydian, Phrygian, and so on—had largely given way to a single type of diatonic scale, with half steps between scale degrees 3–4 and 7–8 (in the major mode) or 2–3 and 7–8 (in the minor mode). "Mode" was now reserved to distinguish between the major and minor forms of this one scale, which could be transposed to any desired key.

Renaissance music was for the most part international in style, but national styles of writing began to emerge over the course of the 17th century. The Italian style was associated with the predominance of melody, a sharply profiled rhythmic shape, and a strong sense of meter. Many commentators considered it serious and weighty. Italian notational practice tended to leave the performer considerable room for improvisation. The French style was typically characterized as "sprightly," "bright," and "lively," strongly influenced by the rhythms of dance but tending toward a fluid sense of melody. French notational practice generally prescribed desired embellishments and grace notes in greater detail than did the Italian. The German style was considered a synthesis of the French and Italian, incorporating elements of both but adding a dimension of contrapuntal gravity.

CONCLUSION

Musicians working in the first decade of the 17th century—the beginning of the Baroque—were keenly aware that music had entered a new era. The emergence of monody opened up possibilities that had been scarcely imaginable only a generation before: opera, madrigals with distinctly separate vocal and instrumental parts, and an emerging conception of chordal harmony, all driven by a fundamentally new attitude toward the relationship between words and music. Over the next 150 years, composers and performers of the Baroque would explore the consequences of these innovations in their ongoing attempts to represent the passions of the human spirit.

SUMMARY OF STYLE DIFFERENCES BETWEEN RENAISSANCE AND BAROQUE MUSIC

	RENAISSANCE	BAROQUE
STYLE	One generally consistent style, dubbed in retrospect the *prima prattica*.	Two styles, the *prima prattica* and the newer *seconda prattica*.
TEXT SETTING	Relatively restrained representation of texts.	Relatively freer projection of texts with greater attention to the declamation of individual words and, on a larger scale, entire sentences.
TEXTURE	Polyphonic, with all voices of essentially equal importance.	Polyphonic or homophonic with a strong sense of polarity between the two outer voices.
RHYTHM	Generally balanced and evenly flowing. A steady pulse (the *tactus*) governs performance, and although this may change within the course of a work, it remains steady for long stretches at a time.	A cultivation of extremes between simplicity and complexity, typically determined in vocal works by the text. The *tactus* gives way to a stronger sense of meter with fixed units of "strong" and "weak" beats.
MELODY	Generally lyrical, rarely virtuosic in an overt manner.	More openly virtuosic, with more opportunities for embellishment by soloists. A growing differentiation between vocal and instrumental idioms.
HARMONY	Primarily modal, with harmony conceived of as a by-product of the interrelationship of voices. Relatively circumscribed treatment of dissonance and voice leading.	Primarily tonal, especially by the end of the 17th century, with harmony conceived of as a progression of vertical sonorities. Relatively freer treatment of dissonance and voice leading.
FORM	Primarily paratactic (A, B, C, D, . . . etc.), with individual subunits of a work more or less sharply demarcated from one another.	Both paratactic and syntactic (i.e., with subunits connected rhythmically, harmonically, and thematically). Formal patterns based on recurring material become increasingly important.
INSTRUMEN-TATION	Vocal works adhere to the a cappella ideal, with the option of instruments doubling voices. Vocal and instrumental idioms are essentially interchangeable.	Composers have the option of writing for voices alone or for voices and instruments together, including independent instrumental parts that complement rather than double the vocal lines. Vocal and instrumental idioms become increasingly differentiated.

Vocal Music, 1600–1650

The *seconda prattica* was driven by new attitudes toward text setting and is thus best exemplified by the vocal music of the early Baroque era. The transformed genre of the madrigal, the entirely new phenomenon of opera, and the sacred music of this period all manifest the commitment of 17th-century composers to new ways of synthesizing text, melody, and rhythm.

SECULAR SONG

In Italy, composers applied the principles of the new practice to the still popular genre of the madrigal. In France, the influence of monody and basso continuo is reflected in the emergence of a new genre, the *air de cour*.

Italy: The Madrigal

The madrigal—any through-composed setting of freely structured verse—remained the preeminent genre of secular vocal music in Italy throughout the first half of the 17th century. The genre encompassed traditional a cappella settings as well as the newer monodies for solo voice and basso continuo. The monodic principle is also at work in the **concertato madrigal,** in which voices of any number combine with instruments, either basso continuo alone, or basso continuo and other instruments. Concertato madrigals represent a kind of synthesis between the single-voiced monody (with basso continuo) and the multivoiced a cappella polyphonic madrigal.

The madrigals of Claudio Monteverdi (1567–1643; see Composer Profile), published in nine books, reflect all the manifestations of the genre in the early Baroque. The madrigals in the first four books (1587, 1590, 1592, 1603) predate the rise of monody and are written in the tradition of such mid- to late-16th-century composers as Willaert, Rore, and Lasso. Basso continuo makes its first appearance in the fifth book (1605), but is structurally essential only in the last five madrigals in the volume. In all the madrigals from Book Six (1614) on, basso continuo is the norm. Indeed, when Monteverdi issued a second edition of Book Four in 1615, 12 years after the first edition, he added a continuo line to each madrigal. Concertato madrigals play an increasingly important role in Monteverdi's output over the final decades of his career, as reflected in the works published in Books Seven (1619), Eight (1638), and Nine (published posthumously in 1651).

Even the early madrigals, written in a traditional polyphonic texture, reflect the emergence of the *seconda prattica*. Monteverdi himself identified two madrigalists of the mid–16th century—Cipriano de Rore and Adrian Willaert (see Chapter 6)—as the originators of the "new practice," on the grounds that both composers had gone out of their way to make their music project the essence of the words being sung. Monteverdi adhered to this principle throughout his own career as a composer of madrigals.

The most serious public dispute about the *seconda prattica* in fact did not center on any collection of monodies, but rather on certain polyphonic madrigals that would later be published in Monteverdi's Fifth Book of Madrigals. The Italian composer and theorist Giovanni Maria Artusi (ca. 1540–1613) attacked Monteverdi's treatment of dissonance in these works as unacceptable, spelling out his objections in considerable detail in a pamphlet issued in 1600 entitled *L'Artusi, ovvero delle imperfettioni della moderna musica* ("The Artusi; or, On the Imperfections of Modern Music"). Artusi knew these madrigals through manuscript copies—Book 5 would not actually be published for another five years—and he took particular exception to Monteverdi's five-voiced *Cruda Amarilli*. He chastised the composer for having violated the precepts of counterpoint as set down by Zarlino. Monteverdi replied with a brief manifesto of his own in the introduction to his Fifth Book of Madrigals, published in 1605. The set opens quite pointedly with *Cruda Amarilli*, the very madrigal Artusi had attacked so sharply. The Artusi-Monteverdi controversy exposed the fundamental differences in outlook between advocates of the "old" and the "new" practice. Artusi, representing the traditional approach, looked first and foremost at the construction of the music, whereas Monteverdi justified the use of unconventional musical techniques with the assertion that the words demand them.

Monteverdi
Cruda Amarilli

The controversies about the nature of the *seconda prattica* were already well underway before the emergence of monody and basso continuo. Indeed, some of the a cappella madrigals of the 17th century count among the most daring and progressive pieces of the entire Baroque era. The jarring dissonances in the opening measures of Carlo Gesualdo's *Moro, lasso, al mio duolo* of 1611 (Example 8-1) project the pain in the words "I shall die, miserable, in my suffering . . ." in an almost visceral way. The descending chromatic harmonies capture the anguish of a man who has lost the will to live. Even without basso continuo, composers of the early Baroque pushed the boundaries of musical practice to previously unimagined extremes.

More typical of their time are the concertato madrigals that appeared in ever-greater numbers over the first three decades of the 17th century. Monteverdi's setting of *T'amo mia vita* published in 1605 exhibits striking differences with Luzascho Luzasschi's setting of the same text issued only four years earlier (Anthology; see Chapter 6). Thanks to the use of the solo voice, Monteverdi is able to distinguish quite clearly between the narrator's memory of the words he has heard from his beloved ("I love you, my life") and his own injunction to the god of love, Amor, to imprint these words on his heart. Because it is a concertato madrigal—a work for voice and instruments that function both together and independently of one another—Monteverdi can distinguish solo passages from polyphonic ones and capture the drama of the poetry in a way that Luzasschi's wholly polyphonic setting cannot.

Monteverdi
T'amo mia vita

Monteverdi's *Zefiro torna e di soavi accenti*, for two tenors and basso continuo, illustrates just how musically elaborate the concertato madrigal had become by the early 1630s. Most of the work rests on a **ground bass,** a short phrase repeated over and over again in the lowest voice. This particular bass pattern, complete in two measures in

Monteverdi
Zefiro torna e di soavi accenti

Composer Profile

Claudio Monteverdi
(1567–1643)

Claudio Monteverdi. *The only indisputably authentic image of Monteverdi appeared on a publication of his music issued shortly after his death. Based on the similarity of that likeness to the portrait here, scholars believe this oil portrait depicts the composer in the mid-1610s, perhaps after he had assumed the position of maestro di cappella at the Basilica of San Marco in Venice.*

Source: Bernardo Strozzi (1581–1644), Claudio Monteverdi, composer (1567–1643), Oil on canvas/Landesmuseum Ferdinandeum, Innsbruck, Austria/©Photograph by Erich Lessing/Art Resource, NY

Monteverdi's career straddled the Renaissance and Baroque, and he mastered both the *prima prattica* and *seconda prattica*. His career falls into two distinct phases, one in Mantua, the other in Venice. In Mantua, he served at the court of the Gonzaga dynasty, writing music to order, including his first two operas, *Orfeo* (1607) and *Ariadne* (1608). The success of these works was such that Monteverdi was soon offered the position of maestro di cappella (director of music) at the Basilica of San Marco in Venice. This was arguably the most prestigious position for any musician in all of Italy, and it allowed him the luxury of writing madrigals and dramatic music as well as sacred music. The surviving correspondence paints a vivid picture of the composer choosing his commissions with care, according to what interested him and how well it paid. When the rulers of Mantua tried to lure Monteverdi back to their court, he replied with a letter diplomatically yet firmly declining the offer:

> I shall . . . submit for Your Lordship's consideration the fact that this Most Serene Republic [Venice] has never before given to any of my predecessors—whether it were Adriano [Willaert] or Cipriano [de Rore], or [Gioseffo] Zarlino, or anyone else—but 200 ducats in salary, whereas to me they give 400. . . . Nor, having done this for me, have they ever regretted it: on the contrary they have honoured me, and honour me continually in such manner, that no singer is accepted into the choir until they ask the opinion of the Director of Music [Monteverdi]; . . . nor do they take on organists or an assistant director unless they have the opinion and the report of that same Director of Music; nor is there any gentleman who does not esteem and honour me, and when I am about to perform either chamber or church music, I swear to Your Lordship that the entire city comes running.

> Next, the duties are very light. . . . Moreover, [the director of music's] allowance is assured until his death: neither the death of a procurator nor that of a doge interferes with it, and . . . if he does not go at the appointed time to pick it up, it is brought round to his

modern transcription, shares no thematic material with the upper voices but instead provides a structural framework that allows the voices above it to unfold freely, without regard to their harmonic underpinnings. The ground bass also provides continuity at those moments when neither of the two tenors is singing (measures 54, 56, 58, 66, etc.). Without the basso continuo, such pauses would simply not be feasible.

house. . . . [T]hen there is occasional income, which consists of whatever extra I can easily earn outside St Mark's of about 200 ducats a year (invited as I am again and again by the wardens of the guilds) because whoever can engage the director to look after their music—not to mention the payment of 30 ducats, and even 40, and up to 50 for two vespers and a mass—does not fail to take him on, and they also thank him afterwards with well-chosen words.[1]

Monteverdi was constantly trying new styles and new genres. In addition to operas for an elite audience at court (such as *Orfeo*), he also wrote works for the new public opera houses that began to open in Venice at the end of the 1630s. In his later life he introduced a new style of writing he called the *genere concitato* to capture emotions that were agitated or bellicose. His music remained a touchstone for all subsequent 17th-century composers.

Principal Works

MADRIGALS Monteverdi's madrigals span almost his entire creative life. Between 1587 and 1638, he published eight numbered books of madrigals along with various miscellaneous collections and pieces. A ninth was published posthumously. The first four books of madrigals are in the traditional polyphonic texture of the Renaissance. Book 5 (1605) introduces basso continuo in its final numbers, and the remaining books all feature basso continuo. These works as a whole reflect a remarkable range of compositional techniques, from polyphony to monody.

DRAMATIC WORKS An appalling proportion of Monteverdi's dramatic music has disappeared. We know that at least some of it was reused or reworked in surviving madrigals (the *Lamento d'Arianna* is all that survives of the opera *Arianna* from 1608, for example), and we have some of the librettos for works whose music has been lost. But for the most part, scholars can only speculate about more than a dozen missing works for the stage, ranging from operas to *balli*, staged dance spectacles with singing.

KEY DATES IN THE LIFE OF CLAUDIO MONTEVERDI

1567 Born in Cremona (northern Italy); baptized May 15

1582 First publication, a set of motets for three voices

1590 Hired as singer and viol player by the Duke of Mantua; becomes music director at the Mantuan court in 1602

1605 Publishes his Fifth Book of Madrigals, which includes several works with basso continuo and a prefatory letter defending the principles of the *seconda prattica*

1607 Composes his first opera, *Orfeo,* for the court at Mantua

1613 Appointed maestro di cappella at the basilica of San Marco, Venice

1643 Dies in Venice on November 29

The operas that have survived are *Orfeo* (1607); *Il Ritorno d'Ulisse in Patria* ("The Return of Ulysses to his Homeland," 1641); and *L'incoronazione di Poppea* ("The Coronation of Poppea," 1642). Most notable among the many smaller dramatic works is *Il Combattimento di Tancredi e Clorinda* (1624), whose libretto is drawn from a well-known epic poem of the day, in which the knight Tancred defeats Clorinda—who is disguised as a man—in battle.

SACRED MUSIC Monteverdi wrote a variety of Masses, hymns, psalms, and motets. By far his best known sacred work is the *Vespers* of 1610, a cycle of 14 movements that uses a variety of styles, old and new.

The repeating bass reinforces the static nature of the pastoral poem. But when the poem shifts abruptly to the first person (measure 113), the ground bass suddenly breaks off and the music slows down through a change in mensuration. For the last line of the poem ("As my fate wills it, I sometimes weep, sometimes sing"), Monteverdi forcefully juxtaposes the contrast between joy and sorrow, setting the final statement of

Example 8-1 Carlo Gesualdo, *Moro, lasso, al mio duolo*, measures 1–8

I die, alas, of my pain, and she who could give me life [kills me and will not help me!]

Note: The unconventional bar-lines in the opening measures follow the edition of Gesualdo's madrigals published in score in Genoa in 1613. **Source:** Carlo Gesualdo, *Moro, lasso, al mio duolo* from *Sämtliche Madrigale von Carlo Gesualdo*, vol. 6, ed. W. Weismann, pp. 74–77. © 1957 VEB Deutscher Verlag für Musik. © 1957 Deutscher Verlag für Musikm Leipzig. Used by permission of the publisher.

the word *piango* ("weep") on a suspension with a jarring dissonance (measures 143–144) whose resolution ushers in the final return of the ground bass with the word *canto* ("I sing").

    The use of variation as a structural device is also evident in *Lasciatemi qui solo* ("Leave Me in Solitude Here"), a strophic monody by Francesca Caccini (1587–ca. 1640; see Composer Profile). The text is a lament—once again, a lover has

Francesca Caccini
Lasciatemi qui solo

Composer Profile

Francesca Caccini
(1587–ca. 1640)

As a renowned virtuoso and composer of monodies and operas, Francesca Caccini followed in the footsteps of her father, the composer and singer Giulio Caccini (see Chapter 7). She was the first woman to compose an opera but achieved even greater fame as one of the most celebrated singers of her time. She also wrote poetry, both in Italian and Latin. Caccini spent most of her career in or around the Medici court in Florence. By the 1620s, she had become the highest paid musician in the family's service. She wrote music for court performances (particularly intermedi) and a great many songs. Her duties also included teaching music and singing to the women of the court; her *Primo libro delle musiche* (1618) is particularly well suited for teaching.

Her only surviving opera, *La liberazione di Ruggiero,* pits a young knight, Ruggiero, against Alcina, a seductive sorceress who puts him under a spell. The work has been revived to critical acclaim in both Europe and the United States in recent years. No authentic likeness of her is known.

Principal Works

Most of Francesca Caccini's works have been lost. She wrote the music for an estimated fourteen court

KEY DATES IN THE LIFE OF FRANCESCA CACCINI	
1587	Born September 18 in Florence
1600	Probably performs in her father's operas in Florence, *Euridice* and *Il rapimento di Cefalo*
1607	Begins independent service within the Medici court in Florence as a singer, composer, and teacher of music
1618	Publishes *Il primo libro delle musiche,* a large collection of monodic songs on both sacred and secular texts
1625	Production of her opera *La liberazione di Ruggiero*
1641	Dies sometime after June 1641

entertainments in Florence during the years 1607 to 1627, including ballets, intermedi, and incidental music to comedies. Her *Primo libro delle musiche* (1618) is a substantial collection of sonnets, madrigals, arias, motets, hymns, and canzonettes, all for solo voice and continuo.

---

been abandoned—that progresses from sorrow to death. The music's basic structural unit is the nine-measure pattern stated at the outset by the bass.

Tradimento ("Betrayal"), a madrigal for soprano and continuo by Barbara Strozzi (1619–1664), daughter of the Venetian poet Giulio Strozzi, illustrates one of the most important of all formal innovations of the Baroque, the **ritornello principle. A ritornello** (the word means "small return" in Italian) is an opening musical idea that returns at several points over the course of a work, usually after contrasting material of some kind. Composers used the ritornello principle to establish a framework of both repetition and variation, and it appears in a great many genres of the Baroque era, vocal as well as instrumental. It would later take on special importance in the genre of the concerto (see Chapter 10).

The ritornello in Strozzi's *Tradimento*—the exclamation "Betrayal!" and the agitated theme associated with it—is both textual and musical. In these recurring outbursts, the

Strozzi
Tradimento

The Doctrine of Affections

The 17th century witnessed the beginnings of what we now think of as modern-day psychology, the study of the human mind and its relationship to the emotions. René Descartes's *The Passions of the Soul* (1649) was the most prominent in a long line of texts that attempted to codify the human passions. Descartes identified six basic affections: admiration (wonder), love, hate, desire, joy, and sadness, and he examined ways in which these states could be induced.

The question of how music reflects and represents these passions was a matter of intense concern throughout the Baroque. The idea that an agitated manner of writing—the *genere concitato*—could evoke feelings of anger and agitation, for example, was one expression of a broad attempt to find musical means for portraying human passions. The various ideas about the relationship between music and emotion that emerged over the course of the Baroque are known today as the *doctrine of affections*.

Most writers of the Baroque adhered to the ancient idea that the passions derived from the physical mixture of the body's four cardinal humors (fluids)—blood, phlegm, yellow bile, and black bile—each of

which governed a particular emotion. In their proper proportion, these were all needed to create a well-balanced disposition. But if one of these elements gained the upper hand, its effect would dominate the whole person. Too much blood (*sanguis* in Latin) made one calm, or sanguine; too much phlegm made one sluggish, or phlegmatic; too much yellow bile made one angry, or choleric; and too much black bile made one melancholy.

Certain types of music, it was believed, could excite the body to produce more blood, phlegm, black bile, or yellow bile, thereby altering the disposition of the listener. The precise mechanism for this was never entirely clear. The German composer and critic Johann Mattheson (1681–1764) suggested that because "joy is an *expansion* of our vital spirits, it follows sensibly and naturally that this affect is best expressed by large and expanded intervals," whereas "sadness . . . is a *contraction* of those same subtle parts of our bodies. It is, therefore, easy to see that the narrowest intervals are the most suitable." Such pronouncements, however, rested more on imagination than scientific observation.

scorned lover swears to kill the object of her (or his?) wrath. The ritornello sections offset more inward and less violent reflections: "My sickness has advanced so / That I have discovered that the thought of being [a prisoner of love] makes me contented."

Strozzi's ritornello captures the physical energy of the scorned lover's fury with rapid-fire repeated notes. This technique, developed by Monteverdi for evoking a mood of bellicose agitation or anger, was known as the **genere concitato**—the "agitated" or "warlike" manner. The flurry of repeated notes outlining a triad that opens *Tradimento*—and recurs with each statement of the ritornello between strophes and at the end—sounds almost like a trumpet fanfare, rousing troops for battle.

France: The *Air de cour*

Like their counterparts in the Florentine Camerata, French academicians of the late 16th century sought to recreate the magical powers of ancient music, but in a manner suited to the qualities of the French language. Jean-Antoine de Baïf (1532–1589) and his followers at the Académie de poésie et musique (Academy of Poetry and Music), founded in 1570, developed a system they called *musique mesurée à l'antique* ("music adapted to the ancient style"). Adherents of this approach tried to adapt French verse to the quantitative principles of Greek and Latin poetry, in which syllables are differentiated by length

Party Music, 1612. *Music has long been associated with drinking and lascivious behavior, as this scene of student music-making and revelry from 1612 suggests. The harpsichordist and the violinist on the right seem especially interested in the arrival of the young ladies, whom their friend at the door is enthusiastically helping down the steps. The lutenist in the right foreground is repairing a broken string. The others (at least, those who are not drinking) are playing and singing from partbooks. Composers did not hesitate to write music for the student market. In 1626, Johann Hermann Schein issued a collection called* Studenten-Schmauss *("Student Banquet"), a collection of songs for five voices written to provide "praiseworthy companionship for wine or beer."*

Source: Kunstsammlungen der Veste Coburg, Germany/ Neg#3740, Inv.#VII, 308, 24

(duration) rather than by weight (accent). Baïf advocated musical settings in which long and short syllables were consistently declaimed in a ratio of 2:1. The musical accompaniment did not rest on basso continuo—a device that spread only slowly throughout Europe and did not become standard until about 1680—but rather on notated tablature for the lute or other similar instruments. Although this type of notation reduced the need for improvisation, the textural clarity of a solo voice with discreet accompaniment is clearly indebted to the principles of monody.

The most important repertory of secular song in early-17th-century France centers on the ***air de cour*** ("courtly air"). Like the madrigal, the *air de cour* was at first polyphonic but eventually evolved into the favored vehicle for solo voice and lute accompaniment. The first published set of this genre appeared in 1571. It includes arrangements of earlier four-part compositions as well as new works in the style of the *voix de ville* (simple strophic verse set to chordal accompaniments). Etienne Moulinié's *Enfin la beauté que j'adore* ("At Last, the Beauty Whom I Adore"), published in 1624, resembles many similar *airs de cour* in its fluid, syllabic declamation of text and its harmonic simplicity and melodic grace, avoiding overt displays of virtuosity. Moulinié (ca. 1600–after 1669) served for many years as director of music to Gaston d'Orléans, Louis XIII's younger brother, and he was one of many French composers of the early 17th century to cultivate the *air de cour,* along with Pierre Guédron (ca. 1570–ca. 1620) and Antoine Boësset (1586–1643).

Moulinié
Enfin la beauté que j'adore

OPERA

Music had played an important role in the theater throughout the Renaissance: plays routinely included songs, dances, and interludes of instrumental music. Shakespeare's dramas, the earliest of which appeared in the 1580s, are full of such musical elements. The so-called **madrigal comedies** of the late 16th century consist of a cycle of madrigals connected by a dramatic theme. The most famous work of this kind, Orazzio

Vecchi's *L'Amfiparnaso* of 1597 (the title means roughly "The Slopes of Mount Parnassus"), is a series of 14 madrigals for five voices that draw on the stock characters of the commedia dell'arte, the Italian tradition of improvised comedy: the dottering merchant (Pantalone), the long-winded doctor (Gratiano), and the young lovers (Isabella and Lucio). But these madrigal comedies seem not to have been staged, and even in their most developed form they represent little more than the songs of a play with the spoken dialogue that might otherwise connect them.

The chief obstacle to composing an opera—that is, a drama sung in its entirety from beginning to end—was the absence of a technique that would permit a single voice to represent an individual character on stage. Monody overcame that obstacle. And another new technique, **recitative,** permitted solo voices to declaim relatively large quantities of text in a rapid yet comprehensible manner. Recitative is a largely syllabic style of singing in which greater emphasis is given to the declamation of the text than to the creation of a melodic line. With recitative, composers could more nearly approximate the inflections of spoken speech even while indicating specific pitches and rhythms to be sung.

Not surprisingly, the three most important composers associated with the Florentine Camerata and the emergence of the *seconda prattica*—Giacopo Peri, Giulio Caccini, and Emilio de' Cavalieri—played central roles in creating the new genre of opera. Peri and Caccini collaborated at first but later competed with one another, with each claiming to have written the "first" opera, even while acknowledging the contributions of Cavalieri. These are the relevant compositions:

◆ *Dafne,* music by Giacopo Peri, text by Ottavio Rinuccini. Produced during carnival season of 1598, at the palace of Jacopo Corsi and also at the Medici court, both in Florence. The music is almost entirely lost.

◆ *Rappresentazione di Anima e di Corpo* ("Representation of the Soul and the Body"), music by Emilio de' Cavalieri, text by Agostino Manni. Produced in Rome, February 1600.

◆ *Euridice,* music by Peri, text by Rinuccini. Produced in Florence, October 1600; score published in February 1601.

◆ *Euridice,* music by Giulio Caccini, text by Rinuccini. Produced in its entirety in December 1602 but published January 1601.

Judging from the accounts of eyewitnesses, these earliest operas did not make a particularly strong impression. Although they mix recitative with polyphonic madrigals, arias (settings of strophic texts), choruses, and instrumental interludes, recitative predominates. Effective as it might be for projecting a text, recitative could not provide sufficient musical variety over time to maintain viewer interest. At least one member of the original audience that took in Peri's *Euridice* in 1600 found this method of singing tedious, "like the chanting of the Passion" in church.[2]

Having established the new style of recitative, composers now faced the challenge of integrating this manner of singing into a work that was both musically and dramatically satisfying. Claudio Monteverdi's *Orfeo* of 1607 is generally acknowledged to be the first opera to have achieved this goal. *Orfeo* takes as its subject the most celebrated musician of ancient myth, Orpheus, whose music was so powerful that it persuaded the gods of the underworld to release Euridice from the realm of the dead. It was certainly not the first opera (as it is sometimes mistakenly called), but it was the first to gain critical acclaim.

Monteverdi
Orfeo

Part of its appeal lies in its keen sense of dramatic pacing, as illustrated in the extended excerpt from Act II in the anthology.

Timbral contrast is one of many devices that gave Monteverdi a crucial advantage over his operatic predecessors. *Orfeo* benefited from the full financial backing of the Mantuan court, which allowed for a large ensemble and elaborate staging. Peri's and Caccini's earlier operas, by contrast, had been produced on relatively small budgets, which limited the number of musicians and the quality of the staging. Monteverdi's score to *Orfeo* calls for almost forty instruments, an astonishing demand at the time. Monteverdi labels these instruments with extraordinary specificity at various points in his score in an attempt to create a distinctive timbre for particular scenes.

Orpheus's celebrated aria in Act III ("Possente spirto"; unfortunately too long to include in the Anthology), is a masterpiece of both vocal and instrumental writing. Here, Orpheus uses voice and lyre in turn to persuade Caron to allow him to cross the River Styx and enter the underworld. Each ritornello between the strophes of this plea has its own sound, each magically drawn from the lyre. Interestingly, it is only after this aria, with his more spontaneous and unaccompanied outburst on the words *Ahi, sventurato amante* ("Ah, unhappy lover that I am"), that Orpheus achieves his goal. Caron had remained unmoved by the carefully planned, instrumentally diverse, and artistically ornamented aria, but he is overwhelmed by the passion of the more immediate and direct appeal that follows.

Orfeo ends with what would become a time-honored device in later opera, the *deus ex machina* (literally, "god from a machine"), in which a god (here, Apollo) descends on a chariot from the skies to rescue the hero. But Monteverdi and his librettist, Alessandro Striggio, avoid an unrealistically happy ending (a temptation that would not be resisted in many later settings of this same fable). Instead of restoring Euridice to life once again,

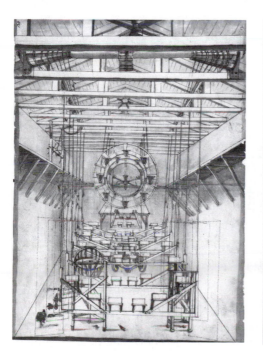

Opera as spectacle. *Machinery played a vital role in creating special effects on the operatic stage. The two illustrations here show the audience's view and the behind-the-scenes machinery used to create the illusion of gods floating through the clouds in a scene from Giovanni Legrenzi's opera* Germanico sul Reno, *as performed in 1675 at the Teatro San Salvatore, Venice.*

Source: A Cloud Scene in Legrenzi's Opera—Res 853 PL. 16 98C 225436 and Res 853 PL. 17 98C 225437/Bibliotheque Nationale de France, Paris

Composer Profile

Heinrich Schütz
(1585–1672)

Born exactly 100 years before J. S. Bach, Heinrich Schütz was the leading German composer of the 17th century and a key figure in transmitting the *seconda prattica* north of the Alps. He mastered the polychoral style of the late Renaissance under the tutelage of Giovanni Gabrieli in Venice, adapted the newly developed technique of recitative to the German language, composed the first German opera, and maintained music at the court of Dresden for many years.

In spite of his progressive tendencies, Schütz believed that a proper grounding in counterpoint—the basis of the *prima prattica*—remained an essential element of compositional instruction. "It is thus," he wrote in the preface to his *Geistliche Chormusik* ("Sacred Choral Music"), a collection of a cappella motets in the style of the *prima prattica,* published in 1648,

> that I have been persuaded to undertake a little work such as the present—without *basso continuo*—as a means . . . of admonishing many composers (in particular, the younger generation of Germans) of the need to crack this tough nut [the intricacies of traditional counterpoint] with their own teeth and to seek out the sweet kernel and foundations of a just counterpoint before progressing to the *stile concertante* [composition with basso continuo]—wishing, in this way, to stand up to their first test. In Italy (true and honest school of all music), when, in my youth, I laid the

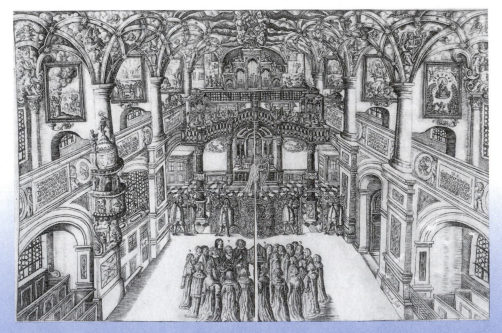

Heinrich Schütz conducts the court chapel of the elector of Saxony. *In this allegorical depiction of Psalm 150 ("Praise the Lord . . . in His sanctuary"), Schütz leads his choristers from a large choir book. An image of King David (author of the Psalms) stands in front of the altar, and an orchestra composed of the instruments listed in Psalm 150 occupies the side and middle balconies just beneath the organ.*

Source: German School (17th century), "Choir" (engraving)/ Bridgeman Art Library

Apollo tells Orfeo that he can see "an image of her loveliness" at all times "in the sun and in the stars." It is a bittersweet ending.

From Florence and Mantua, opera soon took root and flourished in other cities in Italy. Ruling dynasties saw in the genre a way to promote not only their poetic and musical sophistication but also—through dazzling stage displays that we might now think of as

foundations of my profession, it was normal practice for beginners to start by devising and publishing some little work, sacred or secular, without *basso continuo:* as, probably, is still the custom in these southern climes. I have wished to give this account of my personal experience in the study of music (and for the greater fame of our nation) that it be used by each man as he sees fit, and without wishing to discredit anyone.[3]

Schütz served for more than fifty years as Kapellmeister to the elector of Saxony, but his professional life was far from stable. The Thirty Years' War (1618–1648) forced him to flee Dresden at different times, and he spent extended periods in Denmark and Italy over the course of his career.

Principal Works

Aside from his early Italian madrigals, the lost opera *Dafne,* and a lost ballet on the legend of Orpheus, Schütz's output is almost entirely sacred, including works in both Latin and German. These are his best known compositions:

- The *Psalmen Davids* (1619), polyphonic choral works based on texts from the Psalms.

- The *Cantiones sacrae* (1625), a collection of 41 sacred motets.

- The *Symphoniae sacrae,* works for various combinations of voices and instruments published in three volumes over a period of 21 years (1629, 1647, 1650).

- The *Musicalische Exequien* (1636), a cycle of music appropriate for funeral services.

- The *Kleine geistliche Concerte* ("Small Sacred Concertos"), motets for one to five voices with continuo, published in two books (1636, 1639). Of modest scale, they reflect the reduced means of the musical establishment at the Dresden court during the Thirty Years' War.

- The *Geistliche Chormusik* (1648), a set of 29 motets in the *prima prattica.*

- Three Passions (1664–1666), one for the Gospel according to St. Luke, one for the Gospel according to St. John, and one for the Gospel according to St. Matthew.

KEY DATES IN THE LIFE OF HEINRICH SCHÜTZ

1585 Born Köstritz (central Germany) on October 8

1599 Becomes a chorister in the court chapel at Kassel

1609 Sent to Venice by the landgrave of Hesse-Kassel to study under Giovanni Gabrieli; probably meets and possibly studies with Claudio Monteverdi as well

1611 Publishes his first works, a set of five-part Italian madrigals

1612 Returns from Venice and becomes court organist in Kassel

1617 Appointed Kapellmeister to the elector of Saxony at Dresden; remains employed there for the rest of his career

1627 Produces the first German opera, *Dafne* (the music is now lost)

1630s–1640s Compelled by the ravages of the Thirty Years' War to take extended leaves of absence in Copenhagen and Italy

1672 Dies in Dresden on November 6

special effects—their technological prowess as well. Courts began to commission operas routinely for festivals to celebrate weddings (the tangible joining of dynasties), the birth of heirs, birthdays of monarchs, state visits, coronations, funerals, and military victories.

In Rome, the powerful Barberini family built within the walls of its palace a theater seating no fewer than 3,000 spectators. It opened in 1632 with the opera *Sant' Alessio*

("Saint Alexander"), with music by Stefano Landi (1590–1639) and stage designs by Giovanni Lorenzo Bernini (1598–1680), better known as the architect of Saint Peter's Basilica in the Vatican. Like a number of subsequent Roman operas, this one centered on a sacred subject. Pope Urban VIII was himself a member of the Barberini family, and the church—the Jesuits in particular—quickly recognized the power of sung theater to convey moral and spiritual ideas.

Not until 1638, however, with the establishment of the first public opera house in Venice, did the new genre begin to reach beyond the closed circles of court and nobility. Open to any and all who could pay the price of admission, public opera houses were in fact partly supported by the state—a pattern of funding that continues to this day in Europe—but they extended the art of opera to a far wider audience than before.

With the change in audience came changes in production values and musical style. Cost precluded the widespread use of elaborate machinery and staging, focusing increased attention on the singers themselves. In place of lavish scenery, audiences were treated to lavish virtuosity. The musical style began to reflect more the tastes of a wider audience, with greater emphasis on melody. Plots shifted from the mythological to the realistic or historical. Comic elements also found their way onto the stage. Composers and librettists who had once written to flatter and suit the monarchy now had to accommodate broader tastes.

Monteverdi
L'incoronazione di Poppea

A comparison of Monteverdi's *Orfeo*, written for the court of Mantua in 1607, and his *L'incoronazione di Poppea* ("The Coronation of Poppea"), written for the Teatro Grimano in Venice in the season of 1642–1643, illustrates the differences between courtly opera of the early 17th century and public opera of the mid–17th century. *Orfeo*, for all its stylistic variety, is serious from beginning to end, without an ounce of comic relief. *Poppea*, in contrast, mixes high seriousness with comic scenes. It also requires relatively little in the way of chorus and orchestra and has no scenes that call for elaborate sets or machinery. *Poppea*'s very human characters, drawn from history, contrast vividly with the mythic, allegorical characters in *Orfeo*. Nero, the emperor of Rome, is married to Ottavia but hopelessly in love with Poppea, who in turn is married to Ottone. Smitten by his love for Poppea, Nero turns to putty in her hands. At Poppea's urging, he banishes her husband to exile, divorces his own wife, and puts to death the philosopher Seneca for the simple reason that his moralizing is inconvenient for her. Poppea is, in short, a close cousin to Lady Macbeth, a very realistic personality whose lust for power leads her to cut down everything in her path.

As in *Orfeo*, Monteverdi uses a variety of dramatic and musical strategies to create a story that is consistently fast paced. The boundary between recitative and aria, which would become more pronounced in the opera of the later 17th and 18th centuries, is still quite fluid.

SACRED MUSIC

Composers applied the principles of the *seconda prattica* to sacred as well as secular music. Monteverdi's *Vespro della Beata Vergine* ("Vespers for the Blessed Virgin") of 1610, for example, is a veritable compendium of compositional techniques that incorporates both old and new styles. This cycle of 14 different movements includes *prima prattica* polychoral numbers like *Nisi Dominus* for two five-part choirs; the notated organ part essentially doubles the voices and does not play a structurally significant role. At the other end of the compositional spectrum is *Duo Seraphim*, a movement for three soloists and basso continuo, with virtuosity every bit as flamboyant as that found in the madrigal

Zefiro torna. In between are works that blend old-style vocal part writing with instrumental ritornellos (*Ave maris stella*) or with instrumental parts that are structurally essential to the fabric of the work (*Domine ad adjuvandum*).

Heinrich Schütz's *Singet dem Herren ein neues Lied* ("Sing unto the Lord a New Song") owes much to Monteverdi's style. Schütz may or may not have actually studied with Monteverdi in Venice, but he was certainly aware of the older composer's music. The two solo violin lines of this work operate at times in counterpoint to the tenor solo, at times as an antiphonal "choir" of their own. Every verse or half verse of the psalm text (Psalm 96: 1–4) is differentiated by a new musical idea, yet the individual sections are connected through a slow but steady increase in register, rhythmic motion, and melodic intensity. In a series of carefully graduated steps, the listener is moved from stasis to a state of spiritual ecstasy at the end.

Schütz
Singet dem Herren ein neues Lied

Like Monteverdi, Schütz never abandoned the *prima prattica* entirely, particularly for settings of sacred texts. On the contrary, he believed that training in *prima prattica* counterpoint was essential for aspiring composers (see Composer Profile: Heinrich Schütz). Still, even in a polychoral motet like *Saul, was verfolgst du mich?* he incorporates distinct traits of the *seconda prattica*. In a moment of high drama, Saul (later to become the Apostle Paul) is struck blind on the road to Damascus and hears the voice of God calling to him: "Saul, Saul, why dost thou persecute me?" The opening cry rises out of the low depths of the bass, punctuated by the basso continuo, eventually swelling into the combined voices of two four-part choirs, six soloists, and two additional lines for unspecified treble instruments (usually played by violins). The echo of the cry is not just softer but eerily different in timbre (measures 21–23). God's words to Saul continue with a series of lines distributed among the various vocal and instrumental forces. Solo passages alternate with choral and instrument sections. The words rush ahead at times, hold back at others; certain of them (such as *löcken*, "to kick") are emphasized through the use of melisma; others ("Saul") make their effect through simpler declamation. The cumulative effect is stunning as it captures the reverberations of God's words in Saul's mind at the very moment in which Saul is struck blind.

Schütz
Saul, was verfolgst du mich?

CONCLUSION

The first half of the 17th century was a period of rapid and intense change in musical styles. The influence of the *seconda prattica* extended to all genres of vocal music, both secular and sacred, and the new genre of opera moved beyond strictly courtly venues to appeal to a wider public. By 1650, the basso continuo was well on its way to becoming a standard feature of music making throughout the European continent. Further developments in musical style over the next 100 years would build on all these precedents.

Vocal Music, 1650–1750

By the middle of the 17th century, opera had established itself as both a critical and commercial success on the Italian peninsula. France began to develop its own traditions of sung drama around this time, and English composers made their first tentative steps in this direction toward the end of the century. But it was the distinctively Italian phenomenon of opera seria that would dominate the theaters of the continent from the 1680s through the whole of the 18th century. Sacred music was also deeply influenced by opera, not only in the new dramatic (but unstaged) genre of the oratorio, but even in such traditional genres as the motet and the Mass. The cantata, in turn, emerged as the principal genre of sacred music in Protestant Germany.

OPERA

Beyond Italy, opera was slow to develop. France, Spain, and England all enjoyed their own forms of dramatic entertainment, many of them with strong musical elements. But France did not see its first opera until 1662, and even then the new genre failed to win over the court. The reasons were partly political—opera was an imported art, and anti-Italian forces at the court conspired to undermine its introduction into France—but mostly aesthetic. The French nobility found no compelling reason to listen to a drama sung in its entirety. Singing by its very nature takes longer than speaking, which means an opera necessarily has less text than a play of equivalent duration. And with the possible exception of recitative, a sung text is typically more difficult to understand than a declaimed text.

In England, the genre of the **masque** enjoyed a certain vogue in the 17th century. This was a form of entertainment rather like the Florentine intermedi, a mixture of declaimed poetry, songs, scenery, dance, and instrumental music. The first opera produced in England was a **pasticcio** (Italian for "hodgepodge"), a work whose individual parts were written by several different composers. But *The Siege of Rhodes*, produced in 1656, was a critical and commercial failure, largely because the English, like the French, resisted the idea of a drama being sung from beginning to end.

Another reason for opera's lack of appeal compared to the ballet in France and the masque in England may have been that opera was mere spectacle, whereas ballet and masque were participatory events, in which the barriers between stage and audience were fluid or even nonexistent. Members of the court did not just watch these entertainments, they mixed with the performers on stage. How could opera compete with the thrill, for a noblewoman, of dancing with Zeus, or for a nobleman, of dancing with Venus?

France: *Comédie-ballet* and *Tragédie en musique*

The preferred vehicle for musical theater in France for the first two-thirds of the 17th century was the *ballet de cour,* a genre that arose in the early 1580s. Combining song, dance, and instrumental music, these courtly ballets were heavily allegorical, their heroes almost invariably thinly veiled stand-ins for the reigning monarch.

It was an Italian immigrant, Jean-Baptiste Lully (1632–1687; born Giovanni Battista Lulli), who established sung drama in France in the guise of a new genre that was part opera, part ballet. A superb entrepreneur as well as a gifted composer, Lully skillfully negotiated the royal bureaucracy that controlled theatrical productions in France to advance his career. Beginning in the 1660s, he wrote a series of *comédie-ballets* that highlighted the dancing talents of his master, Louis XIV. The *comédie-ballet* was a mixture of spoken drama and dance.

In 1672, through a series of legal maneuvers abetted by his close personal connections with King Louis XIV, Lully purchased a patent from the crown to establish the Royal Academy of Music that gave him the exclusive right to produce sung dramas in France. Then, with the poet Philippe Quinault (1635–1688) and a team of handpicked musicians and stage designers, he created a new operatic genre, the *tragédie en musique* (also known as *tragédie lyrique*), composing and producing one a year between 1673 and 1687. Although supported and financed by the court, these works were accessible to the paying public when performed at the Palais-Royal in Paris, which Lully took over in 1674.

Lully and Quinault drew on classical mythology and chivalric romances for subject matter for their operas, but their plots were widely understood as veiled commentaries (always favorable, of course) on recent events at court. The hero of any given opera was almost invariably understood to be an allegorical counterpart to Louis XIV. In *Armide,* the hero Renaud obeys the call of duty and spurns the enchantment of the sorceress for whom the opera is named.

Lully
Armide

Structurally, a *tragédie en musique* consists of these parts:

◆ An overture that moves from a slow introduction with dotted rhythms to a fast imitative section. The dotted rhythms, associated with royalty, were an homage to the splendor of the king. This form eventually came to be known as the **French overture** and would be adopted by many composers—Italian and German as well as French—over subsequent decades.

◆ An allegorical prologue closely connected to some recent event at the court but always flattering to the king, either explicitly or implicitly.

◆ Five acts of entirely sung drama, each divided into several different scenes.

◆ Many *divertissements* (interludes) within individual acts that provided ample opportunities for displays of dancing and choral song. Instrumental music figured prominently in these divertissements in the form of **symphonies,** a term used at the time to describe any music for a large ensemble.

Composer Profile

Jean-Baptiste Lully
(1632–1687)

The founder of the French operatic tradition was an Italian. Giovanni Battista Lulli—better known by the French version of his name, Jean-Baptiste Lully—was born the son of a poor miller in Florence. He did not arrive in France until the age of 14, but he soon won favor at the court through his talents as a dancer, singer, and violinist. By the end of his life he had established himself as a wealthy cavalier at the French court and the most important figure in the musical world of 17th-century France.

An admiring account of a 1668 performance at the court of Versailles of Lully's ballet *Les fêtes de l'Amour et de Bacchus* ("The Festivities of Amor and Bacchus"), which included vocal passages, gives some indication of the esteem in which the composer was held:

> It may be said that in this work, the Sieur de Lully has discovered the secret of satisfying and charming everyone, for never was there anything so fine or so well devised. If one takes the dances, there is no step that does not speak of the action the Dancers are to perform, or whose accompanying gestures are not as good as words that may be understood. If one takes the Music, there is nothing which does not perfectly express all the passions, delighting the spirit of the Hearers. But what was never before seen is that pleasing harmony of voices, that symphony [i.e., sounding together] of instruments, that delightful union of different choruses, those sweet songs, those tender and amorous dialogues, those echoes, in short, that admirable conduct in every part, in which it might always be seen from the first words that the Music was increasing, and having begun with a single voice, it concluded with a concert of over one hundred persons, seen all at once upon the same Stage, uniting their instruments, their voices and their steps in a harmony and cadence that brings the Play to an end, leaving everyone in a state of admiration that cannot be adequately expressed.[1]

Lully died in service to his profession. While conducting his ensemble, he accidentally struck his foot with the sharp cane he used to pound out the beat. The blow must have been severe because gangrene soon set in, and he died of blood poisoning at the age of 54.

KEY DATES IN THE LIFE OF JEAN-BAPTISTE LULLY

1632 Born in Florence (Italy) on November 28, the son of a miller

1646 Taken to Paris as a page to a cousin of Louis XIV because of his vocal talent

1652 Becomes a ballet dancer in the service of Louis XIV and is soon composing court ballets

1661 Appointed superintendent of music at the French court

1662 Appointed music master to the French royal family

1672 Receives a patent to establish the Royal Academy of Music, essentially an opera house

1687 Dies in Paris on March 22

Lully was one of the first composers whose music continued to be performed long after his death. His works for the stage were presented repeatedly in Germany, Italy, and England in the 18th century, and they remained popular in France for more than a hundred years.

Principal Works

BALLETS Lully's earliest works for the French court were ballets, many of which also incorporated song at various points. His best known are *Le Bourgeois Gentilhomme* (based on Molière's play of the same name) and *Psyché*.

OPERAS At least half a dozen of Lully's operas never left the active repertory of the French stage. Most notable among these are *Cadmus et Hermione*, *Alceste*, *Atys*, *Persée*, *Roland*, and *Armide*.

OTHER GENRES In addition to his dramatic works, Lully also wrote a set of trio sonatas, a setting of the Mass, a Te Deum, and a number of motets.

The vocal portions of each opera move fluidly between the declamatory *récit* (recitative) and the lyrical *air* (aria), mixed with occasional duets, trios, and choruses. Lully used measured but highly supple rhythms to project the fluid prosody of the French language. The music is replete with constantly shifting meters that go largely unnoticed in performance because they match the declamation of the text so well.

Lully's monopoly on sung drama was both a blessing and a curse for the development of French opera. With the best talent of his time at his disposal, he established a model for the genre that would prevail for more than a hundred years. But for the 15 years from 1672, when he secured his royal patent, until his death in 1687, no other composer had any incentive to become proficient at opera. Although later composers like André Campra (1660–1744) and Marin Marais (1656–1728) achieved a certain degree of success in the genre, Lully's operas continued to cast a shadow over the French musical landscape long after his death.

Not until the appearance of the first operas by Jean-Philippe Rameau (1683–1764) in the 1730s did Lully's music find a serious rival on the French stage. Rameau was an unlikely candidate for theatrical success. He had won great fame as a composer of keyboard music and as a theorist, but he did not begin writing operas until he was in his 50s. The great popular success of his *Castor et Pollux* (1737) provoked dismay among Lully's admirers (the Lullistes), leading to a pamphlet war between them and the followers of Rameau (the Ramistes). Like so many of the artistic controversies that arose out of the French court in the 18th century, this one seems to have had less to do with aesthetics than with politics. Rameau himself insisted that he had taken the operas of Lully as his model, but his critics accused him of writing music that was overly intricate and "unnatural," particularly in its rich harmonies. Yet it is precisely this quality that makes his operas so engaging to us today. Ironically, Rameau would be held up as the very embodiment of French music a generation later in yet another controversy, this time between pro-French and pro-Italian operatic camps, the so-called War of the Buffoons (see Chapter 13).

Italy: Opera seria

Opera seria ("serious opera")—so called because of its usually tragic content and in contrast to the later *opera buffa* ("comic opera"; see Chapter 13)—was far and away the most important type of opera cultivated between about 1670 and 1770. Developed in Italy and sung almost exclusively in Italian, opera seria was exported to every corner of Europe. The German-born composer George Frideric Handel, for example, composed and produced some of the finest examples of the genre in London in the early 18th century. Opera seria underwent many changes over the period in which it flourished, but its central conventions remained more or less constant.

The typical opera seria libretto draws its subject matter from Classical antiquity. Rulers are always presented in a favorable light, heroic and magnanimous, placing duty and honor above personal gain. The texts balance the demands of drama and music with a mixture of action (recitative) and reflection (aria). But librettists consistently provided plenty of material for arias, the showcase settings for the great solo singing that audiences flocked to the theater to hear.

The Da Capo Aria.   The large majority of the arias in the typical opera seria are **da capo arias.** The name comes from the indication at the end of the second section: *da capo*—literally, "from the head," or, as we would say today, "from the top," that is, the beginning. Having finished the B section, the performer goes back to the beginning of A

PRIMARY EVIDENCE

The Premise of Opera: A Dissenting Voice

The French nobleman Charles de Marguetel de Saint-Denis, Seigneur de Saint-Evremond (1610–1703), was a soldier and man of letters with strong connections to the British aristocracy. (Like Handel, he would be buried in the Poets' Corner of Westminster Abbey.) In a letter written in 1678 to the Duke of Buckingham, Saint-Evremond takes issue with the very premise of opera: the idea of singing an entire drama from beginning to end.

• • • • •

There is another thing in Operas so contrary to Nature, that I cannot be reconciled to it; and that is the singing of the whole Piece, from beginning to end, as if the Persons represented were ridiculously match'd, and had agreed to treat in musick both the most common, and most important affairs of Life. Is it to be imagin'd that a master calls his servant, or sends him on an errand, singing; that one friend imparts a secret to another, singing; that men deliberate in council, singing; that orders in time of battle are given, singing; and that men are melodiously killed with swords and darts? This is the downright way to lose the life of Representation, which without doubt is preferable to that of Harmony: for, Harmony ought to be no more than a bare attendant, and the great matters of the Stage have introduc'd it as pleasing, not as necessary, after they have perform'd all that relates to the Subject and Discourse. Nevertheless, our thoughts run more upon the Musician than the Hero in the Opera: *Luigi, Cavalli,* and *Cesti,* are still present to our imagination. The mind not being able to conceive a Hero that sings, thinks of the Composer that set the song; and I don't question but that in the Operas at the Palace-Royal, *Lulli* is an hundred times more thought of than *Theseus* or *Cadmus.*

. . . The Grecians made admirable Tragedies where they had some singing; the Italians and the French make bad ones, where they sing all.

Source: *The Letters of Saint-Evremond,* ed. and trans. John Hayward (London: George Routledge & Sons, 1930), pp. 207–9. Used by permission of the publisher.

FOCUS

The Poet of Opera Seria: Pietro Metastasio (1698–1782)

Pietro Metastasio was the quintessential librettist of opera seria. In Greek, *metastasio* means "transformation," and that is exactly what this poet brought to the world of the opera libretto in the early 18th century. Born Pietro Antonio Domenico Bonaventura Trapassi (*trapassi* or *trapassamento* also means "transformation" in Italian), the young poet wrote his first tragedy at the age of 15; his first major success as a librettist came in 1723 with *Didone abbandonata* ("Dido Abandoned"), and from then on he was the favorite librettist of his era. Some of the leading composers of 18th-century opera—Leonardo Leo, Johann Adolph Hasse, Niccolò Jommelli, Antonio Caldara, Giovanni Battista Pergolesi, and Christoph Willibald Gluck—used his texts. All told more than 700 operas are based on Metastasio's librettos. Some of them were set more than 60 times by different composers. One of Mozart's early oratorios, *La Betulia liberata,* and his last opera, *La Clemenza di Tito* ("The Clemency of Titus"), were both set to adaptations of Metastasian texts. A Metastasio libretto provides a clear delineation between recitative and aria, with ample material for the virtuoso arias that gave composers and soloists the opportunity to show their skill, to the delight of opera audiences.

Metastasio did not always approve of the way his arias were set. "The singers of the present times," he noted late in his life, "wholly forget that their business is to imitate the speech of man, with numbers [i.e., rhythms] and harmony. On the contrary, they believe themselves more perfect, in proportion as their performance is remote from human nature."[2]

and continues to the end of that section. Singers were expected to embellish the A section of an aria on its return, transforming long notes into ornaments or runs, altering entire passages, adding new and spectacularly high (or low) notes, and generally rewriting the music to show off their particular vocal strengths.

Within each A and B section, the ritornello principle plays a central role, as the aria *L'empio, sleale, indegno* from Act I of Handel's opera *Giulio Cesare* illustrates. Ptolomey (Tolomeo), co-ruler of Egypt with his sister, Cleopatra, is threatened by the arrival of the conquering Julius Caesar (Giulio Cesare). To appease Caesar, Ptolomey presents him with the severed head of Caesar's Roman rival, Pompey. But Caesar is disgusted by such barbarism and rejects the gift. Ptolomey, informed of Caesar's reaction, is outraged.

The ritornello principle is reinforced by the tonal structure: the A section begins and ends in the tonic, with a contrasting key in between. The B section, in C minor, beginning at the words *Mà perda pur la vita* is even briefer and consists entirely of solo singing with instrumental support; there is no ritornello within this section itself. When considered within the context of the aria as a whole, however, this B section is framed by two ritornello passages: Ritornello 3 from the end of A, and Ritornello 1 from the da capo resumption of the aria's beginning. In a sense, then, the B section as a whole can be seen as a large Solo 3.

The half cadence in measure 58 is a signal to orchestra and audience alike that the **cadenza** is about to begin. From the Italian word for "cadence," the cadenza is a truly soloistic moment, with no accompaniment of the orchestra at all; the soloist instead improvises (or at least gives the appearance of improvising), invariably with great virtuosity. Cadenzas are typically indicated in the score of an aria by a simple fermata sign, and the cadenza in the da capo performance of the A section was expected to be even more flamboyant than in the first.

Handel
Giulio Cesare

Handel, *Giulio Cesare*, Act I, *L'empio, sleale, indegno:* the A section

	Rit. 1	Solo 1	Rit. 2	Solo 2	Cadenza	Rit. 3
Measure	1	12	32	36	58	61
Key	E♭ major	E♭ major	B♭ major	Unstable	V/E♭ major	E♭ major
Harmony	I		V		V/I	I

Handel, *Giulio Cesare*, Act I, *L'empio, sleale, indegno:*
the structure of the whole in performance

A					B	A (da capo)				
Rit. 1	Solo 1	Rit. 2	Solo 2	Rit. 3	Solo 3	Rit. 4	Solo 4	Rit. 5	Solo 5	Rit. 6
I		V		I	vi	I		V		I

Recitative.   By the second half of the 17th century, aria and recitative were becoming increasingly distinct. Opera seria uses *recitativo semplice*—"simple recitative," accompanied only by the basso continuo—for extended passages of prose, as in a monologue or rapid exchanges among characters. This kind of recitative is often known as **secco** ("dry") **recitative.** Although it may indeed seem dry at times, secco recitative helped composers move a plot forward by quickly disposing of large quantities of text. Arias, in contrast, tend to be dramatically static but psychologically quite revealing, allowing characters

PRIMARY EVIDENCE

French versus Italian Opera, 1702

Comparisons between French and Italian culture in all its aspects, including music, were common in the 17th and 18th centuries. The author of this *Comparison between the French and Italian Music and Operas*, François Raguenet (ca. 1660–1722), was a French priest, physician, and historian. He astutely describes the salient differences between the operas of the two nations. The anonymous translation here is from a contemporary English edition (London, 1709).

• • • • •

Our opera's are writ much better than the Italian; they are regular, coherent designs; and, if repeated without the music, they are as entertaining as of our other pieces that are purely dramatick. . . .

On the other hand, the Italian opera's are poor, incoherent rhapsodies, without any connexion or design; all their pieces, properly speaking, are patched up with thin, insipid scraps; their scenes consist of some trivial dialogues, or soliloquy, at the end of which they foist in one of their best airs, which concludes the scene. . . .

Besides, our opera's have a farther advantage over the Italian, in respect of the voice, and that is the bass, which is so frequent among us, and so rarely to be met with in Italy. . . . When the persons of gods or kings, a Jupiter, Neptune, Priam or Agamemnon, are brought on the stage, our actors, with their deep voices, give 'em an air of majesty, quite different from that of the falsettists or the feign'd basses among the Italians, which have neither depth nor strength. Besides, the blending of the basses with the upper parts forms an agreeable contrast, and makes us perceive the beauties of the one from the opposition they meet with from the other, a pleasure to which the Italians are perfect strangers, the voices of their singers, who are, for the most part, castrati, being perfectly like those of their women.

The Italian language is much more naturally adapted to Musick than ours; their vowels are all sonorous, whereas above half of ours are mute, or at best bear a very small part in pronunciation; so that, in the first place, no cadence, or beautiful passage, can be form'd upon the syllables that consist of those vowels, and, in second place, one cannot hear but half the words, so that we are left to guess at what the French are singing, whereas the Italian is perfectly understood. . . .

The Italians are more bold and hardy in their airs, than the French; they carry their point farther, both in their tender songs and those that are more lively, as well as in their other compositions; nay, they often unite styles, which the French think incompatible. The French, in those compositions that consist of many parts, seldom regard more than that which is principal, whereas the Italians usually study to make all the parts equally shining, and beautiful. In short, the invention of the one is inexhaustible, but the genius of the other is narrow and constrain'd. . . .

It is not to be wonder'd that the Italians think our musick dull and stupefying, that, according to their taste, it appears flat and insipid, if we consider the nature of the French airs compar'd to those of the Italian. The French in their airs aim at the soft, the easie, the flowing, and coherent; the whole air is of the same tone, or if sometimes they venture to vary it, they do it with so many preparations, they so qualifie it, that still the air seems to be as natural and consistent as if they had attempted no change at all; there is nothing bold and adventurous in it; it's all equal and of a piece. But the Italians pass boldly, and in an instant from sharps to flats and from flats to sharps; they venture the boldest cadences, and the most irregular dissonances; and their airs are so out of the way that they resemble the compositions of no other nation in the world.

Source: From an anonymous English translation published as *A Comparison between the French and Italian Musick and Operas* (London, 1709).

to reflect on what has just transpired in the recitative. *Recitativo accompagnato*—**accompanied recitative,** supported or punctuated by the full orchestra rather than the basso continuo alone—was reserved for moments of high emotion and drama, such as Julius Caesar's monologue at the tomb of Pompey in Handel's *Giulio Cesare*.

Virtuosity and the Exit Convention.   The da capo aria offered singers the perfect vehicle for demonstrating their vocal prowess. Unfortunately, virtuosity—when it comes in the form of very high or low notes, fast passages, or rapid ornaments—can obscure the intelligibility of the words being sung. The da capo form provides opportunities for multiple restatements, however, so words missed on a first run-through might be picked up on the second.

The demand for virtuosity also led to personal rivalries among singers, resulting in a staging device known as the **exit convention.** After finishing an aria (presumably to great applause), an opera seria character almost always exits. This allows for curtain calls and also prevents one singer from stealing the stage from the next.

The Castrato.   Soprano singers were so highly prized in the 17th and 18th centuries—for male as well as female roles—that young boys with promising voices would sometimes submit themselves or be subjected to castration, which prevented a change of voice at puberty. The effect of a grown man singing in the soprano range was by all accounts electrifying, for the **castrato** combined the high range of the female voice with the physical power of the male voice.

What we now regard as a grotesque practice may have seemed 300 years ago an acceptable sacrifice, considering the compensation. The greatest of the castrati enjoyed celebrity and financial rewards comparable to that of today's pop music stars.

Audiences in the 17th and 18th centuries, it should be noted, viewed castrati with a sense of both awe and amusement. These surgically altered singers were the object of humor and satire as well as adulation. The phenomenon of the castrato contributed to a growing image of opera seria as an "unnatural" art form, which in turn led to major changes in the broader genre of opera in the second half of the 18th century (see Chapter 13).

The Business of Opera.   The establishment of the first public opera houses in Venice in 1638 profoundly influenced the development of the genre. The new audience—at once larger and more heterogeneous—demanded new kinds of performance spaces and imposed a new economics of music on opera. Without the direct support of either the court or the church, opera was forced to establish itself on a for-profit basis.

Opera's major season was carnival, running from roughly just after Christmas until Lent, which begins in late February or March. Carnival was an enormous draw for visitors from all over Europe: it has been estimated that Venice, a city of about 140,000 in 1700, consistently attracted some 30,000 foreign visitors during this one season every year. These visitors wanted entertainment of all kinds, including opera, and they were willing to pay for it. By the end of the century Venice could boast of no fewer than 16 opera houses.

By then, however, the business had long since been taken over by professional impresarios, the equivalent of modern-day Hollywood producers. It was the impresarios who assembled all the necessary pieces—and the capital—to mount new productions of opera.

The impresario invested the money to rent the theater, sell tickets, and hire the many artists required to stage an opera, including librettist, composer, singers, players, stage designers, and costume designers.

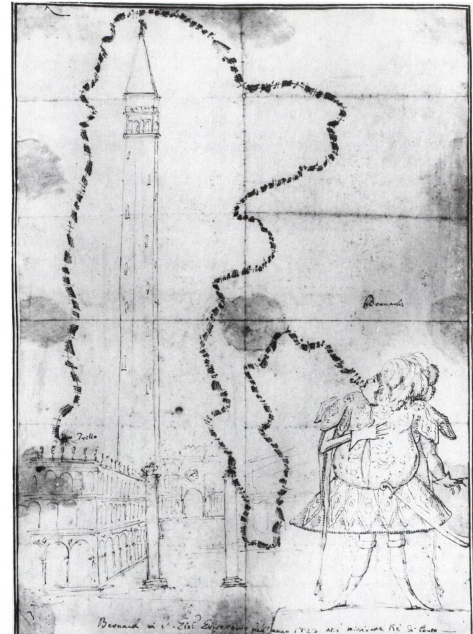

The castrato. *This early-18th-century caricature of the castrato Antonio Maria Bernacchi (1685–1756) lampoons two well-known tendencies of castrati: to put on weight and to sing fantastically elaborate passagework. Here, the music leaps above the bell tower in Venice's St. Mark's Square and explodes in a trill over a nearby building. The music is in fact taken from a melody in the title role of Giovanni Maria Cappelli's* Mitridate re di Ponto *(1723), an opera seria whose libretto would be set to music again almost fifty years later by the young Wolfgang Amadeus Mozart.*

Source: Venezia, Fondazione Giorgio Cini

England: Masque, Semi-Opera, Opera, and Ballad Opera

Like France, England enjoyed a rich tradition of spoken drama, in which music occupied an important if subordinate role. Plays and masques provided what most Englishmen considered ample opportunity for a combination of drama, song, and ballet. Masques began as semi-improvised intrusions into large social festivities by masked and costumed actors; the genre eventually migrated to the stage as a loosely assembled series of vignettes that

Composer Profile

Henry Purcell
(ca. 1659–1695)

KEY DATES IN THE LIFE OF HENRY PURCELL

?1659 Born in London (?)

1669 Becomes a chorister in the Chapel Royal

1679 Succeeds John Blow as organist of Westminster Abbey

1680 Writes his first music for the stage

1689 Composes *Dido and Aeneas,* his only opera

1695 Dies in Westminster (London)

Considering his stature as one of the greatest of all English composers ever to write for the theater, we know remarkably little about Henry Purcell. We are not sure whether his father was Henry Purcell or his brother Thomas Purcell; both were Gentlemen of the Chapel Royal and active at the English court. Details of Purcell's later life are sketchy. Yet we know that when he died his loss was mourned throughout the English musical world.

Purcell contributed songs and instrumental music to dozens of plays and semi-operas, but wrote only one opera, *Dido and Aeneas.* The English musical scene was not hospitable to opera during the 17th century. Commenting on this state of affairs in his letter of dedication to the semi-opera *Dioclesian* (1690), Purcell suggested that an English opera would eventually emerge from a combination of French and Italian characteristics:

> Musick is yet but in its Nonage, a forward Child, which gives hope of what it may be hereafter in *England,* when the Masters of it shall find more Encouragement. 'Tis now learning Italian, which is its best Master, and studying a little of the *French* Air, to give it somewhat more of Gayety and Fashion. Thus being farther from the Sun, we are of later Growth than our Neighbour Countries, and must be content to shake off our Barbarity by degrees.[3]

Purcell himself united the dramatic verve of French *tragédie en musique* with the melodic brilliance of Italian opera seria in *Dido and Aeneas.* That opera's remarkable sense of dramatic pacing leaves us wondering what the history of English opera might have been had its composer lived beyond the age of 36.

Principal Works

THEATER MUSIC Aside from *Dido and Aeneas,* Purcell contributed songs to a great many plays of his day, including dramas by John Dryden, William Congreve, and Thomas D'Urfey as well as various 17th-century adaptations of Shakespeare's plays. *Dioclesian, The Fairy Queen, The Indian Queen,* and *King Arthur* contain enough music to be considered semi-operas rather than merely plays with music.

SONGS Purcell wrote many songs suited for amateur musicians. The most notable collection is *Orpheus Britannicus,* published posthumously by Purcell's widow.

SACRED MUSIC Purcell's duties at Westminster Abbey required him to write many sacred works, particularly anthems. Some of these are in the older polyphonic style, others in a lighter, rhythmically lively style more closely akin to French music of the day.

Henry Purcell. *This engraved portrait appeared on the frontispiece of* Orpheus Britannicus *("The British Orpheus"), a collection of the composer's songs published by Playford of London in 1698, three years after Purcell's death.*

allowed for a colorful mixture of musical and dramatic elements. The playwright Ben Jonson (ca. 1573–1637) collaborated with the artist and stage designer Inigo Jones to produce more than thirty masques during the first three decades of the 17th century.

What came to be known as **semi-operas** flourished in the second half of the 17th century. These were essentially plays with a large proportion of musical numbers, both vocal and instrumental. The English composer Henry Purcell (see Composer Profile) contributed a number of outstanding works in this genre, most notably *Dioclesian, King Arthur,* and *The Fairy Queen.*

But the 17th century was a time of great political unrest in England, and circumstances were not favorable to the introduction of opera from abroad. The commonwealth (1649–1660), under the leadership of the puritan Oliver Cromwell, took a dim view of secular music in all its various forms. But even with the monarchy restored, England remained resistant to opera. "While other nations bestow the name of opera only on such plays whereof every word is sung," the *Gentlemen's Journal* declared in 1692, "experience hath taught us that our English genius will not relish that perpetual singing."

Purcell
Dido and Aeneas

Sung throughout, Henry Purcell's opera *Dido and Aeneas* (1689) is thus an anomaly. One of the very few English operas of its time, its origins and performance history remain shrouded in mystery. We know it was first performed by the students at a school for young ladies in Chelsea (west of London at the time), but the next known performance, in a drastically altered version, did not occur until 1700, and the earliest surviving musical sources date from well after the composer's death. *Dido and Aeneas* may have been suppressed for political reasons, either by Purcell himself or by the authorities, on the grounds of its potentially unflattering commentary on the dual reign of King William, a foreigner, and Queen Mary, daughter of Charles I. The plot, after all, deals with a foreign prince who promises to marry the queen of Carthage, then reneges and abandons her, driving her to suicide.

The foreign prince is Aeneas, a refugee from fallen Troy, who is on his way to Italy with his companions to found the city of Rome in fulfillment of a promise from the gods. They land in Carthage, ruled by Queen Dido. Aeneas and Dido are smitten with one another. She, with great foreboding, knowing his destiny, lets herself be wooed. He pledges to abandon his promised Rome. But when a witch disguised as Mercury, the messenger of the gods, orders him to leave, he obeys and abandons Dido. She, disconsolate, dies, but not before singing an exquisite lament.

Purcell's opera owes much to the French tradition, beginning with the overture, a slow introduction followed by an imitative fast section. The singing moves rapidly and fluently, with a minimum of virtuosity and no da capo arias.

When opera finally conquered England in 1711, it was through a performance of Handel's *Rinaldo,* an opera seria written in Italian by a German. What had once been scorned was now all the rage, at least among the upper classes. Rival opera companies soon sprang up in London. English opera would not emerge again in any substantial fashion for another generation. For the moment, at least, the stage belonged to Handel, Alessandro Scarlatti, Nicola Porpora, Antonio Bononcini, and other foreign-born composers of opera seria.

Gay and Pepusch
The Beggar's Opera

The English aversion to Italian opera never disappeared entirely, however. In 1728, the playwright John Gay (1685–1732) achieved a rousing success with *The Beggar's Opera,* an English-language semi-opera or **ballad opera** that portrayed common criminals rather than mythological figures or historical heroes. Gay set his words to existing tunes and engaged the German-born Johann Christoph Pepusch (1667–1752) to provide the accompaniments. The arrangements are quite simple, and the dialogue is spoken

Notable Opera Composers of the Baroque Era

Of more than a dozen works for the stage written by **Claudio Monteverdi** (1567–1643, see Chapter 8), only three have survived intact, and even those have come down to us in problematic versions. Monteverdi's long career spanned from the earliest days of opera around 1600 to the flourishing of the new public opera houses in Venice in the late 1630s and 1640s.

Francesco Cavalli (1602–1676) studied with Monteverdi and assumed his same post as music director at San Marco in Venice. He wrote more than forty operas in a style similar to that of Monteverdi's later works, mixing recitative and arialike passages fluently.

Marc' Antonio Cesti (1623–1669), a pupil of Giacomo Carissimi (discussed later in the section on sacred music), became music director at the Medici court in Florence in 1660. Only about a dozen of his more than a hundred operas have survived. His most famous work is *Il pomo d'oro* ("The Golden Apple"), a mammoth production in five acts, with 66 scenes, 24 different set designs, 48 different singing roles, and numerous ballets. The premiere in Vienna in 1667 was part of the wedding festivities of Emperor Leopold I of Austria to the Infanta Margherita of Spain. Only a court could have mounted such a lavish production.

Alessandro Scarlatti (1660–1725) was one of the first great masters of opera seria. Like Cesti, he studied with Carissimi. He held numerous positions at various courts in Rome and Naples and wrote an estimated 115 operas, of which about 50 have survived.

George Frideric Handel (1685–1759) played a central role in bringing opera seria to England. His *Rinaldo* (1711) was an instant success, and many subsequent works met with equal or even greater acclaim. Foremost among these are *Radamisto* (1720), *Giulio Cesare* (1723), *Rodelinda* (1725), *Tamerlano* (1732), *Ariodante* (1735), and *Serse* (1738).

Johann Adolph Hasse (1699–1783) studied with Alessandro Scarlatti and was the leading exponent of opera seria in German-speaking lands. His musical style was thoroughly Italian and during his lifetime he was widely regarded as the greatest composer in the genre. Nicknamed "Il Sassone" ("the Saxon") after his German place of birth, he was Metastasio's favorite composer.

---

rather than sung. As the Beggar explains at the outset, "I hope I may be forgiven, that I have not made my Opera throughout unnatural, like those in vogue; for I have no Recitative." The work took on new life in a German adaptation by Bertholt Brecht in 1928 entitled *Die Dreigroschenoper*—"The Three-Penny Opera"—with music by Kurt Weill.

SACRED MUSIC

The demand from religious institutions for new music expanded enormously in the 17th and 18th centuries. The Italian city of Bologna alone had more than 200 churches and chapels, 36 monasteries, and 28 convents by the end of the 18th century. All except the smallest of these had their own chorus and organ. Larger churches, monasteries, and convents routinely presented music by instrumental ensembles as well. Convents took on special importance for music in Italy during the Baroque era. A major increase in the number of these institutions began in the middle of the 16th century and continued well into the 17th. Families sent daughters to convents for a variety of reasons, most commonly economic: the cost of a convent dowry was only a fraction of the cost to marry a daughter into a respectable family. Illegitimate daughters were also frequently sent to convents. By 1600, the city of Milan alone had some 41 convents. And in two-thirds of these the residents cultivated polyphonic music.

Oratorio

Recognizing the power of opera to dazzle and seduce, the Vatican banned its performance in Catholic-ruled lands across the Continent during the penitential seasons of Advent (the four weeks before Christmas) and Lent (the 40 days before Easter).

Beginning around the middle of the 17th century, this operatic void was filled by the new and immediately popular genre of **oratorio.** The term comes from its original place of performance: in Italian, an *oratorio* is a prayer hall. To compensate for the lack of staged action, a narrator often related connective threads of the plot in recitative. The musical vehicles for projecting the drama, which included recitative, da capo aria, and chorus, were otherwise not much different from those of opera. (Ironically, the best known of all oratorios, Handel's *Messiah*—with no narrator, no characters, and no real plot but instead a collection of biblical texts relating to Christ's coming, death, resurrection, and promised return—is thoroughly atypical of the genre.) The performance of an oratorio was both a religious and social event. In his diary entry for March 31, 1715, the German aristocrat Johann Friedrich Armand von Uffenbach describes a performance of Antonio Caldara's oratorio *Abisai* at the palace of Prince Ruspoli, a prominent Roman patron of the arts. Caldara (1670–1736) was a prolific composer of operas (87) and oratorios (32) and one of the most respected musicians of his generation.

> People listened to the excellent voices so attentively that not a fly stirred, except when a cardinal or a lady arrived, since everyone stood up but afterward sat down again in his old place. I found also that all the voices usually heard in operas fell short of these; particularly the one called Mariotgi had something quite extraodinary and uncommonly pleasing in her singing. The leading soprano was the wife of Caldara; to be sure, she was very finished in music and sang the most difficult things with nothing but great skill, yet to me, because of the weakness of her voice, she did not long please as well as the one described above. At about the middle of the concert they had an intermission, and then liquors, frozen things, confectionery, and coffee were brought around in quantity and presented to everyone. Afterward was performed the other half of the concert, which lasted altogether four hours. I would have remained even fourteen days with great pleasure, for I certainly left with genuine astonishment, and I have never in my life heard anything to compare with this.[4]

Carissimi
Jephte

Giacomo Carissimi's *Jephte* (probably written in the second half of the 1640s, certainly before 1650) was one of the most popular of all early oratorios. The Latin-language libretto, based on the book of Judges 11, tells the story of Jephte (also spelled Jephthah), an Israelite general who promises to sacrifice to God the first thing to emerge from his house on his homecoming if God grants him victory in an impending battle. Returning home victorious, Jephte is dismayed to see his only daughter emerge first from his house to greet him. She, virtuously, urges him to fulfill his vow. The work ends with an extended lament by the daughter (who has no name, either in the Bible or in this oratorio) and her companions. This lament, in the view of one mid-17th-century Jesuit observer, "is composed with such skill that you would swear that you hear the sobs and moans of the weeping girls."[5] In Carissimi's setting, a narrator designated as the Historicus—at times a bass, at times an alto—introduces the characters and keeps the plot moving forward in brisk fashion. Except for this narrative device and the fact that it is sung in Latin, *Jephte* is musically indistinguishable from operas of the mid–17th century. Like them, it places a premium on vocal virtuosity and features a quick succession of short movements, some for solo, some for a small group of soloists, others still for chorus.

The new genre of oratorio took root in the Protestant north of Europe as well as in Catholic Italy. German composers were especially keen to set the Gospel narratives of Christ's Passion to music. The chorus played an increasingly important role in these

Bach's autograph score of the St. Matthew Passion.   *The pages shown here include the chorale that recurs throughout the work (top left), the Evangelist's narration of the earthquake that followed Christ's crucifixion (bottom left: notice the rapidly repeated notes in the basso continuo part), and an interjection of the chorus (bottom right). Those portions of the text taken from the Bible are entered throughout in red ink.*

Source: Courtesy of Staatsbibliothek zu Berlin–Preussischer Kulturbesitz, Musikabteilung mit Mendelssohn–Archiv/Mus. ms. Bach P25, S. 140/141

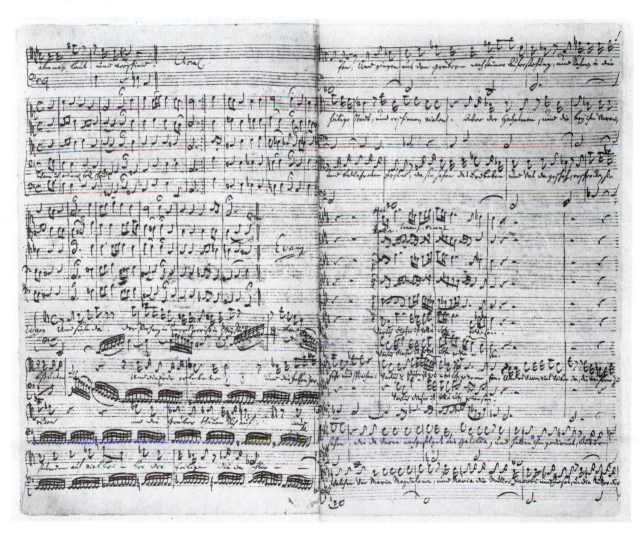

Composer Profile

George Frideric Handel
(1685–1759)

George Frideric Handel. *Handel composes at the clavichord, ca. 1730. His head is shaved so as to better accommodate a wig, but he wears a turban here, partly for warmth and partly because the sight of a man's shaved head in public was considered obscene at the time.*

Source: © Archivo Iconografico, S.A./CORBIS

Although Handel and J. S. Bach were born in the same year within 100 miles of each other, they never met, and their subsequent careers as composers could scarcely have been more different. Bach spent his entire life in central Germany, whereas Handel traveled widely in Europe. After beginning his career near home, Handel moved to Italy in 1706, where he remained for several years, establishing a name for himself as a composer of operas and oratorios.

In 1710, he returned to Germany as music director for the elector of Hanover but soon journeyed to England where a production of his opera *Rinaldo* the following year won great acclaim. In 1712, still in the service of the elector, he took up residence in England, where his music continued to find favor. When the elector ascended the English throne as George I in 1714, Handel was thus perfectly positioned to enjoy the new king's patronage and support. He associated himself with the newly founded Royal Academy of Music in 1720, but like so many operatic enterprises of the time, it eventually foundered due to financial weakness, political intrigue, and quarrels among performers. Handel later helped found another opera series at the King's Theater in 1729, but like the first undertaking, this one was never financially secure. It was also involved in a rivalry with a competing company—the Opera of the Nobility—that set many critical tongues wagging. By the mid-1730s, the composer was devoting more and more of his energies to oratorio, and he abandoned opera altogether in 1741.

Handel was one of the first composers whose music has remained steadily popular with the public and has therefore come down to us in an uninterrupted performance tradition. This is not to say that performance styles have gone unchanged: Mozart, for example, was commissioned to "modernize" the orchestration of *Messiah* to include clarinets in the late 1780s, and in the 19th century, Mendelssohn and Brahms would make similar arrangements of other of Handel's works.

Handel is buried in the "Poets' Corner" in Westminster Abbey, an honor reflecting both the high esteem in which his contemporaries held him and the then relatively new idea that composers were artists on the same level as poets. He was also the first composer to be the subject of a separately published biography, John Mainwairing's *Memoirs of the Late G. F. Handel,* published in London in 1760.

In 1784, 25 years after Handel's death, Westminster Abbey was the scene of an enormous festival dedicated to his music. The historian Charles

Burney wrote the following fond reminiscence of the composer for the occasion:

> The figure of Handel was large and he was somewhat corpulent and unwieldy in his motions; but his countenance, which I remember as perfectly as that of any man I saw but yesterday, was full of fire and dignity, and as such impressed ideas of superiority and genius. He was impetuous, rough and peremptory in his manners and conversation, but totally devoid of ill-nature or malevolence; indeed, there was an original humor and pleasantry in his most lively sallies of anger or impatience, which, with his broken English, were extremely risible. His natural propensity to wit and humor and happy manner of relating common occurrences in an uncommon way enabled him to throw persons and things into very ridiculous attitudes.[6]

Principal Works

OPERAS Handel's *Rinaldo* (1711) was one of the first Italian operas to win public acclaim in London, and the composer was quick to build on this early success. The most acclaimed of his subsequent operas (all in Italian) are *Giulio Cesare* (1724), *Rodelinda* (1725), *Orlando* (1733), *Ariodante* (1735), and *Serse* (1738). Unlike his oratorios, Handel's operas were almost entirely forgotten after his death: only one of them is known to have been performed on a stage anywhere between 1754 and 1920. Thanks to the combined efforts of scholars and musicians, opera lovers have recently begun to rediscover the wonders of this repertory.

ORATORIOS, ODES, AND CANTATAS Handel wrote Italian oratorios early in his career. *Esther* (1732), his first in English and the first oratorio of any kind performed in London, set off a great wave of enthusiasm for the genre there. Many successes followed: *Saul* (1739), *Israel in Egypt* (1739), *Messiah* (1742), *Samson* (1743), *Semele* (1744), *Hercules* (1745), *Judas Maccabeus* (1747), *Joshua* (1748), and *Jephtha* (1752).

Handel also set to music a number of nonsacred texts—odes and serenades—that are very much in the spirit of the oratorio. Among the more notable of these are *Alexander's Feast* and the *Ode for Saint Cecilia's Day* (both set to texts by the poet John Dryden) and *L'Allegro, il Penseroso ed il Moderato* (to a text by John Milton). Less well known but well worth exploring are the many secular cantatas, mostly early works in Italian and mostly for solo

KEY DATES IN THE LIFE OF GEORGE FRIDERIC HANDEL

1685	Born in Halle (central German) on February 23
1697	Becomes assistant organist at Halle Cathedral at the age of 12
1702	Enters law school but leaves after a year
1703	Moves to Hamburg and plays violin in one of the opera houses there
1705	Composes two opere serie, which are produced in Hamburg
1706	Travels throughout Italy, where he continues to write operas and composes his first oratorios
1710	Returns to Germany as Kapellmeister to the elector of Hanover
1711	First visit to England; his opera *Rinaldo* is greeted there with praise
1712	Takes up permanent residence in England
1714	Handel's German patron, the elector of Hanover, becomes King George I of England
1720	Appointed musical director of the new Royal Academy of Music as composer and conductor of operas
1727	Becomes a British subject
1732	Produces his first English oratorio, *Esther,* to great public acclaim
1741	Abandons the stage and turns his attention almost entirely to oratorio
1742	*Messiah* is greeted enthusiastically at its premiere in Dublin
1751	Undergoes a series of unsuccessful operations to save his failing eyesight; later suffers from total blindness
1759	Dies on April 14 and is buried in Westminster Abbey

voice and instruments. Handel drew on these compositions later in life and reworked a number of movements for later operas and oratorios.

SACRED MUSIC At various times and places, Handel wrote music for the Roman Catholic and Lutheran churches, but the bulk of his sacred music, reflecting his long residence in his adopted home, was for the Anglican church. These works include the Chandos Anthems and music for various royal weddings, coronations, and funerals.

ORCHESTRAL MUSIC In addition to his concerti grossi and concertos for organ (see Chapter 10), Handel also wrote several orchestral suites that remain great favorites: three suites called *Water Music*

(written for a royal procession down the River Thames in 1717) and one entitled *Music for the Royal Fireworks,* composed in 1749 to celebrate the Treaty of Aix-la-Chapelle, which ended the War of Austrian Succession.

KEYBOARD AND CHAMBER MUSIC Handel's works for harpsichord are not as often played or studied today as those by Bach, but they were well known during the composer's lifetime. Most of them fall under the category of suites or variations. They were directed primarily at amateurs, as were the sonatas op. 1 (for flute, recorder, oboe, or violin and basso continuo) and the trio sonatas of op. 2 and op. 5.

compositions. Johann Sebastian Bach's *Saint Matthew Passion* and *Saint John Passion* are in effect Lutheran oratorios, combining a narrator (the Evangelist), da capo arias, and choruses, many of which incorporate Protestant chorale melodies. Bach never wrote an opera, but his oratorios give us a sense of what a Bach opera would have sounded like if he had.

George Frideric Handel cultivated the oratorio with particular zeal from the 1730s onward. This was due in large part to the growing disaffection of London audiences with Italian opera around this time. Handel's later oratorios are all in English. Working with his librettists, Handel managed to tap into a growing sense of English nationalism, one manifestation of which was a tacit belief that Old Testament events validated English preeminence. Biblical Israel, in essence, was understood as a metaphor for England, which was enjoying God's favor as Israel had in the past. Besides the generically atypical *Messiah*, Handel's most popular oratorios of his late period include *Israel in Egypt, Judas Maccabeus,* and *Joshua.*

Motet and Mass

The same forces that introduced new possibilities for the madrigal also helped expand options in the realm of nondramatic sacred music. The polyphonic motet continued to thrive throughout the Continent. In Italy, Benedetto Marcello (1686–1739) was admired as much for his sacred music as for his operas. A large body of sacred choral music emanated from England in the 17th century from the pen of such composers as Henry Lawes (1596–1662) and his brother William Lawes (1602–1645), John Blow (1648–1708), and Henry Purcell. In France, the *grand motet* combined vocal soloists, chorus, and orchestra in a series of contrasting movements to a sacred text in Latin. Lully, Michel-Richard Delalande (1657–1726), and François Couperin (1668–1733) all contributed to the genre.

Much sacred music from the latter part of the Baroque era strikes many listeners today as operatic in its dazzling virtuosity. But before the early 19th century, no clear distinction was made between sacred and secular musical styles. Johann Sebastian Bach, for example, transformed any number of movements from secular works written in honor of a monarch into sacred works written in honor of God. Like many sacred compositions honoring Saint Cecilia, the patron saint of music, the Kyrie of Alessandro Scarlatti's *Messa di S. Cecilia* is as florid and virtuosic in its own way as any dramatic music of its time (1720).

We should also keep in mind that a good deal of sacred music was tailored to fit quite practical needs. The long orchestral introduction to Handel's *Zadok the Priest,* for example, allowed the royal procession sufficient time to make its way down the long center aisle of Westminster Abbey for the coronation of King George II in 1727. The effect of the swelling orchestra, the dramatic entrance of the voices, and the arrival of the new king were of such overwhelming effect that the anthem has been used in every British coronation since that time.

Handel
Zadok the Priest

Cantata

Throughout the Baroque era the term **cantata** was applied to many different kinds of vocal works, from sacred to secular. The word itself derives from the Italian *cantare,* "to sing," and it was used to denote both small- and large-scale works, ranging from a solo singer with basso continuo to a large ensemble of chorus, soloists, and instruments. A cantata could be a single movement or multiple movements. Many 17th-century cantatas are works in the tradition of the solo madrigal. J. S. Bach in fact used the designation *cantata* only for his solo cantatas; the broader application of the term originated with 19th-century editors of his works. For works with chorus and orchestra, he more often used terms like *Concerto, Motetto,* or *Kirchen-Stück* ("church piece").

The body of works we now think of as Bach's cantatas embody many different traditions, ranging from motetlike movements and chorale harmonizations for chorus to virtuosic solos and duets, often with the participation of additional solo instruments as well as instrumental ensemble, basso continuo, or both.

The opening chorus of *Jesu, der du meine Seele* ("Jesus, Who My Soul") is a tour de force of Baroque compositional techniques, synthesizing diverse traditions, including ostinato, chorale, ritornello, and motet.

J. S. Bach
Jesu, der du meine Seele, BWV 78

The ostinato passage in this movement is the four-measure figure in the bass line at the opening of the work that descends by half steps from G to D. This descending chromatic fourth, known as the *passus duriusculus* ("painful passage"), had long been associated with moments of anguish. Migrating through various voices and instruments, it is present in almost every measure of the movement.

This first movement is also permeated with the melody of the chorale from which the cantata takes its name. The words and melody of *Jesu, der du meine Seele* would have been familiar to any of the parishioners hearing the first performance of this cantata. The melody falls into distinct phrases and is always presented by the soprano (beginning in measure 21). Thus the chorale melody presents a kind of superstructure above the ostinato figure.

The movement opens with an extended passage for the orchestra alone, with a dotted-rhythm melody running above the ostinato in the bass. The rhythm of this triple-meter melody is reminiscent of the sarabande, a dance common to many instrumental

Composer Profile

Johann Sebastian Bach
(1685–1750)

Born into a family of musicians in central Germany, Bach synthesized European music of his time without ever really leaving home. He held down a succession of different jobs in his early career, including positions as organist (Mühlhausen), as violinist and concert master to a court orchestra (Weimar), and as court composer (Cöthen). Like any good 18th-century composer, Bach wrote what was demanded of him. Thus a great many of Bach's organ works date from his early years at Mühlhausen, and many of the best known orchestral works, including the Brandenburg Concertos, date from the years in Cöthen.

Bach's final position—as cantor of St. Thomas's Church in Leipzig—required him to produce large quantities of music for worship services, and it was here that he wrote the vast majority of his more than 200 cantatas. Had he spread this output out over his full 27 years in Leipzig, the accomplishment would be remarkable enough. But through detailed studies of paper, handwriting, and other evidence, scholars have been able to demonstrate that Bach actually wrote about 150 cantatas within his first 3 years in Leipzig at the rate of roughly one a week. When one considers the tasks involved for Bach—composing the work, writing out the score, supervising the copying of the parts, rehearsing, and performing— and this week after week, all in addition to attending to his duties as a teacher at the church's school, the achievement seems almost superhuman.

The composer was not entirely happy in Leipzig and thought of moving elsewhere. As he confided to a friend in 1730,

> [A]s I find that (1) the duties are by far not so agreeable as they were described to me originally; and (2) that

Johann Sebastian Bach.   *To at least some extent, portraits are often self-portraits, in that the subject routinely chooses the back-drop and props. Here, Bach holds in his hand a copy of his* Canon Triplex, BWV 1076. *The choice of works is revealing: this is a puzzle canon whose three notated voices produce six different voices that can be played in an astonishing variety of permutations. Within the portrait itself, the canon is resolved by creating a new voice, through inversion, out of each of the notated parts. The inversion of the uppermost voice enters at a fourth above; the middle voice enters at a fifth above; and the bass (which is similar to the opening of the bass line in the Goldberg Variations) enters at a fourth below. Each voice works in counterpoint against not only its own inversion, but against the two other themes and their inversions as well. And this is only one of many possible solutions to this canon.*

Source: Stadtgeschichtliches Museum Leipzig

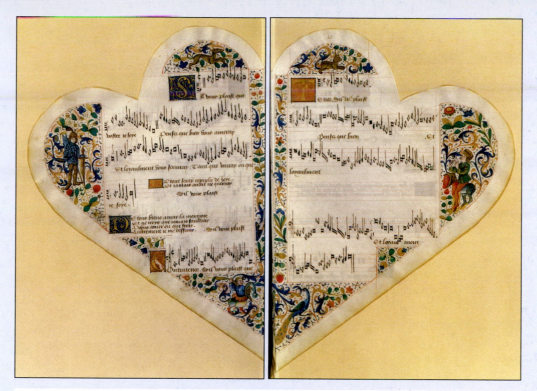

PLATE 7   The Chansonnier Cordiforme. The most famous of all 15th-century chansonniers, this manuscript consists entirely of love songs. It is shaped like a heart when closed, a double heart when opened. None of the works is attributed to a composer in the manuscript, but we know from other sources that it includes music by Du Fay, Binchois, Busnois, and Ockeghem.
[Bibliotheque Nationale de France]

PLATE 8   Music and the fountain of pleasure. From a lavishly illustrated codex on astronomy produced in northern Italy around 1470, this miniature shows the confluence of music, wine, and erotic love. Three different types of musician are shown: singers in the upper left, wind players (performing on the shawm) in the upper right, and a lutenist in the lower right. One of the shawm players is overcome by laughter, a comment on the ludicrousness of this otherwise terribly earnest scene.
["De Sphaera" (Music and the Fountain of Pleasure), MS. lat 209, X.2.14. Biblioteca Estensa Universitaria]

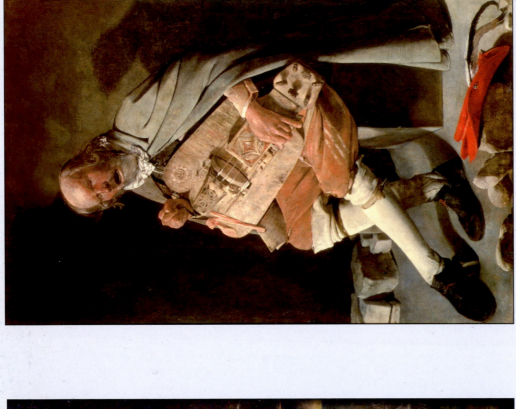

PLATE 10 **The Unwritten Tradition.** Certain instruments, such as the bagpipe and hurdy-gurdy, were invariably associated with the lower classes and the tradition of unwritten music, in contrast to the composed and notated music of the elite. The blind peasant accompanying himself on the hurdy-gurdy is portrayed here with a powerful nobility that suggests a respect for the emotional power of this music. The scene would probably have reminded many viewers of the blind poet Homer, who related the *Illiad* and *Odyssey* in the form of sung verse long before the words were ever written down.
[Georges de la Tour (1593–1652), "The Hurdy Gurdy Player," 1620's, oil on canvas, 162 cm. x 105 cm./Musée des Beaux–Arts, Nantes, France/Giraudon/Bridgeman Art Library]

PLATE 9 **Elisabeth Jacquet de La Guerre.** Renowned as both a composer and harpsichordist, Elisabeth Jacquet (1665–1729) was a favorite of the French royal court from the age of five. She married the organist Marin de La Guerre in 1684 and published her first set of harpsichord pieces three years later. Jacquet de la Guerre was the first Frenchwoman to compose an opera (*Cephale et Procris*, 1694), and she later published sonatas and sacred cantatas as well. She was also in great demand at the court for her improvisations on the harpsichord.
[Francoise de Troy, "Portrait of Elisabeth–Claude Jacquet de la Guerre," (circa 1694–1695), oil on canvas, 47-3/8 in. x 36-3/4 in./Private Collection, London]

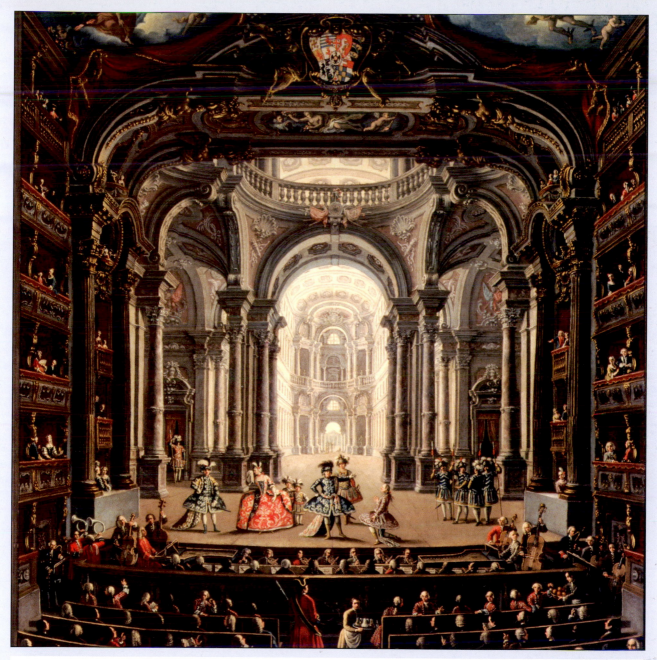

PLATE 11 Opera seria. This scene of a performance of Francesco Feo's *Arsace* (1740) at the Teatro Regio in Turin (northern Italy) has much to tell us about the nature of *opera seria*. The soloist has quite literally taken center stage. In *opera seria*, action was typically suspended for the duration of an aria, allowing the soloist to display his or her talents without fear of competition from anyone else on stage. The orchestra, relatively small by later standards, is typical of its time: 18 string players, two oboists, two hornists (to the far left), and two basso continuo ensembles, one of which directs the orchestra, the other of which accompanies the recitatives. The servers in the aisles and the casual attitude of many of the spectators suggest an atmosphere more like that found in a sporting arena than an opera house today. "I shall have frequent occasion to mention the noise and inattention at the musical exhibitions in Italy," the Englishman Charles Burney would observe in the 1770s. Some members of the audience are talking while others follow the libretto or use a spyglass for a closer look at the stage. The bailiff, weapon in hand, is ready to impose control should the audience become too rowdy. Primarily a symbol of royal power, bailiffs were in fact called upon to exercise their authority from time to time. Stage designs, often extremely elaborate, made use of the most technologically advanced machinery. The back of the stage here has been painted to create the illusion of depth.

[Pietro Domenico Oliviero, (1672–1754), "The Teatro Reale in Turin," oil on canvas/Museo Civico, Turin, Italy/The Bridgeman Art Library]

PLATE 12   The Illusion of Order. In his *Les hasards heureux de l'escarpolette* ("The Pleasant Dangers of the Swing") of 1767, Jean-Honoré Fragognard (1732–1806), a contemporary of Haydn, captures perfectly the kind of artistic playfulness and ambiguity so typical of late 18th-century art. The image works on several levels: it is at once innocent, erotic, and comic. The virtuous-looking young man on the right pushes the young lady on the swing (he uses ropes, for it would be improper actually to touch her). His earnestness contrasts with the rapture of the young man—a rival for her affections?—spying voyeuristically on the scene from the bushes on the left. How are we to understand the young lady's strange expression? Is she aware of the man on the left? Has she lost her shoe by accident, or kicked it off deliberately, and if deliberately, is it to reward or punish her concealed admirer? Much of the music of this era moves back and forth between order and disruption in an analogous manner. The music of Haydn, in particular, is often simultaneously regular and irregular, serious and humorous.

[Jean-Honore Fragonard, (1732–1806), "The Swing," oil on canvas/Musée Lambinet, Versailles, France/Bridgeman Giraudon/Lauros/Bridgeman Art Library]

quite a few of the bonuses attached to the post have been withdrawn; that (3) the cost of living is very high here; and (4) that the authorities are rather strangely hostile to music; that I have to live in a state of almost constant struggle; that envy prevails and vexations are numerous; I find myself, so help me God, compelled to seek my fortune elsewhere. . . .

My salary here is seven hundred thalers, and when there are more burials than usual, the added fees raise this proportionately higher. But whenever the air is a little more healthful, the loss is great. Last year the fees for common burials showed a deficit of a hundred thalers. With four hundred thalers I could support myself in Thuringia more comfortably than here with twice that amount, for the cost of living in Leipzig is exorbitant.[7]

Bach's surviving sons were all successful composers in their own right. Indeed, Carl Philipp Emanuel Bach (1714–1788) would eventually become more famous than his father, even during the elder Bach's lifetime. Johann Christian Bach (1735–1782), sometimes called the "London Bach" because of his eventual home, was one of Mozart's favorite composers. Wilhelm Friedemann Bach (1710–1784), said to be perhaps the most musically gifted of all Bach's sons, met repeated misfortunes in his career and died in poverty.

In contrast to Handel, Bach was largely forgotten as a composer in the decades after his death. Very few of his works were published during his lifetime, and although the *Well-Tempered Clavier* and some other keyboard works continued to circulate in manuscript, the vocal music lay dormant for many years. The first stirrings of a Bach revival came around 1800 with the publication of the first biography of the composer (by Johann Nikolaus Forkel, in 1802) and several of the motets in score. But the big breakthrough came in 1828 when the young Felix Mendelssohn performed the *Saint Matthew Passion* in Leipzig. It was a musical revelation for listeners and composers alike. Western composers began almost without exception to study Bach's music with care and devotion, and his influence remains inescapable even today.

KEY DATES IN THE LIFE OF JOHANN SEBASTIAN BACH

1685 Born on March 21 in Eisenach, Germany, the son of a town musician

1703 Appointed organist at Arnstadt

1705 Walks to Lübeck, some 215 miles away, to hear and meet Dietrich Buxtehude

1707 Appointed organist at a larger church in Mühlhausen

1708 Appointed court organist and chamber musician (later concertmaster) to the Duke of Weimar

1717 Appointed music director at the court of Anhalt-Cöthen; writes many of his works for orchestra (including the Brandenburg Concertos) while in this position

1722 Succeeds Johann Kuhnau as cantor of St. Thomas's School in Leipzig; writes most of his cantatas in this position

1747 Visits his son Carl Philipp Emanuel in Potsdam and improvises for King Frederick II ("The Great"); the improvisation eventually takes the form of *A Musical Offering*

1750 Dies in Leipzig on July 28

Principal Works

CANTATAS Bach wrote an estimated 280 sacred cantatas, of which about 200 have survived; he also wrote about 30 secular cantatas for royal birthdays, marriages, civic occasions, and university ceremonies.

These works are remarkable in both quantity and quality. Bach's productivity was staggering: he composed the bulk of his sacred cantatas in the span of his first three or four years in Leipzig, producing a new one almost every week. These works appeared in three cycles over the years 1723–1724 (first cycle), 1724–1725 (second cycle), and 1725–1727 (third cycle). Bach began work on each cycle with the First Sunday after Trinity and carried each through to the following Trinity Sunday a year later. For the first cycle, he drew on compositions from his years in Weimar and Cöthen, but for the most part he was writing essentially a new work every Sunday. The second cycle is the most systematic of the three, consisting of chorale cantatas, in which the melody of the closing chorale figures into one or more of the work's other movements as well. Bach also wrote cantatas for special Feast Days such as the Feast of Saint John and the Festival of the Reformation.

Bach drew on three different kinds of sources for his cantata texts: (1) the biblical passages to be read in church that particular day; (2) a chorale text associated with that particular day; and (3) a new poetic interpretation of sentiments consistent with that particular day. A typical cantata mixes all of these elements. Like Schütz and many other Protestant German musicians before him, Bach considered himself an interpreter of the sacred word, using music to convey the spiritual meaning of any given text.

Bach explored a variety of instrumental and vocal forces in his cantatas, as well as a variety of formal plans. Some, like *Jauchzet Gott in allen Landen*, BWV 51, are for soloist; others are for soloists and chorus (like *Jesu, der du meine Seele*, BWV 78; see Anthology). All but the earliest cantatas make use of recitative, and many feature prominent instrumental solo parts in one or more movements, such as the trumpet part in *Jauchzet Gott in allen Landen* or the oboe part in the bass aria of *Jesu, der du meine Seele*.

PASSIONS The music for Holy Week—the period leading up to Easter, commemorating the betrayal and crucifixion of Christ—was of particular importance in the German Protestant church. Bach wrote five different settings of the Passion, but only those based on the biblical accounts of Saint Matthew and Saint John survive. These are enormous works featuring a narrator (the Evangelist) and individual characters (Christ, the disciples) that sing texts taken from the gospels. The gospel text settings are interspersed with chorales, recitatives, and arias set to contemporary poetry. In the *Saint Matthew Passion*, Bach sets off the words of Christ by scoring them to a "halo" of stringed accompaniment.

MASS AND MOTETS Bach's seven motets are for a cappella chorus, four of them for double chorus. Some of the surviving performance materials indicate that instruments may have doubled the voice parts on occasion. These works were written on commission for special occasions, probably funerals. He also wrote numerous settings of mass movements, but his one integrated cycle, the great Mass in B minor, consists of a variety of movements culled from works written over a period of some two decades.

CHAMBER MUSIC Bach wrote quantities of chamber music for a variety of instruments. Many of these works are now lost, but most notable among those that survive are the sonatas for harpsichord with viola da gamba (3), violin (6), and flute (2). The three sonatas and three partitas for solo violin remain a touchstone of the violin repertory, demanding great virtuosity within a contrapuntal framework remarkable for a single instrument of this kind. The six suites for solo cello are also a staple of that instrument's repertory.

ORCHESTRAL MUSIC The most famous of Bach's works for orchestra are the six concerti grossi dedicated to the Margrave of Brandenburg, the so-called Brandenburg Concertos. Each is scored differently.

The first and third concertos feature no individual soloist, and the third is for strings alone. The second is a brilliantly scored concerto for trumpet, recorder, oboe, violin, and strings. The fourth features a solo violin and two solo recorders. The fifth incorporates an extended solo section for harpsichord, one of three solo instruments in the work, the others being violin and flute. The sixth's unusual scoring calls for low strings (no violins, no violas) to accompany two solo violas and two solo viola da gambas.

Bach also wrote solo concertos for violin, two violins, violin and oboe, and one to four harpsichords. The four orchestral suites all bear evidence of French influence, particularly in their French overtures; the second of these suites features a solo flute throughout.

ORGAN MUSIC Bach generally made a clear distinction between his harpsichord and organ music, almost invariably drawing on the full resources of the latter instrument in ways that made this music inaccessible to the harpsichord. The organ works span a great many genres, including chorale harmonizations, chorale preludes, toccatas, preludes and fugues, trios, and solo concertos. These last are arrangements of orchestral concertos by Duke Johann Ernst of Saxe-Weimar and by Antonio Vivaldi; BWV 593 is an arrangement of Vivaldi's op. 3, no. 8 (Anthology). Here, as in virtually all other genres, Bach was constantly exploring the works of other composers, both predecessors and contemporaries, to learn new ways of writing music.

HARPSICHORD MUSIC A good deal of the harpsichord music is didactic, intended to serve composers and performers alike: the Two- and Three-Part Inventions, the *Well-Tempered Clavier* (see Chapter 10), the *Clavier-Übung,* and the short pieces from the three *Clavier-Büchlein* ("Little Book of Keyboard Pieces") written for his eldest son, Wilhelm Friedemann Bach, and his second wife, Anna Magdalena Bach. The suite was a genre

of special interest to Bach: his keyboard works of this kind include the so-called English and French suites (each a set of six suites), and the six partitas. He also transcribed many orchestral concertos by Vivaldi and others for harpsichord; the *Concerto in the Italian Taste* (better known simply as the Italian Concerto) is an original work for a single keyboard that imitates the tutti and solo alternations so characteristic of Italian concertos of the time.

CANONIC WORKS AND FUGAL WORKS OF THE FINAL DECADE In the last decade of his life, Bach devoted increasing attention to canonic and fugal works. The *Musikalisches Opfer* ("Musical Offering") is a set of elaborations on a theme given to him personally by Frederick II ("The Great") of Prussia. Bach had been visiting his son Carl Philipp Emanuel in Potsdam in 1747 when the Prussian ruler asked him to improvise a set of variations on a theme of Frederick's invention. Bach complied but also took the "Royal Theme" back to Leipzig and eventually presented the monarch with a dazzling set of variations, including two ricercars, several canons, and a number of works in a free style.

The *Kunst der Fuge* ("Art of Fugue") is a quasi-encyclopedic compilation of fugues on a single basic theme. The cycle remains unfinished. Legend has it that Bach was struck blind when he entered a countersubject on the notes B-A-C-H (that is, B♭, A, C, B♮, "H" being the German term for B♮), but he had been losing his eyesight for some time. The work is written in open score, with no indication of performance medium, and it has been performed on organ and harpsichord, as well as by instrumental ensembles of all sorts.

The so-called *Goldberg Variations* (Anthology; see Chapter 10), the puzzle canon BWV 1076, and the canonic variations on the Christmas hymn *Vom Himmel hoch* (later reworked by Stravinsky in the 20th century) also belong to the final decade of Bach's life.

suites. This material functions as a ritornello throughout the entire movement, returning between the successive entrances of the chorus:

The Ritornello Structure of Bach, *Jesu, der du meine Seele*, BWV 78, Opening Movement

Section	Rit. I	Ch. I	Rit. II	Ch. II	Rit. III	Ch. III	Rit. IV	Ch. IV	Rit. V	Ch. V	Rit. VI
Measure	1	17	37	49	68	73	85	89	99	107	140
Tonality	g				d		F		B♭	→ g	g (G)

Finally, by dividing the text into six distinct sections, each with its own thematic material, and each with its own set of points of imitation, Bach in effect employs the structure of the motet for the choral portions of the opening movement.

Subsequent movements alternate between aria and recitative. The second-movement duet and following recitative and aria pair for tenor (the latter omitted from the Anthology for reasons of space) are masterpieces of word-painting.

Formally, Bach constructs this duet as a da capo aria:

THE DA CAPO ARIA STRUCTURE OF BACH, *JESU, DER DU MEINE SEELE*, SECOND MOVEMENT			
	Section	**Measure numbers**	**Harmony**
A	Ritornello I	1–8	B♭ major
	Solo I	9–42	B♭ major
	Ritornello II	43–50	B♭ major
B	Solo II	51–60	G minor → C minor
	Ritornello III	61–64	C minor
	Solo III	65–80	C minor → D minor
	Ritornello IV	81–82	D minor → F major
	Solo IV	83–98	F major (= V/B♭), A section da capo

The bass aria is a duet between the vocalist and the oboist. This kind of writing for voice and solo instrument occurs frequently in Bach's music. The cantata concludes with a harmonized setting of the chorale tune *Jesu, der du meine Seele*, which had provided the cantus firmus for the opening movement, rounding out the whole to provide a sense of cyclical symmetry.

CONCLUSION

The synthesis of word, rhythm, and pitch that had been so important in the early decades of the Baroque remained equally important at the end of the era, even if musical styles and genres had changed over time. Yet throughout this same period of time, composers devoted more and more of their energies to writing music without words at all. And it is to this instrumental repertory that we turn in Chapter 10.

Instrumental Music, 1600–1750

The same forces that drove changes in vocal music during the Baroque helped transform instrumental music as well. Even though they were working without texts, composers of instrumental music sought to move listeners by writing works that evoked human passions, in keeping with then current beliefs about the relationship between music and emotion. The new emphasis on homophonic texture, a greater sense of rhythmic and melodic freedom, and a strong desire for timbral contrast animates much of the instrumental music written in the 17th and early 18th centuries.

INSTRUMENTS OF THE BAROQUE ERA

Over the course of the 17th century, many instruments began to acquire their modern form, including those of the violin family (violin, viola, and cello), the harpsichord, and a variety of winds and brasses.

The keyboard repertory of the Baroque era reflects the growing size and quality of the instruments themselves. The period from the middle of the 16th century through the early decades of the 18th was a golden age of organ and harpsichord making. The technical advances in instrument building were at once inspired by and inspiring to the composers who wrote for the keyboard.

The clavichord was valued as a particularly expressive instrument because of the control a player could exert over the contact between the striking blade, or tangent, and the string. Because the tangent is attached directly to the key, performers could create a kind of vibrato by moving the finger up and down slightly after a note was struck but still sounding. The Germans called the effect *Bebung,* or "trembling."

Two basic types of harpsichord emerged during the Baroque era, Italian and Flemish. Italian harpsichords generally featured only one keyboard (also called a *manual*), the Flemish two. By the early 18th century, two manuals had become the norm across Europe. Instruments on the whole became larger, louder, and brighter, with an increasing variety of stops. Smaller versions of the harpsichord included the virginal and the spinet. Like the clavichord, these were instruments for the intimacy of the home, limited in the volume of sound they could produce.

For all their versatility, the harpsichord and its plucked string relatives could not produce gradations of volume. The chief technical obstacle was to develop a mechanism that would allow a hammer to strike a string with variable force, but then immediately fall away without ricocheting, so the string could reverberate freely. The Florentine instrument maker Bartolomeo Cristofori (1655–1730) achieved the earliest break-through in this endeavor, building about twenty instruments that he called *gravicembalo col piano e forte* ("harpsichord with soft and loud") between 1709 and 1726. These earli-est pianos—known generally as fortepianos—attracted little attention at the time, how-ever. It was not until about 1760 that the instrument began seriously to challenge the preeminence of the harpsichord (see Chapter 9).

Organ building made great strides during the late 15th and early 16th centuries, but the craft enjoyed its golden age from about 1550 through 1750, particularly in northern Europe, in what is now northern France, Belgium, the Netherlands, northern Germany, Denmark, and Sweden. Important organ builders of this era include Arp Schnitger (1648–1719), who worked in northern Germany, and Gottfried Silbermann (1683–1753), who was active in southern Germany and what is now eastern France. Silbermann was also known for his harpsichords and early pianos. The more monumen-tal instruments of this period feature three or even four manuals, a large independent pedal division, and more than sixty speaking stops. Each of the manuals controlled one or more sets of pipes: the *Hauptwerk* (the Great), the *Brustwerk* (the Breastworks), placed in front of the organist, and the *Rückpositif* (Chair organ, so called because it was sometimes placed under the organist's bench). Churches invested large sums of money in their organs.

The orchestra in the modern sense of the term—an ensemble of players with more than one to a part, at least in the string section—emerged gradually over the course of the Baroque era. In 17th-century Italy, any large church in a major city maintained its own *cappella* consisting of instrumentalists as well as singers. Court orchestras rose to special prominence in France and Germany. The fame of Louis XIV's "24 Violinists of the King"—a core group of 24 string players, augmented by winds and percussion as needed—spread throughout Europe and, like the palace of Versailles itself, became a model for other monarchs to emulate.

The public concert—that is, a concert taking place outside the church or theater and open to the public—remained a relatively unusual phenomenon throughout the Baroque era. Convents and orphanages offered public concerts from time to time, but regular performances in the same locale by the same musicians were quite rare before the 18th century. Taverns and public rooms sometimes sponsored musical performances, and in London, a coal dealer by the name of Thomas Britton offered concerts in his lodg-ings for a decade or so around 1700. He charged admission and aroused great admiration among his contemporaries for his cultural and entrepreneurial spirit in spite of his mod-est social standing. Handel is said to have performed at some of these gatherings.

Amateur societies also offered public performances from time to time. In 1702, the composer Georg Philipp Telemann organized the Leipzig Collegium Musicum, con-sisting primarily of university students, which performed weekly in local coffeehouses. J. S. Bach directed the ensemble during the 1730s and 1740s. The most important venue for public performances in France was the *Concert spirituel* ("spiritual concert") series, founded by Anne Danican Philidor (1681–1728) in 1725.

A student orchestra of the 1740s. *Students from the University of Jena's Collegium Musicum perform in the town square in conjunction with a civic ceremony or festivity of some kind. The music is clearly festive in nature, for the large orchestra includes trumpets and timpani. The harpsichordist, at center, conducts from the keyboard. J. S. Bach led a similar ensemble in nearby Leipzig after 1729; indeed, the orchestra here is similar to that called for in Bach's Fourth Orchestral Suite.*

Source: Museum fur Kunst und Gewerbe, Hamburg, Germany

INSTRUMENTAL GENRES OF THE BAROQUE ERA

Instrumental genres of the Baroque tend to be quite flexible in their terminology. The sonata, concerto, and suite were the most important genres of music for ensembles; the keyboard repertory encompassed sonatas, suites, and a variety of other formal types.

Sonata

The term **sonata** was used quite broadly in the early Baroque era and did not acquire its modern, more specialized meaning until well into the 18th century. In Italian, *sonata* means simply "that which is sounded," meaning played on instruments, as opposed to that which is sung, a *cantata*. The term was something of a catchall for instrumental works of all kinds, including those for a large ensemble with more than one player to a part. In general, a Baroque sonata had no fixed number or order of movements.

By the end of the 17th century, however, one distinctive type of sonata—the **trio sonata**—had acquired a relatively fixed form. As its name implies, a trio sonata has three notated parts: two higher voices above a basso continuo. The basso continuo, although a single musical line, might be realized by two or even more players. The two upper voices were usually written for violins, but composers, publishers, and performers were generally flexible about these designations. Thus the title pages of many published trio sonatas state that the upper voices can be performed by two violins, or two flutes, or two oboes, or any combination of these instruments (violin and oboe, flute and oboe, and so forth). The music, in other words, tends not to be idiomatic to any particular instrument. Because most of these works were written for amateur performers, they tend to be relatively undemanding technically.

By the middle of the 17th century, a distinction had emerged between two different types of trio sonata: the **sonata da camera** and the **sonata da chiesa.** The sonata da camera ("sonata for the chamber") consists of a suite of dances (see later for a discussion

The Art of Embellishment

Instrumental soloists, like vocal soloists, were routinely expected to embellish their musical lines during the Baroque era. The illustration here, from a 1710 edition of a trio sonata by Arcangelo Corelli (op. 5), indicates what that might involve. The bottom line is the basso continuo and the middle line the violin part as Corelli wrote it. The top line, however, purports to show how Corelli himself, a famous violin virtuoso, actually played the line. It was the slower passages in particular that Corelli embellished. On the page shown here, for example, from the middle of op. 5, no. 1, only the passages marked adagio or grave are embellished.

Embellishment also extended to matters of rhythm. Ample evidence suggests, for example, that performers routinely played two notes of equal value in a single beat as if they had been written with unequal values, the first slightly longer than the second. This practice—known by its French name of *notes inégales* ("unequal notes")—is mentioned in more than eighty-five French treatises published between roughly 1550 and 1810, as well as in other treatises from elsewhere across the Continent. But exactly how and when to apply it remains open to considerable debate. None of the evidence that historians have culled from the relevant treatises provides an unambiguous answer. Now as then, it is the performer who must decide for any given work how to put the theory of *notes inégales* into practice.

Source: Edizioni Scelte

of the suite as a genre). The sonata da chiesa ("sonata for the church") was so called because of its suitability for performance within the liturgy. In his *Dictionnaire de musique* of 1703, Sebastian de Brossard points out that the sonata da chiesa is "proper for the Church" because it "usually begins with a serious and majestic movement, suited to the dignity and sanctity of the place." The imitative movements that follow sustain this aura of serious dignity.

The term *sonata* also applied to works for solo instrument (meaning either a solo instrument with basso continuo or a solo keyboard instrument). These ranged from a single movement to multiple movements. For multimovement sonatas of all kinds, composers sought to provide a variety of tempos and effects, but there was otherwise no fixed pattern for a cycle of movements.

Concerto

Like sonata, the term **concerto** had a wide range of meanings during the Baroque era. In the early 17th century, it was applied to works in which any number or combination of diverse musical forces work together, or "in concert." It did not necessarily apply, as it later would, to the opposition of different forces—soloists against orchestra or singers against instrumentalists—although it certainly did not preclude such contrasts.

Only in the last quarter of the 17th century did the opposition between a soloist or soloists and an ensemble emerge as a characteristic feature of the genre, and even then, earlier usage persisted. As late as the 1720s, for example, J. S. Bach gave the designation of "Concerto" to some of his cantatas for soloists, chorus, and orchestra.

The emergence of a genre that highlights the contrasts within its performing forces represents an important new development in the history of music. As with the sonata, several subcategories of concerto had established themselves by the end of the 17th century: the **concerto grosso,** the **solo concerto,** and the **ripieno concerto.**

◆ The concerto grosso features a small group of soloists, the **concertino,** with its own basso continuo, against a larger ensemble known as the **ripieno** (Italian for "full") or **tutti** ("all").

◆ The solo concerto features a single soloist (such as violin, flute, or oboe) or a pair of soloists (two violins or two flutes) against a ripieno ensemble.

◆ The ripieno concerto, which features no soloists at all, reflects the persistence of the earlier understanding of the genre, in which the opposition between contrasting forces within an ensemble plays little or no role. These works have often come down to us with other designations like *sonata* or *sinfonia* as well as *concerto.*

Corelli
Concerto grosso,
op. 6, no. 2

Arcangelo Corelli's concerti grossi are among the earliest works of their kind. Although not published until 1714, a year after the composer's death, at least some of these works were circulating in manuscript in Rome as early as the 1680s. Corelli's concerti grossi feature a ripieno of strings and basso continuo with a concertino (solo ensemble) typical of a trio sonata: two violins and basso continuo. The concertino part is continuous and—as the original title page indicates—can be performed with or without the ripieno forces. The ripieno part, in other words, is not essential to the structural integrity of these works. But without the ripieno, these works lack the timbral variety—the rapid back-and-forth between soloists and ensemble—that gives them their distinctive profile.

The guitar as domestic instrument. *The popularity of the guitar is not a recent phenomenon. The "Spanish" guitar, as it was known in England, was already in wide use by the early 17th century; only in the mid–19th century did it begin to be supplanted, at least to some extent, by the piano. The ability to sing and accompany oneself on the guitar was long considered a desirable social skill, particularly for young ladies. Here, a young woman from the Lake family has chosen to have herself portrayed with the instrument; this image was made sometime around 1660.*

Source: Peter Lely (1619–1680), "Two Ladies of the Lake Family," (c. 1660), (detail)/Tate Gallery, London/Art Resource, NY

The formal structure of these concertos is fluid. The individual movements are not built around recurring themes—ritornelli—like the later concertos of Vivaldi and Bach, but instead move through a series of relatively brief sections that present contrasting thematic ideas in different keys and tempos. The third movement opens with a Grave and moves to a thematically distinct Andante Largo. Harmonically, this movement begins in D minor and ends on V the dominant of F. It leads without a break into the fourth movement, an Allegro in binary form (consisting, that is, of two repeated sections).

A comparison of Corelli's concerti grossi, written in the 1680s, to Antonio Vivaldi's solo concertos, written in the 1710s, illustrates the rapid development of the Baroque concerto. Vivaldi's concertos, reflecting the influence of opera (see Chapter 9), make far greater use of the ritornello principle than do Corelli's. In Vivaldi's concertos, ripieno and solo sections are more clearly differentiated, longer, and fewer than in any given movement of a concerto by Corelli. Thematically, Vivaldi's movements tend to be driven by a **head motif** (also sometimes called a *motto theme*), which further contributes to a sense of thematic continuity.

Vivaldi
Concerto in A minor, op. 3, no. 8

Notable Concerto Composers of the Baroque Era

**F
O
C
U
S**

Arcangelo Corelli (1653–1713), who spent most of his career in Rome, wrote 12 concerti grossi that enjoyed wide distribution in manuscript long before they appeared in print in 1714. A violin virtuoso, Corelli helped establish modern bowing techniques and was one of the first to use double-stopping and chords. According to one contemporary account of his playing, "it was usual for his countenance to be distorted, his eyes to become as red as fire, and his eyeballs to roll as if in agony."[1] Corelli also wrote numerous trio sonatas and a sonata for violin and continuo (see Focus: "The Art of Embellishment").

Giuseppe Torelli (1658–1709) worked mostly in Bologna (Italy) but also spent time north of the Alps. His ensemble pieces in op. 5 (published 1692) are among the earliest ripieno concertos. His op. 6 (1698) includes the earliest known concertos, with the solo part (for violin) explicitly marked as such (nos. 6 and 12). He is best remembered for his trumpet concertos, written after 1701.

Francesco Geminiani (1687–1762) studied with Corelli in Rome and Alessandro Scarlatti in Naples. In 1714, he settled in London and won fame as a violin virtuoso, composer, and teacher. He wrote many concerti grossi in the style of Corelli.

Pietro Locatelli (1695–1764) also studied with Corelli and eventually settled in Amsterdam, where

he gave regular public concerts. He was renowned as a virtuoso violinist as well as a composer. His first concerti grossi appeared in print in 1721.

Antonio Vivaldi (1678–1741; see also the Composer Profile later) was by far the most prolific (and popular) of all concerto composers in his time. He wrote almost 60 ripieno concertos, 350 solo concertos (about two-thirds of which are for solo violin), and 45 double concertos (more than half of which are for two violins).

George Frideric Handel (1685–1759; see also the Composer Profile in Chapter 9) wrote two sets of concerti grossi (op. 3, also known as Oboe Concertos, and op. 6) as well as two sets of concertos for organ (op. 4 and op. 7), which he performed himself between the acts of opera or oratorio performances in the London theaters.

Johann Sebastian Bach (1685–1750; see also the Composer Profile in Chapter 9) studied Vivaldi's concertos carefully and integrated the ritornello principle into a more complex polyphonic texture. His most celebrated concertos are the six dedicated to the Margrave of Brandenburg in 1721 and scored for a variety of solo instruments; one of them (the third) is a ripieno concerto. Bach also wrote three concertos for solo violin, almost a dozen for solo harpsichord, and a half dozen more for two or more harpsichords.

The first movement of Vivaldi's Concerto for Two Violins, op. 3, no. 8, for example, is constructed around four ritornello and three solo sections, as the accompanying table summarizes. The alternation of ritornello and solo is more a general organizing principle than a rigid scheme, however. Almost all of the solo and ritornello sections include interpolations of an opposing texture.

Vivaldi uses only a few thematic ideas, almost all of them presented in Ritornello I, but he alternates them and varies each to spin out a movement that is considerably longer than a typical movement in a concerto grosso by Corelli. And in Vivaldi's work, unlike Corelli's, the solo and ripieno parts are structurally interdependent: the solo part could not sensibly be performed on its own without the ripieno part. Although the soloists do play in unison with the ripieno from time to time (including all of Ritornello I), the two forces often present different thematic material.

Orphan musicians.   *The image here depicts a performance given by girls from several different Venetian orphanages in honor of a visiting Russian dignitary in 1782. Orphanages played a significant role in musical life throughout the 16th through 19th centuries, particularly in northern Italy. In an effort to teach orphans a useful trade, a number of these institutions took on the character of a musical conservatory, teaching young boys and girls to sing and play instruments, often at a high level of accomplishment. Antonio Vivaldi taught violin for many years at the Venetian Hospice of Pity for orphaned girls. Its orchestra was famous throughout the Continent, and the city fathers used it repeatedly as a means of both entertaining and impressing visiting dignitaries. The young women there played from behind a veiled screen—disembodied, as it were, so as not to inspire any less-than-spiritual ideas in the minds of the listeners. Accounts of such performances frequently describe the music as angelic.*

Source: Gabriele Bella (1730–1782), "Concert given by the girls of the hospital music societies in the Procuratie, Venice", oil on canvas/Galleria Querini–Stampalia, Venice, Italy/The Bridgeman Art Library

Vivaldi uses harmonic variety to complement the contrasting textures and instrumentation. Rhythmically, the music pushes forward with a sense of propulsive, headlong energy. There are short pauses (the second beat of measure 4 in the violins, for example), but these are typically covered by forward motion in other voices. This technique, which has been called *motoric rhythm*, became increasingly prominent in late Baroque music. German writers of today refer to it as *Fortspinnung*, or "spinning out," a term that aptly describes the way Vivaldi spins out the material in the opening measure into a longer and longer thread before finally cutting it. Other examples of this propulsive technique may

THE STRUCTURE OF THE FIRST MOVEMENT OF VIVALDI'S CONCERTO IN A MINOR FOR TWO VIOLINS AND ORCHESTRA, OP. 3, NO. 8			
Section	**Harmonic area**	**Measures**	**Thematic ideas**
Ritornello I	i	1–16	Head motif
Solo I	i→III	16–36	Dotted eighth figure
Ritornello II	III→iv	37–47	Repeated sixteenths
Solo II	iv→I	48–65	Dotted eighth figure returns in i
Ritornello III	i	65–71	Head motif returns in I
Solo III	i	71–78	Extension of head motif
Ritornello IV	i	78–93	Extension of head motif

be found in the imitative sections of Corelli's Concerto Grosso, op. 6, no. 2 (the beginning of the second movement, in particular), in the arias in Handel's opera *Giulio Cesare* (Anthology), and in the fugues of J. S. Bach's *Well-Tempered Clavier* (Anthology, discussed later).

Suite

The idea of grouping dance movements in sets of two or three or even more dates to the Renaissance. In the Baroque era, the suite emerged as an even more extended series of dances or dance-inspired movements, usually in the same key, but often varying between major and minor modes. Such groupings went by many different names in the Baroque era, depending on locale. Some works labeled as sonatas are in fact a series of dances (the sonata da camera, for example). The keyboard suite was also known as a *partita* in Germany and Italy, a *lesson* in England, and an *ordre* in France.

Although the number of movements in any given suite is variable, most consist of four to six dances of varying tempo, meter, and character. The basic framework for a suite consists of two moderately fast movements (an allemande and courante) followed by a slow movement (a sarabande), and, at the end, a lively dance in triple meter (the gigue). Movements based on other dance forms, such as the minuet, bourrée, or gavotte, might be substituted or added at will (see table: "Baroque Dance Types Commonly Used in Suites").

As we saw in Chapter 6, these kinds of dances tend to be in binary form. Any dance, in turn, could feature what the French called a *double*, the Germans a *Nachtanz* (literally, "after-dance")—in either case, a second dance paired with the first and based on the same thematic idea. The *double* of the courante in Elisabeth Jacquet de la Guerre's *Pièces de clavecin* is essentially a variation on the original dance. The *double* of the gigue that follows is even more elaborate in its rapid passagework. (See Plate 9 in color insert II for a portrait of the composer.)

Jacquet de la Guerre
Pièces de clavecin

Another type of suite, the **variation suite,** is more tightly organized than other examples of the genre. Expanding on the idea of thematically related dances, the variation

Composer Profile

Antonio Vivaldi
(1678–1741)

A near contemporary of Handel and J. S. Bach, Vivaldi was a prolific composer. Known as the "Red Priest"—because he was redheaded and ordained—he served for many years as director of music at Venice's Ospedale della Pietà (Hospice of Pity), a large orphanage for girls. (See illustration on page 191.) Being the music director of an orphanage might strike us today as a strange job for one of the most famous composers of his time, but the young women at this particular institution were thoroughly trained in musical performance, and to judge from the music Vivaldi wrote for them, they must have been quite talented as well. Although he later worked in Vienna at the court of Charles VI, Vivaldi wrote most of his many concertos while in service to the orphanage in Venice.

Vivaldi's music was widely published and well known throughout Europe during his lifetime. J. S. Bach arranged several of Vivaldi's concertos for the organ, and in the process taught himself how to

Antonio Vivaldi. *This caricature from 1723 by Pier Leone Ghezzi captures a certain levity and mischievousness that characterizes a good bit of Vivaldi's music, which despite its conventional surface is never predictable.*

Source: Courtesy of the Library of Congress

KEY DATES IN THE LIFE OF ANTONIO VIVALDI

1678 Born in Venice on March 4

1703 Becomes violin instructor at the Ospedale della Pietà, an orphanage for girls in Venice

1703 Takes holy orders and becomes a priest

1718 Becomes music director to the court of Mantua

1727 Appointed music director to the court of Charles VI in Vienna

1741 Dies in Vienna; buried on July 28

write concertos "in the Italian style." Bach and Handel may have had greater facility at counterpoint, but Vivaldi was a master of melodic invention and the projection of a sense of drama.

Principal Works

CONCERTOS An old joke among musicians is that Vivaldi did not write 400 concertos, but rather one concerto 400 times. There is a grain of truth in this witticism, to be sure, but the outward similarities of form and structure in these works mask a rich, almost overwhelming variety of approaches to the genre. Vivaldi wrote for a remarkable range of instruments and instrument combinations, including not only violins, oboes, and flutes, but also for more unusual instruments, such as mandolins, lutes, piccolos, and violas d'amore.

OPERAS Vivaldi wrote 46 operas in the opera seria tradition, of which 21 have survived. Rarely performed today, these works were highly regarded by Vivaldi's contemporaries. The success of recent revivals reaffirms this favorable estimation.

SACRED MUSIC Vivaldi's *Gloria* is a staple of the choral repertory, but he wrote a great many other works that are equally rewarding. His output includes 12 motets and more than three dozen various sacred works, as well as two oratorios.

BAROQUE DANCE TYPES COMMONLY USED IN SUITES			
Dance type	Meter	Tempo	Character
Allemande	4/4	Moderate	Flowing; often begins with an upbeat
Bourrée	2/2	Fast	Units begin on fourth beat
Courante	3/4 or 3/8	Fast	Begins with an upbeat
Double	Variable	Variable	Variation on any immediately preceding dance
Gavotte	4/4	Fast	Units begin on third beat
Gigue	6/8	Fast	Often features dotted rhythms
Hornpipe	3/2	Fast	Cadences on third beat
Minuet	3/4	Moderate	Stately
Passepied	3/4 or 3/8	Fast	Light, rapid articulation of notes
Polonaise	3/4	Moderate	Accents on second beat
Sarabande	3/4 or 3/2	Slow	No upbeat; noble
Siciliano	6/8 or 12/8	Moderate	Pastoral; often with dotted rhythms

suite presents a series of contrasting dances based on one basic thematic idea. It is, in effect, a set of variations grouped as a dance suite. Composers who cultivated this subgenre include Johann Hermann Schein (1586–1630) and Isaac Posch (d. 1622), both of whom worked in northern Germany.

The suite was also a favorite medium for program music, that is, instrumental music meant to express a nonmusical story or idea. Some of these programmatic works could be quite graphic. A good example is by Johann Kuhnau (1660–1722), J. S. Bach's immediate predecessor as Kantor of St. Thomas's Church in Leipzig. In his *Musikalische Vorstellung einiger Biblischer Historien, in 6 Sonaten auf dem Claviere zu spielen* (Musical Representations of Several Biblical Stories, in Six Sonatas for the Harpsichord), Kuhnau presented musical depictions of six Bible stories. The first of these illustrates David's victory over Goliath. The key movements are entitled as follows:

Kuhnau
Biblische Historien

The Trembling of the Israelites before the Giant, and Their prayer to God

The Courage of David

The Combat between the Two

The Flight of the Philistines

Musical devices convey not only the predominant affect of each movement but also its sequence of events. Kuhnau even marks in the score the music that represents David whirling his slingshot and the clumsy and dissonant passage that represents Goliath's fall.

An even more graphic example of program music is a movement by Marin Marais (1656–1721) in the Seventh Suite for viola da gamba and continuo published in his *Fifth Book of Pieces for the Viola da Gamba* (1725). Entitled *Le Tableau de l'opération de la taille* ("Representation of an Abdominal Surgery"), the work depicts the removal of a kidney stone from a patient, and the score is marked in graphic verbal detail to match the music: "Here the incision is made. . . . Here the stone is grasped. . . . The blood flows. . . ."

The suite was also an important genre for larger ensembles of instruments. Together with the ripieno concerto, the suite was in fact the principal genre for orchestral music throughout the Baroque era. (The earliest concert symphonies—that is, symphonies written for the concert hall rather than as overtures to theatrical productions—would not appear until the 1720s.) Opera and ballet provided a significant source of music for orchestral suites written in the 17th and 18th centuries, particularly in France.

Many orchestral suites were programmatic. Among them is an extraordinary work by Jean-Féry Rebel (1661–1747) entitled *Les élémens* (The Elements, 1737). The first movement, "Chaos," begins with a chord that strikes even 21st-century ears as chaotic. It is a simultaneous sounding of all the notes in a D-minor scale (D-E-F-G-A-B♭-C♯). The introduction to the first-movement overture, Rebel noted in his preface to the score, "represents the confusion that prevails among the elements before that moment in which, subject to invariable laws, they assume the place prescribed for them by the order of Nature." The bass, he goes on to explain, "expresses the Earth through the tied notes,

Rebel
Les élémens

<table>
<tr><td>

F

O

C

U

S

</td><td>

Musical Rhetoric

Early Baroque theories of expression had been based on the clear projection of the words being sung, but by the early 1700s, many theorists were advancing a new idea: even without a text, a composition could be considered a musical oration, a speech without words. The principal theme, according to this line of thought, corresponds to the principal theme of an orator's speech. Everything that follows in some way elaborates or comments on this main idea, either through variation or contrast.

The idea of musical rhetoric drew heavily on the traditions of ancient Greek and Roman oratory. Music theorists of the early 18th century developed extended systems of parallels between the structures of verbal and musical "speech." Such basic terms as *period* (from the Latin *periodus*, meaning "sentence"), *phrase*, *antecedent*, and *consequent* were transferred to music from the realm of grammar. Many writers went even further to establish systems of musical figures, or tropes, comparable to those used in speech. Such figures could be used in instrumental music and vocal music alike. In vocal music,

they are invariably associated with the words being set at that particular moment. We already encountered one such figure, the *passus duriusculus*, a figure associated primarily with pain and anguish, in the discussion of J. S. Bach's cantata *Jesu, der du meine Seele* (Anthology). Other comparable figures include these:

- *Pathopoeia*, harsh-sounding accidentals used to create a sensation of sorrow or fear

- *Abruptio*, a sudden and unexpected pause or silence

- *Suspiratio*, the breaking up of a melodic line by rests, often associated with gasping, sighing, or extreme agitation

What is particularly significant is not so much the precise definition of individual figures as the growing acknowledgment that instrumental music alone, without the aid of words, might create in listeners the same kinds and degree of effects that had long been considered the exclusive domain of vocal music.

</td></tr>
</table>

played percussively. The flutes, with their rising and falling lines, imitate the flow and murmuring of water. The air is depicted by long-held notes followed by cadences in the piccolos. And finally, the violins represent the active nature of fire through their vigorous and brilliant strokes. . . . I have dared to connect the idea of the confusion of the elements with a confusion of harmony. . . . These notes proceed to a unison in a progression that is natural, and after a dissonance, we hear a perfect chord [i.e., a unison]."

More subtle programmatic elements may be found in the instrumental music of the French *clavecinistes* (keyboard composers), particularly François Couperin, who liked to place provocative (and often enigmatic) titles at the head of individual dance pieces within a suite. His 24th *ordre,* published in the fourth book of his *Pieces for the Harpsichord* (1730), for example, includes movements with intriguing titles such as (in English translation) The Amphibian, The Visionary, and The Mysterious One. These brief programmatic works for keyboard would eventually provide a basis for the important genre of the character piece for piano in the 19th century.

Keyboard Genres

Genres of the Baroque era associated primarily or exclusively with keyboard instruments fall into four broad categories: free, vocal based, dance based, and variations.

Free Genres.   Free genres are based on no preexistent material and adhere to no particular pattern or structure. They can be predominantly imitative, nonimitative, or they can combine both textures within a single work. The most important nonimitative free genres of keyboard music in the Baroque era are the toccata, canzona, fantasia, and prelude (Latin, *praeludium*). The most important imitative genres are the ricercar and fugue.

Frescobaldi
Toccata IX

The Ninth Toccata from Frescobaldi's *Second Book of Toccatas* (1627), although unusually intricate, is nonetheless representative of the genre as a whole. Rapid passagework combined with freedom of form had been characteristic of the toccata since the genre emerged in the 16th century (see Chapter 6). Highly episodic, Frescobaldi's toccata moves rapidly through a variety of textures, registers, rhythms, and meters. Some sections last only a few measures. The rhythms are constantly shifting and at times quite intricate (for example, measures 11, 22, 25); the right and left hands occasionally work in cross-rhythms (measures 56–60, 65); and the passagework, which is distinctly idiomatic to the harpsichord (as opposed to the organ), is dazzling at times (measures 25–26, 50–54). Small wonder, then, that Frescobaldi should add the remark at the very end of this work: *Non senza fatiga si giunge al fine* ("Not without effort does one arrive at the end").

Already well established as a genre for instrumental ensembles in the 16th century, the **canzona** began to evolve into a keyboard genre in the early 17th century. In the process, it lost its connection with vocal models and became an essentially free composition comparable to the toccata. Canzonas and other keyboard genres were often performed in the church. Frescobaldi's *Fiori musicali* ("Musical Flowers") of 1635, for example, includes a "Canzona [to be played] after the Epistle," a "Toccata [to be played] at the elevation of the host," and a "Canzona [to be played] after the Communion."

Buxtehude
Praeludium in
G minor,
BuxWV 149

Virtuosity and structural openness on an even larger scale than in Frescobaldi's toccatas are evident in Dietrich Buxtehude's Praeludium in G minor for organ (BuxWV 149), written sometime between 1675 and 1689. (Throughout the Baroque era, *prelude* and *fantasia* were essentially interchangeable terms indicating a work that adhered to no fixed structural pattern.) Except for the very end, the individual sections

Notable Keyboard Composers of the Baroque Era

F O C U S

Girolamo Frescobaldi (1583–1643) was born in Ferrara, where he studied with Luzzasco Luzzaschi. Except for a brief period in Florence (1628–1634), Frescobaldi spent most of his life in Rome as organist of St. Peter's. He raised the art of idiomatic composition for the organ and harpsichord to new heights. His music was considered daring for its harmonic boldness and technical difficulty. He cultivated virtually every keyboard genre of his era, including the toccata, fantasia, canzona, ricercar, and, above all, the variation.

Samuel Scheidt (1587–1654) is best remembered as the composer of *Tabulatura nova* ("New Tablature"), published in three volumes in 1624 in open score on five-line staves, as opposed to the traditional organ letter tablature or the six-line staves common in other keyboard sources of the time. The set includes chorale preludes, free compositions, and many variations and is stylistically indebted to Scheidt's teacher, Sweelinck.

Johann Jakob Froberger (1616–1667) was born in Germany, studied in Rome with Frescobaldi, and eventually settled in Vienna, where he was court organist. He was among the first composers to write extended keyboard suites.

Dietrich Buxtehude (1637–1707) was the most celebrated organist of his day. He spent most of his early career in Denmark. From 1668 onward he held the prestigious post of organist at the Marienkirche in Lübeck, a prosperous port city on the Baltic in what is now northern Germany.

Johann Pachelbel (1652–1706), known today almost exclusively for his Canon in D (which is actually the first part of a Canon and Gigue), was better known during his own lifetime as an organist and composer of sacred music, including many sets of chorale variations and chorale preludes. He was born in Nuremberg and held prestigious posts in several central German cities, including Eisenach (where J. S. Bach was born in 1685), Erfurt, and Stuttgart, as well as his native Nuremberg.

François Couperin (1668–1733), nicknamed "Le Grand" ("The Great") because of his prowess in organ playing, came from a long line of musicians. Born in Paris, he served most of his adult life as a musician at the courts of Louis XIV and Louis XV. He wrote some 233 pieces for harpsichord and grouped them by tonality in a series of *27 ordres*, which in turn were published in four separate books (1713, 1717, 1722, 1730).

Jean-Philippe Rameau (1683–1764) inherited Couperin's mantle as the greatest organist and harpsichordist in France. The bulk of Rameau's harpsichord music appeared relatively early in his career (three books, published 1706, 1724, and ca. 1729–1730). Like Couperin's suites, Rameau's works include many individual pieces with descriptive and sometimes enigmatic titles. Rameau has justly been called "the creator of the modern science of harmony," for he was the first to codify the modern system of harmony based on triadic chords related to a fundamental bass.

Johann Sebastian Bach (1685–1750; see Composer Profile in Chapter 9) wrote many of his harpsichord works, including the *Well-Tempered Clavier*, as didactic exercises for his children and pupils. He also cultivated the suite. His encyclopedic *Clavier-Übung* ends with the massive *Goldberg Variations*. Bach's organ music includes many chorale-based compositions, free works (toccatas, fugues, fantasias), and variations, most notably the Passacaglia in C minor, BWV 582.

of Buxtehude's Praeludium are clearly articulated, each with its own distinctive theme and texture. Long imitative sections are typical of the prelude and many other free keyboard genres in the 17th century. But imitation is only one of many textures we are likely to encounter in these characteristically varied and unpredictable works. Buxtehude's Praeludium ends with an extended rhapsody that sounds almost improvisational. The formal structure, in short, is paratactic, with each section more or less self-contained.

The breadth of sound, intricate pedalwork, and extended imitative passages of this work are characteristic of a northern European tradition of keyboard composition that flourished in the 17th century. This tradition had its roots in the work of Jan Pieterszoon Sweelinck (1562–1621; see Chapter 6). Buxtehude was Sweelinck's greatest successor, and Buxtehude's greatest successor would be Johann Sebastian Bach, who traveled from Arnstadt to Lübeck in 1704 to hear Buxtehude perform.

Other free genres depend primarily on the elaboration of one or more ideas through imitative counterpoint. These include canon, ricercar, and fugue. The ricercar originated as an improvisatory genre for lute in the early 16th century and evolved into an instrumental counterpart to the polyphonic motet by the middle of the century (see Chapter 6). In the 17th century, it underwent yet another transformation, establishing itself primarily as an imitative genre for keyboard instruments. It eventually came to be associated with particularly strict and learned forms of counterpoint in the *stile antico,* or "old style." The two ricercars in J. S. Bach's *Musical Offering,* a cycle of variations on a theme given to the composer by Frederick the Great, are especially demanding in this regard.

The **fugue** emerged in the 17th century as a keyboard genre in which a single thematic idea is subjected to imitative treatment for the entire length of a work. Johann Pachelbel (1652–1706) was one of the first composers to write fugues in this sense. Before the 17th century, the Latin term *fuga* had been used primarily to mean "canon." A *Missa ad fugam* in the Renaissance, for example, was by definition a canonic Mass.

Fugue is a genre rooted in texture rather than a particular medium or form. There is no typical fugue structure, but most fugues share certain basic elements. A fugue usually begins with a single voice that states the theme, or **subject.** A second voice enters in imitation, presenting the same theme (or a slightly altered version of it), even while the first voice continues. When all the voices have entered and stated the subject at least once, we have reached the end of the **exposition** (not to be confused with the exposition of a sonata-form movement; see Chapter 11). From this point on, a fugue can do just about anything. Composers sometimes branch off into long passages in a relatively free style with little or no imitation. At some juncture, however, the fugue subject will reestablish an imitative structure. The nonimitative free-style passages are called **episodes,** and the new points of imitation are called **middle entries.** Fugues typically consist of a series of alternating middle entries and episodes, for a fugue with no free sections might sound ponderous, and a fugue with no imitation after the exposition would not sound much like a fugue at all.

J. S. Bach
Well-Tempered Clavier

The two books of Bach's *Well-Tempered Clavier* present a rich variety of imitative and nonimitative keyboard pieces. Each book consists of a series of 24 paired preludes and fugues, with one pair in each of the 24 major and minor keys. Bach wrote these two sets in part to demonstrate the viability of **equal temperament,** a system of tuning that allowed keyboard players to play in any key (see Focus: "Equal Temperament"). He organized these works in ascending chromatic order.

In a reflection of Bach's passion for exploring the many possibilities of a single idea, all the preludes and fugues are different from one another. The Prelude in C Major follows a pattern of broken chords in a manner known as **style brisée** ("broken style"), adopted from the arpeggiated ("broken") chords and figures typically found in lute music. Not coincidentally, this piece remains a favorite among guitar players. The Prelude in C minor is in the style of a keyboard toccata, full of rapid figuration. The Prelude in C♯ minor is in the style of a sarabande, a slow dance in triple meter. Some analysts have discerned subtle thematic or motivic links between certain preludes and their associated fugues, but in general these too are musically independent of each other.

Equal Temperament

The G sharp in a mathematically pure Pythagorean E-major scale is slightly higher than the A flat in a pure F-minor scale. Vocalists and string players can adjust for this difference, but keyboard players can't, because on a keyboard, G sharp and A flat are played by the same key. Thus to tune a keyboard in a way that will allow it to play in any of the 24 major and minor keys of the diatonic scale requires a great many slight modifications, or temperaments, away from Pythagorean purity. The system of temperament in use today, called equal temperament, emerged only gradually in the 18th century, when it replaced a variety of older systems of tuning and temperament.

J. S. Bach advocated this system of equal temperament, but many of his colleagues objected to the "impure" sound of the intervals. By the end of the 18th century, however, equal temperament had become the norm, thanks in large part to its adaptability to every key and every conceivable modulation.

Some fugues—especially the longer ones—have more than one subject, and these do not necessarily all appear at the outset. A new subject enters the Fugue in C♯ minor of Bach's *Well-Tempered Clavier,* Book I, for example, in measure 36. Some fugues incorporate one or more **countersubjects,** thematically distinctive material that is used as counterpoint to the principal subject and goes on to play an important role over the course of the fugue as a whole. In the Fugue in B Major, a countersubject appears in the left hand in measures 3–5.

Vocal-Based Genres.   As in the Renaissance, keyboard arrangements of vocal works, particularly chansons, were popular in the Baroque. By far the most important vocal-based genres of keyboard music in the Baroque era were those based on chorale melodies. Protestant chorales provided northern composers with an almost endless source of material for chorale variations, chorale preludes, and chorale fantasias. Chorale preludes were intended to serve as instrumental introductions to the congregational singing of a chorale tune in church. Given this function, these works tend to be brief and relatively straightforward.

Johann Pachelbel's chorale prelude *Magnificat peregrini toni,* written sometime toward the end of the 17th century, is typical in this regard. The chorale tune had been adopted from the Ninth Psalm Tone of the Roman Catholic liturgy (the *tonus peregrinus,* or "pilgrim tone," so called because it moves from one recitation tone in its first half to a different one in its second). In the Protestant services, this melody was commonly associated with the Magnificat, the words uttered by the Virgin Mary when she learns from the annunciating angel that she is to bear the Christ child ("My soul doth magnify the Lord," Luke 1: 47–55). In Pachelbel's setting the tune is stated in its entirety in long notes in the upper voice, with the other voices weaving around it. Antiphonal passagework never obscures the melody in the upper voice. The pièce concludes with a **tièrce de picardie** (**picardy third**)—a major third at the end of a work otherwise in minor mode. Such endings had become commonplace for works in the minor mode by 1700. Evidence suggests that even if a sharpened third was not explicitly notated on the final cadence in a score, performers were expected to provide it—a late vestige of musica ficta (see Chapter 5).

J. S. Bach's chorale prelude on the same melody exhibits a different approach to the genre. Written as part of Cantata 10 in 1724 and published for organ in 1748, this brief work, like the Pachelbel, places the melody in the upper voice in long note values. The three lower voices, however, are considerably more chromatic and intricate than the

Pachelbel
Chorale Prelude on the *Magnificat peregrini toni*

J. S. Bach
Chorale Prelude on *Meine Seele erhebt den Herren*

The minuet as dance. *Courtly dancing was one of the requisite social graces for ladies and gentlemen of the upper classes, and tutors helped demonstrate the steps for each dance. The illustration here shows the proper order of steps for the minuet. Dancing of this kind was extremely formal and stylized; notice the distance between the two figures.*

Source: Jan van der Gucht (1697–1776), K.8. K.7 Book 2 plate IV, The Music Ceremony concluded, the Dance begins: music, dance steps and dancers for a Minuet from Kellom Tomlinson's "Art of Dancing", engraving/British Library, London, UK/The Bridgeman Art Library

lower voices in the Pachelbel. Early in his career Bach was called to task for the way in which he harmonized chorales being sung by parishioners. According to the letter of reprimand, Bach had "made many curious *variationes* in the chorale, and mingled many strange tones in it, and . . . the congregation has been confused by it."[2]

Dance-Based Genres.   A large percentage of keyboard music is based on the principles of dance, often using binary forms, as in the courante and gigue from Elisabeth Jacquet de la Guerre's *Pièces de clavecin* discussed earlier (Anthology). Other common dance types included the sarabande, allemande, and gavotte. These dance movements were sometimes arranged in ordered sequences as a suite; at other times they were gathered more loosely, as in the *ordres* of François Couperin, collections whose individual units could be played either individually or as a whole.

Variations.   Variations on bass line patterns—ground basses—were extremely popular in both vocal and instrumental music of the Baroque. These bass lines are not fixed patterns, and they manifest themselves in a variety of ways over time. The use of a **basso ostinato**—an "obstinate bass," one that is present at all times and simply will not go away—inspired composers in the art of variation, challenging them to make constant repetition appealing through the use of an ever-changing countermelody above it. Many of these basso ostinato patterns derived from popular dances of the time, including the **chaconne** or **passacaglia,** the **passamezzo,** and the **folia.**

J. S. Bach's *Goldberg Variations* offer perhaps the most spectacular example in the entire history of music of the elaborations possible within the framework of a simple bass line. For many years, it was believed Bach wrote this set of harpsichord variations on behalf of one of his pupils, Johann Gottlieb Goldberg, who in turn was employed by a certain Baron von Keyserling. Legend has it that the baron had trouble getting to sleep at night and these variations were designed to help him while away the evening hours. But the story is demonstrably false, because Goldberg was only about 14 years old when Bach wrote this work.

The *Goldberg Variations*, like the *Well-Tempered Clavier* and the late, unfinished *Art of the Fugue*, is an example of Bach's passion for writing encyclopedic works. In the *Well-Tempered Clavier* he explored the permutations of free preludes and imitative fugues in every possible key. In the *Art of the Fugue* he would explore various ways in which different fugal devices can be brought to bear on a single subject. In the *Goldberg Variations* he systematically explored the technique of both variation and canon.

The variations take us through an astonishing set of permutations on a single idea. The source of that idea is elusive. Bach's use of the term *aria* to designate the opening variation draws our attention to the soprano line, but the theme, spelled out here, is actually in the bass:

J. S. Bach's *Goldberg Variations:* **The Structure of the Theme**

Measure	1–8		9–16	
Theme	‖: G-F#-E-D-B-C-D-G		G-F#-E-A-F#-G-A-D :‖	
Tonality	I	I	I	V
Measure	17–24		25–32	
Theme	‖: D-B-C-B-G-A-B-E		C-B-A-D-G-C-D-G :‖	
Tonality	V	vi	ii⁶	I

(margin) **J. S. Bach** *Goldberg Variations*

Bach further concealed the theme with added notes, even on its first presentation in the aria. In the first reprise, the theme's pitches mostly coincide with the longer notes on the downbeats in the bass line (predominantly half notes and dotted half notes); in the second reprise, the notes of the theme do not coincide with the downbeat nearly as often.

Bach uses this bass progression as the foundation for all subsequent variations. In Variation 1, for example, the theme is readily apparent on the downbeat of every measure in the first reprise, but harder to follow in the second reprise.

Another structural device Bach uses throughout this set is a series of canons. Every third variation (Numbers 3, 6, 9, 12, etc.) presents a canon in the two upper voices, creating a trio sonata texture with two high voices and a bass. The bass line operates independently of the canon, although always providing the necessary notes of the theme in the proper order. Each canon, moreover, is written at an interval one step greater than the one before. Thus the first canon (Variation 3) is at the unison: the second voice enters one measure after the first, but at the same pitch. The second canon is composed at the interval of a second (no easy task), with the second voice entering one whole step above the first and a measure behind. The third canon is a canon at the third, and so on.

In a third level of complexity, Bach incorporates a variety of musical styles within the *Goldberg Variations*. Variation 16, for example, which opens the unlabeled second part of the work, is in the style of a French overture. Number 10 is a fugue. Number 7 is a gigue. In addition, the work contains many dazzling passages, as in Variation 14, that require a virtuoso to perform.

As is true of so many works by Bach, the technical intricacies of the *Goldberg Variations* in no way obscure the delightful turns and surprises of the music. We can appreciate the music without knowing how it is put together, but knowing how it is put together can heighten our appreciation of what was, until Beethoven's "Hammerklavier" Sonata of 1819, the longest single work of keyboard music ever published.

CONCLUSION

The quantity and quality of instrumental music written in the Baroque era was without precedent. No previous period in the history of music had seen such an intense cultivation of instrumental genres. In the second half of the 18th century—the Classical era—the genres of sonata, symphony, and concerto would rise to even greater prominence at the hands of such composers as Joseph Haydn and Wolfgang Amadeus Mozart.

DISCUSSION QUESTIONS

1. If the Renaissance marked the re-discovery of ancient Greek culture, in what ways could the early Baroque era be said to constitute a continuation of Renaissance principles?

2. Solo singing had existed long before the Baroque era. Why, then, was the development of basso continuo toward the very end of the 16th century so stylistically important?

3. Why did sung drama—opera—emerge as a genre in the early 17th century and not before?

4. In what way does a *prima prattica* work like Schütz's *Saul* (Anthology) reflect the influence of the *seconda prattica*?

5. Why was opera slow to take hold in France in the 17th century?

6. Should music written during the Baroque era be performed only on instruments of that era, either on originals or on good copies? Why or why not?

7. In what ways are the Baroque concerto and the typical *opera seria* solo aria related?

8. Would a work like Kuhnau's depiction of David's victory over Goliath in his *Musikalische Vorstellung einiger Biblischer Historien* (Anthology) make musical sense without its verbal program?

9. Why did many of Bach's musical colleagues resist the idea of equal temperament?

Part Four
The Classical Era

Prelude

The Classical era in music—roughly 1750 to 1800—corresponds to a period of intense ferment and change in European history. Powerful intellectual currents bearing notions of liberty and progress challenged the established order. Conflict on a global scale among the great powers of Europe undermined the finances of Great Britain and France, loosening Britain's hold on its American colonies and triggering a cataclysmic revolution and the collapse of the monarchy in France. Advances in technology led to the beginning of the Industrial Revolution.

THE AGE OF ENLIGHTENMENT

The 18th century saw the emergence of an intellectual outlook that stressed the power of humanity, through the application of reason, to understand and improve its condition, and the power of the individual, granted sufficient liberty, to use reason in pursuit of

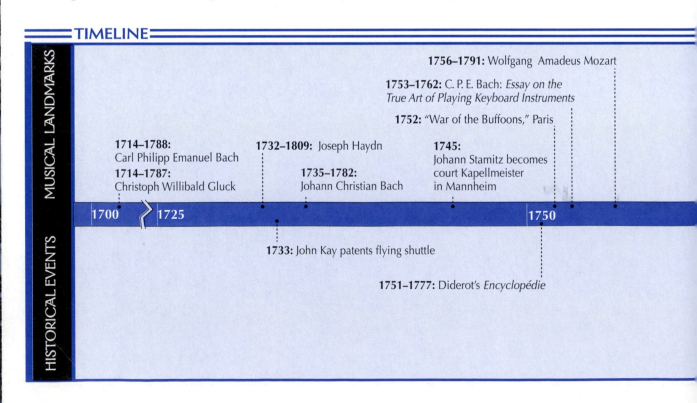

TIMELINE

MUSICAL LANDMARKS

1756–1791: Wolfgang Amadeus Mozart

1753–1762: C. P. E. Bach: *Essay on the True Art of Playing Keyboard Instruments*

1752: "War of the Buffoons," Paris

1714–1788: Carl Philipp Emanuel Bach
1714–1787: Christoph Willibald Gluck

1732–1809: Joseph Haydn

1735–1782: Johann Christian Bach

1745: Johann Stamitz becomes court Kapellmeister in Mannheim

1700   1725   1750

HISTORICAL EVENTS

1733: John Kay patents flying shuttle

1751–1777: Diderot's *Encyclopédie*

self-fulfillment. The advocates of this outlook considered it to be enlightened, and the period in which they flourished is known as the Age of Enlightenment.

Leading figures of the Enlightenment were ready to follow reason wherever it might take them, even if that meant risking their lives and welfare in attacking such established institutions as the monarchy and the church. The leaders of the American Revolution were all steeped in Enlightenment thinking, as reflected in the Declaration of Independence of 1776, a thoroughly Enlightenment manifesto. The French Revolution, with its Enlightenment call for liberty, equality, and fraternity, marked the beginning of a gradual decline in the strict hierarchy of class structure across Europe. The loosening of social hierarchies meant increased opportunities for individuals of talent, who could choose their occupations with greater freedom than ever before.

Consistent with their belief in the power of reason to promote progress, Enlightenment thinkers were deeply committed to the pursuit of scientific knowledge. Quite aside from its potential for practical applications, the understanding of nature was seen as the key to self-enlightenment, a kind of religion in its own right. Scientific knowledge was considered a principal means of overcoming superstition.

The desire to distribute new knowledge made the Enlightenment the great age of encyclopedias. The foremost example was the 33-volume *Encyclopédie*, published in France between 1751 and 1777. This massive compendium, bearing the subtitle *A Systematic Dictionary of Sciences, Arts, and Crafts*, contains approximately 72,000 entries written by more than 140 contributors. Jean-Jacques Rousseau (1712–1778), a composer and Enlightenment thinker, wrote almost all the entries on music for the *Encyclopédie* and would later use them as the basis for his influential dictionary of musical terms, published in 1768. In England, the more modest *Encyclopedia Britannica* first appeared in 1768–1771. The German-language *Brockhaus* encyclopedia began publication in 1796.

The Industrial Revolution, driven by new technology that made manufacturing more efficient and economical, had profound social consequences. Workers operating heavy machinery in large factories increasingly did work that had once been done in the

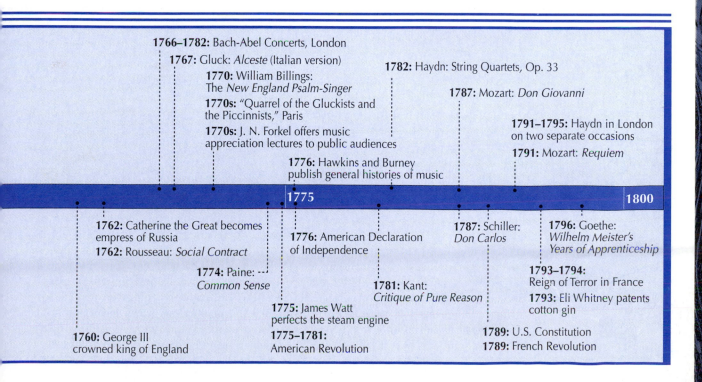

1766–1782: Bach-Abel Concerts, London
1767: Gluck: *Alceste* (Italian version)
1770: William Billings: The *New England Psalm-Singer*
1770s: "Quarrel of the Gluckists and the Piccinnists," Paris
1770s: J. N. Forkel offers music appreciation lectures to public audiences
1776: Hawkins and Burney publish general histories of music

1782: Haydn: String Quartets, Op. 33
1787: Mozart: *Don Giovanni*
1791–1795: Haydn in London on two separate occasions
1791: Mozart: *Requiem*

1775   1800

1762: Catherine the Great becomes empress of Russia
1762: Rousseau: *Social Contract*
1774: Paine: *Common Sense*
1760: George III crowned king of England
1775: James Watt perfects the steam engine
1775–1781: American Revolution
1776: American Declaration of Independence
1781: Kant: *Critique of Pure Reason*
1787: Schiller: *Don Carlos*
1789: U.S. Constitution
1789: French Revolution
1796: Goethe: *Wilhelm Meister's Years of Apprenticeship*
1793–1794: Reign of Terror in France
1793: Eli Whitney patents cotton gin

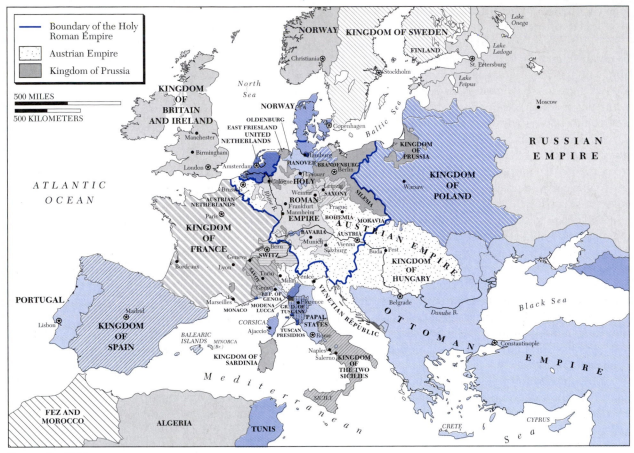

Europe in 1763

home. Cities grew up around these new factories, often in the most haphazard fashion. Squalid living conditions and poor sanitation were commonplace, as were outbreaks of communicable diseases like tuberculosis, typhoid fever, and cholera. But as national economies increased in size and scope, more and more workers followed job opportunities from the agrarian countryside to the industrialized city.

MUSIC IN ENLIGHTENMENT SOCIETY

Both directly and indirectly, music benefited from Enlightenment ideals and the many advances in commerce, technology, and transportation during the 18th century. Reflecting the Enlightenment impulse to produce encyclopedic compendiums of knowledge, the first comprehensive histories of music date to the Classical era. Technological advances in engraving improved the efficiency of music publishing, and the music trade became truly international in the second half of the 18th century. Improved manufacturing techniques made musical instruments like the piano increasingly affordable to middle- and upper-middle-class households. The growth of cities and entrepreneurial enterprise, particularly in England, was accompanied by an increasing demand for public concerts and an increase in the number of venues in which to hold them.

FOCUS

Music in the French Revolution

The French Revolution marks a new chapter in the use of music by the state. The ideals of the Revolution—liberty, equality, fraternity—called for an approach to music that was essentially public and nonelitist. The revolutionary government encouraged the singing of songs by enthusiastic crowds as a way to spread revolutionary ideology in much the same way that Martin Luther had used the congregational singing of hymns to spread the word of the Reformation in the 16th century.

The French Revolution had not one but two anthems. *Ça ira* ("This Shall Be"), with its denunciation of the aristocracy ("We'll string up the aristocrats! Despotism will die, Liberty will triumph. This shall be, this shall be!"), was sung endlessly by the crowds in the streets. *La Marseillaise,* composed in 1792 by Claude-Joseph Rouget de Lisle, an army captain, became the French national anthem on July 14, 1795, the sixth anniversary of the Revolution. Its capacity to inspire revolutionary ardor led several subsequent regimes—including those of Napoleon, Louis XVIII (after 1815), and Napoleon III (in the 1850s and 1860s)—to ban its performance. It would be reinstated as the French national anthem in 1879.

But the government's role went well beyond encouraging the use of one or two songs. The annual festivals commemorating the anniversary of the revolution made music a participatory event, not merely a spectacle for the entertainment of audiences. These enormous, open-air gatherings featured numerous secular hymns and political songs. Various constitutions of the new state were actually set to music—mostly to well-known tunes—for the express purpose of disseminating their content in a way the common person could understand.

The new government also established a national Conservatory of Music to train composers, performers, and teachers, who were, in turn, to create, perform, and propagate music for the national festivals and for the army. The agenda of the new institution was unabashedly nationalistic. The composer François-Joseph Gossec (1734–1829) argued for the establishment of such a school as a bulwark against those "foreign musicians, who, having no attachment to our country, corrupt our language and pervert our taste. . . . It is therefore advantageous—or to put it better, necessary—that we have a truly national music, and to achieve this end we need an Academy of Music." Gossec later became the conservatory's first director.

In the end, the goals of the French government were far loftier than its accomplishments. Within a few years, Paris was once again attracting foreign musicians of talent, and the emphasis on political music soon declined. But the use of music, even for a brief period, as a tool of the state would provide a powerful model for subsequent revolutions and regimes throughout the world.

Audiences also wanted to know more about the music being performed at these concerts. Enterprising publishers rushed to fill this need with a steadily increasing number of music periodicals. In the 1770s, the German composer and theorist Johann Nikolaus Forkel (1749–1818) delivered a series of public lectures that represent one of the earliest attempts to educate the general public in music appreciation. Audiences also wanted to learn about composers themselves. John Mainwaring's *Memoirs of the Late G. F. Handel* (1760) was the first separately published biography of a composer. Several biographies of Wolfgang Amadeus Mozart appeared shortly after his death in 1791. This trend reflects the emergence of composers as cultural icons, their growing independence from aristocratic patronage, and their growing dependence on a paying public. When Joseph Haydn arrived in London the same year as Mozart's death, his reputation preceded him. Earlier in his career he had been a liveried servant for his aristocratic employer; now he was welcomed into the highest levels of society. By the time he returned permanently to Vienna in 1795, he had become a cultural hero and national

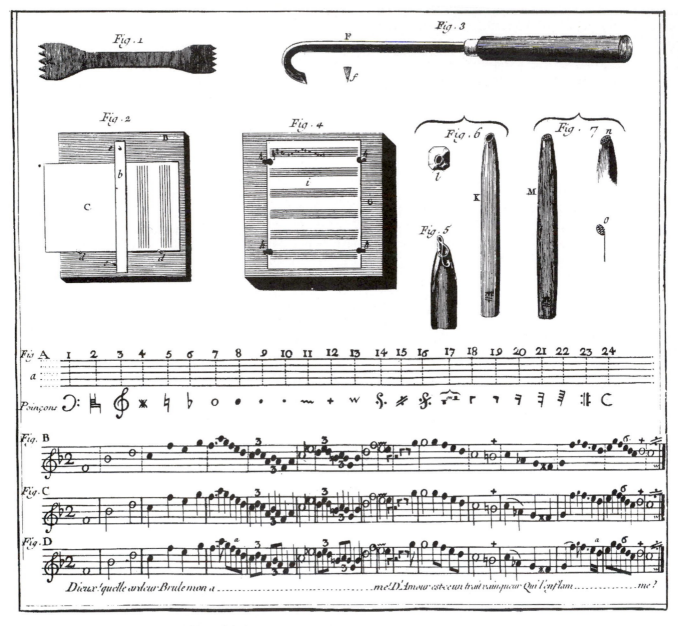

Music engraving *Music engraving, although not new in the 18th century, made tremendous advances during this time and became the preferred method for publishing music. It offered the advantages of mass production while at the same time allowing for a considerable degree of freehand notation. This plate from Diderot's* Encyclopédie *illustrates the process of music engraving. The tool labeled Fig. 1 was used to engrave staves. Fig. 2 shows two staves engraved on a metal plate. The straight edge (labeled b) kept the stave engraving tool straight as it was drawn against the plate. Various punches (Fig. 5, Fig. 6, and Fig. 7) produced standard notational elements. The punch labeled Fig. 5, for example, created the treble clef sign. The notes could be either punched or drawn freehand.*

Source: Library of Congress

treasure (see "The composer as a cultural hero: Haydn's farewell performance," Plate 14 in color insert III).

Despite these trends, most music was still performed for the courts and residences of the royalty and aristocracy during the second half of the 18th century. The variety and quality of music at any given court thus depended entirely on the tastes and financial resources of the titled patron who presided over it. Composers likewise remained mostly dependent on the patronage of the nobility and church for their livelihoods. Haydn was fortunate to have a princely employer committed to music making of high quality who had the resources to pay for it. He was able to live independently later in his career only because he had become an international celebrity. Other composers, like Mozart, were not so lucky. Independent by default because he was unable to secure a lucrative appointment, Mozart cobbled together an income from a variety of sources. He taught piano and composition, gave concerts from time to time, wrote works on commission, and sold the rights to works of all kinds to various music publishers. He was finally granted a minor position at the Imperial court in Vienna late in life, but the income it provided was insufficient to support him and his family.

Vienna thrived as a musical center during the Classical era because it was home to many noble and aristocratic families with the resources and the desire to maintain their own musical ensembles. As the capital of the Austrian Empire, it was also home to many foreign embassies, each seeking to impress the others with sophisticated music. Haydn, who had lived in Vienna during the winter months for most of his career, moved there after the death of his long time patron in the 1790s. Mozart moved there in the early 1780s to take advantage of its opportunities and in search of an appointment at the Imperial court. By the time the young Ludwig van Beethoven (1770–1827) arrived in 1792, Vienna had established a well-earned reputation for welcoming musicians and composers of talent. Aristocratic patrons vied for Beethoven's services, in part because they liked his music, in part to demonstrate their own cultural sophistication.

The Art of the Natural

Like all the other period labels we have encountered so far, the label *Classical* was applied retrospectively. In this case, the designation dates to the middle of the 19th century. It was then that music historians began to look back on the late 18th century as a musical golden age that produced works of enduring value, hence "classical."

The term *classical* also refers to Greek and Roman antiquity and the aesthetic values associated with it—balance, proportion, clarity, and naturalness. In this sense the term is aptly descriptive, because late-18th-century composers and audiences did indeed value these qualities in music. This was an era that on the whole preferred understatement to overstatement, clarity to obscurity. Although composers had long since given up the idea of recreating the music of antiquity, they found broad parallels between their musical ideals and the sculpture and architecture of ancient Greece and Rome, which for the most part avoided excessive ornamentation and decoration.

MUSIC AND THE IDEA OF NATURE

The ideal work of art, according to the predominant aesthetic of the 18th century, must imitate nature in some way. Beginning around 1730, the increasing appeal of nature and the natural created a climate in which the ornate gave way to the simple, the opulent to the straightforward. By the middle of the 18th century, the emphasis had shifted from the musical expression of the affect inherent in a poetic, dramatic, or religious text to a more straightforward, "natural" representation of the passions. The music critic Johann Mattheson (1681–1754; see Focus: "The Emergence of Tonal Harmony," in Chapter 7) singled out Bach's cantata *Ich hatte viel Bekümmernis,* BWV 21, for special ridicule with this mocking transcription of the text underlay in one movement:

"I, I, I, I had much grief, I had much grief, in my heart, in my heart. I had much grief, etc., in my heart, etc., etc., I had much grief, etc., in my heart, etc., I had much grief, etc., in my heart etc., etc., etc., etc., etc. I had much grief, etc., in my heart, etc., etc." Then again: "Sighs, tears, sorrow, anguish (rest), sighs, tears, anxious longing, fear and death (rest) gnaw at my oppressed heart, etc." Also: "Come, my Jesus, and refresh (rest) and rejoice with Thy glance (rest), come, my Jesus (rest), come, my Jesus, and refresh and rejoice . . . with Thy glance this soul, etc."[1]

Bach, like many composers of his generation, had repeated the same words many times over to give full expression to their associated musical affect. But during the 18th century, this kind of attention to individual words, basic to so much Baroque vocal music, came to be viewed with increasing distaste. By the time Bach died, even his sons considered his music old-fashioned. It was too ornate, too elaborate—in a word, too artful.

At the same time, 18th-century critics recognized that music, as an art, is distinct from nature, and requires technique and craft. Music that seems natural and effortless, in other words, requires art and effort. According to the aesthetic theory of the time, this dichotomy between art and nature plays itself out in the person of the artist, who must combine genius (nature) with technique (art) and bring both to bear on the raw material of nature to produce a work of enduring quality.

Haydn drew a sharp distinction between the (natural) invention of a melody and its (artificial) working out. When asked late in his life how he went about composing, Haydn responded,

> I sat down [at the keyboard] and began to fantasize, according to whether my mood was sad or happy, serious or playful. Once I had seized an idea, my entire effort went toward elaborating and sustaining it according to the rules of art. . . . And this is what is lacking among so many of our young composers; they string together one little bit after another, and they break off before they have barely begun, but nothing remains in the heart when one has heard it.[2]

The genius of inspiration—the idea—is an essential first step in the process, but it is not an end in itself.

FORM AND STYLE IN THE CLASSICAL ERA

The hallmarks of Classical style began to emerge as early as the 1720s, becoming increasingly evident around the middle of the century. Music historians have used several terms to describe the stylistically diverse music of the decades between the 1720s and the 1750s. Some call it *Preclassical,* but this term carries an unfortunate (if unintended) value judgment, suggesting the music of this time is somehow not yet up to the standards of the full-fledged Classical style. Others, borrowing from art history, use the terms **Galant** and **Rococo.** Both imply a sense of grace and elegance, aptly capturing the more transparent textures evident in many works of this time.

Empfindsamkeit—German for "sensibility"—describes a characteristic aesthetic associated with the new style. In the 18th century, to be a person of sensibility of "sentiment," as it was also called, was to be attuned to nuance and detail, delighting in small things. The author Laurence Sterne mocked this aesthetic in his 1768 novel *A Sentimental Journey through France and Italy,* in which the central character is so sensitive to details that he remains blind to larger and more consequential events. The term is nevertheless fitting for much of the music written around the middle of the 18th century, which tends to focus on detail and avoid thick textures and grandiose gestures.

One early marker of the Classical style is the emergence of genuine homophony—in which a subordinate voice or voices support a single prominent melodic line—as opposed to the continuo homophony of the Baroque era. More and more, the melodic

PRIMARY EVIDENCE

Nature Is the Best Dictator

Many accounts of the compositional process from the Classical era address the connections and tensions between nature and art. In his "Introduction to the Rules of Musick" published at the beginning of his collection *The New England Psalm-Singer* (1770), the Boston-born composer William Billings sums up the matter quite neatly.

• • • • •

Perhaps it may be expected by some, that I should say something concerning the Rules for Composition; to these I answer that *Nature is the best Dictator,* for all the hard dry studied Rules that ever was prescribed, will not enable any Person to form an Air any more than the bare Knowledge of the four and twenty Letters, and strict Grammatical Rules will qualify a Scholar for composing a Piece of Poetry, or properly adjusting a Tragedy, without a Genius. It must be Nature, Nature must lay the Foundation, Nature must inspire the Thought. But perhaps some may think I mean and intend to throw Art intirely [*sic*] out of the Question, I answer by no Means, for the more Art is display'd, the more Nature is decorated. And in some sorts of Composition, there is dry Study requir'd, and Art very requisite. For instance, in a *Fugue,* where the Parts come in after each other, with the same Notes; but even there, Art is subservient to Genius, for Fancy [i.e., fantasy, imagination] goes first, and strikes out the Work roughly, and Art comes after, and polishes it over. . . . Therefore . . . for me to dictate, or pretend to prescribe Rules of this Nature for others, would not only be very unnecessary, but also a great Piece of Vanity.

Source: William Billings, "Introduction to the Rules of Musick," from his *The New England Psalm-Singer* (1770), in *The Complete Works of William Billings,* vol. 1, p. 32, ed. Karl Kroeger (© 1981 American Musicological Society and the Colonial Society of Massachusetts).

focus moved to the top line and the bass line ceased to function as an independent voice. Over the course of the Classical era, the basso continuo largely disappeared. Not coincidentally, the two genres in which it did survive—sacred music and, in opera, secco recitative—were among the most stylistically conservative.

The increasing prevalence of homophony, however, did not mean the end of counterpoint. Many composers continued to cultivate canon and fugue. And even within essentially homophonic textures, more subtle forms of counterpoint became increasingly prevalent in the 1770s and 1780s with the emergence of the **obbligato accompaniment,** in which secondary voices contribute material essential to a work's musical fabric. Although subordinate to the melody, these accompanimental voices establish their own distinctive profile. For example, in the opening of Haydn's String Quartet in C Major, op. 33, no. 3 (Anthology; discussed again in Chapter 12), the principal melodic line lies firmly in the first violin part, but the second violin, viola, and cello contribute material that, although apparently subordinate at first (measures 1–3), becomes motivically distinctive as it progresses (measures 4–6).

Periodic phrase structure, basic to the dance music repertories of earlier eras, became increasingly common in all musical genres of the Classical era. The more or less symmetrical juxtaposition of antecedent and consequent musical statements is found in operas, songs, symphonies, concertos, and all forms of chamber music from the second half of the 18th century. Related to this development was a shift away from paratactic forms, in which discrete thematic ideas follow each other in sequence (A, B, C, D), to syntactic forms, in which a few thematic ideas are manipulated in various ways over an entire movement. The most important new syntactic structure to emerge in the Classical era was *sonata form,* described later in the chapter, which, like periodic phrase structure, has its roots in the structure of earlier dance and dance-related music. Another new syntactic structure, **rondo form,** described in Chapter 12, became popular in the 1780s, particularly for instrumental finales. Composers regularly exploited both forms, often with great ingenuity and wit, creating patterns that were at once distinctive and easily recognizable.

Another characteristic of Classical style, this one emerging around the middle of the 18th century, was a relative slowing of **harmonic rhythm**—that is, the rate of harmonic change within an individual phrase or series of phrases. In most music of the Baroque era, harmonies often change from beat to beat; this is much less common in music of the Classical era, when harmonic shifts tend to occur less frequently, only once or twice in a measure, for example. This change reflects the growing emphasis on homophony, which demanded a decrease in the distinctiveness of all voices other than the melody. As composers came to rely increasingly on areas of broad harmonic contrast and repetition in large-scale forms, the polarity between tonic and dominant became particularly strong during the Classical era. In the binary and ritornello structures of the Baroque era, in contrast, the return to the tonic often occurs just before the end of a movement. In the larger-scale structures of the Classical era like sonata form and rondo form, such a brief return of the tonic would sound incomplete and unsatisfying.

The Illusion of Order

The sense of balance and proportion that characterizes the Classical style is equally countered by an undercurrent of asymmetry and irregularity. Just as syncopation is possible only within a defined metrical pattern, so too did the naturalness favored by 18th-century aesthetics make room for a subversion of balance and proportion. The apparent order on the surface of much of this music often covers a more complex subsurface.

This illusion of order is captured in Jean-Honoré Fragonard's well-known painting of 1767 entitled *The Pleasant Dangers of the Swing* (Plate 12 in color insert II.) At first glance, this painting appears to depict an orderly scene of simple and innocent playfulness, a young man pushing a young woman on a swing. Closer inspection, however, reveals an undercurrent of sexual tension. Similar contrasting levels operate in music as well: what we hear on the surface may seem orderly and straightforward, yet below the surface—often not so very far down—the music is turbulent and unpredictable. Haydn, Mozart, and their contemporaries wrote music that abounds with irregularity, humor, and irony.

The Classical era is often misunderstood as an age in which composers were somehow shackled by rules. This view, like the label *Classical* itself, arose in the 19th century. But there were in fact no rules to follow or break, only conventions to observe or bend. The young Beethoven who arrived in Vienna in 1792 was considerably more conservative than the elderly Haydn, who in his time was renowned for his idiosyncratic wit and unpredictability. During his own lifetime Haydn was repeatedly compared to Laurence Sterne, the author of *Tristram Shandy,* one of the most anarchical works in all of English literature. Sterne uses—and at the same time breaks—every known convention of narrative, repeatedly making his readers aware they are reading a book. Much of the music written during the Classical era, as we will see, adopts this same approach. In a style that was supposedly natural—at least on the surface—we are repeatedly reminded of the artifice behind the effect.

The end of the Classical era is difficult to pinpoint. Some historians extend the period to the death of Beethoven in 1827; others prefer to treat Beethoven's late style

Harmony as a structural principle.   *Johann Philipp Kirnberger's* Die Kunst des reinen Satzes in der
Musik *("The Art of Strict Musical Composition," 1771–1779) devotes considerable attention to the relationship between voice leading and harmony, arguing that "all music which cannot be reduced to a natural progression of both kinds of fundamental chords"—that is, triads and seventh chords—"is composed
unintelligibly, hence incorrectly and contrary to the strict style of composition." To illustrate the importance
of harmony within even the most contrapuntal structures, Kirnberger reduces the B-minor fugue from Book
I of J. S. Bach's* Well-Tempered Clavier *to a series of harmonic progressions. The uppermost system shows
Bach's original (measures 66–67); the middle system shows a skeletal reduction of all parts with a figured
bass; the next-to bottom line shows a slightly different figured bass, including all dissonances; and the bass
line at the bottom shows the harmony reduced to its fundamental components as defined by Rameau (triads
and chords of the seventh). Although such a reduction might seem unremarkable today, Kirnberger's
method manifests a fundamental shift in theoretical thought from the Baroque to the Classical era.*

Source: Courtesy of the Library of Congress

The original title page from Mozart's "Musical Joke." *"A Musical Joke for Two Violins, Viola, Two Horns, and Bass, written in Vienna on the 14th of June, 1787 by W. A. Mozart. Op. 93," published by Johann André in 1802. The artwork fits the music perfectly, for in this sextet Mozart lampoons many of the conventions of Classical style. The part writing is intentionally faulty at times, rhythms and harmonies are displaced, and the closing fugue never quite gets off the ground. Buyers are nevertheless assured that this publication has been "edited according to the original manuscript of the author." By the end of the 18th century, consumers were beginning to demand editions of works that were accurate and genuine—that is, written by the composer named on the title page and not by someone else. André knew the exact date of composition because he had acquired many of Mozart's manuscripts, including his personal thematic catalog, from the composer's widow, Constanze.*

Source: Dover Publications, Inc.

(from about 1815 onward) as part of the Romantic era. Still others have argued that the Classical and Romantic eras together constitute a single stylistic epoch. The end date used in this book, 1800, is based less on changes of style than on changes in attitudes toward the nature of music, the profession of the composer, and the perceived role of music in society. As we see in Chapter 14, these new attitudes fundamentally changed the way music was produced and consumed.

The Emergence of Sonata Form

The most important formal innovation of the Classical era was **sonata form.** Although the term for it dates to the middle of the 19th century, this structural device had become firmly entrenched by the late 18th century. It applies to the organization of individual movements in a variety of genres—including sonatas, symphonies, and quartets—not to any sonata, symphony, or quartet as a whole.

Sonata form is essentially an expanded binary form that always modulates within the first reprise and usually involves more than one theme. The first reprise is called the **exposition** because it exposes the thematic ideas that will be manipulated in the second reprise. The exposition begins with one or more themes in the tonic, or primary key area, followed by a transitional modulation to one or more themes in the secondary key area, usually the dominant (if the movement is in a major key) or the relative major (if the movement is in a minor key). The thematic material first stated in the primary key area is conventionally labeled P (or 1P, 2P, and so on, if there are multiple themes in this key). The thematic material first stated in the secondary key area is conventionally labeled S (or 1S, 2S, and so on). The transitional material, which can have its own themes, is conventionally labeled T.

The first part of the second reprise is called the **development** because it develops the thematic ideas of the exposition. Harmonically, the development tends to be unstable and can move to almost any key other than the tonic. The harmonic instability and unpredictability of the development is counterbalanced by the **recapitulation**—the second part of the second reprise—which reestablishes the tonic. The onset of the recapitulation is usually marked by a simultaneous return to the tonic key and a restatement of the opening theme of the exposition (1P). A recapitulation typically follows the order of the exposition, sometimes closely, sometimes freely, but always with one important difference: the thematic material (S) that was first stated in the secondary key is now restated in the tonic. In other words, the recapitulation, unlike the exposition, does not modulate, but remains in the tonic, providing a sense of harmonic balance and stability. The effect is to resolve the movement's harmonic contrasts and bring it to a satisfying close. Some sonatas conclude with a **coda** (Italian for "tail") after the recapitulation. Codas, like tails, range from short to long, but they always end on the tonic.

A typical sonata-form movement, then, might be diagrammed as follows:

Sonata Form

Section	Exposition		Development	Recapitulation	(Coda)
Themes	‖: 1P 2P . . . T	1S 2S . . . :‖:	any theme(s) from exposition	1P 2P . . . T 1S 2S . . . :‖	
Key	I or i	→ V or III	unstable	I or i	I or i

In practice, no two manifestations of sonata form are entirely alike. The only constant elements are the modulation from a primary to a secondary key area in the exposition, a departure from these harmonic areas in the development, and the simultaneous return of the opening idea and the primary key area in the recapitulation. These predictable conventions provided listeners with easily recognized signposts with which they could orient themselves within a sonata form movement.

The first movement of Georg Matthias Monn's Symphony in B Major is an early example of sonata form. Probably written around 1740, the symphony exhibits both Baroque and Classical features. The first movement begins with two four-measure phrases in which the figure stated in the first phrase by the first violins is repeated in the second phrase by the second violins. This kind of sequential repetition is characteristically Baroque. The bass line, however, is decidedly un-Baroque, in that it provides harmonic underpinning but very little in the way of an independent voice. With its steady drumlike rhythm and repetition of single notes for up to two measures, the bass line also acts to slow the harmonic rhythm of the movement.

Monn
Symphony in
B Major

The First Movement of Monn's Symphony in B Major

Section	Exposition				Development			Recapitulation			
Themes	‖:1P	2P	T	1S :‖:	1P	2P		1P	2P T		1S :‖
Measure	1	9	19	26	33	39		59	67 79		86
Key	I			V	V	ii (unstable)		I			

The exposition sets out two different themes in the tonic (1P and 2P), another within the transition from the tonic to the secondary key area (T), and another (1S) in the secondary key area, F♯ major, the dominant of B. The development begins with 1P but now in the dominant. (Note that themes retain the identity assigned them in the exposition throughout a movement as a whole, regardless of the key in which they might subsequently appear.) The development then circulates through a series of harmonies, none of which establishes an area of clear stability. From measure 39 until the end of the development, a variant of the musical idea 2P predominates. At measure 59, the recapitulation begins with the return of the opening theme (1P) in its original key. At measure 67, we hear what is recognizably 2P, but in a different form. Beginning in measure 79 we hear a variant of the transitional theme (T), which this time remains in the tonic, leading to a restatement of 1S (measure 86), likewise in the tonic. The movement has no coda and ends with the recapitulation.

Not all binary form movements from this period bear the hallmarks of sonata form. Most of Domenico Scarlatti's one-movement sonatas for keyboard lack a clear recapitulation. The Sonata in D Major, K. 492, written in the 1750s toward the end of the composer's life (1685–1757), features two areas of harmonic stability (tonic and dominant) in the first reprise but lacks a clear return of the opening idea in the tonic within the second reprise. The material originally presented in the dominant, however, is restated in the tonic in the second reprise, beginning in measure 91.

Domenico Scarlatti
Sonata in D Major,
K. 492

Like the first movement of Monn's symphony, Scarlatti's sonata features mixed elements of Baroque and Classical styles. The periodic phrase structure, relatively slow harmonic rhythm, and transparent textures look forward, whereas the virtuosic runs (measures 35–42, 91–97) and sequential passages (measures 10–16, 36–42, etc.) are more characteristic of the earlier part of the 18th century.

Binary form is not the only historical antecedent to sonata form. Another is the ritornello structure of the typical Baroque aria or concerto. Like sonata form, the ritornello structure features a modulation from a primary to a secondary key area, followed by a period of harmonic instability and a return to the tonic at the end. Thus a work like the first movement of Johann Stamitz's Symphony in D Major, op. 3, no. 2 (ca. 1752–1755), although it more closely follows a ritornello structure, can also be analyzed in terms of sonata form. Consistent with ritornello structure, two statements of the opening theme in the tonic (measure 5, measure 103) flank a middle statement of the same theme in the dominant (measure 53), with contrasting material in between. Following the pattern of sonata form, the opening section of the movement progresses from tonic to dominant; the music then moves to a different key area (measure 77) before returning to the tonic (measure 87). The return of the opening theme (measure 103) does not coincide with the return of the tonic, however, and in this sense, the recapitulation is diffused. Many movements from the mid–18th century feature such mixed elements of old (ritornello) and new (sonata) forms, however. Even in the later decades of the 18th century, composers frequently departed from the standard conventions of sonata form.

Stamitz
Symphony in D Major, op. 3, no. 2

Relationship of Ritornello Structure and Sonata Form in the First Movement of Stamitz's Symphony in D Major, op. 3, no. 2

Ritornello Structure	Rit. I						Rit. II					Rit. III	
Sonata form	Exposition						Development			Recapitulation			
Themes	1P	2P	1T	2T	1S	2S	1P	2P	2T	1S	2S	1P	2P
Measure	5	13	18	29	37	44	53	61	77	87	94	103	111
Key	I				V		V	IV		I			

By the 1760s, sonata form had established itself as the structural framework for the first movements of most instrumental works, and for some slow movements and many finales as well. Except for concertos, the influence of ritornello structure had largely disappeared. The opening movement of Johann Christian Bach's Keyboard Sonata in D Major, op. 5, no. 2, first published in 1766, is typical for its time, and not just from the standpoint of form. It is also an excellent example of the kind of music that appealed to the prevailing aesthetic at mid-century of sensibility (*Empfindsamkeit*). The simple, straightforward melodies, textures, and rhythms create a movement that is unpretentious in the best sense of the word. The first movement of this sonata offered what 18th-century critics perceived as a natural form of expression that was unforced, without overt displays of contrapuntal, rhythmic, or textural artifice.

J. C. Bach
Sonata in D Major, op. 5, no. 2

The sharp contrast between this movement by J. C. Bach and a work like his father Johann Sebastian Bach's *Goldberg Variations*, written only 25 years earlier, illustrates the generation gap that divided Classical from Baroque style. In the opening air of the *Goldberg Variations*, the theme is in the bass and remains there through all subsequent

Mannheim's "Orchestra of Generals"

Johann Stamitz (1717–1757) wrote his Symphony op. 3, no. 2, for his orchestra at the court of Mannheim, in southwestern Germany. The ensemble was renowned for its virtuosos. The critic and historian Charles Burney, who experienced firsthand almost every major ensemble of his time, wrote that this orchestra had "more solo players and good composers . . . than perhaps . . . any other orchestra in Europe; it is an army of generals, equally fit to plan a battle as to fight it." Another contemporary observer, C. D. F. Schubart, observed that "its forte is like thunder, its crescendo like a waterfall, its diminuendo is like a distant plashing brook, its piano like a breath of spring." In the 1770s, Mozart sought to find a position at the Mannheim court. He failed, but he did meet Constanze Weber, his future wife, there.

In the early 20th century, the German music historian Hugo Riemann championed the composers of what he called the "Mannheim School"—Stamitz, Franz Xaver Richter (1709–1789), Ignaz Holzbauer (1711–1783), and others—for their forward-looking orchestral scoring: extended crescendos (evident in Stamitz's symphony in the opening measures), tremolos, and an advanced integration of winds and strings. More recent research has shown that many of these devices originated in Italy and were transmitted to Mannheim through prominent operatic composers of the day.

variations; the melody in the soprano is of only momentary significance. In the opening measures of the son's work, in contrast, the lowest voice consists of repeated figurations on a series of triadic harmonies. This **Alberti bass**—so called because it was a favorite device of an otherwise obscure Italian composer named Domenico Alberti (1710–ca. 1740)—provides harmonic support for the melody in the upper voice but is not itself very engaging. The frequent repetition of the same broken chord necessarily leads to a harmonic rhythm slower than that typically found in music from the Baroque era. J. C. Bach's sonata also avoids the kind of sequential repetition so basic to much of his father's music.

Typically for music of the 1760s, the dimensions of J. C. Bach's movement are relatively small. The exposition presents only one theme in the primary key area (1P, measures 1–8), and the transitional theme (T) suggests a move away from the tonic as early as its second measure (with the A♯ in the bass at the end of measure 10) before cadencing clearly on V of V in measure 18. The first theme in the secondary key area (1S, beginning in measure 19) presents a strong contrast to the opening theme, and the exposition as a whole ends with a clearly articulated cadence (measure 42). During the development, the themes appear in fragments. The end of 1S, for example, appears at the beginning of the development in measure 43, and the beginning of T can be heard in measure 48. In measure 60, the harmony reaches what later theorists would call a "point of furthest remove" from the tonic, in this case B minor. The music then gathers itself for a retransition back to the tonic and the opening theme, which arrives with great emphasis at measure 77, the beginning of the recapitulation. In typical sonata form fashion, the themes are presented in the same order as in the exposition, but this time all in the tonic and with only small variations and embellishments.

Sonata form appealed to composers and listeners alike. Composers used it as a framework for large-scale movements incorporating multiple and often contrasting thematic ideas. Audiences, too, benefited from hearing ideas presented in a more or less predictable order and fashion. An 18th-century listener hearing a work like J. C. Bach's Sonata op. 5, no. 2, for the first time, for example, could readily apprehend the overall structure of the opening movement based on its adherence to the conventions of sonata

Composer Profile

Carl Philipp Emanuel Bach (1714–1788) and Johann Christian Bach (1735–1782)

Today, Johann Sebastian Bach's reputation overshadows that of his children, but in the late 18th century this was not the case. Indeed to the extent the senior Bach was known at all, it was primarily as the father of Carl Philipp Emanuel Bach (the "Berlin Bach") and Johann Christian Bach (the "London Bach"). The two were actually half brothers. Carl Philipp was the second surviving son

C. P. E. Bach. *Carl Philipp Emanuel Bach (center) drops in on Christoph Christian Sturm, one of the leading clerics in the city of Hamburg, who in turn is having his portrait done by the artist Andreas Stöttrup. The scene thus represents a meeting of art, music, and poetry. Sturm had written a number of poems on religious themes that C. P. E. Bach would later set to music.*

Source: Andreas Stoettrub, pen and ink-wash sketch, 1774, showing Bach and Sturm. Hamburger Kunsthalle, C. P. E. Bach. Bildarchiv Preussischer Kulterbesitz.

KEY DATES IN THE LIFE OF CARL PHILIPP EMANUEL BACH

1714 Born in Weimar on March 8, second surviving son of J. S. Bach

1723 Moves with his family to Leipzig and continues to study music under his father

1740 Appointed chamber musician and clavecinist to Frederick the Great at the court in Berlin

1753–1762 Publishes his *Essay on the True Art of Playing Keyboard Instruments*

1767 Succeeds Telemann as music director of the principal church in Hamburg

1788 Dies in Hamburg, December 14

of Maria Barbara Bach, who died in 1720; Johann Christian was the youngest surviving son of Anna Magdalena Bach, whom Johann Sebastian had married in 1721. Both boys, along with their many siblings, learned to perform and compose from their father, but they developed distinctive styles consistent with their times. Carl Philipp, after all, was a near contemporary of Gluck, whereas Johann Christian was actually three years younger than Haydn.

In 1740, C. P. E. Bach was appointed chamber musician and clavecinist to the court of Frederick II ("The Great") at Potsdam, just outside Berlin. The post gave him the freedom and resources to compose and perform in an almost ideal setting. One of his colleagues was Johann Joachim Quantz, the greatest flutist of his time and a composer of wide renown. In 1752, Quantz published what was then the definitive treatise on flute technique. The following year, C. P. E. Bach published the first volume of a two-volume treatise on harpsichord technique. Both treatises have considerable information on composition and aesthetics. In 1750, C. P. E. Bach sought to succeed his recently deceased father as Kantor of St. Thomas's Church in Leipzig, but the town council there rejected his application. In 1767, he assumed the duties of music director for the city of Hamburg, succeeding another celebrated musician of the time, Georg Philipp Telemann (1681–1767). Bach's responsibilities in this new capacity included providing music for the city's five main churches, so not surprisingly, he wrote most of his sacred music during these last years of his life. C. P. E. Bach rivaled his father's prodigiousness.

Johann Christian Bach lived for a time in Milan (in northern Italy) but in 1762 moved to London, where he served as music master to Queen Charlotte, the wife of King George III. His graceful compositions,

Johann Christian Bach. *Unlike his father, who never traveled outside central and northern Germany, Johann Christian Bach was a true cosmopolite who felt equally at home in Germany, Italy, and England. During his years in London, from 1762 until the end of his life, he enjoyed the patronage of the royal family, particularly Queen Charlotte, wife of George III. This connection led to a commission for the portrait shown here from one of the leading artists of the time, Thomas Gainsborough (1727–1788).*

Source: © Archivo Iconografico, S.A./CORBIS

KEY DATES IN THE LIFE OF JOHANN CHRISTIAN BACH

1735 Born in Leipzig on September 5, the eleventh and youngest surviving son of J. S. Bach

1750 After his father's death, continues his musical studies with his brother Carl Philipp Emanuel Bach, in Berlin

1754 Appointed music director to Count Antonio Litta in Milan, Italy

1762 Moves to England and is soon appointed music master to Queen Charlotte

1782 Dies in London, January 1

---

most of which are within the technical grasp of amateur performers, enjoyed great popularity in their time. The "London Bach" wrote in almost every genre of his era: opera, oratorio, sacred music, symphony, chamber music, and above all keyboard music. When the young Mozart visited the English capital with his father Leopold in 1764–1765, J. C. Bach played a key role in introducing them to fellow musicians and influential patrons.

Principal Works of Carl Philipp Emanuel Bach

C. P. E. Bach composed in almost all the same genres as his father, but was perhaps most prolific in his works for keyboard. These include sonatas, concertos, trio sonatas, and many individual pieces such as rondos, fantasias, and dance movements. He also wrote symphonies, songs, and many large-scale works for chorus and orchestra, including passions, oratorios, and motets.

Principal Works of Johann Christian Bach

J. C. Bach was renowned in his lifetime not only as a composer of keyboard music, particularly sonatas and concertos, but also as one of the leading composers of opera seria, of which he wrote more than a dozen. He wrote symphonies, concertos, and much sacred music as well.

form. In this sense, sonata form functions more as a broad outline than a strict plan, rather like the form of a murder mystery, with its predictable sequence of characters and events: a crime, followed by a series of clues unraveled by an investigator sorting through a string of suspects, and ending with a solution. Yet no two sonata form movements are exactly alike, just as no two murder mysteries follow exactly the same plot, even though they follow the same general and predictable outline.

The Fantasia

To appreciate the function of formal conventions in a structure like sonata form, it helps to consider the one genre without any: the fantasia. For a composer to designate a work or movement a fantasia was to alert listeners that it would provide them with no predictable framework. In the 18th century, theorists often claimed the fantasia had "no theme." This is not literally true, of course, in that every fantasia has at least one theme, and most of them have quite a few. What theorists meant by this claim is that the fantasia typically lacks a *central* theme around which the work as a whole is organized. Eighteenth-century theorists also liked to compare the fantasia to that part of the compositional process identified with inspiration, the invention of ideas. Haydn himself said that when he began to compose, he sat down at the keyboard and *fantasized* until he latched on to a theme.

C. P. E. Bach
Fantasia in C minor

In this sense, the fantasia is like a search for themes, often opening with rhapsodic, quasi-improvisatory flourishes on the triad. At the beginning of Carl Philipp Emanuel Bach's Fantasia in C minor (originally published as the finale to a three-movement keyboard sonata in 1753), we hear a series of broken arpeggios and seemingly aimless passagework. The music conveys a mood of contemplation. Indeed, it struck the poet Heinrich Wilhelm von Gerstenberg as grappling with issues of life and death, inspiring him to set an elaborate text to this music based on the celebrated soliloquy in Shakespeare's *Hamlet* ("To be, or not to be: that is the question . . ."). Gerstenberg later set a second text to it as well, this one based on the dramatic moment when Socrates drinks poison rather than compromise his ethical principles. One reason for the serious reaction this work provoked is its dramatic trajectory: it begins with a mood of resigned contemplation, becomes agitated, recedes to a lyrical tone (the Largo section), and concludes with agitated force (Allegro moderato).

Like many fantasias of the time, C. P. E. Bach's is full of abrupt changes and unexpected events. It also features long stretches without any bar lines, emphasizing the rhythmic freedom with which it is to be performed. The notated meter at the opening—allegro moderato—seems almost irrelevant. Only in the middle section do we hear a recognizable theme in a recognizable meter; but this proves transitory.

CONCLUSION

What we now think of as the Classical style emerged gradually over the course of several decades during the middle of the 18th century: many works from this period resist easy stylistic classification. But by the 1760s, an aesthetic of naturalness had come to predominate, favoring lighter textures, slower harmonic rhythms, and periodic phrase structure.

SUMMARY OF STYLE DIFFERENCES BETWEEN MUSIC OF THE BAROQUE AND CLASSICAL ERAS		
	BAROQUE	**CLASSICAL**
STYLE	Two styles, the *prima prattica* and the newer *seconda prattica*.	Sacred music tends to be somewhat more conservative, preserving basso continuo and imitative writing, but most music is written in what was then called the modern style.
TEXT SETTING	Relatively freer projection of texts with greater attention to the declamation of individual words.	Greater emphasis on sense of natural declamation; less focus on the projection of individual words.
TEXTURE	Polyphonic (in the *prima prattica*) or homophonic (in the *seconda prattica*) with a strong sense of polarity between the two outer voices ("continuo homophony").	Predominantly homophonic, especially in the early years of the Classical era, although with increasing use of nonimitative counterpoint ("obbligato accompaniment") in later decades.
RHYTHM	A cultivation of extremes between simplicity and complexity, typically determined in vocal works by the text. The tactus gives way to a stronger sense of meter with fixed units of "strong" and "weak" beats.	Periodic phrase structure predominates, but this supposedly natural symmetry is often inflected by subtle irregularities.
MELODY	More openly virtuosic, with more opportunities for embellishment by soloists. A growing differentiation between vocal and instrumental idioms.	Predominantly lyrical, with emphasis on periodic phrase structure. Virtuosity remains an option, but an aesthetic of naturalness predominates.
HARMONY	Primarily tonal, especially by the end of the 17th century, with harmony conceived of as a progression of vertical sonorities. Relatively freer treatment of dissonance and voice leading.	A relatively slower harmonic rhythm, with limited and carefully controlled use of dissonance. The growing polarity of tonic and dominant allows composers to create movement-length forms on the basis of large-scale areas of harmonic stability.
FORM	Both paratactic and syntactic, that is, with subunits connected rhythmically, harmonically, and thematically. Increasing use of ostinato patterns, binary form, and the ritornello principle.	Syntactic forms predominate, particularly binary form and its outgrowth, sonata form; rondo form becomes increasingly popular in finales after 1780. The only significant paratactic form is the set of variations on a theme.
INSTRUMENTATION	Composers have the option of either a cappella or concertato scoring, the latter with independent instrumental parts that complement rather than double the vocal lines. Vocal and instrumental idioms become increasingly differentiated.	A clear distinction between vocal and instrumental parts becomes the norm. The nucleus of the modern orchestra (strings, winds, brass, percussion) emerges as the standard ensemble for large instrumental works.

Instrumental Music in the Classical Era

Public demand for instrumental music grew steadily over the course of the Classical era, driven in part by the increasing internationalization of the music publishing trade, in part by the growing affluence of middle- and upper-middle-class musical amateurs. These amateurs sought out the latest chamber music, and publishers were there to sell it to them. A string quartet by Mozart printed in Vienna would now be readily available in, say, London or Paris. And composers kept publishers and musicians alike supplied with a remarkable outpouring of new works.

THE LANGUAGE OF INSTRUMENTAL MUSIC

Since antiquity, theorists and musicians had considered vocal music superior to purely instrumental music. Most Enlightenment thinkers who had something to say about music concurred in this evaluation. Jean-Jacques Rousseau, for example, writing in the 1760s, criticized instrumental music on much the same grounds as Plato had more than two thousand years before. Without words, Rousseau argued, music could please the senses, but it could not embody concepts or reason:

> The words to be sung usually provide us with the means to determine the object being imitated, and it is through the touching sounds of the human voice that this image awakens in the depth of our souls the sentiment it is intended to arouse. . . . To understand what all the tumult of sonatas might mean . . . we would have to follow the lead of the coarse painter who was obliged to write underneath that which he had drawn such statements as "This is a tree," or "This is a man," or "This is a horse." I shall never forget the exclamation of the celebrated Fontenelle, who, finding himself exhausted by these eternal symphonies, cried out in a fit of impatience: "Sonata, what do you want of me?"[1]

At the same time, instrumental music was gaining respect. Although it lacked vocal music's ability to convey meaning, commentators agreed that it nonetheless constituted a "language of the heart," governed by its own rules of syntax and rhetoric. The idea that instrumental music had a syntax and rhetoric of its own, analogous to the syntax and rhetoric of language, emerged, as we saw, in the early 1700s (see Focus: "Musical Rhetoric," in Chapter 10). By the second half of the century, this idea had become widely accepted.

In 1787, the composer and theorist Heinrich Christoph Koch (1749–1816) published a textbook on composition in which he taught students how to construct melodic sentences from two- to four-measure-long phrases. According to Koch, just as a linguistic sentence consists of a subject and predicate, the basic components of a musical sentence, or melody, are a subject phrase followed by a predicate phrase. Koch shows a variety of techniques for expanding simple musical sentences, then shows how to join musical sentences into larger units of musical syntax—paragraphs—that cohere by virtue of their common melodic material.

According to Koch and other theorists, an entire movement must carefully combine elements to produce what was called "unity in variety"—a sufficient degree of contrast within an integrated whole. To burden a short movement, for example, with four "completely different melodic units," Koch argued, would create so much variety that it "would destroy a still more basic element of the piece, namely its unity and symmetry."

A key concept in the Classical analysis of instrumental music in rhetorical terms is that of the *Hauptsatz* (German for "head sentence," or more idiomatically, "topic sentence"). The inner coherence of an instrumental work, according to Classical theorists, depends on the way the composer manipulates and sustains the *Hauptsatz*. They compared its function to that of a gospel reading for a church sermon. Just as all the points in a well-structured sermon always relate directly or indirectly to the reading, so all the thematic material in an instrumental movement relate directly or indirectly to the *Hauptsatz*.

FORM AND GENRE IN THE INSTRUMENTAL MUSIC OF THE CLASSICAL ERA

The most important genres of the Classical era—sonata, string quartet, symphony, concerto—consisted of three or four movements that provided distinct contrasts of tempo. First and last movements were normally fast; the middle movement (or one of the middle movements) was slower. Slow movements could take many forms: sonata form, theme and variations, and ternary (ABA) are the most common.

In four-movement cycles, one of the interior movements (usually the third) was almost always a **minuet.** This kind of movement was often rollicking and sometimes downright boisterous, adding a touch of levity to what might otherwise be a mostly serious work. Derived from a Baroque dance form, the minuet is always in triple meter and almost always consists of two juxtaposed binary forms. The first of these binary forms is called the **minuet proper,** and the second is called the **trio.** At the end of the trio, the minuet proper is repeated, as in a da capo aria. The trio often presents a contrasting mood and typically has a distinct theme or themes of its own; it might also be in a different key or mode.

Finales, too, can take on a variety of forms, the most common of which are sonata form and (particularly from the 1780s onward) **rondo,** a type of movement associated largely with finales and found in many different instrumental genres, including symphonies, string quartets, concertos, and sonatas. Like the minuet, the rondo derives from a Baroque dance form, used for a lively round dance. Rondos appear in many guises, but they always involve the alternation of a recurring theme with contrasting material. In the simplest terms, this pattern can be diagrammed as ABACADA, with A representing the opening, recurring idea (often called the **refrain**), and B, C, and D representing contrasting ideas (known as **episodes,** or **couplets**).

The opening theme, or refrain, of a rondo movement is typically brief and catchy. It is almost always a closed, self-contained unit consisting of an antecedent and consequent phrase with a cadence in the tonic. The first contrasting episode, or couplet, tends to be brief, thereby giving listeners an early return to the refrain. Longer digressions from the refrain usually appear later in a movement.

As with sonata form, composers used the basic rondo structure as a point of departure for any number of related formal schemes. They might, for example, have bundled more than one contrasting episode between refrains to create a pattern like ABACDAEFBA. They also overlaid aspects of sonata form on the rondo to create what eventually came to be known as **sonata-rondo form.** In this synthesis, the first episode (B) is presented in a secondary key, like a theme in the secondary key area of a sonata-form exposition; when this theme reappears toward the end of the movement, it is transposed to the tonic, as in a sonata-form recapitulation. In general terms, then, a sonata-rondo form might look like this:

Sonata-Rondo Form

Theme	A	B	A	C	A	B	A
Key	I	V	I	X (unstable)	I	I	I

In practice, movements rarely follow this form strictly. Rondo, like sonata form, provided composers with a general framework for the presentation of ideas, not an unchangeable design.

Sonata

The sonata remained the quintessential domestic genre of instrumental music in the Classical era. The keyboard sonata, in particular, flourished throughout the second half of the 18th century, thanks to the growing availability of the piano.

The keyboard sonata by Johann Christian Bach (op. 5, no. 2; Anthology), discussed in Chapter 11, is typical of the genre at mid-century. It is light textured and small in scale, can be played equally well on harpsichord or piano, and places only limited technical demands on the performer.

Haydn
Piano Sonata in C minor, Hob. XVI:20

The same cannot be said of Haydn's Sonata in C minor, Hob. XVI:20, published in 1771, only four years later than Bach's. This three-movement work is indicative of the increasing scale of late-century sonatas. Compared to Bach's it is longer, more varied musically and emotionally, and more demanding of the performer. Reflecting Haydn's fascination with the possibilities of the newer instrument, it also exploits the dynamic capabilities of the piano to great effect. A harpsichord, for example, would be incapable of the rapid shifts from *forte* to *piano* in measures 13–14.

The first eight measures of the sonata also illustrate Haydn's ability to create irregular patterns even within the constraints of periodic phrase structure. The opening two measures present a standard tonic to dominant progression, leading the listener familiar with this kind of pattern to expect the next two measures to lead back from the dominant to the tonic, completing a closed unit. But Haydn delays the **half-cadence** (a cadence on the dominant) by repeating the turning figure sequentially to create an antecedent phrase of four rather than two measures. The next two measures (5–6) reiterate the tonic, but this time in a lower register—register will be a very important compositional element in this movement—and after a surprise flourish in measure 6, the music returns to the tonic in measure 8. This initial point of harmonic and rhythmic closure, however, is not very strong. The composer does not yet want the music to come to a complete stop, so he creates the expectation of continuity by placing the tonic cadence on the third beat of the measure rather than the downbeat and also by leaving it harmonically "empty"— that is, as unharmonized octave C's. We may be at the end of a sentence, Haydn is telling us, or even of a paragraph, but certainly not the end of a chapter or an entire work. In one sense, then, this opening eight-measure unit fulfills all our expectations about melodic and rhythmic structure. The first four measures take us from the tonic to the dominant, and the second four bring us back to the tonic. Haydn, however, has manipulated the inner workings of this larger progression in ways that are full of small surprises. Again, the music is rather like Fragonard's painting of the girl on the swing—it seems simple on the surface but on close inspection reveals subtle complications.

Haydn's sonata also features a style of writing that some commentators today refer to as **Sturm und Drang** ("Storm and Stress"). The term comes from the title of a play written in the late 18th century and applies to a small but significant body of music written during the late 1760s and early 1770s by such composers as Haydn, Mozart, Gluck, and Johann Baptist Vanhal (1739–1813). The characteristics of Sturm und Drang music include a predilection for the minor mode and such extreme gestures as large melodic leaps, jagged syncopations, and sudden dynamic contrasts. The overall result is a sense of heightened emotional intensity and drama. Haydn wrote several works that fit this description during the late 1760s and early 1770s, including, in addition to the Piano Sonata in C minor, the Symphonies nos. 45 in F# minor and 49 in F minor and the String Quartet in F minor, op. 20, no. 5. Mozart's Symphony in G minor, K. 183, and his Quartet in D minor, K. 173, both of which were written in the early 1770s, also fit the Sturm und Drang label.

String Quartet

Although composers had written chamber works for four instruments during the Baroque era—some trio sonatas, for example, fall into this category—the string quartet is new to the Classical era. Two features in particular distinguish it from most earlier genres. Its performance forces—two violins, a viola, and a violoncello—are all from the same family, giving it a homogeneous timbre, and it has no basso continuo line. Although manuscript copies of some early string quartets include a figured bass, the cello and viola lines together provide the necessary harmonic underpinning that in earlier times would have been supplied by the basso continuo.

The limited timbral variety of the string quartet posed a special challenge to composers but also contributed to the genre's prestige. Contemporaries compared a good quartet to an intimate conversation among a close group of friends, in which the participants exchange ideas. It was a domestic genre, designed for performance in the house or salon to a small and select audience. During the Classical era, string quartets were rarely performed at public concerts. Some of Haydn's string quartets may have been performed publicly in London in the 1790s, but this would have been an exception.

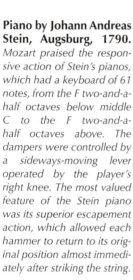

Piano by Johann Andreas Stein, Augsburg, 1790.
Mozart praised the responsive action of Stein's pianos, which had a keyboard of 61 notes, from the F two-and-a-half octaves below middle C to the F two-and-a-half octaves above. The dampers were controlled by a sideways-moving lever operated by the player's right knee. The most valued feature of the Stein piano was its superior escapement action, which allowed each hammer to return to its original position almost immediately after striking the string.

Source: Collection of the Music Instrument Museum, City Museum of Munich/ Musikinstrumentenmuseum im Münchner Stadtmuseum-Inv. #88-13

String quartets of the Classical era typically consist of three, four, or five movements, with the four-movement format emerging as the standard in Haydn's works around the late 1760s. The quartets of Haydn and Mozart surpass those of their contemporaries in textural richness and technical difficulty, qualities that did not always impress critics. Mozart's quartets in particular came under fire for being overly elaborate and complex. One anonymous critic complained that Mozart "aims too high in his artful and truly beautiful writing, in order to become a new creator, so that little is gained for feeling and for the heart. His new quartets for two violins, viola, and cello, which he has dedicated to Haydn, are certainly too highly seasoned—and what palate can endure this for long?"[2]

Haydn
String Quartet in C Major, op. 33, no. 3

The first movement of Haydn's String Quartet in C Major, op. 33, no. 3, illustrates his characteristic textural richness. In one sense, the repeated notes in the second violin and viola parts in the opening measures are clearly accompanimental. The pulsing rhythm and unchanging pitch seem to be preparing us for the entry of a more engaging melodic line, which does indeed begin to emerge in the first violin in measure 2. Yet the surprising changes of pitch in this seemingly innocuous pulsing figure give it a growing significance: the C and E in the opening measures shift to F and D in measure 7, and B♭

and D in measure 13. What appears to be a subordinate figure emerges as a motivic idea in its own right, blurring the boundary between melody and accompaniment. That boundary is similarly ambiguous in the interaction between the first violin and the cello from measures 18 to 26. Are the two parts exchanging the melody from measure to measure, or is the cello figure merely accompanying the longer note values of the violin's melody? What these examples illustrate is the truly obligatory nature of the obbligato accompaniment in this quartet. Blending counterpoint with homophony, Haydn has created a texture in which accompaniment and melody are inextricably linked.

The lively second movement of this quartet, which Haydn labeled "scherzo," follows the typical structure of a minuet, with measures 1 to 34 constituting the minuet proper, measures 35 to 51 the trio. (Why Haydn chose to call this movement and its counterparts in the other quartets in op. 33 scherzos rather than minuets is not clear.) The duet between the first and second violin in the trio provides another example of the blending of homophony and counterpoint. The first violin clearly carries the melody within this simple two-voiced texture, but the second violin line provides nonimitative counterpoint to the melody.

The slow third movement of Haydn's quartet is in **sonata form with varied reprise.** In this variant of sonata form, the exposition is not repeated note for note, but instead written out and changed in subtle ways. The varied reprise in this particular movement begins with the return to the tonic in measure 30 and a restatement of the opening theme with new melodic embellishments, especially in the first violin. The modulation to the dominant, confirmed in measure 14 in the first statement of the exposition, is repeated in the second statement in measure 43, again with an elaboration in the first violin part. The effect is similar to that of a da capo aria, in which the singer was expected to embellish a reprise the second time through. In this case, however, Haydn specified the embellishment, rather than leaving it up to the performer. After a short development section (measures 59–64), the music returns to the tonic (measure 65) at the onset of the recapitulation, which repeats the themes of the exposition, but this time all in the tonic.

The last movement, a rondo, illustrates one of Haydn's favorite devices in this form—to incorporate thematic material from the opening refrain (the A section) within a contrasting episode. The A section (measures 1–22) and the B section (measures 23–36) are clearly distinct. The material in measures 37 to 72, however, which leads back to a second statement of A, is as long as the A and B sections combined and based on material from A. By manipulating harmonies and fragmenting the thematic material into increasingly small units, Haydn makes the return to A at measure 72 a significant event, even though it offers no thematic contrast to what precedes it. What, then, is the formal status of the material in measures 37 to 72? Because it is based on thematic material from A, it could be considered a statement of A within a typical rondo structure. Functionally, however, it is more like an extended retransition—a return to the opening idea—or even (in sonata-form terms) a development section. The finale as a whole can also be analyzed as a type of sonata-rondo form, as in the following diagram:

Sonata-Rondo Form in the Fourth Movement of Haydn's String Quartet in C Major, op. 33, no. 3

Theme	A	B	retransition	A	B	retransition	A	Coda
Measure	1	23	37	72	93	107	125	147
Key	I	vi	x (unstable)	I	i	x → V	I	

These overlapping interpretations of a single movement reflect the way Haydn, like many composers of the Classical era, manipulated established conventions, working within the parameters of these forms but never constrained by them.

Symphony

In the early decades of the 18th century, the terms *symphony* and *overture* were synonymous. Sometime around the 1720s, however, these one- or three-movement works (fast-slow-fast) began to appear outside the theater, independent of any opera or oratorio for which they had originally been written. The earliest independently composed symphonies are believed to have been written in the 1720s by the Italian composer Giovanni Battista Sammartini (1701–1775). The concert symphony was cultivated intensely throughout the Classical era: composers across Europe wrote a staggering number of such works for performance at courts, in churches, and increasingly in public concerts (see Focus: "The Rise of the Public Orchestral Concert"). One recent scholar has catalogued more than twelve thousand symphonies written between roughly 1720 and 1810.

The quality of orchestras varied widely within Europe, but their size grew steadily during the second half of the 18th century. Haydn's symphonies, which span some four decades from the 1750s through the 1790s, provide a convenient reflection of this trend. His early symphonies typically call for strings (first and second violins, violas, cellos, double basses) and two oboes, with an occasional flute (sometimes two) or a pair of bassoons, or both. Relatively few of these early symphonies call for horns, trumpets, or timpani. From the late 1760s on, two horns became standard. By the mid-1780s, trumpets and timpani were routinely added to the mix. Haydn was relatively slow to accept clarinets into the orchestra, but in his last four symphonies, written in the mid-1790s, he included them as well. Mozart, in contrast, had scored clarinets into his symphonies of the late 1780s, and the Belgian composer François-Joseph Gossec (1734–1829) had been using them since the 1770s.

Like other composers, Haydn also used special instruments or combinations of instruments from time to time to give a distinctive color to individual symphonies. In his Symphony no. 22 in E♭ Major (nicknamed "The Philosopher" by a later generation of listeners), for example, he substitutes two English horns for the oboes. His Symphony no. 39 in G minor, from the late 1760s, uses four horns. And in his Symphony no. 100 in G Major from 1794 ("Military"), he incorporates a number of so-called Turkish instruments for special effect at certain points. (These instruments, which include the bass drum, cymbal, tambourine, and triangle, were associated with the style of Turkish music.)

Although we tend to think of the Classical symphony as a four-movement form (fast-slow-minuet-fast), these works, the early ones in particular, actually display considerable variety in the sequence and number of movements. Many of Haydn's early symphonies, for example, have only three movements, a pattern derived from one of the genre's antecedents in the theater—the so-called **Italian overture**—which consisted of three movements in the order fast-slow-fast. (Many Classical era operas featured overtures of this kind.) In addition, the finales of early symphonies are not always fast. Some are minuets or in the minuet style.

By the early 1770s, the concert symphony had begun to distinguish itself from other genres of instrumental music by its lofty tone as well as the number of performers it required. The first movements of "the best chamber symphonies," according to the composer and critic Johann Abraham Peter Schulz (1747–1800),

contain grand and bold ideas, free handling of compositional techniques, apparent irregularity in the melody and harmony, strongly-marked rhythms of various sorts, powerful bass melodies

The Rise of the Public Orchestral Concert

F
O
C
U
S

The first regularly scheduled public concerts of orchestral music date to the Classical era. The range and nature of offerings, however, varied from city to city.

London, with a variety of concert-producing organizations, enjoyed Europe's most active and publicly accessible musical life. The Bach-Abel Concerts, organized jointly by Johann Christian Bach and Carl Friedrich Abel, flourished from 1766 to 1782. The Concerts of Ancient Music, founded in 1776, were unusual for its time in that they played no music less than twenty years old and was particularly committed to music by Handel. The Professional Concerts (1783–1793) were organized by the Italian Muzio Clementi and the Germans Wilhelm Cramer and Johann Peter Salomon. In 1786, Salomon formed his own organization and five years later brought Haydn to London. Occasional concerts organized for special events provided yet another venue for the public consumption of music. Less formal but no less important were the many performances held in the city's "pleasure gardens"—a sort of genteel amusement park—that appealed to a still wider audience.

The focus of musical life in Paris continued to be the court and the residences of the aristocracy. The public *Concerts spirituel* series and the *Concerts de la Loge Olympique* were nevertheless important

institutions in prerevolutionary Paris. It was for the latter of these that Haydn was commissioned to write his "Paris" symphonies (nos. 82–87) in 1785–1786.

Vienna, where private orchestras thrived in the 1780s and 1790s, followed much the same pattern as Paris. There were, however, a few regular public concert series, and occasional concerts open to a paying public also became increasingly common during this period. Mozart, for example, organized and performed in a number of such concerts in the 1780s, often playing his own piano concertos. His father, Leopold Mozart, reported approvingly to his daughter after one such event, "a great many members of the aristocracy were present. Each person pays a gold sovereign or three ducats for these concerts. Your brother is giving them in the Mehlgrube [a local theater] and pays only half a gold sovereign each time he uses the hall. The concert was magnificent and the orchestra played splendidly."[3]

In Berlin, concert life outside the court was relatively slow to develop. The opera was open to the public, but instrumental music enjoyed little support. A civic choral society, the *Singakademie*, played an important role in reviving the music of Johann Sebastian Bach in the early 19th century and provided a model for other German cities to follow in establishing their own amateur musical societies.

and unisons, concerting middle voices, free imitations, often a theme handled fugally, sudden transitions and shifts from one key to another, which are the more striking the weaker the connection is, bold shadings of *forte* and *piano*, and particularly the *crescendo*, which has the greatest effect when used with a rising melody and its climax. To this is added the art of weaving all the voices in and out of one another in such a way that all parts, when played together, create a single melody that is incapable of accompaniment, but rather one in which every voice is making its own particular contribution to the whole. Such an Allegro in a symphony is like a Pindaric ode: it elevates and moves the soul of the listener in the same way, and it requires the same spirit, the same sublime imagination, and the same knowledge of art to be fully appreciated.[4]

The powerful, sudden, and wholly unexpected drumroll that opens Haydn's Symphony no. 103 in E♭ Major illustrates what critics like Schulz had in mind when they wrote of the sublime in music. It would have struck contemporary listeners as loud, bizarre, and portentous, surely a signal announcing some great event, but what kind of event? It gets our attention but not necessarily our sympathy. The musical idea that follows is dark, fragmented, and difficult to grasp, like a painting of a scene shrouded in mist. Only later will we realize that what we are hearing is a premonition of themes to come.

**Haydn
Symphony no. 103**

Interior of a Brass Instrument Workshop in Paris, ca. 1760. *The scale of this workshop is small compared to the instrument factories of the mid–19th century. In the 18th century, instruments were made by licensed masters who took on journeymen and apprentices learning their trade. Workshops like this one had no external source of power. Pounding, shaping, and polishing were all done entirely by hand.*

Source: Dover Publications, Inc.

The opening theme in the low strings reinforces the mysterious air of this slow introduction. The first two measures sound very much like the opening of the *Dies irae* ("Day of wrath") from the plainchant Mass for the Dead (see Example 12-1). (Thirty-five years later, Hector Berlioz would use the complete *Dies irae* melody in the finale of his *Symphonie fantastique;* see Chapter 15).

The slow introduction ends with what contemporary audiences must surely have perceived as a bizarre pounding on the notes G and A♭ (measures 35–39). But what sounds dark and ominous at the end of the slow introduction is immediately transformed into a bright and airy theme at the beginning of the Allegro con spirito that follows. Progressions like this—from somber to bright, dark to light, obscurity to clarity—are another manifestation of what 18th-century critics considered sublime. The sudden deflection from the dominant of C minor to E♭ Major is likewise another portent of things to come, this time of the many other sudden and unexpected modulations that abound in this symphony.

Example 12-1 Plainchant Sequence *Dies irae* from the Mass for the Dead.

Di - es ir - ae, di - es il - la, Sol - vet   sae - cu - lum   in fa - vil - la

Day of wrath, day that will dissolve the world in ashes

As is typical of slow introductions in general, the slow introduction to Symphony no. 103 follows no established conventions of form; instead, it represents something along the lines of a fantasia. It nonetheless shares important elements with the body of the first movement that follows. The down-and-up half-step motion of the *Dies irae*–like theme in the introduction, for example, resurfaces in the opening theme of the Allegro con spirito. The opening drumroll itself prefigures a remarkable number of themes in the first movement (and the symphony as a whole) that incorporate repeated notes. Among these are the principal theme of the sonata-form section of the movement (measures 39–40) and the transitional theme beginning at measures 58–59. The opening idea of the finale also features repeated notes, as does the theme of the second reprise of the minuet.

Concerto

As in the Baroque era, the concerto was the principal genre for instrumental virtuosos to showcase their talents during the Classical era. Concertos for keyboard—harpsichord or piano—were an important new addition to the repertory of the late Baroque and early Classical eras. Johann Sebastian Bach was one of the first to write concertos for the harpsichord, and his sons followed in his footsteps. Like the sonata (but unlike the symphony after about 1770), most concertos of the Classical era are in three movements (fast-slow-fast), without a minuet.

The ideals of spontaneity and improvisation exerted a powerful influence on the concerto genre. Cadenzas in every movement, particularly the first, were expected to be (or at least appear to be) moments of intense improvisation, giving performers free rein to exercise their fancy. Although Mozart wrote out many of his own cadenzas, these were presumably for friends and students. Not until Beethoven's last piano concerto, written in 1809, did composers begin to write obligatory cadenzas, and even then only sporadically.

The first movements of many concertos of the Classic era, including Mozart's piano concertos, employ a variant of sonata form called **double-exposition concerto form.** As the name implies, this structural convention presents two expositions, the first for the full orchestra (the tutti exposition) and the second for the soloist (the solo exposition). The tutti exposition does not modulate and remains essentially in the tonic throughout. The solo exposition begins in the tonic and then moves to the secondary key area, as in a conventional sonata-form exposition (I to V or i to III). Development and recapitulation proceed along the lines of conventional sonata form, at least harmonically, with the addition of an opportunity for a solo cadenza toward the end of the recapitulation.

Double-Exposition Concerto Form

Section	Tutti exposition	Solo exposition	Development	Recapitulation	Cadenza & coda
Key	tonic	tonic → secondary	unstable	tonic	tonic

The first movement of Mozart's Piano Concerto no. 1, based on Johann Christian Bach's Keyboard Sonata in D Major, op. 5, no. 2 (discussed in Chapter 11), illustrates the relationship between sonata form and double-exposition concerto form. For the first eight measures, Mozart closely follows Bach's sonata (Anthology), adding additional accompaniment in the inner voices (second violins and violas) but making no structural changes. At the beginning of the transition, however (measure 9), when the sonata modulates to the dominant, the concerto stays in the tonic. Mozart then abbreviates much of

Mozart
Piano Concerto in D Major, K. 107, no. 1

Composer Profile

Joseph Haydn
(1732–1809)

Haydn's father made wagon wheels for a living, but his family and their neighbors in the village in which he was born recognized the boy's musical talent and sent him to Vienna when he was 8 years old. There he sang in the choir at St. Stephen's Cathedral and absorbed the repertory of the late Baroque and early Classical eras. When Haydn's voice broke, he was no longer of any use to the chorus at St. Stephen's and was, by his own account, thrown out on the street. He survived by giving music lessons and eventually drew the attention of the aristocratic Morzin family, who hired him as their music director in 1758. Three years later, he was lured away by Prince Paul Anton Esterházy, who was in the process of assembling what by all accounts was one of the best orchestras in Europe at the time. Prince Paul Anton died in 1762, but his brother and successor, Prince Nikolaus, was willing to spend even *more* money on music.

Haydn was thus in an ideal position to create new music. Late in life, he told one of his biographers, "My Prince was satisfied with all of my works and I received applause. As the director of an orchestra, I could make experiments, observe what elicited or weakened an impression, and thus correct, add, delete, take risks. I was cut off from the world, no one in my vicinity could cause me to doubt myself or pester me, and so I had to become original." A lesser composer might easily have fallen into a comfortable routine, churning out symphonies, sonatas, and quartets according to his patron's requirements, but Haydn imposed astonishing demands on himself. Beyond certain outward similarities, every one of his works seems to define its own issues and standards.

Haydn's first contract with the Esterházy family required him to "compose such music as His Serene Highness may command, and neither to communicate such compositions to any other person, nor to allow them to be copied, but he shall retain them for the exclusive use of His Highness, and not compose for any other person without the knowledge and gracious permission of His Highness." He was obliged to "appear daily . . . in the antechamber before and after midday, and inquire whether His Highness is pleased to order a performance of the orchestra." Haydn was also required "to instruct the female vocalists, in order that they may not forget in the country what they have been taught with much trouble and expense in Vienna."[5]

In spite of all this, Haydn soon became more famous than even he himself realized. Unscrupulous publishers in Paris pirated his music or placed his name on music that others had written. Haydn nevertheless spent most of his professional life writing music on demand. When his prince became obsessed with the baryton, a curious instrument rather like a viola da gamba, Haydn set to work writing literally dozens of trios for baryton, viola, and cello. When the prince was bitten by the opera bug and built a new opera house a few years later, Haydn dutifully composed new operas year after year.

The death of Prince Nikolaus in 1790 opened a new chapter in the composer's life. Johann Peter Salomon, a German-born impresario living in London, persuaded Haydn to make two extended tours to England, where he composed symphonies, songs, and a number of works for piano. After he returned to Vienna for good in 1795, he produced two highly successful oratorios (*The Creation* and *The Seasons*), a handful of Masses, and several of his finest string quartets.

Principal Works

SYMPHONIES Haydn's 106 authentic symphonies span almost his entire career. Some of the early ones are openly programmatic (nos. 6, 7, and 8 bear the subtitles "Morning," "Noon" and "Night," respectively). Others are based on plainchant themes: the Symphony no. 26, for example, uses themes from a widely performed plainchant setting of the Lamentations of Jeremiah. Still others are downright bizarre. The most famous of these is the so-called "Farewell" Symphony in F♯ minor—one of only two known

KEY DATES IN THE LIFE OF JOSEPH HAYDN

1732 Born in Röhrau (Austria) on March 31.

1740 Sent to Vienna, where he sings in the choir at St. Stephen's Cathedral.

1748 Forced to leave St. Stephen's; ekes out a living giving music lessons; composes first works.

1758 Appointed music director to Count Morzin in what is now the Czech Republic.

1761 Appointed assistant music director to Prince Paul Anton Esterházy in Eisenstadt.

1766 Becomes music director to Prince Nikolaus, Paul Anton's successor.

1790 Prince Nikolaus dies and Haydn leaves for England.

1791–1792 First English tour. Feted as a genius; receives an honorary degree from Oxford University.

1793–1794 Back in Vienna, gives lessons in harmony, counterpoint, and composition to Beethoven.

1794–1795 Second English tour; finishes the last of his twelve "London" symphonies.

1796–1801 Writes his final works, including the last quartets, two oratorios, and several Masses.

1801 Suffers the first of several strokes.

1809 Dies in Vienna on May 31.

with the widest possible audience. Examples include the drum stroke in the slow movement of the "Surprise" Symphony (no. 94), the tick-tock of the slow movement of the "Clock" (no. 101), and the opening of the slow movement of Symphony no. 98, which begins like "God Save the King," only to continue in a different fashion. At the premiere, some members of the audience must surely have begun to rise when they heard it, only to sit down foolishly a moment later.

Haydn Composing at the Clavichord. *This painting is consistent with what Haydn himself said of the way he composed: "I sat down [at the keyboard] and began to fantasize, according to whether my mood was sad or happy, serious or playful. Once I had seized an idea, my entire effort went toward elaborating and sustaining it according to the rules of art." The blank music paper underneath the inkwell, juxtaposed with the work now on the stand, suggests a work in progress. Haydn was an extremely prolific composer and proud of his ability to write quickly and efficiently.*

Source: Bildarchiv der Oesterreichischen Nationalbibliothek

18th-century symphonies in this key—in which the musicians exit one by one in the finale. Haydn was apparently trying to remind Prince Nikolaus that his musicians had stayed too long at Esterháza in the summer of 1772 and were eager to return to their families in Eisenstadt.

Many of Haydn's "London" symphonies (nos. 93–104) feature a gimmick guaranteed to resonate

STRING QUARTETS Haydn played an important role in the emergence of the string quartet as a genre during the 1750s and 1760s. Even his earliest quartets (from the mid-1750s) have no need of a supporting basso continuo: the four voices alone combine to create the necessary sonorities and harmonies. Altogether, he wrote 67 complete and indisputably authentic string quartets. The set known as "Opus 3" is probably not by Haydn.

KEYBOARD SONATAS Haydn's career coincides with the rise of the piano as the principal instrument of domestic music making. The earliest of his 36 surviving sonatas were written with the harpsichord in mind, but from the mid-1760s onward, he was clearly attracted to the piano's greater dynamic range.

SACRED MUSIC When he returned from England to Vienna in 1795, Haydn was still officially in the employ of the Esterházy family, even though his orchestra had long since disbanded. For several years in a row, Prince Nikolaus's successor commissioned Haydn to write a setting of the Mass Ordinary in honor of his wife's birthday. These late Masses contain some stunning vocal writing and music every bit as dramatic as the late symphonies. *The Creation*, an oratorio, also dates from this last period of Haydn's career.

what J. C. Bach had presented in the secondary key area, adding a cadential figure of his own (measures 24–28) to close out the tutti exposition. All this time the soloist has been playing as a member of the basso continuo, filling in harmonies according to Mozart's figured bass.

The soloist assumes an altogether different function in the solo exposition, which begins at measure 29. Now the melody moves to the piano, the accompaniment moves to the strings, and the basso continuo drops out altogether. In the solo exposition Mozart also follows J.C. Bach's sonata much more closely, modulating to the dominant on the transitional theme (measures 37–46) and staying there to introduce all the themes J.C. Bach had presented in the secondary key area. (In retrospect, we can now see why Mozart abbreviated the tutti exposition: the music would have stayed in the tonic for far too long in proportion to the movement as a whole.)

The first movement of this concerto can also be analyzed in terms of ritornello structure, a form that Mozart never wholly abandoned in his concertos. As in a Baroque concerto, the movement as a whole consists of alternating tutti and solo sections. The contrasting tutti and solo sections are easy to identify in the score with a quick look at the keyboard part: figured bass notation—indicating the solo instrument is acting as a basso continuo—signals a tutti section; the absence of figured bass notation signals a solo section. Mozart appears to have composed the cadential figure first heard at measures 24–28 precisely in order to demarcate tutti from solo sections. The tutti sections are brief in comparison to the solo sections, but they nevertheless articulate the individual sections of the whole. In the diagram here, the labels applied to the themes in the tutti exposition (which does not modulate) are based on the appearances of these themes within the solo exposition (which does modulate).

Mozart
Piano Concerto in
E♭ Major, K. 271

These same patterns of double-exposition concerto form and ritornello structure are equally evident in Mozart's later concertos, including the Piano Concerto in E♭-Major, K. 271 (1777). The very opening of this concerto reminds us (yet again) that composers were constantly playing with conventions, for here the soloist enters quite unexpectedly as a soloist almost at once (measures 2–7) before receding back into the framework of the basso continuo. (The subsequent marking of *tasto solo* indicates the soloist is to play

XCIII.

Concerto a Cembalo obligato Con Stromenti.

I.R. Schellenberg delin.   W: IV IV IV.   I.R. Holzhalb sculps.

A Keyboard Concerto, 1777. *Mozart was the first man to perform a keyboard concerto in public in Vienna. Before then, women virtuosos dominated this genre in the concert hall. The setting here happens to be domestic: a small and exclusive audience in a private setting. Some in the audience are listening, others conversing.*

Source: Zentralbibliothek Zurich

only the notes indicated, not any harmony above it, until the resumption of the figured bass markings in measure 12.)

To modern ears, accustomed to concertos that showcase the soloist, it may seem strange to hear the soloist shift repeatedly from foreground to background. The modern conception of the soloist's role, however, did not begin to emerge until the early 19th century in the piano concertos of Beethoven and did not become dominant until later in the century with the concertos of such composers as Weber, Mendelssohn, Chopin, and

The Structure of Mozart's Piano Concerto in D Major, K. 107, First Movement

Ritornello structure	Rit. I				Solo 1						Rit. 2
Double-exposition concerto form	Tutti exposition				Solo exposition						
Theme	P	[T	1S	5S]	P	T	1S	2S	3S	4S	5S
Measure	1	9	17	24	29	37	47	54	59	62	70
Key	I				I	→	V				

Ritornello structure	Solo 2				Rit. 3	Solo 3						Rit. 4
Double-exposition concerto form	Development				Recapitulation						Cadenza	Coda
Theme	1S	T	4S	1S	P	T	1S	2S	3S	4S	(improvisation on earlier themes)	5S
Measure	75	80	84	93	105	113	120	128	132	135	143	147	148
Key	unstable		V		I							

Schumann. During the Classical era, although the soloist certainly was given opportunities to shine, the relationship between soloist and orchestra was more collaborative.

From a thematic point of view, Mozart's Piano Concerto K. 271 is tightly organized: almost every idea relates in some fashion to the opening theme, or *Hauptsatz* (Example 12-2a). The three most distinctive elements of the opening idea (1P) are the arpeggiated upward leap (marked with an X in Example 12-2a), the threefold repetition of the B♭ (y), and the stepwise progression from the first scale degree (E♭) up to the fifth scale degree (B♭) and back down again (z). As early as measure 7, Mozart begins to manipulate these elements. The second theme in the primary key area (2P; Example 12-2b) emphasizes the repeated B♭ in its first half, the stepwise motion from E♭ to B♭ and back down again in its second half. The theme labeled 3P (Example 12-2c) expands on the upward arpeggiated figure (X) found in 1P. With its opening half note, 1S (Example 12-2d) picks up on the original rhythm of 1P; the upper notes of 1S outline yet another stepwise progression from the tonic to the fifth scale degree (here, in the key of B♭, the span from B♭ to F). The next theme presented in the secondary key area, 2S (Example 12-2e), syncopates the rhythm of themes 1P and 1S.

Mozart's music in general, and his piano concertos in particular, are renowned for their abundance of thematic ideas, in contrast to the music of Haydn, who tended to develop a smaller number of ideas more thoroughly. Yet Mozart's abundant themes are almost invariably linked in some way. Like all composers of his era, he took care to assure both unity and variety in his music.

Example 12-2 The thematic ideas in the first movement of Mozart's Piano Concerto in
E♭ Major K. 271.

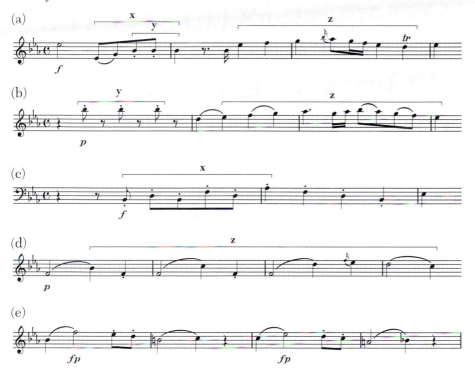

CONCLUSION

Composers of instrumental music working in the second half of the late 18th century
developed or refined a variety of genres and forms that would remain in use
throughout the 19th and even 20th centuries. The string quartet and symphony took
their place alongside such established genres as the sonata and concerto. Sonata form,
rondo, and double-exposition concerto form provided broad frameworks for the
presentation of musical ideas. By 1800, instrumental music had established itself as a
language without words. Theorists borrowed from the terminology of grammar and
rhetoric (period, phrase, antecedent, consequent) to suggest that even without words,
music could function as a language in its own right.

Vocal Music in the Classical Era

In spite of the rising status of instrumental music in the Classical era, vocal music, bolstered by the Enlightenment's emphasis on reason and rational persuasion, retained its traditional position of aesthetic supremacy. Without a text, instrumental music could appeal only to the emotions (the so-called language of the heart), whereas vocal music—sacred or secular—could appeal to both heart and mind at once.

The opera house, in particular, was a center of intense musical activity—and controversy—at any court or in any city with claims to cultural prominence. Opera's high status in the cultural hierarchy made it a subject of great critical interest and a magnet for the most talented singers, composers, stage designers, and poets of the day. Like movie stars today, these people often found themselves the focus of gossip and adulation.

Unfortunately, very few operas of the Classical era are performed with any regularity today. Other than the operas of Mozart and a handful by Christoph Willibald Gluck (1714–1787), the bulk of this enormous repertory remains largely unknown to all but a few specialists.

THE RISE OF OPERA BUFFA

As early as the 1720s, a new style of opera was beginning to emerge in Italy. **Opera buffa**—comic opera—featured many elements not found in opera seria. Its subject matter was humorous rather than serious. The libretto of the typical opera buffa centered on everyday characters rather than heroes, rulers, and gods. Singers included basses (largely absent in opera seria) but not castrati.

Opera buffa gave more emphasis to ensemble singing (duets, trios, quartets), again in contrast to opera seria, which featured mostly solo arias. Opera buffa also avoided da capo arias and other opportunities for elaborate vocal improvisations. Melodies were on the whole simple and straightforward, with increasing evidence of periodic phrase structure.

The origins of opera buffa lie in the tradition of the **intermezzo,** a work intended for performance between the acts of a larger (serious) opera. Giovanni Battista Pergolesi's intermezzo *La serva padrona* ("The Maidservant as Mistress") was written in 1733 and first performed in Naples between the acts of an opera seria also written by Pergolesi. Over time, this intermezzo, and others like it, became so well known that they were performed alone rather than between the acts of other works, thus giving rise to opera buffa as a separate genre.

La serva padrona tells the story of a maidservant who, through guile and cunning, becomes mistress of the household in which she had been employed. In contrast to the elaborate cast of characters found in many opere serie of the time, Pergolesi's intermezzo makes do with only two singers, Uberto (a bass), the master of the house, and Serpina (a soprano), the maidservant. (The character of Vespone, a manservant, is entirely mute and limited to mime.) In his opening aria, "Aspettare e non venire," Uberto expresses impatience with Serpina for failing to bring him his morning hot chocolate. Devoid of elaborate runs or opportunities for embellishment, the aria typifies what audiences of the time considered a more natural style. The music features a relatively slow harmonic rhythm and predominantly homophonic textures with frequent unisons in the strings. The vocal line consists of short melodic phrases organized around the principles of phrase structure. The work as a whole points toward the lighter style of the mid–18th century.

Pergolesi
La serva padrona

OPERA WARS

Admired in some quarters, reviled in others, opera buffa provoked controversy throughout Europe. Advocates considered it a breath of fresh air that would reinvigorate a genre grown otherwise stale; opponents considered it an affront to established traditions.

The debate raged with particular virulence in France. The dispute known as the War of the Buffoons (*Guerre des Bouffons*) was ignited by the debut of Pergolesi's *La serva padrona* in Paris in 1752 in a performance by a troupe calling itself the Bouffons ("the Comedians"). In an era when political dissent was severely limited, this dispute had implications far beyond the immediate issues at hand. Like many other artistic and philosophical controversies, it provided an opportunity for competing social groups to jockey for influence and a pretext for some to question established authority without directly confronting it. The War of the Buffoons pitted partisans of King Louis XV against those of Queen Marie, defenders of French culture against advocates of Italian style, and the entrenched aristocracy against the intellectual bourgeoisie. The king and his conservative followers sought to uphold the traditions of the French *tragédie lyrique* as represented by the stately, serious works of Lully and Rameau (see Chapter 9). Their opponents sought to use the model of opera buffa to promote a new, lighter style of musical theater in France. The philosopher and amateur composer Jean-Jacques Rousseau weighed in with his own *Le devin du village* ("The Village Soothsayer") of 1752, an opera in French about a shepherd and a shepherdess that drew on the conventions of Italian opera buffa. With its simple, unpretentious music, the work was immensely popular.

The traditionalists ultimately lost the War of the Buffoons, and in its aftermath, French composers began to incorporate elements of comic opera into their works. The most notable among them was André Grétry (1741–1813), who came to be called "the French Pergolesi." By the 19th century, comic opera would emerge as a mainstay of French musical culture.

Opera nevertheless remained a forum for public controversy in prerevolutionary Paris. In the late 1770s, another heated debate erupted, this one dubbed the Quarrel of the Gluckists and Piccinnists. Once again the debate pitted Italian against French culture, although in this case the composers at the center of the dispute—Christoph Willibald Gluck and Niccolò Piccinni—were both foreigners. Piccinni was an Italian composer who came to Paris in 1776. Gluck, who was born in the Bohemian region of the Austrian Empire and spent most of his professional life in Italy and Vienna, moved to Paris in 1773. The Parisian music-loving public saw Gluck as a worthy successor to Lully and Rameau in the French tradition of *tragédie lyrique;* Piccinni, in turn, was perceived to represent the Italian tradition of opera seria.

A riot at Covent Garden Theater. *Although today we tend to think of opera as an elite art, earlier audiences in many locales considered it popular entertainment. In London, the King's Theatre catered to a higher social class, but Drury Lane and Covent Garden attracted a more diverse audience. Here, at Covent Garden, members of the audience storm the stage because of management's refusal to admit spectators at half price after the intermission. The musicians are beating a hasty retreat for the door leading under the stage. The opera being performed, Artaxerxes by Thomas Arne (1710–1788), was one of many 18th-century works based on so-called Turkish themes (the era's term for anything Middle Eastern). At the time, Britain and other European nations were consolidating their empires abroad, and the public was fascinated with representations of exotic locales and peoples.*

Source: English School (18th Century), "Riot at Covent Garden" (engraving)/Bridgeman Art Library

GLUCK AND THE REFORM OF OPERA

While the new genre of opera buffa challenged its dominance from without, opera seria was also facing challenges from within. A growing number of poets, composers, and critics maintained that the time-honored conventions of opera seria, designed to showcase the virtuosity of individual singers, were unnatural impediments to dramatic action.

In response, several composers deliberately set out to reform opera seria to make it more natural and dramatically coherent. Notable composers working in this direction include Niccolò Jommelli, Tomasso Traetta, and, most prominently, Christoph Willibald Gluck (see "Composer Profile: Christoph Willibald Gluck"). In many respects, Gluck's aesthetic (see Primary Evidence: Gluck's Operatic Manifesto") closely resembles the principles of the Florentine camerata (see Chapter 7), whose members insisted that the words should be the mistress of the music and not vice versa.

Many of the characteristic features that distinguish so-called reform opera from opera seria are evident in Gluck's *Alceste*. The overture, which sets the tone for the action to come, flows directly into the opening scene. Aria and recitative are for the most part readily distinguishable, but the boundaries between the two are far less pronounced than in opera seria. Recitative is accompanied, rather than secco. And although the vocal

Gluck
Alceste

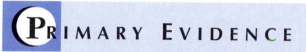

PRIMARY EVIDENCE

Gluck's Operatic Manifesto

Gluck's preface to the published score of *Alceste* is a manifesto of his artistic beliefs. *Alceste* was sufficiently different from all previous operas, in Gluck's own view, as to warrant careful explanation.

• • • • •

When I began to write the music for *Alceste,* I resolved to free it from all the abuses which have crept in either through ill-advised vanity on the part of the singers or through excessive complaisance on the part of composers, with the result that for some time Italian opera has been disfigured and from being the most splendid and most beautiful of all stage performances has been made the most ridiculous and the most wearisome. I sought to restrict the music to its true purpose of serving to give expression to the poetry and to strengthen the dramatic situations, without interrupting the action or hampering it with unnecessary and superfluous ornamentations. So I have tried to avoid interrupting an actor in the warmth of dialogue with a boring intermezzo or stopping him in the midst of his discourse, merely so that the flexibility of his voice might show to advantage in a long passage, or

that the orchestra might give him time to collect his breath for a cadenza. I did not think I should hurry quickly through the second part of an air, which is perhaps the most passionate and most important, in order to have room to repeat the words of the first part regularly four times or to end the aria quite regardless of its meaning, in order to give the singer an opportunity of showing how he can render a passage with so-and-so many variations at will; in short, I have sought to eliminate all these abuses, against which sound common sense and reason have so long protested in vain.

I imagined that the overture should prepare the spectators for the action, which is to be presented, and give an indication of its subject. I believed further that I should devote my greatest effort to seeking to achieve a noble simplicity; and I have avoided parading difficulties at the expense of clarity. I have not placed any value on novelty, if it did not emerge naturally from the situation and the expression. . . . My maxims have been vindicated by success, and the universal approval expressed in such an enlightened city [Vienna] has convinced me that simplicity, truth and lack of affectation are the sole principles of beauty in all artistic creations.

Source: Hedwig and E. H. Mueller von Asow, eds., *The Collected Correspondence and Papers of C. W. Gluck* (London: Barrie and Rockliff, 1962), pp. 22–4. Used by permission of St. Martin's Press.

Composer Profile

Christoph Willibald Gluck
(1714–1787)

Like Handel before him, Gluck was a cosmopolitan composer who seemed to be at home almost anywhere in Europe. He was born in the Bohemian region of the Austrian Empire to German-speaking parents, studied music in Italy, and lived at various times in London, Copenhagen, Vienna, and Paris.

Gluck achieved extraordinary success in Paris, where many of his Italian operas were presented in revised French versions. Like other 18th-century composers, however, Gluck composed on commission, and even in the midst of writing the most

Gluck composes. *Gluck is seated at the clavichord, a small, intimate instrument traditionally associated with the studio rather than the salon or concert hall. His gaze—directed upward to the muses for inspiration—suggests that he is composing and not performing. Note the similarity of this image to Haydn composing at the keyboard (Chapter 12).*

Source: Joseph Siffrede Duplessis (1725–1802), "Christoph Willibald at the spinet", 1775, oil on canvas, 99.5 cm. × 80.5 cm./Kunsthistorisches Museum, Vienna, Austria/The Bridgeman Art Library

KEY DATES IN THE LIFE OF CHRISTOPH WILLIBALD GLUCK

1714 Born in Erasbach (then part of Austria, now in the Czech Republic) on July 2.

1736 Moves to Vienna, plays violin for Prince Lobkowitz (a member of the same family that would support Beethoven), and later travels extensively in Italy.

1741 Composes his first opera, *Artaserse,* in the tradition of opera seria. Travels extensively, including important stays in Paris and London.

1767 Premiere of *Alceste,* in Vienna.

1773 Moves to Paris; becomes embroiled in the 'Quarrel of the Gluckists and Piccinists.'

1779 In poor health; returns to Vienna.

1787 Dies in Vienna on November 15.

famous of his reform operas (*Orfeo ed Euridice,* 1762; *Alceste,* 1767; *Iphigénie en Aulide,* 1774; *Iphigénie en Tauride,* 1779), he continued to write opere serie as the occasion demanded. Although he wrote some trio sonatas that were widely performed in his day, Gluck devoted himself mostly to opera and was known then and is remembered now as one of the greatest of all composers for the stage. In the 19th century, Richard Wagner (see Chapter 17) looked on Gluck, not Mozart, as his principal forerunner, because Gluck, like Wagner, was striving for a synthesis of music and drama.

Principal Works

Aside from a set of six trio sonatas and some ballets, Gluck's output is almost entirely vocal. He wrote dozens of operas, some in Italian, some in French; many exist in versions in both languages. His most acclaimed operas include *Demofoonte* (1742), *Orfeo ed Euridice* (1762), *Alceste* (1767), *Iphigénie en Aulide* (1774), *Armide* (1777), and *Iphigénie en Tauride* (1779).

roles for the soloists are demanding, they are by no means ostentatious. There are no da capo arias, no long melismas, and there is far less repetition of text within an aria. In keeping with principles of ancient Greek tragedy, the chorus reflects the perspective of the community as a whole, transcending that of any individual character.

Very much in the tradition of opera seria, the libretto is based on a Greek legend, that of Queen Alceste's extraordinary devotion to her husband, King Admetus. When the dying Admetus learns from an oracle that he will be saved if another mortal agrees to die in his place, Alceste resolves to sacrifice herself for him. Admetus recovers and Alceste is summoned to the underworld, but Hercules, with the blessing of Apollo, brings her back and she is restored to life.

In the excerpt that appears in the anthology (from Act II, scene iii) Admetus learns that Alceste is the one who will die for him and he pleads with her to change her mind. (The opera was originally performed in Italian in Vienna in 1767; the excerpt in the anthology is from the French version Gluck prepared for performance in Paris in 1776.) In this scene, Gluck skillfully weaves together accompanied recitative, chorus, aria, and duet into a musically continuous dramatic sequence.

Gluck's approach to opera was soon imitated by other composers seeking a more natural approach to the genre. Still, conventional opera seria did not disappear overnight. On the contrary, it continued to flourish well into the 19th century. Mozart's last completed opera, *La Clemenza di Tito* (1791), for example, was an opera seria, with the title role written for a castrato. Gioacchino Rossini (1792–1868) was still writing in the genre in the 1820s. Even Gluck himself wrote several opere serie in the last decades of his life.

MOZART AND THE SYNTHESIS OF OPERATIC STYLES

Of all the genres in which Mozart worked—and he wrote in virtually every genre of his day—his operas are justly celebrated as his greatest achievements. And of all the opera composers of his day, he stands out for two accomplishments: his ability to create psychologically complex characters and his ability to synthesize and transcend the boundaries of buffa, seria, and other operatic styles. Mozart was a keen student of human behavior, with a sharp and a wicked sense of humor. The characters in his most celebrated operas—nobles and commoners alike—are believable, three-dimensional human beings, not the heroic but essentially two-dimensional nobles who populate an opera seria like Handel's *Giulio Cesare*, or even Gluck's *Alceste*, or the stock servants and peasants who predominate in the typical opera buffa. (See "Composer Profile: Wolfgang Amadeus Mozart.")

In his early operas, those written before he moved to Vienna in 1781, Mozart tried his hand at a variety of styles and traditions, including opera seria (both conventional and in Gluck's reform style), opera buffa, and singspiele (German-language plays with songs, akin to modern-day musicals). He was thus ideally positioned to synthesize the previously separate serious and comic strands of musical drama, which he did in four late operas: *Le Nozze di Figaro*, *Don Giovanni*, *Così fan tutte*, and *Die Zauberflöte*. The three of these he wrote in collaboration with the librettist Lorenzo da Ponte (1749–1838)—*Le Nozze di Figaro*, *Don Giovanni*, and *Così fan tutte*—are generally considered his greatest, in no small part because their texts and music probe so deeply into that great central human concern: love and war between the sexes.

The plot of *Don Giovanni* is based on the legend of Don Juan, a nobleman and notorious libertine. Da Ponte's libretto is both comic and serious, pitting men against women and nobles against commoners. The title character is at once malevolent and alluring, a man who openly flaunts conventional morality, pursuing instead his own pleasure under the guise of "liberty." At the beginning of the opera he slays the Commendatore

Mozart
Don Giovanni

Composer Profile

Wolfgang Amadeus Mozart
(1756–1791)

Wolfgang's father Leopold was a competent composer in his own right and renowned in his day as the author of the most important treatise of his time on violin method. Wolfgang was a child prodigy who began composing before he was 5. When he was 6, Leopold began taking Wolfgang and his talented sister Anna (also a keyboard player) on concert tours throughout Europe.

In addition to performing, Mozart would also listen, attending whatever concerts he could. In Rome, for example, he heard Gregorio Allegri's *Miserere,* an early-17th-century work for double choir that had traditionally been reserved for exclusive performance by the papal choir. Afterward, Mozart wrote out the work from memory. In this way, city by city, country by country, the young Mozart absorbed almost everything Europe had to offer in the way of music. As a result, he could later write to his father, matter-of-factly and without boasting, that he "could write in any style" he chose.

It must have been painful for him, as an adult, to see key appointments go to lesser composers. He had to teach composition to supplement his income, and his efforts to secure a steady position at the Habsburg court in Vienna did not bear fruit until the last years of his life, when he was given a minor, essentially part-time position that entailed little more than writing new dances for New Year's galas and other celebrations.

Why was Mozart not more popular in his own time? He was certainly well known, and some of his music—most notably his operas *Le Nozze di Figaro* and *Don Giovanni*—were tremendously successful. But much of his music was perceived to be too complicated, too full of artifice. "Too many notes," the Emperor Joseph II is said to have complained after hearing one of Mozart's operas. Other composers, although they held Mozart in high regard, agreed that the complexity of his music sometimes put it beyond the grasp of contemporary audiences.

KEY DATES IN THE LIFE OF WOLFGANG AMADEUS MOZART

1756 Born in Salzburg (Austria) on January 27.

1763–1771 Undertakes a series of trips with his father to England, Holland, France, Germany, and especially Italy.

1769 Appointed concertmaster at the court in Salzburg.

1770s Continues travels across the European continent but is unable to secure a satisfactory position.

1779 Returns to Salzburg to his previous position as concertmaster and becomes court organist as well, but he detests the provinciality of his native town.

1781 Against the protests of his father, moves to Vienna to seek a position there, earning money by giving concerts and lessons, and through sales of his published works.

1782 Marries Constanze Weber.

1785 Dedicates a set of six string quartets to his friend Joseph Haydn.

1791 Dies in Vienna on December 5.

Ironically, Mozart's popularity seems to have been rising just before he died. His singspiel *Die Zauberflöte* (1791) was a great hit, and he was finally beginning to make inroads at the Habsburg court.

There is a myth about Mozart that composition was effortless for him. Like most myths, it is based on an element of truth. Mozart wrote an astonishing quantity of music, especially considering that he died just short of his 36th birthday. He often packed more melodies into a single movement than most of his contemporary composers used in an entire composition. From time to time in his letters, he mentions works he has already composed in his head but "not yet written down." He is said to have composed the overture to *Don Giovanni* the night before the first performance. And unlike Beethoven a generation later, he did not labor through multiple drafts of a single idea. However, he abandoned an enormous number of works before making very much progress on them. One recent scholar has estimated that for every work he completed he abandoned two. And although Mozart did have a remarkable ability to work out ideas in his head before committing them to paper and a quick sense of what would and would not work once he actually began writing down a musical idea, he nonetheless did sometimes revise and re-revise.

Principal Works

SYMPHONIES Mozart wrote 41 symphonies, but even though the early ones are full of delightful surprise, it is mostly the later ones that are performed with any frequency today. Unlike Haydn, who had a standing orchestra at his disposal, Mozart had no incentive to compose symphonies regularly. He apparently composed his last three symphonies (nos. 39, 40, 41), all in 1788, with an eye toward the kind of trip to London that Haydn would undertake a few years later. In many respects, these last three symphonies are even larger and more ambitious than Haydn's "London" symphonies. Mozart was much quicker than Haydn to integrate the clarinet into the orchestra. With the finale of the Symphony no. 41 in C Major, K. 551 ("Jupiter"), he established the important precedent for later composers, most notably Beethoven, of placing a symphony's emotional and intellectual weight more in the finale than the first movement.

STRING QUARTETS AND QUINTETS Mozart wrote 27 string quartets, including the 6 dedicated to Haydn and published in 1785. His late quartets are remarkable for their transparent textures. In them all four instruments participate as more or less equal partners to an extent that would not be equaled until Beethoven's middle- and late-period quartets. The cello part is especially prominent in Mozart's last three quartets (K. 575, 589, 590), which he apparently intended to dedicate to the king of Prussia, who was an accomplished cellist.

Mozart turned to the string quintet (a quartet with a second viola) relatively late in life. His two works in this genre, the Quintet in G minor (K. 515) and Quintet in C Major (K. 516), are worthy counterparts to his last two symphonies in the same keys (K. 550 and K. 551).

SOLO AND CHAMBER WORKS FOR PIANO In addition to 19 sonatas for solo piano, Mozart also wrote several keyboard duets, variations, fantasias, rondos, and minuets. He also wrote 36 sonatas for violin and piano, 6 piano trios, 2 piano quartets, and a quintet for piano and winds.

CONCERTOS Mozart's earliest piano concertos are not original works, but rather arrangements of existing sonatas or sonata movements by a variety of composers, both well known (J. C. Bach, C. P. E. Bach) and not so well known (H. F. Raupach, L. Honauer). He wrote the bulk of his 23 original piano concertos during his years in Vienna, where they provided a way to showcase his talents as a composer and performer. His correspondence reveals that he was calculating about the effects of these works on his audience. After finishing a set of three concertos in Vienna, for example, Mozart wrote to his father in Salzburg that the works were "a happy medium between what is too easy and too difficult" for listeners. "They are very brilliant, pleasing to the ear, and natural, without being vapid. There are passages here and there from which connoisseurs alone can derive satisfaction; but these passages are written in such a way that the less learned cannot fail to be pleased, though without knowing why."[1] In addition to piano concertos, Mozart also wrote five concertos for violin, four for horn, one for clarinet, one for bassoon, two for flute, and one for flute and harp.

OPERAS Mozart explored every subgenre of opera available to him in his time. *Idomeneo*, K. 366, written for the court at Munich in 1781 and later revived in Vienna, reflects the influence of Gluck's operas. *La Clemenza di Tito*, K. 621, written for the coronation of Emperor Leopold II in Prague in 1791, is in the tradition of opera seria; its text is an adaptation of a much earlier libretto by Metastasio (see Chapter 9). The male lead in both of these work featured a castrato. Mozart's *singspiele*—German-language plays with songs—include *Die Entführung aus dem Serail* ("The Abduction from the Seraglio"), K. 384, and *Die Zauberflöte* ("The Magic Flute"), K. 620. The latter is a fairy-tale opera that had a wide-reaching influence on 19th-century German opera. The three operas Mozart wrote in collaboration with the librettist Lorenzo da Ponte—*Le nozze di Figaro* ("The Marriage of Figaro"), K. 492, *Don Giovanni*, K. 527, and *Così fan tutte* ("All Women Do It Like That"), K. 588—represent an intriguing mixture of buffa and seria styles.

MASSES AND OTHER SACRED WORKS Mozart's duties in Salzburg in the 1760s and 1770s required him to write considerable quantities of sacred music: settings of the Mass and Vespers as well as shorter texts, such as psalms and offertories. In the last year of his life, Mozart received a private commission to write a Requiem but died before he could finish it.

The Mozart family. *This portrait of Mozart's family was painted around 1780, shortly before his departure from Salzburg to Vienna. The family would never again be together for more than brief visits thereafter. Leopold Mozart (1719–1787), holding the violin, presides. Mozart's sister Anna (1751–1829) sits with her brother at the piano. Nannerl, as her family called her, was also a noted keyboard performer. Mozart was the first composer to write music for four hands that required the performers to cross hands, as he and Nannerl are doing here. Maria Anna Mozart—Leopold's wife and Wolfgang and Nannerl's mother—died in 1778, but this painting reproduces a portrait of her hanging on the wall. A statue of Apollo holding a lyre occupies a place of prominence in an alcove in the wall.*

Source: Painting, Baroque, 18th Century. Della Croce, Johann Nepomuk (18th), "The Mozart Family" (1780–1781). Oil on canvas. 140 × 186 cm. Mozart House, Salzburg, Austria. Erich Lessing/Art Resource

(Commandant), the father of Donna Anna, a woman who has just fought off the Don's attempted assault. At the end of the opera, the statue of the Commendatore consigns the unrepentant Don to the flames of hell.

The overture and first three scenes of *Don Giovanni*, which together constitute some 20 minutes of continuous music and seamless dramatic action, demonstrate the way Mozart integrates buffa and seria elements. True to the principles of Gluck's operatic creed, Mozart uses the overture to set the tone of the opera as a whole, with its unpredictable juxtaposition of tragedy and farce. The opening chord, slow tempo, and heavy dotted rhythms convey a sense of ominous foreboding, and indeed this same music returns in Act II when the statue of the dead Commendatore comes to life. The sinuous chromaticism in measures 11–15 and 23–26 intensifies the ominous mood, giving the impression that this is a deeply serious opera. But in measure 31, at the beginning of the longer, sonata-form second section of the overture, the tempo becomes faster and the mood changes abruptly: chromatic lines give way to triadic melodies, gravity to lightness, minor to major, polyphony to homophony. In a broad sense, these contrasting sections symbolize opposite moral poles. The slow introduction represents the world of the Commendatore in which law prevails, crime is punished, and damnation is the sure

consequence for unrepented sin. The lighter second portion of the overture represents the world of Don Giovanni, with his devotion to pleasure and liberty.

The overture segues directly into the first scene. Leporello, the servant of Don Giovanni, stands guard outside a nobleman's house while the Don attempts to seduce yet another woman. Even before Leporello sings a single note, the music announces he is a commoner: the opening theme, which Leporello picks up when he begins his aria-monologue, bounces back and forth between tonic and dominant. There is nothing sophisticated about this theme harmonically, rhythmically, or melodically. Leporello is complaining to himself about the wicked ways of his master while at the same time longing to be a "gentleman" himself. With its relentlessly syllabic text underlay and vehement repetitions of "No, no, no," the aria sounds appropriately comical.

THE STRUCTURE OF THE OPENING SEQUENCE OF MOZART'S *DON GIOVANNI*

	Vocal number	Key	Type	Dramatic action
Overture		D minor/major	Instrumental	Slow introduction and sonata form. Leads directly into Scene i.
Scene i	1: Introduction	F major	Aria-monologue	Leporello alone.
		B♭ major	Duet/Trio	Don Giovanni and Donna Anna enter. The two noble characters struggle, singing in imitative counterpoint. Leporello stands safely apart, commenting, in the bass, in his own diatonic and decidedly nonimitative way.
		G minor	Duet	The Commendatore enters and Donna Anna exits. The Commendatore challenges Don Giovanni to a duel.
		D minor	Instrumental	Sword fight between the Commendatore and Don Giovanni
		F minor	Trio	Slow death of the Commendatore. The Commendatore, Don Giovanni, and Leporello each expresses his own thoughts in what amounts to three simultaneous monologues. Leads directly into Scene ii.
		G major B♭ major	Secco recitative	Don Giovanni and Leporello alone. Exit from stage, but with an immediate musical segue into Scene iii.
		D major	Secco recitative	Donna Anna returns with Don Ottavio and servants.
	2: Recitative and duet	G minor	Accompanied recitative	Donna Anna reacts to her father's death; Don Ottavio directs removal of the corpse.
		D minor	Duet	(a) Alternation between Donna Anna, who swears revenge, and Don Ottavio, who offers consolation; (b) Both characters swear revenge in true duet fashion, singing simultaneously.

But as in the overture, the juxtaposition of comedy and tragedy occurs without warning. Leporello's monologue segues into a frantic duet between two members of an altogether different class: the noblewoman Donna Anna and the nobleman Don Giovanni. Donna Anna pursues the unknown man (Don Giovanni), who attempts to escape unrecognized. Almost at once, the duet becomes a trio as Leporello joins their agitated exchange with more of his melodically simple line, this time commenting on the action and predicting his master's philandering will bring his own ruin.

A new dramatic unit begins with the arrival of the Commendatore, Donna Anna's father. He demands a duel with the unknown intruder. Don Giovanni reluctantly accepts and deals the Commendatore a mortal wound. Again, Leporello comments on the scene as it transpires before him, this time with an even greater sense of gloom. There follows a brief dialogue in secco recitative between Don Giovanni and Leporello, after which they exit. We then move directly into another dramatic unit, still with no real break in the music. Donna Anna returns, having summoned the aid of her kindhearted but rather boring fiancé, Don Ottavio. During the accompanied recitative that follows, they discover her father's body and she faints. Don Ottavio revives her so efficiently, however, that she is soon able to launch into her part of a powerfully dramatic duet ("Fuggi, crudele, fuggi") at the end of which they swear together to avenge her father's death. The music, agitated and virtuosic, comes from the world of opera seria. Mozart fuses the reflective power of aria (Donna Anna's shock at the death of her father) with the interchange of duet (Don Ottavio's promise of consolation and revenge), all interrupted at unpredictable moments by powerful outbursts of accompanied recitative.

Leporello's "Catalogue Aria." *This early 19th-century engraving shows the scene from Act I of Mozart's* Don Giovanni *in which the servant, Leporello, reveals to Donna Elvira the long list of names of his master's prior loves. Don Giovanni himself can be seen slipping away in the background.*

Source: Courtesy of the Library of Congress

Clearly, Mozart wanted to create a sense of dramatic continuity for the entire opening sequence of events, for it is only now, at the end of this extended duet, that he gives the audience its first opportunity to applaud. The arias and ensembles are not, as is so often the case in opera seria, reflections on events that have already happened. On the contrary, they are part of the action, propelling it forward. The events of the drama, in other words, move through the music.

One of the devices Mozart uses to structure this extended series of units is tonality (see table). The sequence begins and ends in D minor, and the choice of key in between is closely coordinated with the drama unfolding on stage. Each dramatic unit has its own distinctive key, different from yet related to the one before and the one after. Although we have no letters from Mozart detailing the creation of *Don Giovanni,* his concern with tonal design is evident in a letter written to his father in 1781 while working on *Die Entführung aus dem Serail* ("The Abduction from the Seraglio"). Describing a particular aria he had composed for the character Osmin, Mozart wrote that

In working out the aria I have . . . allowed Fischer's beautiful deep notes to glow. . . . And because Osmin's rage increases throughout, the allegro assai (which comes just at the moment when the aria seems to have reached its end) is of necessity in a totally different meter and key, thereby allowing it to make the best possible effect. For a man who finds himself in such a towering rage will overstep all bounds of order, moderation, and propriety and completely forget himself; and in just this manner, so must the music, too, forget itself. But because the passions, whether violent or not, must never be expressed to the point of arousing disgust, and as music, even in the most hair-raising situations, must never offend the ear, but must please the listener, or in other words must always remain *music,* so I have chosen a key that is not foreign to F (the key of the aria) but one related to it—not the nearest, D minor, but the more remote A minor.[2]

SACRED MUSIC

Almost every major composer of the Classical era wrote music for the church. Within the boundaries of the Holy Roman Empire, however, political factors limited the possible outlets for sacred music after 1780, when the Emperor Joseph II became the empire's sole ruler. Influenced by Enlightenment principles, the emperor instituted extensive reforms intended to limit the hereditary privileges of the nobility, strengthen the state bureaucracy, and restrict the influence of the church. His ecclesiastical reforms extended to music. Elaborate Masses requiring full orchestra, chorus, and soloists were no longer welcomed. Instead, the court encouraged simpler, more chordal settings of the liturgy. As a result, many composers—including Haydn and Mozart—abandoned the field of sacred music altogether until after Joseph II's death in 1790, when the restrictions were relaxed or dropped altogether. Even then, however, the church continued to struggle with the proper role of music in the liturgy. By the end of the 19th century, the Vatican was trying to steer its followers away from elaborate concert-style Masses on the grounds that they were overly secular.

In their orchestration, melodic style, and demand for vocal virtuosity, the sacred works of Haydn, Mozart, and others are indeed sometimes hard to distinguish from their secular theatrical works. On the whole, however, church music remained relatively conservative during the Classical era, retaining the basso continuo long after it had been abandoned in the concert hall, and well after it was still necessary from a strictly technical point of view. Sacred music also preserved more of the tradition of strict counterpoint than was customary in either the theater or the chamber. Certain sections of the Mass, such as the end of the Gloria and Credo, were often set as elaborate fugues in what was called the *stile antico,* the "old style," featuring subjects in long note values and written in alla breve meter.

Mozart
Requiem, K. 626

The Introit of Mozart's unfinished *Requiem,* K. 626, is a good example of the synthesis of older and newer styles often found in the sacred music of the Classical era. For this movement, Mozart drew on the opening chorus from Handel's *Funeral Anthem for Queen Caroline,* HWV 264, written in 1737, and available to Mozart in Vienna through Baron Gottfried van Swieten, a nobleman who took a special interest in the works of Handel and J. S. Bach. For the section beginning with the words "Te decet hymnus Deus in Sion" ("To thee, Lord in Zion, we sing a hymn"), Mozart brings in an even older source of sacred music, Gregorian chant. Here, in the soprano, he introduces the Ninth Psalm Tone (see Chapter 1), also associated in German-speaking lands with the Magnificat, another hymn of praise to God. The concluding "Dona eis pacem" ("Grant them peace") section brings back the opening theme ("Requiem aeternam") but now combines it with a new countersubject. Mozart's *Requiem* has been surrounded in controversy since the time of its composition. It was known at the time that Mozart had died before he could complete the work, yet it was in his widow Constanze's interest to portray the efforts of the various collaborators who finished it—mostly students of her late husband—as inconsequential. Scholars have been trying to sort out Mozart's work from those of others since at least the 1820s. There is no dispute, however, about the opening half of the work, including the Introit, because it has been preserved in manuscript in the composer's own hand.

SONG

If the sonata was the quintessential domestic instrumental genre in the Classical era, the song was the quintessential domestic vocal genre. Because songs were financially lucrative for composers and publishers alike, the Classical song repertory is enormous, but most of it remains unexplored today.

Zelter
Kennst du das Land?

Carl Friedrich Zelter's "Kennst du das Land?" ("Do You Know the Land?") offers a good example of the kind of song writing that flourished throughout the Classical era. The setting is strophic and largely syllabic. Both the vocal and piano parts are straightforward and technically undemanding. The range of the vocal line barely exceeds an octave. The text is from Goethe's widely read novel *Wilhelm Meisters Lehrjahre* ("Wilhelm Meister's Years of Apprenticeship"), the story of a young man's coming of age. Wilhelm is an aspiring actor who falls in with an odd assortment of characters, one of whom is a mysterious young girl named Mignon. She has no family, and Wilhelm becomes something of a father figure to her, but there is a powerful erotic tension beneath the surface of their relationship. From time to time throughout the novel, Mignon sings songs, of which Goethe gives only the words. Zelter (1758–1832) was one of the first composers to set these texts to music, and Goethe expressed his pleasure with Zelter's settings of his texts. But as we shall see (Chapter 16), many later composers were also drawn to this and other texts by Goethe that are not nearly so straightforward.

Billings
Wake Ev'ry Breath

William Billings's "Wake Ev'ry Breath," the opening song of his *New-England Psalm-Singer* (1770) illustrates what in its time was called a "social song"—that is, one intended to be sung by many voices at a social gathering like the one depicted on the frontispiece to his collection, which is reproduced here. Participants at this kind of gathering were generally not affluent enough to hire musicians, so they made their own

Women as musical performers in the church.
The priest is celebrating Mass at the high altar, but almost every eye in the (largely male) congregation is riveted on the female soloist. Even the musicians (especially the trumpeter in the opposite gallery) seem lost in admiration. The appeal is both physical and aural. This illustration first appeared in a Protestant tract in 1784 and reflects the view among at least some Protestant denominations that music in church, when performed by women, distracted the congregation from the liturgy. The Catholic church, in contrast, was more open to women performers, particularly in the Austrian Empire before 1790. The Empress Maria Theresa herself once sang the soprano part in a Mass written by Michael Haydn (Joseph's brother), and Mozart apparently wrote the virtuosic soprano line in his Mass in C minor, K. 427 (417a) for his wife, Constanze.

Source: Bildarchiv der Oesterreichischen Nationalbibliothek

Social song. *This frontispiece to William Billings's* The New-England Psalm-Singer *(1770) was engraved by the silversmith Paul Revere (1735–1818), better known for his ride from Boston to Lexington on April 18, 1775. It shows a group around a table performing the canon "Wake Ev'ry Breath" (Anthology). Music was an important element in most social gatherings, both in Europe and in the colonies of North America. The performance here is not in a church, but in a home.*

Source: CORBIS BETTMANN

music. Social singing was a tradition brought to the American colonies from England, which had long cultivated imitative part-songs of various kinds. Catches tended to be humorous, whereas glees were generally more folklike in nature; the texts of canons usually addressed moral or religious subjects. Billings (1746–1800), a native of Boston, was one of the first American-born composers to achieve international fame. He was largely self-taught, and his musical style, although indebted to English precedents, exhibits a certain roughness that gives it great energy. Billings's part-song *Chester* ("Let tyrants shake their iron rod/And slav'ry clank her galling Chains/we fear them not we trust in God/ New England's God for ever reigns") became an unofficial anthem of the American Revolution.

CONCLUSION

V ocal music—opera, sacred music, and song—maintained its traditional position of aesthetic superiority throughout the Classical era. Opera, in particular, was considered the highest of all musical genres and became increasingly accessible to a wider public, particularly in cities like London and Vienna. Although opera seria remained the favored subgenre at European courts, opera buffa appealed to a wider audience. Mozart, in particular, was able to integrate seria and buffa styles in a series of operas that fundamentally shaped the future of the genre.

DISCUSSION QUESTIONS

1. How has the idea of "naturalness" been evoked at various times in music history, up to and including the Classical era?

2. What distinguishes sonata form from binary form?

3. Many writers of the late 18th century compared the string quartet to a conversation among four rational individuals. Judging from a work like Haydn's String Quartet in C major, op. 33, no. 3 (Anthology), how valid is this comparison?

4. How does double-exposition concerto form integrate sonata form and the ritornello principle?

5. How do Gluck's principles for the "reform" of opera compare to the efforts of the Florentine Camerata in the late 16th century to create a genre of sung drama?

6. What effect did Haydn's career—the circumstances of his employment as a composer—have on the genres in which he wrote?

7. In what ways does Mozart's *Don Giovanni* retain certain elements of *opera seria?*

8. Many writers of the late 18th century conceived of instrumental music as a language, with syntactic structures analogous to linguistic phrases and sentences. How valid is this analogy?

Major Composers
of the Classical Era

FRANCE

The celebrated Swiss-French philosopher and novelist **Jean-Jacques Rousseau** (1712–1778) devoted considerable energies to music. He was an ardent advocate of Italian music and rather an outcast in France. He wrote most of the articles on music for the *Encyclopedia* and an important dictionary of musical terms (1768). His opera *Le devin du village* ("The Village Soothsayer," 1752) enjoyed great popularity in France well into the 19th century. Rousseau advocated a natural style in music that excluded elements he considered artificial, such as counterpoint and overly elaborate harmony or dissonance.

François-Joseph Gossec (1734–1829) and **André-Ernest-Modeste Grétry** (1741–1813) both gained fame as composers of opera. Gossec, who was Belgian but spent most of his life in Paris, was also active in the establishment of the Paris Conservatory in the years after the French Revolution. Grétry was widely credited with establishing the tradition of French comic opera that would thrive in the 19th century under such composers as Auber, Adam, and Boieldieu.

GREAT BRITAIN

Charles Avison (1709–1770) is best remembered for his many concertos for a variety of instruments. **Thomas Arne** (1710–1788), the composer of the tune to "Rule, Britannia," also wrote many masques and operas. **William Boyce** (1711–1779) published *Cathedral Music,* a monumental collection of sacred works in three volumes, from 1760 to 1778. He also wrote symphonies, sonatas, operas, and songs.

ITALY

Although born in the same year as Handel and J. S. Bach, **Domenico Scarlatti** (1685–1757) wrote in a style that in many ways looks forward to the lighter textures of the Classical era. Only a small fraction of his nearly 600 sonatas were published during his lifetime. These are single-movement works mostly in binary form, ranging from the technically simple to the highly demanding. The son of Alessandro Scarlatti (see Chapter 9), he spent his last three decades in the service of the Spanish court in Madrid, and it was there that he wrote the bulk of his harpsichord music.

Baldassare Galuppi (1706–1785), **Niccolò Jommelli** (1714–1774), and **Tomasso Traetta** (1727–1779) were hailed in their time as masters of Italian opera. Galuppi has been called "the father of Italian comic opera"; Jommelli and Traetta preceded Gluck in the movement to reform opera (see Chapter 13). **Domenico Cimarosa** (1749–1801) composed almost 80 operas in the span of 29 years. He served for almost a decade as court composer in St. Petersburg, Russia.

Giovanni Battista Sammartini (1701–1775), his brother **Giuseppe Sammartini** (ca. 1693–ca. 1750), and **Luigi Boccherini** (1743–1805) are best remembered for their instrumental music. G. B. Sammartini was active in Milan and was one of Gluck's teachers. His most important works are his concert symphonies, some of which date from the 1730s, making them among the earliest works of this kind. Giuseppe Sammartini lived for many years in London, where he played oboe and conducted various ensembles. Boccherini, the leading cello virtuoso of his day, spent many years in the service of the Spanish court in Madrid. Among his many chamber works are 125 string quintets, works of great beauty and formal ingenuity.

Antonio Salieri (1750–1825) and Muzio Clementi (1752–1832), born in Italy, gained fame elsewhere. Salieri was court composer in Vienna and wrote many operas. Clementi spent most of his adult life in England, gaining renown as a piano virtuoso, composer, publisher, and piano manufacturer. His most celebrated compositions are the sonatas for piano.

THE AUSTRIAN EMPIRE

Christoph Willibald Gluck (see Composer Profile in Chapter 13), Joseph Haydn (see Composer Profile in Chapter 12), and Wolfgang Amadeus Mozart (see Composer Profile in Chapter 13) are the most prominent among a remarkable number of musicians born in the Austrian empire during the 18th century. Georg Matthias Monn (1717–1750) wrote many instrumental works that fall stylistically somewhere between Baroque and Classical (see Chapter 10 and Anthology). Monn's Harpsichord Concerto would later be transcribed by Arnold Schoenberg for cello and orchestra (1933). Johann Georg Albrechtsberger (1736–1809) was a prolific composer of sacred music as well as chamber music; Beethoven studied counterpoint with him in the 1790s. Carl Ditters von Dittersdorf (1739–1799) was similarly prolific. His works include a series of 12 programmatic symphonies based on episodes from Ovid's *Metamorphoses*. Michael Haydn (1737–1806), the younger brother of Joseph Haydn, worked largely in Salzburg and was a close friend of the Mozart family. A symphony long attributed to Mozart (no. 37) was actually written by Michael Haydn. The Viennese composer Johann Baptist Vanhal (or Wanhal) (1739–1813) suffered a similar misattribution; until the 20th century several of his symphonies were wrongly thought to be by Joseph Haydn.

GERMANY

In Prussia, Princess Anna Amalia (1723–1787) and her brother, Frederick II ("The Great," 1712–1786), sponsored a remarkably active musical life at the court in Potsdam, just outside Berlin. The princess composed several instrumental works and chorales, but is best remembered for assembling an astonishing musical library that included many works by J. S. Bach. Frederick was an accomplished flutist and wrote a number of flute sonatas and concertos. His court flutist, Johann Joachim Quantz (1697–1773), contributed even more music for this instrument and wrote an important treatise on playing the flute. Another important court employee was Carl Philipp Emanuel Bach. His younger brother Johann Christian Bach enjoyed the favor of the English court in London. (See Chapter 11 for a Composer Profile on the Bach brothers.)

A native of Hamburg, Johann Adolf Hasse (1699–1783) gained renown as a composer of Italian operas that were popular throughout Europe. He also wrote many oratorios, Masses, and other sacred works. He spent his later years at the Saxon court at Dresden.

Johann Stamitz (1717–1757) was the most prominent composer and musical director of the Mannheim School, the remarkable musical establishment assembled and funded by the elector Carl Theodor from the 1740s into the 1780s (see Chapter 11). Stamitz was also one of the first composers to write a symphony that used clarinets and among the first consistently to employ the four-movement format in his symphonies. His sons Carl (1745–1801) and Anton (1750–1796) were composers at the same court.

NORTH AMERICA

Musical life in England's American colonies, and later in the United States, during the Classical era was dominated by European music. William Billings (1746–1800) of Boston was one of the country's first native-born composers. He wrote a great deal of sacred music that was extremely popular in its time. His publications include *The New-England Psalm-Singer* (1770; see Anthology) and *The Continental Harmony* (1794).

Part Five
The 19th Century

Prelude

The 19th century was a period of unprecedented change in Western society. The population of the world's major powers increased by more than 150 percent, and the political boundaries of Europe were redrawn several times over. Many European nations established overseas empires, and the United States grew from an outpost at the edge of civilization to a world power reaching from the Atlantic to the Pacific. In the late 19th century, economic hardship, religious persecution, and population growth combined to impel millions of Europeans, especially from southern and eastern Europe, to leave their homes and seek opportunity in other parts of the world. Most of the migrants went to the United States and other countries in the Western Hemisphere. Technological developments fundamentally altered commerce, travel, and the exchange of information.

TIMELINE

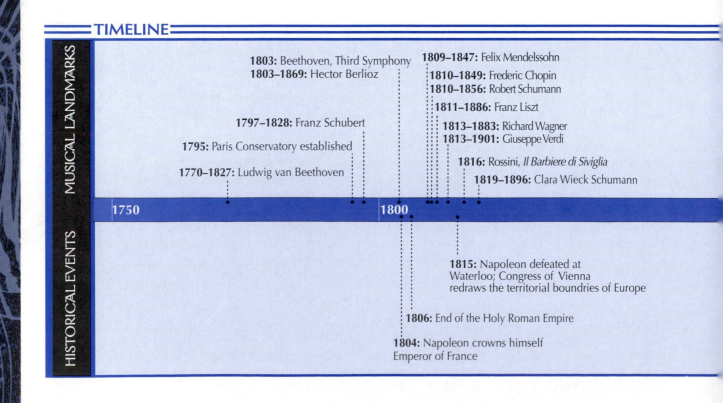

MUSICAL LANDMARKS

1803: Beethoven, Third Symphony
1803–1869: Hector Berlioz

1809–1847: Felix Mendelssohn

1810–1849: Frederic Chopin
1810–1856: Robert Schumann

1811–1886: Franz Liszt

1813–1883: Richard Wagner
1813–1901: Giuseppe Verdi

1797–1828: Franz Schubert

1816: Rossini, *Il Barbiere di Siviglia*

1795: Paris Conservatory established

1770–1827: Ludwig van Beethoven

1819–1896: Clara Wieck Schumann

1750   1800

HISTORICAL EVENTS

1815: Napoleon defeated at Waterloo; Congress of Vienna redraws the territorial boundries of Europe

1806: End of the Holy Roman Empire

1804: Napoleon crowns himself Emperor of France

PROGRESS AND DISLOCATION

The Industrial Revolution that began in the 18th century accelerated rapidly in the 19th, with profound social, economic, and political consequences. Technological advances in transportation and communication—particularly the railroad and telegraph—changed daily life in basic ways. Science and technology combined to change daily life as well. New fertilizers and new machines like reapers and tractors increased agricultural yields. A new understanding of the causes of disease led to the development of vaccines and the sterilization of instruments used in surgery. Major cities in Europe and the United States began constructing water and sewage systems, substantially reducing the spread of disease.

Technological advances fed a growing belief in the inevitability of progress, the conviction that every passing year would bring new improvements to life. But for much of the population, this progress came at a heavy price. Industrialization produced disorienting social change. Europe's population increased dramatically during the 19th century. Millions migrated from the countryside in search of work, swelling the populations of the newly industrialized cities. Many factory workers lived in overcrowded, unsanitary housing and worked in dangerous conditions for low wages and with tenuous job security.

IDEAS AND IDEOLOGIES

In the wake of the French Revolution, the rationality of the Enlightenment gradually gave way to a new mode of thought loosely known as **Romanticism.** In general, the Romantic outlook respected reason but, in contrast to the rationalism of the Enlightenment philosophes, did not believe reason could solve all human problems. Romantics valued the individual and the subjective over the universal, the emotional and spiritual over the rational. They revered nature and glorified the creative genius of the artist for

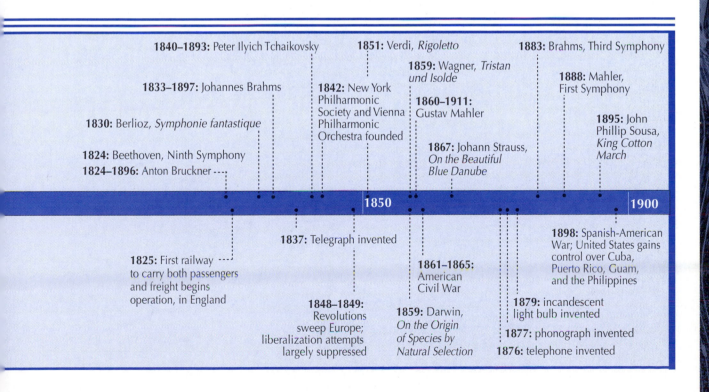

1840–1893: Peter Ilyich Tchaikovsky

1851: Verdi, *Rigoletto*

1883: Brahms, Third Symphony

1859: Wagner, *Tristan und Isolde*

1833–1897: Johannes Brahms

1842: New York Philharmonic Society and Vienna Philharmonic Orchestra founded

1888: Mahler, First Symphony

1860–1911: Gustav Mahler

1830: Berlioz, *Symphonie fantastique*

1895: John Phillip Sousa, *King Cotton March*

1867: Johann Strauss, *On the Beautiful Blue Danube*

1824: Beethoven, Ninth Symphony

1824–1896: Anton Bruckner

1850

1900

1837: Telegraph invented

1898: Spanish-American War; United States gains control over Cuba, Puerto Rico, Guam, and the Philippines

1825: First railway to carry both passengers and freight begins operation, in England

1861–1865: American Civil War

1848–1849: Revolutions sweep Europe; liberalization attempts largely suppressed

1859: Darwin, *On the Origin of Species by Natural Selection*

1879: incandescent light bulb invented

1877: phonograph invented

1876: telephone invented

the glimpse it offered of a world quite different from the world of reason. In this respect the Romantic outlook favored music, particularly instrumental music, because it was by far the most abstract of the arts and as such allowed for the greatest play of the imagination.

Romanticism often went hand in hand with nationalism, another relatively new ideology in the early 19th century. Across the European continent, more and more peoples began to embrace the idea that their true identity derived from a common language and culture, including shared literary and musical traditions. For centuries, Germany and Italy had been little more than abstractions, but with the rise of nationalism, both emerged as independent states in the second half of the 19th century.

Enlightenment ideals of equality, religious toleration, economic freedom, and representative government lived on in another important early-19th-century ideology, that of political liberalism. In general, political liberals sought to promote constitutional government and laissez-faire economic policies based on the ideas of the Enlightenment era economist, Adam Smith. For the most part, liberals represented the interests of the increasingly prominent wealthy middle class against the traditional power of monarchs and aristocrats.

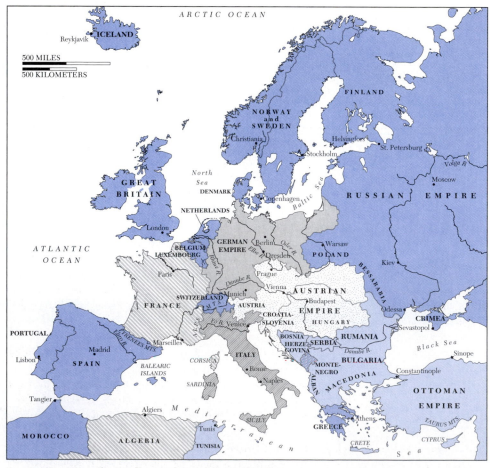

Europe in 1871, after Italian and German Unification.

By the middle of the 19th century, the social dislocations and poverty associated with the early stages of industrial capitalism were nourishing other ideological movements—socialism and Marxism—that posed a more potent challenge than liberalism to the established order throughout Europe. Karl Marx's (1818–1883) advocacy of radical social reform and the elimination of capitalism would inspire revolutionary movements for a century and a half. Less radical approaches to social reform led to the establishment of trade unions throughout Europe and the Americas.

Science, in addition to the technological wonders it spawned, also confronted Western society with troubling new implications. Charles Darwin's (1809–1882) theory of evolution by natural selection, combined with evidence from geology of the great age of the earth, was as unsettling to long-held assumptions about humanity's origins as was the Copernican theory some three centuries earlier to long-held assumptions about the place of the earth in the solar system.

THE MUSICAL WORLD OF THE 19TH CENTURY

The wide-ranging political, social, and economic changes that occurred during the 19th century had correspondingly wide-ranging consequences for the arts. From a strictly commercial point of view, music achieved a scale never before imagined, thanks to advances in music printing, the manufacture of instruments, the growth of public concerts, music journalism, music education, transportation, and the enormous growth of the population in general.

Political change had a direct effect on the way composers made a living. By the middle of the 19th century, private orchestras had all but disappeared because aristocratic patrons, like those in whose palaces Haydn and Beethoven had given the premieres of various symphonies, could no longer maintain them. Concerts became increasingly public as more and more cities established civic orchestras. The salons of aristocrats and wealthy professionals and merchants remained an important venue for chamber music and song in the upper levels of society, but the middle-class family and home took on new importance in the early 19th century as a source of private music making. The ability to read and perform music, in the minds of many, was a sign of a well-rounded education. Middle-class families took pains to see that their children, especially their daughters, could play the piano and sing.

As aristocratic patronage declined, the sale of printed music became an increasingly important source of income for composers. Fortunately, technological advances in paper manufacturing and lithography substantially lowered the cost of music printing, and advances in communication and transportation further expanded the market for published music. Still, few composers could rely exclusively on music sales; most had to find additional work to make ends meet.

No matter how they earned their living, composers benefited from the immense growth in the production and consumption of music across all levels of society. Public education became increasingly widespread over the course of the century, with a corresponding increase in musical literacy as well as general literacy. This helped make the 19th century the era of the amateur musical society. Even small cities that lacked a civic orchestra usually had a variety of amateur musical organizations. Brass bands were a source of considerable pride for many small villages, particularly in England and Wales. Choral societies became popular in Great Britain and Germany, spawning a vast repertory of choral music—most of it a cappella—by composers as diverse as Felix Mendelssohn, Schumann, Franz Liszt, and Brahms. Although this music is seldom performed today, it

— Farmer Giles & his Wife shewing off their daughter Betty to their Neighbours on her return from School —

The perils of domestic music making.   *Over the course of the 19th century, it became a social necessity for any household with aspirations to a higher social standing to own a piano. Daughters were routinely taught to play, and often sing, at a modest level of accomplishment. The cartoon here, from 1809, is entitled "Farmer Giles and Wife Showing off Their Daughter Betty to Their Neighbours on Her Return from School."*

Source: James Gillray, British (1757–1815), "Farmer Giles and his Wife showing off their daughter Betty to their neighbors on her return from School", 31.8 × 47.8 cm/Fine Arts Museums of San Francisco, Achenbach Foundation for Graphic Arts, 1963.30.32811

sold well in its time. Amateurs also gathered at music festivals to perform large-scale works, particularly symphonies and oratorios. These festivals were participatory events, not passive spectacles, and their success was measured not so much in terms of musical quality (which by all accounts varied greatly), but by the number and diversity of the participants, who often traveled a considerable distance to attend.

In addition to the intrinsic joy of performing, many amateur performers were motivated by the belief that music making is a wholesome and uplifting pursuit that strengthens social bonds. Indeed, many factory owners encouraged workers to form musical groups for precisely this purpose.

National governments recognized the role of music in the politics of culture and began to assume responsibility for musical education. The establishment of the state-funded Paris Conservatory in the 1790s spawned dozens of imitators across the Continent

PRIMARY EVIDENCE

Music and the State

For most European governments, the identification and fostering of musical talent was a matter of national importance not to be left to the whims of economic circumstance. The Czech composer Antonín Dvořák (1841–1904) was one of many composers and musicians who benefited from this outlook. The government in his native Bohemia supported several outstanding conservatories, often providing promising students—Dvořák was one of them—with full scholarships. When Dvořák visited the United States in the 1890s, he was struck by the lack of state support for music education. In this extract from an article he wrote for *Harper's New Monthly Magazine* in 1895, he criticizes this lack of support as short-sighted, comparing it unfavorably to the system that nurtured him.

• • • • •

Not long ago a young man came to me and showed me his compositions. His talent seemed so promising that I at once offered him a scholarship in our school [the private National Conservatory of Music, in New York, where Dvořák was teaching at the time]; but he sorrowfully confessed that he could not afford to become my pupil, because he had to earn his living by keeping books in Brooklyn. Even if he came on but two afternoons in the week, or on Saturday afternoon only, he said, he would lose his employment, on which he and others had to depend. I urged him to arrange the matter with his employer, but he only received the answer: "If you want to play, you can't keep books. You will have to drop one or the other." He dropped his music.

In any other country the state would have made some provision for such a deserving scholar, so that he could have pursued his natural calling without having to starve. With us in Bohemia the Diet each year votes a special sum of money for just such purposes, and the imperial government in Vienna on occasion furnishes other funds for talented artists. Had it not been for such support I should not have been able to pursue my studies when I was a young man. Owing to the fact that, upon the kind recommendation of such men as Brahms, Hanslick, and Herbeck, the Minister of Public Education in Vienna on five successive years sent me sums ranging from four to six hundred florins, I was able to pursue my work and to get my compositions published, so that at the end of that time I was able to stand on my own feet. This has filled me with lasting gratitude towards my country.

Such an attitude of the state towards deserving artists is not only a kind but a wise one. For it cannot be emphasized too strongly that art, as such, does not "pay," to use an American expression—at least, not in the beginning—and that the art that has to pay its own way is apt to become vitiated and cheap.

Source: Antonin Dvořák, "Music in America," *Harper's New Monthly Magazine* 90 (1895): 429–34.

over the next 50 years. Virtually every government recognized that it needed a body of civic-minded musicians, composers, and music educators, and that it should establish the institutions to educate such individuals. Unlike most European nations, the United States never embraced the idea of a national conservatory. This was due in part to the nation's decentralized system of higher education, in part to the perception that music is less important to national development than such disciplines as engineering, medicine, and the law (see Primary Evidence: "Music and the State").

The Age of the Tone Poet

The greatest changes in music during the early decades of the 19th century were not primarily in matters of style but rather perception. Composers and audiences alike began to conceive of music and hear it—instrumental music in particular—in a radically new manner. Instrumental music, precisely because it was free from the confining strictures of language, was now regarded as capable of conveying ideas and emotions too profound for mere words.

Composers, responding to this changing perception, began to see themselves as well in an entirely new way. Beethoven reflected this trend when he dubbed himself a "tone poet," an artist who creates poetry with notes rather than words. The public, in turn, began to see great composers as divinely inspired high priests of art who could provide glimpses into a loftier, more spiritual world.

ROMANTICISM AND THE NEW PRESTIGE OF INSTRUMENTAL MUSIC

The term *romantic* derives from the name of a literary genre—the romance—that first emerged in the medieval era. A romance tells a long story in verse or prose. (As such, the genre is a forerunner to the novel, and indeed the word for "novel" in both German and French is *roman*.) Unlike other literary forms, such as epic or lyric poetry, the romance is largely free of structural or narrative conventions. It was because of this association with relatively freer narrative expression that the genre gave its name to an artistic movement—Romanticism—that values imagination and personal expression.

With its stress on imagination, Romanticism was closely associated with the philosophical outlook known as **Idealism,** a system of thought based on the premise that objects in the physical world are a reflection of ideas in the mind.

For many 19th-century Idealist philosophers and critics, instrumental music—because it is intrinsically abstract—was the art form that most approximates the disembodied realm of ideas.

By 1810, E. T. A. Hoffmann proclaimed instrumental music to be "the most romantic of all the arts—one might almost say, the only genuinely romantic one—for its sole subject is the infinite." Hoffmann included Haydn and Mozart among the "Romantic composers" not on the basis of their style but because their music provided a glimpse into the realm of "the spirit world." Eight years later, the German philosopher Arthur Schopenhauer (1788–1860) was arguing that "if music is too closely united to the words, it is striving to speak a language which is not its own." For it is not in the nature of music to "express this or that particular and definite joy, this or that sorrow, or pain, or horror, or delight, or merriment, or peace of mind," but rather "joy, sorrow, pain, horror, delight, merriment, peace of mind *themselves*, to a certain extent in the abstract, their essential nature, without accessories, and therefore without their motives."[1] Music, in other words, should not descend to the level of words.

THE COMPOSER AS HIGH PRIEST

With art in general and music in particular now perceived as a window on the realm of the infinite and spiritual, the social status of composers rose enormously. In the Classical era, the composer had been viewed essentially as an artisan providing goods made to order. By the 1830s, the composer had taken on the aura of a divinely inspired creator, a demigod. There was much talk in the early 19th century about "Art-Religion." This referred not so much to the worship of art as to the revelation of the divine through the medium of art. Composers emerged as the high priests of this new religion, for they dealt with the most abstract (and thus the most revealing) of all the arts.

The composer, according to Schopenhauer, was like a clairvoyant or sleepwalker, someone who in a half-conscious, half-dreaming state "reveals the innermost nature of the world . . . in a language his reasoning faculty does not understand."

The listening public sought insight into the working methods of composers as never before. Beethoven's sketches commanded high prices in the marketplace. The public also wanted to know more about the composers themselves, and biographies about them began to appear in great numbers. Composers, too, were more likely to write about themselves and their art. Berlioz, Schumann, Liszt, and Wagner all wrote prose as well as music. Composers were also far more likely than ever before to incorporate autobiographical elements into their music.

Given the new perception of the composer as a divinely inspired creator, it is scarcely surprising that performers and listeners would begin to place more weight on the accuracy and authority of published scores. Authoritative editions of composers' collected works began to appear for the first time in the 19th century, including the complete works of Beethoven, Schubert, Schumann, and Wagner.

The most revered composers became cultural heroes, bringing honor to their native cities, which, in turn, felt obligated to erect statues in their honor. Salzburg erected its statue of Mozart in 1842, Leipzig completed its monument to J. S. Bach in 1843, and Bonn unveiled its statue of Beethoven in 1845. The funerals of Haydn (1809) and Beethoven (1827) in Vienna were state occasions. Richard Wagner, later in the century, became a cult figure whose influence extended far beyond music. His most devoted followers adopted not only his radical political views but even his vegetarian dietary practices.

ORIGINALITY AND HISTORICAL SELF-CONSCIOUSNESS

Artists and critics of the 19th century were obsessed with the idea of originality. Whereas earlier composers had often recycled themes or even entire movements into new works, composers of the 19th century were far less inclined to engage in this practice. Earlier composers would have been pleased to have their style likened to that of an acknowledged master. Now composers sought to find their own distinctive voice and express it in music unlike any heard before.

As we have seen in Chapter 11, earlier composers routinely integrated originality and convention. The Romantics chose to interpret and portray their innovations as a rejection of convention, as an act of artistic liberation. Every Romantic artist saw himself or herself blazing a unique path to truth.

In an odd way, however, the cult of originality made composers more aware of the musical past than their predecessors had been. One could not be original, after all, in a vacuum. Composers studied earlier music carefully with an eye toward doing something different. The music of the past also began to be heard in the concert hall and opera house with unprecedented frequency. Before the 19th century, it would have been unusual to hear the music of a composer from a previous generation. There were exceptions, of course. Lully's operas were still favorites in Paris a hundred years after his death and Handel's oratorios continued to be performed regularly in England throughout the Classical era and beyond. In the early 19th century, however, works by earlier composers became staples in the active repertoire, beginning with the later symphonies and quartets of Haydn and Mozart and the operas of Gluck and Mozart. By the end of the century, it would have been difficult to find a concert without at least one work from an earlier era. With newer and older works now on the same program, younger composers were inevitably compared not only to their contemporaries, but to masters of earlier generations as well.

By the middle of the 19th century, consciousness of the past took on a new form, that of **historicism,** in which composers openly embraced the forms and styles of earlier generations while presenting them in original ways. Anton Bruckner (1824–1896), for example, whose symphonies used some of the most advanced chromatic harmonies of his time, wrote a number of sacred choral works and Masses in an intentionally anachronistic idiom, one that the unsuspecting ear might mistake briefly for that of Palestrina (see Chapter 17, Anthology). Brahms, appropriating a theme from a cantata by J. S. Bach, openly incorporated the archaic form of the passacaglia into the finale of his Fourth Symphony (see Chapter 18).

Interest in early music led musicians and scholars to seek out otherwise forgotten repertories, leading to the recovery of quantities of music from the medieval era, the Renaissance, and the Baroque period. In 1828, Felix Mendelssohn became the first musician to conduct J. S. Bach's *Saint Matthew Passion* since Bach's death. Mendelssohn's rediscovery inspired the editing and publication of other works by Bach as well. By the end of the century, almost all of Bach's music had been carefully edited and published in a sumptuous edition. Handel, Schütz, and earlier composers such as Lassus and Palestrina enjoyed the same process of rediscovery in the 19th century.

THE NEW DICHOTOMY BETWEEN ABSOLUTE AND PROGRAM MUSIC

The growing prestige of instrumental music as an abstract art created a critical backlash around the middle of the 19th century. The composers and critics involved in this reaction maintained that music could achieve its highest potential only through a synthesis

The virtuoso as idol.   *Throughout the 19th century, the great musical virtuosos and composers were perceived as endowed with divine, superhuman powers. This satirical drawing of the great Polish composer and pianist Ignace Jan Paderewski (1860–1941) from ca. 1895 also reminds us that the public's fascination with long-haired musicians began long before The Beatles. One newspaper of the time reported that "three New York ladies have embroidered musical phrases from [Paderewski's] Minuet on their stockings." In his 1892–1893 concert tour of the United States, Paderewski traveled in his own private railcar along with his secretary, valet, manager, chef, two porters, his Steinway piano, and his piano tuner. The grotesquely exaggerated hand stretch, covering the entire keyboard, betrays the mixture of awe and derision with which the public viewed its virtuosos: awe at their seemingly superhuman powers, derision at their "trained seal" status.*

Source: Caricature of Ignace Jan Paderewski from John Mansfield Thomsons "Musical Delights: A Cavalcade of Cartoon and Caricature (London: Thames and Hudson, 1985) pg. 35

PRIMARY EVIDENCE

Liszt on the Superiority of Program Music

Franz Liszt, along with Richard Wagner, was a leader in the battle to legitimize program music. In an extended essay on Berlioz's symphony *Harold en Italie,* he identifies the key distinction between the "purely musical composer" (that is, one dedicated to the idea of absolute music) and the more engaged composer who wrestles with ideas extending beyond music.

• • • • •

In so-called Classical music, the recurrence and thematic development of themes are determined by formal rules that are considered inviolable, even though its composers possessed no other prescription for these processes than their own fantasies. These composers arranged the formal layout of their works in a manner that some would now proclaim as law. In program music, by contrast, the recurrence, variation, and modification of motifs are determined by their relationship to a poetic idea. Here one theme does not beget another according to any formal laws; the motives are not a consequence of stereotypical similarities or contrasts of timbre; coloration in itself does not determine the grouping of ideas. Although certainly not ignored, all exclusively musical considerations are subordinated to the treatment of the subject at hand. Accordingly, the plot and subject of this symphonic genre demand an engagement that goes beyond the technical treatment of the musical material. The vague impressions of the soul are elevated to definite impressions through a defined plan, which is taken in by the ear in much the same manner in which a cycle of paintings is taken in by the eye. The artists who favor this kind of art work enjoy the advantage of being able to connect with a poetic process all those affects which an orchestra can express with such great power.

Source: Franz Liszt, *Gesammelte Schriften*, vol. 4, ed. L. Ramann, (Leipzig, 1882), 49–50, 69. Transl. MEB

with other arts, including the arts of the word. Richard Wagner led the attack on what he derisively termed **absolute music,** meaning music that was cut off from the larger world of words and ideas. (The prefix *ab* in *absolute* derives from the Latin word for "separate" or "disconnected.") Wagner's criticism of absolute music echoed the view of 18th-century critics toward instrumental music: he valued its ability to move the passions but considered it too abstract to carry true meaning. Only with the "fertilizing seed" of the word, Wagner argued, could music realize its full potential. This "fertilizing seed" could take the form of a program or programmatic text—like that which Berlioz wrote for his *Symphonie fantastique*—or better still, a text to be sung.

The term *absolute* was soon embraced as a label for purely instrumental music even by its proponents, but with a different, positive, interpretation. To them, pure instrumental music was absolute in its ability to transcend earthly life, rising above mundane, everyday existence. This usage reflected Idealist philosophy, in which *absolute* had been used as a noun to convey the idea of the infinite. The most influential advocate of this view of absolute music in the middle of the 19th century was the Viennese critic Eduard Hanslick (1825–1904; see Primary Evidence: "Hanslick on the Superiority of Absolute Music").

Unlike Wagner and Liszt, who wrote forcefully in favor of program music, none of the composers of stature who favored absolute music took pen to paper in its defense. Johannes Brahms, for example, one of the most prominent practitioners of absolute music, preferred, according to one of his close associates, "to polemicize with works of music rather than with words."[2] The debate itself was charged with political overtones. Wagner and Liszt claimed for themselves the mantle of progressivism, calling their work "The Music of the Future," whereas Hanslick (and by association, composers like Brahms) were associated with the forces of conservatism.

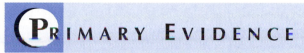

PRIMARY EVIDENCE

Hanslick on the Superiority of Absolute Music

Eduard Hanslick's *On the Beautiful in Music*, first published in 1854, was the manifesto of the musical conservatives who believed in the sanctity of absolute music. Hanslick (1825–1904) argued that music could not in its own right express emotions. By this he did not mean that music is incapable of moving the listener, but rather that beauty in music flows from its ability to project "forms animated through sound."

· · · · ·

The nature of beauty in a musical composition is specifically musical. By this we understand a beauty that is independent and in no need of any external content. It is a beauty that lies entirely in the notes and in their artistic interweaving. The meaningful connections of inherently pleasing sounds, their concords and discords, their departure and arrival, their eruption and subsiding—this is what comes before our spiritual perception in free forms and pleases us as beautiful. . . .

If we now ask what is to be expressed with this musical material, the answer is: Musical Ideas. A complete musical idea is already self-sufficient beauty; it is an end in itself and in no way merely a means or the material for the presentation of emotions or thoughts.

The sole and exclusive content and object of music are forms animated through sound.

. . . It is extraordinarily difficult to describe this self-sufficiently beautiful in music, this specifically musical beauty. Because music has no prototype in nature and expresses no conceptual content, it can be discussed only either in dry technical terms or through poetic fictions. Its kingdom is truly "not of this world." All the fantastic descriptions, characterizations, and paraphrases of a musical work are figurative or wrong. What in accounts of every other art is merely descriptive is already metaphorical in music. Music demands to be perceived simply as music; it can be understood and enjoyed only in terms of its own self. . . .

Source: Eduard Hanslick, *Vom musikalisch-Schönen* (Leipzig: R. Weigel, 1854). Transl. MEB

The question of instrumental music's meaning remained a central topic of debate throughout the 19th century. A new generation of composers, critics, and audiences saw merit in both points of view. Many composers were ambivalent on the matter or changed their opinions gradually. Even Wagner began to realize that absolute music was really not so empty after all. And Liszt, the great champion of program music, issued one of his most significant works, the Sonata in B minor, with a generic title, refusing to provide his followers with indications about any extramusical "meaning" despite repeated requests. Berlioz tried (unsuccessfully) to suppress the detailed program of his *Symphony fantastique;* Brahms, who remained aloof from open debate on the issue, incorporated certain programmatic elements into at least some of his works, although he never revealed these connections to a wider public. The literary critic Walter Pater (1839–1894) summed up the matter neatly when he declared that music's ability to embody form without the burden of specific content was the envy of poetry and painting, and that "all art constantly aspires towards the condition of music."[3] Such an attitude acknowledges music's unique ability to transcend the representation of objects or ideas while also allowing for the incorporation of nonmusical elements.

NATIONALISM

While composers and critics debated the relative merits of program and absolute music for conveying meaning, some noted that music's meaning could at times be political. Writing in 1898, for example, the American critic James Huneker declared that "the most profound truths, the most blasphemous things, the most terrible ideas, may be incorporated within the walls of a symphony, and the police may be none the wiser. It is its freedom from the meddlesome hand of the censor that makes of music a playground for great brave souls."[4]

Nationalist sentiments and aspirations in particular lent themselves to musical expression, notably in the work of composers from eastern Europe. Chopin, for example, whose native Poland was under Russian control, made a nationalistic statement with the mazurkas and polonaises—both traditional Polish dance forms—that he wrote while living in Paris as part of the Polish exile community. This nationalistic element was not lost on listeners. Schumann pointed out as early as 1837 that if the czar of Russia "knew what a dangerous enemy threatened him in Chopin's works, in the simple tunes of his mazurkas, he would forbid this music. Chopin's works are cannons buried in flowers."[5]

Russia itself was in the process of becoming a major European power, and with its vast empire straddling Europe and Asia was seeking to define a national identity that would both relate it to and distinguish it from its neighbors to the west. In response, many Russian composers sought to create a distinctively Russian musical idiom based on the melodic and harmonic inflections of Russian folk music. In 1836, Mikhail Glinka (1804–1857) wrote an opera—*Ivan Susanin* (also known as *A Life for the Tsar*)—that was an early landmark in this endeavor. Based on a story from Russian history, it has a Russian libretto, and the score, although following the conventions of contemporary Italian opera, incorporates elements from Russian folk music. Glinka's precedent inspired many later Russian composers, most notably Alexander Borodin (1833–1887) and Modeste Mussorgsky (1839–1881). Borodin's orchestral work *In the Steppes of Central Asia*, for example, incorporates two folk songs and employs such features of Asian music as the pentatonic whole-tone scale. Mussorgsky's opera *Boris Godunov* (1869; revised 1872), like Glinka's *Ivan Susanin*, draws its story from Russian history and includes folk songs and folk-song-like elements in the music.

Throughout Europe and the Americas, many 19th-century composers cultivated styles of writing that in some way drew on the folk idioms of their respective nationalities: Verdi in Italy, Wagner in Germany, Dvořák in Bohemia (now the Czech Republic), and Gottschalk in the United States (see Chapter 16).

Composers sometimes used folk music from lands not their own to add an exotic flavor to their music, to pay homage to another nationality, or to indulge in the general Romantic interest in folk culture. The Italian composer Giuseppe Verdi, for example, incorporated what he thought to be Egyptian musical elements into his opera *Aida* (1871), which is set in ancient Egypt; the work was written to commemorate the opening of the Suez Canal and had its first performance in Cairo. Brahms, who came from the northern German city of Hamburg, used a Hungarian idiom in his various Hungarian Dances. Antonin Dvořák incorporated what he thought to be elements of Native American music into his Symphony no. 9, subtitled "From the New World." He did this in part to encourage American composers to forge their own national idiom.

THE GROWING DIVISION BETWEEN ART AND POPULAR MUSIC

It was during the 19th century that musicians, composers, and the music-consuming public began to draw a distinction between *art music* and *popular music*. The terms, it turns out, are misleading and impossible to define musically in any consistent way (see Appendix 4: "The Concepts of Art and Popular Music"). Still, their emergence reflects real changes in social attitudes toward music and the economics of the music business.

Before the 19th century, composers routinely wrote music to suit their immediate audiences. Mozart, for example, wrote two entirely different works for the stage in the final months of his life: *Die Zauberflöte* ("The Magic Flute"), a Singspiel, for a middle-class theater in Vienna, and *La Clemenza di Tito* ("The Clemency of Titus"), an opera seria commissioned for the celebrations surrounding the coronation in Prague of Emperor Leopold II as king of Bohemia. *La Clemenza di Tito,* although admired in its time and into the 19th century, never had a substantial audience. At least some numbers from *Die Zauberflöte,* however, became so popular that to this day many Germans believe they are folk songs and are surprised to discover they were actually written by Mozart. In Mozart's time, these two works would have been performed before audiences of different social levels in decidedly different kinds of theaters. By the end of the 19th century, however, an opera house would present both operas to the same audience. The works themselves had not changed, but rather the attitudes toward them.

This shift in attitudes can be traced to changing assumptions about the nature and purpose of music. Accepting their status in the Romantic imagination as high priests of the new religion of art, at least some 19th-century composers no longer felt obliged to take their audiences into account, at least not directly. Listeners, in turn, came increasingly to accept that it was their job to understand a composer's music, not the composer's job to make it accessible to them. At the same time, undemanding music was becoming increasingly accessible to the broad public. One audience, the audience for music as art, saw it as a means to spiritual enlightenment. The other audience, the audience for what was considered popular music, saw it as a source of entertainment.

Economic factors reinforced this division. With the decline of royal and aristocratic patronage and the growth of an educated middle class, orchestras and opera houses became increasingly reliant on income from ticket sales, which in turn drove them to stage music with broad popular appeal. Publishers, too, recognized there was serious money to be made in music that could be easily performed and readily absorbed, the kind of music that before the 19th century would have been part of the orally transmitted unwritten tradition. The development of recording technology in the 20th century would make this music ever more pervasive.

Concert manners—a revealing index of attitudes toward music—also changed considerably over the course of the 19th century. In earlier times, audiences felt free to respond openly at musical performances whenever moved to do so. Mozart, writing to his father from Paris in 1778, describes how he had marked a crescendo in an orchestral work in such a way as to solicit applause from the audience and how the audience had responded on cue. "What a fuss the oxen here make of this trick!" Mozart observed, half amused, half pleased with the effect. What is particularly revealing in his comment is the assumption that listeners would express their delight without inhibition in the middle of a performance. Such outbursts are still common today at jazz, rock, and country music concerts but not in the realm of the concert halls where Mozart's music is now performed.

By 1900, a little more than a hundred years after Mozart's death, outbursts in the middle of a concert performance had become rare, and even applause between movements was becoming the exception rather than the rule. The new behavior was certainly more respectful to fellow listeners and to the music itself, but it put a damper on the kind of spontaneity that so amused Mozart. For all practical purposes, the concert hall had become a temple, a sanctuary that fostered devotion and contemplation. But there was a price: the rituals of concert decorum that made music easier to hear by

The expansion of musical literacy.   *With a look of weary resignation, the tavern keeper realizes that removing the music stands has not discouraged his clients from continuing with their music making. (The dog seems particularly distressed about this.) Instruction in basic music literacy became a part of the school curriculum in many European nations after 1800, and these amateurs are reading music, not performing from memory. The part-song for men's chorus, a now largely forgotten genre, was popular in the 19th century. Schubert, Schumann, and Brahms all contributed to it. The guitar was ubiquitous in domestic music making; its portability gave it an advantage over the piano. Transported to a comparable scene from today, this group would no doubt be listening to recorded music.*

Source: Bildarchiv der Oesterreichischen Nationalbibliothek

reducing distractions also made the listening experience more passive and self-conscious. In the dance hall and music hall, in contrast, audiences continued to respond to performances spontaneously and vocally.

MUSIC IN THE 19TH CENTURY: A STYLISTIC OVERVIEW

The growing drive toward originality opened up a wide variety of options in every element of music: texture, melody, harmony, rhythm, and form. Almost every major composer sought to cultivate a style that was uniquely his or her own.

Textures ranged from the simple homophony of a song like Schubert's *Wanderers Nachtlied* (Anthology, discussed in Chapter 16) to the extreme complexity of a Mahler symphony (Anthology, discussed in Chapter 18). Beethoven introduced a rich array of textures in his late quartets that later composers would explore further. In his String Quartet, op. 130, for example (Anthology, discussed in Chapter 16), all four voices contribute on an essentially equal basis to the fabric of the whole in a way that sounds more like an intimate conversation among friends—the metaphor 18th-century observers had used to characterize the ideal string quartet—than any previous work in the genre.

Melodic structures similarly range from the simple to the complex. Periodic phrase structure persists but becomes increasingly less apparent and regular over the course of the century. The principal theme of the first movement of Berlioz's *Symphonie fantastique* (Example 14-1) reflects this trend. It begins with a clear antecedent-consequent structure based on units of 4 + 4 but then dissolves into a series of repeated fragments that enter at ever higher pitches, mirroring the obsessive mental state of the artist who is the subject of the symphony's program. The harmonic direction, rhythmic structure, and thematic content do not follow any conventional pattern after the first eight measures.

Example 14-1 Berlioz, *Symphonie fantastique*, first movement, measures 72–111: the initial appearance of the principal melody.

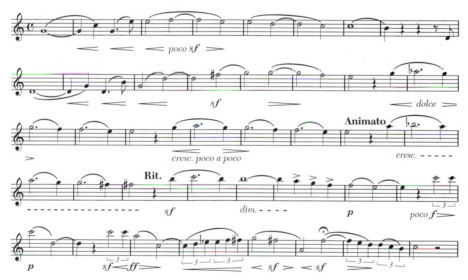

Over the course of the century, harmonies became increasingly chromatic. By the end of the 19th century, chromaticism was no longer reserved for inflections between various points of stability, but had become a legitimate idiom in its own right—open ended, ambiguous, and unstable in the best sense of all these terms. Franz Liszt's *Nuages Gris* ("Gray Clouds") from 1881 (Anthology, discussed in Chapter 16) exemplifies this new approach.

As harmonies became increasingly chromatic, rhythm became increasingly complex. Even the initially regular rhythm of the principal idea in the first movement of Berlioz's *Symphonie fantastique* (Example 14-1) is accompanied by a metrically irregular, impulsive figure. On the final page of his Ballade in G minor, op. 23 (Anthology, discussed in Chapter 16), Chopin introduces passages in rhythmic groupings of 29 and 39 notes over the span of two measures each, followed by groupings of 21 and 28 notes within individual measures (measures 246–255). Such passages cannot be played with rhythmic exactitude; instead, Chopin uses these large groupings to indicate that performers can present them freely and not in strict meter.

Composers continued to structure works according to such formal conventions of the Classical era as sonata form, scherzo (minuet), and rondo, but because of the demand for originality and innovation, they often downplayed or disguised their presence. Thus in many 19th-century sonata-form movements, particularly those written toward the end of the century, the distinctions between exposition and development or between development and recapitulation can be hard to hear.

Cyclical coherence became increasingly important to composers for multi-movement instrumental works. Compared to the subtle connections late-18th-century composers sometimes created between movements (see Chapter 12), the connections between movements in 19th-century works tend to be more overt. Probably the best known example of such an overt thematic link is the short-short-short-long rhythmic motif that opens Beethoven's Fifth Symphony and is repeated in various transformations in every movement. The idea that a multi-movement cycle should be built around a central thematic idea reflects the increasingly prevalent view that artworks should appear organic, as if they grew from a single seed. E. T. A. Hoffmann, for example, praised Beethoven's Fifth Symphony for the unity that underlies its seeming chaos. Only on closer examination, he pointed out, would listeners discover that the symphony, like a "beautiful tree" with all its "buds and leaves, blossoms and fruits" had grown "out of a single seed." Wagner's music dramas, with their interconnected network of thematic motifs (see Chapter 17), are a late-19th-century manifestation of this organic analogy.

Although virtuosity was certainly not new in the 19th century, composers of the time began to cultivate it to a degree that had been largely lacking in the music of the Classical era. Much of the music from this period lies beyond the technical ability of all but the most skillful performers.

Orchestral writing became so demanding that conductors became a necessity. Up until the 1820s, most orchestras were conducted by the concertmaster—the principal first violinist—or the keyboard player within the basso continuo. But the increasing complexities of orchestral textures, the tendency toward more fluid changes in tempo, and the growing intricacies of rhythm created a need for a single individual—someone not playing an instrument—to coordinate and direct the ensemble.

Rehearsals, long an exception, became the rule. Above one particularly demanding orchestral passage in the first movement of his *Symphonie fantastique* (1830), Berlioz entered this note: "The following eleven measures are extremely difficult. I cannot recommend strongly enough to conductors that this passage be rehearsed many times and with the greatest care. . . . It would be good to have the first and second violins study their parts alone at first, then with the rest of the orchestra."[6] Here, in effect, Berlioz has invented the sectional rehearsal.

CONCLUSION

Stylistic changes between the music of the Classical era and the music of the early 19th century were neither sudden nor pronounced. Changing attitudes toward the nature and function of music in the early decades of the new century, however, exercised a profound long-term influence on the development of musical styles. Composers, seeking an original voice, developed idioms that were distinctively individual. The range of compositional choices expanded enormously in all elements of music.

PLATE 13   The composer as a cultural hero. Haydn last appeared in public at a performance of his oratorio, *The Creation*, in Vienna on March 27, 1808, just a few days before the composer's 76th birthday. Haydn, seated at the center, receives a gift from Princess Marie Hermenegild, wife of Prince Nicolaus Esterházy, scion of the family that Haydn had served for so many years. Trumpeters play a fanfare during the presentation, and all eyes are on the composer. The Viennese public, including even the aristocracy and nobility, acknowledged Haydn as a cultural hero. Such a scene would have been unthinkable during the many decades in which Haydn was in daily service to the Esterházy family; by 1808, attitudes toward composers had changed considerably.
[Copyright by Direktion der Museum der Stadt, Wien]

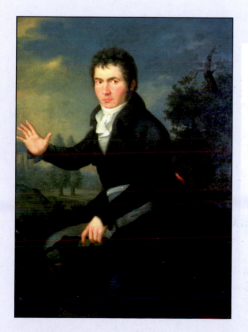

PLATE 14   Beethoven as Orpheus. Anyone who sat for a portrait in Beethoven's time took great care in selecting and arranging the setting and surrounding objects. A portrait, after all, was one of the principal means by which one projected one's self to society as a whole. (People often pose for photographic portraits in the same way today, in a setting or with an object that best captures their personality.) This portrait, painted by Willibrord Joseph Mähler in 1804 or 1805, shows Beethoven with his back to a scene of darkness and turmoil moving toward green, sunlit fields. In his left hand he holds a lyre-guitar, a fashionable instrument of the day. The lyre is traditionally associated with Apollo and (especially) Orpheus, who had great musical powers, so the implication here is that Beethoven is a modern-day Orpheus. Only a few years later, E. T. A. Hoffmann would open his celebrated review of Beethoven's Fifth Symphony by reminding readers how the lyre of Orpheus—instrumental music—had opened up a spirit realm otherwise closed to mortals. Not coincidentally, this portrait presents a much more handsome-looking Beethoven than any other contemporary likeness.

[Willibrord Joseph Mähler, (1778–1860), "Ludwig van Beethoven," 1804, oil on canvas/Historisches Museum der Stadt Wien, Austria/The Bridgman Art Library]

PLATE 15   Schubert in his circle of friends. This curious watercolor— *The Original Sin* ("Der Sündenfall"), watercolor by Leopold Kupelwieser (1821)—shows a gathering of Schubert's circle of friends engaged in a pantomime. The artist, Leopold Kupelwieser, by the door, poses as the "Tree of Knowledge" while the poet Franz von Schober plays the serpent. The couple in front of him represents Adam and Eve, who are about to be driven from the Garden of Eden. Schubert, seated at the keyboard in the foreground, has interrupted his playing to look on. But why are so few members of the audience actually looking at the pantomime? The figure opposite Schubert is the poet Joseph Spaun, who gazes intently at the composer, seemingly oblivious to the pantomime. The similarity in posture between Schubert and the dog behind him is too obvious to be coincidental, but what is its significance? On the whole, this watercolor gives a sense of the kind of obscure symbolism favored by Schubert's circle, many of whom belonged to a group that called itself the "Nonsense Society."

["Leopold Kupelwieser, (1796–1862) "The Family of Franz Peter Schubert (1797–1828) playing games"/Historiches Museum Der Stadt, Vienna/The Bridgeman Art Library]

PLATE 16   Richard Wagner at His Home in Bayreuth. This richly symbolic scene—painted by W. Beckmann—shows Wagner in the last year of his life at the center of an admiring circle of intimates, all eyes on him. The composer, standing, is reading from the libretto of his latest (and last) work, *Parsifal*, which received its premiere in Bayreuth in 1882, the same year in which this group portrait was executed. On the wall above his left shoulder is a portrait of the great German philosopher Arthur Schopenhauer, who had singled out music as the greatest of all the arts because it alone could capture the essence of the universe. Wagner's position suggests that he and his works embody Schopenhauer's ideas. Sitting to the composer's right is his wife, Cosima Liszt Bülow Wagner. A portrait of Cosima leans against the back wall, above her head. On the floor behind her is a painting of one of the sets from *Parsifal*, the Temple of the Grail. The first figure to Wagner's left is his father-in-law, Franz Liszt, who seems to be conducting an imaginary orchestra from a manuscript, probably the score of *Parsifal*, in his lap. Wagner's hands overlap Liszt's, symbolizing the important links—both familial and artistic—between these two musical giants of the 19th century. The third seated figure, Hans von Wolzogen, was a disciple of Wagner who wrote many pamphlets identifying the leitmotivs in Wagner's music dramas.

[Anonymous, "Wagner with Liszt, and Liszt's daughter, Cosima"/Wagner Museum, Bayreuth, Germany/The Bridgeman Art Library]

PLATE 17 Liszt at the Piano. A number of celebrated figures listen to Liszt perform in this idealized scene painted in 1840 by Josef Danhauser. On the far left is Alexandre Dumas, the author of *The Three Musketeers* and *The Count of Monte Cristo*. To his left is the novelist George Sand, who was Chopin's mistress at the time. In keeping with the male persona of her pseudonym (her real name was Amandine-Aurore-Lucile Dudevant) she often dressed in men's clothing and smoked cigars. Standing behind Sand and Dumas is Victor Hugo, best known as the author of *Notre Dame de Paris* and *Les Misérables*. His drama *Le roi s'amuse* was the basis for the libretto to Verdi's *Rigoletto* (see Chapter 17). Standing against the wall, in front of a portrait of Lord Byron, the quintessential Romantic poet, are Niccolò Paganini (left) and Giaocchino Rossini (right). Paganini was to the violin what Liszt was to the piano, both as a composer and as a performer. Rossini had retired from opera by the time this painting was done, but his Parisian salon continued to attract the leading figures in all the arts. On the floor leaning her head against the piano is Liszt's mistress, Marie d'Agoult (1805–1876). Like her friend George Sand she was a writer, and she also wrote under a male pseudonym (Daniel Stern). She bore three children by Liszt, including a daughter, Cosima, who married Richard Wagner. With her back turned to us, Marie d'Agoult alone is focused on Liszt. The others gaze into space. Liszt himself seems to be looking past the bust of Beethoven on the piano to the infinite sky beyond. The painting as a whole, by showing literary and musical figures together, wonderfully represents music's ability to unite the arts. But it also illustrates music's ability to transcend the word—Dumas, Hugo, and Sand, the three literary figures, have all been interrupted in their reading—and to direct attention to a higher realm.

[Staatliche Museen zu Berlin, Stiftung, Preussischer Kulterbesitz, Nationalgalerie]

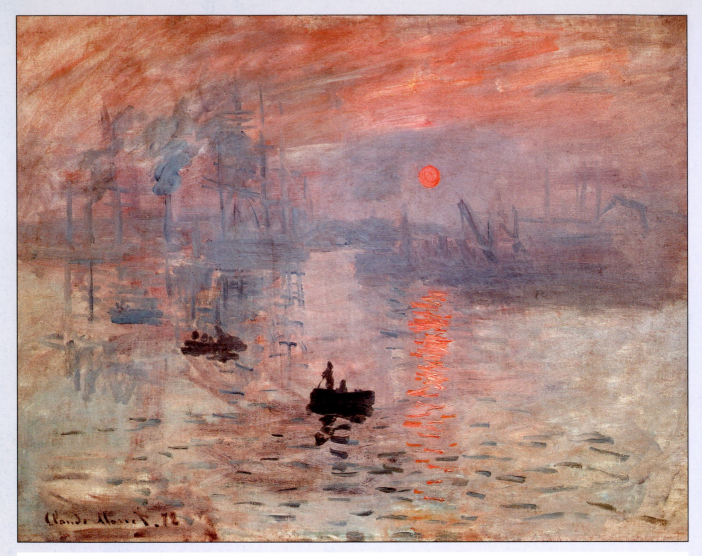

PLATE 18 Impressionism. Impressionist paintings command big money in the auction house nowadays, but the style was widely rejected when it first came onto the scene in Paris in the mid-1870s. One critic, writing of an exhibition in which this 1872 painting—Claude Monet's *Impression: soleil levant* (Impression: Sunrise)—appeared, complained that Monet, Renoir, Cezanne, and others were "impressionists in that they do not render a landscape, but the sensation produced by the landscape. The word itself has passed into their language: in the catalogue, the *Sunrise* by Monet is called not landscape, but *Impression*. Thus they take leave of reality and enter the realms of idealism." Another critic of the time was even less charitable: "Wallpaper in its embryonic state is more finished than that seascape." Musical impressionism, similarly concerned more with color than with line, also met with resistance for a time; one critic declared that Debussy's *Prélude à l'Après-midi d'un faune* was "to a work of music what an artist's palette is to a finished painting."

[CORBIS BETTMAN]

SUMMARY OF STYLE DIFFERENCES BETWEEN MUSIC OF THE CLASSICAL ERA AND 19TH CENTURY

	CLASSICAL	19TH CENTURY
STYLE	Sacred music tends to be somewhat more conservative, preserving basso continuo and much imitative writing, but most music is written in what was thought of at the time as the modern style.	Composers seek to develop a distinctly personal style; originality becomes paramount in all genres.
TEXT SETTING	Greater emphasis on sense of natural declamation, less focus on the projection of individual words.	A wide range of options from the simple to the ornate emerges.
TEXTURE	Predominantly homophonic, especially in the early years of the Classical era, although with increasing use of nonimitative counterpoint (obbligato accompaniment) in later decades.	The polyphonic and homophonic coexist, with composers drawing on whichever approach best suits their immediate needs.
RHYTHM	Periodic phrase structure predominates, but this supposedly natural symmetry is often inflected by subtle irregularities.	Periodic phrase structure continues in the works of certain repertories (dance, march), but on the whole becomes increasingly less obvious over the course of the century.
MELODY	Predominantly lyrical, with emphasis on periodic phrase structure. Virtuosity remains an option, but an aesthetic of "naturalness" predominates.	Ranges from the simple to the complex.
HARMONY	A relatively slower harmonic rhythm on the whole, with relatively limited and carefully controlled use of dissonance. The growing polarity of tonic and dominant allows composers to create movement-length forms on the basis of large-scale areas of harmonic stability.	Becomes increasingly chromatic over the course of the century, which makes harmonic simplicity unusual.
FORM	Syntactic forms predominate, particularly binary form and its outgrowth, sonata form; rondo form becomes increasingly popular in finales from the 1780s onward. The only paratactic form of significance is the set of variations on a theme.	The large-scale formal conventions of the Classic era continue in use, but often in a manner that obscures their presence. Cyclical coherence becomes an increasingly important issue within multi-movement works.
INSTRUMENTATION	A clear distinction between vocal and instrumental parts becomes the norm. The nucleus of the modern orchestra (strings, winds, brass, percussion) emerges as the standard ensemble for large instrumental works.	The distinction between vocal and instrumental writing becomes even more pronounced. The orchestra grows in both size and instrumental variety.

Orchestral Music, 1800–1850

The growing prestige of instrumental music in the early decades of the 19th century created new demands for orchestral genres of all kinds. The symphony and concerto became increasingly substantial in length and tone, and the new genre of the concert overture provided an important new format for program music. Performed by a large body of musicians before a large audience, these genres distinguished themselves both in scope and content from the more private spheres of chamber music, song, and short pieces for solo piano.

BIGGER HALLS, BIGGER AUDIENCES, AND LOUDER INSTRUMENTS

With the decline of royal and aristocratic patronage in the first half of the 19th century, orchestral music became an increasingly public genre. Concert impresarios, dependent on ticket sales for revenue, sought bigger venues to boost profits. Audiences grew in size, and concert halls grew larger to accommodate them. Whereas most 18th-century symphony audiences had numbered around two to four hundred, many concert halls built during the 19th century could seat a thousand or more, and the audiences that filled them were more socially diverse than before.

These economic trends had important aesthetic implications for orchestral music. The larger halls required a new approach to orchestral sound. Ensembles grew substantially in size, particularly the string sections. The design of stringed instruments was also modified to increase the volume of sound they produced.

The development of valve technology for brass instruments beginning about 1815 increased the possibilities for orchestration and texture. Keyed valves allowed players to adjust an instrument's tubing length easily, and thus its natural overtone sequence, permitting them to play chromatic intervals cleanly within the instrument's full range.

THE SYMPHONY

By 1800, the symphony had established itself as the most prestigious of all instrumental genres, in part because of its size and length—four movements for a large orchestra—and in part because of its distinctly public nature.

Standard scoring around 1800, the year of Beethoven's First Symphony, consisted of double winds (flutes, oboes, clarinets, bassoons), two horns, two trumpets, timpani, and strings. New instruments were introduced into the genre steadily over the course of the century. Trombones, which had traditionally been restricted to the realms of church and theater, appear in the finale of Beethoven's Fifth Symphony, the "Storm" movement of his Sixth, and the finale of his Ninth. Instruments normally reserved for special effect, such as the piccolo, contrabassoon, bass drum, triangle, and cymbals (as, for example, in Haydn's Symphony no. 100 ("Military") and the finale of Beethoven's Ninth) became increasingly common. With so many timbral options, sonority itself became a distinctive feature of the genre, which made every major 19th-century symphonist feel compelled to some extent to create a distinctive orchestral sound.

Because the symphony required the more or less equal participation of many instruments in a large ensemble, critics came to view it metaphorically as an expression of communal spirit. Shortly before his death in 1883, Wagner distinguished between Beethoven's sonatas and quartets, in which "Beethoven makes music," and his symphonies, in which "the entire world makes music through him."[1]

The understanding of the symphony as a genre of universal import helps explain the readiness of 19th-century commentators to associate specific symphonies with extramusical ideas. Sometimes composers themselves provided these associations, with a title (like Beethoven, who called his third symphony *Eroica*, or "heroic") or a detailed program distributed at performances (like Berlioz for his *Symphonie fantastique*). But even works with no such explicit extramusical theme were presumed nonetheless to have some transcendent meaning. Beethoven, for example, gave no hint of any programmatic idea on the score for his Fifth Symphony. The public, however, was quick to accept what Anton Schindler, Beethoven's personal secretary, claimed was Beethoven's explanation for the symphony's famous opening—"Thus fate knocks at the door"—despite Schindler's questionable veracity. E. T. A. Hoffmann and others had already perceived in this symphony an allegory of struggle leading to victory, and Schindler's supposedly eyewitness account merely reinforced this perception.

Beethoven's Symphonies

Beethoven's nine symphonies encompass a wide range of compositional approaches. Indeed, his symphonies are so varied that it is impossible to single out any one of them as typical. Almost all of them explore some fundamentally new approach to the genre. With the Third Symphony, for example, he extended the reach of the genre into the moral, social, and philosophical realms for the first time. The work's title, *Eroica*, evokes the ethical and political ideals associated with the French Revolution. In the second movement, labeled "Funeral March," Beethoven confronts death itself.

The Fifth Symphony (1808)—with its thematic transformation of a prominent rhythmic motive (the famous short-short-short-LONG of the work's opening), its blurring of movement boundaries (between the two final movements), and the return of an extended passage from one movement (the third) within the course of another (the fourth)—makes explicit strategies of cyclical coherence that had long been latent in earlier music. In the Sixth Symphony (*Pastoral;* 1808), Beethoven explores the potential of instrumental music to represent objects and ideas. Each of the work's five movements bears a programmatic title related to images and feelings inspired by the countryside. The verbal clues about the music's meaning range from the vague to the astonishingly specific. The first movement, for example, bears only the heading "Awakening of Happy Thoughts Upon Arriving in the Countryside," but the slow movement, "Scene by the Brook," ends with an evocation of birdcalls that Beethoven actually labels by species: nightingale, cuckoo, and quail. The Seventh Symphony (1812), perhaps the most popular of all Beethoven's symphonies in the 19th century, eschews programmatic headings but explores orchestral sonorities and rhythms with unparalleled intensity.

With the Ninth Symphony (1824), Beethoven fused vocal forces into a symphonic framework. The use of a chorus and soloists to sing a portion of Friedrich Schiller's poem *An die Freude* ("To Joy") in the last movement was unusual and controversial at the time. As we have seen, it suggested to some critics an acknowledgment of the expressive limits of

Beethoven cancels the original title of the *Eroica* Symphony. *Beethoven, who initially idealized Napoleon Bonaparte as an enlightened ruler, became enraged when he learned that Napoleon had accepted the title of emperor. From the title page of the autograph score of the Eroica Symphony, it is clear that Beethoven crossed out the words* intitolata Buonaparte *after* Sinfonia grande *("Grand Symphony entitled Bonaparte"). In his typically sloppy fashion, though, Beethoven left just enough of the words around their edges to make the original still readable. The title page shows an odd mix of Italian (the title itself) and French ("Louis van Beethoven"). Both were more fashionable than German at the time. Only later in life would Beethoven begin to give titles, tempos, and expressive markings in his native language. This reflects the rise of German as a literary language as well as a growing German nationalism, which first emerged around 1800 in part as a response to Napoleon's invasion of German-speaking lands.*

Source: Ludwig van Beethoven. Symphonie Nr. 3 Op. 55, "Sinfonia Eroica". Titelblatt der Partitur—Abschrift mit eigenhandigen. Bemerkungen Beethoven. Archiv der Gesellschaft der Musikfreunde in Wien.

purely instrumental, or absolute, music. But like the Third Symphony, it confirmed the status of the symphony as a vehicle for the expression of ideas extending well beyond music.

If most of Beethoven's symphonies are innovative, the *Eroica* nevertheless stands out as a work of singular historical significance. First performed in 1805 in the Viennese palace of its dedicatee, Prince Lobkowitz, the *Eroica* breaks new ground in many respects. The first movement, although it is in sonata form, is of an unprecedented length; at 691 measures it dwarfs any previous sonata-form first movement. In the slow movement, Beethoven became the first composer to make symphonic use of the **march,** a military form in duple meter characterized by a strong, repetitive beat for keeping soldiers in orderly formation. The third movement of the *Eroica* epitomizes the transformation of the 18th-century minuet—a courtly dance—into the **scherzo** (Italian for "joke"). Although the term had been used for dance-inspired movements before, the designation became standard in the 19th century. Like the *Eroica*'s third movement, scherzos tend to be faster and longer than minuets; this particular scherzo has a written-out return of the opening section, that is, it is not a straightforward da capo form after the middle-section trio. The finale, consisting of a series of variations on a theme, is proportionately substantial and complex yet at the same time readily accessible. The work as a whole, moreover, has an overarching musical trajectory, reflected in the similarity between the opening themes of the first movement and the finale. The finale, in other words, is more than the last movement of the work: it represents a culmination of the whole. Critics seeking to describe the effect of this musical trajectory have consistently described it as a passage from struggle (first movement) and death (second movement) to rebirth (third movement) and triumph (fourth movement). That this work could evoke such profound associations is both a tribute to the power of Beethoven's music and a reflection of the high regard for instrumental music as a vehicle for the expression of abstract ideas in the Romantic aesthetic.

Beethoven
Symphony no. 3
(*Eroica*)

The Symphony after Beethoven

With its vocal finale, Beethoven's Ninth Symphony provoked a crisis of confidence among composers. How, they wondered, could anyone surpass Beethoven's accomplishments in this genre? By 1830, the future of instrumental music—the symphony in particular—had become a topic of intense debate. In 1835, Robert Schumann wrote that after Beethoven's Ninth, there was reason to believe the dimensions and goals of the symphony had been exhausted. Schumann declared Felix Mendelssohn to have won "crown and scepter over all other instrumental composers of the day," but noted that even Mendelssohn had "apparently realized that there was nothing more to be gained" in the symphony and was now working principally within the realm of the concert overture, "in which the idea of the symphony is confined to a smaller orbit."[2] (The *Overture to a Midsummer Night's Dream,* discussed in the next section, is the kind of work Schumann had in mind here.)

Richard Wagner maintained that the Ninth Symphony was effectively the end of the genre. With it Beethoven had demonstrated what Wagner considered the "futility" of absolute music.

You strive for naught when to satiate your trifling, egoistic desire to produce new works you would deny the cataclysmic significance of Beethoven's Last Symphony. Even your stupidity, which allows you to claim that you do not understand this work, will not save you! Do what you will: look past Beethoven, fumble after Mozart, gird your loins with Sebastian Bach; write symphonies with or without choruses, write Masses, oratorios—those sexless embryos of Opera!—make songs without words, operas without texts. You shall bring into this world nothing that has true life within itself.[3]

Composer Profile

Ludwig van Beethoven
(1770–1827)

Beethoven's contemporaries were quick to note the striking contrast between the man and his music. "Whoever sees Beethoven for the first time and knows nothing about him." wrote an observer in 1797, "would surely take him for a malicious, ill-natured, quarrelsome drunkard who has no feeling for music. . . . On the other hand, he who sees him for the first time surrounded by his fame and his glory, will surely see musical talent in every feature of an ugly face."[4]

Beethoven's tendency to isolate himself from society grew with his increasing deafness, the first signs of which he acknowledged privately around the age of 30. It is unclear exactly what caused this deafness, but in the remarkable document known as the "Heiligenstadt Testament"—which Beethoven wrote in 1802 and kept hidden until his death in 1827—he reveals the pain it caused him.

> Oh you men who think or say that I am malevolent, stubborn or misanthropic, how greatly do you wrong me. You do not know the secret cause which makes me seem that way to you. . . . But, think that for 6 years now I have been hopelessly afflicted, made worse by senseless physicians, from year to year deceived with hopes of improvement, finally compelled to face the prospect of *a lasting malady*. . . . If at times I tried to forget all this, oh how harshly was I flung back by the doubly sad experience of my bad hearing. Yet it was impossible for me to say to people, "Speak louder, shout, for I am deaf." Ah, how could I possibly admit an infirmity in the *one sense* which ought to be more perfect in me than in others, a sense which I once possessed in the highest perfection, a perfection such as few in my profession enjoy or ever have enjoyed.

His despair, he goes on, drove him almost to suicide. "It was only *my art* that held me back," he concedes. "Ah, it seemed to me impossible to leave the world until I had brought forth all that I felt was within me."[5]

Born in Bonn in 1770, Beethoven grew up in a musical household. His father was a singer at the court there, and his grandfather had been Kapellmeister. But his father was alcoholic, and the young Beethoven had to take on adult responsibilities at an early age. He was appointed assistant organist at the court in 1784 and also played viola in the theater orchestra. Recognizing the young man's talent as a composer, the elector of Bonn (the city's ruler) arranged for him to go to Vienna to study with Haydn in 1792. Count Ferdinand Waldstein, another early supporter of the young composer, wrote prophetically in Beethoven's notebook before his departure for Vienna: "With the help of assiduous labor, you shall receive Mozart's spirit from Haydn's hands."[6] Mozart had died less than a year before (in December 1791).

Although the image of Beethoven receiving the spirit of Mozart from the hands of Haydn has become fixed in the public imagination, the composer himself did not create an immediate sensation when he arrived in Vienna, nor did he get along particularly well with Haydn. When Beethoven sent supposedly new works back to Bonn a few years later, these were exposed as compositions that he had mostly already written before he had left for Vienna. Beethoven nevertheless managed to attract the attention of an important group of aristocratic patrons in Vienna who would provide him financial support in various ways for most of the rest of his life. When Jerome Bonaparte, Napoleon's brother, offered Beethoven a lucrative position as Kapellmeister in Kassel in 1808, a group of these aristocrats pooled their resources to keep the composer in Vienna by creating what amounted to a trust fund for him, a large sum of money that generated enough interest to provide a regular income. The last 15 years of Beethoven's life were not happy, however. Inflation ate into his income, he suffered from chronic poor health (his liver, pancreas, and intestines seem to have given him particular problems), his deafness became increasingly worse, and he became embroiled in a bitter custody battle with his sister-in-law over her son Karl, whose father was Beethoven's deceased brother. Beethoven held his sister-in-law in low regard, as did the courts, which awarded him custody of the boy in 1816. But Beethoven was not well prepared to become the single parent of a teenager, and constant struggles involving the boy over the next decade, both in and out of court, took their toll both emotionally and financially.

It is commonly (but erroneously) believed that Beethoven's music was misunderstood in his own lifetime. On the contrary, his music was extremely popular. Some of his more unconventional works, such as the *Eroica* Symphony, were not well understood at first, but this may have been because they were poorly performed as much as anything else. By 1810, Beethoven was already recognized as the greatest living composer of instrumental music. When he died in 1827, he had become a national hero. Throngs of mourners attended his funeral hoping to catch a last glimpse of the great tone poet.

Beethoven's Three Styles

Around the middle of the 19th century, critics and historians began to divide Beethoven's musical works into three broad style periods: early (to about 1802), middle (from roughly 1802 until 1815), and late (1815–1827). Although some disagreement has arisen about just when each of these periods begins and where certain works fit, this division has proved remarkably useful over time because it does reflect certain broad changes in Beethoven's style.

EARLY PERIOD   Like any aspiring composer, Beethoven took the works of acknowledged masters, especially Mozart and Haydn, as his model. Still, such early works as the Piano Sonatas op. 10 and op. 13 (*Pathétique*) or the Second Symphony are hardly mere imitations of earlier composers or styles. We hear in them an original voice that is unquestionably Beethoven's.

MIDDLE PERIOD   On the whole, however, it is the works of the middle period that are generally recognized as quintessentially Beethovenian: the *Waldstein* and *Appassionata* Piano Sonatas, the *Razumovsky* String Quartets, the Third through Eighth Symphonies, the Third through Fifth Piano Concertos, the Violin Concerto, and the opera *Fidelio*. The middle period style is often called "heroic" because of its evocation of struggle and triumph, as in such works as the Third Symphony (subtitled *heroic*), the Fifth Symphony, and the Third *Leonore* Overture.

KEY DATES IN THE LIFE OF LUDWIG VAN BEETHOVEN

1772   Born December 16 in Bonn (Germany).

1782   Appointed assistant organist at the court in Bonn.

1792   With financial support from the elector of Bonn and other benefactors, goes to Vienna to study with Haydn.

1801   Acknowledges to a few close friends the onset of deafness.

1802   Writes the Heiligenstadt Testament, revealing his tumultuous inner life and near suicidal despair over his growing deafness.

1809   Declines offer from the king of Westphalia to become music director to the court there; leverages the offer to secure a fixed annual income from the pooled resources of several Viennese patrons, on the condition that he stay in Vienna.

1812   Writes passionate love letter to the "Immortal Beloved," probably Antonie Brentano.

1815   With increasing deafness, withdraws into an ever-smaller circle of friends and assistants.

1816–1820s Fights a bitter legal battle with his sister-in-law over the custody of his nephew Karl. The struggle occupies a great deal of the composer's time and energy.

1827   Dies in Vienna on March 26.

LATE PERIOD   In the last 12 years of his life, Beethoven became increasingly withdrawn from society and his music became increasingly introspective. With only occasional exceptions (most notably the Ninth Symphony), he abandoned the heroic style for one that many subsequent critics have found to be more enigmatic yet no less moving. Above all, the late works are characterized by an exploration of musical extremes in such areas as form, proportion, texture, and harmony. The finale of the Ninth Symphony, for example, conforms to no conventional pattern at all, and with its unprecedented choral conclusion it incorporates voices into what had been a purely instrumental genre. Exploring extremes of length, Beethoven wrote some of his longest works—the Ninth Symphony, the *Hammerklavier* Piano Sonata op. 106—as well as some of his briefest, such as the almost cryptic piano works he (ironically) labeled *Bagatelles,* or "little bits of nothing." In the late style we also find extremes of texture, ranging from the simple to the extraordinarily complex. Many movements have the directness of song (such as the *Cavatina* from the String Quartet op. 130); others explore the intricacies of fugue at great length. Finally, in the late period, Beethoven exhibits an increasing sense of harmonic freedom and a kind of raw emotion in tone that is something new in music. In the middle of the *Cavatina* in the String Quartet op. 130, for example, Beethoven moves from E♭ to C♭ major and tells the first violinist to play the lyrical melody in a manner that is *beklemmt*—literally, "caught in a vise." And indeed, the music sounds like an operatic heroine so emotionally devastated that she is gasping for breath. Beauty is no longer the primary consideration. What is primary now is psychological truth.

Principal Works

SYMPHONIES Although the first two symphonies are distinctive in their own right, they operate within the traditions of the genre as transmitted by Haydn and Mozart. In contrast, the Third Symphony—the *Eroica*—is a truly revolutionary work, not only because of its size (almost twice as long as any symphony before) but also because of its structural complexity, its treatments of the orchestra, the weight of its finale, and what might be called its ethical dimension, its engagement with the idea of heroism. (Beethoven's symphonies are considered at length in this chapter.)

PIANO SONATAS Like the symphonies, Beethoven's 32 piano sonatas explore a remarkable variety of styles. Many of these works are known by nicknames that have no connection with the composer. Op. 27, no. 1, for example, became the *Moonlight* Sonata because it reminded one critic of moonlight on a lake. The designation *Appassionata* for op. 57 derives from the passionate tone of the outer movements of the work. The name of the *Tempest* Sonata (op. 31, no. 2) comes from Anton Schindler (1795–1864), Beethoven's personal secretary, who fabricated many stories about the composer. Schindler claimed that when he asked Beethoven about the poetic program behind this sonata, the composer growled, "Go read Shakespeare's *Tempest*." (Even if the report is true, did Beethoven mean it seriously?) Other nicknames have a more solid foundation. The *Waldstein* Sonata (op. 53; discussed in Chapter 16) is in fact dedicated to Count Waldstein. And Beethoven himself, in an indisputable example of the effect of events in his life on his work, named Sonata op. 81a *Les Adieux* ("The Farewell") to commemorate the departure, exile, and

In contrast to Wagner, other composers saw the Ninth as an aberration, a onetime experiment, and indeed, the surviving sketches for the symphony Beethoven was working on when he died suggest it would have been purely instrumental.

As it turned out, it was the French composer Hector Berlioz (1803–1869) who would be most widely acclaimed as Beethoven's true heir, not because he imitated Beethoven, but because each of his three symphonies was so strikingly original and different from anything heard before. With his brilliant and original orchestration, his fresh approach to the grand scale of the genre, and his ability to blend music and narrative, he demonstrated for subsequent composers that it was possible to follow Beethoven's spirit of originality without directly imitating him. The symphonies of Liszt and Mahler, in particular, are deeply indebted to the legacy of Berlioz.

Berlioz
Symphonie fantastique

All three of Berlioz's symphonies are programmatic to varying degrees. The first of them, the *Symphonie fantastique* of 1830, as already mentioned, is based on a detailed program of Berlioz's own invention. Inspired by the composer's infatuation with an

return of his pupil and patron, Archduke Rudolph, who had been forced into exile by the arrival of French troops in Vienna. The late sonatas (opp. 101, 106, 109, 110, 111) enjoy a special place in the piano repertory. Op. 106 (the *Hammerklavier*) has been called the "Mount Everest of the Piano" because of its size and technical difficulty, particularly in the fugal finale. The last of these sonatas, op. 111, is in two movements, which prompted the original publisher to inquire whether or not the composer had neglected to send him the finale.

STRING QUARTETS AND OTHER CHAMBER WORKS
Beethoven wrote his first set of string quartets, op. 18, under the shadow of Haydn, the acknowledged master of the genre at the time. At least one of these works, however (op. 18, no. 5), takes a quartet by Mozart (K. 464) as its model. Beethoven's next set of quartets, published in 1808 as op. 59, is altogether different: larger, more difficult, and full of the heroic style associated with the Third and Fifth Symphonies. The three works as a whole are known as the *Razumovsky* Quartets by virtue of their dedicatee, the Russian ambassador to the Austrian Empire, who was also one of Beethoven's most important patrons in Vienna. All of the subsequent quartets were substantial enough to be issued individually. The *Harp* Quartet, op. 74 (so called because of its many arpeggiated pizzicato figures in the first movement) still belongs to the middle period, but op. 95 (1810) cannot be classified so easily. Many critics consider it one of the first works in the late style.

The five late quartets (opp. 127, 130, 131, 132, and 135) constitute some of the most demanding music of the 19th century, both technically and aesthetically. Indeed, for much of the 19th century, these works were seen as manifestations of Beethoven's extreme sense of isolation from the external world and were more respected than loved. In the 20th century they came to be appreciated as probing explorations of the human psyche, providing inspiration for such diverse composers as Schoenberg, Bartók, Stravinsky, and Carter.

In addition to the string quartets, Beethoven also wrote ten sonatas for violin and piano, five for cello and piano, six piano trios, five string trios, and various other chamber works in a variety of combinations for strings, winds, and piano. All of these were popular in their day and have endured as staples of the chamber repertoire.

VOCAL MUSIC Beethoven wrote a great deal more vocal music than most people realize. Several dozen songs, more than a hundred folk-song arrangements, two substantial settings of the Mass ordinary, several secular cantatas and miscellaneous works for chorus and orchestra, an oratorio (*Christ on the Mount of Olives*), an opera (*Fidelio,* originally entitled *Leonore* and revised several times), and almost fifty canons for various numbers of voices. Given this considerable output, it must have galled Beethoven that his contemporaries almost always qualified their praise by calling him the greatest living composer of *instrumental* music.

actress named Harriet Smithson, the program relates the increasing emotional turmoil of a young musician as he realizes the woman he loves is spurning him (see Primary Evidence: "Berlioz's Program for the *Symphonie fantastique*"). The emotional trajectory of the symphony is thus almost the reverse of Beethoven's Ninth. Beethoven's symphony moves from a turbulent first movement to a joyous finale; the *Symphonie fantastique*, in contrast, moves from a joyous first movement, which evokes of the young musician's first infatuation, to a dark finale, labeled "Dream of a Witches' Sabbath," which evokes the image of the musician's beloved dancing demonically at his funeral. The sounding of the *Dies irae* ("Day of Wrath") from the well-known plainchant Mass for the Dead within the finale serves as a dark counterpoint to Beethoven's theme for the vocal setting of Schiller's "Ode to Joy" in the finale of the Ninth. Instead of a vision of heaven, we are given a vision of hell and the triumph of evil.

Not everyone found Berlioz's program for his *Symphonie fantastique* helpful. Robert Schumann, in an otherwise favorable review of the work, argued that the movement

PRIMARY EVIDENCE

Berlioz's Program for the *Symphonie fantastique*

Berlioz was for many years adamant about the importance of the program: "At concerts where this symphony is to be performed," he once declared, "it is essential that this program be distributed in advance in order to provide an overview of the dramatic structure of this work." The program exists in two versions. The one given here is from the published score of 1845; a later edition presents the entire story as an opium-inspired dream that is part of an unsuccessful suicide attempt. In the end, however, Berlioz rejected both programs, wearied no doubt by the lavish attention given his prose at the expense of his music. The frequent ellipses in the program are Berlioz's own. The *ranz des vashes* is a shepherd's call, frequently associated with reed instruments in orchestral compositions of this era. The *Dies irae* in the last movement is a chant sung during the Mass for the Dead. The text is apocalyptic. It is safe to say that every member of Berlioz's original audience would have recognized this melody (and its implicit text) at once.

· · · · ·

(1) Dreams—Passions. The author imagines that a young musician, afflicted with that malady of the spirit called the *vague des passions* by one well-known writer, sees for the first time a woman who embodies all the charms of the ideal being of his dreams, and he falls hopelessly in love with her. By bizarre peculiarity, the image of the beloved always presents itself to the soul of the artist united with a musical idea that incorporates a certain character he bestows to her, passionate but at the same time noble and shy.

This melodic image and its source pursue him ceaselessly as a double *idée fixe*. This is the reason for the persistent appearance, in every movement of the symphony, of the melody that begins the opening Allegro. The transition from this state of melancholic reverie, interrupted by a few spasms of unfounded joy, to one of delirious passion, with its animations of fury, jealousy, its return to tenderness, its tears, its religious consolations—this is the subjection of the first movement.

(2) A Ball. The artist finds himself in the most varied situations in the middle of the tumult of a party, in the peaceful contemplation of the beauties of nature. But everywhere—in the city, in the countryside—the cherished image of his beloved presents itself to him and troubles his spirit.

(3) Scene in the Countryside. Finding himself in the countryside one evening, he hears in the distance two shepherds conversing with each other through a *ranz des vaches*. The pastoral duet, the scenic setting, the light rustling of the trees sweetly swayed by the wind, some reasons for hope that have lately come to his knowledge—all unite to fill his heart with unaccustomed tranquility and lend a brighter color to his fancies. He reflects upon his isolation; he hopes that he will not be lonely too much longer. . . . But if she should be deceiving him! . . . This mixture of hope and fear, these thoughts of happiness troubled by certain dark presentiments constitute the subject of the Adagio movement. At the end, one of the shepherds resumes the *ranz des vaches;* the other no longer responds. . . . Distant noise of thunder . . . solitude . . . silence. . . .

(4) March to the Scaffold. Convinced that his love has been ignored, the artist poisons himself with opium. The dose of the narcotic is too weak to kill him and plunges him into a sleep accompanied by the most horrible visions. He dreams that he has killed the woman he loved, that he is condemned, led to the scaffold, and is to witness his own execution. The procession moves to the sound of a march at times somber and fierce, at times brilliant and solemn, in which the muffled noise of the heavy footsteps is followed without any transition by the noisiest outbursts. At the end of the march, the first four measures of the *idée fixe* reappear like a final thought of love interrupted by the fatal blow [of the guillotine].

(5) Dream of a Witches' Sabbath. He sees himself at the Sabbath, in the middle of a frightening troupe of ghosts, sorcerers, monsters of every kind, all gathered for his funeral rites. Strange noises, groans, bursts of laughter, distant cries to which other cries seem to respond. The beloved melody reappears, but it has lost its noble and shy character. It is nothing more than the melody of a common dance, trivial and grotesque; it is she who comes to join the Sabbath. . . . A roar of joy at her arrival. . . . She throws herself into the diabolical orgy. . . . Funeral knell, burlesque parody of the *Dies irae*. Witches' Round Dance. The dance and *Dies irae* combined.

Source: Berlioz's program to the first edition of the full score of the *Symphonie fantastique* (1845).

titles alone would have been sufficient. German listeners in particular, Schumann argued, disliked having their thoughts "so rudely directed," all the more so given their "delicacy of feeling and aversion to personal revelation." But Berlioz, Schumann rationalized, "was writing primarily for his French compatriots, who are not greatly impressed by refinements of modesty. I can imagine them, leaflet in hand, reading and applauding their countryman who has depicted it all so well; the music by itself does not interest them."[7]

Whatever their response to the program, listeners were universally impressed by the work's orchestration. More than any composer before or since, Berlioz expanded the sound of the orchestra. Berlioz's handling of the orchestra was also unusually forward looking for 1830. At the beginning of the *Symphonie fantastique*, for example, he calls for the high winds to play *pp*, then *ppp*, and then to decrescendo, presumably to an inaudible level. And in the fourth movement, the "March to the Scaffold," he introduces a brass sound never before heard in the concert hall: massive, forceful, and rhythmically charged. Berlioz also peppers his scores with instructions of a hitherto unknown specificity. The *Symphonie fantastique* is also notable for its realism: Berlioz avoids prettifying ugly or grotesque themes, representing them instead with what were, for the time, harsh-sounding musical devices.

THE CONCERT OVERTURE

The **concert overture** grew out of the 18th-century tradition of performing opera overtures in the concert hall, independently of the operas for which they had been written. By the early 19th century, the overture had emerged as a work of instrumental music in a single movement connected in some way with a known plot. Overtures themselves became increasingly dramatic, none more so than Beethoven's *Leonore* Overture no. 3 (op. 72a, 1806), one of four different overtures Beethoven wrote for his opera *Fidelio* (entitled *Leonore* in its original version). The plot of *Fidelio* involves faithful love and political injustice. Florestan, imprisoned for his political beliefs by Don Pizarro, a wicked governor, languishes in jail. To free him, his wife, Leonore, disguises herself as a man, takes the name Fidelio ("Faithful One"), and gains the confidence of Florestan's jailer. After long months of menial work, she is finally allowed to take a few scraps of bread and some water to the dungeon that houses the "most dangerous" of all the jail's prisoners, Florestan. But just as she is about to spring her husband free, Don Pizarro appears, intent on killing Florestan. Leonore intervenes and reveals her true identity. Just then an enlightened state minister arrives, saves the couple, frees the rest of the prisoners, and punishes Pizarro.

Beethoven's *Leonore* Overture no. 3 wordlessly encapsulates this drama. It opens with a darkly chromatic slow introduction in C minor before moving to a buoyant Allegro in C major. The end of the turbulent development reenacts the arrival of the minister with an offstage trumpet fanfare, and the recapitulation provides the climactic moment of triumph. The blaze of C major at the end of the overture reflects the release of all the political prisoners.

Why did Beethoven reject this overture? It is certainly one of his most dramatic instrumental works, but this was precisely the problem. By synthesizing the emotional unfolding of the entire story—gloom, hope, despair, rescue, jubilation—Beethoven had created an overture that made the opera itself something of an anticlimax. The instrumental overture had outgrown its function, and Beethoven wisely published it as a separate work. In its place, he composed a much shorter, less dramatic, but effective overture for *Fidelio*, the one played before the opera in performances today.

Composer Profile

Hector Berlioz
(1803–1869)

Berlioz, admired today as one of the most original of 19th-century composers, was an outsider almost all of his life. Born in a rural province of southern France, he had to fight to make his way in the bitterly partisan world of Parisian musical politics. By the time he won the grudging admiration of his countrymen, he was nearing the end of his life, and he was never embraced in his native France the way he was in Germany.

Berlioz's father, a physician, sent his son to Paris to study medicine. The young Hector wrote home regularly to report on the progress of his course work and just as regularly to ask for more money. In fact, however, the youth had largely given up attending classes and was busy immersing himself in the local musical scene. This charade could not continue indefinitely, of course, and Berlioz eventually found himself on his own. In 1826, he enrolled in the Paris Conservatory, whose teachers considered him talented but willful and undisciplined. Every year the Conservatory held a contest among its composition students for an award—the coveted Prix de Rome—that automatically opened doors of opportunity for the winner. Berlioz yearned for the prize but failed to win it several years in a row. Finally, in desperation, he resigned himself to writing in a style he knew the judges would like, and he won in 1830.

During this same period, Berlioz was composing the stunningly original *Symphonie fantastique.* The woman who inspired this work, the subject of its thematic *idée fixe* and the object of Berloz's infatuation, was the Irish actress Harriet Smithson, whom he first saw in a performance of Shakespeare's *Hamlet* in 1827. He eventually met and married her, but the marriage did not last.

After his return to Paris in 1832, Berlioz struggled to get a commission from the Opéra, the city's most prestigious musical institution, but the politics of artistic patronage conspired against him on repeated occasions. He turned to music journalism to supplement his income, and his reviews still make fascinating reading.

KEY DATES IN THE LIFE OF HECTOR BERLIOZ

1803 Born at Côte-Saint-André (southern France) on December 11.

1821 Goes to Paris to study medicine so he might follow in the footsteps of his father, a physician.

1826 Abandons medicine and enrolls in the Paris Conservatory, where he is as unhappy with the instructors as they are with him.

1826–1829 Applies unsuccessfully for the coveted Prix de Rome; all three of his compositions for this competition are rejected.

1830 Wins the Prix de Rome with a more conventional composition.

1833 Marries Harriet Smithson, an Irish actress whom he has worshipped from a safe distance for many years and who was the inspiration for his *Symphonie fantastique* (1830). The marriage is a disaster, however, and ends in 1840. He later remarries.

1842 Makes the first of several successful tours of Germany, where his symphonies are greeted with greater enthusiasm than in France.

1843 Publishes his *Treatise on Instrumentation and Orchestration,* a work that would subsequently go through many editions and be translated into many languages.

1852 Appointed librarian of the Paris Conservatory, an honorary post but one that acknowledges his place in the musical world of France.

1869 Dies in Paris on March 8.

In later decades, Berlioz received greater acclaim from abroad, particularly from Germany and Russia, than at home in France. In 1843, he published a groundbreaking textbook on orchestration that took into account the new possibilities of the orchestra's changing instruments. The text would later be revised by that other 19th-century master of orchestration, Richard Strauss, and is still in use in many music conservatories.

Principal Works

SYMPHONIES AND CONCERT OVERTURES Berlioz's three major symphonies rank among the greatest works of their kind in the 19th century. Each is utterly different from the other, but all have a literary foundation: The *Symphonie fantastique* (1830) follows a prose program of Berlioz's own invention. *Harold en Italie* (1834) draws on Byron's epic poem *Childe Harold's Pilgrimage,* and *Roméo et Juliette* (1839) is based on Shakespeare's *Romeo and Juliet.* It was the novelty and variety of these various approaches to the genre that led Berlioz's German contemporaries to hail him as Beethoven's true successor.

The works of a variety of authors, from Shakespeare to Sir Walter Scott, inspired Berlioz's concert overtures. These include *Waverly* (1828), *Les francs-juges* (1828), *King Lear* (1831), *Rob Roy* (1832), and *Le Corsaire* (1844). Building on Beethoven's accomplishments in this genre, Berlioz's overtures are important forerunners to the symphonic poems that Liszt and Richard Strauss would compose later in the century.

OPERAS Although admired, Berlioz's two operas have never achieved widespread popularity. *Benvenuto Cellini* (1838) traces the life of the celebrated Renaissance sculptor. *Les Troyens* ("The Trojans," 1859) is based on the story of the Trojan War. Only the second half of this work was ever performed during Berlioz's lifetime; the complete opera was not produced in its original French until 1920, and then not in Paris, but in Rouen.

VOCAL MUSIC Berlioz wrote several unstaged vocal works that are difficult to classify but always dramatic in spirit. These include the massive *Requiem* (1837), which calls for antiphonal orchestras and choruses; *L'Enfance du Christ* ("The Infancy of Christ," 1854), a "sacred trilogy"; and *La Damnation de Faust* (1846), an *opéra en concert* ("concert opera"). *Lélio, or the Return to Life* (1831), a sequel to the *Symphonie fantastique,* is a unique mixture of orchestral music, chorus, song, and melodrama. In 1841, building on the tradition of the French chanson, Berlioz invented a new genre with his song cycle for voice and orchestra, *Les nuits d'été* ("Summer Nights," 1841).

The shock of the loud: Berlioz conducts (1846). *Like any caricature, this one builds on an element of truth. Audiences in the 19th century found Berlioz's orchestras enormous, his music staggeringly loud. Berlioz was also among the first virtuoso conductors. Until roughly 1830, ensembles had been led by the principal first violinist, the concertmaster, or by a keyboard player seated at the piano or harpsichord. By 1850, the conductor had come to be seen as a true interpreter of the music at hand, not merely as someone who kept the ensemble together. Weber, Mendelssohn, and Louis Spohr, like Berlioz, were esteemed as both conductors and composers.*

Source: Andreas Geiger (1765–1856), "A Concert of Hector Berlioz (1803–1869) in 1846", engraving/Musée de l'Opera, Paris, France/The Bridgeman Art Library.

Composer Profile

Felix Mendelssohn
(1809–1847)

Mendelssohn was born into a prominent family whose fame was unconnected to music. His grandfather, Moses Mendelssohn, was one of the leading philosophers of his day, and his father, Abraham Mendelssohn, was a very successful banker in Berlin. Abraham converted to Christianity and added "Bartholdy" to the family's name, hence the designation Felix Mendelssohn Bartholdy (often with an erroneous hyphen).

Felix was the greatest child prodigy of his age, both as a composer and as a pianist. The prestigious Singakademie of Berlin performed his setting of the 19th Psalm in 1819, and the young child traveled across Europe in much the same way as Mozart had half a century before. By the time he was 17, he had already written the Octet for strings op. 20 and the *Overture to a Midsummer Night's Dream,* op. 21. He also excelled as a conductor. In 1828, on the hundredth anniversary of its premiere, he led a hugely successful performance of J. S. Bach's *Saint Matthew Passion,* a then-forgotten work he had helped rediscover.

Mendelssohn was closely attached to his sister, Fanny (1805–1847), who was a talented pianist and composer in her own right. After her marriage in 1829, she published several books of songs and many short piano pieces under the name Fanny Mendelssohn Hensel. She shared her brother's interest in the music of J. S. Bach and remained his closest musical confidante until her sudden death at the age of 41. Biographers have speculated, in fact, that her brother's intense grief hastened his own sudden demise later that same year.

Mendelssohn's death occasioned prolonged public mourning across Europe, and numerous writers speculated on the bleak future of music without him. Within a decade, however, he had become the favorite target of ridicule by musicians who thought of themselves as progressive. To these figures, particularly Wagner, Mendelssohn represented the most conservative elements of music. In the 1930s and 1940s, Mendelssohn became the object of vicious attacks from Germany's Nazi regime because of his Jewish ancestry.

Mendelssohn never rebelled against anything and was the darling of both Prussian and English royalty, and in this respect he does not fit the

KEY DATES IN THE LIFE OF FELIX MENDELSSOHN

1809 Born February 3 in Hamburg.

1819 Becomes member of Berlin Singakademie; its director, Carl Friedrich Zelter, introduces the young Mendelssohn to Goethe in 1821, initiating a friendship that would continue until the poet's death in 1832.

1826 Composes his *Overture to A Midsummer Night's Dream.*

1828 Conducts Bach's *Saint Matthew Passion* with the Berlin Singakademie on March 11, almost exactly a hundred years after the work's premiere; the work, essentially unknown to 19th-century audiences, sparks renewed interest in Bach's music.

1829 Makes the first of ten trips to England, where he becomes the most beloved composer of his generation, helped in part by the favor and patronage of Queen Victoria and Prince Albert.

1836 Becomes conductor of Leipzig Gewandhaus Orchestra, which he builds into the leading orchestra of Europe. Also initiates a series of "historical concerts" with music of composers by previous generations.

1843 Helps establish the Leipzig Conservatory, which soon becomes the leading institution of its kind in Germany and second in prestige only to the Paris Conservatory.

1847 Dies in Leipzig after a brief illness on November 4.

popular image of the Romantic composer. Yet his private letters reveal a far more complex personality than is generally recognized.

Principal Works

SYMPHONIES AND OTHER ORCHESTRAL WORKS Mendelssohn wrote several symphonies for strings in his youth and arranged one of them for full orchestra in 1824 as his First Symphony, op. 11. Later, however, he repudiated this and several other works in the genre, including his *Reformation* Symphony (1832), whose finale includes the melody from Martin Luther's famous hymn "A Mighty Fortress is Our God." Mendelssohn allowed only a few performances of the *Italian* Symphony in the mid-1830s, which has since become his most popular, and appears never to have been completely satisfied with it. The *Scottish* Symphony, op. 56 (1842), was the one work in the genre Mendelssohn allowed to be published. (Although first performed as a symphony, the *Lobgesang* of 1840 was later redesignated a symphony-cantata.)

The concert overtures have fared even better with audiences than the symphonies. Three of them—*The Hebrides* (also known as *Fingal's Cave*), *A Midsummer Night's Dream,* and *The Fair Melusine*—are staples of the orchestral repertory today. In these works, Mendelssohn combined programmatic elements with symphonic writing on a smaller scale, and his contributions in this area exercised a profound influence on later composers of symphonic poems. The Violin Concerto in E minor, op. 64, remains a touchstone of the repertory. The two piano concertos, widely performed in their time, have not fared as well.

CHAMBER WORKS Aside from the youthful Octet op. 20, Mendelssohn's chamber music—piano trios, string quartets, and string quintets—is not performed as much as it deserves. The early string quartets, opp. 12 and 13, are among the few works of their kind written under the direct influence of Beethoven's late quartets. The later chamber music, in particular, features a distinctly personal idiom that integrates counterpoint and lyricism.

PIANO WORKS The 48 *Lieder ohne Worte* ("Songs without Words"), published in eight separate books, were enormously successful in their time. The piano

sonatas and various other miniatures combine brilliance with substance.

VOCAL MUSIC The oratorios *Paulus* (1836) and *Elijah* (1846) enjoyed extraordinary popularity in the 19th century, particularly in England. Choral societies there were quick to add these works to their repertories alongside the oratorios of Handel, which served as Mendelssohn's principal model in the genre. The choral writing, inspired by Bach as well as Handel, is among the most powerful and moving of the entire 19th-century repertory. Mendelssohn also wrote many works for a cappella chorus, some of them in a deliberately archaic style, evoking the music of earlier composers such as Palestrina and Bach.

Felix Mendelssohn. *In contrast to the many likenesses of Beethoven that portray him as a fiery individualist, this portrait of Mendelssohn done by J. W. Childe in 1829 portrays him as a gentleman. Mendelssohn's lack of personal rebelliousness has contributed to his image as a talented but somehow safe composer, not willing to assault tradition in the manner of his near-contemporaries Berlioz, Liszt, and Wagner. Mendelssohn is shown here on the first of his ten trips to England, where he was idolized both as a composer and as a conductor.*

Source: Staatsbibliothek zu Berlin, Stiftung Preussischer Kulturbesitz

Inspired by Beethoven's example, other composers began writing overtures expressly for the concert hall. Felix Mendelssohn wrote his *Overture to A Midsummer Night's Dream* when he was 17 years old as a stand-alone work; only later did he compose additional movements to make the work suitable as incidental music for a theatrical production of Shakespeare's play. Unlike Beethoven's *Leonore* Overture no. 3, the piece does not recount the drama in brief. Instead, Mendelssohn presents a succession of themes representing the play's main characters. One of the ways Mendelssohn captures the sometimes chaotic magical spirit of the midsummer night's forest is through the simultaneous use of disparate dynamics. At measure 294, for example, he brings in the horns *fortissimo, "con tutta la forza"* ("with all force"), even as the strings and high winds maintain their elfin *pianissimo* figure.

Mendelssohn himself outlined the work's thematic associations in a remarkable letter of February 15, 1833, to his publisher. The composer is reluctant to equate the music and the stage action directly, yet he cannot deny they are connected.

> It is not possible for me to indicate the course of ideas in this composition for the printed concert program, for this course of ideas *is* my overture. . . . I would prefer it if on the printed program you would summarize only this content and said nothing further about my music, so that it can simply speak for itself, if it is good; and if it is not good, then no explanation will help at all.[8]

Mendelssohn wrote many other popular concert overtures in addition to the *Overture to A Midsummer Night's Dream.* These include *The Hebrides* (also known as *Fingal's Cave*), which conjures up a landscape off the Scottish coast; *Calm Seas and a Prosperous Voyage,* which is based on a poem of the same title by Goethe; and *The Fair Melusine,* which reflects a folktale about a mermaid who takes on human form.

Over the course of the 19th century, a great many commentators created programs for instrumental works that had none, often in an attempt to make the difficult and highly abstract art of instrumental music more approachable to untrained listeners. The need for such clues was driven at least in part by the growing formal, harmonic, and rhythmic complexity of the music. Listeners perplexed by Mahler's First Symphony in the last decade of the 19th century, for example, accused the composer of having suppressed the work's program (which in fact is precisely what he had done). The work would have been far more intelligible, they insisted, had its story been revealed to them.

THE CONCERTO

The 19th century was the age of the great instrumental composer-virtuoso. The violinists Niccolò Paganini (1782–1840), Joseph Joachim (1831–1907), and Pablo de Sarasate (1844–1908) all wrote concertos for themselves, as did the pianists Beethoven, Chopin, Mendelssohn, Clara Schumann, Brahms, Liszt, and Edvard Grieg (1843–1907). As with Vivaldi and Mozart, the concerto provided the ideal vehicle for a composer-performer to show off his or her talents in both fields at once.

Most 19th-century concertos maintained the three-movement fast-slow-fast format of the Classical era. With the decline of basso continuo in the late 18th century, however, the role of the soloist in the concerto changed significantly. No longer obligated to support or play along with the ensemble during tutti sections, the soloist instead waited in silence before making a grand entrance. Unlike the symphony and concert overture, the concerto remained a mostly nonprogrammatic genre, at least on the surface. Few composers openly associated their concertos with extramusical ideas, yet audiences could not help but hear drama in the interplay between soloist and orchestra.

The interplay between soloist and orchestra in the second movement of Beethoven's Fourth Piano Concerto, op. 58, illustrates this kind of drama quite vividly. The soloist and the orchestra—limited in this movement to the strings—engage in an extended dialogue that moves from confrontation to resolution. The strings open with a loud unison figure characterized by dotted rhythms and staccato articulation. The piano responds with an utterly different kind of statement, a lyrical, hymnlike theme that Beethoven marks *molto cantabile*. To underscore the timbral difference between soloist and orchestra, Beethoven calls on the pianist to play the entire movement *una corda* ("one string")—that is, using one of the pedals to shift the entire keyboard action so the hammers strike only a single string.

At least some listeners have interpreted this movement as a musical reenactment of part of the myth of Orpheus and Euridice. Although Beethoven himself left no direct evidence to support this interpretation, accounts by friends and acquaintances suggest that it is at least plausible. And as a painting he commissioned of himself suggests (see "Beethoven as Orpheus," Plate 14 in color insert III), Beethoven apparently did think of himself as a modern-day Orpheus.

In its breadth of sound and susceptibility to programmatic interpretation, this movement also illustrates the growing influence of the symphony on the concerto in the 19th century. A result of this trend was to increase the role of the orchestra without diminishing the demand for soloistic virtuosity. The piano concertos of Schumann, Grieg, and Brahms are openly symphonic in scale and tone, as are Brahms's concertos for violin (op. 77) and for violin and cello (the Double Concerto, op. 102). Indeed, Brahms's First Piano Concerto, op. 15 (1854), began life as a symphony; only after he began to sketch out its basic ideas did Brahms decide to fashion it into a concerto.

Beethoven
Piano Concerto
no. 4, op. 58

CONCLUSION

The dimensions of orchestral music expanded in almost every conceivable respect in the first half of the 19th century. Orchestras grew in size and volume, symphonies and concertos became longer, and instrumental music in general took on the task of transcending the realm of mere sound. Beethoven's symphonies, in particular, served as a catalyst in transforming attitudes toward the scope of instrumental music, demonstrating to the listening public the ability of music to convey ideas and images without a text. Following Beethoven's lead, later composers like Mendelssohn also developed the emerging genre of the concert overture, a programmatic orchestral work in a single movement. Before 1800, vocal music had always been considered aesthetically superior to instrumental music. By the 1830s, this was no longer the case. Precisely because of its independence from words, instrumental music—above all, the symphony—was increasingly perceived as the highest form of the musical art.

Chapter 16

Piano Music, Chamber Music, Song

Beethoven's Piano Sonatas
and String Quartets

Song

The Character Piece

I n contrast to orchestral genres, the repertories of piano music, chamber music, and song occupied a more private sphere. These smaller scale genres were performed largely in social gatherings in homes or salons rather than in public concerts. The phenomenon of the solo piano recital before a paying public did not begin to emerge until the end of the 1830s.

BEETHOVEN'S PIANO SONATAS AND STRING QUARTETS

Beethoven
Piano Sonata in C
Major, op. 53
(*Waldstein*)

The gulf between music written for amateurs and professionals expanded greatly during the 19th century. Beethoven's piano sonatas, although widely admired, were repeatedly criticized during his lifetime for their technical difficulty. His Sonata in C Major, op. 53, completed in 1804 and dedicated to Count Waldstein, an early patron from Bonn, may seem relatively undemanding compared to later works, but its rapid passagework and broken octave scales put it beyond the reach of most amateurs at the time it was written. In a break with what had become standard practice in the Classical era, the exposition of the first movement modulates to the mediant (E major, which later becomes E minor) instead of the dominant (G major). This kind of modulation reflects the increasing chromaticism of 19th-century harmonic practice and the consequent erosion of the polarity between tonic and dominant that had characterized the formal structures of the mid-to-late 18th century. Later composers working within the conventions of sonata form would often modulate to keys other than the dominant or relative major.

While looking forward in terms of its technical demands and harmonic structure, the *Waldstein* also looks back for thematic inspiration, illustrating Beethoven's ability to transform a predecessor's idea into an entirely new creation. The opening bears striking parallels to Haydn's String Quartet op. 33, no. 3 (Anthology, discussed in Chapter 12).

Like his piano sonatas, Beethoven's string quartets also reflect the trend toward increasing technical difficulty. Good amateurs could readily have performed the six quartets he published as op. 18 in 1801, but not the three substantially longer quartets he published as op. 59 in 1808. Beethoven's late quartets—opp. 127, 130, 132, and 135, composed between 1824 and 1826—are among the most challenging works he wrote in any genre, for performers and listeners alike. Contemporary listeners had never heard anything quite like the opening of the Quartet in B♭ Major, op. 130. The music is full of unexpected starts and stops. What appears at first to be a slow introduction, for example, turns out to be an integral part of the sonata-form exposition. And instead of modulating to the expected dominant (F) in the exposition, Beethoven dramatically overshoots it (measure 51) and lands instead in the unlikely key of G♭ (♭VI, measure 55). Subsequent movements are full of formal and technical surprises.

The original finale of op. 130 was an enormous fugue that Beethoven later published as a separate work with its own opus number, the *Grosse Fuge* ("Great Fugue," op. 133). This work has justly been called Beethoven's equivalent to *The Art of Fugue,* Johann Sebastian Bach's compilation of fugues on a single theme. It is no coincidence that it should have originally been intended to provide the capstone to a work so thoroughly occupied with issues of texture. In its place, Beethoven wrote a shorter finale in which an apparently simple opening, based on a kind of folklike dance, becomes increasingly complex, with a remarkable multiplicity of textures.

Beethoven
String Quartet in B♭
Major, op. 130

SONG

Like many of his later compositions, Beethoven's String Quartet op. 130 was not particularly well received at first. Most contemporary performers and listeners preferred less demanding music. This explains in part the enormous popularity of the genre of song for solo voice and piano in the first half of the 19th century.

German composers cultivated this genre with such intensity that it is often designated by its German name, the **Lied** (pronounced "leet"; the plural, **Lieder,** is pronounced like the English word "leader"). The rise of German poetry, the growing availability of the piano, and the idealization of domesticity and the family converged to give the Lied its newfound prominence.

Performed by only two musicians in a room of modest size before a select audience, the song is a genre in which the slightest inflections of harmony, dynamics, and register can have great effect. In contrast to a monumental genre like the symphony, the song calls for heightened sensitivity from composers, performers, and listeners. Its popularity reflects a belief that simplicity can be profound, that a universe of emotions can be encapsulated within a work of small dimensions.

From the perspective of form, songs generally fall into one of three categories: strophic, modified strophic, or through composed. In *strophic form*, the simplest of the three, each verse (strophe) of a poem is set to the same music. In **modified strophic form,** as in a variation on a theme, the music varies from strophe to strophe—with melodic embellishment, for example, or alteration of texture or harmony—but remains otherwise recognizably the same. A *through-composed* song, in contrast, has no recognizable pattern of repetition, and often no repetition at all.

Song composers in the 19th century were judged according to the extent to which their music enhanced the words of the poems they set. The repetitive rhythmic insistence of Franz Schubert's *Erlkönig* ("Elf-king") reflects the content and iambic meter of

Schubert
Erlkönig,
Prometheus, and
Wanderers
Nachtlied

F O C U S

The Piano

The piano grew in almost every respect over the course of the 19th century. By 1900, its compass had increased from five octaves to the now-standard 88 keys. A substantial increase in the size of the frame and various improvements in escapement action made it possible for a single instrument to combine both lightness and power. Leather hammer coverings were eventually replaced with felt, producing a thicker, heavier sound. Improvements in damper pedals and the addition of a shifting pedal to allow hammers to strike only one string for each note (una corda) increased timbral variety. The introduction of a one-piece cast-iron frame increased both durability and sound volume.

When pianos began to be mass produced in the second quarter of the 19th century, their cost dropped, and by the 1850s they had become standard fixtures in middle- and upper-class homes. Every home with any pretensions to culture had one, and every daughter in such a home was almost certain to have been subjected to piano lessons at some point in her upbringing. As a result, the market for piano teachers and piano music was enormous. The popularity of the instrument also made it feasible for composers (and publishers) to disseminate music in other genres—operas, symphonies, concertos, and even string quartets—in the form of piano reductions.

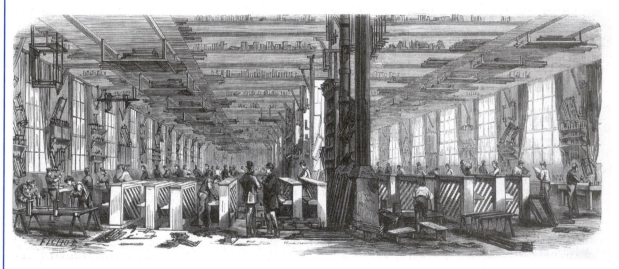

Piano manufacturing. *The mass manufacture of pianos in the 19th century made the instruments considerably more affordable. The upright models being assembled here in the Parisian piano factory of Pleyel around 1845 were designed to fit into the smaller spaces of middle-class homes. The contrast of scale with 18th-century methods of instrument production is striking (see illustration, "Interior of a brass instrument workshop in Paris, ca. 1760" in Chapter 12).*

Source: Mary Evans Picture Library Ltd.

Goethe's strophic poem. Schubert, however, goes beyond this rhythmic device to magnify the poem's emotional force in his modified-strophic setting. *Erlkönig* tells a chilling tale of a father riding home with his feverish son in his arms. The boy hears the Elf-king calling to him with seductive blandishments and cries out in fear as his father tries vainly to calm him. When they arrive, the boy is dead in his father's arms. The poem has four voices— a narrator, the Elf-king, the boy, and the father—and Schubert gives each of them a distinctive character through the strategic use of key, mode, texture, and register.

Free verse, as is found in a poem like Goethe's *Prometheus,* calls for a flexible musical structure. Schubert's through-composed setting emphasizes the declamatory tone and irregular rhythms of the poetry.

A brief poem of a single strophe like Goethe's *Wanderers Nachtlied* ("Wanderer's Night Song") elicited from Schubert an intense attention to detail. The limited melodic motion and straightforward rhythms of the opening capture the sense of calm that pervades the text ("Above all summits is calm . . .") and make the subsequent syncopation (measures 5–8) all the more pronounced. The repeated horn call–like figures in measures 9–13 take on added importance through repetition. In so brief a setting, every gesture carries added weight. Even the one-measure epilogue in the piano (measure 14) resonates with significance, given the remarkably small scale of this work.

Schubert also helped establish the genre of the **song cycle,** a collection of songs ordered in such a way as to convey at least the outline of a story or idea. His *Die schöne Müllerin* ("The Beautiful Daughter of the Miller"), to texts by Wilhelm Müller, is a series of 20 songs that tell the story of a journeyman miller who falls in love with his master's daughter but is spurned and eventually commits suicide. Other cycles, such as Robert Schumann's *Dichterliebe,* op. 48, are more loosely structured in terms of text but carefully organized in terms of tonality and other musical parameters.

Different composers were often drawn to the same text, bringing to it a variety of interpretations that reflect changing styles and expanding musical options. Carl Friedrich Zelter's late-18th-century setting of Goethe's poem *Kennst du das Land?* ("Do You Know the Land?" Anthology), for example, is relatively straightforward, with a limited melodic range and restrained chromaticism. Later settings—like those by Schubert, Schumann, and Hugo Wolf—have more intricate vocal lines, richer textures, and increasingly chromatic harmonies that reflect the 19th century's ever-expanding harmonic vocabulary. Wolf's setting, in particular, illustrates the move away from the aesthetic of simplicity among composers of the latter part of the 19th century. His *Mignon,* composed in 1888, reflects none of the strophic elements of the original poetry but is instead wholly through composed, with multiple changes of tempo and key.

Clara Wieck Schumann's *Liebst du um Schönheit* ("If You Love for Beauty") is more typical of the song at mid-century, however. It remains well within the technical grasp of amateur musicians and places its focus squarely on the voice. The text, by Friedrich Rückert, speaks of the kind of idealized love that appealed to middle-class households.

This kind of sentimentality was also popular in the United States, where songs for voice and piano were cultivated with special intensity. Particularly in the first half of the 19th century, Americans had relatively little opportunity to hear large professional musical ensembles, increasing the appeal of music that could be performed in a domestic setting. By far the most important 19th-century American songwriter was Stephen Foster (1826–1864). Born in Pennsylvania, he initially worked as a bookkeeper, but eventually supported himself entirely from the sale of his music, the first American composer to do so. Although he spent most of his adult life in Cincinnati, Pittsburgh, and New York City, he is indelibly associated with the pre–Civil War South because of his contribution to the subgenre of the **minstrel song.** Typically performed by white performers in blackface, minstrel songs purported to represent African American slave life. There were black troupes, but most of these formed after the Civil War. A minstrel ensemble generally included a tambourine, castanets ("bones"), banjo, and fiddle. The shows often portrayed African Americans with demeaning caricatures and exaggerated dialect, helping reinforce and perpetuate racial stereotypes. Foster's songs, although sentimental, usually portrayed his subjects with compassion and dignity. At least some of these songs have been performed by such 20th-century African-American singers as Paul Robeson and Marilyn Horne. The minstrel tradition, moreover, to the extent that it indeed featured and popularized music with characteristically African-American syncopations, was one

Schubert, Robert Schumann, and Wolf
Settings of Goethe's *Kennst du das Land?*

Clara Wieck Schumann
Liebst du um Schönheit

Composer Profile

Franz Schubert
(1797–1828)

Schubert was born into a musical family and received his early training from his father (a schoolmaster), his brother, and the organist of his parish church. In 1808, he gained a place in the Imperial court choir, and with it, admission to the prestigious Imperial and Royal City College. While there, he studied composition with Antonio Salieri, the court Kapellmeister.

As a composer, Schubert followed very much in the footsteps of Mozart in Vienna: he never managed to secure a position as a composer at the court in spite of his talent; he was forced to give music lessons to make ends meet; and he died young, at the age of 31. Unlike Mozart, however, Schubert never achieved operatic success, in spite of repeated efforts to write a theater hit. His greatest talents lay in the realm of song, where he had an extraordinary ability to match texts with melodies ranging from the lyrical to the dramatic, the simple to the intricate. He found ample opportunity to perform his songs within his circle of friends, which included many poets and singers. His reputation as a songwriter attracted the attention of Beethoven and helped secure him a more or less open arrangement with the Viennese publisher Cappi and Diabelli to publish any new songs he might compose. Unfortunately, this fame and the potential for financial security it promised came only a few years before the composer's untimely death.

Schubert was incredibly prolific. In the year 1815 alone, he composed no fewer than 144 songs. In the 1820s, he turned more and more toward instrumental music, particularly piano sonatas, quartets, piano trios, and symphonies. He composed more songs toward the end of his life, however, and the publisher Haslinger issued a posthumous set under the title of *Schwanengesang* ("Swansong").

For almost a century and a half, the predominant image of Schubert was that of a dreamy, introverted Romantic who was more or less indifferent to events and persons around him and who lived only for his music. The recent work of several musicologists, however, has given us a far more complex image of the composer. Schubert was apparently an intensely sensual man of uncertain sexual orientation. He belonged to a group of artists who called themselves "The Nonsense Society" and who enjoyed playing practical jokes and creating enigmatic images of one another. One of these, a watercolor titled *Der Sündenfall* ("The Original Sin"), is reproduced in color insert III, Plate 15.

Principal Works

SYMPHONIES Schubert took Haydn, Mozart, and, later, Beethoven, as models for his instrumental music, confessing to a friend in 1824 that he was working his way toward a large-scale symphony by composing string quartets. At the time, in fact, he had already completed the two remarkable movements of his so-called *Unfinished* Symphony in B Minor (D. 759) and sketched portions of a third. In the last year of his life, he completed his Symphony in C Major, (D. 944, "the *Great*"), a masterpiece that points toward a remarkably distinctive approach based less on principles of thematic manipulation and counterpoint than on melody, color, and large-scale harmonic design. Both the *Great* and the *Unfinished* remained essentially unknown, however, until their rediscovery and first public performances in 1839 and 1865, respectively. As with Mozart, we can only speculate about the kinds of works Schubert might have written had he lived longer.

STRING QUARTETS AND OTHER CHAMBER WORKS Two of Schubert's best known chamber works incorporate slow movements related to his songs. The 12th

KEY DATES IN THE LIFE OF FRANZ SCHUBERT

1797 Born January 31 in Lichtenthal (now a part of Vienna).

1808 Becomes a singer in the Imperial court choir at Vienna; later receives composition lessons from Antonio Salieri, the court Kapellmeister.

1813 Becomes an elementary school teacher in the school his father directs.

1815 Composes the song *Erlkönig,* later published in 1821 as his op. 1. Prepublication performances establish a reputation that leads to the sale of a remarkable 300 copies within the first 18 months.

1820s Tries repeatedly, without success, to secure a position at the court in Vienna. Meager income from private lessons and sales of his songs leaves him always on the edge of poverty.

1828 Dies in Vienna of typhoid on November 19 and is buried near Beethoven, testifying to the belated recognition of his enormous talent.

PIANO SONATAS AND MISCELLANEOUS WORKS FOR PIANO As a composer of instrumental music, Schubert is inevitably compared to Beethoven, but Schubert's distinctive voice is abundantly evident in his works. By his late 20s—which is to say, toward the end of his life—he had even managed to achieve a distinctive approach toward sonata form, based on the large-scale juxtaposition of broad harmonic areas, as opposed to Beethoven's characteristic intensive manipulation and fragmentation of thematic ideas. The *Wanderer* Fantasy, D. 760, consists of four movements played without interruption, all of them based on a theme derived from Schubert's song of the same name. Miscellaneous works for solo piano include marches and dances, as well as the *Impromptus* and *Moments musicaux,* both of which bear a certain resemblance to song in both tone and form. Performers of four-hand piano music particularly prize Schubert's contributions to that repertory.

SONGS Had Schubert written only a handful of the hundreds of songs he did, he would still be honored as the greatest composer of all time in this genre. His choice of poetry varies widely from some of the best ever written in the German language (by Goethe and Schiller) to some that is mediocre at best. Whatever their quality, however, Schubert always managed to elevate the texts he set. A few dozen songs have emerged as perennial favorites, such as *Gretchen am Spinnrade* (set to a text from Goethe's *Faust*), *Der Lindenbaum, An Schwager Kronos,* and *Die Forelle*. The two song cycles, *Die schöne Müllerin* ("The Beautiful Daughter of the Miller") and *Die Winterreise* ("The Winter Journey"), have also achieved enduring popularity, in part because they combine the miniature essence of the genre with a larger scale plot. His less well-known songs and many part-songs deserve greater exposure than they have had. Recordings today group many songs together, encouraging listeners to play through many at a time. Schubert, however, intended them, like all miniatures, to be savored individually.

of the 15 string quartets, D. 810, is known as *Death and the Maiden* because its slow movement is a set of variations on Schubert's own song of the same name. The *Trout* Quintet, D. 667, for violin, viola, cello, double bass, and piano, features a set of variations on his song *Die Forelle* ("The Trout"). The two late piano trios are remarkably expansive works that point toward the scope of his Symphony in C Major, "the Great."

African-American minstrels, ca. 1860s. *A rare photograph of four African-American musicians from some time around the 1860s, playing the tambourine, violin, banjo, and castanets ("bones").*

Source: James Bollman

of the roots of ragtime, a genre that became immensely popular in the early 20th century (see Chapter 20). Among Foster's most famous minstrel songs are *Oh! Susanna, My Old Kentucky Home, Camptown Races, Old Folks at Home,* and *Massa's in the Cold, Cold Ground.*

Foster also wrote many **parlor songs** (so called because of their place of performance, the 19th-century equivalent of today's living room). The texts are invariably strophic and sentimental, as in Foster's *Beautiful Dreamer.* The simplicity and melodic straightforwardness of these songs is very much in keeping with the aesthetic of the German Lied in the first half of the century, with its emphasis on naturalness and directness. Although billed as his last song on early editions—the work was first published after the composer's death—*Beautiful Dreamer* was in fact written in 1862, when Foster was still turning out songs at the rate of about two a month.

The **mélodie,** as the song was known in France, was cultivated by such composers as Berlioz, Charles Gounod (1818–1893), Jules Massenet (1842–1912), Ernest Chausson (1855–1899), and above all Gabriel Fauré (1845–1924). Berlioz's *Nuits d'été* ("Summer Nights") of 1840–1841 is the earliest French song cycle, and when the composer

Foster
Beautiful Dreamer

A raucous crowd at a Jenny Lind song recital, 1845. *Jenny Lind (1820–1887) was widely regarded as the greatest singer of her generation. She toured the United States from 1850 to 1852, under the sponsorship of P. T. Barnum, who is better remembered today for his circuses than his concerts. Barnum billed Lind as "The Swedish Nightingale" and was undoubtedly inspired by the circuslike atmosphere of scenes like the one caricatured here, which depicts Lind in Hamburg five years before her first American tour. The few women in the audience are pointedly not applauding, whereas the men, in a frenzy not unlike that seen at rock concerts today, clamber over the seats to get closer to the stage. The caption reads: "We are blessed! We are transported! Madame Lind has made our heads spin!" According to his contract with Lind for her American tour, Barnum was to pay her $1,000 for every performance, plus expenses. But when Lind discovered the first concert grossed $28,000, she demanded $1,000 per concert, plus half the receipts over $3,000, plus expenses, and Barnum capitulated. The tour ultimately grossed more than $712,000, earning Lind $175,000. At the time, the president of the United States earned $25,000 a year.*

Source: Museum of Hamburg History

orchestrated the set in 1856, it marked the beginning of a new genre, the orchestral song. This type of composition would later be cultivated by the Germans Hugo Wolf and Gustav Mahler.

In Russia, the most important composers of song included Mikhail Glinka (1804–1857), Alexander Dargomyzhsky (1813–1869), and Modeste Mussorgsky (1839–1881). Russian composers often incorporated folklike elements into their songs, repeating or varying slightly a folklike melody, for example, or using characteristically Russian chromatic and modal inflections. Mussorgsky's *V chetyrjokh stenakh* ("In Four Walls"), from the song cycle *Bez solnca* (1874, "Sunless"), illustrates the ever-expanding

Mussorgsky
V chetyrjokh stenakh

The Salon

The salon was a vital forum for music making in the 19th century, particularly chamber music, piano music, and song. The setting—the residence of a wealthy host or hostess—was small enough to be intimate yet large enough to exercise influence on a city's broader musical life. On occasion, a host or hostess might engage a single artist to perform for the assembled guests: many contemporary accounts of Chopin's playing derive from performances he gave in salons. Countess Marie d'Agoult, Liszt's longtime companion, recalls the more common system for arranging the musical entertainment in a Parisian salon in the mid-1820s. Anyone throwing a party catered the artists, in effect, along with the food. In this case, the musical caterer was Rossini.

•••••

Composers and singers still had their place apart; in spite of the eagerness to have them, they appeared in the salons only on the footing of inferiors. If someone wanted to give a fine concert, he sent to Rossini, who, for a recognized fee—it was small enough, only 1500 francs if I recollect rightly—undertook to arrange the program and to see to its carrying out, thus relieving the master of the house of all embarrassments in the way of choice of artists, of rehearsals, and so on. The great maestro himself sat at the piano all evening accompanying the singers. Generally he added an instrumental virtuoso—Herz or Moscheles, Lafont or Bériot, Nadermann (the leading Paris harpist), Tulou (the king's first flute), or the wonder of the musical world, the little Liszt. At the appointed hour they arrived in a body, entering by a side door; in a body they sat near the piano; and in a body they departed, after having received the compliments of the master of the house and of a few professed dilettantes. The next day the master sent Rossini his fee and believed he had discharged his obligations toward them and him.

Source: Marie d'Agoult, *Mes Souvenirs*, quoted in Arthur Loesser, *Men, Women, and Pianos: A Social History* (New York: Simon & Schuster, 1954), p. 344.

presence of chromaticism in music from the later decades of the 19th century, as well as Mussorgsky's penchant for a naturalistic kind of declamation that fits well with his often dark and brooding texts.

THE CHARACTER PIECE

The **character piece,** a new genre associated almost exclusively with the piano, is the instrumental counterpart to the song. A work of relatively small dimension, it seeks to portray and explore the mood or "character" of a particular person, idea, situation, or emotion. Sometimes these are specified, sometimes not. The character piece tends to be brief, sectional, and fairly simple in construction. Many follow an ABA, AAB, or ABB pattern.

Mendelssohn
Lieder ohne Worte

By its very nature, the character piece operates on the border between programmatic and absolute music. Mendelssohn's provocatively titled *Lieder ohne Worte* ("Songs without Words,") invites—indeed challenges—performers and listeners to imagine the nature of the words that the composer leaves so pointedly absent. Mendelssohn himself was reluctant to elaborate on these works, letting them suggest the possibility of concrete interpretation while remaining abstract. In an eloquent answer to a friend who had asked for descriptive titles for several of these pieces, Mendelssohn emphasized the inadequacy of words to capture the spirit of music:

There is so much talk about music, and so little is said. I believe that words are not at all up to it, and if I should find that they were adequate I would stop making music altogether. People usually complain that music is so ambiguous, and what they are supposed to think when they hear it is so unclear, while words are understood by everyone. But for me it is exactly the opposite—and not just with entire discourses, but also with individual words; these, too, seem to be so ambiguous, so indefinite, in comparison with good music, which fills one's soul with a thousand better things than words. What the music I love expresses to me are thoughts not too *indefinite* for words, but rather too *definite*.[1]

Chopin's Mazurka op. 17, no. 4 (1833), is one of many 19th-century character pieces modeled on a particular dance—in this case, the mazurka, a Polish peasant dance in triple meter, often with an accent on the second or third beat. The work is harmonically ambiguous in several ways. It opens with three three-note chords that do not follow a harmonic progression in any conventional sense. The focus, instead, appears to be the motion of the middle note in each chord, the only one of the three to change. The progression B-C-D within the framework of the F and A in the outer voices prefigures a harmony that will prove repeatedly elusive. The cadence at the end of measure 4 can be read as an F-major chord in first inversion (A-C-F), but the absence of B♭ gives the work more a modal sound, either Lydian (a scale on F without the B♭) or Aeolian (a scale on A with no accidentals). The chromatic descent of linked thirds beginning in measure 9 (F♯–D♯ followed by F♮–D♮) further undermines the sense of a strong tonal center. Chopin creates the expectation of a strong cadence on A minor at the downbeat to measure 13, but delays it until measure 20. And even then, he gives us just enough stability in A minor to make us think we know where we are going and the piece has a tonal center. The middle section of this work, by contrast (measures 61–92), hammers away at A-major triads so relentlessly that it seems to take all the energy it can muster to move to a dominant harmony even briefly. But with the return of the opening section at measure 93, we are thrust back into the realm of harmonic ambiguity. At the end of the piece, Chopin repeats the opening sequence of harmonically ambiguous chords followed by an A-C-F triad, giving us a conclusion but no harmonic closure. A harmonically ambiguous opening had many distinguished precedents. One need think only of such works as Mozart's 'Dissonant' Quartet, K. 465, or Haydn's Symphony no. 103 ('Drumroll'; Anthology). But a harmonically ambiguous close like this one was a phenomenon essentially new to the 19th century.

As a work for solo instrument, this mazurka and other character pieces like it allowed for considerable rhythmic freedom in performance. By all accounts, Chopin himself took many rhythmic liberties when playing his own music, so many that Berlioz accused him of not being able to play in time.

Chopin and other pianists of the day also made considerable use of **tempo rubato** (literally, "robbed time"), a performance tradition that involved subtle accelerations and decelerations in tempo and at times complete independence of the hands, with the "singing" hand moving in a freer rhythm against the steady beat of the accompaniment. Carl Mikuli, one of Chopin's students, described his teacher's playing in this way:

> In keeping time Chopin was inexorable, and some readers will be surprised to learn that the metronome never left his piano. Even in his much maligned *tempo rubato*, the hand responsible for the accompaniment would keep strict time while the other hand, singing the melody, would free the essence of the musical thought from all rhythmic fetters, either by lingering hesitantly or by eagerly anticipating the movement with a certain impatient vehemence akin to passionate speech.[2]

Character pieces were usually too brief to be published separately, and so works like Chopin's nocturnes, polonaises, and waltzes, or Mendelssohn's *Songs without Words* were issued typically in collections of three, four, or more individual pieces. Occasionally, however, composers organized a set of character pieces as a coherent cycle. Chopin's 24

Chopin
Mazurka in A minor, op. 17, no. 4

Chopin
Preludes, op. 28

Composer Profile

Frédéric Chopin
(1810–1849)

The son of a French father and a Polish mother, Chopin never felt quite at home anywhere. Poland had lost its always precarious independence in the late 18th century and during Chopin's youth was mostly under Russian domination. After early training in his homeland, Chopin set out on a European tour in 1830. Kept abroad by an ultimately abortive nationalist uprising in Poland, Chopin settled in France, never to return to his homeland. Polish nationalism continued to smolder after the uprising, particularly among the nation's exile community. Chopin's own deep affection for his native land is reflected in his cultivation of such national dances as the polonaise and mazurka.

Thanks in part to the large number of Polish expatriates in Paris, Chopin was able to circulate in the highest levels of Parisian society. He made a good living from teaching and the sale of his music, as well as from the occasional public concert, although he avoided these as much as he could, especially in his later years. His fame allowed him to charge far more than the going rate for piano lessons. In 1837, he began a decade-long liaison with the novelist Amandine-Aurore Lucile Dudevant (1801–1876), better known by her pen name, George Sand. The relationship eventually went sour, but for a time at least, Sand helped provide Chopin more freedom and time to compose than he would have had otherwise. In 1838–1839, the two wintered on the island of Majorca, off the Spanish coast in the Mediterranean. During their stay, Chopin took ill and was diagnosed with tuberculosis by local doctors. Chopin refused to believe them. In a letter to a friend, he wrote,

I have been sick as a dog these last two weeks; I caught cold in spite of 18 degrees of heat [65 degrees Fahrenheit], roses, oranges, palms, figs, and three most famous doctors of the island. One sniffed at what I spat up, the second tapped where I spat it from, the third poked around and listened how I spat. One said I had died, the second that I am dying, the third that I shall die. . . . I could scarcely keep them from bleeding me. . . . All this has affected the Preludes [op. 24], and

KEY DATES IN THE LIFE OF FRÉDÉRIC CHOPIN

1810 Born near Warsaw on February 22.

1825 Publishes first piano works.

1831 After touring central Europe, gives first concert in Paris and soon afterward settles there, living off lessons, performances, and the publication of his works.

1837 Meets the novelist George Sand and begins a decade-long relationship with her.

1838 Suffering from tuberculosis, spends the winter with Sand on the island of Majorca in the Mediterranean.

1849 Dies in Paris on October 17 and is buried between Cherubini and Bellini.

God knows when you will get them. . . . Don't tell people that I've been ill; or they'll make up a tale.[3]

Despite his poor health, Chopin continued to compose steadily until the last months of his life.

Principal Works

SOLO PIANO The bulk of Chopin's output consists of works for solo piano. In addition to the mazurkas and preludes already discussed, these include the following:

◆ Nocturnes. These "night pieces," characterized by lyrical melody and a relatively clear homophonic texture, follow no particular fixed form. The genre itself was relatively new, related to the tradition of the serenade, an "evening song" performed outside a loved one's window. The nocturne as a character piece was first introduced into the piano repertory by the Irish composer John Field (1782–1837).

◆ Etudes. Chopin's two books of "Studies," op. 10 and op. 25, each consisting of 12 numbers, reflect the composer's devotion to strict technique and his abhorrence of the standard finger exercises that were so common in his time. Each of the etudes addresses a particular technical challenge—such as scalar runs, three-against-two rhythms, or rapid broken arpeggiations—but presents that challenge in a form that sounds like anything but a mechanical exercise.

◆ Polonaises. Chopin created many highly stylized versions of this Polish dance. The polonaises have generally heavier textures than those of Chopin's other music.

◆ Waltzes. These, too, are stylized pieces, not meant for dancing. They vary widely in character, tempo, and dimension.

◆ Sonatas. The earliest, op. 4, is a youthful work, but the two later ones are substantial four-movement works. Robert Schumann, in an otherwise favorable review of these later works shortly after their publication, questioned their cyclical coherence and accused Chopin of having smuggled "four of his dearest children" into a single work under the guise of composing a "sonata." With their uncharacteristically dense textures, these show Beethoven's influence more than any of Chopin's other works.

◆ Ballades. The four ballades are among the most celebrated works of the 19th-century piano repertory. Technically demanding and inherently dramatic, each gives the impression of telling a different kind of story. Long thought to be associated with the ballads of the Polish poet Adam Mickiewicz (1798–1855), these works adopt a distinctly narrative approach with clearly delineated episodes of contrasting character.

◆ Scherzos. The four scherzos are large-scale works, like the ballades, but without their narrative qualities. The scherzos also feature more repetition of extended sections. As is characteristic of the scherzo form, they are in triple meter and approximately ABA form. But although *scherzo* many mean "joke" in Italian, these works are not particularly joking.

◆ Impromptus. These few works (there are only three) are lighter in tone, as their name suggests,

than those in the other genres Chopin cultivated. The *Fantasie-Impromptu* of 1835 remained unpublished during the composer's lifetime but has become a perennial favorite since then.

◆ Individual piano pieces. In addition to pieces in the genres just listed, Chopin also wrote several independent works of substantial proportion. These include the *Barcarolle*, the *Berceuse* ("Cradle Song," a fascinating compositional study on a gently rocking ostinato bass figure, in keeping with the title), the *Bolero* (inspired by Spanish music), and the *Fantasie*.

OTHER WORKS All Chopin's other works involve the piano with other forces. These include two piano concertos, the Sonata for Cello (op. 65), The Piano Trio (op. 8), and some posthumously published songs on Polish texts.

Chopin. *One of the earliest known photographic images of any composer, this daguerreotype, made in 1849, reveals both energy and weariness. Chopin died later the same year from the tuberculosis that had sickened him for so long.*

Source: CORBIS BETTMANN

Composer Profile

Robert Schumann
(1810–1856)

Clara Wieck Schumann
(1819–1896)

The partnership of Robert Schumann and Clara Wieck reflects the evolving pattern of relationships between men and women in 19th-century society. The two married out of love, against her father's wishes, and they forged a musical partnership throughout their 16 years of marriage, which ended only with Robert's death in 1856. They concertized widely—Robert conducting, Clara performing on the piano—throughout Europe. Indeed in many respects Clara was more famous as a virtuoso than Robert was as a composer.

Robert Schumann

A pianist by training, Schumann quite naturally began his compositional career with a series of piano works. But in 1840, he shifted almost exclusively to song and in 1841, to orchestral music; chamber music followed in 1842, oratorio in 1843. These successive pursuits of a single genre have sometimes been interpreted as evidence of a manic-depressive personality and a foreshadowing of the debilitating mental illness of his last years. It seems equally plausible that these periods of intense engagement with a particular genre were the result of Schumann's systematic effort to broaden his scope as a composer.

Schumann was also one of the most influential critics in the history of music. His collected journalistic writings fill two thick volumes and have shaped the way we think and write about music today. He founded and edited for a decade the *Neue Zeitschrift für Musik* ("New Journal of Music"), which quickly established itself as the most important journal of its kind and is still published today. Schumann and his colleagues took on the more conservative elements of the musical establishment with an "us versus them" attitude, dubbing themselves the *Davidsbund*, the "Band of David," because they saw themselves fighting the numerically superior but aesthetically deficient "Philistines." Schumann was one of the first to extol Berlioz's *Symphonie fantastique,* and he was the first major critic to recognize publicly the compositional genius of both Chopin and Brahms.

To give voice to different points of view in his reviews, and in general to represent different aspects of his own persona, Schumann invented several fictional characters: the exuberant, extroverted Florestan; the more circumspect and introverted Eusebius; and the sagacious Magister Raro, who sometimes mediates between the other two. Schumann attributes the opening of his review of *the Symphonie fantastique,* for example, to Florestan, and its detailed account of the work's technical structure to Eusebius. All three characters are drawn from the fiction of Schumann's favorite novelist, Jean Paul (Johann Paul Friedrich Richter, 1763–1825).

Schumann's last years were turbulent. He accepted the directorship of the municipal orchestra at Düsseldorf in 1850, but the arrangement was mutually unsatisfactory. Advancing signs of mental instability forced him to resign in 1853, and thereafter his condition deteriorated rapidly. In 1854, he attempted suicide by throwing himself into the Rhine and was confined to an institution. In his last months he rarely recognized visitors.

Clara Wieck Schumann

Clara was the daughter of Robert's own piano instructor, Friedrich Wieck, but the courtship was not an easy one. Wieck did not want his daughter to marry a composer and journalist, particularly one of such limited financial means as Schumann. In the middle of an extended series of legal battles with her father, the couple eloped. Until her father eventually reconciled himself to the marriage, Clara found herself in often heartbreaking conflict with him. At one point she had to go to court to get back from him a piano she herself had paid for. Finding herself a widow when only in her mid-30s, she went on to establish a highly successful career as a soloist and teacher. Her performances of Beethoven's sonatas and concertos, Chopin's piano pieces, and her husband's compositions were legendary in their time. She developed a close relationship with Johannes Brahms, 14 years

KEY DATES IN THE LIFE OF ROBERT SCHUMANN

1810 Born in Zwickau (Saxony, in central Germany) on June 8.

1828 Studies law at Leipzig, later at Heidelberg, but eventually abandons law for music.

1830 Moves to Leipzig and lives with his piano teacher, Friedrich Wieck.

1832 Injures his hands through a device intended to promote independence of the fingers; forced to abandon a performance career, he turns increasingly to journalism and composition.

1834 Co-founds the *Neue Zeitschrift für Musik.*

1840 Marries Clara Wieck.

1841 Produces or begins five major works for orchestra.

1842 Writes three string quartets, a piano quartet, and a piano quintet.

1850 Moves to Düsseldorf to become the city's musical director.

1853 Meets the 20-year-old Johannes Brahms and proclaims the young composer's talent to the world in the celebrated essay "New Paths." First signs of growing mental instability.

1854 Attempts suicide and is confined to an asylum at Endenich, near Bonn.

1856 Dies at Endenich on July 2.

KEY DATES IN THE LIFE OF CLARA WIECK SCHUMANN

1819 Born in Leipzig on September 13.

1828 After studying piano with her father, gives her first public recital.

1832–1839 Gives concert tours throughout Germany, Austria, and France; studies with Robert Schumann.

1840 Marries Schumann against her father's wishes; concertizing over the next 16 years includes an extended tour of Russia.

1856 Moves to Berlin with her children after her husband's death; continues concertizing.

1878–1882 Directs the piano division of the Hoch Conservatory of Music in Frankfurt.

1896 Dies in Frankfurt on May 20.

Principal Works of Robert Schumann

SYMPHONIES AND OTHER ORCHESTRAL WORKS Like almost every other composer of his generation, Robert Schumann struggled against Beethoven's legacy in the symphony, eventually opting for a smaller scale, less monumental approach to the genre. His four numbered symphonies have gained in prestige over the years. The myth that Schumann was an incompetent orchestrator is also beginning to disappear, thanks to recent performances on period instruments, which reveal a clarity of texture and counterpoint that had been obscured by later transformations of the orchestra, not to mention numerous retouchings at the hands of conductors like Felix Weingartner and Gustav Mahler. Schumann's other works for orchestra include the *Overture, Scherzo, and Finale,* op. 52, several concert overtures, and the ever-popular Piano Concerto in A minor, op. 54, written for and widely performed by his wife, Clara Wieck Schumann. The Cello Concerto in A minor, op. 129, is one of the few late works to have gained general acclaim.

younger, who helped her manage her affairs during the difficult last years of her husband's life.

Clara's compositional output is relatively modest in quantity, consisting primarily of short piano pieces and songs, but it is of a consistently high quality. Her one large-scale work is a piano concerto. Later in life, she edited the first complete edition of her husband's works.

CHAMBER MUSIC In 1842, his "year of chamber music," Schumann wrote three string quartets, op. 41, the Piano Quartet, op. 47, and the Piano Quintet, op. 44. To this remarkably intensive output, he later added three piano trios and various other works for combinations of piano and strings or winds.

PIANO MUSIC Schumann's piano music, particularly the early works from the 1830s, established his reputation as a composer, and these works remain central to the piano repertory. Outstanding among them are *Papillons* ("Butterflies"), op. 2; the *Davidsbündlertänze* ("Dances for the Brotherhood of David"), op. 7; *Carnaval*, op. 9 (discussed in this chapter); the *Symphonic Etudes*, op. 13, a set of etude-variations on an original theme; and *Kreisleriana*, op. 16, evoking the mystical world of E. T. A. Hoffmann's fictional Kapellmeister, Johannes Kreisler. Perhaps surpassing even these in greatness, however, is the monumental *Fantasie*, op. 17, the proceeds from which Schumann donated to the erection of a statue of Beethoven in Bonn.

SONGS Marriage to Clara in 1840 coincided with a remarkable outpouring of song, including the cycles *Liederkreis*, op. 24, and *Dichterliebe* ("Poet's Love"), op. 48, both to texts by Heinrich Heine; another *Liederkreis*, op. 39 (to texts by Joseph von Eichendorff); and *Frauenliebe und leben* ("Woman's Love and Life"), op. 42, to texts by Adelbert von Chamisso. *Dichterliebe*, in particular, explores the many subtle techniques by which a series of miniatures can be linked in a larger cycle. Stylistically, Schumann's songs continue the tradition cultivated by Schubert, albeit with the more pronounced chromaticism we would expect from a later composer. Schumann also gave the piano a more prominent role. Although instrumental preludes had long been a common feature in songs, Schumann cultivated the idea of allowing the piano to continue after the voice has stopped, providing a kind of wordless commentary on the text that has gone before.

VOCAL MUSIC Most of Schumann's choral music is forgotten today, but in its time, the oratorio *Das Paradies und die Peri* was hugely popular, as were a number of compositions for men's, women's, and mixed choruses, both with and without orchestra. The decline in the reputation of these works is in part social, for Schumann's music provided important repertory for the widespread choral societies of his time. He himself founded and conducted one such group in Dresden in the late 1840s. With the decline of such choral societies in the 20th century, this and similar music by Schubert, Mendelssohn, and even Brahms has unfortunately fallen into obscurity.

Principal Works of Clara Wieck Schumann

Clara Schumann worked in many of the same genres as Robert Schumann, even before their marriage. She composed songs, part-songs, and several works of chamber music, the most notable of which is the Piano Trio in G minor, op. 17 (1846). She also wrote a Piano Concerto in A minor in 1836, ten years before her future husband's piano concerto in the same key.

preludes, for example, follow the circle of fifths to move systematically through the 24 major and minor keys of the twelve-note scale (from C major and A minor to G major and E minor, and so forth). The homage to J. S. Bach's *Well-Tempered Clavier* is unmistakable (Anthology; see Chapter 10). The first prelude, in C major, imitates the broken chordal writing in the corresponding prelude of the first book of Bach's collection and uses harmonic progressions to create a sense of overall shape. And even though Chopin's preludes lack fugues, many of them explore unusual possibilities of voice leading. In the A-minor Prelude, for example, a back-and-forth half-step motion in one voice is framed by another voice making leaps of a tenth.

Robert and Clara Schumann (1850). *He gazes with admiration at his wife, who by now is recognized as one of the great virtuosos of her time. She sacrificed much of her early career to help raise their children but was able to concertize fairly extensively from about 1845 onward. Clara's innate grace and Robert's innate awkwardness are amply evident in this revealing dual portrait. Even before his final illness, Robert was a notoriously uncomfortable conversationalist, whereas Clara, by all accounts, could captivate any gathering. Upright pianos like the one in this picture were a 19th-century innovation that lowered costs and made it possible to fit pianos into small spaces.*

Source: Art Resource/Reunion des Musées Nationaux

Although composers in the generations after Beethoven never abandoned the multi-movement sonata entirely, it gradually gave way to larger scale forms in a single movement such as the ballade, cultivated by Chopin, Liszt, Brahms, and Fauré, and the scherzo, cultivated by Chopin and Brahms. At least some of these longer character pieces were substantial enough to be published separately. Chopin's Ballade in G minor, op. 23, written between 1831 and 1835, is an extended work with many elements of sonata form.

It was long believed that Chopin based each of his four ballades on one of the poetic ballads of the 19th-century Polish poet Adam Mickiewicz, but no evidence supports this belief. Indeed, like Mendelssohn with his *Songs without Words*, Chopin gives no indication that the ballades had any textual inspiration at all. Yet each section of his Ballade in

Chopin
Ballade in G minor, op. 23

Composer Profile

Franz Liszt
(1811–1886)

Liszt is a figure who seems to pop up everywhere. He crossed paths with virtually every major musician in the generations from Beethoven through Brahms and played an important role in the careers of such diverse personalities as Berlioz, Paganini, Chopin, and Wagner. He was extraordinarily generous with his time and energy toward younger composers and performers. He was also a man of enormous contradictions. Liszt cultivated his image as a Hungarian composer (his *Hungarian Rhapsodies* for piano are perennial favorites), but his native language was German, and he learned Hungarian only toward the end of his life. After living a life full of earthly pleasures, he took holy orders in his mid-50s and assumed a new identity as Abbé Liszt.

Physical appearance was part of his mystique: the imposing height, aquiline nose, swept back hair, and graceful hands all contributed to an air of suavity and mystery that captivated audiences. The Countess Marie d'Agoult (1805–1876, better known by her pen name, Daniel Stern) was Liszt's mistress in the late 1830s and the mother of his three children. She recalled her first impressions of the young artist in this way:

> A tall figure, excessively thin, a pale face with large sea-green eyes in which glistened swift flashes of light like waves catching the sunlight, features at once suffering and powerful, a hesitant step which seemed less to tread the floor than glide over it, an absent-minded and uneasy look, like that of a ghostly visitant for whom the hour of returning to the shades is about to sound—that was how I saw before me this young genius. . . .
>
> In politics as in religion Franz detested moderation and boldly embraced extreme opinions. He despised bourgeois royalty and middle-of-the-road government, and prayed for the reign of justice; which, he explained to me, meant the Republic. With the same restiveness he turned to innovations in the arts and letters which threatened the old disciplines. . . . All the proud or desperate revolutionaries of romantic poetry were the companions of his sleepless nights. With them he enthused in proud disdain of the conventions; like them he shuddered under the hated yoke of those aristocracies which had no foundation in genius or virtue.[4]

Liszt revolutionized the art of the recital and indeed gave the phenomenon its very name. *Recitals* had previously been confined to the sphere of oratory (as in a "recital of facts"). Playing on the image of music as a language in its own right, Liszt transferred the term to musical performance. He also turned the piano sideways on the stage so the audience could see his dramatic profile. When possible, he even placed two pianos on stage facing one another and alternated between them so all of the audience could see his hands (and profile) at some point. Liszt also developed the idea of putting selected members of the audience, usually aristocratic women, in a semicircle around him at the back of the stage, occasionally chatting with them between numbers. His audiences, men and women alike, consistently spoke of being "transported" by his playing. So great were the passions generated by Liszt's playing that the poet Heinrich Heine coined the term "Lisztomania" to describe a condition having "every resemblance to an infectious disease."[5] (For a portrayal of a Liszt recital, see "Liszt at the piano," in color insert III, Plate 17.)

For all this solitary splendor on the stage, Liszt was actively involved in the broader musical world of his day. Through his composing, conducting, and writing, he became one of the two central figures (along with his eventual son-in-law, Richard Wagner) on what many saw as the "progressive" side of the struggle against musical "conservatives."

Principal Works

SYMPHONIES AND SYMPHONIC POEMS Liszt's two symphonies represent a synthesis of symphony and symphonic poem. The *Faust-Symphonie* of 1854

KEY DATES IN THE LIFE OF FRANZ LISZT

1811 Born near Ödenburg (Hungary), in what was then part of the Austrian Empire.

1821 Moves with family to Vienna and begins study of the piano with Carl Czerny, one of the leading virtuosos of his day and a friend of Beethoven.

1827 Moves to Paris and continues to amaze audiences with his dazzling performances on the piano.

1830s Concertizes extensively and publishes many works for piano.

1848 Becomes music director at the court of Weimar and turns more and more to writing for the orchestra.

1861 Moves to Rome but continues extensive travels.

1865 Receives minor holy orders by decree of Pope Pius IX and becomes an abbot.

1870 Daughter Cosima marries Richard Wagner, further intensifying his already well-established support of that composer.

1886 Dies in Bayreuth on July 31.

own emotional transformation through love; Mephistopheles, in turn, has no significant theme of his own but instead consistently distorts and disfigures themes heard in earlier movements. The symphony concludes with a brief section for tenor and chorus based on the closing scene from Part II of Goethe's *Faust*. The *Symphonie zu Dantes Divina commedia* of 1856, also in three movements, similarly concludes with a brief vocal section that culminates a trajectory leading from struggle (*Inferno, Purgatorio*) to paradise. The text is taken from the Magnificat.

Liszt called his early one-movement works for orchestra *overtures* because at the time of their composition there was no better designation by which to describe them. In the mid-1850s, however, he coined the terms *symphonic poem* and *tone poem* to convey their alliance with some kind of literary program or idea.

PIANO WORKS Liszt's piano music covers an enormous range, from large-scale works like the Sonata in B Minor to miniatures, most of it beyond the technical reach of amateurs. Many of the character pieces relate to texts, like the *Sonnets after Petrarch,* or to places, like the *Années des pèlerinages* ("Years of Pilgrimage"), which take the listener on a series of wide-ranging journeys. Programmatic ideas behind Liszt's piano music are as likely to be sacred ("Saint Francis of Assisi Preaches to the Birds") as demonic (the various "Mephisto" Waltzes). The *Transcendental etudes* are even more technically difficult than Chopin's *Etudes*. Liszt also transcribed for solo piano all of Beethoven's symphonies and numerous songs by Schubert. His paraphrases on contemporary operas were in great demand during his lifetime.

VOCAL MUSIC The four Masses, Requiem, three oratorios, and numerous works for chorus and orchestra, although they constitute an important portion of the composer's output, are for the most part forgotten today. Liszt's more than sixty songs for voice and piano occasionally find their way into performances but largely await rediscovery.

(revised 1857) consists of what he called three "character pieces" reflecting the three central figures in Goethe's *Faust*: Faust, Gretchen, and Mephistopheles. In this work, Liszt used what would later come to be known through Wagner's music dramas as *Leitmotivs,* a network of interrelated musical ideas that convey some sort of extramusical idea. The motives associated with Faust in the first movement, for example, become palpably softer and gentler in Gretchen's movement, mirroring Faust's

G minor has a particular affect, varying from resigned to catastrophic, and the piece projects an overall sense of narrative direction. The work also conveys a sense of creative improvisation. Like the singer of ballads as described by Goethe, Chopin "has so thoroughly internalized his pregnant subject—his characters, their actions, their emotions—that he does not know how he will bring it to light. . . . He can begin lyrically, epically, dramatically and proceed, changing the forms of presentation at will, either hastening to the end or delaying it at length."[6]

Ambiguity and complexity were not the only interests of 19th-century composers. Many also wrote music in a disarmingly simple style. Robert Schumann's cycle of character pieces entitled *Kinderszenen* ("Scenes from Childhood"), op. 15 (1838), evoke the ancient idea that truth is to be found in the unspoiled innocence of childhood. *Träumerei* ("Reveries") and *Der Dichter spricht* ("The Poet Speaks") are two well-known works from this set: they are technically quite straightforward yet every bit as profound as the more openly virtuosic and sophisticated character pieces of their time.

Robert Schumann
Carnaval, op. 9

Schumann's *Carnaval*, op. 9 (1835), is a cycle of character pieces ranging from the simple to the complex, linked by the common theme of Carnival, the brief season of revelry immediately preceding the penitential season Lent.

Like the season for which it is named, many of the movements of Schumann's *Carnaval* contain elements of intrigue, impersonation, excess, and downright nonsense. Schumann embeds musical riddles and autobiographical references within individual movements. The key to the riddle is to be found in the German names for the notes of each motivic idea. Adding "s" to any note name in German designates it as flat. Thus E♭ is "Es" and A♭ is "As." In addition, Germans designate B♭ with the letter "H." With this in mind, we can see that one of the sequences (E♭-C-B-A) spells "Schumann" in an abbreviated form, and the other two (A♭-C-B and A-E♭-C-B) spell "Asch":

E♭	C	B	A		A♭	C	B		A	E♭	C	B
Es	C	H	A		As	C	H		A	Es	C	H
S	c	h(um)	a(nn)		As	c	h		A	s	c	h

"Schumann," obviously, is Schumann's own name; Asch is the hometown of Ernestine von Fricken, who was Schumann's fiancée when he wrote *Carnaval*. But Schumann uses the mask of music to say things he would not otherwise have ventured to acknowledge openly. Consider, for example, the trio of movements labeled "Chiarina," "Chopin," and "Estrella." Chiarina was the nickname of the 15-year-old Clara Wieck, the daughter of his own piano teacher. Schumann would later marry Clara, but when he wrote *Carnaval* he was engaged to Ernestine, whose nickname was Estrella. In a gesture clearly anticipating the inevitable end of his engagement to Ernestine, Schumann marks "Estrella" to be played *con affetto* ("with affection") and, in pointed contrast, marks "Chiarina" to be played *passionate* ("passionately"). The two women in question surely grasped the significance of these indications. The two movements are mediated by one named after Chopin, a composer Schumann greatly admired, who had paid personal visits to both Clara and Robert in September 1835.

Liszt
Galop de bal

Gottschalk
The Banjo

Most mid-19th-century piano works were not quite so elaborate or laden with meaning as *Carnaval*. More typical is Franz Liszt's *Galop de bal* (ca. 1840), which places relatively limited demands on the performer, and with its relentless accents, evokes the frenzy of the ballroom. The galop was a fashionable group dance of this period that often provided the climax to an evening's entertainment. Louis Moreau Gottschalk's *The Banjo* captures the spirit of the quintessentially American instrument. Gottschalk (1829–1869) was born in New Orleans. With the rhythmic vitality of *The Banjo* he anticipates the

The title page to Louis Moreau Gottschalk's *The Banjo* (1855). *The fanciful artwork, with its rustic lettering, conjures up images of the American backwoods, in keeping with the work's subtitle, "An American Sketch." Note the international distribution of this seemingly provincial work: France, Spain, England, Germany, Italy, and Portugal. Gottschalk (1829–1869), a native of New Orleans, studied in Paris, where his pianism was praised by both Chopin and Berlioz. After his return to the United States in 1853, he became one of the nation's most popular soloists.*

Source: Dover Publications, Inc.

ragtime style that would become popular in the early years of the 20th century (see Chapter 20).

Like the song, the character piece became increasingly chromatic in the latter part of the 19th century. Liszt's *Nuages gris* ("Gray Clouds"), written in 1881 but unpublished at the composer's death five years later, opens with a rising fourth, followed by a rising augmented fourth and a descending G-minor triad in measure 2. In its context, this triad sounds neither particularly triadic nor like a triad in the tonic (which it is). Throughout this brief piece, Liszt alludes to the tonic through the leading tone of F♯ without actually presenting any strong statement of G minor. Even the final chord juxtaposes a G–B♮ dyad with an open A–E fifth in the lower voices. The music seems to float like the clouds evoked in its title, with little sense of any forward motion. In this respect, it anticipates the Impressionist style of the late 19th and early 20th centuries (see Chapter 20).

Liszt
Nuages gris

CONCLUSION

Chamber music, song, and music for solo piano found a ready market in 19th-century households. The growing affordability of the piano made this instrument the new focus of music making in the home. Sonatas and other works for solo piano, as well as songs for voice and piano, became a staple of the domestic repertory. The emergence of German as a literary language gave composers new texts to set by such prestigious poets as Goethe and Schiller. The character piece for piano, in turn, provided an instrumental counterpart to song, a miniature genre with strong suggestions of programmatic content but without an explicit text.

Dramatic and Sacred Music

In spite of the growing significance of instrumental music in the 19th century, the large-scale genres of vocal music—opera, operetta, and sacred music—maintained their long-standing aesthetic prestige. Opera, in particular, was still considered by many critics and listeners to be the pinnacle of the musical art, for it combined drama (the libretto), music (the score), and the visual arts (scenery, costume) in a single genre. It continued to attract the finest singers and many of the most talented composers of the day, and it was by far the most financially lucrative of all genres. Through ticket sales, printed scores, and the prospect of future commissions, a hit opera was a composer's surest path to fame and success. Operetta, a lighter form of musical drama, usually featuring spoken dialogue as well as singing, commanded an even wider following among the public. Sacred music, in turn, became increasingly varied in scope, ranging from monumental settings of the Mass and Requiem in the most modern style to smaller scale motets strongly influenced by the idiom of the late Renaissance.

OPERA

Since its emergence in the early 17th century, opera had been periodically rocked by controversies that pitted the demands of music against the demands of drama. Melodic structure and vocal virtuosity had rarely meshed with dramatic realism or the clear declamation of texts, and over the course of the 19th century, particularly from the 1840s onward, composers of all nationalities pursued new approaches to reconciling these conflicting agendas. By the end of the century, their efforts had fundamentally changed the genre of opera, but in ways that were different in Italy, France, and Germany.

Italy in the Early 19th Century: Rossini

The first three decades of the 19th century are often referred to as the "Age of Beethoven," but it would be more accurate to call this period the "Age of Rossini and Beethoven." Like Beethoven in the realm of instrumental music, Gioacchino Rossini (1792–1868) enjoyed unquestioned preeminence in the world of opera in the first half of the 19th century. Rossini was internationally famous as an opera composer by the age of 21. Between 1815 and 1823, he composed 20 new operas, including a critically acclaimed setting of Shakespeare's *Othello* in 1816. He toured the Continent extensively, scoring successes in Vienna, Paris, and London. In 1829, he won renewed acclaim with his opera *Guillaume Tell* ("William Tell"), which fuses Italian lyricism into the tradition of French grand opera. He wrote opera serie (*Tancredi, Otello, Semiramide*) as well as opere buffe (*Il Barbiere di Siviglia, La Cenerentola,* the latter based on the story of Cinderella). For reasons that remain unclear, he then abruptly retired from the world of opera at the age of 37, composing only a few nonoperatic pieces thereafter. He spent the remainder of his life in Florence, Bologna, and Paris, where he became a fixture in the salons. Rossini helped establish a style of Italian opera known as **bel canto**—literally, "beautiful singing." The term refers to a vocal technique that emphasizes lyrical melodic lines, legato phrasing, and a seemingly effortless vocal technique, even in passages of great technical difficulty. Orchestral accompaniment in 19th-century bel canto opera is typically discreet, limited to harmonic underpinning with little or no counterpoint. The emphasis throughout is on the voice. Although not every aria or every role in a bel canto opera conforms to this style, the ideal of beautiful production lies at the aesthetic core of all these works.

Rossini's *Il Barbiere di Siviglia* ("The Barber of Seville," 1816), the most popular of his many operas, integrates the traditions of opera buffa into the style of bel canto. The barber of the title is Figaro, a buffa-like character whose profession brings him into contact with people at the highest levels of Seville's society, making him an ideal go-between—a "factotum," as he calls himself. Over the course of the opera, Count Almaviva (disguised as a student) uses Figaro to help him win the hand of Rosina, who is also being pursued by a certain Doctor Bartolo. The drama unfolds in a series of madcap antics full of mistaken identities, disguises, and secret notes.

Rossini
Il Barbiere di Siviglia

In this opera it is the music more than the words that informs us of the essential nature of the characters. Figaro's opening number, for example, *Largo al factotum* ("Make way for the factotum"), does a marvelous job introducing the title character. He half complains, half boasts that his services are in such demand among people of quality that he is always busy. Constantly repeating the same lines of text, Figaro works himself into a frenzy, imitating people calling him—"Figaro! Figaro!"—in that famous three-note melody (just before rehearsal no. 35) that has come to be indelibly associated with his character. "One at a time!" he half shouts to himself in response.

Rosina's *Una voce poco fa* ("A voice a short while ago") is very much in the bel canto tradition and draws an equally sharp characterization. Like many arias of this period, it consists of two sections, a slow opening and a lively conclusion, known as the **cabaletta.** Rosina sings while writing a letter to Lindoro, who is in fact Count Almaviva in disguise. After declaring Lindoro her chosen suitor, she professes to be "docile, respectful, and obedient." The music, however, gives the lie to this claim, changing from reserved to lively and spontaneous in the cabaletta as she goes on to sing, "But if you push me the wrong way, I'll be a viper, and the last laugh will be on you." By the time she returns to her profession of docility, the feistiness of the music has infected the orchestra, leaving no doubt that the music, not the words, represents Rosina's true character.

Italy at Mid-century: Verdi

Verdi
Rigoletto

In the generations after Rossini, composers devoted increasing attention to issues of dramatic integrity. Giuseppe Verdi (1813–1901) was the leading composer of Italian opera in the generation in the middle of the 19th century, and his *Rigoletto* exemplifies several key characteristics of the new approach to the genre: dramatic realism, the use of the *scena* (scene) as the unit of dramatic organization, and dramatically justified virtuosity.

Dramatic Realism.   Verdi was fiercely committed to the idea of realism on the stage and struggled throughout his life to find librettos of high literary quality. For *Rigoletto*, he used an adaptation of the play *Le roi s'amuse* ("The King Amuses Himself") by the French writer Victor Hugo (1802–1885), one of the greatest playwrights of his age. Verdi worked closely with the Italian dramatist Francesco Piave (1810–1876) to adapt Hugo's stage play into a suitable libretto. The opera's plot revolves around the Duke of Mantua, a notorious womanizer; his humpbacked court jester, Rigoletto; Rigoletto's daughter and only child, Gilda; and a wronged father's curse. The Duke's courtiers resent Rigoletto's malicious wit and plot to humiliate him. Rigoletto has been keeping Gilda in seclusion, allowing her out only on Sunday to attend church. The courtiers discover her, but mistake her for Rigoletto's mistress, and plot to abduct her for the Duke's pleasure. But the Duke, disguised as a young student, has already approached her on her Sunday outings and has determined on her as his next conquest. In the opening sequence, Rigoletto belittles Count Monterone, who has come to denounce the Duke for seducing his daughter. As he is led off to prison, Monterone turns on Rigoletto and the courtiers and hurls a curse at them all, but singling out Rigoletto in particular. When the courtiers abduct Gilda and bring her to the Duke, Rigoletto attributes his misfortune to Monterone's curse. Discovering the Duke has had his way with Gilda, Rigoletto hires an assassin to kill his master. But Gilda, in love with the Duke despite his faithlessness, saves his life by sacrificing herself at the last moment to the assassin's knife. When Rigoletto realizes what has happened, he cries out in despair, "Ah, the curse!"

Verdi and Piave encountered serious obstacles from government censors in their effort to bring *Rigoletto* to the stage in Venice. Both Hugo's play and Piave's adaptation present royalty in an unflattering light, featuring, as they do, a philandering ruler who hides behind the protection of his lofty position in society. Almost as problematic was the character of Rigoletto himself. In an age when the physically disabled were thought unsuitable subjects for a drama, it was daring indeed to feature a hunchback in an opera's title role.

Larger Units of Dramatic Organization.   Although Verdi uses many of the traditional elements of Italian opera (such as arias, duets, choruses, and accompanied recitative), he consistently incorporates these into a larger dramatic unit of multiple elements. Verdi was not the first to take this approach to dramatic organization. It was already being used by Gluck and Mozart in the 18th century and was particularly prominent, as we saw in Chapter 13, in the opening sequence of Mozart's *Don Giovanni* (Anthology). It is also found in works by Rossini and his contemporaries, such as Gaetano Donizetti (1797–1848) and Vincenzo Bellini (1801–1835). But Verdi and other mid-century composers expanded on this approach to create increasingly extended spans of music and drama uninterrupted by scenery changes or obvious opportunities for applause.

In *Rigoletto* this practice results in greater dramatic realism. Verdi's means of expression are remarkably economical. Avoiding an extended overture, he opens instead with a brief, somber instrumental Prelude that sets the tone of this deeply tragic opera. The opening bars introduce the motif associated with Monterone's curse. Although we do not yet know its meaning, we recognize at once the dark character of the music. The effect is similar to that of the theme that begins the overture to Mozart's *Don Giovanni*, a theme later associated with the Commendatore's death and subsequent vengeance. Indeed, *Rigoletto* is in many ways Verdi's homage to Mozart's opera. Both concern the fate of a libertine and his victims.

The extended opening unit of music—labeled simply "N[umber] 2. Introduction"— unfolds continuously yet consists of eight discrete yet interconnected subsections, in each of which the music underscores the dramatic action.

The next unit of action, (Act I, no. 6), a duet between Rigoletto and the assassin Sparafucile, is compact, but the subsequent "Scene and Duet" (Act I, no. 7) is more complicated. The "scene" is a monologue in which Rigoletto muses on his deformity,

	Measure	Tempo	Text	Dramatic action
STRUCTURE OF VERDI'S *RIGOLETTO*, ACT I, NO. 7				
Scene	1–11	Adagio	"Pari siamo . . ."	Rigoletto muses on the similarities between himself and Sparafucile, the assassin.
	12–14	Adagio	"Quel vecchio maladevimi!"	Rigoletto: "That old man has laid a curse on me!" Return of the "curse" motif.
	15–29	Allegro/Adagio	"O uomini! o natura!"	Curses his deformity and fate.
	30–40	Moderato	"Questo padrone mio . . ."	Rigoletto thinks of the Duke, who is "young, powerful, and handsome."
	41–51	Allegro	"Oh dannazione!"	Curses the Duke and all the members of his court. "If I am evil, it is only because of you!"
	52–57	Andante	"Ma in altr' uomo qui mi cangio . . ."	"But here I change into another man." Rigoletto arrives home.
	58–68	Andante/ Allegro	"Quel vecchio . . ."	Unwelcome memory of Monterone's curse.
Duet	69–116	Allegro	"Figlia!"	Gilda enters, and Rigoletto embraces her.
	117–124	Adagio	"Se mi volete . . ."	Rigoletto reminds Gilda never to leave the house; he has never revealed to her his true identity as jester; she knows him only as her father.
	125–202	Andante	"Deh non parlare"	Rigoletto tells Gilda that she is his sole consolation in life; Gilda is moved by his suffering.
	203–242	Andante	"Già da tre lune"	Gilda asks why she must always remain at home, allowed to leave only to attend church on Sunday. Rigoletto, constantly fearful that she will be abducted, thinks he hears a prowler; it is Giovanna, the family's servant.
	243–343	Allegro	"Ah! veglia, o donna . . ."	Rigoletto implores Giovanna to protect Gilda.

his malicious wit, and his contempt for the Duke and his courtiers. In his extended duet with Gilda, Rigoletto reveals another, more compassionate side to his character (see Table: "Structure of *Rigoletto*, Act I, No. 7").

The final duet within the duet has its own internal structure. It is, in effect, a series of variations on a single theme and follows the traditional pattern of love duets: he sings, she sings, and then finally they both sing, and in this respect, Verdi adheres to convention. But he also slips in important plot developments within the duet. At measure 279, Rigoletto hears a prowler—the Duke, it turns out—and interrupts himself to launch into an agitated inquisition of Gilda's nursemaid, Giovanna. Thus we have a dramatic dialogue in the middle of the duet (Rigoletto: "No one has followed her from church?" Giovanna (lying): "Never!" and so on). Meanwhile, the Duke himself has been listening in on all this and realizes the woman he has been pursuing (Gilda) is the daughter of his court jester (Rigoletto) and interjects a few asides to express his astonishment at this revelation. With his fears calmed, Rigoletto resumes his duet with Gilda, who sings a glorious descant to his original melody (measure 303). The protracted farewell provides the traditional cabaletta, an extended concluding section that accelerates as it nears the end of this very long unit of music.

Liszt
Rigoletto: Konzert-Paraphrase

Dramatically Justified Virtuosity. The music in *Rigoletto* requires virtuoso singing, but Verdi never introduces virtuosity for its own sake. Arias never interrupt the flow of the drama and always reflect the character of the singer. The Duke's brilliant vocal displays, for example, reflect his pompous strutting, just as Gilda's soaring yet delicate and airy lines reflect her fragile innocence and key moments of emotional ecstasy.

The celebrated Quartet from Act III, following the Duke's famous aria *La donn' è mobile* ("Women are always changing"), illustrates Verdi's remarkable ability to convey contrasting emotions simultaneously. Verdi is the only composer ever to have rivaled Mozart in this regard. The Quartet (no. 16) presents two scenes simultaneously. One is inside the inn where Sparafucile plans to murder the Duke; the other is outside. Inside,

Opera and Politics

F O C U S

As in previous eras, the influence of opera extended beyond the purely musical into the realm of social and political expression. The opera house was a meeting place for socialites and businesspeople and a forum for the often symbolic dramatization of political and moral ideas. State censors scrutinized *Rigoletto* for subversive ideas because they knew that composers, librettists, and audiences all were prone to interpret events on the stage as a kind of allegorical commentary on current events. Early in the century, Beethoven struggled with Viennese authorities over his politically charged *Fidelio*, which advocated freedom of political speech. Daniel-François-Esprit Auber's *La muette de Portici* ("The Deaf Girl of Portici") was the likely catalyst for a popular uprising that erupted in Brussels when it was performed there in 1830. The plot, about

a peasant revolt in Naples in 1647, was apparently enough to ignite the smoldering passions of the populace. Verdi's *Un ballo in maschera* ("A Masked Ball") in 1859 encountered more resistance from the censors in Naples than *Rigoletto* had from the censors in Venice. The Neapolitan censors prohibited the performance of the opera because it was based on the real-life assassination of King Gustavus III of Sweden. Only when Verdi and his librettist changed the time and place of the opera's setting to remote colonial Massachusetts and the victim to a fictitious Earl of Warwick did the censors relent. And when George Bernard Shaw interpreted Wagner's *Der Ring des Nibelungen* as an allegory for the struggles during the 19th century among the competing forces of capitalism, socialism, and anarchy, his views were taken very seriously indeed.

the Duke tries to seduce Maddalena, Sparafucile's sister. She resists but finds him charming nonetheless. Outside, Gilda and Rigoletto witness the goings on inside. Rigoletto asks his daughter if she does not finally realize what a scoundrel the Duke is; she watches in stunned disbelief and anguish. Verdi meshes the contrasting emotions of these four characters in a manner that is astonishingly intricate without sounding complex. The music seems to fall into place simply.

The power of this quartet, one of the most contrapuntally sophisticated passages in all opera, made it also one of its most popular. In 1860, Liszt published a concert paraphrase for piano that itself gained popular renown.

The quartet from Act III of Verdi's *Rigoletto*.   *This ensemble manifests one of the powers of opera to do what spoken drama cannot: convey contrasting emotions simultaneously. Inside the tavern, the Duke is seducing Maddalena; outside, Gilda watches and listens in horror while her father, Rigoletto, asks if she is not now convinced that the man she loves (the Duke) is in fact a libertine. The room above (only the bottom of the window is visible here) is where the Duke will retire for the night and sing the reprise of his famous aria* La donn' è mobile. *Near the end of the opera, when Rigoletto hears the Duke singing again, he thinks at first it is a dream; but he quickly discovers it is in fact his daughter who has been murdered and not the Duke.*

Source: CORBIS BETTMANN

Composer Profile

Giuseppe Verdi
(1813–1901)

Little in Verdi's early life suggests his later greatness. He showed musical talent as a child but failed the entrance examination for the Milan Conservatory. He turned instead to private teachers and immersed himself in the study of harmony and counterpoint. Verdi then secured a series of conducting posts in his native Busseto, a relatively small community. His first opera, *Oberto*, scored a success at one of Europe's leading opera houses, La Scala in Milan, in 1840, opening further opportunities in the theater. Two years later, Verdi enjoyed even greater success with *Nabucco* (1842). The opera's chorus of the captive Israelites in Babylon (*Va, pensiero*) became one of the unofficial anthems of the simmering Italian uprising against the occupying Austrian forces, helping secure Verdi's place, at age 30, within the great tradition of Italian opera. Verdi himself became swept up in the political struggles of the day when he was voted into the newly constituted Italian parliament in 1860.

The remainder of Verdi's long life revolved around a series of commissions. He was at home in both Italy and France but spent the majority of his time in Milan. Visitors who recorded their impressions of Verdi almost invariably spoke of the man's modesty and self-effacing nature. A few years before his death, he established a home for retired musicians unable to support themselves and consigned all his royalties for 30 years after his death to this institution.

Principal Works

OPERA The operas fall roughly into three periods. The works through the 1840s (including *Oberto*, *Nabucco*, *Ernani*, *Macbeth*, and *Luisa Miller*) build on traditions established by his predecessors. The middle-period works, beginning with

KEY DATES IN LIFE OF GIUSEPPE VERDI

1813 Born near Busseto (northern Italy) on October 10.

1832 Applies to the Milan Conservatory but is rejected for lack of technical knowledge; studies privately instead.

1839 His first opera, *Oberto,* is greeted warmly at La Scala in Milan, one of Italy's leading opera houses.

1840s Establishes his reputation in Italy with a series of operatic successes, most notably *Nabucco, Macbeth,* and *Luisa Miller.*

1850s and 1860s Achieves international fame with *Rigoletto* (1851), *Il Trovatore* (1853), *La Traviata* (1853), *Un ballo in maschera* (1859), and *Don Carlos* (1867, in French).

1871 Premiere of *Aïda,* commissioned for the opening of the Suez Canal and first performed in Cairo.

1887 Persuaded to come out of retirement to write two last operas on Shakespearean themes: *Otello* and *Falstaff* (1893).

1901 Dies in Milan on January 27.

France: Grand Opéra and Opéra Comique

French opera of the 19th century divides into two broad categories, each with its own tradition. Grand opéra emphasized story lines drawn from historical subjects and typically featured lavishly expensive stage designs, ballets, and large choral numbers. Works written in the tradition of grand opéra tend to be long and are almost invariably in five acts.

Rigoletto (1851), include some of the composer's most popular operas—*Il Trovatore*, *La Traviata*, *Un ballo in maschera*, *La forza del destino*, and *Aïda*—which all remain staples of the operatic repertory. But Verdi was never content to remain within established formulas, and he was consistently able to make the operatic conventions of his day sound fresh and original. His style ranged from the utterly straightforward (homophonic texture, strophic form) to the astonishingly complex (polyphonic textures, through-composed forms). In his late works—*Otello* (1887) and *Falstaff* (1893)—he integrated the orchestra into the vocal texture to an unprecedented degree and at the same time developed a formal approach that considerably reduced the number of such recognizable units as arias and duets. Many contemporaries saw this change as a concession to Wagner's principles of music drama (discussed later). But anyone familiar with Verdi's earlier works can recognize the continuing development of tendencies already present in his earlier works.

SACRED MUSIC When Rossini died in 1868, Verdi conceived of asking 13 different Italian composers to contribute one movement each to a setting of the Requiem Mass. Verdi wrote the last movement, "Libera me," but the plan did not otherwise bear fruit. When he learned of the death of Alessandro Manzoni (1785–1873), poet and novelist, Verdi resolved to complete the Requiem himself. The result, his *Messa da Requiem*, premiered one year to the day after Manzoni's death. Its theatricality—the furor of the "Dies irae" is particularly famous—has led more than one wit to term it "Verdi's best opera." The *Four Sacred Pieces* were published in 1898; the first of these, *Ave Maria*, is composed on what the composer called the "enigmatic scale"—of C-D♭-E-F♯-G♯-A♯-B-C—which is neither major nor minor nor even wholly diatonic, given the interval of three half steps between D♭ and E. Even the 85-year-old Verdi was open to chromatic experimentation.

Verdi. *When preparing a new opera for production, Verdi's attention to detail was legendary. He coached the singers, kept or had made copious notes on staging and scenery, and devoted great care to historical detail. Although he could not attend the premiere of Aïda in Cairo in 1871, he made sure the stage designs were supervised by August Mariette, a renowned Egyptologist of the day.*

Source: Library of Congress

Although always sung in French, they were written by composers from across the Continent: the Italians Rossini and Gaspare Spontini (1774–1851), the German Giacomo Meyerbeer (1791–1864, born Jakob Beer), and the French Daniel-François-Esprit Auber (1782–1871) and Jacques-François-Fromental-Elie Halévy (1799–1862). Meyerbeer was acknowledged as the unrivaled master of the genre. A protégé of Rossini, he wrote works that appealed to the public love of spectacle combined with frequent evocations of the supernatural, especially in his most popular work, *Robert le diable* ("Robert the Devil," 1831). Grand opéra was a true institution of the political establishment. Commissions were given as much on the basis of personal contacts as on talent; intrigue was rampant.

The city's other two leading opera houses, the Opéra Comique and the Théâtre Lyrique, offered alternatives to the grand style. In spite of its name, the genre known as opéra comique was not always comic. But it allowed for spoken dialogue and placed far less emphasis on ballet, stage design, and crowd scenes. Composers like Charles Gounod (1818–1893), Bizet, and Jules Massenet (1842–1912) all contributed to this genre. Among the works still performed today are Gounod's *Faust*, Bizet's *Carmen*, and Massenet's *Manon*. The fate of Bizet's *Carmen* illustrates the gulf between the two worlds of French opera. In its original form, the work could not be presented at the prestigious Opéra. But shortly after Bizet's death, his friend Ernest Guiraud set the spoken dialogues to music in the form of recitative and added a ballet scene to Act IV, drawing on music from other works by Bizet. In this guise—and still translated into Italian—*Carmen* became one of the most popular operas of all time.

Germany: Weber to Wagner

German opera had been slow to develop before the 19th century. Italians and French had dominated the German stage, both as composers and as performers. Most of the dramatic works even of the German-speaking composers Haydn and Mozart had Italian texts. The most important exceptions were Mozart's *Die Entführung aus dem Serail* ("The Abduction from the Seraglio") and *Die Zauberflöte* ("The Magic Flute"). Like Beethoven's later *Fidelio*, these works were *Singspiele*—that is, written in German, with spoken dialogue and only occasional accompanied recitatives.

Carl Maria von Weber (1786–1826) caused a sensation in 1821 with yet another work of this kind, *Der Freischütz*, the story of a hunter who strikes a bargain with the devil to win a shooting contest that in turn will allow him to marry the woman he loves. *Freischütz* is something of a Faust story with a happy ending, and Weber's setting captured the imagination of his contemporaries. The "Wolf's Glen Scene" at the end of Act II won special praise, with its electrifying combination of music and special effects, including diminished sevenths played on low tremolo strings, an offstage chorus, shadowy figures, and a burning wagon wheel careening across the stage. Audiences also responded to the folklike arias, choruses, and dance scenes elsewhere in *Freischütz*. Weber's sudden death at the age of 39 cut short what would have certainly been a brilliant career, but his works inspired the next generation of German composers to write stage works in their native tongue.

The most important of Weber's successors was Richard Wagner (1813–1883). Like so many composers of his generation, Wagner was committed to making opera more dramatically realistic, but the approach he eventually settled on differed radically from that of Weber, Verdi, or for that matter any other figure in the history of the genre.

Wagner rejected traditional opera on the grounds that in it the libretto, the drama, served as little more than a pretext for the music, and more specifically, for virtuosic singing. Traditional opera, according to Wagner, suffered from a fatal flaw: neither of its constituent elements—text and music—could stand on its own, without the other. In other words, a staged, spoken performance of a typical opera libretto would be dramatically unsatisfactory, whereas a performance of an opera's score, without its text, would be musically incoherent.

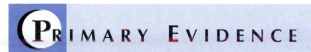

Source: Reproduced in *Shaw on Music*, ed. Eric Bentley, pp. 114–5, which in turn quotes *The World*, January 17, 1894.

George Bernard Shaw on the Advantages of Opera over Drama

The playwright George Bernard Shaw (1856–1950) worked for many years as a music critic. His writings are always witty and often insightful. This passage, from an essay written in 1894, goes to the heart of Wagner's ability to integrate music and words and the advantages of music drama over traditional spoken drama.

• • • • •

Wagner regarded all Beethoven's important instrumental works as tone poems; and he himself, though he wrote so much for the orchestra alone in the course of his music dramas, never wrote, or could write, a note of absolute music. The fact is, there is a great deal of feeling, highly poetic and highly dramatic, which cannot be expressed by mere words—because words are the counters of thinking, not of feeling—but which can be supremely expressed by music. The poet tries to make words serve his purpose by arranging them musically, but is hampered by the certainty of becoming absurd if he does not make his musically arranged words mean something to the intellect as well as to the feeling.

For example, the unfortunate Shakespeare could not make Juliet say:

O Romeo, Romeo, Romeo, Romeo, Romeo;

and so on for twenty lines. He had to make her, in an extremity of unnaturalness, begin to argue the case in a sort of amatory legal fashion, thus:

O Romeo, Romeo, wherefore art thou Romeo?
Deny thy father and refuse thy name,
Or, if thou wilt not, etc., etc., etc.

It is verbally decorative; but it is not love. And again:

Parting is such sweet sorrow
That I shall say goodnight till it be morrow;

which is a most ingenious conceit, but one which a woman would no more utter at such a moment than she would prove the rope ladder to be the shortest way out because any two sides of a triangle are together greater than the third.

Now these difficulties do not exist for the tone poet. He can make Isolde say nothing but "Tristan, Tristan, Tristan, Tristan, Tristan," and Tristan nothing but "Isolde, Isolde, Isolde, Isolde, Isolde," to their hearts' content without creating the smallest demand for more definite explanations; and as for the number of times a tenor and soprano can repeat "Addio, addio, addio," there is no limit to it.

The Elements of Wagnerian Music Drama

Wagner struggled with the "error of opera" for decades but eventually arrived at a solution he considered so revolutionary that it represented not merely a new kind of opera, but an entirely new genre altogether, the **music drama.** In spite of its outward similarity to opera, Wagnerian music drama rests on premises and elements not ordinarily found in earlier forms of opera.

The Ideal of the *Gesamtkunstwerk*.   Wagner summarized his approach to his art with an imposing term—*Gesamtkunstwerk*—that is actually a conjunction of three German words:

Gesamt, meaning "synthesized, unified, whole, complete, self-contained"

Kunst, meaning "art" (that is, the arts in general, including music, poetry, and gesture or movement)

Werk, meaning "work" (of art)

A *Gesamtkunstwerk* was one in which all the requisite elements were at once both self-sufficient yet inextricable from one another. Thus the music should cohere as in a symphony by Beethoven, the drama should be as compelling as a drama by Goethe, and these two elements, music and drama, should be mutually motivating.

Drama as "Deeds of Music Made Visible."   Inspired by such works as Beethoven's Third and Fifth Symphonies, and particularly the *Leonore* Overture no. 3 (see Chapter 15), Wagner sought to transfer the power of instrumental music into the theater by establishing "genuine drama on the basis of absolute music." In a particularly memorable turn of phrase, Wagner called the drama—the events transpiring on the stage—"deeds of music made visible." What happens on the stage, in other words, is a tangible reflection of what is going on in the orchestra pit. By the same token, what happens in the orchestra pit is the musical manifestation of the actions on stage. Ideally, then, we should be able to follow the course of a Wagnerian music drama through the music alone, by tracing the fate of its various musical ideas. These musical ideas would eventually come to be known as *Leitmotivs*.

The Leitmotiv.   Literally, a "leading motive," a **Leitmotiv** is a brief musical idea connected to some person, event, or idea in a music drama. Opera composers had long used specific musical motifs as tags for specific dramatic themes, bringing them in repeatedly at appropriate points in a plot. The curse motif in Verdi's *Rigoletto* is a perfect example of this well-established practice of musical reminiscence. What distinguishes Leitmotiv from reminiscence in Wagner's music dramas is (1) the musical metamorphosis of these ideas over time according to the dramatic situation, and (2) the musical and dramatic interrelationship of these motifs within a broad network of thematic ideas. A Leitmotiv, then, is a musical figure capable of growth, development, and transformation.

Wagner
Tristan und Isolde

The network of Leitmotivs in Wagner's *Tristan und Isolde* illustrates the way these thematic ideas work. Based on an ancient legend that had circulated in various forms throughout northern Europe, *Tristan und Isolde* tells a story of ill-fated love. Tristan, a knight in the service of King Mark, has been given the task of bringing the Irish princess Isolde back to Cornwall, on the western coast of England, where she is to marry Mark, against her will. But Tristan and Isolde have already met: she had nursed him back to health some years before, and Tristan now feels torn between his debt to her and his allegiance to King Mark. The two vow to drink poison and kill themselves before their ship lands in Cornwall, but Brangaene, Isolde's maidservant, substitutes a love potion for the poison. Tristan and Isolde fall madly in love, yet they must hide their passion from all others, especially King Mark. In Act II, the lovers contrive a pretext to meet alone: Tristan drops back from a hunting party and returns to the castle under cover of night. But their deception is revealed, a fight ensues, and in the closing Act III, Tristan dies of the new wounds he has suffered. Isolde, overcome with grief, sinks lifeless upon his corpse, uniting the two lovers in death.

In their simplest forms, the motifs in this opera have a one-to-one relationship with corresponding onstage actions. Wagner makes sure, for example, that we will associate the motif in Example 17-1 with the potion that causes Tristan and Isolde to fall in love. We hear it first at the beginning of the Prelude, but as with the curse motif that begins the Prelude to *Rigoletto*, we do not yet know its implications.

We do hear a sense of longing in its celebrated dissonance, beginning with what has come to be known as the "Tristan chord" (F-B-D♯-G♯ on the downbeat of measure 2 in Example 17-1). Commentators have often cited the progression from this chord to the end of the motif as signaling the beginning of the end of traditional harmony.

Example 17-1 The "love potion" motif, with the "Tristan chord" highlighted.

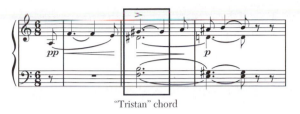

"Tristan" chord

Wagner assaults the modern ear.   *Much of the controversy surrounding Wagner's music in his own lifetime concerned his penchant for massive orchestration and highly chromatic harmonies. As one irate listener wrote to the editors of the English* journal Musical World *in 1876, "Enough already has been done in the present century to lead the public away from the laws of nature. It may be original to have interminable successions of discords which don't resolve, but it is a matter of taste whether such proceedings are an improvement on the pleasurable sensations of man. Vinegar, mustard, and cayenne-pepper are necessary condiments in the culinary art, but I question whether even the Wagnerites would care to make their dinner of these articles only. When sound taste begins to fail, eccentricity will take its place. Let the young student beware of its malignant influence."*

Source: Leonard de Selva/CORBIS BETTMANN

Within the course of the Prelude, Wagner fragments, extends, transposes, inverts, and otherwise manipulates this basic idea over and over again. The rising minor chromatic third first heard in measures 2–3 assumes special importance. Following the model of thematic elaboration provided by the instrumental music of Beethoven, Wagner manipulates a fragment of this theme (Example 17-2a, first measure; Example 17-2b) by using repetition, harmonic and melodic variation, and silence to enrich each successive statement. The Prelude as a whole follows no established convention of large-scale form.

Having developed at least some of the intrinsically musical potential of the Prelude's central thematic idea, Wagner establishes its dramatic significance by bringing it back toward the end of Act I, at the crucial moment when Tristan and Isolde drink what they believe is a death potion. But what makes the technique of Leitmotiv different from the convention of isolated reminiscences is the manner in which the thematic transformations of these motifs relate to the events of the drama. When we listen to Act II more

Example 17-2a and b Subsequent transformations of the "love potion" motif.

(a)

(b)

Example 17-3 "Love's longing."

Example 17-4 "Bliss."

closely, we realize the distinctive chromatic rise in the "love potion" motif has actually been present for quite some time in a variety of guises—sometimes rising, sometimes falling—going all the way back to the Prelude to Act I.

The motif known as "love's longing" (Example 17-3) represents yet another manipulation of the rising chromatic third. Here, the melodic trajectory is reversed: the chromatic line moves downward and is supported by a clearly outlined triadic base. The feeling here is more confident, more directional, as befits the dramatic situation. This motif dominates the tension that builds toward an event Isolde knows will happen: Tristan's return. Still another metamorphosis of this motif (Example 17-4) emerges when Tristan finally arrives: the theme becomes more joyous, rising in its opening to a high note before descending,

Example 17-5 "Death."

Death-destined head! Death-destined heart!

rather than descending from the very start. Such changes, subtle but effective, have led more than one commentator to accord this idea a separate identity, associating it with the idea of "bliss," which is of course the desired consequence of longing. The musical and dramatic parallels function in tandem.

Another prominent Leitmotiv in *Tristan und Isolde* (Example 17-5) is associated with death (*Tod* in the German text). Like the "love potion" motif, the "death" motif is chromatic and harmonically unusual. (Wagner often used chromatic themes or unusual harmonic progressions to evoke conditions of pain, such as love and death.) Although the "death" motif manifests itself in many different ways, its characteristic harmonic feature is the juxtaposition of two otherwise distant chords (such as A♭ major and A major, as in Example 17-5), combined with a distinctive rhythm of LONG-LONG-short-LONG.

The labels we have been using to identify these Leitmotivs, although useful for analyzing Wagner's music, can lead us to think of them (incorrectly) as fixed entities, both musically and in terms of their dramatic associations. Probably for this reason, Wagner himself almost never explicitly identified any of these themes. More important is to recognize how Wagner works his Leitmotivs into an ever-evolving web of complementary and contrasting musical and dramatic relationships that can sustain a work lasting many hours in performance.

The Relationship of Voice and Orchestra.   Wagner's Leitmotivs are sometimes sung, but more often they appear in the orchestra alone. In traditional opera, in contrast, the voice carries the melody while the orchestra provides the accompaniment. Constant repetition of text is likewise common in traditional opera. Indeed text set to ornate vocal lines often has to be repeated if it is to be understood. Wagner abhorred this practice, and it was his desire to make the text intelligible that prompted him to shift the melodic element from the voice to the orchestra. Doing so allowed him to have the characters on stage sing in a declamatory manner lying between aria and recitative. A typical Wagnerian vocal line, considered without any accompaniment at all, is not nearly as lyrical as a vocal line by Verdi, but the texture of Wagner's writing allows the words to come through with remarkable clarity. His design for the opera house in Bayreuth (illustrated here) also helps the vocal line to project through and above a large orchestra.

The Structure of the Dramatic Text.   Unlike most composers of opera, Wagner wrote his own librettos, developing in his mind (and occasionally committing to paper) the musical motifs to be associated with particular moments of the drama. Wagner was also careful to avoid distinctions between verse and prose in his librettos. Traditionally, arias had been written in metrical verse, recitative in prose. In his effort to eliminate what he considered the arbitrary and disturbing disjunction between recitative and aria, Wagner wrote his librettos in a consistently free poetic style that avoided any suggestion of metrical (and thus also melodic and musical) regularity. He did not, however, turn to entirely free verse, employing instead an alliterative poetic device called *Stabrheim* that had been cultivated in certain repertoires of German poetry of the Middle Ages. *Stabrheim* literally means "staff rhyme"—staff in the sense of a shepherd's crook, something that gathers together loose elements. What it gathers, though, is not rhyme (which typically occurs within an established metrical pattern) but rather the initial or internal sounds of two or more different words. For example, here are the words Isolde uses to command her servant to extinguish the light in Act II of *Tristan und Isolde* (beginning at measure 304):

Lösche des Lichtes letzten Schein!
Dass ganz sie sich neige, winke der Nacht!
Schon goss sie ihr Schweigen durch Hain und Haus,
schon füllt sie das Herz mit wonnigem Graus.
O lösche das Licht nun aus,
lösche den scheuchenden Schein!
Lass' meinen Liebsten ein!

(Extinguish the last glow of the light!
So that night might approach fully, give her [the night] a signal!
She has already poured her silence on field and house,
She already fills the heart with blissful horror.
Oh, extinguish the light,
Put out the frightening glow!
Let my lover in!)

Endless Melody.   Another concept central to Wagner's theory of music drama is what he called "endless melody." By "endless," Wagner meant fluidly continuous. His music dramas include units comparable to arias, but at least until the end of an act, these elide smoothly into subsequent material. Wagner thus keeps his music moving from the beginning to the end of an act, leaving the audience no opportunity to applaud in between. Indeed in two instances—the original version of *Der fliegende Holländer* (1841) and *Das Rheingold* (1854)—an entire work moves continuously from beginning to end without a break. "Endless" does not, as some of Wagner's critics suggested, mean interminable. His music dramas are no longer than the typical grand operas of his time.

By "melody," Wagner had in mind something different from what the term is commonly understood to mean. He differentiated "true melody" from what might be called filler. He abhorred the empty figuration that played such an important role in the Italian opera of his time and even in the instrumental music of Mozart. He sought to avoid virtuosity for virtuosity's sake, stressing the need for true melody at all times in both orchestral and vocal parts.

In practice, Wagner was not always entirely rigorous in applying his theories of music drama. There are recognizable numbers—arias, even strophic songs—woven into the fabric of his music from time to time. Once he had demonstrated the viability of his new approach, he seems to have felt free to use more traditional forms in his later music dramas. Wotan's farewell to Brünnhilde at the end of *Die Walküre*, the soaring love duet between Siegfried and Brünnhilde at the end of *Siegfried*, and the trio of revenge in Act II of *Götterdämmerung* are all in the tradition of 19th-century Italian and French opera. The playwright George Bernard Shaw (1856–1950), an ardent Wagnerite, placed the whole of

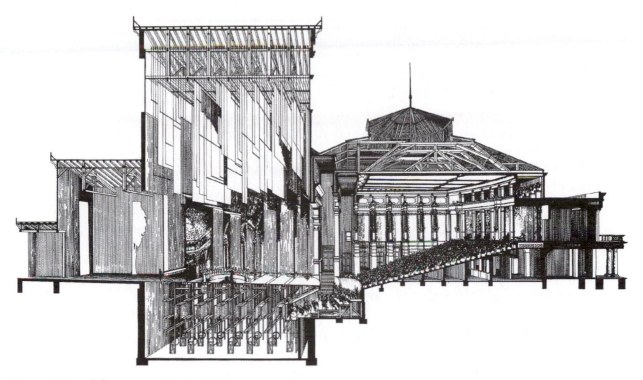

Cross section of the Bayreuth Festspielhaus.   *In addition to writing his own librettos and music, Wagner designed his own theater, the "Festival Drama House," in Bayreuth, a small municipality halfway between Munich and Berlin. The design puts most of the orchestra beneath the stage. This ingenious device brings the audience closer to the stage and also projects the sound of the orchestra more directly toward the audience, creating a better blend of voices and the orchestra within the hall. The acoustics in Bayreuth have long been considered ideal for the integration of orchestral and vocal lines so characteristic of Wagner's music dramas.*

Source: © 2003 Yale University Press/Spotts, *Bayreuth: A History of the Wagner Festival* (1994), image p. 9

Götterdämmerung with its vast sets, large choral numbers, and extended ensembles, squarely within the tradition of grand opera.

On the whole, however, Wagner's method of integrating music and text opened important new vistas for opera. His influence extended well beyond his lifetime, leaving a deep imprint on the operas of Richard Strauss, Arnold Schoenberg, Alban Berg, and even Giaccomo Puccini (see Chapter 21).

OPERETTA

Around the middle of the 19th century, the lighter genre of **operetta** began to establish itself. As the diminutive suffix suggests, this form of musical theater operated on a smaller scale than opera. It usually mixed spoken dialogue with sung numbers and dealt invariably with humorous and lighthearted subjects. Operetta was also more likely than opera to be composed or at least performed in the vernacular. Thus separate traditions of operetta developed in France, Germany, Italy, and even England, scarcely a bastion of operatic composition in the 19th century.

Composer Profile

Richard Wagner
(1813–1883)

"Wagner," one historian recently observed, "is the most controversial artistic figure of all time." Such a claim might well seem like an exaggeration at first, but it is difficult to think of any other artist who has aroused such powerful feelings of support and opposition over such a long period of time. Musically, politically, and personally, Wagner has been worshiped by some, reviled by others.

Born in Leipzig, Wagner aspired early to a career as a composer and conductor. He immersed himself in the music of Beethoven and put bread on his table by writing music criticism. A series of increasingly prestigious positions as a conductor of opera in Germany culminated in his appointment as Kapellmeister in Dresden in 1843. Wagner would have been assured success had he stayed in this prestigious position the rest of his life, for he had outstanding resources at his disposal there.

The Revolution of 1848 changed everything. Wagner fought on the barricades, in effect seeking to overthrow the very regime that employed him. A warrant was issued for his arrest and he fled to Switzerland, where he lived in exile for the next decade, composing, among other works, *Tristan und Isolde*. He eventually won the support of King Ludwig II of Bavaria, who spared no expense to support the composer and his art. It was around this time, in the mid-1860s, that Wagner became intimate with Cosima Liszt von Bülow, the daughter of Franz Liszt and the wife of the conductor Hans von Bülow. Wagner, Cosima, and von Bülow lived for a time in a bizarre ménage à trois, with all three devoted to Wagner's art. Eventually, Cosima divorced von Bülow and married Wagner, by whom she had already borne three children.

The final phase of Wagner's life centered around Bayreuth, a small city roughly halfway between Munich and Berlin, the respective capitals of Bavaria and Prussia. "Germany" had only recently become a political reality, and it was Wagner's aim to build in Bayreuth a *Festspielhaus*—a "festival drama house"—that would unify Germany culturally as well. Wagner oversaw every detail of the building and the performances to be held within it. Thus, when the *Ring* received its premiere there in 1876, Wagner could legitimately claim not only to have written the libretto and the music, but to have built the opera house as well. He died in Venice in 1883.

As a critic, Wagner was one of the most prolific and influential of all composers who have also written about music. In addition to his early reviews, he wrote program notes, pamphlets, numerous essays, an autobiography, and an especially important (if long-winded) three-volume treatise entitled *Opera and Drama* (1850).

A painting by W. Beckmann reproduced in Plate 16, color insert III shows Wagner at home in Beyreuth surrounded by family and other intimates.

Principal Works

In his early years, Wagner wrote in a variety of genres, including song, sonata, and quartet; he even tried his hand at the symphony on more than one occasion. But the young composer soon recognized that his talents and interests lay in the realm of theater music, and from the 1840s onward, almost all his most significant works are operas—or, as he called his later works, "music dramas." Dates in parentheses here represent the date of first performances.

EARLY OPERAS Wagner used a number of models for his early operas, drawing particularly on the works of Rossini, Donizetti, Weber, and Heinrich Marschner for *Die Feen*, a fairy-tale opera; *Das Liebesverbot*, a comic opera based on Shakespeare's *Measure for Measure*; and *Rienzi*, a grand opera based on a contemporary novel about a tribune of the Roman Empire.

THE ROMANTIC OPERAS *Der fliegende Holländer* ("The Flying Dutchman," 1843) is based on the Norse legend of the sea captain who is condemned to eternal wandering and who will find rest, and death, only through the love of a woman. Every seven years, the Dutchman lands ashore to seek his salvation, which he ultimately finds in a woman named Senta. The most famous number in the opera is Senta's ballad in Act II, in which she tells the story of the Dutchman and becomes transported by her own narrative.

Tannhäuser (1845) is an opera about the minnesingers, medieval Germany's equivalent of the French troubadours and trouvères (see Chapter 1). Once again, Wagner deals with the redemptive power of a woman's love and the title character's struggle between sensual pleasure and religious faith.

Lohengrin (1850) also draws on Germanic legend. Lohengrin, a knight of mysterious origins, makes a dramatic appearance just in time to defend the honor of Elizabeth, who has been falsely accused of murdering her brother. Lohengrin makes only one demand of Elizabeth: that she accept him for who he is and not demand to know his name or his lineage. Elizabeth accepts this condition, and Lohengrin defeats her accuser in a duel, thereby winning her hand in marriage. But plotting by the defeated accuser and his sister eventually drives Elizabeth mad with curiosity, and she puts the fateful question to Lohengrin just before they are to be married. (The famous wedding march known as *Here Comes the Bride* is from this opera.) In *Lohengrin*, we sense that Wagner is on the edge of making the breakthrough from traditional opera to the music drama.

THE MUSIC DRAMAS *Tristan und Isolde* (1865) draws on a medieval legend to tell the story of the tragic love triangle of Tristan, Isolde, and King Mark. As in so many of Wagner's works, redemption comes only through death.

Die Meistersinger von Nürnberg (1868), like *Tannhäuser*, deals with the minnesingers of medieval Germany, but in a much more lighthearted vein. In this thinly veiled account of Wagner's own battle with his critics, Beckmesser, a pedant, insists that songs must always be written according to the rules while other characters show him just how dry and stale such an approach is. Wagner weaves a love story around all of this, but for once no one dies in the end.

Wagner worked on the libretto for *Der Ring des Nibelungen* ("The Ring of the Nibelungs," 1876) from the late 1840s through the mid-1850s before

KEY DATES IN THE LIFE OF RICHARD WAGNER

1813 Born in Leipzig (Germany) on May 22.

1831 Studies composition with Theodor Weinlig, cantor of the *Thomasschule* and thus an indirect successor to J. S. Bach.

1832 Publishes first composition, a piano sonata, and writes a symphony, both strongly influenced by the music of Beethoven.

1833–1843 Takes on a series of increasingly responsible positions in German opera houses (Würzburg, Königsberg, Riga), with a three-week stint in debtors' prison (1840).

1843 Appointed music director at the Royal Opera House in Dresden, one of the most coveted positions of its kind in Germany.

1848–1849 Participates actively in the Revolution; a warrant is issued for his arrest, and he flees to Switzerland.

1850s While in exile, writes *Tristan und Isolde*, begins composing *Der Ring des Nibelungen*, and writes several important treatises on music.

1864 Receives support from the new king of Bavaria, Ludwig II ("Mad Ludwig"), who supports Wagner financially with public funds, much to the dismay of the Bavarians and the members of Ludwig,s court.

1868 First contact with the philosopher Friedrich Nietzsche, who at first supports Wagner and later turns against him.

1870 Marries Cosima Liszt von Bulow, who keeps a detailed diary that records the remainder of the composer's life in astonishing detail.

1872 Cornerstone laid for the Festspielhaus in Bayreuth. The central work on the dedicatory concert is Beethoven's Ninth Symphony, the work Wagner considered the cornerstone for the "Music of the Future."

1876 The Bayreuth Festspielhaus opens with the first complete performance of the *Ring* cycle.

1883 Dies in Venice on February 13.

setting the text to music. He interrupted his work for some seven years in the late 1850s and early 1860s to compose *Tristan* and *Meistersinger*. Although some of the works in the *Ring* cycle were premiered individually, the cycle as a whole received its debut at the newly opened Festspielhaus in Bayreuth in 1876. The plot, based on various legends from Norse mythology, is intricate and highly symbolic, revolving around a web of conflicts that pits love against both power and duty. The *Ring* consists of four separate works performed ideally on four successive days: *Das Rheingold*, *Die Walküre*, *Siegfried*, and *Götterdämmerung*.

In *Parsifal* (1882), Wagner turned again to medieval legend. The title character is the "perfect" fool, an innocent who discovers the truths of life, self-denial, and love (both sacred and profane) through the Fellowship of the Grail. It was Wagner's wish that *Parsifal* never be performed anywhere except at Bayreuth. Fortunately, this wish has been disregarded.

Operetta grew out of the long tradition of songs with plays. In 18th-century Germany, these were known as *singspiele* (literally, "song plays") and included such works as Mozart's *Die Entführung aus dem Seraglio* and *Die Zauberflöte*, both of which were written to German texts. This tradition continued with later works like Johann Strauss's *Die Fledermaus* ("The Bat," 1874) and Franz Léhar's *Die lustige Witwe* ("The Merry Widow," 1905). In France, the operettas of Jacques Offenbach (1819–1880) were enormously popular. A transplanted German, Offenbach wrote more than ninety works of this kind, the most famous of which is *Orphée aux enfers* ("Orpheus in the Underworld," 1858), a farce on the ancient Greek legend in which Eurydice is quite happy to be in Hades. The work includes the famous "can-can" music danced by spirits of the underworld.

Gilbert and Sullivan
Pirates of Penzance

No English composer for the stage has achieved the enduring renown of Sir Arthur Sullivan (1842–1900), who, in partnership with the librettist Sir William S. Gilbert (1836–1911), created a long string of box office successes that continue to fill theaters today. Gilbert and Sullivan's *Pirates of Penzance* (1879) illustrates both the similarities and differences between 19th-century opera and operetta. It draws heavily on the principal forms of opera, with numbers that are easily recognizable as arias, duets, ensembles, and even accompanied recitatives. At the same time, the work manages to poke fun at almost every one of these very same conventions. The General's famous patter song ("I am the Very Model of a Modern Major General") is entertaining enough in its own right and even more so when we realize it is a parody of a model established by Rossini. In addition to the humor inherent in the song's rapid declamation, it is also incongruous to see a supposedly noble figure of authority like a general performing in a manner usually reserved for servants like Leporello in Mozart's *Don Giovanni* or Rossini's Figaro.

SACRED MUSIC

The growing importance of instrumental music and the fierce debate about the nature of opera during the 19th century have tended to obscure the many important works of sacred music written during this time. As with other genres, settings of the Mass grew considerably in length: Beethoven's *Missa solemnis*, op. 123, and Bruckner's Mass in F minor both run well over an hour in performance. Schubert, Weber, Mendelssohn, Schumann, and Liszt also contributed to this repertory. Settings of the Requiem enjoyed special favor in the 19th century, most notably at the hands of Berlioz, Verdi, and Fauré. The first two are particularly theatrical, combining chorus and orchestra (and in Berlioz's work, multiple orchestras) to great effect.

The oratorio also flourished, allowing composers a chance to write sacred vocal music to librettos of their own choosing. The oratorios of Handel remained the model for virtually all 19th-century composers, including Beethoven (*Christ on the Mount of Olives*), Mendelssohn (*Elijah, Paulus*), Berlioz (*L'enfance du Christ*), and Brahms (*A German Requiem*, set to biblical texts). These works combine large choruses (almost always with at least one extended fugue), solo arias, and solo ensembles, mixed with recitative.

Over the course of the 19th century, the Catholic church became increasingly uncomfortable with what it perceived to be the overly virtuosic and operatic nature of music written for the liturgy. These misgivings are reminiscent of the objections raised at the Council of Trent in the mid-16th century about the "profane" nature of sacred music (see Chapter 6). A number of 19th-century composers allied themselves to what came to be known as the **Caecilian movement,** named after the patron saint of music, which sought to restore Gregorian chant and the style of 16th-century a cappella polyphony as the ideals of church music. During the 1830s, the Benedictine monks of Solesmes, France, began to prepare critical editions of Gregorian chant, and a number of composers cultivated a self-consciously archaic style modeled on the polyphonic sacred works of the late Renaissance. Bruckner's motet *Virga Jesse floruit*, for example, is indebted to what was broadly known as the "Palestrina style" in its rhythms and textures, even if its harmonies are highly chromatic from time to time. No one would mistake this for a work by Palestrina, yet Palestrina's influence is undeniably evident in this and many other sacred works of the period.

Bruckner
Virga Jesse floruit

CONCLUSION

In spite of the growing prestige of instrumental music, vocal music more than maintained its hold on the musical world of the 19th century. In Italy, Giuseppe Verdi developed an approach to opera that strove to create a greater sense of dramatic realism by integrating text and music to an unprecedented degree. In Germany, Richard Wagner sought to fuse operatic and symphonic idioms in a new genre he called the music drama, in which the dramatic coherence of the music coming from the orchestral pit was as important as the dramatic coherence of the words and gestures unfolding on the stage. Operetta, a lighter form of opera with spoken dialogue between the musical numbers, attracted even wider audiences. And although the importance of the church as a patron of new music declined somewhat in the 19th century, composers of this era produced a remarkable range and quantity of sacred music, from monumental works in the most advanced idiom to small-scale compositions reflecting the influence of Renaissance masters.

Chapter 18

Orchestral Music, 1850–1900

T he civic orchestra, a permanent ensemble located in a single city and giving a regular schedule of public concerts season after season, became the predominant musical institution for orchestral music in the second half of the 19th century. Few such ensembles had existed before this time. The orchestra Haydn conducted in England in the 1790s was assembled expressly for him and disbanded after he left; London had no organization providing regular concerts until the establishment of the Philharmonic Society in 1813. Vienna—home to Mozart, Beethoven, and other prominent composers— offered only occasional concerts performed by mostly ad hoc ensembles until the establishment of the Vienna Philharmonic in 1842. The New York Philharmonic was likewise established in 1842. The leading orchestra of Paris in the 1820s and 1830s was that of the Conservatory. By the end of the century, however, every city with any claim to cultural significance could boast its own opera company and civic orchestra. Smaller cities housed both in a single building, whereas larger, more affluent cities built separate structures for each.

MUSIC FOR DANCING AND MARCHING

The concert hall was not the only important venue for orchestral music in the 19th century. Others included the dance hall, music hall, and parade ground. Dance halls and music halls served up food, drink, and music in varying proportions to clients from all classes of society. Dance, which offered unmarried couples the opportunity for physical contact at a time when it was otherwise frowned on, was a vital element in the rituals of courtship, and music was indispensable for dance. The most popular dances in the 19th century were the quadrille (a type of square dance), the polka (a lively dance in duple meter), and, above all, the waltz, which originated in Vienna in the last decades of the 18th century and swept all Europe in the first decades of the 19th. Much of its popularity was due to the nature of the dance itself. It was one of the first socially acceptable dances that allowed partners to hold each other in a relatively close embrace, with the man's hand on his partner's back.

The popularity of the waltz was boosted by the memorable music written for it by such composers as Joseph Lanner (1801–1843) and the two Johann Strausses, father (1804–1849) and son (1825–1899). All three hailed from Vienna, a city that became

Dance fever, 1839. The Grand Galop of Johann Strauss, *engraving by A. Geiger after J. C. Schöller. The "Grand Galop" was a favorite finale of dance events, a group activity in which partners could hold one another tightly while moving at dizzying speeds. The pace was clearly too much for the couple in the left foreground of this illustration. A pileup looms behind them as they stumble to the ground. (Is she more upset to have fallen or to have discovered her partner was wearing a toupee?) The single young men clustered in the middle look on with envy. The orchestra, conducted by Johann Strauss the elder (1804–1849, father of the "Waltz King"), plays on the balcony, with the bass drum occupying a place of special prominence.*

Source: Engraving by A. Geiger, after J. C. Schöller: "Der Grosse Galopp von Johann Strauss"/LW 74.285 Res. C(R)/Inv. Nr. 57.835/Bildarchiv der Oesterreichischen Nationalbibliothek, Vienna

Der große Galop von Joh. Strauß.

Composer Profile

Peter Ilyich Tchaikovsky
(1840-1893)

Tchaikovsky was a late bloomer. The son of a mining inspector in the Ural Mountains, he entered the St. Petersburg Conservatory at the age of 21, having already secured a position as a government clerk. Within five years, however, he was teaching harmony at the Moscow Conservatory. A wealthy widow, Nadezhda von Meck, provided him with a long series of generous commissions that allowed him to resign his teaching position in 1878 and devote himself entirely to composition. Remarkably, Tchaikovsky never met his patroness, preferring instead to keep the relationship on an idealized plane through an extensive correspondence. By the time Madame von Meck withdrew her support in the late 1880s, Tchaikovsky had achieved wealth and fame on his own.

As a conductor, Tchaikovsky traveled widely across Europe. Tchaikovsky embraced his Russian heritage but did not make a display of it, unlike some of his contemporaries, who made a point of writing explicitly nationalistic music. Stylistically, Tchaikovsky was an internationalist, blending Russian, French, Italian, and German traditions with his remarkable gift for melody.

Tchaikovsky was an intensely private individual, subject to repeated bouts of depression. The circumstances surrounding his death have long been

KEY DATES IN THE LIFE OF PETER ILYICH TCHAIKOVSKY

1840 Born in Votinsk, Russia, the son of a mining inspector in the Ural Mountains.

1850 Moves with his family to St. Petersburg, capital of Russia.

1861 Enters the St. Petersburg Conservatory; studies composition with Anton Rubinstein.

1866 Appointed professor of harmony at Moscow Conservatory.

1875 Attends opening of Wagner's Festspielhaus at Bayreuth and writes musical criticism for a Moscow newspaper.

1878 Resigns from the Moscow Conservatory and devotes himself entirely to composition.

1891 Makes concert tour of the United States.

1893 Dies in St. Petersburg on November 6.

controversial. He died apparently of cholera during an epidemic of the disease in St. Petersburg. Some maintain that he knowingly drank contaminated water, effectively committing suicide, but nothing in

---

inextricably linked in the public mind with the waltz. The younger Strauss's *On the Beautiful Blue Danube* (1867) is representative of the genre. It consists of an extended introduction followed by a series of individual waltzes (numbered 1, 2, 3, etc.), each with its own thematic idea and some with their own introductions (marked *Eingang* ["entry"] in the score). This modular structure allowed ensembles to repeat any individual waltz as often as needed. At the same time, Strauss was careful to integrate the sequence of dances into a coherent whole. The introduction (written in A major but heard as the dominant of D) establishes the tonic key of D major for most of the waltzes. The fourth waltz modulates to F major for the sake of harmonic variety, and an extended coda brings the work to a close in the tonic and reprises the theme of the opening waltz.

Strauss
An der schönen blauen Donau

Typically for dance music, each of the individual waltzes within *An der schönen blauen Donau* is built on units of 4 or 8 measures, which join to create larger units of 16 or 32 measures, and most of the waltzes follow a simple ABA pattern. This kind of

his correspondence suggests he was unusually depressed at the time.

Principal Works

BALLETS AND OPERAS Even had he written nothing else, Tchaikovsky's ballets would be enough to justify his fame as a composer. *Swan Lake* (1876), *Sleeping Beauty* (1889), and *The Nutcracker* (1892)

all became immediate staples of the repertory. Nineteenth-century Russia looked westward to France as its principal cultural model, but Russian achievements in the realm of ballet eventually surpassed those of France. Tchaikovsky also wrote many operas, only a few of which are well known today, most notably *Eugene Onegin* (1879) and *Queen of Spades* (1890).

SYMPHONIES, OVERTURES, CONCERTOS Tchaikovsky's six completed symphonies are remarkable for their lyricism, orchestration, and dramatic tone. Formally, they broke no new ground, although the last, the *Pathétique,* ends with a long slow movement that is full of heroic resignation rather than triumph. Tchaikovsky also cultivated the symphonic poem, although he preferred the more traditional designation of "overture" for these works. The celebrated *1812 Overture,* written to commemorate the Russian victory over Napoleon's invading army, incorporates the French and Russian national anthems and concludes with a blast of cannons. The First Piano Concerto and the Violin Concerto are among the most enduringly popular works of their kind.

Tchaikovsky. *When Tchaikovsky toured the United States in 1891, he helped inaugurate the newly built Carnegie Hall in New York City. His second tour was sponsored, in part, by the Knabe & Co. Piano Manufactory of Baltimore, at the time the third largest piano manufacturer in the world.*

Source: Library of Congress

rhythmic and structural predictability was essential for the function of social dance and would become the basis for many forms of dance or dance-related genres in the 20th century, including ragtime, the blues, and even rock and roll.

Music halls offered a mixture of instrumental and vocal works together with comedy, vaudeville routines, and animal acts. *Ta-Ra-Ra-Boom-de-ay,* still used in circuses today, is a typical music hall song of the 1890s.

The march, like dance music, was written to coordinate physical movement—in this case, of soldiers. In the hands of such masters as the American composer John Philip Sousa (1854–1932), however, the march became a genre for the bandstand as well as the parade ground. Like Strauss's waltzes, Sousa's marches are invariably modular in structure and build on units of 4, 8, 16, and 32 measures. But Sousa's marches are less concerned with issues of tonal closure; in fact, he often ends his marches in the subdominant. *King Cotton,* for example, begins in E♭ major but closes in A♭ major.

Sousa
King Cotton March

THE BALLET

Accounts of theatrical dance go back as far as the Renaissance, and ballet had played an important role in opera since the very beginnings of that genre around 1600. Ballet nevertheless assumed unprecedented importance in the 19th century. It began to provide the main attraction for entire evenings of public entertainment in Paris in the 1870s.

France, which had always been preeminent in the field of dance, continued to lead the way in the 19th century, as ballet became an increasingly public genre, moving outside the patronage of the courts. The most prominent French ballet composers of the period were Adolphe Adam (1803–1856) and Léo Delibes (1836–1891). Adam's *Giselle* (1841) and Delibes's *Coppélia* (1870) remain staples of the ballet repertoire.

In the last third of the century, the Russian composer Peter Ilyich Tchaikovsky (1840–1893) emerged as the preeminent ballet composer. Tchaikovsky's lyrical melodies

F O C U S

The Programmatic Sources for Liszt's Symphonic Poems

Liszt drew on a variety of extramusical sources for his symphonic poems, from specific poems to historical events to general ideas.

Title	Extramusical associations
Ce qu'on entend sur la montagne (1849)	Poem by Victor Hugo ("That Which Is Heard on the Mountain")
Tasso (1849)	Poem by Johann Wolfgang Goethe
Heroïde funèbre (1850)	Funeral march
Prometheus (1850)	The myth of Prometheus
Mazeppa (1851)	Poem by Victor Hugo
Festklänge (1853)	Marriage celebration ("Festival Sounds")
Orpheus (1854)	The myth of Orpheus
Les préludes (1848; revised 1854)	Poem by Alphonse de Lamartine
Hungaria (1854)	The dream of an independent Hungary
Die Ideale (1857)	Poem by Friedrich Schiller ("The Ideals")
Die Hunnenschlacht (1857)	Painting by Wilhelm von Kaulbach ("The Battle of the Huns")
Hamlet (1857)	Shakespeare's play
Von der Wiege bis zum Grabe (1882)	Painting by Mihály Zichy ("From Cradle to Grave")

and rich orchestrations combined to make his *Swan Lake* (1876), *Sleeping Beauty* (1889), and *The Nutcracker* (1892) among the most enduringly popular works of their kind. *The Nutcracker*, based on the well-known story by E. T. A. Hoffmann, combines a real-life plot with fairy-tale fantasy. In Act I, a mysterious inventor named Drosslemeyer gives a young girl, Clara, a magical nutcracker as a present. At night the nutcracker comes to life and leads an army of toy soldiers into battle with an army of mice. When Clara saves the Nutcracker's life, he transforms into a handsome young man. In Act II, the transformed Nutcracker takes Clara on a magical journey that ends in the Land of Flowers where they meet the Sugar Plum Fairy. The divertissements of Act II allow Tchaikovsky to construct a series of loosely connected vignettes, each of which presents the characteristic sound (or what at least was believed at the time to be the characteristic sound) of a variety of exotic lands. The musical exoticism of all these dances held particular appeal for audiences of the late 19th century at a time when the European world was claiming dominion over vast portions of the earth.

Tchaikovsky
The Nutcracker

THE SYMPHONIC POEM

By 1850, Berlioz, Mendelssohn, and Schumann had all contributed important works to the symphonic repertory. Yet widespread skepticism remained about the continuing viability of the genre. Richard Wagner had proclaimed the death of the symphony and many composers, like him, avoided the genre altogether. Others, like Brahms, as we will see, took it on despite its historical freight. Still others negotiated a middle ground in the genre of the symphonic poem.

Liszt coined the term **symphonic poem** (*Symphonische Dichtung*) in 1854 as a new name for what had traditionally been called a concert overture (see Chapter 15). By the 1830s, the traditional designation had become a misnomer because works in this genre were no longer overtures in any meaningful sense of the word. Although usually programmatic and only one movement long, they were written for the concert hall, not as an opening for a play or opera. The new term caught on quickly because it captured the main characteristics of the genre: symphonic and poetic. The programmatic source for a symphonic poem could range from the vague to the specific and might be reflected in the music in anything from a very general to a very particular way. A list of the extramusical associations for Liszt's 13 symphonic poems (see Focus: "The Programmatic Sources for Liszt's Symphonic Poems") gives some idea of the variety of programmatic sources composers turned to for inspiration.

Richard Strauss (1864–1949) succeeded Liszt as the acknowledged master of the symphonic poem, combining his gifts as an orchestrator with his genius for joining symphonic forms and story lines. Strauss's symphonic poems include *Also sprach Zarathustra* (loosely based on a treatise of the same name by the poet and philosopher Friedrich Nietzsche), *Don Juan* (based on a poem by Nicholaus Lenau), *Don Quixote* (based on the novel by Cervantes), and the quasi-autobiographical *Ein Heldenleben* ("A Hero's Life").

These expansive, opulent works epitomize the late 19th century's love of grandeur, particularly in their exploitation of the ever-expanding resources of the modern orchestra. It was Strauss who revised Berlioz's influential treatise on orchestration (see Composer Profile: "Hector Berlioz," in Chapter 15) and he did so in part to account for the expanded size of the orchestra and the new instruments (such as the tuba and saxophone) that had been added to it since Berlioz's day. The forces Strauss calls for in his symphonic poems represent the orchestra at its peak—or, as some critics would have it, at its most overblown. In *Don Juan* (1889), for example, he called for the following:

3 Flutes (one doubling on piccolo)	3 Trombones
2 Oboes	Tuba
English horn	3 Timpani
2 Clarinets	Triangle
2 Bassoons	Cymbals
Contrabassoon	Glockenspiel
4 Horns	Harp
3 Trumpets	Strings

Strauss was careful to use these forces judiciously, frequently dividing them into smaller units and reserving the full ensemble for special effect.

THE SYMPHONY

With its perceived ability to give voice to communal feeling (see Chapter 15), the symphony proved itself a particularly fertile genre for composers seeking to introduce nationalistic elements into their music. This inclination was particularly prominent among eastern European composers. Antonin Dvořák, who was trained and worked within an essentially German environment, drew extensively on the dance rhythms and melodic inflections of popular music from his native Bohemia, particularly in his later symphonies. In his last work in the genre, subtitled "From the New World" (1893), he includes the musical impressions he took from his various tours to the United States, especially to a Native American reservation in Iowa. In Russia, such composers as Nikolai Rimsky-Korsakov, Peter Ilyich Tchaikovsky, Mily Balakirev, and Alexander Borodin were quick to incorporate into their symphonies such nationalistic elements as modal inflections and folk-inspired rhythms. Their orchestrations also tend to reflect the rich tradition of the Russian brass ensemble.

Several important American composers also used the symphony as a vehicle for nationalistic expression. Anthony Philip Heinrich, who emigrated to the United States from Bohemia in the first decade of the 19th century, incorporated such tunes as *Yankee Doodle* and *Hail, Columbia* into his *Columbiad: Grand American National Chivalrous Symphony* (1837). Like Dvořák many decades later, Heinrich was fascinated with the music of Native Americans, as is reflected in his *Manitou Mysteries, or The Voice of the Great Spirit*, subtitled *Gran sinfonia misteriosa-indiana* (1845). Despite its unusual title, the work follows a traditional four-movement format, with a rondo finale. Louis Moreau Gottschalk's *La Nuit des tropiques: Symphony No. 1* (1859), in contrast, is a two-movement work that integrates rumba and fugue toward the end of its finale. The *Gaelic* Symphony by Amy Beach (1896) uses Irish melodies. These and other American symphonies of the 19th century remain little known but are well worth investigating.

In an effort to take the genre of the symphony in new directions, several prominent composers created works that draw on elements from other genres. Outstanding examples include hybrids with the concerto (Berlioz's *Harold en Italie*, Lalo's *Symphonie espagnole*); cantata (Mendelssohn's *Lobgesang*, Félicien David's *Le Desert* and *Christoph Colombe*, the latter two bearing the designation *ode-symphonie*); opera

(Berlioz's *Roméo et Juliette*); and even the symphonic poem (Liszt's *Faust-Symphonie*, each of whose three movements the composer called a "Character Sketch," the first for Faust, the second for Gretchen, the third for Mephistopheles).

The symphonic character of many pieces lying nominally outside the genre is also evident in works such as Rimsky-Korsakov's *Sadko* (1867; revised 1869 and 1891), subtitled "Symphonic Pictures," and Debussy's *La Mer* (1898), subtitled "Three Symphonic Sketches," in which the remnants of symphonic form are clearly discernible: a slow introduction to a fast opening movement, followed by a scherzo and a fast culminating finale. Symphonic form and breadth are also frequently evident in concertos. The concertos of Schumann, Brahms, and Dvořák, for example, all display a symphonic tone, avoiding virtuosity for its own sake and more fully integrating soloist and orchestra than earlier concertos.

Brahms and the Challenge of the Past

Still other composers, most notably Johannes Brahms and Antonin Dvořák, continued to write symphonies in the traditional four-movement pattern. Brahms in particular embraced his musical heritage, openly aligning himself with the traditions of composers like Bach, Haydn, Mozart, Beethoven, Schubert, and Schumann. But he did so with considerable ambivalence, for like all 19th-century composers, he felt compelled to demonstrate creative originality. Approaching the age of 40, Brahms despaired of ever writing a symphony. When asked whether he would, he confided to a friend, "You have no idea how it feels . . . when one always hears such a giant marching along behind." The "giant" was of course Beethoven. In his First Symphony, Brahms introduced a triumphant lyrical theme in the finale that closely resembles the "Ode to Joy" in the finale of Beethoven's Ninth. When someone pointed this resemblance out to the composer, Brahms is said to have replied, "Yes indeed, and what's really remarkable is that every jackass notices it at once."

Despite the inhibiting effect of Beethoven's long shadow, Brahms was able to write four symphonies that each bear his own distinct stamp. As with Beethoven, his symphonies have no common formula; each takes a different conceptual approach to the genre. In general, Brahms sought to avoid making the symphony even more monumental than it had already become. The relatively diminutive inner movements of his First Symphony, for example, serve almost as interludes to the outer movements, and the last movement of the Second Symphony breaks with the tradition of the finale as a grandiose symphonic culmination.

The imposing set of variations in the finale of his Fourth Symphony, however, stands well within a tradition set down in the last movement of Beethoven's *Eroica*. But here, Brahms reaches past Beethoven to an even earlier tradition, that of J. S. Bach. On one level, the structure of this finale is quite simple: it is a series of 30 variations, each eight measures long and based on the same eight-measure theme. Within this relatively simple, potentially restrictive, framework, Brahms introduces a stunning variety of thematic ideas, textures, harmonies, and colors. The theme is based on the ostinato subject of the finale of Bach's Cantata no. 150 (Example 18-1), a work that Brahms knew well. (Bach used the ostinato technique in a similar fashion in the first movement of Cantata no. 78, *Anthology*, discussed in Chapter 9). Within this self-imposed structure of variations on

Brahms
Symphony no. 4

Example 18-1 Ostinato theme of Bach, Cantata no. 150, finale (transposed).

Composer Profile

Johannes Brahms
(1833-1897)

Like Beethoven, Brahms was from the northern part of Germany—Hamburg—and chose to spend most of his adult life in Vienna. The decisive moment of his career came at the age of 20, when Robert Schumann declared him the new messiah of music. Schumann did not merely predict future greatness for Brahms; he declared him to be already in full command of his artistic powers ("fully armored, like Minerva from the head of Cronus," as Schumann put it). This pronouncement proved both a blessing and a curse. Thanks to Schumann's stature, it gave Brahms immediate recognition, but its extraordinary language burdened him with unrealistic expectations. Critics predisposed to dislike his music (that is, the followers of Liszt and Wagner) were quick to belittle Brahms's first works for falling short of those expectations.

Stung by these early assaults, Brahms soon developed a thick skin. For the rest of his life, he more or less ignored his critics and moved forward as he alone saw fit. His music cannot be easily classified as either "progressive" or "conservative." In many ways, it was both at the same time. In the 20th century, Arnold Schoenberg, one of the most radical composers of his generation, hailed Brahms as one of the most progressive composers of the late 19th century, primarily because of Brahms's ability to reveal the rich potential of a seemingly simple germinal idea. Many critics in Brahms's own lifetime found his music texturally and harmonically complicated, structurally intricate, and difficult to comprehend.

Brahms was nevertheless deeply committed to building on and rejuvenating the works of the great composers of the past, from the recent Schumann, Beethoven, Mozart, and Haydn to the more distant Bach, Handel, and Schütz of the Baroque era, and the even more distant Palestrina of the Renaissance. In an era remarkable for its emphasis on novelty and originality, Brahms thus embraced the musical past. In contrast to Liszt and Wagner, he refused to accept that music could or should be subordinate to any other art.

In keeping with these beliefs, Brahms worked in the traditional genres of instrumental music:

KEY DATES IN THE LIFE OF JOHANNES BRAHMS

1833 Born in Hamburg (Germany), May 7.

1847 Gives first public concert as a pianist.

1853 On tour with the violin virtuoso Joseph Joachim, meets both Liszt and Schumann. Schumann introduces the young Brahms to the world as the new messiah of music.

1862 Moves to Vienna, where he spends most of the remaining years of his life. Makes his living subsequently almost exclusively from conducting and from sales of his own compositions.

1876 Finishes First Symphony; declines an honorary doctorate from Cambridge University but accepts one from Breslau University.

1897 Dies in Vienna on April 3 and is buried alongside Beethoven and Schubert in Vienna's Central Cemetery.

symphony, concerto, string quartet, piano trio, piano quartet, piano quintet, string sextet, and sonatas for many combinations of instruments. He also applied the principles of sonata form more openly than almost any other composer of the late 19th century. This is not to say that Brahms's sonata-form movements are predictable—he manipulated the conventions of the form in the same spirit as had Haydn and Beethoven.

Brahms found another outlet for his historicism as a music editor. He prepared many new editions (often without credit or payment) of music by Handel, Bach, Mozart, Schubert, and Schumann. His friends included many prominent music scholars who were helping launch the first substantial effort to publish critical editions of past composers.

Principal Works

SYMPHONIES AND OTHER ORCHESTRAL WORKS Brahms struggled off and on for more than twenty years to write a first symphony. Throughout the 1860s and early 1870s he produced a small but steady stream of orchestral works. These include the two Serenades (1858, 1860), and the *Variations on a Theme of Haydn* (1873; more recent scholarship has revealed that the tune is in fact probably not by Haydn, although Brahms had every reason to think it was). After finally finishing his First Symphony in 1876, he produced three more in relatively quick order: no. 2 in D major (1877), no. 3 in F major (1883), and no. 4 in E minor (1885). Each is different from the others, yet all four fall squarely within the symphonic tradition.

Brahms's later orchestral works include two overtures: the *Academic Festival Overture* (1880), written as a thankful gift to the University of Breslau for conferring an honorary doctorate on him, and the *Tragic Overture* (1881), a work for the concert hall. "One laughs, one cries," Brahms noted of these two works.

CONCERTOS Although few in number, Brahms's concertos helped define the genre in the second half of the 19th century. The two piano concertos (1854, 1881), the Violin Concerto (1878), and the "Double" Concerto for violin and cello (1887) are all symphonic in scope and tone. These works demand great virtuosity on the part of the soloist, yet the solo part never seems arbitrarily difficult.

CHAMBER WORKS Brahms cultivated chamber music with an intensity unmatched by any other composer of his generation. His output includes three violin

sonatas, two cello sonatas, two clarinet sonatas, three piano trios, trios for horn, cello, and piano and for clarinet, cello, and piano, three string quartets, three piano quartets, a piano quintet, a clarinet quintet, and two string sextets. All of these works are technically demanding and lie well beyond the range of the average amateur musician.

PIANO MUSIC Brahms established his early reputation both as a pianist and as a composer. His op. 1, in fact, is a piano sonata with strong echoes of Beethoven's *Hammerklavier* Sonata, op. 106. But with op. 5, he abandoned the solo piano sonata and turned instead to variations, producing sets based on themes by Schumann, by Handel, and by Paganini. Later in life, he cultivated the character piece, even though he gave these generic names such as Capriccio, Rhapsody, Intermezzo, or the utterly neutral designation of *Klavierstück* ("Piano Piece"). Brahms pointedly avoided references to external ideas or objects in these works, presumably to distance himself from other 19th-century composers for the piano like Chopin or Liszt. Brahms's late piano pieces include some of his most beautiful and moving compositions.

SONGS Considering how many songs Brahms wrote, it is surprising that so relatively few remain in the active repertory today. In addition to the standard settings for voice and piano, there are also a number of vocal duets and quartets. Brahms also arranged a number of German folk songs for publication.

VOCAL MUSIC The *German Requiem* (1868), written to texts selected from the Bible, is a staple of the choral repertory. Less well known but every bit as appealing are such works as the *Alto Rhapsody* (1869) and *Nänie* (1881). Brahms also wrote music for men's, women's, and mixed choruses that is little known but deserves wider exposure. He also wrote his share of occasional music, such as the *Triumphlied* of 1871 to celebrate the German victory in the Franco-Prussian War of 1870–1871.

Brahms (right) and Johann Strauss, Jr. (1894) *Brahms admired the art of the "Waltz King" deeply. He once wrote the opening theme of the* Blue Danube Waltz *on a lady's fan and underneath it added the words* Leider nicht von Brahms *("Not by Brahms, unfortunately"). The contrast between these two men in appearance and style of dress is striking, especially when we realize the dapper Strauss was almost eight years older than Brahms. When this photograph was taken, Strauss was 69, Brahms 61.*

Source: CORBIS BETTMANN

Composer Profile

Gustav Mahler
(1860–1911)

When Gustav Mahler was a child, he was reportedly asked what he wanted to be when he grew up. "A martyr" was the young boy's reply. Mahler certainly got his wish. In spite of his acknowledged brilliance as a conductor, he would eventually be driven from his post as music director of the Vienna Opera, and his contemporaries would dismiss his compositions, mostly symphonies and songs, as little more than a harmless sideshow. "My time will yet come," Mahler predicted, and again correctly. For almost five decades after his death, the composer's symphonies were considered monstrous curiosities, championed only by a small group of devoted followers. Thanks to the advent of long-playing records and such outstanding conductors as Jascha Horenstein, John Barbirolli,

Working Holiday. *Mahler is shown here on holiday in the Austrian Alps in the summer of 1908 with the younger of his two daughters, Anna (1904–1988), who would go on to become an accomplished sculptor. Because he devoted most of the year to conducting, Mahler could focus on composing only during the summer. He typically wrote new works while on holiday and left matters of revision and orchestration for fall, winter, and spring.*

Source: Bildarchiv der Oesterreichischen Nationalbibliothek

and above all Leonard Bernstein, Mahler's music began to gain a huge following in the early 1960s. Today he is acknowledged as one of the towering figures of late-19th- and early-20th-century music.

This belated recognition has much to do with the nature of Mahler's music, which most of his contemporaries found to be a confused mixture of incompatible styles and idioms. But it is precisely this juxtaposition of the serious and comic, the sublime and the banal that seems so appealing today. This deep sense of conflict is very much an extension of Mahler's own personality: he struggled throughout his life with the question of life after death, and in one way or another translated this issue into all of his symphonies. He was also torn between his Jewish heritage and the Catholic faith, to which he converted in 1897. There has been considerable debate about the sincerity of this conversion. Anti-Semitism was so rampant in Austria that Mahler would not, as a Jew, have been able to assume the directorship of so prestigious an institution as the Vienna Opera. At the same time, the theological promise of life after death made Christianity deeply appealing to Mahler. He ended his life as a pantheist, finding manifestations of God and eternal life in all things.

Mahler's extended tours of the United States in the years 1907 to 1911 reflect the growing cultural power of the United States in the late 19th and early 20th centuries. He was appointed principal conductor of the Metropolitan Opera in New York, then of the New York Philharmonic Society. Organizations like these now had the financial resources to attract musicians of the highest stature from across the Atlantic. Although Mahler struggled constantly with the management of both institutions, he helped raise the artistic standards of American musical life immeasurably.

Principal Works

SYMPHONIES Like Beethoven, Mahler consistently rethought the nature of the genre every time he began a new symphony. These works nevertheless fall into several broad categories:

- The *Wunderhorn* Symphonies (nos. 1–4). Each of these incorporates thematic material from at least one of his *Wunderhorn* songs (see later), and three of the four incorporate voices as well. The First,

---

KEY DATES IN THE LIFE OF GUSTAV MAHLER

1860 Born in Kalischt, Bohemia (then part of Austrian Empire; now in the Czech Republic) on July 7.

1880–1888 Obtains increasingly responsible conducting positions in a number of opera houses, including Ljubliana, Olmütz, Kassel, and Leipzig.

1888 Appointed music director at the Royal Opera in Budapest. Conducts from fall through spring and devotes summer vacations to composing.

1897 Appointed music director of the Vienna Court Opera, the most prestigious institution of its kind in the Austrian Empire and arguably in all of Europe.

1901 Marries Alma Schindler (1879–1964), an aspiring composer of songs; Mahler at first prohibits her from composing, then relents and promotes her music enthusiastically.

1907 Forced out of his position as music director of the Vienna Court Opera in spite of critical acclaim for his artistic accomplishments; accepts offer to become principal conductor of the Metropolitan Opera in New York.

1908 Appointed principal conductor of the New York Philharmonic Society.

1911 After several years of slowly declining health, dies in Vienna.

---

the only purely instrumental work of the group, follows the pattern of struggle to triumph established in Beethoven's Fifth and Ninth Symphonies, as does the second (*Resurrection*), which includes a grandiose choral finale. The fourth and fifth movements of the Third Symphony are vocal, but the slow finale is instrumental. The Fourth Symphony's finale is a *Wunderhorn* song for voice and orchestra, but the entire work operates on a smaller scale than any of the previous three.

◆ The Middle-Period Symphonies (nos. 5–7). These are strictly instrumental works, independent of earlier songs. The Fifth follows a trajectory from struggle to triumph; the Sixth (*Tragic*) is equally heroic but ends in the minor mode. The Seventh ends with an almost maniacally joyful rondo in C major, but only after working its way through an inner movement that Mahler marks *schattenhaft* ("shadowy").

◆ The "Symphony of a Thousand" (no. 8). So-called (with some exaggeration) because of its large performance forces, this work is unique within Mahler's output. The symphony is in two movements, each with soloists and chorus. The first is a setting of the Latin hymn *Veni creator spiritus* ("Come creator spirit"), the second a setting of scenes from the end of Part II of Goethe's *Faust,* concluding with the celebrated line "The eternal-feminine draws us ever onward" (*Das Ewig-Weibliche zieht uns hinan*). These seemingly disparate texts are in fact closely related, as are the musical themes of these two enormous movements.

◆ The Late Symphonies (nos. 9 and 10 and *Das Lied von der Erde*). These works mark a turn away from the triumphalism of most earlier works. An air of quiet resignation dominates all of these late works, including even their finales. Mahler had a fear of writing a Ninth Symphony, knowing that Beethoven, Schubert, and Bruckner had all died without completing a Tenth. Mahler thought to avoid this by not numbering what would have been his ninth symphony, calling it instead *Das Lied von der Erde* ("The Song of the Earth"), a "Symphonic Song Cycle for Tenor and Alto" based on a German translation of Chinese poetry. His subsequent Ninth Symphony, however, would indeed prove to be his last finished work. Both *Das Lied* and the Ninth end with long, slow elegiac movements, and the last measure of *Das Lied* remains harmonically open, a C-major triad juxtaposed with the note A. Several subsequent composer-scholars have produced their own completions of the Tenth, left unfinished at the composer's death.

SONGS Mahler stands at the end of the entire 19th-century tradition of song, integrating Schubert's lyricism with the chromaticism of Wagner and Wolf. In addition to numerous miscellaneous songs for voice and piano, Mahler wrote three major cycles for voice and orchestra: *Des Knaben Wunderhorn* ("Youth's Magic Horn") and *Lieder eines fahrenden Gesellen* ("Songs of a Wayfarer") are settings of German folk poetry, whereas the *Kindertotenlieder* ("Songs on the Death of Children") are based on texts by the poet Friedrich Rückert.

a theme, Brahms integrates the principle of sonata form, though not in a strict sense, because the movement lacks the essential modulation to a secondary key. With this finale of his last symphony, Brahms seems to be reminding the musical world that old forms are capable of rejuvenation, that it is possible to search for the new without abandoning tradition entirely.

Example 18-2 Brahms's ostinato theme for the finale of his Symphony no. 4.

"Noise" invades the symphony. *Mahler's use of cowbells, an anvil, and bunched twigs (applied to the timpani) in his Sixth Symphony of 1905 evoked howls of derision in many critical circles. (The sleigh bells had been used in the Fourth Symphony; the ratchet is fictional.) The caption reads, "Heavens, I've forgotten the automobile horn! I'll have to write another symphony."*

Source: Courtesy Henry-Louis de la Grange

The Symphony at the End of the Century: Mahler

Straddling the 19th and 20th centuries are the symphonies of Gustav Mahler (1860–1911). Although his later symphonies, particularly the Ninth (1910) and unfinished Tenth, anticipate 20th-century idioms and approaches to the genre, his First Symphony (1888) is a decidedly 19th-century work. Like many of Beethoven's symphonies, it follows a trajectory from struggle to triumph.

The funereal third movement of Mahler's First Symphony careens wildly from the beautiful to the grotesque, the sincere to the ironic. Mahler himself once suggested that the entire movement was inspired by a well-known illustration, reproduced here, showing wild animals bearing a hunter to his grave. By writing a funeral march into his symphony, Mahler is of course directly linking it to the funeral march in the second movement of Beethoven's *Eroica*. But the ironic tone of this music, inspired by a grotesque ceremony in which the hunted bury the hunter, mocks the somberness of the earlier work.

Some critics (many of them motivated by anti-Semitism) criticized the passage beginning in measure 39 for its "Jewish" or "eastern" qualities. The sound world evoked here is that of the Klezmorim, the professional Jewish musicians of eastern Europe, what we refer to today as **klezmer** music, characterized by a steady oompah sound in the

Mahler
Symphony no. 1

The world turned upside down. *Gustav Mahler once revealed that this well-known woodcut had inspired the slow movement of his First Symphony. The image is one of a world turned upside down: animals bury the hunter. The weeping and mourning are of course deeply ironic and provide an important clue to the nature of the third movement's funeral march, which is at times sincere, at times sardonic.*

Source: Moritz von Schwind. *How Animals Bury the Hunter* (Wie die Tiere den Jäger begraben). Woodcut 1850. Reproduced in Gerhard Pommeranz-Leidtke, Moritz von Schwind, Mahler und Poet (Vienna and Munich: Anton Schroll, 1974), Ill. no. 24

bass (here, in low strings, bass drum, and cymbals) and rhythmically free winds above. Chromatic passages in thirds, exaggerated accents, repeated half steps back and forth, and the prominence of the shrill-sounding E♭ clarinet all contribute to what many critics dismissed as the music of peasants, not suited to the lofty realm of the symphony.

The contrast between the funeral marches of Beethoven's Third Symphony and Mahler's First manifests the enormous changes music had experienced in less than a century. Beethoven's music is earnest, sincere, unself-conscious; Mahler's, by contrast, combines hauntingly beautiful melodies with passages that fairly drip with irony. Mahler's subsequent symphonies manifest similar contrasts of tone, at times deadly serious, at times lighthearted and remote. All of his symphonies are large-scale works: unlike Mendelssohn, Schumann, and Brahms, he built on the monumental aspect of the genre as embodied above all in Beethoven's Ninth Symphony, but also in Schubert's *Great* C-Major Symphony, D. 944, and the symphonies of Bruckner.

CONCLUSION

Music for the orchestra assumed many forms in the second half of the 19th century: functional music for dancing and marching, the stylized dance of the ballet, the programmatic symphonic poem, and—in its most expansive manifestation—the symphony, a genre capable of being presented or interpreted with or without programmatic associations. Civic orchestras proliferated toward the end of the century, further strengthening the importance of the symphony and symphonic poem within the social network of music.

DISCUSSION QUESTIONS

1. What factors account for the sudden rise in the prestige of instrumental music in the early 19th century?

2. Why did Beethoven refer to himself as a "tone poet" (*Tondichter*)?

3. What elements distinguish Beethoven's Symphony no. 3 (*Eroica*) from all earlier symphonies?

4. What kinds of new musical institutions emerged in the 19th century and why?

5. What musical features distinguish *public* genres like the symphony, concerto, and symphonic poem from the more *private* genres of song, character piece, and chamber music?

6. How did Wagner's theory of the music drama differ from previous approaches to opera?

7. How did the orchestra change over the course of the 19th century?

8. In what ways did historicism manifest itself musically in the 19th century?

9. Why did the concept of absolute music first arise in the 19th century?

10. Why did critical editions of composers' complete works first begin to appear in large quantities in the 19th century and not earlier?

Major Composers
of the 19th Century

FRANCE

Berlioz (see Composer Profile, Chapter 15) and the Polish expatriate **Chopin** (see Composer Profile, Chapter 16) were the most prominent of many illustrious French composers in the 19th century. **Luigi Cherubini** (1760–1842) was highly esteemed for his operas and sacred music. **Charles Gounod** (1818–1893), **Georges Bizet** (1838–1875), and **Jules Massenet** (1842–1912) were among the leading theatrical composers of France in the second half of the century. Gounod's best known work is *Faust;* Bizet's fame rests largely on *Carmen,* one of the most popular operas of all time. Massenet's *Manon* and *Werther* continue to be staged today.

César Franck (1822–1890) was born in Liège (now a part of Belgium) but became a French citizen in 1873. He was one of the great organ virtuosos of his century. His one symphony, in D minor, is a staple of the concert repertory. **Camille Saint-Saëns** (1835–1921) worked in virtually every genre of his era and was immensely prolific. He lived such a long life that, despite the immense vitality of his work, he eventually came to be identified with musical conservatism in France. His Symphony no. 3, which includes a prominent part for the organ, remains popular, as does his opera *Samson et Dalila.*

Eduard Lalo (1823–1892) is best remembered today as the composer of the *Symphonie espagnole,* for violin and orchestra; his opera *Le Roi d'Ys* is occasionally performed as well. **Gabriel Fauré** (1845–1924) ranks as one of the great song composers of the 19th century; his chamber music and choral music, especially the Requiem, are also significant. **Vincent d'Indy** (1851–1931) and **Ernest Chausson** (1855–1899) both wrote masterfully for the orchestra. Like many of their French contemporaries, they also fell under the spell of Wagner, succumbing to what came to be known in France as *Wagnerisme.* D'Indy is best remembered for his *Symphony on a French Mountain Air,* which incorporates a French folk song. He also wrote an important composition manual and founded the Schola Cantorum in 1896 in an attempt to revive the plainchant repertory. Chausson's most frequently performed works are his *Poème* for violin and orchestra and his one symphony.

GREAT BRITAIN

The piano virtuoso and composer **John Field** (1782–1837) was born in Dublin but spent most of his adult life on the Continent. His nocturnes influenced the young Chopin. **Charles Villiers Stanford** (1852–1924), also born in Ireland, and **Charles H. H. Parry** (1848–1918) contributed much to the repertory of sacred music. **Sir Arthur Sullivan** (1842–1900) is best known for his collaborations with the lyricist William Schwenk Gilbert (1836–1911). Together, Gilbert and Sullivan wrote a string of enormously successful operettas, the most beloved of which are *H.M.S. Pinafore, The Pirates of Penzance, Iolanthe, The Mikado, The Yeomen of the Guard,* and *The Gondoliers.* Sullivan also wrote the music to the hymn *Onward, Christian Soldiers.*

ITALY

Only slightly younger than **Rossini, Gaetano Donizetti** (1797–1848) and **Vincenzo Bellini** (1801–1835) also worked largely in the field of opera, emerging from Rossini's shadow after his abrupt retirement in 1829. Donizetti's most celebrated operas include

L'Elisir d'amore, Lucrezia Borgia, Lucia di Lammermoor, and *Don Pasquale.* Bellini's most frequently performed works for the stage are *Il Pirata, La Straniera, La Sonnambula,* and above all, *Norma.* Italian opera composers working in the wake of **Verdi** (see Composer Profile, Chapter 17) include **Pietro Mascagni** (1863–1945) and **Ruggiero Leoncavallo** (1858–1919). They are inseparably linked in the mind of the musical public by two one-act operas that are frequently performed on the same bill: Mascagni's *Cavalleria rusticana* and Leoncavallo's *I Pagliacci.*

SPAIN

Fernando Sor (1778–1839), the most celebrated guitar virtuoso of the 19th century, wrote many short pieces for that instrument. **Pablo de Sarasate** (1844–1908) was to the violin what Sor was to the guitar; his most popular work is *Zigeunerweisen,* on gypsy-style themes. **Isaac Albéniz** (1860–1909) and **Enrique Granados** (1867–1916) count among Spain's first nationalistically inclined composers; both also won fame as pianists. Albéniz's best known work is *Iberia,* a suite for piano. Granados's most popular composition is his piano suite *Goyescas,* each of whose movements is associated with a specific painting or etching by the Spanish artist Francisco Goya.

GERMANY AND AUSTRIA

Beethoven (see Composer Profile, Chapter 15) cast a long shadow over his contemporaries. Most prominent among these are two who are best known today for their work in opera: **Carl Maria von Weber** (1786–1826) and **Heinrich Marschner** (1795–1861). Both created works rich in special effects and fairy-tale atmospheres. In addition to *Der Freischütz* (see Chapter 17), Weber also wrote *Euryanthe* and *Oberon.* Marschner gained fame through such works as *Der Vampyr* ("The Vampire") and *Hans Heiling.* Both composers exercised considerable influence on **Wagner** (see Composer Profile, Chapter 17).

   Ludwig Spohr (1784–1859) worked in a variety of genres, composing six symphonies, ten operas, and four oratorios. He was regarded as one of the leading musicians of his day, excelling as violinist, conductor, and composer. Like **Mendelssohn** (see Composer Profile, Chapter 15), **Schumann** (see Composer Profile, Chapter 16), and **Brahms** (see Composer Profile, Chapter 18), Spohr wrote a number of important symphonies, as did the Austrian **Anton Bruckner** (1824–1896). Bruckner was associated in the public mind with Wagner because of his penchant for large orchestras and advanced chromaticism, but Bruckner devoted himself largely to symphonies (nine of them numbered) and sacred music. **Carl Loewe** (1796–1869) and **Hugo Wolf** (1860–1903) are best known for their songs. Loewe, a near contemporary of **Schubert** (see Composer Profile, Chapter 16), cultivated the ballad with particular intensity.

   Richard Strauss (1864–1949) belongs equally to the 19th and 20th centuries. Along with **Mahler** (see Composer Profile, Chapter 18), Strauss was deeply influenced by the works of **Liszt** (see Composer Profile, Chapter 16), Wagner, and Bruckner. Strauss was also one of the great conductors of his generation. He favored the genres of opera and symphonic poem in particular. His works for the stage include *Elektra, Salome,* and *Der Rosenkavalier.* At the time of its premiere in 1907, *Salome* was considered particularly daring, not only because of its advanced chromaticism but also its erotically charged subject matter. Most of Strauss's symphonic poems date from the earlier decades of his career: among the most often performed are *Till Eulenspiegel's Merry Pranks, Don Juan, Death and Transfiguration, Thus Spake Zarathustra,* and *Don Quixote,* the last a series of "variations on a knightly theme" for solo cello and orchestra. Even Strauss's most bitter critics conceded that he was one of the greatest orchestrators of all time, and it is only fitting that he should have produced a new edition of Berlioz's *Treatise on Orchestration,* bringing it up to date to reflect more recent developments in the orchestra.

SCANDINAVIA

Niels Gade (1817–1890) was a protégé of Felix Mendelssohn, who conducted Gade's First Symphony in Leipzig in 1843. Gade went on to become a leading figure in Denmark's musical life. The Norwegian **Edvard Grieg** (1841–1907), one of the celebrated piano virtuosos of his day, achieved renown not only through his performances, but also through his own compositions. His Piano Concerto remains a favorite in the repertory of 19th-century concertos.

BOHEMIA

Bedřich Smetana (1824–1884) and **Antonin Dvořák** (1841–1904), both natives of Bohemia (now part of the Czech Republic), grew up in what at the time was part of the Austrian Empire. Smetana's *The Bartered Bride* was the first Czech opera to register international success; his orchestral suite *Má Vlast* ("My Country") continues to enjoy great popularity. Dvořák blended Bohemian images and sonorities with a more mainstream middle-European tradition. He is sometimes called the "Bohemian Brahms," and Brahms was in fact one of Dvořák's greatest promoters. He wrote in a wide variety of genres, including opera, symphony, song, piano music, string quartets, and piano trios. His extended visit to the United States brought him into contact with music of Native Americans and African Americans. He urged American composers to develop a distinctly national style by drawing on these indigenous idioms and even provided an example of how this might be done in his own Symphony in E minor ("From the New World").

RUSSIA

Mikhail Glinka (1804–1857) was one of the first Russian composers to gain international fame. While studying in Italy as a young man, he experienced "musical homesickness," the desire to hear music that was distinctively Russian. His two great operas, *A Life for the Czar* and *Ruslan and Ludmila,* inspired several subsequent generations of Russian composers, including the group known as "The Five": **Mily Balakirev** (1836–1910), **César Cui** (1835–1919), **Alexander Borodin** (1833–1887), **Modeste Mussorgsky** (1839–1881), and **Nikolai Rimsky-Korsakov** (1844–1908). Many Russian composers considered **Peter Illich Tchaikovsky** (see Composer Profile, Chapter 18) too foreign in training and outlook to belong to this group of nationalists. Russian musical idioms are especially evident in such works as Balakirev's symphonic poem *Islamey;* Borodin's *In the Steppes of Central Asia* (also a symphonic poem) and his opera *Prince Igor;* and Mussorgsky's unfinished operatic masterpiece *Boris Godunov* and his celebrated piano suite *Pictures at an Exhibition* (later orchestrated by Maurice Ravel). Rimsky-Korsakov, the dean of Russian composers at the end of the century, won renown with such orchestral works as *Scheherezade* and *Le Coq d'or* and also wrote an important treatise on orchestration. As an educator, he lent guidance and support to a great many younger Russian composers, including Igor Stravinsky.

UNITED STATES

Lowell Mason (1792–1872) wrote many hymns and sacred works still in use today, but his greatest legacy is as an educator. Mason worked tirelessly to ensure that children be taught to read music in the schools; his efforts paralleled a similar movement in Europe.

Mason himself eventually became superintendent of music in the Boston public school system, but his impact extended far beyond New England.

Dan Emmett (1815–1904) played in minstrel bands and wrote both the words and music to *Dixie,* the unofficial anthem of the Confederate States of America during the Civil War. **Stephen Foster** (1826–1864) was unquestionably the greatest of all 19th-century songwriters in America. He earned his early reputation as a composer of minstrel songs (discussed in Chapter 16). Foster's first great hit, *Old Folks at Home* ("Way Down upon the Swanee River . . ."), sold some forty thousand copies in its first year. Several of his songs became so popular that many people believed them to be folk songs.

Anton Philip Heinrich (1781–1861), Bohemian by birth, was one of the first composers to write in a self-consciously American idiom, often drawing on Native American themes. He wrote hugely ambitious works with such titles as *Complaint of Logan the Mingo Chief, Last of His Race* and *The Mastodon: A Grand Symphony in Three Parts for Full Orchestra,* whose finale bears the title "Shenandoah, a Celebrated Oneida Chief." **Louis Moreau Gottschalk** (1829–1869) also worked American inflections into many of his works, including *The Banjo* (Anthology). A showman as well as a musician, he always made a ceremony of taking off his white gloves before he played in public.

Many composers born in the United States went to Europe for their training, among them **John Knowles Paine** (1839–1906), who taught at Harvard, and **Horatio Parker** (1863–1919), whose pupils at Yale included the young Charles Ives (see Composer Profile, Chapter 20). Another New Englander, **Amy Beach** (1867–1944), was the first American woman to gain recognition as a significant composer of large-scale works. Her compositions include the *Gaelic Symphony,* based on Irish folk melodies, and a Mass in E♭.

Part Six
The 20th Century

Prelude

The most striking aspect of music in the 20th century is its stylistic diversity. By the end of the century, composers, performers, and listeners had more access to more different kinds of music than ever before, thanks largely to technological advances in travel and communication. Either firsthand or through recordings, people could experience entire repertories of music that in previous eras would have remained unknown to them. Musical styles that had once existed only in the form of unwritten folk traditions could now be disseminated through recordings and broadcasts. These in turn expanded the musical vocabulary of composers working within the written tradition. The spirit of the age was one of innovation, and in pursuit of innovation many composers rejected—or at least tried to reject—tonality, up until this time one of the most basic elements in all of Western music. Still other composers embraced tradition. The result, by the end of the century, was a musical landscape that was either hopelessly fragmented or abundantly diverse, depending on one's point of view.

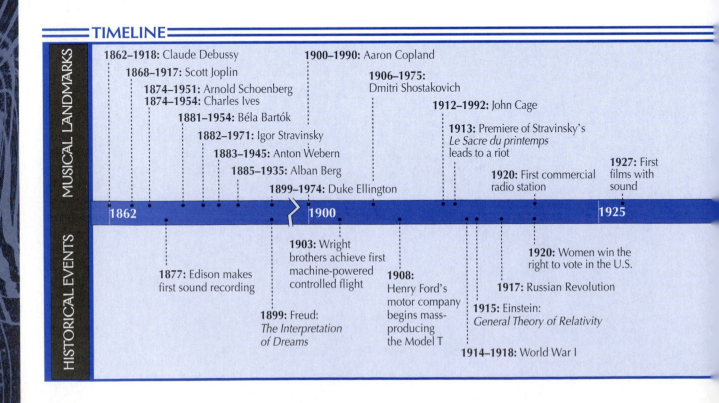

TIMELINE

MUSICAL LANDMARKS

1862–1918: Claude Debussy
1868–1917: Scott Joplin
1874–1951: Arnold Schoenberg
1874–1954: Charles Ives
1881–1954: Béla Bartók
1882–1971: Igor Stravinsky
1883–1945: Anton Webern
1885–1935: Alban Berg
1899–1974: Duke Ellington

1900–1990: Aaron Copland
1906–1975: Dmitri Shostakovich
1912–1992: John Cage
1913: Premiere of Stravinsky's *Le Sacre du printemps* leads to a riot
1920: First commercial radio station
1927: First films with sound

1862　　**1900**　　**1925**

HISTORICAL EVENTS

1877: Edison makes first sound recording
1899: Freud: *The Interpretation of Dreams*
1903: Wright brothers achieve first machine-powered controlled flight
1908: Henry Ford's motor company begins mass-producing the Model T
1914–1918: World War I
1915: Einstein: *General Theory of Relativity*
1917: Russian Revolution
1920: Women win the right to vote in the U.S.

The world itself was far more diverse in 2000 than it had been 100 years earlier. The sprawling overseas empires of the United Kingdom, France, Spain, Portugal, Belgium, and the Netherlands disappeared almost completely in the years between 1945 and 1970. Even in Europe, new states asserted their independence from traditional rulers. The number of sovereign nations in the world as a whole grew from 55 in 1900 to 192 in 2000.[1]

Wars, revolutions, and long-term international conflicts changed the political landscape of the globe at several junctures during the 20th century. In 1914, the growing territorial rivalries among the European powers culminated in World War I, which would leave some 10 million dead in its wake. The United States joined the conflict against Germany and Austria-Hungary in 1917 and helped turn the tide of battle. The Treaty of Versailles (1919) redrew the map of Europe, based on the principles of self-determination, and laid the groundwork for the League of Nations, headquartered in Geneva.

World War I also helped precipitate the Russian Revolution. In March 1917, after teetering on the edge of dissolution for more than a decade, the Russian monarchy collapsed when Czar Nicholas II was forced to abdicate. The provisional government that replaced the monarchy was in turn overthrown by Nikolai Lenin's Bolshevik party in October of that same year. Lenin thereby succeeded in establishing the renamed Soviet Union as the first communist state, run in theory by the people themselves—the proletariat—but in fact controlled by a handful of party bureaucrats.

By the mid-1920s, most of the world had entered what would become a long-term economic depression. Economic uncertainty in Germany undermined that nation's fledgling attempt at democratic rule and contributed to Adolf Hitler's rise to power in the early 1930s. The United States, which enjoyed an economic boom during the 1920s, plunged into the Great Depression following a precipitous collapse in prices on the New York Stock Exchange in October 1929. By 1932, one-third of the American work force was unemployed.

War broke out again in 1939 when Hitler's Germany invaded Poland. World War II (1939–1945), which pitted the Axis powers (Germany, Italy, Japan) against the Allies

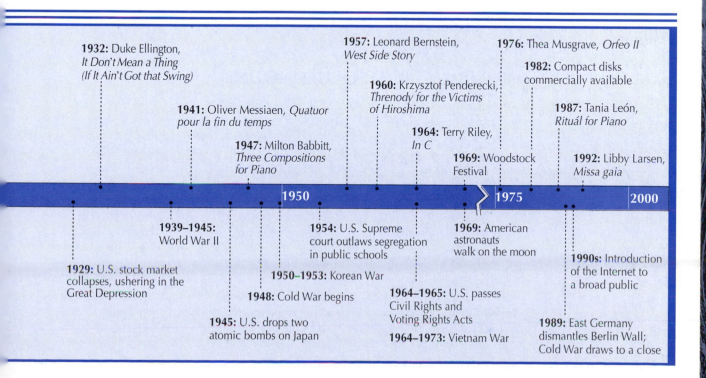

(Great Britain, France, the Soviet Union, and, after 1941, the United States), was the bloodiest and most far-flung conflict in history. It left an estimated 50 million dead, provided cover for the attempted extermination of all the Jews by the German Nazi regime, and ended with the detonation of two atomic bombs over Japan in August 1945. The United Nations was founded that same year to help avoid international conflicts.

Although the United States and the Soviet Union fought as allies against Germany, they rapidly became enemies after the end of World War II. The Soviet Union translated its battlefield victories in eastern Europe into a sphere of influence that gave it control over the satellite states of Poland, East Germany, Czechoslovakia, Hungary, Romania, and Bulgaria. Tensions between the communist nations of this Eastern bloc (led by the Soviet Union) and the Western bloc (led by the United States) threatened to explode into war at many points in the four decades after World War II. However, the threat of mutual annihilation through nuclear weapons helped prevent a third world war. Because the two superpowers—the United States and the Soviet Union—never confronted one another directly on the battlefield, this period came to be known as the cold war. One of the most striking symbols of the war was the Berlin Wall, erected by East German authorities in 1961 to prevent the mass exodus of their population to the West.

The cold war featured many indirect confrontations between the two superpowers. Among the most significant of these were the Korean War (1950–1953) and Vietnam War (1964–1973), in both of which the United States and its allies fought proxies of the Soviet Union. Both wars reflected the American strategy of containment, by which Western nations sought to limit the global spread of communism.

Confronted with a collapsing economy in the mid-1980s, Premier Mikhail Gorbachev (b. 1931) sought to promote economic reform and greater political openness in the Soviet Union. By the late 1980s, however, the Soviet Union was losing control of its satellite states in eastern Europe. The dismantling of the Berlin Wall in 1989 and the reunification of Germany a year later signaled the beginning of the end for Communist Party domination of the Soviet Union and most other communist states in eastern Europe, and with it, the end of the cold war.

THE IMPACT OF RECORDED SOUND

The emergence of sound recording in the late 19th century marks the most important development in the transmission of music since the introduction of music printing by movable type in the early 16th century. Thomas Edison created the first known recording of any kind—his recitation of "Mary Had a Little Lamb"—in his laboratory in Menlo Park, New Jersey, in 1877. Edison's metal (and later, wax) cylinders eventually gave way to the shellac disk, played on a turntable moving at the rate of 78 revolutions per minute (rpm). By 1910, these 78 rpm disks had become standard features of well-to-do households. The great Italian tenor Enrico Caruso (1873–1921) was one of the recording industry's first superstars: at the peak of his career, he was earning $115,000 a year from recordings alone, the equivalent of almost $2 million today. His success on the stage fueled sales of his recordings, and the popularity of his recordings further boosted his success on the stage.

Recordings had an enormous impact on composers as well, shrinking the distance between musical cultures. Lacking access to recordings, the only way Claude Debussy could hear a Javanese gamelan in Paris in the late 19th century was to witness a performance of an ensemble specially organized for the world's fair that took place there in 1889 (the same fair, incidentally, that gave us the Eiffel Tower). A hundred years later,

The technology of early sound recording.   *Until the development of useful microphones in the mid-1920s, amplification remained a fundamental obstacle to making recordings. Orchestras had to work in cramped settings and rely on megaphone-like devices to convey the music directly onto disk. Tapes and the possibilities of editing would not emerge until the 1940s. In this image from 1919, the English composer Edward Elgar conducts his Cello Concerto; the soloist is his compatriot Beatrice Harrison (1892–1965), the first woman cellist ever to give a solo performance at Carnegie Hall in New York.*

Source: © Hulton-Deutsch Collection/CORBIS BETTMANN

a composer in Paris could place an order through the Internet for compact disk recordings of three dozen different gamelan ensembles and have them delivered to her door within a few days. Recording technology also changed the very notion of what constitutes a work of music. By the 1960s, composers as diverse as Milton Babbitt or John Lennon and Paul McCartney of the Beatles were creating works that could not be performed by musicians in a live setting but existed solely in recorded form.

MODERNISM: THE SHOCK OF THE NEW

Modernism was a phenomenon that affected all the arts in the 20th century, including literature and painting as well as music. It is not a style in its own right but rather an attitude, one that gave rise to a variety of important styles. Modernism is the self-conscious striving for novelty at almost any cost, based on a conviction that the new must be as different as possible from the old. Since at least the Renaissance, artists have consciously sought to create new kinds of art, and in this sense modernism has long been a driving force in the creative process. But in the 20th century, the quest for novelty took on unprecedented centrality, involving the outright rejection of what had long been fundamental elements: rhyme and meter in poetry, linear narrative in literature, representation and perspective in painting (see the paintings by Pablo Picasso and Jackson Pollock in color insert IV), and ornament in architecture. Each generation had what it thought of as its **avant-garde.** The term is French for "vanguard," the first troops to engage the enemy in battle. As such it conjures the image of a small band of artists waging war against the conservative tastes of resistant audiences. In all the arts in the 20th century, those in the avant-garde—modernists—considered it their duty to lead art in new directions.

In music, the most obvious manifestations of modernism were an abandonment of conventional forms and of tonality. But modernism also cast a long shadow over many aspects of the art: impressionism, expressionism, atonality, serial composition, aleatory music—all confronted listeners with the challenge of the New. Even the less overtly confrontational idioms of neoclassicism, minimalism, and postmodernism can be understood as reactions against modernism. In its most extreme form, modernism sought to erase all links to the past. "Creators must look straight ahead," the composer and conductor Pierre Boulez (b. 1925) once famously declared. "It is not enough to deface the Mona Lisa because that does not kill the Mona Lisa. All the art of the past must be destroyed."

But even in destroying the past, composers had to confront the past. Novelty, after all, could only be measured against what had already been done. John Cage, perhaps the most quintessentially modernist of all 20th-century composers, summed up this paradox neatly in the form of an anecdote:

> Once in Amsterdam, a Dutch musician said to me, "It must be very difficult for you in America to write music, for you are so far away from the centers of tradition." I had to say, "It must be very difficult for you in Europe to write music, for you are so close to centers of tradition."[2]

The gulf between new and old became wider and wider as the century progressed. To be sure, audiences had confronted so-called difficult music before the 20th century, but in the early decades of the century a number of younger composers posed an unprecedented challenge when they started writing music without a tonal center. Most listeners found the new idiom difficult to follow, and many reacted with overt hostility. Arnold Schoenberg and his followers in Vienna, weary of having their concerts disrupted, formed their own Society for Private Musical Performances, withdrawing themselves from public scrutiny altogether. Audiences became less confrontational after World War II as the rage of earlier listeners eventually cooled, partly through acceptance of new sounds but also partly through indifference.

For much of the 20th century, what came to be known as "difficult" music—music not particularly popular with the general listening public—enjoyed a certain prestige within the community of musical artists. A great many composers took comfort in Ralph Waldo Emerson's pronouncement that "To be great is to be misunderstood." Popular success, in fact, became suspect in certain circles. This is especially evident in the case of a composer like Leonard Bernstein, who wrote so-called difficult music as well as music of wide appeal, most notably his Broadway musicals *Candide* and *West Side Story*. Even when criticizing the isolation of difficult music in the mid-1960s, Bernstein felt compelled to adopt an apologetic tone:

> As of this writing, God forgive me, I have far more pleasure in following the musical adventures of Simon & Garfunkel or of The Association singing "Along Comes Mary" than I have in most of what is being written now by the whole community of "avant garde" composers. . . . Pop music seems to be the only area where there is to be found unabashed vitality, the fun of invention, the feeling of fresh air. Everything else suddenly seems old-fashioned: electronic music, serialism, chance music—they have already acquired the musty odor of academicism.[3]

Bernstein had already begun to experience a certain degree of disdain from colleagues who were accusing him of selling out to popular tastes, and he was well aware that his comments were likely to antagonize a good many of his peers. To be popular, in the view of these avant-garde artists, was to be shallow. Compositional complexity was a correlative of quality, and if an audience didn't "get it," the fault lay with the audience.

The widespread acceptance of such a perspective was new in the 20th century. Earlier composers—Haydn and Verdi, for example—had seen little if any conflict between popularity and musical integrity. But in the end it is pointless to blame either composers or listeners for this state of affairs. Audiences have always listened to the music that moves them, and at no point in history had there ever been so many listeners, or so large a menu of musical styles from which to choose, as at the end of the 20th century.

Chapter 19

The Growth of Pluralism

The diversity of 20th-century musical styles was a source of both pleasure and anxiety for composers and listeners alike. The proliferation of styles during this era can be viewed from several different perspectives, all of which reflect broader trends in society as a whole.

FROM FRAGMENTATION TO DIVERSITY

At the beginning of the 20th century, Western nations dominated much of the globe, and Western peoples presumed for themselves a corresponding cultural superiority. The United States proudly proclaimed itself a social melting pot in which people from all over the world could blend into a homogeneous society. By the end of the century, the melting pot metaphor had changed to that of a mosaic—that is, many individually distinct units combining to create a larger whole. The shift in the imagery used to describe society is revealing, for the mosaic metaphor rejects the idea that diverse cultures can (or should) be homogenized into a single mainstream. What had previously been seen as fragmentation, a source of weakness, was now recognized as diversity, a source of strength.

Attitudes toward music in Western culture of the 20th century reflect a similar transformation in outlook. In the early and even middle decades of the century, music that did not conform to the mainstream idiom of tonal music was widely condemned. The tonally unconventional works of Arnold Schoenberg and the rhythmically unconventional works of Igor Stravinsky were seen in part as a rebellion against the social status quo, which in a sense they were, and performances of this music occasionally led to riots in the concert hall, as the cartoon on the next page illustrates. Rhythmically charged music like ragtime (in the 1900s and 1910s), jazz (1920s and 1930s), and rock and roll (1950s and 1960s) also touched off their share of controversy. Part of this animosity was motivated by racial prejudices and generational conflicts, but, as in the case of Schoenberg and Stravinsky, the music offended listeners primarily because it was perceived to threaten the existing social order, a concern that cultural observers have expressed at many times throughout history. Plato, for example, had warned more than two thousand years before that "a new type of music is something to beware of as a hazard of all our fortunes. For the modes of

"The Next Concert by Schoenberg in Vienna."
Schoenberg continues to conduct even though pandemonium has broken out. The figure on the floor at the bottom center appears to be Schubert, suggesting that Schoenberg's music is an affront not only to his contemporaries but to Viennese composers of the past as well. The image caricatures an actual event, the Viennese "Scandal Concert" of March 31, 1913, in which a performance of Alban Berg's Altenberg Lieder, *op. 4, led to an open revolt of the audience. One of the organizers of the concert was arrested for striking the operetta composer Oscar Straus, who at the trial glibly remarked that the punch to his head "seemed to be the most harmonious sound of the entire evening."*

Source: Phaidon Press Limited

music are never disturbed without unsettling of the most fundamental political and social conventions." This mistrust of new music was still common in the first half of the 20th century.

In the later decades of the century, however, audiences became more and more inclined to take a pluralistic, live-and-let-live attitude, embracing the music they liked and simply ignoring any they found objectionable. By the 1980s, Western society as a whole was embracing a greater diversity of musical idioms than at any point in its past.

Technology helped, particularly in the United States. In the 1950s, most Americans could tune in only two or three national television networks. When Elvis Presley and the Beatles appeared on *The Ed Sullivan Show,* in 1956 and 1964, respectively, their audiences included viewers of all ages, from children to adults. This weekly show was designed to offer something for everyone: comedians, acrobats, magicians, and musicians of all kinds, from Maria Callas singing scenes from Puccini's *Tosca* to Bo Diddley singing *Bo Diddley.*

By the mid-1980s, the rise of cable television had made the concept of the variety show obsolete. With so many channels to choose from, viewers could focus not only on specific shows but entire networks devoted to specialized interests. Radio stations developed even more highly focused niche audiences. With so many television and radio broadcasts available, musical groups were no longer competing for a common audience, and listeners were content to leave one another more or less alone. It was not only possible but relatively easy for listeners of one generation to be wholly unaware of the music of another. A dominant culture with a dominant set of norms was replaced by cultural pluralism.

The multiplicity of musical styles in the 20th century can be found even within the works of individual composers. Here are some examples:

◆ **Scott Joplin** (1868–1917), known during his life as the "King of Ragtime" because of his enormously popular piano rags (see Chapter 20), integrated the style of ragtime into the classical genre of opera. Although a concert production of his *Treemonisha* (1911) failed to arouse great interest during Joplin's lifetime, the work was successfully revived in a staged performance in 1972 and won a special posthumous Pulitzer Prize in 1976.

◆ **George Gershwin** (1898–1937) moved easily between popular song (*Swanee*, *Let's Call the Whole Thing Off*) and the traditional genres of the opera house and concert hall with works that frequently incorporate jazz idioms (see Chapter 22). *Rhapsody in Blue* (1924) is in effect a one-movement concerto for piano and jazz orchestra, and the opera *Porgy and Bess* (1935) draws on African American sources.

◆ **Duke Ellington** (1899–1974) defies categorization (see Chapter 20). He wrote popular songs, dance numbers for big bands, sacred music, and works for orchestra. Songs like *Sophisticated Lady* and *It Don't Mean a Thing (If it Ain't Got That Swing)* stand side by side in his output with works like *Harlem*, commissioned by Arturo Toscanini for the NBC Symphony Orchestra, and *Black, Brown, and Beige*, a symphonic poem that runs some 45 minutes in performance.

◆ **Frank Zappa** (1940–1993) pursued an astonishing variety of musical styles, writing for rock bands as well as for orchestras. His *Dog Breath Variations*, for example, began life on *Uncle Meat* (1969), an album recorded with his rock group The Mothers of Invention; Zappa subsequently refashioned the work on two occasions, once for orchestra and once for a smaller wind ensemble.

◆ **Jim Morrison** (1943–1971) crossed many boundaries both as a performer and as a composer. His 1967 recording of the *Alabama Song* from Kurt Weill's *Aufstieg und Fall der Stadt Mahagonny* (Anthology, discussed in Chapter 22) introduced an entire generation of rock aficionados to a German opera written in the 1920s. Morrison's eleven-minute *The End*, released on the same album, extended both the textual and musical expectations of what a rock group could do.

◆ **Keith Jarrett** (b. 1945) has cultivated a wide range of styles both as a performer and composer. Although associated primarily with jazz, he has explored jazz-rock, new age, and classical repertories as well. His own improvisations resist categorization.

In spite of such personal diversity, marketing dictated that musical works—and specifically, recordings—be packaged in such a way as to target specific audiences and tastes. Categories and subcategories created for marketing purposes inevitably shape the way we hear the music.

Marketing also plays a basic role in what kinds of music listeners hear in the first place. The Polish composer Henryk Gorecki (b. 1933) rocketed to fame in the mid-1990s when his Third Symphony was marketed in England as a pop recording in 1994; it rose to number six on the charts for a time. When Samuel Barber's highly chromatic *Adagio for Strings* appeared on Hollywood film soundtracks—*Elephant Man* (1980) and *Platoon* (1986), among others—it became a worldwide hit with listeners who had never before heard of Samuel Barber.

THE PAST CONFRONTS THE PRESENT

The listening public's interest in new idioms was not confined to new music. The rediscovery of what has come to be known as early music—generally speaking, music written before 1700—opened up an entirely new section of the musical menu. Earlier repertories that had for all practical purposes been inaccessible to the music public became readily available through scores, performances, and above all recordings. The works of Dufay, Josquin, and Monteverdi, for example, had all languished in obscurity for centuries and were virtually unknown in 1900; by 2000, at least some of them had become very well known indeed.

Arnold Dolmetsch (1858–1940) was in many respects the father of what in his time was called the early music movement. He was one of the first and certainly the most visible of a number of musicians in the late 19th and early 20th centuries who began performing on instruments that had remained essentially dormant for a century or more, such as the harpsichord, clavichord, spinet, viola da gamba, viola d'amore, and a variety of wind and percussion instruments. In the years between 1950 and 1980, a number of outstanding groups sprang up that specialized in what came to be known as period instruments, either originals or accurate copies of instruments contemporary to the repertory being performed.

By the late 1970s, Josquin, Dufay, and Machaut had joined Bach, Beethoven, and Brahms in the record (and later CD) stores. Even Gregorian chant hit the charts in the mid-1990s. To a certain extent, the early music movement has satisfied the desire of listeners for new repertories without recourse to newly composed music.

Some composers found new sounds in instruments of the past. Although the harpsichord had never disappeared entirely, it enjoyed a renaissance in the early 20th century

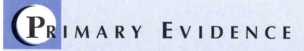

PRIMARY EVIDENCE

"This Ugly Game of Idolizing the Past"

In response to a questionnaire distributed in 1984 by the International Music Council, the eminent German avant-garde composer Karlheinz Stockhausen (b. 1928) railed against the preoccupation of artists and the recording industry with music of the past to the exclusion of music of the present. At no time before the present, Stockhausen argued, has the public ever been so absorbed with music of prior generations and so unconcerned with new music. Here he proposes a program of change.

• • • • •

What can be done: Shake up the leading interpreters in the world, ask them to refuse to serve any longer the machinery of composer-stripping, financial exploitation of dead composers through established gangs of cultural manipulation and "music marketing"; insist that they serve musical evolution: help vulnerable new musical organisms rather than living from a 300-year-old bank account of musical literature; spend at least 50% of their time rehearsing and performing new works; fight for progress and refuse to continue this ugly game of idolizing the past.

Source: Karlheinz Stockhausen, "To the International Music Council," *Perspectives of New Music*, vol. 24, no. 1 (1985): 44.

through works like Manuel da Falla's *Harpsichord Concerto*. Many popular recording artists, among them the Beatles and singer Tori Amos, also made use of the instrument in their recordings. Paul Hindemith, in turn, wrote several pieces for the viola d'amore, an instrument that had not been in general use since the Baroque era. Sonorities, forms, and styles of earlier times inspired still other composers of the 20th century. Many works by the Estonian composer Arvo Pärt (b. 1935), for example, are indebted to the textures and sonorities of 13th-century polyphony. The American composer Ellen Taaffe Zwillich (b. 1939), in turn, has written works from time to time that openly evoke the forms and styles of the Baroque, such as her *Concerto Grosso* (1985) and Partita, for violin and string orchestra (2000).

RECORDED VERSUS LIVE MUSIC

Until the late 19th century, music had always been a quintessentially social art, one that brought people together in the same space to share the experience of performing and hearing music.

We are so accustomed to sound recordings today that it is difficult to recapture the sense of alienation this technology created when it was new. In the early 20th century, many believed something intangible was lost, that recordings changed the very nature of the musical experience for the worse. The absence of a performer, some charged, robbed music of its expressive and emotional power. The opportunity to hear a given piece as often as desired, whenever desired, was thought to reduce the immediacy of the musical experience.

The availability of recorded music in general also made music a more passive experience. Making music for oneself and one's friends became a far less common activity than it once was, and the number of community choruses and bands declined markedly.

An outspoken advocate of recorded music was the Canadian pianist Glenn Gould (1932–1982), who shunned public performances for most of his mature career, arguing that he "could better serve music in a recording studio than in a concert hall."[1] Although Gould's stance may have been extreme, his point remains an important one. The musical possibilities of the recording studio are in many respects considerably greater than those of the live stage. In the studio it is possible to overdub tracks and modify sounds in myriad ways. It is even possible to make music without any performer at all—at least in the traditional sense—by using prerecorded sounds such as the singing of birds or whales, or with a preprogrammed electronic synthesizer, or by sampling snippets of other recordings.

The ready availability of recordings also altered listener expectations, making many listeners less tolerant of wrong notes, flawed tuning, or other imperfections in live performances. By the end of the century, more and more live performances were integrating recorded sounds, even to the point of overdubbing the lead singers themselves. The distinctions between recorded and live music became increasingly fuzzy in the last decades of the 20th century.

AUTHENTICITY

The tendency to view music not as a source of entertainment, but as a source of insight into a higher, more spiritual realm, grew throughout the 19th century and reached new extremes in the 20th, particularly in the repertory of the concert hall. The idea of performing a work of music in a manner that reflected the composer's original intentions became more important than ever. Reasonably good editions prepared in the 19th century were replaced with scrupulously prepared editions in the 20th (see Appendix 2: A Guide to Musical Editions). Editorial techniques rose to a level worthy of biblical scholars, and indeed the output of Bach (or Mozart, or Beethoven, among others) was treated for all intents and purposes as if it were holy writ. Many performers took up the cause of historical authenticity as well, not only by using period instruments, but by performing them in a manner consistent with practices that were current in the composer's own time. These techniques included different kinds of vibrato, articulation, and attack, as well as various approaches to tempo, dynamics, and phrasing. These historically informed performances were a revelation to listeners. The way Bach's cantatas and Handel's oratorios were performed at the end of the 20th century was substantially different from the way they had been presented in 1900, or even 1950—and, most would agree, far more representative of what the composers originally intended.

But historical authenticity exacted a price. Repertories shrank in scope. Large orchestras were less inclined to play Bach's Brandenburg Concertos and Orchestral Suites in the second half of the 20th century than they had been in the first because these works were not written for modern instruments or such large ensembles. Pianists were less likely to perform the music of Bach, or even Haydn and Mozart, in their recitals in 2000 than 50 years before because the modern piano is not authentic to the period of those composers. Except for encore pieces, instrumentalists of all kinds dropped most arrangements of works not originally composed for their instruments from their repertories. Concerts and recordings became far less heterogeneous in the second half of the

(P)RIMARY EVIDENCE

Authentic Spontaneity

Many critics have dismissed much of the popular repertory as trivial and shallow because of its supposed simplicity. But equating complexity with quality and simplicity with cheapness denies the driving force that ultimately gives music its ability to move the human spirit. Rock music, for example, is often deprecated for its harmonic, rhythmic, textural, and textual simplicity and for its unrefined directness of emotion. Yet these are the very same qualities valued in the song repertory of the late 18th and early 19th centuries. With its loud volume, insistent rhythms, and glorification of the sensuous, rock music often generates an experience that can overwhelm the listener. As the musician and critic Robert Palmer (1945–1997) reminds us, however, the rock concert is in many respects the closest thing we have nowadays to the Dionysian frenzies of ancient Greece, wild celebrations of physical and spiritual ecstasy in the name of Dionysus, the god of wine.

• • • • •

And that's the beauty of rock and roll. The lifestyle can be perilous, the rate of attrition remains high, but the survivors can go on practicing and perfecting their craft while the younger generation's best and brightest assume the Dionysian mantle and get on with the main program, which is liberation through ecstasy. Somewhere, in some sleazy bar or grimy practice room or suburban garage, young musicians wielding guitars or turntables, drum kits or beat boxes, sequencers or samplers, are creating the music for tomorrow's rock and roll revelry. Now that women have belatedly been accepted as guitarists, bassists, drummers, songwriter-auteurs, and "not just another pretty face," we're witnessing the birth of a whole new style of rock and roll frenzy and transcendence. Even the media overkill surrounding the much-hyped "riot grrrls" can't rob the term of its Dionysiac import. Don't let the faux-Apollonians fool you. As rockers, we are heirs to one of our civilization's richest, most time-honored spiritual traditions.

We must never forget our glorious Dionysian heritage.

Source: Robert Palmer, *Rock & Roll: An Unruly History* (New York: Harmony Books, 1995), p. 155.

20th century. Orchestras differentiated more and more between "standard" and "pops" concerts, with increasingly little repertory crossing boundaries. This kind of division discouraged breadth of taste.

In other repertories, authenticity took on a different form. Many jazz and rock vocalists cultivated a sound considered emotionally authentic precisely because it ran counter to the standards of cultivated voice production. Voices that by an earlier aesthetic might sound strained, distorted, or not entirely in tune were no longer automatically criticized as defective. To the contrary, a "realistic" sound—unvarnished by training and practice—was taken to be a reflection of the performer's emotional authenticity.

THE USES OF MUSIC IN 20TH-CENTURY SOCIETY

Technological advances in the reproduction and dissemination of sound created a wealth of new potentials—and pitfalls—for music in 20th-century society. Music was used on a scale and in places that could not have been imagined a century before. Indeed, the largest single event in human history, the Live Aid concert held July 13, 1985, to raise money for famine relief in Ethiopia, was focused on music. The concert featured almost a hundred different artists and groups, including Bob Dylan, Joan Baez, Phil Collins, U2, Mick Jagger, Eric Clapton, Neil Young, David Bowie, Paul McCartney, Elton John, the Beach Boys, The Who, Sting, and the Four Tops. It was staged simultaneously in London (Wembley Stadium) and Philadelphia (John F. Kennedy Stadium) and broadcast live over 14 satellites to an estimated 1.6 billion people in 160 countries. Music was a powerful unifying force in this global undertaking. "Maybe for the first time since Man left the African Rift Valley we began to talk in a common language, and that language, bizarrely, turned out to be pop music," proclaimed organizer Bob Geldof a decade after the event.[2]

In truth, there was nothing at all bizarre about the idea of music uniting people of different nationalities or of using music to raise money for worthy charities. Haydn had conducted a number of performances in London in the 1790s to support needy musicians in their old age, and Liszt had given recitals in 1838 to benefit victims of a recent flood on the Danube River. But 20th-century technology made it possible to disseminate music, and raise money, on an unprecedented scale.

Music and the State

Since the time of Plato (see Prologue), governments have recognized the ability of music to move the emotions of entire populations, and with the increased reach the new technologies of amplification, recording, and broadcasting made possible, music took on an even more significant role in political life in the 20th century. Instrumental music was particularly susceptible to varied political interpretation. The fate of Beethoven's symphonies in 20th-century Germany offers a good case in point. They were used by every element of the political spectrum, from the extreme right (Nazis) to the extreme left (communists) and every party in between, before, during, and after World War II. Ironically, they were even used by Germany's enemies: the opening motif of the Fifth Symphony served as a sonic icon of Allied resistance throughout World War II. That this was music written by a German composer made it difficult for German troops to suppress its use as a kind of code among partisan resisters, who could rightly claim they were merely "whistling something by Beethoven."

Nazi Germany was quick to suppress certain kinds of music like jazz, because of its non-Aryan origins, and twelve-tone composition (see Chapter 21), because of its failure to connect with the supposedly "natural" idioms of the people. The Soviet Union also struggled with nontraditional musical styles. In the decade or so after the revolution of 1917, the communist government encouraged experimentation, and the avant-garde flourished. But by the early 1930s, the regime had changed its stance. Josef Stalin encouraged native composers to produce music that was accessible to the masses, and that was informed, at least to some degree, by folk music. Absolute music—particularly abstract, complex music—came under special censure as formalist on the grounds that it was written without an eye toward its emotional effect on average citizens. At one time or another during the period 1930 to 1970, Dimitri Shostakovich, Serge Prokofiev, and many other composers came under attack from the government for writing overly formalist music. Serial composition (see Chapter 21), without a tonal center, was discouraged and openly derided by political leaders. As late as the 1960s, the premier of the Soviet Union, Nikita Khrushchev, condemned it as a threat to the "wholesomeness" of socialist ideals, declaring, "our people can't use this garbage as a tool of their ideology."[3]

The American government never became embroiled in musical politics to such a degree. No president ever offered an opinion one way or the other about serial composition, and the government as a whole never invested very heavily in any of the arts. Efforts to establish a national conservatory of music in the 1920s failed for lack of funds and were never seriously revived. The founding of the National Endowment for the Arts in the early 1960s represented a modest step in the direction of government patronage of the arts, yet although this agency helped many programs and individuals, its funding for music was never substantial enough to provoke a national political debate over any music it did fund.

Music and Race

Music played a vital role in the ongoing struggle for racial justice throughout the world, particularly in the United States. Ragtime, jazz, and rock were closely associated with African-American culture when they first arrived on the musical scene, yet all were quickly embraced and cultivated by white people as well. All three genres had to overcome considerable resistance, much of it either blatantly or subtly racist. Yet the appeal of this music ultimately transcended racial lines, even if the process was slow.

Ragtime, jazz, rock—all of these increasingly brought black and white performers and audiences together at a time when American society and most of its institutions were racially segregated.

With the progress of the civil rights movement beginning in the 1940s and the end of legal segregation in the 1960s, the black-white divide in jazz and rock, although it remained present, became less pronounced. When rap music, a new idiom rooted in the black experience, emerged in the 1990s, it encountered, like its predecessors, a round of racially tinged criticism. And like its predecessors, it too was soon adopted by white musicians.

Music and Protest

Composers and performers of the 20th century continued the long tradition of using music to assert their opposition to the status quo. Kurt Weill and his librettist Bertolt Brecht collaborated to produce a series of stage works ridiculing capitalism and middle-class values; Alban Berg took up the cause of society's outcasts with his opera *Wozzeck* (Anthology, discussed in Chapter 21).

A 1938 jam session.
More than any other kind of music, jazz promoted racial integration, for audiences as well as performers. Here the celebrated clarinetist Artie Shaw jams with Duke Ellington and drummer Chick Webb in 1938. At the time, most American institutions, including the military and schools—not to mention housing, restaurants, and hotels—were segregated either by law or in practice.

Source: Photograph by Charles Peterson, courtesy of Don Peterson

Such messages did not depend on texts alone. Jimi Hendrix's distorted rendition of *The Star-Spangled Banner* on an electric guitar at the Woodstock Festival in 1969, although wordless, was universally understood as an act of protest. The melodic distortions, heavy electro-acoustic feedback, and the free flights of improvisation helped turn the national anthem into a statement of dissent.

The protest music of three movements in the 20th century stands out in particular: that of the labor movement, especially in the decades 1910 to 1950; that of the civil rights movement of the 1950s and 1960s; and that associated with the opposition to the Vietnam War from the mid-1960s through the early 1970s.

Music Therapy

Music has been used to cure illnesses since ancient times, as suggested by the biblical story of David curing Saul of his melancholy by playing the harp (see Prologue). It was not until the 20th century, however, that music therapy established itself as an acknowledged protocol for the treatment of psychological, physical, and cognitive problems. Doctors treating wounded and traumatized soldiers after World War I noticed that patients exposed to music or given a chance to make music tended to recover more rapidly and more fully than those who were not. The first professional association of music therapists in the United States was established in 1950, the outgrowth of an expanding body of scientific literature that had substantiated the positive effects of music on the physical and mental health of individuals.

In clinical settings, music therapy has proved particularly important in helping patients suffering from neurological disorders like Alzheimer's and Parkinson's diseases. Scientists believe that music's therapeutic effects relate to its ability to enhance the processes by which the brain reorganizes cerebral functions that have been damaged by disease or injury. By the 1990s, music therapy was also being used as an agent of social change, as at the Pavarotti Music Centre in the city of Mostar in Bosnia-Herzegovina. Funded by the singer Luciano Pavarotti, the centre uses music making as a means of bridging ethnic and religious divides.

Ambient Music

Ambient music—background music—is the sonic equivalent of architecture in that its primary purpose is to shape actions and attitudes rather than to be a focus of attention. Music had been used to create moods and influence human behavior long before the 20th century, but the idea of using it in the background, and not as the immediate focus of listeners' attention, was unimaginable before the rise of recording technology.

It was the genius of George Owen Squier (1865–1934) to see the commercial applications of ambient music. He founded what eventually became the Muzak Corporation in 1922 and initially marketed the service to private homes, charging $1.50 per month for three channels. But Squier soon discovered that carefully programmed music—mostly soft-edged arrangements of well-known tunes—could increase productivity in the workplace and make customers spend more time in retail outlets or less time in restaurants, thereby increasing turnover and boosting sales. Although few listeners were aware of the presence of ambient music at any given moment, by 2000, it had become the most commonly heard source of music in the entire world, with more than 100 million listeners daily. And almost none of them, as its critics pointed out, could turn this music off.

The idea of creating new works designed to function specifically as ambient music caught the imagination of a number of talented composers in the last quarter of the 20th century. This kind of ambient music is characterized by widely spaced textures, consistently soft dynamics, and an extremely subdued sense of rhythm or pulse. The English composer Brian Eno (b. 1948) maintained that his *Music for Airports* (released in 1978) was "intended to induce calm and a space to think. Ambient music must be able to accommodate many levels of listening attention without enforcing one in particular; it must be as ignorable as it is interesting."[4]

MUSIC IN THE 20TH CENTURY: A STYLISTIC OVERVIEW

The history of Western music in this era follows a trajectory of ever-expanding possibilities. Anyone who composes music today can choose from an unprecedented array of options in every element of the art. Indeed, styles vary so markedly from genre to genre, within genres, and even within the work of many individual composers that it is no longer possible to identify a lowest common denominator of style.

Musical textures in the 20th century ranged from the extremely simple to complex. No single genre or style can be associated exclusively with any particular texture.

Rhythm, like other musical elements, manifested itself in a variety of possibilities. Dance music, as in all previous eras, relied on a steady beat. Ragtime, jazz, country music, and rock all evolved from dance idioms and accordingly built on a steady rhythm. Ragtime and jazz tended toward syncopated rhythms, sometimes quite intricate.

Melody varied greatly according to genre, the intended audience, and the function of the work at hand. The melodic variety evident in much music of the late 19th century continued to grow, supplemented by increasing use of nondiatonic scales such as whole tone and pentatonic. At the same time, many composers at the end of the century were still writing in a diatonic idiom not terribly different from that of Mozart and Haydn. But this was a choice made consciously and not for lack of options.

Harmony was widely perceived in the first two-thirds of the 20th century as a defining element of style. Critics tended to categorize composers according to their preferred harmonic idiom, and when a new piece was performed, accounts invariably mentioned its place on the spectrum between tonality and atonality. (Atonal music, discussed in Chapter 21, is characterized by the lack of any tonal center. It emerged early in the century in the works of several innovative composers.) In spite of important developments in other areas like rhythm, timbre, and form, it was harmony that emerged as the chief battleground in the debate over musical modernism. Indeed, the controversy over harmony in the early decades of the 20th century bears many remarkable similarities to the debate over the merits of the *prima prattica* and the *seconda prattica* in the years around 1600 (see Chapter 8). In both instances, new and old styles continued to flourish side by side.

Form also ranged from the simple to the complex. Composers who chose to work within the tonal idiom were generally more inclined to use such traditional forms as sonata form, rondo, and ABA. Those working outside the tonal idiom typically preferred to use dynamics, texture, and orchestration rather than harmony and thematic ideas as the basis of large-scale structures. Serial composition (see Chapter 21), based on the manipulation of a basic series of notes throughout a work, provided important structural alternatives for composers working outside the tonal idiom. Minimalism (see Chapter 23) and aleatoric music (see Chapter 23) offered even more radical approaches to form.

Instrumentation expanded beyond the realm of acoustic instruments to include electronically generated sounds through such instruments as the electric guitar, the synthesizer, and the computer (see Chapter 23). The synthesizer and computer provided composers the opportunity to control with precision the basic elements of pitch, vibrato, and timbre.

CONCLUSION

As in the early decades of the Baroque era, composers working at the end of the 19th century and the beginning of the 20th had the option of writing in both "Old" and "New" styles. Thanks to the rapid emergence and evolution of new technologies, however—in sound recording, radio and television broadcasting, and computers—the range of idioms available to composers expanded dramatically over the course of the 20th century. The result, by the end of the century, was a stylistic pluralism that made it impossible to identify anything resembling a musical mainstream.

SUMMARY OF STYLE DIFFERENCES BETWEEN MUSIC OF THE 19TH CENTURY AND 20TH CENTURY		
	19TH CENTURY	**20TH CENTURY**
STYLE	Composers seek to develop a distinctly personal style; originality becomes paramount in all genres.	An even greater variety of compositional styles; originality remains paramount in most genres.
TEXTURE	The polyphonic and homophonic coexist, with composers drawing on whichever approach best suits their immediate needs.	A wide range of options, from monophony to complex polyphony.
RHYTHM	Periodic phrase structure continues in the works of certain repertories (dance, march), but on the whole becomes increasingly less obvious over the course of the century.	A continuation and intensification of the same tendencies evident in the 19th century.
MELODY	Ranges from the simple to the complex.	From the simple to the complex, with added possibilities derived from nondiatonic scales, such as whole tone, pentatonic, quarter tone, and so on.
HARMONY	Becomes increasingly chromatic over the course of the century, which in turn makes harmonic simplicity a potentially unusual feature.	In addition to the idioms inherited from before, atonality—the absence of a tonal center—emerges as one of many compositional options.
FORM	The large-scale formal conventions of the Classical era continue in use, but often in a manner that obscures their presence. Cyclical coherence becomes an increasingly important issue within multi-movement works.	Conventional forms remain important in the work of some composers; others avoid these forms at all costs.
INSTRUMENTATION	The distinction between vocal and instrumental writing becomes even more pronounced. The orchestra grows in both size and instrumental variety.	Amplification and the electronic production of sound open new dimensions in timbre. Through the use of a synthesizer, any audible wave length can be reproduced precisely.

The Search for New Sounds, 1890–1945

The two generations of composers working between approximately 1890 and 1945 confronted and challenged many of the most basic stylistic premises of Western music, including triadic harmony, traditional forms, and conventional timbres. The result of these challenges was a variety of new approaches to self-expression through sound.

IMPRESSIONISM

The movement known as **impressionism** represents one of the earliest attempts to explore fundamentally new approaches to music. The term was first used in painting to designate the style of a group of painters, among them Claude Monet, Edouard Manet, Pierre-Auguste Renoir, and Edgar Degas, who used an accumulation of short brush strokes instead of a continuous line to produce not so much a representation of an object as a sensation—an impression—of it. (See Monet's painting *Impression: Sunrise*, Plate 18 in color insert III. The name of the movement derived from the title of this painting.)

In impressionist painting, color takes precedence over line. Similarly, the impressionist style in music is based on a blurring of distinct harmonies, rhythms, and forms. It also makes greater use of color (timbre) than any previous style of music. The number of composers thought of today as impressionists is relatively small—the most prominent are Claude Debussy (1862–1917) and Maurice Ravel (1875–1937)—but their influence on later composers and later styles was considerable.

Musical impressionism can be broadly characterized as follows:

◆ Form: Impressionist music for the most part avoids the kind of goal-oriented structures that had dominated music of the preceding century or more. These works flow instead from one moment to the next, building and receding in tension but without the same sense of striving toward resolution. They tend to be structured less around harmony and thematic ideas than around masses of sound.

◆ Harmony: Although impressionist composers never abandon tonality, they use ninth, eleventh, and thirteenth chords to an unprecedented degree. They also draw occasionally on nondiatonic scales such as the whole tone and pentatonic, creating sounds evocative of East Asia.

◆ Voice leading: Individual voices often move more or less independently of one another, without strict regard to the traditional rules of voice leading. Parallel fourths, fifths, and octaves contribute to the distinctive sound of impressionism.

◆ Rhythm: The rhythms of impressionist music tend to be fluid, often avoiding any definite sense of meter and preferring instead an elusive sense of motion that at times moves forward and at times seems to hang in suspension.

◆ Timbre: Impressionist composers drew new sounds out of the piano and orchestra alike. Debussy once declared that Beethoven had written in an overly percussive style for the piano; he advocated a style that treats the piano as an "instrument without hammers," with a tone that is more lyrical, intimate, and sensuous.[1] Debussy and Ravel were both renowned for their orchestrations, which rely frequently on techniques that distribute thematic ideas throughout the entire fabric of the orchestra.

Debussy hated the term *impressionism*, particularly when used to describe his music. He insisted he was more concerned with making "something new—realities—as it were: what imbeciles call 'impressionism.'"[2] His objection rests on the belief that our sensory perceptions, our impressions of the world, in fact construct their own kind of reality, an alternative to a conscious and supposedly objective, external reality that may not even exist in the first place. This attitude was not a new one: the Romantics of the early 19th century had embraced the idea of music as a means of conveying an alternate reality, but the impressionists extended the inward turn of the eye (and ear) still further.

Debussy's music also resonates with the French poetry of his day. Poets like Charles Baudelaire (1821–1867), Stéphane Mallarmé (1842–1898), Paul Verlaine (1844–1896), and Arthur Rimbaud (1854–1891) relished the sound of language for sound's sake and were not constrained by syntax or logic. These poets, who became known as symbolists, envied music's ability to suggest without stating, to construct forms without the burden of representation, and they sought to recreate this in their poetry. In place of narrative in their works—a linear progression of ideas—we find a succession of images, often connected only loosely. In place of description, we find symbols, allusions, suggestions.

Debussy's music takes a comparable approach to sound. His *Prélude à l'Après-midi d'un faune* ("Prelude to an Afternoon of a Faun," 1894) was actually inspired by a symbolist poem, Stéphane Mallarmé's *L'Après-midi d'un faune* (1876). Evocative and at times obscure, Mallarmé's poem captures the ruminations of a mythological faun, a half man, half goat who remembers—or did he only dream about?—his erotically charged encounter with a pair of wood nymphs. The opening line reads, "Those nymphs, I want to make them permanent," and the rest of the poem floats between dream and consciousness. Illusion and reality are indistinguishable.

For traditionally minded listeners of the late 19th century, Debussy's *Prélude à l'Après-midi d'un faune* was an enigma. They found the lack of clearly defined themes, the successions of seventh chords (measures 48–49), and the parallel fifths (measure 102)

Debussy
Prélude à l'Après-midi d'un faune

primitive in the worst sense of the word. Almost thirty years after the work's premiere, Camille Saint-Saëns (1835–1921), one of the leading French composers of his generation, wrote privately to a friend that he could make little sense of the work:

> The need to be new at any price is an illness of our era. . . . The public. . . now applauds a work in which the trumpets violently present to your ears a succession of fourths and fifths. It is a return to the earliest attempts at harmony. This is no longer music.
>
> The *Prelude to the Afternoon of a Faun* has a pleasing sonority, but one finds in it scarcely anything that could properly be called a musical idea. It is to a work of music what an artist's palette is to a finished painting. Debussy has not created a style; he has cultivated an absence of style, of logic, and of common sense.[3]

But others found in this "absence of style" an inspiration, a new approach to music that opened the door to writing in a manner that was decidedly modern. Although no single work can be said to represent the birth of modernism, Debussy's *Prélude à l'Après-midi d'un faune* epitomizes the assault on traditional elements and attitudes that characterizes a great deal of music written at the end of the 19th century and the beginning of the 20th.

CHALLENGES TO TONALITY

Debussy
Voiles

For all its chromaticism and harmonic ambiguities, Debussy's *Prélude à l'Après-midi d'un faune* stands well within the tonal tradition: it ends squarely in the key of E major. But his later *Voiles*, published in the first book of *Preludes for the Piano* in 1910, goes beyond the traditions of even advanced chromatic harmony. *Voiles* is full of parallel octaves and fifths, and its harmonies are obstinately nondirectional. Its supple rhythms add to a sensation of constant fluidity, as does its form. Although the work follows an ABA pattern in its broadest outlines, with A returning at measure 58, critics disagree as to whether the B section starts at measure 23, 37, or 55. Here as elsewhere, Debussy's music is delightfully ambiguous. Even the title has two possible meanings: "sails" or "veils."

More importantly, *Voiles* also illustrates the increasing use of nontraditional scale forms in the early decades of the 20th century. Debussy constructs the melodic ideas of this work primarily from **whole-tone** (Example 20-1) and **pentatonic scales** (Example 20-2).

A growing number of composers in the early 20th century also turned—or perhaps more appropriately, returned—to modal scales. English composers particularly fond of modal writing included Ralph Vaughan Williams, Benjamin Britten, and the songwriting team of John Lennon and Paul McCartney, whose *Norwegian Wood* (1966) uses the Mixolydian mode.

The **octatonic** scale was another important source of new sounds for composers of the early 20th century. It alternates between half and whole steps and contains within itself all possible intervals, from the minor second to the major seventh. Although the octatonic scale had been used on occasion in the 19th century for coloristic effect (by Liszt,

Example 20-1 Whole-tone scale.

Example 20-2 Pentatonic scale.

Example 20-3 Octatonic scale used in measures 1–5 of Béla Bartók, *Diminished Fifth.*

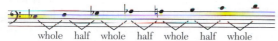

whole   half   whole   half   whole   half   whole

Mussorgsky, and Rimsky-Korsakov, among others), it became an important element for such later composers as Alexander Scriabin, Debussy, Stravinsky, Maurice Ravel, and Béla Bartók. Because of its symmetrical construction and strict alternation between half and whole steps, this scale, too, tends to subvert the idea of a tonal center. Bartók's short piano piece *Diminished Fifth,* from Book 4 of his *Mikrokosmos,* repeatedly juxtaposes two **tetrachords** (four-note units) that together make up the octatonic scale outlined in Example 20-3.

Bartók
Diminished Fifth

The possibilities of harmonies based on unconventional scales were almost limitless. In Russia, Alexander Scriabin (1872–1915) promoted what he called his "mystic chord," consisting of augmented and diminished fourths arranged in the sequence (from bottom to top) C–F♯–B♭–E–A–D. In the United States, Charles Ives (1874–1954), independently of Scriabin, was also experimenting with the idea of **quartal harmonies,** chords built on the interval of a fourth rather than a third. His song *The Cage* (1906) is based entirely on such chords. The unsettling text, about a leopard pacing in his cage, receives an appropriately repetitive and unsettling melody whose relentless up-and-down progression creates a kind of cage in its own right. The accompaniment provides little sense of direction, at least not within the expected conventions of triadic harmony. This brief song, in effect, is in no key at all.

Ives
The Cage

Ives's *The Things Our Fathers Loved* (1917), a song written to a text by the composer himself, plays with traditional harmony in a different way by stringing together a series of tunes from popular songs but joining and harmonizing them in an extremely unusual manner, often in the "wrong" key. *Dixie,* at the very beginning, merges imperceptibly into *My Old Kentucky Home,* followed by *On the Banks of the Wabash* (at the words "I hear the organ on the Main Street corner"), the hymn tune *Nettleton* ("Aunt Sarah humming Gospels"), *The Battle Cry of Freedom* ("The village cornet band, playing in the square. The town's Red, White and Blue"), *In the Sweet Bye and Bye* ("Now! Hear the songs!") through the end of the text. The harmonizations of these tunes, all of them familiar to Ives's contemporaries, create a strange sense of distance. The familiar becomes unfamiliar, and the way in which one melodic fragment flows into the next, always to words from a different source, seems very much in keeping with the literary technique of the stream of consciousness developed by the modernist author James Joyce. The net result is a song that insists on its modernity even while celebrating (and quoting from) songs of the past.

Ives
The Things Our Fathers Loved

The conflict between traditional and nontraditional harmonies is particularly acute in Ives's *The Unanswered Question* (1908), in which the solo trumpet and the small ensemble of flutes seem to occupy an entirely different sphere from the strings, which speak in slow, measured, choralelike tones, using the tonal language of conventional triads. Dissonance in the strings is carefully controlled and resolved: the entire string part, in fact, looks and sounds almost like a student essay in species counterpoint. The solo trumpet, by contrast, repeatedly poses a five-note figure that implies no harmonic center at all (B♭–C♯–E–E♭–C, or, in some instances, ending with a B♭ instead of a C). The winds, in turn, are even more tonally diffuse and grow rhythmically more independent. The work ends with a serene, perfect authentic G-major triad, yet the sensation it creates is not one of resolution.

Ives
The Unanswered Question

Composer Profile

Claude Debussy
(1862–1918)

Debussy's life straddled two centuries—he was born during the American Civil War and died a few months before the end of World War I—yet he is widely regarded as the first great composer of the 20th century. The inevitable association with the label of impressionism tends to obscure the genuine novelties of his music: no other single figure of his era did more to expand the possibilities of form, harmony, voice leading, and timbre.

In all this, Debussy developed a style of writing that provided a model for countless subsequent composers seeking to overthrow the cultural domination of 19th-century German music, particularly that of Beethoven, Brahms, and Wagner. Yet he remained curiously aloof from the musical scene of his day. He held no formal posts after his youth, appeared in public only sporadically as a pianist or conductor, and left behind no direct pupils. He nevertheless had many imitators (*Debussyistes,* as they were known), and his death was widely mourned throughout the musical world. Prominent composers, including Igor Stravinsky, Béla Bartók, Paul Dukas, Manuel de Falla, Maurice Ravel, and Erik Satie, contributed short pieces to the commemorative volume issued as *Le tombeau de Claude Debussy* in 1920.

Principal Works

PIANO MUSIC The *Suite bergamasque* (1890–1905) includes the celebrated *Claire de lune.* Debussy wrote *The Children's Corner* (1908) in a deceptively simple style: like all great works for children, it offers something to young and old alike. Its title and the titles of its individual movements are all in English, a

KEY DATES IN THE LIFE OF CLAUDE DEBUSSY

1862 Born in the Parisian suburb of St.-Germain-en-Laye, August 22.

1872 Admitted to the Paris Conservatory at the age of 10.

1880 Becomes the piano teacher for the children of Nadezhda von Meck, the patroness of Tchaikovsky; travels through Switzerland, Italy, and Russia, where he becomes familiar with the works of Mussorgsky.

1884 Wins the Prix de Rome, the highest compositional prize of the Paris Conservatory.

1888 Visits Bayreuth and falls briefly under the spell of Wagner's music, but struggles against this tradition over the decade, even though its influences remain evident in Debussy's only completed opera, *Pelléas et Mélisande.*

1889 Hears Javanese gamelan at the Paris Exposition and begins to experiment with new, non-Western approaches to timbre, form, and harmony.

1901 Begins writing music criticism for a Parisian journal in an attempt to pay debts.

1907 Begins a series of tours throughout Europe as a conductor and pianist.

1918 Dies in Paris on March 25.

nod to the propensity of affluent French families to hire English nannies. Each of the 24 *Préludes* (in two books, 1910 and 1913) bears a descriptive title that

---

In his foreword to the score of *The Unanswered Question,* Ives gave some hint as to the symbolism behind these contrasting elements:

The strings play *ppp* throughout with no change in tempo. They are to represent "The Silence of the Druids—Who Know, See and Hear Nothing." The trumpet intones "The Perennial Question of Existence," and states it in the same tone of voice each time. But the hunt for "The Invisible Answer" undertaken by the flutes, and other human beings, becomes gradually more

appears at the end of each piece: *The Sunken Cathedral* and *The Girl with the Flaxen Hair* are two of many well-known works in this set. Each of the

twelve *Etudes* (1915), implicit homages to Chopin, addresses a particular technical challenge (repeated notes, arpeggios, octaves, etc.) without sounding like an exercise.

ORCHESTRAL MUSIC Debussy was a master of orchestration from the very beginning. His *Prélude à l'Après-midi d'un faune* (1894), *Nocturnes* (1899), *La Mer* ("The Sea," 1905), and *Images* (1908) are all staples of the orchestral repertory. He avoided the symphony as a genre, even though traces of the form are evident in the three-movement cycle *La Mer*.

DRAMATIC MUSIC Although *Pelléas et Mélisande* (1902) is the only opera Debussy actually completed, he labored on several others throughout his life, including settings of two stories by Edgar Allan Poe, *The Devil in the Belfry* and *The Fall of the House of Usher. Jeux* (1913), a ballet with a scenario that takes place on a tennis court, was written for Diaghilev's Ballets Russes (see Focus: "Sergei Diaghilev") and performed in the same year as Stravinsky's *Le Sacre du printemps*.

CHAMBER MUSIC Debussy's String Quartet (1893) is the most frequently performed of all French quartets. Toward the end of his life, Debussy set out to write a series of six sonatas for different combinations of instruments. Unfortunately, by the time of his death he had completed only three of these works: the Sonata for Flute, Viola, and Harp (1915); the Cello Sonata (1915); and the Violin Sonata (1917).

Debussy and Stravinsky. *This photo, taken around 1912 by the composer Erik Satie, documents a meeting of two of the greatest composers of the 20th century. Stravinsky, 20 years younger than his French colleague, owed much to Debussy's style, particularly in matters of form and timbre. Debussy, in turn, consulted Stravinsky about the orchestration of his ballet* Jeux, *which, like Stravinsky's* Le Sacre du printemps, *was produced for the Ballets Russes of the Russian impresario Sergei Diaghilev. Debussy acknowledged Stravinsky's present of a score of* Le Sacre *with these words: "It is a special satisfaction to tell you how much you have enlarged the boundaries of the permissible in the empire of sound."*

Source: CORBIS BETTMANN

SONGS Debussy's songs continue the rich tradition of the French *mélodie* fostered before him by Fauré, Gounod, Franck, and Massenet, among others. Debussy was particularly drawn to the texts of such symbolist poets as Charles Baudelaire, Paul Verlaine, and Stéphane Mallarmé. He cultivated melodic lines that combine sinuous melody with a declamatory style; the piano is an equal partner throughout.

active, faster and louder through an *animando* [animatedly] to a *con fuoco* [with fire]. This part need not be played in the exact time position indicated. It is played in somewhat of an impromptu way; if there be no conductor, one of the flute players may direct their playing. "The Fighting Answerers," as the time goes on, and after a "secret conference," seem to realize a futility, and begin to mock "The Question"—the strife is over for the moment. After they disappear, "The Question" is asked for the last time, and "The Silences" are heard beyond in "Undisturbed Solitude."[4]

It is revealing that Ives should choose to represent this metaphysical debate through a simultaneous contrast of the musical old (conventional harmony and regular rhythms within a single tempo) and the musical new (unconventional harmony and irregular rhythms within shifting tempos). Like other modernist composers of the early 20th century, Ives felt the need to challenge listeners out of what he perceived to be their all-too-comfortable habit of listening to "beautiful" music—listeners who, like the Druids of *The Unanswered Question*, are content within themselves and oblivious to all that is around them.

PRIMITIVISM

Modernism's rejection of tradition assumed many forms in the early 20th century. One of the most powerful of these was **primitivism.** *Primitive* is often used as a derogatory term, but as an aesthetic movement in the early 20th century, primitivism was considered a positive, purifying force in all the arts. The impetus behind primitivism was a rejection of the self-imposed, arbitrary conventions of Western culture. Primitive peoples, what the Enlightenment philosopher Jean-Jacques Rousseau had called "noble savages," were uneducated and unrefined but for that very reason all the more genuine and pure. The primitive was regarded as a source of both beauty and strength, representing a stage of civilization unthreatened by decadence and self-consciousness. In painting, primitivism manifested itself in the work of the group of artists known as the *fauves*—the "wild beasts"—who used a seemingly crude kind of draftsmanship, coupled with bold, unrealistic colors. These artists owed much to Paul Gauguin (1848–1903) and Henri Rousseau (1844–1910; see Plate 19 in color insert IV).

Musical primitivism manifested itself in many ways over the course of the 20th century, particularly in the work of composers who sought to elevate rhythm to a level of unprecedented importance. Composers associated with primitivism also tended to abandon or substantially alter such "civilized"—arbitrary—concepts as voice leading, triadic harmony, and the major and minor forms of the diatonic scale.

Stravinsky
Le Sacre du printemps

All of these traits are evident in Igor Stravinsky's ballet *Le Sacre du printemps* ("The Rite of Spring," 1913), subtitled "Pictures from Pagan Russia." By rejecting traditional harmonic progressions, timbres, and above all rhythms, Stravinsky was able to create a score that reflected the same kind of raw, elemental relationship between humans and nature that is represented on stage through the story of the dance. The ballet's story centers on a pre-Christian ritual that welcomes the coming of spring and offers in thanks to the gods a human sacrifice—primitive and uncivilized to be sure, but consequently all the more elemental and powerful. Stravinsky elevated the role of rhythm in this ritual in a number of ways, sometimes through complexity, sometimes through simplicity. Just before the moment of sacrifice at the end of the piece, audiences hear a passage in which the meter shifts no fewer than eight times in the span of only 12 measures (Example 20-4).

In Part I (Adoration of the Earth), the passage beginning at measure 88 is equally unpredictable, even though it is based on a series of repeating eighth-note chords. Stravinsky strips the music of all harmonic and melodic variety. The orchestra, in effect, functions as a kind of giant, polychordal drum, repeating the same chord 32 times in succession (Example 20-5). By marking each iteration with a down bow, Stravinsky eliminates the slight alternation of strong and weak that is often perceptible from standard back-and-forth (down-up) bowing, and by placing accents at irregular intervals, he eradicates any sense of a rhythmic pattern.

Example 20-4 Stravinsky, *Le Sacre du printemps*, Sacrificial Dance (rhythm only).

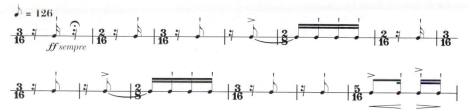

Source: Passage mm. 1–12 (1913 edition, rhythm only), Stravinsky *Sacre du printemps*, Sacrificial Dances, in *Aspects of twentieth-century music* by Richard DeLone et al.; Coordinating editor, Gary E. Wittlich. Prentice-Hall, 1975, p. 220. *The Rite of Spring* (1913), Copyright 1921 by Edition Russe de Musique. Copyright assigned 1947 to Boosey & Hawkes for all countries of the world. Reprinted by permission.

Example 20-5 Measures 1–8 after no. 13.

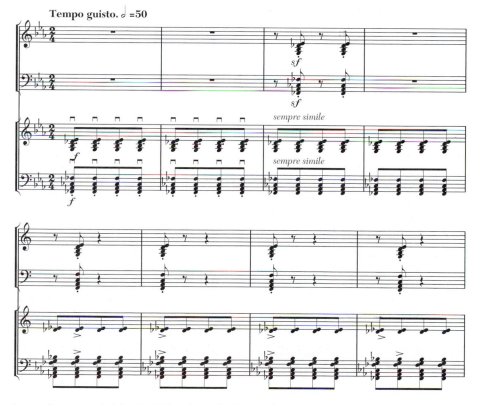

Source: Passage mm. 1–4 after No. 13 from Stravinsky, *Le Sacre du printemps*, "Danse des Adolescentes" from *Twentieth-century music: a history of musical style in modern Europe and America* by Robert P. Morgan (New York: W. W. Norton, 1991), p. 98. *The Rite of Spring* (1913), Copyright 1921 by Edition Russe de Musique. Copyright assigned 1947 to Boosey & Hawkes for all countries of the world. Reprinted by permission.

Composer Profile

Charles Ives
(1874–1954)

Ives was a true American original whose music incorporates many of the idioms blended in the melting pot of late-19th-century American society. As a youth in Danbury, Connecticut, he absorbed a wide variety of musical traditions: the orchestral repertory of the concert hall, hymns in church, band music at community gatherings like the Fourth of July, and popular songs in the parlors of the town's homes. Ives worked all of these styles into his own music at various times, often in the same work. And all this was merely a part-time hobby, for Ives's real profession was in the insurance business.

George Ives, the composer's father and first teacher, was a bandmaster in the Civil War and a musical eccentric in his own right who at times experimented with polytonality and quarter-tone tuning. At Yale, Charles Ives studied with a very different kind of teacher, Horatio Parker, one of the leading American composers of his era but for all intents and purposes a European composer in outlook and idiom. German trained, Parker wrote in the style of Mendelssohn, Schumann, and Brahms, and Ives absorbed the finer points of this tradition. But Ives's String Quartet no. 1, written as an undergraduate, shows his interest in other idioms as well. Subtitled *A Revival Service,* it is full of references to popular hymns of the day. The first movement is based on the hymn tune *From Greenland's Icy Mountains* by another American composer, Lowell Mason.

After graduation, Ives entered the insurance business but continued to write music in his spare

KEY DATES IN THE LIFE OF CHARLES IVES
1874 Born October 20 in Danbury, Connecticut.
1894 Enters Yale University, where he studies composition with Horatio Parker, one of the leading American composers of the day.
1898 Graduates from Yale and enters the insurance business.
1907 Establishes an insurance firm of his own in partnership with George Myrick and plays an important role in developing the modern industry of life insurance.
1918 Suffers heart attack and begins a long period of ill health that will last until his death.
1922 Publishes and distributes to friends, at his own expense, 114 Songs.
1947 Receives the Pulitzer Prize for his Third Symphony, written in 1911.
1954 Dies May 19 in New York City.

time. If a composer "has a nice wife and some nice children," he once asked, "how can he let them starve on his dissonances?"[5] But he more or less stopped composing in his early to mid-40s after his health began to fail. Ives achieved only modest fame as a composer during his lifetime, in part because of the advanced idiom of his style, in part because he

---

The **polytonal** harmony of this same passage posed further challenges to early listeners. Contrasting triads are juxtaposed simultaneously, with each of four instrumental groups—two sets of horns, high strings, low strings—playing its own chord.

For all its aesthetic primitivism, Stravinsky's *Le Sacre du printemps* is extremely intricate. The orchestra used to create its so-called primitive sounds is enormous, even by the standards of the early 20th century, and is in fact the product of hundreds of years of development and innovation.

But Stravinsky often uses the instruments in unconventional ways to create an *impression* of rawness. The very opening of the ballet illustrates this point quite

never really promoted himself. Many of his more important works were not performed publicly until long after they had been composed. The String Quartet no. 2, for example, was written in 1913 but not performed in public until 1946, and his Symphony no. 2 (1902) had to wait almost fifty years for its premiere in 1951. But Ives's fame and influence have grown steadily since the 1950s, and in many ways his music was an inspiration to later composers, in part for his readiness to combine

contrasting idioms, and in part because of his irreverence toward the seriousness of "high art."

Principal Works

ORCHESTRAL MUSIC In spite of their eccentricities, the five symphonies (four with numbers, one titled *Holidays*) stand well within the tradition of the genre as an expression of broad, communal sentiment. Ives also wrote a number of programmatic works for orchestra, including *Three Places in New England* and *The Unanswered Question*.

PIANO AND CHAMBER MUSIC Ives's Piano Sonata no. 2—subtitled *Concord, Mass., 1840–1860* and inspired by the writings of fellow New Englanders Emerson, Hawthorne, the Alcotts, and Thoreau—is widely regarded as one of his finest works in any genre. Ives published the work at his own expense in 1919. In addition to two string quartets, Ives also wrote four violin sonatas, a trio for violin, clarinet, and piano, and a piano trio.

VOCAL MUSIC In 1922 Ives collected and published at his own expense a volume entitled *114 Songs* for distribution to friends free of charge. These works, like his many compositions for chorus, range from exceedingly simple to exceedingly complex.

Ives the Revolutionary: graduation portrait, Yale University, 1898. *Beneath the conventional clothing and demeanor lay an undergraduate seething at the strictures of musical convention. Ives had studied music at Yale with Horatio Parker, who was only 11 years older than Ives but already one of the most celebrated American composers of his generation. Parker was of the Old School—which is to say, the school of German tradition; Ives, in turn, came to Yale having already experimented with polytonality and quarter-tone tunings. The relationship of pupil and teacher was predictably strained.*

Source: Courtesy of Yale University Music Library

well. The high range of the bassoon makes the instrument sound strained, and the disconnected entrances of the other winds contribute to a sensation of hearing the orchestra in an inarticulate, almost chaotic state. We do not hear the traditions of Bach, Beethoven, or Brahms in these measures, but a more elemental, unrefined means of expression.

Textures in *Le Sacre du printemps* are correspondingly complex. The passage beginning at figure 11, for example, presents no fewer than 18 distinct and rhythmically unique ideas all at the same time. Although layered textures were certainly cultivated in the 19th century, nothing had ever approached this degree of intricacy. For most orchestras, the challenge of performing passages like this lies not in the notes themselves, but in the rhythms and the coordination of so many independent parts.

The audience rioted at the premiere of *Le Sacre du printemps*, in Paris in May 1913. As the composer himself later recalled:

> The complexity of my score had demanded a great number of rehearsals, which [Pierre] Monteux had conducted with his usual skill and attention. As for the actual performance, I am not in a position to judge, as I left the auditorium [to stand backstage in the wings] at the first bars of the prelude, which had at once evoked derisive laughter. I was disgusted. These demonstrations, at first isolated, soon became general, provoking counter-demonstrations and very quickly developing into a terrific uproar. During the whole performance I was at [the choreographer Vaslav] Nijinsky's side in the wings. He was standing on a chair, screaming "sixteen, seventeen, eighteen"—they had their own method of counting to keep time. Naturally, the poor dancers could hear nothing by reason of the row in the auditorium and the sound of their own dance steps. I had to hold Nijinsky by his clothes, for he was furious, and ready to dash on to the stage at any moment and create a scandal. [The impresario Sergei] Diaghilev kept ordering the electricians to turn the lights on or off, hoping in that way to put a stop to the noise. That is all I can remember about that first performance. Oddly enough, at the dress rehearsal, to which we had, as usual, invited a number of actors, painters, musicians, writers, and the most cultured representatives of society, everything had gone off peacefully, and I was very far from expecting such an outburst.[6]

But the riot soon turned to Stravinsky's advantage. Within a few short months, audiences across Europe were greeting *Le Sacre du printemps* with great enthusiasm, and the initial rejection of the work served to rally all artists of modernist tendencies. They saw in this incident a vindication of artistic vision in the face of conservative public tastes. Audiences, in turn, became less likely to express their opinions in quite such a physical fashion and began to become increasingly tolerant of modernism in general.

F O C U S

Sergei Diaghilev

Few nonmusicians exerted such an enormous effect on 20th-century music. As a producer, an impresario, Sergei Diaghilev (1872–1929) assembled teams of artists that included painters, dancers, choreographers, conductors, and composers. Finding just the right mix of talent could yield impressive results, and Diaghilev scored success after success in the first three decades of the 20th century. The "Russian Ballet" did in fact consist largely (but not exclusively) of Russian dancers, but the list of other artists Diaghilev engaged at various times includes many of the early 20th century's most distinguished figures:

♦ **Composers** Erik Satie, Igor Stravinsky, Sergei Prokofiev, Claude Debussy, Maurice Ravel, Darius Milhaud, Francis Poulenc, Manuel de Falla

♦ **Artists and stage designers** Pablo Picasso, Léon Bakst, Juan Gris, Georges Braque, Max Ernst, Juan Miró, Giorgio de Chirico

♦ **Dancers** Vaslav Nijinsky, Tamara Karsavina, Léonide Massine, George Balanchine, Anna Pavlova, Serge Lifar

Diaghilev's troupe cultivated many different styles of dance, but he is best remembered for his abandonment of the classical traditions of dance, moving away from graceful movements and women dancing *en pointe* (on the point of their toes) and toward a more vigorous, athletic kind of dance. The choreography for Stravinsky's *Le Sacre du printemps* exemplifies this new approach to ballet.

RAGTIME, JAZZ, AND COUNTRY MUSIC

Primitivism manifested itself more forcefully in the early 20th century in repertories heard outside the concert hall than those heard in it. The most important of these—ragtime, jazz, and country music—all developed in the United States.

Ragtime

Ragtime, which grew out of the largely unwritten tradition of African American dance, flourished at the end of the 19th century and in the early decades of the 20th. The music is usually in duple meter and based on units of 8 or 16 measures. Syncopation is prevalent throughout, thrown into relief by the steadiness of the bass line typically heard in the banjo music of minstrel shows (see Chapter 16). A piece in ragtime style typically follows the form of a march: three or four different themes, each running to 16 measures, with connecting material between sections. In ragtime, the opening theme is often repeated after the second theme. The structure of Joplin's *Maple Leaf Rag*, for example, follows the typical ragtime pattern of AA BB A CC DD.

Joplin
Maple Leaf Rag

Like its successors jazz and rock, ragtime met with considerable resistance, couched in complaints about its syncopated ("loose") rhythms and the purportedly loose morals of those who played and listened to it, but often grounded in unvarnished racism. One commentator, writing on the eve of World War I, called ragtime "a pernicious evil and enemy of true art," and urged readers to

> take a united stand against the Ragtime Evil as we would against bad literature, and horrors of war or intemperance and other socially destructive evils. In Christian homes, where purity of morals is stressed, ragtime should find no resting place. Avaunt with ragtime rot! Let us purge America and the Divine Art of Music from this polluting nuisance.[7]

Middle- and upper-class white listeners saw ragtime as irresistibly primitive in the positive sense: spontaneous and genuine, in contrast to what many viewed as the overly refined and decadent idioms of the concert hall and opera house. Charles Ives, who railed against the overly refined nature of the European tradition, also wrote a set of ragtime dances.

This distinctly American idiom soon captured the imagination of European artists as well. Stravinsky became familiar with the style during World War I and wrote *Ragtime for Eleven Instruments* (1917). Debussy's *Golliwog's Cakewalk*, from his *Children's Corner Suite* (1908), captures the rhythms of the style perfectly, even if the harmonies are at times distinctly chromatic. The cakewalk was a popular dance that featured prominently in minstrel shows of the 19th and early 20th centuries and were themselves a source of the ragtime style. Debussy adds a touch of irony to his work by incorporating into it (measures 61–63) an oblique reference to the celebrated "Tristan" chord of Wagner's *Tristan und Isolde* (see Chapter 17). He instructs the performer to play this passage haltingly, and "with great emotion," only to answer the quotation with a series of jaunty, disjointed eighth notes.

Debussy
Golliwog's Cakewalk

Jazz

The same kind of rhythmic liveliness so characteristic of ragtime is also prevalent in **jazz.** The term has been used to cover such an enormous range of musical styles that attempts at a concise definition seem futile. The trumpeter Louis Armstrong (1900–1971) once famously answered the question, "What is jazz?" by saying, "Man, man, if you gotta ask, you'll

Composer Profile

Igor Stravinsky
(1882–1971)

Stravinsky occupies a central place in the history of 20th-century music not only because of the quality of his works but also because of their remarkable range and variety. He was a true cosmopolitan who at various times called Russia, France, Switzerland, and the United States home. Like almost every composer of his generation, he absorbed the chromaticism and bombast of late Romanticism, but he went on to explore other idioms as well, including primitivism, Neoclassicism and, in the last 15 years of his life, even serial composition. His detractors called him a "musical chameleon," but the epithet does not give due credit to his remarkable ability to assimilate new styles and approaches to music. The phases of his career break down roughly in this way:

◆ Russian period. Like almost every other composer of his generation, Stravinsky began writing in a style of advanced chromaticism. The early ballets written for Diaghilev—*L'oiseau de feu* ("The Firebird"), *Petrouchka*—belong very much to the traditions of the 19th century. *Le Sacre du printemps* and *Les Noces* ("The Wedding") both mark a turn to primitivism; neither uses Russian folk melodies, but in their modal inflections, polytonality, and impulsive rhythmic vitality, both capture the spirit of what Stravinsky called "Pagan Russia."

◆ Neoclassical period. In the period after World War I, Stravinsky changed styles, moving toward a greater economy of both means and expression (see Chapter 22). The intensity of *Le Sacre* gave way to the cool detachment ("objectivity") of the Octet, the Concerto for Piano and Winds,

Pulcinella (another Diaghilev ballet, based on preexistent 18th-century material), the *Symphony in C,* the *Symphony in Three Movements,* the *Symphony of Psalms,* and the opera *The Rake's Progress.*

◆ Serialist period. Prompted in part by his personal assistant, Robert Craft, Stravinsky began studying serial music in the early 1950s and was drawn to the works of Anton Webern in particular. His own serial compositions using this technique include the ballet *Agon* (1957, only partly serial), *Threni* (1958), and the *Requiem Canticles* (1966).

Even during his lifetime Stravinsky was widely considered one of the century's two greatest composers (the other was Schoenberg). He always seemed to stay one step ahead of everyone else, reinventing himself at various points along the way. In spite of his avowed modernism (more than one critic dubbed him "Modernsky"), his music found a relatively wide following among concertgoers. Although he had no direct students, his influence on subsequent generations of composers was profound.

For a picture of Stravinsky, see Composer Profile: "Claude Debussy," where there is a photograph of him with Debussy.

Principal Works

BALLETS AND OTHER ORCHESTRAL WORKS Stravinsky made his early mark in the world through his ballets, particularly *L'oiseau de feu* (1910), *Petrouchka* (1911), *Le Sacre du printemps* (1913), and *Les Noces* (1920), all produced for Sergei Diaghilev's Ballets Russes in Paris. All three use striking orchestral effects, and the combined brilliance of their music and choreography soon propelled Stravinsky into the forefront of modernist composers. His later ballets include *Apollon Musagète* (1928), commissioned by

never know." Armstrong's response is at once evasive and revealing: he recognized that the term cannot be confined to a list of specific musical characteristics. Along these lines, more than one jazz musician has defined the art "not as a what, but a how." Jazz, in this view, is not so much a style of playing as an attitude, an approach toward music that embraces improvisation and rhythmic and intonational freedom, along with a general acceptance that the musical work exists in performance rather than in the form of a written score.

KEY DATES IN THE LIFE OF IGOR STRAVINSKY

1882 Born June 17, son of the famous bassist Feodor Stravinsky, in Oranieneburg, near St. Petersburg.

1903 While studying law, begins private lessons with Nikolai Rimsky-Korsakov, the leading Russian composer of his day.

1910 Premiere of the ballet *L'oiseau de feu* in Paris, commissioned by the Russian impresario Sergei Diaghilev.

1911 Moves to Paris and produces a string of stunningly successful ballets for Diaghilev: *Petrouchka* (1911), *Le Sacre du printemps* (1913), *Le Rossignol* (1914), *Pulcinella* (1920), *Les Noces* (1923).

1925 First American tour; he receives many commissions from American patrons and institutions from this point onward.

1934 Becomes a French citizen.

1939 Leaves France, settles in Hollywood, and becomes an American citizen in 1945.

1939–1940 Delivers (in French) the Charles Eliot Norton Lectures at Harvard University, largely ghost-written by the composer Roland-Alexis Manuel Lévy.

1950–1962 Tours and conducts widely, including a return to the Soviet Union in 1962, where he is welcomed warmly.

1971 Dies in New York on April 6 and is buried in Venice, near Diaghilev.

the Elizabeth Sprague Coolidge Foundation and premiered in Washington, D.C., at the Library of Congress; *Perséphone* (1934), with recitation and chorus, to a text by André Gide; *Jeu de cartes* ("Card Game," 1937); and *Orpheus* (1948).

The reputation of the ballets tends to overshadow that of the symphonies, all of which are significant works in the history of the genre: the *Symphony for Winds* (1920, written in memory of Debussy), the *Symphony in C* (1940), the *Symphony in Three Movements* (1945), and above all the *Symphony of Psalms* (1930) for chorus and orchestra, commissioned by the Boston Symphony Orchestra. Stravinsky also wrote several significant (and quite individual) concertos: for piano and winds (1924), for violin (1931), for clarinet and swing band (the *Ebony Concerto,* 1946), for chamber orchestra (the Dumbarton Oaks Concerto, 1938), and for string orchestra (the Concerto in D, 1947).

VOCAL AND DRAMATIC WORKS *L'Histoire du soldat* ("The Soldier's Tale," 1918) is scored for narrator and seven instrumentalists and written in Stravinsky's Neoclassical style, as is the "opera-oratorio" *Oedipus Rex* (1927), based on Sophocles' drama, which can be performed either in concert or as a theatrical piece. *The Rake's Progress* (1951), acknowledged by most to be Stravinsky's greatest opera, set to an English-language libretto by W. H. Auden and Chester Kallman, was inspired by a series of engravings by the 18th-century English artist William Hogarth; the work traces the decline and fall of a libertine.

CHAMBER WORKS In addition to the Octet (1923), Stravinsky wrote a number of small-scale works for chamber ensembles: the *Duo concertante* for violin and piano, The Septet for piano, strings, and winds (1954), and an instrumental arrangement of three madrigals by the Renaissance composer Gesualdo (1960).

Like ragtime, jazz originated in the largely unwritten traditions of African-American dance and song, combined with other diverse influences such as marching band music, hymnody, and improvisatory storytelling. In the 1920s, it appealed as modernist art by virtue of its emphasis on rhythm, its freedom of improvisation, and what was perceived to be a kind of purity of spontaneous expression, seemingly devoid of calculated artifice.

Composer Profile

Scott Joplin
(1868-1917)

Scott Joplin was not the first African-American composer, nor was he the first composer of ragtime music, but he was without question the most famous on both counts in his time. As a musician, he was largely self-taught and earned his early living by playing the piano in saloons, brothels, and music halls. His *Maple Leaf Rag* propelled him to instant fame: the piece sold 75,000 copies in its first six months and would eventually sell more than a million.

In spite of these successes, Joplin struggled to achieve his greatest dream, which was to integrate ragtime into the established forms of opera. The music to his first opera, *A Guest of Honor,* is lost, and if the work was performed publicly at all, it received little notice. Joplin published a piano-vocal score of a second opera, *Treemonisha,* at his own expense in 1911, but it was not well received in a concert performance of 1915. Its first staged performance did not take place until 1972, when it opened to rave reviews in Washington, D.C. Today we would call Joplin a crossover artist; audiences of his own time seem not to have been prepared to make the jump. Joplin's failure to break into the

KEY DATES IN THE LIFE OF SCOTT JOPLIN
1868 Born November 24 in Texarkana, Texas.
1882 Leaves home and earns a living in St. Louis and other towns by playing the piano in brothels, saloons, and variety halls.
1896 Settles in Sedalia, Missouri; enrolls in harmony and composition courses at George R. Smith College for Negroes.
1899 Publishes *Maple Leaf Rag* and achieves instant fame.
1907 Moves to New York City; begins work on his opera *Treemonisha* two years later.
1911 Publishes *Treemonisha* at his own expense; the work is performed in concert in 1915 but does not reach the stage until 1972.
1917 Dies April 1 in New York City.

prestigious realm of opera was also doubtless due to racial prejudices against ragtime. As in the later cases of jazz and rock and roll, however, white

The **blues** were a particularly important force in the development of jazz. The text of a blues song is by definition a lament, bemoaning poverty, social injustice, fatigue, or, most famously of all, lost love. This type of song originated in the South among enslaved African Americans and their descendants. Early recorded examples preserve the artistry of such individuals as Ma Rainey (1886–1939) and Blind Willie Johnson (1902–1947). Later artists who cultivated the blues include Howlin' Wolf (Chester Arthur Burnett, 1910–1976), Muddy Waters (McKinley Morganfield, 1915–1983), and B. B. King (b. 1925). The standard instrumental version of a blues song rests on a repeated harmonic pattern of 12 measures in 4/4 time, which in turn is divided into three groups of 4 measures each. A series of variations on this pattern is known as the **12-bar blues form.** A typical harmonic progression within a single 12-measure unit might look something like this:

Measure number	1	2	3	4	5	6	7	8	9	10	11	12
Harmony	I				IV		I		V		I	

musicians were quick to adopt the style: Irving Berlin scored great success with such works as *Alexander's Ragtime Band* (1911). Joplin's popularity enjoyed a revival in 1974 when arrangements of his music were used in the soundtrack to the movie *The Sting.* Today, his piano pieces are acknowledged, as one critic has observed, as the American counterparts to Chopin's mazurkas and Brahms's

waltzes, both in musical quality and in the manner in which each captures the spirit of its time and place.

Principal Works

Aside from two operas (see above), various songs, waltzes, and marches, Joplin's output consists of about fifty piano rags.

A drawing of Scott Joplin and the title page from an early edition of his Maple Leaf Rag. *Joplin rocketed to fame with the publication of this work in 1899. Legend has it that the publisher, John Stark, heard Joplin playing it in the Maple Leaf Club, a saloon in Sedalia, Missouri, and later offered him $50 plus royalties on the work. Maple Leaf Rag eventually sold more than a million copies.*

Source: (left) © 2000 CORBIS BETTMANN; (right) Getty Images Inc.—Hulton Archive Photos

This basic structure, like that of the basse danse forms of the Renaissance (see Chapters 5 and 6), leaves room for enormous variation. Harmonies can be altered, enriched, or made to move at a faster speed, and melodies can easily be changed to accommodate the text. In performance, a blues song is fluid in spite of its underlying structure. Vocalists are free to improvise, and the text, even if metered, can be declaimed irregularly, stretching the music to accommodate any number of syllables at any given point. The characteristic sound of the blues is shaped by the **blue note,** the slightly lowered third or seventh degree in the major scale. For an example of this, listen to the first "ain't" in *It Don't Mean a Thing* as performed by Duke Ellington's band.

Dippermouth Blues, as recorded by Joe Oliver and his Creole Jazz Band in 1923, is a good example of an instrumental blues number. After an introduction of four measures, the music falls into nine sections, each consisting of 12 measures and based on the principal tune. Each of these sections is known generically as a **chorus.** The first two of these choruses are performed by the full ensemble, followed by two featuring the clarinetist Johnny Dodds. Sections 5 and 8, again for full ensemble, frame a pair of sections with

Composer Profile

Duke Ellington
(1899-1974)

Ellington always struggled with musical labels. He resisted being categorized as a "jazz musician" and wrote in a variety of styles reflecting, at various times, the influences of the big band sound, swing, bop, cool jazz, rock, and many kinds of classical music. In his own way, Ellington synthesized as many styles as Stravinsky. But in the case of Ellington, critics were slow to accept this variety. When "The Duke" began to explore larger forms and more classically inspired idioms, disappointed listeners accused him of "abandoning jazz." Ellington himself insisted that "there are simply two kinds of music, the good kind and the other kind."[8]

In any event, Ellington was widely hailed in the 1930s as the leading jazz composer of his time. For almost fifty years, he was able to assemble and direct a remarkable group of musicians who toured the country and eventually the world. They could (and did) function as a dance band, but they went far beyond this. Their celebrated Carnegie Hall concert of 1943 included the premiere of *Black, Brown, and Beige,* a tone poem tracing the history of African Americans and suggesting, metaphorically, the eventual integration of American society. The concert concluded with the presentation of a plaque signed by Kurt Weill, Aaron Copland, Marian Anderson, Leopold Stokowski, and others. The entire event symbolized a bridging of both racial and musical barriers, although many of Ellington's subsequent audiences, particularly in the South, would remain segregated until the 1960s.

Like his near contemporary, Aaron Copland, Ellington was hugely feted toward the end of his life, receiving the Presidential Medal of Freedom (1969) and some seventeen honorary degrees. The U.S. State Department sponsored a tour of the Soviet Union in 1970 at a period of intense tension between the two superpowers. In spite—or more likely because—of the Soviet government's tendency to discourage jazz, Ellington and his group were wildly received there: at some concerts, tickets sold for eight times their face value.[9]

Principal Works

SONGS Ellington's most celebrated songs (many of which he wrote in collaboration with his colleague Billy Strayhorn) include *Mood Indigo, Don't Get Around Much Anymore, I Got it Bad (And That Ain't Good), Prelude to a Kiss,* and *Satin Doll.* Ellington made multiple arrangements of all his songs, both with and without lyrics.

INSTRUMENTAL MUSIC Harlem and *Black, Brown, and Beige* are tone poems that take as their subject the history of African Americans. Ellington also wrote extended works that highlighted his own instrumentalists, such as *Echoes of Harlem* and *Concerto for Cootie,* both created for his principal trumpeter, Cootie Williams. The 1932 recording of *It Don't Mean a Thing (If It Ain't Got That Swing)* illustrates a typical Ellingtonian arrangement that allows successive members of his group to shine.

KEY DATES IN THE LIFE OF DUKE ELLINGTON

1899 Born Edward Kennedy Ellington on April 29 in Washington, D.C.; later nicknamed "Duke" because of his personal elegance and bearing.

1923 Moves to New York City and forms his first band.

1939 Begins collaborating with the songwriter and arranger Billy Strayhorn; together the two create some of the band's most memorable hits.

1943 First of several concerts at Carnegie Hall.

1965 First of a series of "Sacred Concerts," events for which Ellington wrote new music to sacred texts.

1970 Tours Soviet Union under the sponsorship of the U.S. Department of State as a "goodwill ambassador."

1974 Dies in New York on May 24.

solos by the group's leader, the trumpeter Joe "King" Oliver. A final section for full ensemble and a brief two-measure conclusion bring the work to its close. This pattern of a full ensemble alternating with a series of featured soloists, is basic to the structure of many jazz numbers in performance.

Duke Ellington's *It Don't Mean a Thing (If It Ain't Got that Swing)*, written in 1932, represents jazz in the "Swing Era" of the 1930s and 1940s. Swing rhythm features a hard meter but a subtle avoidance of cadences and downbeats, with the soloist placing notes either just ahead or just behind the beat in a way that heightened the music's rhythmic suppleness. Swing was also dominated by the sound of what were called big bands, relatively large ensembles consisting of piano, drums, double bass, and a large complement of winds: saxophones (often five—two altos, two tenors, one baritone) and groups of three or four trumpets, trombones, and clarinets. Many of these bands also featured a vocal soloist. Each group sought to establish its own distinctive sound through its orchestration, often dictated by the leader's instrument and tastes—Duke Ellington's piano, Harry James's trumpet, Glenn Miller's trombone, Artie Shaw's clarinet.

Ellington
It Don't Mean a Thing

Formally, the original song version of Ellington's *It Don't Mean a Thing* consists of an 8-measure instrumental introduction, followed by a 2-measure **vamp,** a short progression of chords that can be repeated indefinitely before the entrance of the voice. The **verse** ("What good is melody . . .")[10] consists of 16 measures (2 × 8) that end on a half cadence leading to the song's chorus or principal melody. The chorus itself consists of four units of 8 measures each whose thematic content follows the pattern AABA. This pattern is so common in 20th-century song that it has come to be known as **song form.** The contrasting B section (here, from the words "It makes no diff'rence" through "ev'rything you got") is often known as the **bridge** because it connects statements of the A theme.

When Ellington recorded this number with his band in 1932, he substantially reworked the form of the piece. The recorded version omits the introduction and begins with 10 measures of the vamp, in which the singer (Ivie Anderson) uses her voice as an instrument, singing syncopated nonsense syllables against the steady beat of the bass in a technique known as **scat singing.** The 32-measure verse, expanded from the song's 16-measure version, is allotted to a solo muted trombone. The voice, in turn, presents the chorus in its full 32-measure form. At this point, the instruments take over with a series of quasi-improvised solos. In rehearsal, Ellington and his group would have planned who would play these solos and in what order. Beyond this, each instrumentalist was free to improvise at will, knowing in advance the basic chord progressions with which the band would support him. In this particular performance, we hear only one extended solo, given to the saxophonist (Johnny Hodges), who varies thematic elements of both verse and chorus. The full band then plays the opening of the chorus; the vocalist returns with the bridge passage, and the work concludes with the syncopated "doo-wah" fragmented on the muted brass.

Other performances of this same work by Ellington vary the number and sequence of the soloists, the order in which verse and chorus are first presented, the final cadence, and countless other features large and small. Jazz performances by their very nature represent a fusion of composed and improvised elements.

Country Music

Like jazz, country music embraces a variety of styles and represents the synthesis of many different musical traditions, most of them unwritten. The most important of these are Anglo-American folk song, hymnody, and traditional dance tunes. As early as the 17th century, country dancing in England was a lively type of social dance accompanied by one or two fiddles. Unlike courtly dance, these steps—reels, jigs, hornpipes, and the like—were often fast and physical. Transplanted to the American colonies, these musical traditions were cultivated with particular intensity in the rural South. The singing and playing style of country music was decidedly uncultivated; its energetic and sometimes rough-edged quality gave it an emotionally authentic quality.

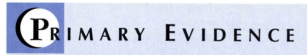

PRIMARY EVIDENCE

Jazz and the Question of Stylistic "Purity" (1943)

Winthrop Sargeant, a highly influential music critic of the mid–20th century, was deeply sympathetic to jazz (he wrote a book on the subject in 1938), but his sympathy had a patronizing edge. The appeal of jazz, Sargeant argued, lay in its directness and simplicity. He was alarmed that jazz in its so-called "pure" form was beginning to mix too much with other styles of composition and thereby lose its essential, primitive, quality. What bothered Sargeant was what would trouble many others over subsequent decades, whether they admitted it or not: jazz was evolving in new directions, not remaining what it had once been. Ellington responded gracefully but with force.

• • • • •

Sargeant's Critique

The mistake of the fashionable jazz aesthetes has been to take jazz out of the simple sidewalk and dance hall milieu where it belongs and pretend that it is a complex, civilized art. In its own surroundings, jazz need make no apologies. It is the most vital folk music of our time; it is distinctly and indigenously American, and it speaks a new, infectious dialect that is fresher than anything of the sort Europe has evolved in centuries. It is, I think, something of a pity that, in a watered-down commercial form, jazz has virtually drowned out every other form of American popular music. . . . Curiously enough, the mass-produced, commercialized product is also tending to swamp what is left of real, improvised jazz. It is already obvious that the fresh, ingenuous type of jazz the Negroes of New Orleans and Chicago played a generation ago is unlikely ever to be heard again except in phonograph records. Thus, the original spring of jazz has run dry—and for very logical reasons. The musical dialect of jazz, like verbal dialects, owes its development to its remoteness from standardized education. One of its most important ingredients has been the rather colorful awkwardness—the lack of technical polish—with which it is played. And that awkwardness, when genuine, is the fruit of ignorance.

Jazz appeared in the first place because the poor Southern Negro couldn't get a regular musical education, and decided to make his own homemade kind of music without it. His ingenuity has proved him to be one of the world's most gifted instinctive musicians. But as his lot improves, and with it his facilities for musical education, he is bound to be attracted by the bigger scope and intricacy of civilized concert music. Give him the chance to study, and the Negro will soon turn from boogie woogie to Beethoven.

Ellington's Response

Mr. Sargeant has evidently not been exposed to some of the more intelligent jazz, nor is he aware of the amazing musical background of some of our foremost composers and arrangers, in the popular field. . . .

He says that "harmony in jazz is restricted to four or five monotonous patterns," and names the blues, to substantiate this strange statement. I would be interested in knowing how he has managed to arrive at his classifications. Everyone knows that the blues is built upon a set pattern, as is, for example, the sonnet form in poetry. Yet this hasn't seemed to limit poetry to four or five monotonous patterns, nor, do I think is jazz so limited. . . .

Most of all, I was struck by Mr. Sargeant's concluding statement, that given a chance to study, the Negro will soon turn from boogie woogie to Beethoven. Maybe so, but what a shame! There is so much that is good in a musical expression in the popular field.

Source: Winthrop Sargeant, "Is Jazz Music?" *American Mercury* 57 (1943): 403–9; Duke Ellington, "Defense of Jazz," *American Mercury* 57 (1944): 124. Courtesy Enoch Pratt Free Library. H. L. Mencken Collection.

Long known simply as "old-time" or "mountain" music, country music was performed by and appealed to a largely rural population. Unlike piano rags and popular songs of the early 20th century, country music was played on such instruments as the fiddle, banjo, guitar, mandolin, autoharp, and double bass—all of them readily mobile and capable of being played outdoors, in contrast to the piano, a parlor instrument associated more closely with the urban middle classes. Country musicians were for the most part not professionally trained.

With the rise of radio in the 1920s, the popularity of country music began to extend well beyond the South. On November 28, 1925, station WSM in Nashville, Tennessee, began broadcasting a program called *The WSM Barn Dance* and its first performer, 77-year-old "Uncle" Jimmy Thompson, who claimed he could "fiddle the bugs off tater vine," was old enough to have fought in the Civil War.[11] The show changed its name to *The Grand Ole Opry* in 1928 to emphasize its distinction from the "high" art of grand opera. Yet as an institution, The Grand Ole Opry functioned very much like the great opera houses of Europe, for its impresarios launched many a career. By the late 1930s the weekly show, now performed before a large studio audience, was being broadcast nationwide.

Foggy Mountain Breakdown, as recorded by Lester Flatt, Earl Scruggs, and the Foggy Mountain Boys in 1949, represents the country music subgenre of **bluegrass,** which emerged in the 1940s and whose characteristic sound is an acoustic string ensemble of banjo, guitar, fiddle, and double bass. The banjo is picked (as opposed to strummed), and vocals tend to be pitched in the upper end of the singer's register, creating what has been described as a "high, lonesome sound." The characteristic syncopation of bluegrass anticipates the downbeat slightly, in contrast to jazz, in which performers often play just slightly behind the beat. The resulting rhythms are propulsive and infectious—"folk music with overdrive" as one commentator described it. In *Foggy Mountain Breakdown,* Scruggs demonstrates his renowned technique of three-finger banjo picking. The virtuosity is dazzling, even within the relatively simple harmonic and metrical confines of this particular number. The piece also reveals formal similarities with the basic patterns of many jazz numbers: soloists take turns improvising variations on a given theme or harmonic pattern. Like jazz, bluegrass and other forms of country music provided performers with a framework for improvisation.

Flatt and Scruggs
Foggy Mountain Breakdown

NATIONALISM

Musical nationalism, like primitivism, was driven by a desire to return to cultural roots through a musical idiom connected to the people. Already evident in the 19th century (see Chapter 14), musical nationalism took on new importance in the 20th with the growing political and cultural aspirations of ethnic groups throughout Europe and the Americas. The Austro-Hungarian Empire, ruled by the Habsburg dynasty from its German-speaking capital of Vienna, provides a good example of the ethnic diversity within a single political entitity. In 1900, the Habsburgs governed an empire that encompassed portions or all of what are now Austria, Hungary, the Czech Republic, Slovakia, Croatia, Slovenia, Bosnia, Herzegovina, Serbia, Romania, Poland, and even Italy. Yet each of these regions had its own language and culture, and music was an important means of asserting ethnic identity.

When Béla Bartók set out into the field to record the melodies sung and played by peasants (see the photograph in Composer Profile: "Béla Bartók"), he was thus attempting to capture not only a repertory of songs but also the very identity of the ethnic groups singing them. Bartók and others like him were driven in part by the belief that folk song represents the untarnished purity of preindustrial society.

Composer Profile

Béla Bartók
(1881–1945)

Alongside his conventional training as a pianist and composer, Béla Bartók developed an intense interest in the folk musics of central and eastern Europe. He took advantage of recent developments in recording technology to make what we would now call field recordings, and his published transcriptions attempt to capture nuances of singing and playing not normally notated in concert repertory. Bartók had a keen ear for the more fluid sense of pitch and meter in the unwritten tradition, along with its flexible rhythms and distinctive timbres.

This kind of music eventually worked its influence on Bartók's own compositions. He wrote his earliest works in the style of Brahms, but from about 1905 onward most of his music incorporates at least some elements that give it an ethnic sound. For Bartók, the idioms of the people offered a source of inspiration and tradition that was at once genuine and a departure from the established (and predominantly German) tradition of Bach, Haydn, Mozart, Beethoven, and Brahms. Bartók sometimes used folk tunes more or less directly, adding harmonies; on other occasions he created original tunes with folk-like inflections.

Leaving his position at the Royal Academy of Budapest, Bartók emigrated to the United States in 1940, but his music did not at first generate much interest in North America beyond a small group of dedicated enthusiasts. His *Concerto for Orchestra* (1944), however, commissioned by Serge Koussevitsky, the conductor of the Boston Symphony Orchestra, soon established itself as one of the most popular of all 20th-century orchestral works. Unfortunately, the composer died of leukemia less than a year after its premiere.

KEY DATES IN THE LIFE OF BÉLA BARTÓK

1881 Born March 25 in Nagyszentmiklós, in the Transylvania region of Hungary (now Romania).

1899 Enters the Royal Academy of Music in Budapest and studies both piano and composition.

1905 Begins collaboration with the composer Zoltán Kodály to collect folk music of central and eastern Europe; continues to travel to remote regions to record and transcribe the songs and instrumental music of many different ethnic groups.

1907 Appointed piano instructor at Royal Academy of Music, Budapest.

1922 Tours London and Paris, performing his own music and accompanying a number of noted violinists.

1927–1928 Makes his first tours of the United States and the Soviet Union.

1934 Commissioned by the Hungarian Academy of Sciences to prepare an edition of some thirteen thousand Hungarian folk songs; the work would be completed and published posthumously.

1940 Emigrates to the United States and settles in New York; receives an honorary degree from Columbia University.

1941 Takes position as research fellow at Columbia to pursue folk song studies; receives several major commissions for new compositions.

1945 Dies in New York on September 26.

Principal Works

ORCHESTRAL WORKS Music for Strings, Percussion, and Celesta (1937) and Concerto for Orchestra (1944) are two of the most popular of all 20th-century orchestral works. The Violin Concerto (1939) and the Third Piano Concerto (1945) have also established themselves in the repertory. Other works for orchestra include the Concerto for Two Pianos and Orchestra (1942, an arrangement of his own Sonata for Two Pianos and Percussion) and the Viola Concerto (1945, completed by his pupil Tibor Serly).

VOCAL AND DRAMATIC WORKS Bluebeard's Castle (1911), an opera in one act, and the ballets The Wooden Prince (1917) and The Miraculous Mandarin (1919) are admired but have not achieved the popularity of some of the orchestral works.

CHAMBER MUSIC The six string quartets rank among the greatest in the literature. As in the case of Beethoven, we can trace the composer's development from early to late styles in these works, which explore an astonishing variety of forms, tones, and instrumental techniques. Bartók's two sonatas for violin and piano, as well as a sonata for solo violin, are also significant additions to the repertory.

PIANO MUSIC In the tradition of J. S. Bach, Bartók wrote many pedagogical works for his own children and pupils, most notably Mikrokosmos, a set of 153 progressive works, many of them influenced by his work as a collector of traditional musics. His Allegro barbaro and his many Hungarian and Romanian dances for piano also incorporate folklike elements.

Bartók records in the field (1908).
Bartók was one of the first researchers to make field recordings of folk musicians. His recordings and transcriptions of music from across eastern Europe remain a valuable source of information for ethnographers. In Bartók's day, the musical traditions of the remote villages he visited were still relatively untouched by the growing influence of urbanization, radio, and recorded sound. The villagers are dressed in their Sunday finest: this is, after all, a memorable day in the life of the village. But their garb manifests a more subtle problem faced by field workers who go out to collect "authentic" data. The formality of the occasion might well affect the nature of the performance. Would a villager dressed in his Sunday finest sing for an outsider with a strange recording device in exactly the same way as when dressed in ordinary work clothes singing in an everyday setting?

Source: CORBIS BETTMANN

For modernist composers, folk music offered important stylistic alternatives to the traditions of conventional melody and harmony. Bartók and his colleague Zoltán Kodály (1882–1967) found an altogether different set of melodic possibilities in the folk music of various ethnic groups they collected throughout central and eastern Europe. The two made frequent use of distinctively ethnic characteristics in their own music. They often incorporated irregular rhythms and meters and generally avoided the conventions of functional harmony, preferring instead to substitute intervals of the second, fourth, and seventh in favor of the traditional triad. They also drew on a variety of nondiatonic scales, including whole tone and pentatonic.

Bartók
Six Dances in Bulgarian Rhythm

Bartók in particular favored the kind of irregular meters that characterize a good deal of the folk music of eastern Europe. The first of his *Six Dances in Bulgarian Rhythm* from his *Mikrokosmos,* Book 6, for example, is built on a metrical pattern notated as follows:

$$\frac{4+2+3}{8}$$

This kind of meter is sometimes referred to as complex meter, and although it ostensibly had its origins in folk music, it found its way into much modernist music as well.

Nor were Bartók and Kodaly alone in such ventures. Charles Ives worked many traditional American melodies not only into his songs, but also his symphonies and string quartets. George Gershwin, in turn, regarded jazz as "an American folk music; not the only one but a very powerful one which is probably in the blood and feeling of the American people more than any other style." Gershwin's *Rhapsody in Blue* (1924), for piano and orchestra, was one of the earliest of many works by American composers to integrate the jazz idiom into the repertory of the concert hall. Igor Stravinsky, drawing on recent Russian scholarship of the time, adapted several published folk melodies to great effect in *Le Sacre du printemps.* The English composer Ralph Vaughan Williams (1872–1958) made his own intensive study of English folk song and frequently incorporated such melodies into his own music.

Milhaud
Saudades do Brasil

Composers could, of course, also freely adapt the music of cultures not their own. The French composer Darius Milhaud (1892–1974) drew on Latin American tunes and dance rhythms in his *Saudades do Brasil* ("Nostalgia for Brazil," 1921). These dances integrate popular dance rhythms into a harmonic idiom that is delightfully unpredictable. Milhaud's use of polytonality distinguishes his music from the sounds we would be likely to hear in the streets of, say, Rio de Janeiro; yet the rhythms are true to life enough to provide the music with a decidedly Brazilian flavor.

NEW TIMBRES

In addition to rhythm and pitch, many modernist composers of the early 20th century sought novelty in timbre, through new instruments or new ways of playing old instruments.

Cowell
The Banshee

Although the 20th century brought relatively few technical changes to the piano itself, composers developed many novel ways of using the existing instrument. In *The Banshee* (1925), Henry Cowell (1897–1965) calls on the performer to manipulate directly by hand the strings inside the instrument. The unearthly effect is unlike anything anyone had heard before this time. The eerie quality of the sound fits with the work's title. In Cowell's own words, a banshee is "a woman of the Inner World . . . who is charged with the duty of taking your soul into the Inner World when you die. . . . She has to come to the outer plane for this purpose, and she finds the outer plane very uncomfortable and unpleasant, so you will hear her wailing at the time of a death in your family."[12]

In some of his other works for piano, like *Advertisement* (1914), Cowell pioneered the use of tone clusters, directing that adjacent keys be struck with the forearm, flat of the hand, or some object of an appropriate shape, such as a block of wood. This technique foreshadowed the sounds of the "prepared piano" devised by one of Cowell's pupils, John Cage (1912–1992), who in the 1940s began placing objects like paper clips and pieces of rubber and wood on the strings to produce unusual sounds.

Edgard Varèse's *Ionisation* (1931) is another seminal work reflecting the growing range of sounds available to 20th-century composers. The title (the French word for "atomic fission") comes from the world of nuclear physics, and the timbre is appropriately abstract and challenging. *Ionisation* is the first major composition to have been written entirely for percussion. Most of the 37 instruments have no definite pitch at all: four tam-tams, gong, cymbals, three different sizes of bass drum, bongos, snare drums, guero ("scraper"), slapsticks, Chinese blocks, claves ("rhythm sticks"), triangle, maracas ("shakers"), sleigh bells, castanets, tambourine, anvils, and two sirens. The entrance of pitched instruments (piano, celesta, chimes) toward the end of the work creates a strange sensation, for by this point listeners have somehow grown accustomed to the sound of no pitches of any kind.

Not everyone shared Varèse's enthusiasm for the new, and like a good many modernist pieces, *Ionisation* alienated its share of critics. One of them—writing anonymously—had this to say about the work's premiere, in New York's Carnegie Hall, in 1933:

> Varèse's latest effort, played twice, contains almost nothing of traditional tonal quality, being scored for various gatling-gun species of percussion, a dolorous and quaintly modulated siren, sleigh bells and an ingenious instrument that imitated the voice of an anguished bull. Toward the end of this strange work, which moved even earnest devotees of the musically esoteric to smiles, there was a slight undercurrent of the lyrical in some muted tones of a piano and a celesta.[13]

Although such reviews make for entertaining reading today, we should not lose sight of the genuine difficulties posed by a work like *Ionisation.* No one had ever heard a work of this size written almost entirely without fixed pitches, and it conformed to no established convention of form or genre.

CONCLUSION

The early decades of the 20th century witnessed a series of radical challenges to established musical conventions. Claude Debussy, Igor Stravinsky, and Charles Ives, each in his own way, developed strikingly original approaches to such basic elements of music as melody, harmony, rhythm, and form. Primitivism emerged as a driving force in all the arts, but nowhere more strongly than in music, which embraced the elemental rhythms of Stravinsky's ballets and Scott Joplin's ragtime piano pieces. The emotional authenticity of jazz and country music also spoke directly to audiences weary of an art that to their minds had become overly refined. Along similar lines, folk music—the unwritten tradition—offered fresh alternatives to composers interested in exploring new approaches to melody, harmony, and rhythm. The musical idioms of eastern European peoples recorded by Béla Bartók and others provided an important source of inspiration to composers looking for new sounds. Still other composers, like Henry Cowell and Edgard Varèse, extended the range of timbres inherited from the 19th century, either through performing on old instruments in new ways or through the cultivation of instruments that had not previously been used in the concert hall. The sound of the early 20th century, in short, was decidedly new.

Beyond Tonality

Around the turn of the 20th century, as we have seen, several prominent composers were exploring extended chromaticism as an alternative to triadic harmony based on the major and minor diatonic scales. Among these composers were Gustav Mahler (particularly in his later works, such as the Ninth and unfinished Tenth Symphonies and *Das Lied von der Erde*), Hugo Wolf, and Richard Strauss (especially in the operas *Elektra* and *Salome*), as well as Claude Debussy. Indeed, the chromatic harmonies of Wagner's *Tristan und Isolde* (see Chapter 17) no longer seemed so radical by 1908 when Debussy poked fun at the celebrated "Tristan" chord by quoting it—quite out of context—in his own *Children's Corner Suite* (see Chapter 20).

None of the elements characteristic of early-20th-century extended chromatic harmony was new. Augmented triads, extended sonorities built on thirds (9th, 11th, and 13th chords), unresolved dissonances, nonharmonic tones, nonfunctional bass lines, enharmonicism, fleeting or merely implied tonicization, parallel voice leading—all of these can be found in the music of the mid– to late 19th century. What *was* new at this time was the substantially greater prominence given to all these kinds of features.

The boundary between extreme chromaticism and **atonality**—the absence of a tonal center—is often difficult to identify. By the time he had completed his Chamber Symphony, op. 9, Schoenberg was beginning to recognize that chromatic harmony was approaching the point at which distinctions between dissonance and consonance had become almost meaningless. At some point, logically, the extended avoidance of a tonal center becomes the absence of a tonal center.

ATONALITY

The opening of Schoenberg's Chamber Symphony in E major, op. 9 (1906) provides a good illustration of the limits of traditional chromatic tonality (Example 21-1). The initial chord builds up gradually out of a series of fourths rather than thirds (G-C-F-B♭-E♭-A♭). This sonority resolves to an F-major chord in measure 4 through an augmented sixth chord on G♭ (a French sixth) that includes an additional A♭. The goal of this progression is clearly tonal: there is nothing ambiguous about the second chord in measure 4. But the manner in which the music arrives at this harmony makes the triadic sonority seem all the more isolated and out of place, as if it is the consonance that is dissonant. The tonal basis of the work is further confused by the following four measures, which open with a different series of fourths (D-G-C-F-B♭-E♭) that then move through a series of whole-tone chords in descending parallel motion. The sense of a goal-oriented functional harmony is so remote here that its very presence is called into doubt. Once again, the resolution (vii⁷/E with an added D, moving to E major) sounds almost out of place, even though it is perfectly correct according to the standards of traditional harmony and voice leading.

Schoenberg knew he was in the process of saying farewell to tonality: the third movement of his earlier Second String Quartet, op. 10 (1908), had incorporated a lengthy quotation from the children's song *Ach, Du lieber Augustin* (better known in English as "Did you ever see a lassie go this way and that way?"), in which the relentless repetition of tonic and dominant harmonies dissolves into banality. Schoenberg wanted

Example 21-1 Schoenberg, Chamber Symphony in E major, op. 9 (1906), measures 1–8.

to wean the public from its entrenched familiarity with tonality and explore, in the words sung by the solo soprano who enters in the finale to the Second String Quartet, the "air of other planets." The public, for the most part, was reluctant to travel with him.

Partly independently, partly in conjunction with his pupil-colleagues Anton Webern and Alban Berg, Schoenberg persisted in advancing what he called "the emancipation of the dissonance." In a truly atonal idiom, Schoenberg argued, dissonances would no longer be considered a "spicy addition to dull sounds" but instead the "natural and logical outgrowths" of a musical "organism."[1] Schoenberg hated the term *atonality,* on the grounds that it defined an idiom in terms of what it was not. "I am a musician," Schoenberg declared, "and I have nothing to do with the atonal. Atonal might well mean simply: something that corresponds in no way to the essential nature of tones. . . . A piece of music will always be tonal, at least in the sense that there must be some kind of a relationship from one tone to the next."[2] He advocated calling such music *pantonal,* but the term never caught on.

The impetus toward atonality was more than merely technical. Schoenberg, Webern, and Berg were searching for a new way of writing music whose emotional impact would be more direct and immediate than anything available in the vocabulary of extended chromaticism. Atonality, as it turned out, was particularly well suited to the aesthetics of **expressionism,** a broad artistic movement of the time that sought to give voice (expression) to the unconscious, to make manifest humanity's deepest and often darkest emotions. Expressionism is related to primitivism in that both attempt to strip away the veneer of so-called civilized behavior and reveal the darkest recesses of human emotion. In Freudian terms, expressionist art bypasses the ego, the conscious self, and aims straight for the id, the unconscious repository of basic instincts and drives. Expressionism in all its forms—in literature, painting, cinema, and music—rejects conventional techniques of representation, favoring instead devices that exaggerate and distort.

Expressionist art is not a means of escaping the human condition, but rather of confronting it. The quintessential act of expressionism is the scream (see "The Scream," Plate 20 in color insert IV), an utterance that is not a word, a product of civilization, but rather an intense, spontaneous reaction to something that has caused pain or fear. Indeed, the Austrian poet and critic Hermann Bahr (1863–1934) defined expressionism precisely in terms of this act: "Man screams from the depths of his soul; the whole era becomes a single, piercing shriek. Art also screams, into the deep darkness, screams for help, screams for the spirit. This is expressionism."[3]

Schoenberg, who was deeply sympathetic to expressionist art, and whose own paintings are very much within the expressionist idiom (see the photograph of him with his self-portraits in the Composer Profile), was drawn to the surreal, violent, and eerie imagery in Albert Giraud's *Pierrot lunaire,* a cycle of 21 poems that had recently been translated from their original French into German. Schoenberg's 1914 setting of this cycle for soprano and instrumental ensemble is one of the most widely admired works of musical expressionism and one of the earliest works of atonal music to achieve a wide following.

Schoenberg
Pierrot lunaire

Pierrot is one of the stock masked characters from the commedia dell'arte, and *Pierrot lunaire* draws on the mask as a metaphor for the human manners that conceal deeper emotions. Pierrot himself is the melancholy, moonstruck clown who lives in a state of constant longing. The atonality of no. 7 ("The Sick Moon") makes the moon seem far more ill than any tonal idiom could. Schoenberg projects the violence of the text in no. 14 ("The Cross")—whose first line reads "Holy crosses are the verses on which poets bleed to death"—by having the voice make leaps of ninths, diminished and augmented octaves, and other nontriadic intervals, thereby undermining any sense of a tonal center.

PRIMARY EVIDENCE

"The Last Word in Musical Anarchy"

Schoenberg's *Pierrot lunaire* (1912) posed a challenge to many if not most of its first listeners. The American music critic Arthur M. Abell (1868–1958) filed this review from the work's London premiere.

• • • • •

His music to Albert Giraud's fantastical poems entitled "The Songs of Pierrot Lunaire" is the last word in cacophony and musical anarchy. Some day it may be pointed out as of historical interest, because representing the turning point, for the outraged muse surely can endure no more of this; such noise must drive even the moonstruck Pierrot back to the realm of real music. Albertine Zehme, a well known Berlin actress, dressed in a Pierrot costume, recited the "Three Times Seven" poems, as the program announced, while a musical, or rather unmusical, ensemble consisting of a piano, violin, viola, cello, piccolo and clarinet, stationed behind a black screen and invisible to the audience, discoursed the most ear splitting combinations of tones that ever desecrated the walls of a Berlin music hall. Schoenberg has thrown overboard all of the sheet anchors of the art of music. Melody he eschews in every form; tonality he knows not and such a word as harmony is not in his vocabulary. He purposely and habitually takes false basses and the screeching of the fiddle, piccolo and clarinet baffled description. The remarkable part of this whole farce is that Schoenberg is taken seriously. He even has adherents who rally round his standard and swear by his muse, declaring that this is music of the future. Otto Taubmann, the critic of the Börsen Courier, expressed the feelings of all sane musicians when he wrote, "If this is music of the future, then I pray my Creator not to let me live to hear it again."

Source: Arthur M. Abell, review in *The Musical Courier*, November 6, 1912.

By setting a series of relatively short poems in *Pierrot lunaire*, Schoenberg was able to circumvent one of the more pressing challenges of writing within the new atonal idiom: how to construct large-scale musical forms in the absence of tonality. The tonal system, after all, had provided the basic framework for most musical forms for several centuries. It is no coincidence, then, that most of the atonal works from the early decades of the century are relatively brief, and that many of them are vocal. The texts of these works provide a certain degree of structural coherence in the absence of traditional tonality.

Sprechstimme, the style of singing called for throughout *Pierrot lunaire*, reinforces the surreal quality of the text and music. *Sprechstimme* (literally, "speech-voice," with "voice" understood here in the sense of "singing") is neither speech nor song, but a means of declamation somewhere between the two. Unlike speech, in *Sprechstimme* the vocalist must articulate specified pitches and rhythms. Instead of sustaining a pitch as in the conventional method of singing, however, the performer allows the pitch to drop rather in the same way one's voice drops with the enunciation of a spoken word. *Sprechstimme* is indicated by means of standard notes with a small "x" through the stem.

The atonal idiom of *Pierrot lunaire* also provided Schoenberg with an effective foil for the limited use of tonality. The final number of the cycle (no. 21, "O Ancient Scent") speaks of the intoxicating "ancient scent" that comes "from the time of fairy tales," and throughout this finale, the composer's music is more nearly tonal for longer stretches than at any other point in the entire cycle. At the very end of *Pierrot*, the moonstruck clown wistfully longs for the age of tonality, the age of childhood and fairy tales, but seems to realize this is only a dream, that there is no turning back now.

Composer Profile

Arnold Schoenberg
(1874–1951)

Schoenberg was a tortured soul, an outsider who longed to be accepted yet never felt comfortable within the establishment. Widely perceived as a radical, he saw himself as a traditionalist extending the heritage of Bach, Beethoven, and Brahms. Born Jewish, he converted to Christianity, then later back to Judaism. An Austrian by birth, he moved back and forth between Vienna and Berlin, finally emigrating to the United States when the Nazis assumed power in Germany. (It was in the United States that he changed the spelling of his name from Schönberg to Schoenberg.)

His work falls into three broad periods:

◆ Early (advanced chromaticism). Schoenberg's early works explore the outer limits and reaches of chromaticism. Lush harmonies, thick textures, and an almost constant avoidance of cadences characterize such works as *Verklärte Nacht* ("Transfigured Night"), a tone poem for string sextet; *Gurrelieder,* a cantata of enormous proportions; the Quartet in D minor, in one large movement; the Chamber Symphony no. 1 in E major, op. 9; and many songs.

◆ Middle (atonal). Around 1908, Schoenberg abandoned tonality altogether and declared the "emancipation of the dissonance." Principal works of the atonal period include the String Quartet no. 2 (whose finale features a solo soprano singing the words "I breathe the air of other planets"); the Piano Pieces op. 11 and op. 19; *Pierrot lunaire;* the monodrama *Erwartung* ("Expectation," for soprano and orchestra); and the *Five Orchestral Pieces,* op. 16.

◆ Late (serial). Dissatisfied with the lack of a more structured formal principle by which to organize his atonal works, Schoenberg eventually developed the method of 12-tone serial composition (discussed later) in which no note is repeated until all other 11 pitches of the scale have been stated. His earliest attempts at serial composition

KEY DATES IN THE LIFE OF ARNOLD SCHOENBERG

1874 Born in Vienna on September 13.

1894 Begins private composition lessons with Alexander Zemlinsky; performs in local music halls to earn money.

1910 Appointed teacher of composition at the Vienna Academy.

1911 Finishes his treatise on harmony, dedicated to the recently deceased Gustav Mahler, one of his early supporters; moves to Berlin, where he teaches at the Stern Conservatory.

1912 Premiere of *Pierrot lunaire,* which causes a sensation.

1918 After serving in the Austrian military during World War I, settles once again in Vienna and organizes the Society for Private Musical Performances, to which only selected listeners are invited.

1925 Appointed professor at the Prussian Academy of Arts in Berlin.

1933 Dismissed from his position in Berlin because of his Jewish ancestry and emigrates to France and then the United States, where, after a year in Boston, he settles in Los Angeles.

1935 Appointed professor of music at the University of Southern California; begins teaching a year later at the University of California at Los Angeles; becomes an American citizen in 1941.

1951 Dies on July 13 in Los Angeles.

date from around 1920, and within a few years he was applying this method in almost all his music. The principal serial works include the String Quartets nos. 3 and 4; the *Variations for*

Orchestra; the opera *Moses und Aron;* and the String Trio.

With Stravinsky, Schoenberg was widely regarded as one of the two great composers of the 20th century. No one, however, ever accused him of being a "musical chameleon," as Stravinsky had been called. Even those who did not care for his music respected his uncompromising pursuit of artistic principles. His influence, moreover, extended well beyond his two most famous pupils, Anton Webern and Alban Berg. Every subsequent generation of composers has studied Schoenberg's music carefully, and in this sense he stands as one of—and arguably *the*—most influential composers of the entire century.

Schoenberg and his self-portraits. *Over the course of many years, Schoenberg painted dozens of self-portraits, and in every one it is the eyes that capture our attention. In his paintings as in his music, Schoenberg was less interested in conventional ideas of beauty than in psychological truth. He once described his style of painting as "making music with colors and forms." This fascinating photograph, taken in Schoenberg's Los Angeles home, juxtaposes the 75-year-old composer with three of his own paintings, all done in the year 1910. Clockwise from upper left: (1)* Blue Self-Portrait; *(2)* Green Self-Portrait; *(3)* The Red Gaze. *Not captured in this black-and-white photograph is the intensity of the red eyes in the third painting.*

Source: Copyright 1981 Richard Fish, Photographer

Principal Works

DRAMATIC WORKS The unfinished opera *Moses und Aron,* based on the book of Exodus, is in many respects Schoenberg's masterpiece; it is also a veiled autobiography of the composer himself. Moses, the lawgiver, strives to elevate the people of Israel by transmitting the word of God. But Moses (a speaking role in the opera) cannot persuade with the fluency and eloquence of the young Aaron (a lyric tenor). Many critics have seen in this constellation a parallel with Schoenberg and his pupil Berg, whose atonal and 12-tone music was for most listeners more lyrical and accessible than Schoenberg's. Late in his life, Schoenberg also turned to the genre of the monologue with orchestra in such works as *Kol nidre,* the *Ode to Napoleon,* and *A Survivor from Warsaw.*

ORCHESTRAL MUSIC The *Five Orchestral Pieces* and the *Variations for Orchestra* are atonal and serial, respectively. The Violin Concerto and Piano Concerto are later compositions.

PIANO MUSIC The *Three Piano Pieces,* op. 11, and *Six Piano Pieces,* op. 19, are brief but important works in the development of the atonal idiom. Schoenberg turned to the piano again in developing his 12-tone method of composition, most notably in the Piano Suite, op. 25, which openly adopts the forms, but not the style, of a Baroque dance suite (see Chapter 10). The Piano Pieces op. 33a and 33b use combinatoriality (see Chapter 23).

CHAMBER MUSIC *Verklärte Nacht,* for string sextet (later arranged for string orchestra), is a tone poem based on the story of a woman's confession of infidelity. Written in a lush, post-Wagnerian style, it is the most frequently performed of all Schoenberg's works. The five string quartets (1897, 1905, 1908, 1927, 1936; the first is not numbered) offer a good way to trace the various periods of Schoenberg's compositional career, as do the two chamber symphonies (1906, 1939).

WRITINGS Schoenberg's writings are among the most important in the field of 20th-century theory. He wrote a massive treatise on harmony, and through his lectures, teaching, and analytical essays he exerted considerable influence on subsequent generations of composers, theorists, and listeners.

Webern
Five Pieces for String Quartet, op. 5, no. 4

Early composers writing atonal works without a text had to find other means to structure them. Anton Webern's *Five Pieces for String Quartet,* op. 5 (1908), is a series of miniatures that concentrates its resources into a remarkably intense form of expression. Like most atonal works, it uses a limited number of building blocks that usually consist of four or five notes—sometimes fewer, sometimes more, but rarely very many more. These units tend to avoid triads, both in their linear (melodic) and vertical (harmonic) alignments. Webern, like Schoenberg and Berg, saw himself as a traditionalist who continued in the manner of Beethoven and Brahms by manipulating motivic ideas in a process that Schoenberg called "developing variation." Although the extreme brevity of the movements in Webern's op. 5 makes it difficult to hear this process, at least on first listening, this music does in fact rest on the manipulation of a few thematic ideas that are laid out at the beginning and sustained through to the end.

Berg
Wozzeck

By far the most successful atonal work of the early 20th century—both critically and commercially—was Alban Berg's opera *Wozzeck,* completed in 1922 and premiered in Berlin in 1925. The libretto, drawn from selected scenes of the drama *Woyzeck* by the Austrian playwright Georg Büchner (1813–1837), traces the mental and physical deterioration of a simple army soldier, who is treated abysmally by everyone: his captain, his doctor, and the woman by whom he has fathered a child. In the end, he goes mad and murders Marie, the mother of his young son.

Set Theory and the Analysis of Atonal Music

Atonal music—works like Webern's *Five Pieces for String Quartet,* neither tonal nor 12-tone—seemed for a long time resistant to anything approaching systematic analysis. The American theorist Allen Forte (b. 1926) was the most prominent among a number of critics working in the 1950s and 1960s to develop a method for examining this kind of music. In what came to be called *set theory,* Forte proposed a system for identifying and clarifying the relationship of the relatively small units (*cells* or *sets*) that together provide the building blocks for a typical atonal composition. These sets can consist of anywhere between two and ten pitch classes (a pitch class is any manifestation of a particular pitch, regardless of register; thus the pitch class A–F can be used for units that go either down a major third or up a minor sixth—or down a tenth, and so on). A finite number of set types—220 to be exact—can be created out of all the various combinations of pitch classes (see table).

In analysis, these combinations of differing size are identified by a series of numbers reflecting the prime form of the set, beginning with 0 (the lowest note of the set) and moving upward by half step, in much the same way that 12-tone rows are identified numerically. Thus the tetrachord set C-D♯-F-G would be called 0–3–5–7, because D♯ is three half steps above C, F is five half steps above C, and G is seven half steps above C. Sets can be presented either simultaneously (as a "chord") or successively (as a "melody"). Example 21-2 shows the two tetrachords of the opening set of Webern's op. 5, no. 4.

Looking at the score, we can see that set A is presented in the two upper voices in measure 1, set B at the beginning of measure 2. The pitches of set A recur on the final half beat of measure 2; set B appears as a melodic line in the first violin in measures 3–4, then again in the second violin (measure 4) transposed down a fifth. Identifying pitch-class sets can be a hit-or-miss process at times: some sets occur only once or twice in a piece and cannot really be considered to have structural importance. The identification of sets can nevertheless be extremely helpful for making audibly coherent a work of music that might otherwise seem shapeless, even after repeated hearings.

Number of pitches in set	Name of type of set	Number of possible combinations
2	Dyad	6
3	Triad	12
4	Tetrachord	29
5	Pentachord	38
6	Hexachord	50
7	Septachord	38
8	Octachord	29
9	Nonachord	12
10	Decachord	6
		Total: 220

Example 21-2 Two tetrachords from the opening of Webern's *Five Pieces for String Quartet,* op. 5, no. 4.

A				B			
0	1	5	6	0	1	6	7

Composer Profile

Anton Webern
(1883–1945)

Webern's music tends to be extremely concentrated and brief. The orchestral *Passacaglia,* op. 1, lasts about ten minutes in performance, but no subsequent work has more than five minutes of continuous music. A set of his complete works issued on long-playing records in the 1960s took up only four disks. This aphoristic quality strips music to its bare essentials. In much of his work, Webern never calls for a dynamic level louder than *piano,* and he uses silence more often and more effectively than any composer before him. Listening to this music is like listening to a brilliant speaker who wastes no words and speaks in a whisper: we strain to hear every detail, every nuance.

Born into an aristocratic family, the future composer completed a doctoral degree in historical musicology at the University of Vienna in 1906. His dissertation was on the second volume (1555) of the *Choralis Constantius* by the Renaissance composer Heinrich Isaac (see Chapters 5 and 6). Webern was fascinated by the constructive techniques of Renaissance music, particularly its elaborate canons. During this time, he also studied composition privately with Arnold Schoenberg, and together teacher and pupil explored the possibilities of atonal composition and, later, serial composition.

Webern's death is shrouded in mystery. While visiting his daughter and son-in-law in a small

KEY DATES IN THE LIFE OF ANTON WEBERN

1883 Born December 3 in Vienna.

1906 Receives Ph.D. in musicology from the University of Vienna with a dissertation on the Renaissance composer Heinrich Isaac.

1908–1914 Conducts theater orchestras in various cities in Austria and Germany.

1915–1916 Serves as a volunteer in the Austrian Army in World War I but is discharged because of poor eyesight.

1918 Helps run the Society for Private Musical Performance until its demise in 1921; begins giving private lessons in composition.

1926 Meets the poet Hildegard Jone and from this point on sets only her texts to music.

1933 The Nazis prohibit performances of Webern's music, and he is forced to lecture in secret and work as a proofreader for his Viennese publisher, Universal Edition.

1945 Dies September 15 in Mittersill, Austria, shot by an American soldier.

Austrian village shortly after the end of World War II, he stepped outside to enjoy his first cigar in months, only to be shot and killed by an American sentry

Berg used a series of traditional instrumental forms to structure his opera, identifying them explicitly in the score. He insisted, however, that "there must not be anyone in the audience who . . . notices anything about these various fugues, inventions, suites and sonata movements, variations and passacaglias. Nobody must be filled with anything except the idea of the opera." The congruence of musical and dramatic form within each scene and across each act is extremely effective. In the opening scene of Act I, a suite, Berg uses exactly the same device used by Verdi in the opening scene of *Rigoletto* (see Chapter 17): a series of dances, each with a particular symbolic meaning.

PLATE 19   Primitivism in painting. Musical primitivism had parallels in the visual arts. Henri Rousseau (1844-1910) painted fantastical visions that often juxtapose humans and nature. Here, in *Femme se promenant dans une forêt exotique* (Woman Walking in an Exotic Forest), completed in 1905, the exotic nature of the subject, the simplicity of line, and the bold colors of the flowers all suggest that true power resides not in the civilized woman—a relatively small figure in this painting—but in the tropical forest with its improbably oversized plants. Like Stravinsky's music for *Le Sacre du printemps*, Rousseau's art is sophisticated, conveying a sense of raw power, unrefined and elemental.

[Henri J. F. Rousseau (1844–1910), "Woman Walking in an Exotic Forest," 1905, oil on canvas/The Barnes Foundation, Merion, Pennsylvania, USA/The Bridgeman Art Library]

PLATE 21 Modernism in painting: Cubism. Modernist developments in music in the first decade of the 20th century have striking parallels in other arts. Atonality, for example, has often been compared to cubism, an artistic movement of the same period that went out of its way to violate the conventions of representation, especially perspective. Cubism emerged between 1907 and 1914 in the work of Pablo Picasso (1882–1963), contemporary with the earliest atonal works by Schoenberg and his pupils. In cubism, objects that are often only barely recognizable appear disassembled and re-assembled with all sides of an object showing at once, as if on a flat plane. As in this 1911 painting by Picasso— *Man with a Violin*—no one perspective has priority, just as no key has priority in atonal music. The effect can be disturbing or refreshing—or both at the same time.

[Pablo Picasso (Spanish) "Man with a Violin" ©1911–12, oil on canvas 39-3/8 x29-7/8 in. Philadelphia Museum of Art: Louise and Walter Arensberg Collection. ©1998 Estate of Pablo Picasso/Artists Rights Society (ARS), New York]

PLATE 20 Edvard Munch (1863–1944), *The Scream* (1895). The image has become a cultural cliché but still has the power to move those who take the trouble to look at it with fresh eyes. Munch's woodcut anticipates expressionism, an artistic movement that sought to bring to the surface unconscious thoughts and visceral emotions. The image was inspired by a poem by the Norwegian poet Arthur von Franquet, which reads: "I was walking with two friends./The sun was singing./The sky was red as blood, a sense of melancholy came over me./I stopped, sick and tired unto death./Above the dark fiord and the city there was blood and tongue-like flames./My friends continued onward./But I stayed behind, trembling and anxious./It was as if a scream were tearing through nature."

[Edvard Munch, "The Scream," 1893. Casin on paper, 91 x 73 cm. Nasjonalgalleriet, Oslo. ©2003 The Munch Museum/The Munch-Ellingsen Group/Artists Rights Society (ARS), New York/ADAGP, Paris. Scala/Art Resource, NY]

PLATE 22 Modernism in painting: Abstract expressionism.
Abstract expressionism is nonrepresentational, making its effect through the interplay of shapes and colors. This painting— Number 1, 1950 (*Lavender Mist*)—is by Jackson Pollock, one of the leading abstract expressionist painters of his generation. Pollock began working in his "drip and splash" style in the late 1940s, applying paint with objects other than brushes and often simply by pouring it onto his canvases. The resulting style avoids any single point of emphasis and any hierarchy of shapes or forms. The immediacy and raw energy conveyed by this technique have often been compared to the literary and musical manifestations of expressionism.

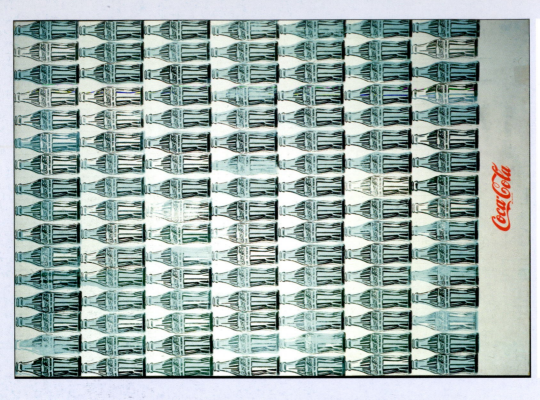

PLATE 24   Minimalism in painting. "Art," Andy Warhol once famously observed, "is what you can get away with." His *Green Coca-Cola Bottles* (1962) combines the daily objects of pop art with the subtle variations of minimalism. What at first glance seems to be unchanging repetition is in fact a series of similar but not identical objects; no two are exactly alike. Like minimalist music, minimalist art focuses our attention on small-scale changes of detail.

[Andy Warhol, American (1930–1987). "Green Coca-Cola Bottles," 1962. Oil on canvas, 82-1/4" x 57" (209.6 x 144.8 cm). Collection of Whitney Museum of American Art. ©2000 Whitney Museum of American Art. ©2001 Andy Warhol Foundation for the Visual Arts/ARS, New York. ©The Coca Cola Company. All rights reserved]

PLATE 23   Pop Art and Postmodernism. Pop Art was one of several movements that emerged in the 1950s and 1960s as a revolt against modernism, particularly abstract expressionism. This 1965 painting—*The Melody Haunts my Reverie*—is by Roy Lichtenstein. Pop Art typically blurs the distinction between art and everyday life by repackaging common images—like those found in comic books—in a new manner, forcing us to look at "throw away" objects more carefully. Although widely reviled when it appeared (*Life* magazine once nominated Lichtenstein as "Worst Artist in the World"), Pop Art helped break down the perceived gulf between "high" and "low" art, and indeed between life and art in general. In this sense, it bears distinct parallels to the work of John Cage and other experimental composers who sought to bridge comparable gaps in music. The title of this particular work evokes a line from Hoagy Carmichael's celebrated love song *Stardust* (1927).

[Roy Lichtenstein (1923–1997). "Reverie," from the portfolio *11 Pop Artists*, Volume II, 1965, color serigraph on paper, 27-1/8 x 23 in./Smithsonian American Art Museum, Washington, D.C./Art Resource, NY/©Estate of Roy Lichtenstein]

who was part of the Allied force occupying Austria at the time. The soldier claimed self-defense and pointed out that Webern was outside after curfew, but it seems unlikely that the diminutive, middle-aged Webern could have posed any threat.

Principal Works

ORCHESTRAL MUSIC The *Passacaglia,* op. 1, reveals Webern's early interest in strict forms and his gift for orchestration. His *Variations,* op. 30, reward careful analysis for the elaborate application of 12-tone devices. Webern's scoring for orchestra is extraordinarily transparent; he once said the sound of a full orchestra caused him physical pain.

CHAMBER MUSIC Webern preferred to work within the smaller scale genres of string quartet and song; even his one symphony is scored for a chamber ensemble and is quite brief. The Five Movements for String Quartet, op. 5, are celebrated for their conciseness and economy of expression, as are the Six Bagatelles, op. 9. The String Quartet, op. 28, is a 12-tone work.

VOCAL MUSIC Webern, along with his teacher Schoenberg, worked through many of the problems of atonality within the genre of song. He favored contemporary poets such as Stefan George, Georg Trakl, and Rainer Maria Rilke; he wrote several texts of his own as well. From 1926 onward, however, he set exclusively the texts of Hildegard Jone (1891–1963), a fellow Austrian whose texts greatly appealed to Webern's sense of an inherent connection between nature and art. Jone's poetry also provided the texts for the two cantatas.

Anton Webern and Alban Berg. *Anton Webern (right) and Alban Berg were Arnold Schoenberg's two most prominent students and colleagues. At the time this photograph was taken in 1912, both had essentially broken their musical ties with tonality and were beginning to explore the possibilities of the atonal idiom.*

Source: © UNIVERSAL EDITION

Some critics, predictably, lambasted Berg's *Wozzeck. Wozzeck* nevertheless became a critical and commercial success almost overnight, opening to great acclaim in 17 cities in Germany between 1926 and 1933. Audiences in Prague, Petrograd (St. Petersburg), Paris, Philadelphia, and New York welcomed the work enthusiastically. When the National Socialists under Adolf Hitler came to power in Germany in 1933, however, Berg's music—along with all other atonal and serial music—was repressed and eventually banned from public performance. In the years after World War II, *Wozzeck* quickly reestablished itself as a staple of the operatic repertory.

Opera in the Early 20th Century

In the early decades of the 20th century, opera continued to thrive in the hands of such composers as Richard Strauss, Alban Berg, Giaccomo Puccini, and Leoš Janáček. From the perspective of form, most of these composers were descendants of Wagner in one way or another, emphasizing musicodramatic continuity even while preserving (in most cases) units still recognizable as arias, duets, and so on. Stylistically, opera was as diverse as the music of the 20th century itself, ranging from the atonal expressionism of Schoenberg's *Die glückliche Hand* (1913), to the tonal lyricism of Puccini's *Turandot* (1926), to the jazz-inspired harmonies and rhythms of Gershwin's *Porgy and Bess* (1935).

Among the more notable operatic composers of this period are the following:

Giaccomo Puccini—*La bohème* (1896), *Tosca* (1900), *Madama Butterfly* (1904), *La fanciulla del West* (1910), *Turandot* (1926)

Leoš Janáček—*Jenůfa* (1904); *Kátya Kabanová* (1921), *Věc Makropulos* (1926)

Richard Strauss—*Salome* (1905), *Elektra* (1909), *Der Rosenkavalier* (1911)

Arnold Schoenberg—*Erwartung* (1909), *Die glückliche Hand* (1913), *Moses und Aron* (1932)

Alban Berg—*Wozzeck* (1925), *Lulu* (1937)

Paul Hindemith—*Cardillac* (1926, rev. 1952), *Mathis der Maler* (1935)

Kurt Weill—*Aufstieg und Fall der Stadt Mahagonny* (1927), *Die Dreigroschenoper* (1928)

George Gershwin—*Porgy and Bess* (1935)

Igor Stravinsky—*The Rake's Progress* (1951)

SERIAL COMPOSITION

For more than a decade, between roughly 1908 and the early 1920s, Schoenberg, Webern, and Berg struggled to find a means of creating large-scale atonal structures. Berg's use of traditional instrumental forms in *Wozzeck* was part of this effort, but the new idiom of atonality required a correspondingly new approach to form as well.

In response to this need, Schoenberg developed the technique of **serial composition** in the early 1920s. Serial composition is based on the premise that an established unit of music—most often a **row,** or **series** (hence the term *serial*), of 12 different pitches—can be varied repeatedly in such a way as to provide the structural basis for an entire work. A composer using this approach could integrate the row and any of its many possible permutations into established formal conventions—variations, sonata-form movements, rondos, and so on—but such forms were not essential to the structural integrity of the work, which was ensured by the constant presence of the row in one guise or another. Serial composition provided composers seeking to break away from traditional tonality with the means to construct large-scale forms that were structurally coherent despite the absence of a tonal center.

Twelve-tone serial composition, also known as **dodecaphony** (from the Greek *dodeca,* meaning "12"), uses as its basic unit a row of 12 different pitches drawn from the 12 pitches of the chromatic octave (C, C♯, D, D♯, etc., up through B). Schoenberg identified three principal functions of the 12-tone row: (1) to avoid creating the impression of a principal note, which in turn might suggest a "tonic" key area; (2) to unify the composition motivically; and (3) to "emancipate" the dissonance, that is, to eradicate any distinction between consonance and dissonance. It is important to distinguish between the theory and practice of 12-tone composition. In theory, 479,001,600 different basic rows are possible (this number is 12! or $12 \times 11 \times 10 \times 9 \times 8 \times 7 \times 6 \times 5 \times 4 \times 3 \times 2 \times 1$). In practice, composers pay careful attention to the musical qualities of the row, generally avoiding intervals or sequences of intervals that might suggest a key area, such as a succession of thirds or of pitches in a diatonic scale. In the strictest applications of 12-tone composition, no pitch is repeated until all other 11 pitches have been stated in that particular iteration of the row. In practice, composers applied this system with considerable flexibility, often repeating a particular pitch before moving on to another one.

There are four basic forms of any given row, each of which can be transposed to start on any of the 12 chromatic pitches in the diatonic scale:

◆ Prime (P) is the basic form of the row.

◆ Inversion (I) is the row played upside down: a rise of a major third in the prime form of the row becomes a fall of a major third; a fall of a minor second in the prime form becomes a rise of a minor second, and so on.

◆ Retrograde (R) is the row played backward, beginning with the last note and ending with the first.

◆ Retrograde Inversion (RI) is the inverted form of the row's retrograde.

These different permutations of a single row are readily evident in Schoenberg's *Piano Suite,* op. 25, an early serial work, written in 1923. The prime form of the row consists of the pitches E-F-G-C♯-F♯-D♯-G♯-D-B-C-A-B♭. A matrix shows at a glance all the 48 possibilities of this row in the transposed versions of P, I, R, and RI (Example 21-3).

Schoenberg
Piano Suite, op. 25

By convention, the **pitch class** on which each form of the row begins is designated by a number. (Theorists use the term *pitch class* to designate any set of notes—any A, any B, any C, and so on—regardless of its register.) The Prime form of the row would thus be P-0; the Inverted form beginning on 4 (that is, four half steps above the original note of P-0) would be I-4; the Retrograde Inverted form beginning on 8 would be RI-8; and so on. By the same token, the pitches of the rows themselves can also be designated numerically. Thus the basic row of Schoenberg's op. 25 (P-0) can be identified as 0–1–3–9–2–11–4–10–7–8–5–6. (Some analysts use the series of numbers 1 through 12, but most American writers on music have tended toward the system using 0 through 11, and it is this latter system that is used here.)

At first glance, such a compositional system might seem like little more than the equivalent of a musical crossword puzzle. But it is important to remember that all forms of composition, and especially the so-called strict forms such as canon and fugue, involve self-imposed limitations. It is equally important to remember that in spite of all these limitations, the composer retains enormous control over the course of a serial work, because the number of ways in which the row can be permuted and combined with other iterations of the same row is virtually infinite. In his *Piano Suite,* op. 25, Schoenberg limited himself to just eight different versions of the row, as outlined in Example 21-4.

For Schoenberg, the idea behind serial composition was deeply rooted in tradition. He maintained that every worthy piece of music, regardless of idiom, was a "working out" of a basic musical idea. This idea was more than just a theme: it could incorporate harmonic, contrapuntal, rhythmic, registral, timbral, and dynamic elements as well. All of Schoenberg's own music manifests this basic process of what he called "developing variation," the process by which an idea grows and evolves over the course of a movement or entire work. It was in this sense that Schoenberg saw himself as the heir to the traditions of Beethoven and Brahms, who had also created large-scale musical structures through the unfolding of relatively simple motives and ideas.

Schoenberg's premise of the musical idea and its unfolding continues the 19th-century tradition of **organicism,** which lies at the heart of an enormous amount of

Example 21-3 The matrix of the row for Schoenberg's *Piano Suite,* op. 25. The prime form in its original transposition (P-0) reads from left to right across the top row.

INVERSIONS ↓

P/I	0	1	3	9	2	11	4	10	7	8	5	6	
0	E	F	G	C#	F#	D#	G#	D	B	C	A	B♭	0
11	D#	E	F#	C	F	D	G	C#	A#	B	G#	A	11
9	C#	D	E	A#	D#	C	F	B	G#	A	F#	G	9
3	G	G#	A#	E	A	F#	B	F	D	D#	C	C#	3
10	D	D#	F	B	E	C#	F#	C	A	A#	G	G#	10
1	F	F#	G#	D	G	E	A	D#	C	C#	A#	B	1
8	C	C#	D#	A	D	B	E	A#	G	G#	F	F#	8
2	F#	G	A	D#	G#	F	A#	E	C#	D	B	C	2
5	A	A#	C	F#	B	G#	C#	G	E	F	D	D#	5
4	G#	A	B	F	A#	G	C	F#	D#	E	C#	D	4
7	B	C	D	G#	C#	A#	D#	A	F#	G	E	F	7
6	A#	B	C#	G	C	A	D	G#	F	F#	D#	E	6
	0	1	3	9	2	11	4	10	7	8	5	6	

PRIMES → (left) RETROGRADES ← (right)

↑ RETROGRADE INVERSIONS

Source: Matrix of the row for Schoenberg, *Piano Suite* Op. 25. From *Materials and techniques of twentieth-century music* by Stefan Kostka, 2nd ed., Prentice Hall, © 1999, p. 201. Reprinted by permission of Pearson Education, Inc., Upper Saddle River, NJ.

theoretical and analytical work in the 20th century. The primary goal of organicist analysis is to demonstrate the manner in which the many different elements immediately audible on the musical surface—contrasts in theme, timbre, harmony, rhythm, and so on—manifest a deeper coherence. The musical work was often seen as a living form, an organism, and many analysts perceived the challenge to be that of identifying what might be called the DNA of the work at hand, the blueprint behind the finished composition.

Dodecaphony was more a principle than a style. Schoenberg, Webern, and Berg each developed their own personal ways of applying the technique of serial composition, even though their followers lumped them together under the rubric of the "Second Viennese School" (following the earlier triumvirate of Haydn, Mozart, and Beethoven, who also worked in Vienna).

Webern's application of serial technique was the most complex and concentrated of the three. Many listeners perceive his music as cryptic and aphoristic; it has been said his compositions are to music what haiku is to poetry. He tended to work with subunits of

Example 21-4 Forms of the row actually used in Schoenberg's *Piano Suite,* op. 25.

Source: Forms of the row actually used in Schoenberg's *Piano Suite* Op. 25, from *Twentieth-century music: A history of musical style in modern Europe and America* by Robert P. Morgan © 1926, renewed 1953 by Universal Edition A.G., Vienna. Reprinted with permission.

the 12-tone row, small motifs of three or four notes. Very often, the first few notes of a row will be transformed in some way to create the remainder of the row. The row of his String Quartet, for example, consists of three different statements of the same pitch-class set, one of which spells out the notes "B-A-C-H." He relished the challenge of synthesizing serial technique with such contrapuntal and constructivist devices as canons, mirror canons, and passacaglias.

Berg tended to take a more liberal approach to serial composition than either Schoenberg or Webern. The first movement of his *Lyric Suite* for string quartet, for example, uses three different (yet related) rows, and not all of its six movements are serial: only the outer movements are entirely dodecaphonic. The third movement is serial in its outer sections but not in its trio, and only the trios of the fifth movement are written using the 12-tone method. Berg manipulates the basic row of the work (Example 21-5a) in ingenious ways. He divides it into two **hexachords** (groups of six notes) and derives two "new" rows from these notes by rearranging their order (Examples 21-5a and b).

Berg
Lyric Suite

Example 21-5 Berg, *Lyric Suite,* the row (a) and two derivations (b and c).

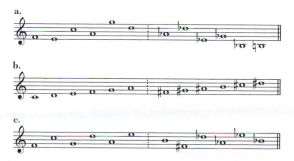

Source: Alban Berg, Lyric Suite, the row (a) and 2 derivations (b and c) from *Twentieth-century music: a history of musical style in modern Europe and America* by Robert P. Morgan. (New York: W. W. Norton. 1991), p. 190. © 1927 Universal Edition A.G., Vienna. © renewed. All Rights Reserved. Used by permission of European American Music Distributors LLC, sole US and Canadian agent for Universal Edition A.G., Vienna.

Composer Profile

Alban Berg
(1885–1935)

1885 Born in Vienna on February 9.

1904 Begins compositional studies with Arnold Schoenberg.

1913 The premiere of Berg's *Altenberg Lieder,* op. 4, creates an uproar in the concert hall.

1915 Drafted into the Austrian army but declared unfit for active service because of severe and chronic asthma.

1918 Helps establish, with Schoenberg and Webern, the Society for Private Musical Performances.

1925 Premiere of *Wozzeck* in Berlin; in spite of many scathing reviews, the work soon gains acceptance and assures Berg's financial security for his remaining years.

1930 Appointed to the Prussian Academy of Arts, a testimony to the impact of *Wozzeck* on his contemporaries.

1935 Dies December 24 in Vienna from blood poisoning induced by an infected bee sting.

Of the three members of the Second Viennese School, Berg stands out as the composer whose music is in many ways the most accessible. In spite of early opposition, his atonal opera *Wozzeck* has established itself as one of the only operas of its kind that can draw audiences in the same way as the operas of Verdi and Wagner. Berg's lyrical gifts and his uncanny ability to capture the dramatic moment with just the right sound contribute to his stature as one of the great opera composers of music history. As did Schoenberg and Webern, Berg began composing in a lush, post-Wagnerian style of extreme chromaticism, broke with the principles of tonality more or less completely around 1909, and then adopted the serial method in the mid-1920s. In his application of 12-tone technique, Berg tended to be rather more free than Schoenberg and especially Webern, yet he was particularly attracted to the idea of retrograding large sections of music, as in the return of the A section of the third movement of the *Lyric Suite.* This kind of large-scale retrograde structure is often associated in his music with some kind of emotional negation or reversal. Indeed, his music is full of secret programs and encrypted messages.

Berg was not a prolific composer. He suffered from ill health for much of his life, yet the works he left behind are more than sufficient in quality to ensure his place as one of the great masters of the atonal and serial idioms.

(See Composer Profile: "Anton Webern" for a photograph of Berg with Webern.)

Principal Works

Dramatic Works Wozzeck remains the most frequently performed of all atonal operas, indeed perhaps of all atonal works of any kind. Its ability to draw even listeners otherwise hostile to this idiom has proven extraordinary. *Lulu,* Berg's other 12-tone opera, is even more ambitious but remained unfinished at the composer's death. It was completed by the Austrian composer and scholar Friedrich Cerha and premiered in its full form in 1979.

Orchestral Music The atonal Violin Concerto is one of the few works of its kind that have thrived in the concert hall. Berg also made several arrangements of music from his *Lyric Suite, Wozzeck,* and *Lulu* that helped expose these larger works to a greater number of listeners.

Chamber Music In addition to one string quartet (op. 3) and the *Lyric Suite,* Berg wrote an important Chamber Concerto for piano, violin, and 13 wind instruments; it is not a 12-tone work.

Songs Most of Berg's songs are early works for piano and voice. The *Five Orchestra Songs on Postcard Text by Peter Altenberg* (1912) display the composer's uncanny ability to shape texts and orchestral colors with melodic lines.

The tonal implications of Example 21-5b are particularly clear; this is the kind of row that Schoenberg and Webern avoided. For the third movement, Berg exchanges the pitches 3 (A) and 9 (G♭) in P-0 (Example 21-5a) and transposes the whole up a fourth to create a "new" primary row for this movement. The importance of this change is that it creates a row in which the notes A-B♭-B-F appear in succession: this tetrachord held intense personal meaning for the composer because its notes spelled out the initials of his lover and himself. By rotating this newly derived row, that is, by beginning it on a pitch other than 0, Berg makes this tetrachord particularly clear. Every voice in the third movement's opening, for example, plays some version of this grouping.

CONCLUSION

The boundaries between extreme chromaticism and atonality became blurred in the music of certain composers working in the early decades of the 20th century, most notably Arnold Schoenberg, Anton Webern, and Alban Berg. Dissatisfied with the difficulties of creating coherent larger scale works in the absence of tonality, Schoenberg developed the idea of serial composition in the early 1920s, based on transpositions and permutations of a basic row or series of notes. Webern and Berg developed serial composition in their own individual ways. Although many composers and listeners refused to embrace these new idioms, the abandonment of tonality introduced a new range of musical options that would be widely explored in subsequent decades.

The Tonal Tradition

For all the importance of atonality and serial composition in the 20th century, many of the era's leading composers continued to work within the tonal tradition. Stravinsky, Bartók, Prokofiev, Shostakovich, Copland, and others all extended the bounds of the traditional harmonic idiom but retained the idea of a tonal center. For some composers, this was almost a matter of faith. The noted German composer Paul Hindemith (1895–1963) believed:

> Music, as long as it exists, will always take its departure from the major triad and return to it. The musician cannot escape it any more than the painter his primary colors or the architect his three dimensions. In composition, the triad or its direct extensions can never be avoided for more than a short time without completely confusing the listener. If the whim of an architect should produce a building in which all those parts which are normally vertical and horizontal (the floors, the walls, and the ceilings) were at an oblique angle, a visitor would not tarry long in this perhaps "interesting" but useless structure. It is the force of gravity, and no will of ours, that makes us adjust ourselves horizontally and vertically. In the world of tones, the triad corresponds to the force of gravity. It serves as our constant guiding point, our unit of measure, and our goal, even in those sections of compositions which avoid it.[1]

NEO-CLASSICISM AND THE "NEW OBJECTIVITY"

Atonality, primitivism, and expressionism fostered their own counterreactions in the early decades of the 20th century. The most important of these was an aesthetic movement known as **Neoclassicism,** the deliberate imitation of an earlier style within a contemporary context. ("Classic" in this sense refers to anything from the distant past, not specifically to the Classical era or to so-called classical music in general.) The idea of writing in a deliberately old-fashioned style, or in a manner openly influenced by a much earlier style, was scarcely new in the 20th century. Still, the movement known as Neoclassicism took on a special significance by virtue of its pointed rejection of such modernist developments. Neoclassicism is characterized by a return to the tonal idiom, a return to conventional genres and forms, and a return to the ideal of absolute music—that is, music not connected with a text or program. Neoclassic music tends toward transparent textures and lighter orchestration, and avoids grandiose or bombastic gestures.

Neoclassicism reached its height in the 1920s and 1930s, in the wake of World War I. Disillusioned by this devastating conflict, many artists and audiences took pleasure in the vaguely nostalgic sense evoked by Neoclassical music. "Back to Bach" and "The New Simplicity" became slogans. The new music did not sound like Bach, of course, nor was it necessarily harmonically simple; but it certainly sounded more like Bach (or other earlier composers) than the works of the day that attempted to overthrow the centrality of triadic harmony.

The Gavotta from the *Classical Symphony*, op. 25 (1917), by Sergei Prokofiev (1891–1953) offers a good example of Neoclassicism. Prokofiev preserves the characteristic form and rhythms of the gavotte but transforms the melody and harmony in ways that are distinctively 20th century.

Prokofiev
Classical Symphony

Stravinsky is another prominent composer associated with Neoclassicism. As for Prokofiev, Neoclassicism was one of many styles he embraced over a long career. Stravinsky's ballet *Pulcinella* (1920) is based on themes from early-18th-century works attributed to Pergolesi (see Chapters 9 and 13); it was later discovered the music had in fact been written by a lesser-known composer of the day, but the important point is that Stravinsky drew on material from a much earlier era. Other Neoclassical works by Stravinsky include the Concerto for Piano and Winds (1924) and the *Symphony in C* (1940; note the designation of key). Like *Pulcinella*, these works embrace pointedly old-fashioned idioms even while incorporating features that make them unmistakable products of their time. Other composers associated with Neoclassicism include Paul Hindemith and Aaron Copland (1900–1990), whose ballet *Appalachian Spring* (discussed later) ends with an elaborate and decidedly tonal fantasy on a Shaker hymn tune.

Related to Neoclassicism is an outlook known as the "new objectivity." Today, we might think of it as the aesthetic of "cool"—music that is detached, unsentimental, and perhaps even slightly surreal. Part of Neoclassicism's appeal lay in its tendency toward understatement: if the quintessential act of expressionism is the scream, then the quintessential act of the "new objectivity" is the raised eyebrow. Irony was a favorite device of Neoclassicism in all the arts.

A similar attitude of detachment is evident in many of the works of the German composer Kurt Weill (1900–1950), who collaborated with the playwright Bertolt Brecht (1898–1956) on several stage works in the 1920s. These productions often emphasized the distance between characters, their words, their music, and the audience. Speaking in the third person (a verbal technique of distancing), the composer announced, "Brecht and Weill have investigated the question of music's role in the theater. They have concluded that music cannot further the action of a play or create its background. Instead, it achieves its proper value when it interrupts the action at the right moments."[2]

Weill's first collaboration with Brecht was *Aufstieg und Fall der Stadt Mahagonny* ("Rise and Fall of the City of Mahagonny," 1927), a satire on capitalism that takes place in a fictional city (Mahagonny) in which the only crime is poverty. Everything is legal as long as it can be paid for. The *Alabama Song*, sung by Jenny (a prostitute) and her six cohorts, assumes the outward form of a traditional aria, with a declamatory introduction and a soaring conclusion, but the words are surreal ("Oh! Moon of Alabama we now must say goodbye./We've lost our good old mama and must have whisky oh you know why.")[3] and, oddly enough for an opera otherwise in German, the text of this number is in English. All this creates a sense of distance—objectivity—that is magnified by the discordant sound of the honky-tonk-style accompaniment.

Weill
Aufstieg und Fall der Stadt Mahagonny

ORCHESTRAL MUSIC

The genres of symphony and symphonic poem continued to flourish in the 20th century. The symphony retained its essential character as a large-scale work in multiple movements, and many of the most prominent composers of the century turned to this genre at one time or another. The symphony proved an especially important vehicle for musical nationalism. Prokofiev and another Russian composer, Dmitri Shostakovich (1906–1975), used folk or folklike inflections in many of their symphonies, as did the Finnish composer Jan Sibelius, the English composer Ralph Vaughan Williams (1872–1958), the Americans Charles Ives, Roy Harris (1898–1979), and Aaron Copland (1900–1990), and the Mexican composer Carlos Chavez (1899–1978). Neoclassicists were also attracted to the symphony. Examples include Prokofiev's openly retrospective *Classical Symphony*, op. 25 (discussed earlier), and Stravinsky's *Symphony in C* (1940) and *Symphony in Three Movements* (1945), which are among the composer's most important orchestral works.

Despite this continued vitality, however, the symphony no longer occupied the position of central importance it had in the 19th century. The idea of musical pluralism extended to genres as well as styles, and composers of instrumental music in the 20th century were no longer expected to prove their abilities and accomplishments by writing a symphony. Atonal and serial composers, focused as they were on breaking with the past, largely avoided the genre, in part because it carried with it such an imposing tradition. The use of atonality, moreover, posed problems of large-scale formal organization that were difficult to solve at first; most early atonal works, as we have already seen, operated on a fairly small scale. Anton Webern's Symphony, op. 21 (1928), a 12-tone work, is really more an anti-symphony, written for chamber ensemble (one player to a part) rather than orchestra, and in two movements rather than the customary four. Like all of Webern's music, the work is quite brief: the entire symphony takes less than ten minutes to perform.

The symphonic poem, like the symphony, appealed primarily to composers whose style remained within the tonal idiom. Debussy, after completing the *Prélude à l'Après-midi d'un faune* (see Chapter 19), would go on to *Nocturnes* and *La mer* ("The Sea"), a three-movement work that resembles a symphony in all but name but whose programmatic movement headings evoke specific images of the sea. Later composers who cultivated the symphonic poem include the following:

Paul Dukas—*The Sorcerer's Apprentice* (1897)

Alexander Scriabin—*Poem of Ecstasy* (1908), *Prometheus* (1910)

Charles Ives—*Holidays* (1904, 1909–1913)

Gustav Holst—*The Planets* (1917)

Sergei Rachmaninoff—*The Isle of the Dead* (1909)

Ottorino Respighi—*The Fountains of Rome* (1917), *The Pines of Rome* (1924)

Darius Milhaud—*The Bull on the Roof* (1919)

George Gershwin—*An American in Paris* (1928)

Bartók
Music for Strings, Percussion, and Celesta

Still other composers wrote large-scale works for orchestra that avoided programmatic and generic associations altogether. Béla Bartók's *Music for Strings, Percussion, and Celesta* (1936) suggests no programmatic elements and avoids aligning itself with the tradition of the symphony, even though its four movements follow an essentially symphonic format. The work is written for an unusual combination of instruments: a double string orchestra (including harp), celesta (a keyboard instrument that mimics the sound of small bells), and a battery of percussion instruments (timpani, piano, xylophone, bass drum, side drum, cymbals, tam-tam).

The work is tightly integrated, with all four movements deriving their principal thematic ideas from the fugue subject of the opening movement. The third movement is structured around the principle of a symmetrical or **arch form,** by which the music progresses toward a midpoint and then more or less retraces its steps. This particular movement centers on measures 49–50, which present an essentially retrograde form of measures 47–48. The music "turns" this moment. On the whole, the movement can be broken down as follows:

	A	B	C	D	E	D	C	B	A
Measure	1	6	20	35	45	65	74	77	80

The proportions are not strict—Bartók was seldom pedantic about such matters—but the overall impression is one of growth, development, climax, and return to an original state.

FILM MUSIC

Film music was a new genre altogether in the 20th century. Although motion pictures were invented in 1891 by Thomas Edison, they did not begin to feature sound until 1927. Dialogue in silent movies was limited to what could be displayed in writing on the screen, with live music provided in the theater by an organist, pianist, small instrumental ensemble, or even (for especially important showings) an orchestra. With the advent of talkies, however, recorded music could be incorporated directly into the film itself, and producers soon discovered it was cheaper and more effective to commission music that would correspond precisely to the events and emotions being portrayed on the screen than to provide live music for every showing.

The challenge of writing for film was similar to that of writing for opera, with the key difference that composers were almost always asked to write music to fit a scene that had already been shot and whose timing was thus fixed. But by the middle of the 1930s a number of highly skilled composers were taking on this challenge. Among the more prominent who ventured into the world of cinema were the English composers Ralph Vaughan Williams, William Walton, and Benjamin Britten; the Frenchmen Darius Milhaud and Georges Auric; and the Americans Bernard Herrmann (1911–1975), Elmer Bernstein (b. 1922), Henry Mancini (1924–1994), and John Williams (b. 1932). From the 1930s onward, émigré composers from central and eastern Europe were particularly successful in this field—in fact, some of the most seemingly American films were set to music by artists who had spent relatively little time in the United States. The music for the Civil War epic *Gone with the Wind* (1939), for example, is by the Austrian Max Steiner (1888–1971); Russian-born Dimitri Tiomkin (1899–1979) created the score for one of the most famous of all Westerns, *High Noon* (1952). Erich Wolfgang Korngold (1897–1957), a brilliant child prodigy and a composer of symphonies and operas in his native Vienna, spent much of his life after 1934 in Hollywood, where he produced the music for such films as *The Adventures of Robin Hood* (1938) and *The Sea Hawk* (1940).

Prokofiev
Alexander Nevsky

Sergei Prokofiev's cantata *Alexander Nevsky* (1938) uses music he had written for the film of the same name directed by Sergei Eisenstein. The film is based on the true story of Grand Duke Alexander of Novgorod, who defeated the Swedes on the River Neva (hence "Nevsky" is his popular name) in the year 1240 and went on to repel an army of Teutonic knights in 1242 in a battle that took place on the frozen surface of Lake Chudskoye. In the film's climactic scene, the ice breaks and swallows the invaders. In 1939, Prokofiev turned his brilliant score for this movie into a cantata for mezzo-soprano, chorus, and large orchestra. The rousing fourth movement of this work (*Arise, People of Russia*), like much of the rest of the score, integrates folk-song-like melodies (of Prokofiev's own invention) with a harmonic idiom that is essentially triadic. The occasional

PRIMARY EVIDENCE

Socialist Realism

The leadership of the Soviet Union worked for decades to encourage composers to write in a style accessible to a wide audience. In the pronouncement here, Tikhon Khrennikov (b. 1913), a prominent Russian composer who served as musical adviser to the Red Army during World War II and was secretary general of the Union of Soviet Composers during the late 1940s and early 1950s, denounces the "decadent" tendencies of Western music. Khrennikov reserves special scorn for his own countrymen who have turned away from writing music for "the people" in favor of a more intellectual style.

• • • • •

It was established that repeated directives of the Party on the problems of art were not carried out by the majority of Soviet composers. All the conversations about "reconstruction," about switching of composers to folkways, to realism, remained empty declarations. Almost all composers who worked in the field of large forms kept aloof from the people, and did not enjoy popularity with the broad audiences. The people knew only songs, marches and film music, but remained indifferent towards most symphonic and chamber music. . . . Soviet people, in their letters to concert organizations and to the Radio Committee, often voiced their perplexity and at times their protests against the incomprehensible and complicated music of a number of Soviet composers. . . .

The Central Committee of the All-Union Communist Party (Bolsheviks) points out in its Resolution that formalistic distortions and anti-democratic tendencies have found their fullest expression in the works of such composers as Shostakovich, Prokofiev, Khachaturian, Popov, Miaskovsky, Shebalin, and others. In the music of these composers we witness a revival of anti-realistic decadent influences calculated to destroy the principles of classical music. These tendencies are peculiar to the bourgeois movement of the era of imperialism: the rejection of melodiousness in music, neglect of vocal forms, infatuation with rhythmic and orchestral effects, the piling-up of noisy ear-splitting harmonies, intentional illogicality and unemotionality of music. All these tendencies lead in actual fact to the liquidation of music as one of the strongest expressions of human feelings and thoughts. . . .

The musical art of the people and, above all, Russian folk songs were not favored by the aforementioned composers. When occasionally they turned toward folk melodies they arranged them in an over-complex decadent manner alien to folk art (as in Popov's *Third Symphony on Spanish Themes,* and in some arrangements of Russian folk songs by Prokofiev).

All these creative faults are typical expressions of formalism.

Formalism is a revelation of emptiness and lack of ideas in art. The rejection of ideas in art leads to the preachment of "art for art's sake," to a cult of "pure" form, a cult of technical devices as a goal in itself, a hypertrophy of certain elements of the musical speech at the price of a loss of integrity and harmoniousness of art.

Source: Tikhon Khrennikov, quoted in Nicolas Slonimsky, *Music Since 1900,* 4th ed. (New York: Charles Scribner's Sons, 1971), pp. 1364, 1365. Used by permission of The Gale Group for Scribner. © 1971 Macmillan Reference USA.

modal and chromatic inflections are extremely limited, for this was music written to appeal to mass audiences and their spirit of patriotism. This kind of writing was actively promoted by Soviet authorities under the banner of what they called **socialist realism,** a readily accessible style that evokes the music of the people in an overwhelmingly optimistic tone (see Primary Evidence: "Socialist Realism").

The Soviet government was quick to recognize the potential of film and film music to galvanize patriotic fervor. The state itself financed Eisenstein's *Alexander Nevsky* in the late 1930s at a time when German invasion appeared imminent: the film's plot is deeply nationalistic and transparently anti-German. Soldiers of the Red Army were actually used as extras in the movie.

BALLET

Ballet enjoyed two "golden ages" in the 20th century. The first came in Paris in the years before World War I through the work of Sergei Diaghilev's Ballets Russes (see Chapter 20) and the American Isadora Duncan (1878–1927), another pioneer of modern dance. The second took place in the middle of the century in New York City through the work of choreographers like George Balanchine (1904–1983, a pupil of Diaghilev); Martha Graham (1893–1991) and Agnes DeMille (1909–1993), both of whom worked with Aaron Copland); Merce Cunningham (b. 1919), who collaborated for many decades with John Cage; and Jerome Robbins (1918–1998), who choreographed the original stage and film versions of Leonard Bernstein's *West Side Story* (see later).

Copland's *Appalachian Spring* (1944) is in many respects the American counterpart to Stravinsky's *Le Sacre du printemps*: both works involve springtime rituals in rural societies, and both draw on folk idioms for their musical materials. The scenario of Copland's ballet revolves around a wedding in the Pennsylvania countryside in the early 19th century: a man and woman build a house; a preacher and his followers praise God; and the work concludes with a set of variations on the Shaker hymn tune *Simple Gifts* (Example 22-1). The influence of Stravinsky is clear: the folk-derived melodies, polytonal harmonies, orchestration, the shifting meters, propulsive rhythms—at times irregular, at times ostinato—all owe much to the work of the Russian master. Yet Copland's work is no mere imitation. In *Appalachian Spring* he created one of the most enduring

Copland
Appalachian Spring

Example 22-1 Shaker hymn *Simple Gifts*.

'Tis the gift to be sim - ple, 'tis the gift to be free, 'tis the

gift to come down where you ought to be. And when we find our-selves in the

place just right, 'twill be in the val - ley of love and de - light.

Source: Shaker hymn "Simple Gifts" from Yudkin *Understanding Music,* 3rd ed., p. 376 (Prentice Hall). Reprinted by permission of Pearson Education, Inc., Upper Saddle River, NJ.

musical emblems of the American experience, a work that has appealed to a wide range of audiences ever since the time of its premiere.

CHAMBER MUSIC

Chamber music appealed to composers working in a broad variety of styles. The string quartet maintained its traditional status as the most prestigious of all chamber genres: Schoenberg, Webern, and Berg all wrote atonal and serial works for this medium; Bartók and Shostakovich produced an impressive body of quartets within an essentially tonal idiom.

Messiaen

Quatuor pour la fin du temps

Other composers explored less conventional groupings of instruments, sometimes out of necessity. The French composer Olivier Messiaen (1908–1992) wrote his *Quatuor pour la fin du temps* ("Quartet for the End of Time") to be performed by fellow inmates in a prisoner-of-war camp in Germany during the early years of World War II, where the only instruments at his disposal were a clarinet, a violin, a cello, and a rickety piano. Although many inmates interpreted its title as an allusion to the end of their time in prison, the composer himself insisted the true inspiration for the work came from Chapter 10 of the New Testament book of Revelation, in which an angel causes time to cease at the end of the world. Messiaen compared the opening movement, "Liturgy of Crystal," to "the harmonious silence of the firmament." The **harmonics** in the cello help create a particularly light, ethereal timbre: by touching the string lightly wherever a lozenge-shaped note is indicated, the cellist creates a pitch—a harmonic overtone—that actually sounds two octaves higher than the notated pitch.

But the "End of the Time" in the work's title is most directly evident in its organization of rhythm. The four voices operate on entirely different rhythmic levels: the violin and clarinet, which by the composer's own account reflect the songs of a nightingale and blackbird, respectively, are free, random, unpredictable. The cello and piano, in contrast, adhere to strict rhythmic and melodic patterns. The cello presents a 15-note melody eight and a half times over the course of the movement (Example 22-2). But because the

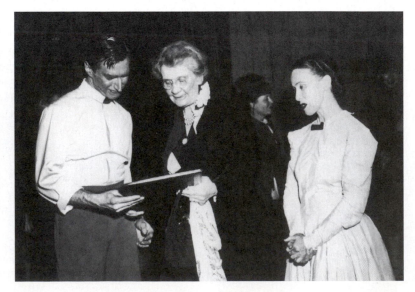

Elizabeth Sprague Coolidge. *Elizabeth Sprague Coolidge (1864–1953) was the single most important patron in the history of American music. She and the foundation that bears her name commissioned an astonishing array of masterpieces from 20th-century composers of all nationalities, including Béla Bartók (String Quartet no. 5), Samuel Barber (Hermit Songs), Aaron Copland (Appalachian Spring), George Crumb (Ancient Voices of Children), Arnold Schoenberg (String Quartets nos. 3 and 4), Igor Stravinsky (Apollon musagète), and Anton Webern (String Quartet, op. 28). Coolidge is shown here with the two principal dancers at the premiere of Copland's* Appalachian Spring *(1944), Erik Hawkins and Martha Graham. Graham also choreographed the ballet.*

Source: Courtesy of The Library of Congress

Example 22-2 Messiaen, *Quatuor pour la fin du temps,* first movement, cello line (sounding pitch), measures 2–8.

Source: Passage, movement 1, cello line (sounding pitch), mm. 2–8, from Messiaen, *Quatuor pour la fin du temps.* In Anthony Pople, *Messiaen: Quatuor pour la fin du temps* (Cambridge University Press, 1998), p. 21. Reprinted with permission of Cambridge University Press.

melody begins before the downbeat and ends after it, these repetitions are rhythmically different with every iteration of the theme.

The rhythmic pattern of the melody is palindromic—the same forward as backward—or as Messiaen himself called it, **nonretrogradable rhythm.** This is not obvious at first because the note values begin in the middle of the rhythmic sequence: time, after all, has been going on before the piece begins. There are several ways to construct a palindromic sequence out of this line. If we count eighth-note values beginning six notes from the end of Example 22-2, for example, we find the following pattern, which is identical forward and backward:

1 1 3 1 1 4 4 3 4 4 1 1 3 1 1

The piano's rhythm of 17 note values, although not palindromic, is also repeated many times. As in the case of the cello, the rhythmic pattern begins and ends in the middle of two different measures and thus shifts constantly in relation to the bar line. Thematically, the piano repeats a sequence of 29 chords throughout, but the thematic and rhythmic patterns do not coincide. This structure resembles that of the medieval isorhythm (see Chapter 3), in which a melodic pattern (*color*) is played against an independent rhythmic pattern (*talea*). Although Messiaen himself was well aware of isorhythm, he maintained that his more immediate sources were the rhythmic structures of certain Hindu modes.

This movement also reminds us just how remote a work can be removed from the framework of triadic harmony. Although many of the piano's 29 chords incorporate triadic harmonies, they also have multiple additional nonharmonic tones.

The String Quartet no. 8 of the Russian composer Dmitri Shostakovich is also heavily autobiographical. "When I die," Shostakovich wrote to a friend, "it's hardly likely that someone will write a quartet dedicated to my memory. So I decided to write it myself." The work is saturated with a musical motif the composer himself identified as his musical monogram: the notes D-E♭-C-B, which in the German system of notation (see Chapter 16) spell D-S (= Es = E♭)-C-H (= B♮), shorthand for **D**mitri **Sch**ostakovich, the German transliteration of the composer's name. The piece as a whole is full of quotations from Shostakovich's operas, symphonies, and chamber works; it also includes snippets from Siegfried's funeral music in Wagner's *Götterdämmerung* and the first movement of Tchaikovsky's Sixth Symphony. The latter two are directly associated with the idea of death, as is the recurring *Dies irae* plainchant melody, the same tune used by Berlioz in the finale of his *Symphonie fantastique* (see Chapter 14).

Shostakovich dedicated his Eighth Quartet "to the memory of the victims of fascism and war"—that is, to the victims of the struggle against Nazi Germany in World War II—a sentiment wholly acceptable to Soviet authorities. But several of the composer's friends

Shostakovich
String Quartet no. 8

Composer Profile

Aaron Copland
(1900–1990)

Copland belonged to the generation of American composers that came of age in the 1920s and 1930s, a generation consumed with the idea of American music. Like so many of his contemporary colleagues, he was trained in the European tradition, studying composition with Nadia Boulanger in Paris and analyzing, under her guidance, a wide range of music by such composers as Monteverdi, Bach, Mahler, and Stravinsky. Some of Copland's music is extremely demanding for listeners and performers alike. Examples include the *Piano Variations* (1930), the 12-tone Piano Quartet (1950), and the *Piano Fantasy* (1957). Yet he never lost what might be called a populist touch, more evident in such works as *Appalachian Spring*, *Billy the Kid*, *Rodeo*, *A Lincoln Portrait*, and *Fanfare for the Common Man*. He also wrote music for a number of Hollywood films, including *Our Town* and *Of Mice and Men*. The appeal of Copland's music transcends generations. The filmmaker Spike Lee used several of his works in the soundtrack to *He Got Game* (1998). "When I listen to Copland's music," Lee explained,

KEY DATES IN THE LIFE OF AARON COPLAND
1900 Born November 14 in Brooklyn, New York.
1921–1924 Studies in Paris with Nadia Boulanger.
1924 Returns to New York and becomes a leading member of what was known as the "New Music" scene.
1940 Becomes head of the composition department at the Berkshire Music Center at Tanglewood in Lenox, Massachusetts, a position he would hold every summer through 1965.
1951–52 Delivers the Charles Eliot Norton lectures at Harvard, later published as *Music and Imagination*.
1960s Tours, conducts, and lectures extensively throughout the United States and Europe.
1990 Dies December 2 in North Tarrytown, New York.

have since asserted the work was Shostakovich's "suicide note," that the composer planned to swallow an overdose of sleeping pills after finishing this work, so depressed was he at having been forced to join the Communist Party. In the final movement, the DSCH motif appears as a counterpoint to a quotation from the last scene of Shostakovich's opera *Lady Macbeth of the Mtsensk District* (1934, banned by the Soviet government) in which prisoners are being transported to Siberia. This could easily have been Shostakovich's own fate had he not agreed to join the Communist Party. Shostakovich used the ambiguity of the music as a shield for his own self-expression.

SONG

Even as many composers of the mid–20th century developed new harmonic idioms—both tonal and atonal—others continued to work within the boundaries of traditional triadic harmony. This trend is seen most remarkably in the genre of song, particularly in the United States. Although they are generally classified as popular rather than art music

"I hear America, and basketball is America. It's like he wrote the score for this film."[4]

Over the last 40 years of his life, Copland was showered with a string of honors and awards: a Pulitzer Prize for *Appalachian Spring*, an Oscar for the score of the movie *The Heiress* (1950), the Presidential Medal of Freedom (1964), and a long series of honorary degrees from universities including Princeton, Brandeis, Wesleyan, Temple, Harvard, Rutgers, Ohio State, New York University, and Columbia.

In addition to his work as a composer, Copland was also a superb lecturer and writer on music. His *What to Listen for in Music* remains a model of its kind, and his many essays for the journal *Modern Music* from the 1920s and 1930s have admirably withstood the test of time.

Principal Works

BALLETS AND OTHER ORCHESTRAL WORKS Copland's best known works are his ballets, particularly *Billy the Kid* (1938, for the choreographer Lincoln Kirstein), *Rodeo* (1942, for Agnes de Mille), and *Appalachian Spring* (1944, for Martha Graham). His *Lincoln Portrait* (1942), for narrator and orchestra, is also frequently performed, as is his *Fanfare for the Common Man* (1942).

SONGS The *Twelve Poems of Emily Dickinson* (1950) are widely admired. The *Old American Songs* are arrangements of American folk songs and as such another manifestation of Copland's populist side.

CHAMBER MUSIC *Vitebsk* (1929), for piano trio, is a "Study on a Jewish Theme." The Piano Quartet (1950) and Nonet for Strings (1960) reflect the more demanding aspects of Copland's musical personality, as do the *Piano Variations* of 1930.

Aaron Copland and Dmitri Shostakovich. *Shostakovich (left) and Copland meet at the Cultural and Scientific Conference for World Peace, held at the Waldorf-Astoria Hotel in New York in March, 1949.*

Source: Frank Driggs Collection

(see Appendix 4: "The Concepts of 'Popular' and 'Art' Music"), the songs of George Gershwin, Irving Berlin, Cole Porter, and Duke Ellington in fact stand in a direct line of descent from those of Schubert, Schumann, Brahms, and Wolf.

Songs like Porter's *Night and Day* and Ellington's *Sophisticated Lady* reflect the traditions of the 19th-century lied in remarkable ways. The harmonic vocabularies of these works, although essentially tonal, are richly chromatic and far from straightforward. The poetry is elegant and witty, the melodies unforgettable, and the union of the two represents the genre at its best. In Porter's *Night and Day*, the juxtaposition of the wandering chromatic line in the bass against the repeated Bb of the voice establishes the underlying tension between longing and insistency. Finally, after 35 iterations of Bb, the vocal line itself begins to rise and fall chromatically, gradually, languorously: the longing has become infectious. We do not feel a strong sense of tonic until the word "one" in the clinching phrase ". . . you are the one"[5] (measure 23).

Ellington's *Sophisticated Lady* uses advanced melodic and harmonic chromaticism to project the idea of a woman who has assumed a worldly attitude toward life and love. Melodic chromaticism and rhythmic irregularity emphasize the woman's exterior life

Cole Porter
Night and Day

Ellington
Sophisticated Lady

Dmitri Shostakovich
(1906–1975)

Shostakovich remains one of the great enigmas of 20th-century music. He labored for most of his life under the repressive regime of the Soviet Union and had to be extremely careful about what he said and wrote, both in words and in music. We are not even sure if he wrote the book that claims to be his memoir. The key question about *Testimony*, first published in the West in 1979, is the degree to which the composer differed with the communist regime. Like other citizens of the Soviet Union, he could not voice negative opinions openly without risking punishment, and this makes it difficult to distinguish between what he believed and what he was compelled to say.

Perhaps no other major composer of the 20th century was as indebted to Beethoven. Shostakovich was attracted to the same genres—symphony, sonata, concerto, quartet, opera—and much of his music follows the same emotional trajectory characteristic of much of Beethoven's music: struggle leading either to triumph or resignation. Shostakovich never abandoned tonality, yet his idiom is distinctly innovative for its time.

Principal Works

ORCHESTRAL MUSIC The 15 symphonies are among the most impressive body of works of their kind by any 20th-century composer. They range from the heroic (nos. 5 and 7) to the resigned (nos. 13, 14, 15). The concertos (two each for piano, for violin, and for cello) are among Shostakovich's most popular compositions.

CHAMBER MUSIC The 15 quartets, written between 1938 and 1974, exhibit a remarkable range of styles, tones, structures, and instrumental technique. They will almost certainly become better known to a wider audience over time. The Piano Trio and Piano Quintet are already widely performed.

PIANO MUSIC The *24 Preludes and Fugues* are modeled in certain respects on Bach's *Well-Tempered Clavier* and deserve wider performance, as do the many miscellaneous works for solo piano, such as the Preludes, the two sonatas, and the *Aphorisms*.

OPERAS *Lady Macbeth of the Mtsensk District* (1934) drew the ire of Soviet authorities, not only because

---

KEY DATES IN THE LIFE OF DMITRI SHOSTAKOVICH

1906 Born September 25 in St. Petersburg (Russia).

1919 Enters the conservatory in his native city and studies piano and composition.

1926 Achieves international reputation with the premiere of his First Symphony.

1936 The opera *Lady Macbeth of the Mtsensk District* elicits a furious assault from Soviet authorities, who condemn the work as decadent, a "bedlam of noise." Rehabilitates himself with Soviet authorities with his Fifth Symphony and later (1942) with his Seventh Symphony, which supposedly depicts the defeat of the German army at the hands of the Soviets.

1949 Serves as a delegate to the Cultural and Scientific Congress for World Peace, in New York, but the U.S. State Department forces the entire Soviet delegation to leave the country prematurely.

1957 Elected as a secretary of the Union of Soviet Composers.

1959 Tours the United States and attends the world premiere of his Cello Concerto in Philadelphia.

1962 Pressured by the Soviet government to alter the text of his Symphony no. 13, commemorating the death of Jews in Kiev during World War II.

1966 Awarded two of the Soviet Union's highest honors, the Hero of Socialist Labor and the Order of Lenin.

1975 Dies August 9 in Moscow.

---

of its dissonant musical idiom, but also because it presented such dramatic themes as murder, suicide, and adultery, behaviors inconsistent with what the regime perceived to be the ideals of Soviet art. Shostakovich's earlier opera, *The Nose* (1930), reveals the composer's deep sense of the humorous and grotesque.

Notable Song Composers of the 20th Century

◆ **Irving Berlin** (1888–1989): *Alexander's Ragtime Band, Always, Blue Skies, Puttin' on the Ritz, How Deep Is the Ocean, Marie, God Bless America, White Christmas, There's No Business Like Show Business, Easter Parade*

◆ **Cole Porter** (1891–1964): *Night and Day, Anything Goes, All through the Night, Love for Sale, Begin the Beguine, Just One of Those Things, I've Got You under My Skin, Don't Fence Me In, In the Still of the Night*

◆ **George Gershwin** (1898–1937): *Swanee, Strike Up the Band, I Got Rhythm, Someone to Watch over Me, Embraceable You, Love Is Here to Stay, Let's Call the Whole Thing Off, They Can't Take That Away from Me;* and the opera *Porgy and Bess,* which includes *Summertime, I Got Plenty o' Nuttin, It Ain't Necessarily So, Bess, You Is My Woman Now,* and *A Woman Is a Sometime Thing*

◆ **Hoagy Carmichael** (1899–1991): *Stardust, Georgia on My Mind*

◆ **Richard Rodgers** (1902–1979): The musicals *Oklahoma!, South Pacific, Carousel, The King and I, The Sound of Music, Flower Drum Song*

◆ **Harold Arlen** (1905–1986): *Stormy Weather, It's Only a Paper Moon,* and all the songs for *The Wizard of Oz,* including *Over the Rainbow*

◆ **Henry Mancini** (1924–1994): *Moon River, Days of Wine and Roses,* all music for the *Pink Panther* movies

◆ **Burt Bacharach** (b. 1928): *Raindrops Keep Fallin' on My Head, Walk on By, What the World Needs Now*

◆ **Bob Dylan** (b. 1941): *Blowin' in the Wind, Mr. Tambourine Man, Like a Rolling Stone*

◆ **John Lennon** (1940–1980) and **Paul McCartney** (b. 1942): *I Want to Hold Your Hand, Yesterday, Lucy in the Sky with Diamonds, A Day in the Life, Let it Be*

◆ **Carole King** (b. 1942): *Natural Woman, Up on the Roof, Will You Still Love Me Tomorrow?*

◆ **Paul Simon** (b. 1942): *Sounds of Silence, Mrs. Robinson, Bridge over Troubled Waters*

◆ **Joni Mitchell** (b. 1943): *Woodstock, Big Yellow Taxi, Chelsea Morning, From Both Sides Now*

◆ **Elton John** (b. 1947): *Your Song, I Guess That's Why They Call It the Blues, Candle in the Wind*

◆ **James Taylor** (b. 1948): *Carolina in My Mind, Country Road, Fire and Rain, Lo and Behold, Your Smiling Face*

◆ **Allan Menken** (b. 1949): Songs from *Little Shop of Horrors, The Little Mermaid, Beauty and the Beast, Aladdin*

of glamor and uncaring attitude ("Smoking, drinking, never thinking of tomorrow, nonchalant . . . ").[6] Only with the final word of the text—cry—does the music arrive at its long-avoided resolution on the tonic. The chromaticism, in the end, is revealed as a mask covering the woman's true feelings.

Like many songs of this era, *Night and Day* and *Sophisticated Lady* have been subjected to countless arrangements, vocal and instrumental. Within three months of the film's premiere, more than thirty artists had recorded the song. Within twenty-five years, the number had surpassed a hundred. And no two recordings are alike: the performance tradition of a song like *Night and Day* allows—and in fact encourages—performers to take considerable liberties with its rhythm, text, orchestration, harmonies, words, and even its melody. As in jazz, improvisatory freedom plays such a basic role in this kind of music that the idea of an authentic text loses all relevance.

OPERA AND MUSICAL THEATER

In the second half of the 20th century, although most opera houses relied principally on works of the past, a handful of composers—Benjamin Britten, Michael Tippett, Gian Carlo Menotti, Philip Glass, and John Adams—produced new works that attracted wide followings. The revival of even earlier repertories, particularly the operas of Monteverdi and Handel, offered another kind of novelty to the public as well.

The most vital form of musical drama throughout the 20th century was the Broadway musical, a genre that took its name from the New York City street on which many of the most prominent musical theaters are located. A direct descendant of the singspiel or operetta—a play with songs—the Broadway musical is a commercial venture that requires considerable capital. A hit show can bring handsome returns to investors, driving theaters to produce musicals that can attract audiences willing to pay high prices for good seats. Some shows have had runs that would be the envy of any opera: Andrew Lloyd Webber's *Cats* ran for some 7,485 performances between 1982 and 2000; revivals of earlier musicals like Richard Rodgers's *Oklahoma!* and Jerome Kern's *Show Boat* testify to the continuing appeal of older repertory.

Many of the most successful musicals of the 20th century, like their operatic counterparts in the 19th, combined entertainment with social commentary. Here are some outstanding examples:

◆ *South Pacific* (1948, music by Richard Rodgers, lyrics by Oscar Hammerstein II), which addresses interracial love against the backdrop of World War II.

◆ *My Fair Lady* (1956, music by Frederick Loewe, lyrics by Alan Jay Lerner), based on George Bernard Shaw's play *Pygmalion,* which deals with class warfare as waged through the weapon of language.

◆ *Miss Saigon* (1989, music by Claude-Michel Schönberg, lyrics by Richard Maltby, Jr., and Alain Boublil), based loosely on Puccini's *Madame Butterfly,* which considers the aftermath of the American military involvement in Vietnam.

◆ *Rent* (1996, music and lyrics by Jonathan Larson), a reinterpretation of Puccini's *La Bohème* that confronts the problem of AIDS.

Bernstein
West Side Story

Leonard Bernstein's *West Side Story* (1957) focuses on the problem of gang warfare between Puerto Ricans (the Sharks) and whites (the Jets) in New York City. The libretto, by Stephen Sondheim (who would go on to compose many hit musicals of his own), was unusually gritty and realistic by the standards of its time. It draws liberally on Shakespeare's *Romeo and Juliet,* featuring a pair of lovers from rival groups and ending in the death of one of them.

Tonight is a quartet very much in the tradition of *Bella figlia del l'amore* from Verdi's *Rigoletto* (see Chapter 17). Dramatically, both revolve around the feeling of anticipation: the Sharks and Jets await their climactic conflict; the sultry Anita knows she will get "her kicks" that night ("He'll walk in hot and tired, so what? Don't matter if he's tired, as long as he's hot.")[7]; and the two lovers, Tony and Maria, await their meeting ("Tonight, tonight won't be just any night."). The number builds gradually and becomes increasingly contrapuntal as it progresses, with a lyrical love duet between Tony and Maria that unfolds above the animosity of the rival choruses. Bernstein uses a jazzlike orchestration, a rapid alternation of duple and triple meters, and even *Sprechstimme* at one point to give the music a decidedly modern sound. But the overall shape of the movement—contrasting emotions expressed simultaneously—owes much to the traditions of 19th-century opera.

CONCLUSION

The tonal idiom thrived throughout the whole of the 20th century in every genre of music, particularly the symphony and symphonic poem, the new genre of film music, ballet, song, and musical theater. Some composers were content to remain within the idiom of extended chromaticism inherited from the late 19th century. Others expanded the limits of tonality beyond triadic harmonies and the diatonic scale. Yet all these composers remained committed to the principle of writing works with a tonal center of some kind. Tonal and atonal music thus coexisted in much the same way that the *prima prattica* and *seconda prattica* had flourished side by side in the 17th century.

New Currents after 1945

The end of World War II marked a decisive turning point not only in world history, but in music as well. The war had been a catastrophic experience: the majority of the 50 million killed in the conflict were civilians and included the estimated 6 million victims of the Nazi Holocaust. The atomic bombs dropped on Japan in 1945 opened an era in which humans became capable of destroying virtually all life on earth. People everywhere sought to turn away from these horrors and make a fresh start; artists in all fields were no exception. In the light of the recent past, the New became all the more appealing, setting off what amounted to a second, postwar wave of modernism.

THE QUEST FOR INNOVATION

Penderecki
Threnody for the Victims of Hiroshima

One work written in direct response to the war indicates just how far composers were willing to go in their quest for innovation. Moved by the devastation of Hiroshima, the Polish composer Krzysztof Penderecki (b. 1933) sought to express the grim reality of nuclear war in his *Threnody for the Victims of Hiroshima* (1960). Finding conventional sonorities and textures inadequate to capture the event and its aftermath, Penderecki calls in his score for unique combinations of sounds from an orchestra consisting of 52 stringed instruments (24 violins, 10 violas, 10 cellos, 8 double basses). At times the string players are asked to create sharp, percussive sounds by snapping strings against the fingerboard. At other times they must produce a different kind of percussive sound by striking the body of the instrument with the fingertips. Penderecki's score often grants considerable freedom to the performers. He asks individual players at several points to play simply "the highest note possible," and at other points he directs different groups of instruments to play with vibrato at different rates of speed, indicated only generally by the size of the wavy line in the score; the precise speed is left up to individual players. On still other occasions, individual performers are free to choose from a group of four different notational sequences and perform the chosen group "as rapidly as possible." The work features no meter and no bar lines: durations are indicated by timings that run underneath the bottom of each system of the score.

Other elements of the score, however, are extremely precise. Penderecki uses microtones— intervals smaller than a half step in the diatonic scale—at many points in the score. Western musicians had long been aware of microtones, but principally as a theoretical idea (see Prologue: Antiquity). It was not until the 20th century that composers like Ives, Bartók, Berg, Copland, and Ligeti began to use microtones in their works. Penderecki's *Threnody* explores these possibilities to an unprecedented degree, concluding with a massive quarter-tone cluster of tones and microtones spanning two octaves and played by all 52 instruments.

The form of Penderecki's *Threnody* offers a comparable mixture of precision and imprecision. Like Varèse's *Ionisation* (see Chapter 20), the work is structured around sonorities, dynamics, and textures rather than themes or key areas.

COMBINATORIALITY

In the late 1920s, Arnold Schoenberg had discovered that certain 12-tone rows embody special features. He pointed out that a limited number of rows were **combinatorial.** A row is said to be combinatorial if one of its hexachords—its first six or last six notes, commonly referred to as hexachords A and B—can be combined with one of the hexachords of an inverted, retrograde, or retrograde inverted form of the same row without producing any duplication of pitches.

The row for the first of Milton Babbitt's *Three Compositions for Piano* (1947) illustrates this property (see Example 23-1). Here, P-0 is combinatorial with R-6. In other words, hexachord A of P-0 combines with hexachord B of R-6 to produce all 12 pitches. The order of the pitches is different than in P-0, but combinatoriality is concerned only with the content of the individual (and combined) hexachords, not the actual sequence of the pitches. The complementary hexachords of the two forms (hexachord B of P-0 and hexachord A of R-6) are also combinatorial.

Schoenberg first developed the use of combinatorial rows in his *Variations for Orchestra,* op. 31 (1928), and in his *Piano Pieces,* op. 33a (1929). Combinatoriality eventually became his preferred method of 12-tone composition, but Berg and Webern never really embraced the technique.

Babbitt
Three Compositions for Piano

Example 23-1 Row forms used in Babbitt's *Three Compositions for Piano*, no. 1.

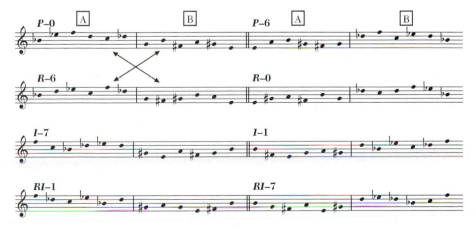

Source: From George Perle, *Serial Composition and Atonality,* Sixth Edition, Revised. Copyright © 1991 The Regents of the University of California. Reprinted with permission of the University of California Press.

Schoenberg's students and followers in the United States took up the idea with special fervor in the years after World War II. Combinatoriality allowed these composers to align different set forms to sound at the same time without risking simultaneous or nearly simultaneous iterations of the same pitch class. By exploiting the combinatorial properties of this row, Babbitt and others were able to create multiple statements of the 12-tone row not only horizontally (in individual voices) but also vertically through the alignment of two different forms of the row sounding simultaneously. In the opening measures of the *Three Compositions for Piano*, no. 1, for example, we find the basic row both horizontally and vertically:

◆ Horizontally—the left hand in measures 1–2 presents P-0 in its entirety; the right hand presents P-6 in its entirety.

◆ Vertically—taking both voices together, all 12 pitches appear in measure 1; all 12 appear again in measure 2, in measure 3, and so on.

INTEGRAL SERIALISM

In the years immediately after World War II, Olivier Messiaen and Milton Babbitt, working independently of each other, developed ways of extending the parameters of serial composition beyond pitch to include such elements as rhythm and dynamics as well. This approach soon became known as **integral** or **total serialism.**

Babbitt's *Three Compositions for Piano* (1947) is one of the earliest and most celebrated of all works to use integral serialism. In addition to manipulating the combinatorial properties of the row, Babbitt serializes the elements of rhythm, dynamics, and register as well. Using the sixteenth note as the unit of measure, he establishes a basic pattern of 5, 1, 4, 2 (that is, five sixteenth notes, followed by one sixteenth note, and so on) and "inverts" the rhythmic structure by subtracting these values from 6. Thus the rhythmic matrix of the work looks like this:

P = 5, 1, 4, 2

I = 1, 5, 2, 4

RI = 4, 2, 5, 1

R = 2, 4, 1, 5

Prime forms of the pitch row, regardless of the transposition, are always presented in the P rhythm (5, 1, 4, 2), inverted forms of the pitch row in the I rhythm (1, 5, 2, 4), retrograde inverted forms in the RI rhythm, and retrograde forms in the R rhythm. Rhythmic durations are articulated by disrupting the pattern of continuous sixteenth notes, either through rests or through slurred notes that create rhythms of longer duration.

Dynamics are also determined by precompositional choices.

P = *mp* (*pp* in measures 49–56)

I = *f* (*mp* in measures 49–56)

RI = *p* (*ppp* in measures 49–56)

R = *mf* (*p* in measures 49–56)

The structure of the work as a whole is highly symmetrical. This is most immediately evident in a comparison of its opening and closing sections:

Section 1 (measures 1–8):

R.H.	P-6	R-0	RI-7	I-1
L.H.	P-0	RI-1	I-7	R-6

Section 6 (measures 49–56):

R.H.	P-0	RI-1	I-7	R-6
L.H.	RI-7	I-1	P-6	R-0

Close examination reveals comparable (and more intricate) symmetries between sections 2 (measures 9–18) and 5 (measures 39–48) and between sections 3 (measures 19–28) and 4 (measures 29–38).

Messiaen's *Mode de valeurs et d'intensités* ("Mode of Durations and Intensities"), published in 1949, is not quite as systematic, but it treats both pitch and rhythm in serial fashion. In this, one of four "Rhythmic Etudes," Messiaen uses three different 12-tone rows, each in its own register (high, medium, low), spanning a total of 36 different notes. Each of the 36 notes is assigned a unique rhythmic value, from a thirty-second note to a dotted whole note. Dynamic markings (from *ppp* to *fff*) and articulation (accent, staccato, a short vertical line, a wedge, or no marking at all) are aligned with specific notes as well, although not in a unique one-to-one correspondence as with the rhythmic values.

Messiaen himself did not pursue integral serialism or even serialism itself much further in subsequent years, but his work in this area exercised great influence on a generation of younger composers, most notably Pierre Boulez (b. 1925) and Karlheinz Stockhausen (b. 1928). In the end, however, integral serialism proved more important as a concept than as an application. In later years, Boulez considered this approach as part of a larger attempt to work through the burdens of tradition tonal, as well as atonal, serial as well as nonserial:

> After the war [World War II], we felt that music, like the world around us, was in a state of chaos. Our problem was to make a new musical language, seeking out what was good from the past, and rejecting what was bad. Around 1950, and for the following three years, we went through a period of seeking out total control over music. The serial process, which originated with Schoenberg and was refined in Webern, pointed out the way. What we were doing, by total serialization, was to annihilate the will of the composer in favor of a predetermining system. . . . But total control, like the total lack of control, can lead to chaos. Gaining this control was a necessary step in our development, because of our need to transubstantiate our musical heritage. But once there, we were at the zero point as composers. Now we could begin. Our process since about 1955 has been to enlarge and generalize what we had acquired through the period of atomization. In that way, we could gain a freedom through conquest, not merely through *laissez-faire*.[1]

By the end of the century, however, the prestige of integral serialism and serialism in general had declined greatly. Composition students continued to learn how to write serial music, but this was no longer considered *the* technique for new music. Pluralism had made it only one of many options available to composers wishing to move beyond tonality.

ALEATORY MUSIC

Whereas integral serialism stressed a high degree of structure and control, **aleatory music** took precisely the opposite approach, with chance playing a leading role. The term *aleatory* comes from the Latin *alea* meaning "die" (the singular of "dice"), and aleatory music involves (at least metaphorically) a "roll of the dice"—that is, chance. The

℗RIMARY EVIDENCE

"Who Cares If You Listen?"

When Milton Babbitt's essay "Who Cares If You Listen?" first appeared in 1958 it soon became the flashpoint of a larger debate about the difficulties audiences were experiencing with modern music. The provocative title—imposed on the author by the editors of *High Fidelity*—suggests that Babbitt and his colleagues had no concern for listeners. But Babbitt's real argument is that some composers need to be able to work in an environment that allows them to explore new ideas the same way scientists conduct experiments in their laboratories. Such an environment, Babbitt argued, is to be found in the university. There, free from commercial pressures, composers would be able to help music develop beyond its current state.

• • • • •

Why should the layman be other than bored and puzzled by what he is unable to understand, music or anything else? It is only the translation of this boredom and puzzlement into resentment and denunciation that seems to me indefensible. After all, the public does have its own music, its ubiquitous music: music to eat by, to read by, to dance by, and to be impressed by. Why refuse to recognize the possibility that contemporary music has reached a stage long since attained by other forms of activity? The time has passed when the normally well-educated man without special preparation could understand the most advanced work in, for example, mathematics, philosophy, and physics. Advanced music, to the extent that it reflects the knowledge and originality of the informed composer, scarcely can be expected to appear more intelligible than these arts and sciences

to the person whose musical education usually has been even less extensive than his background in other fields. But to this, a double standard is invoked, with the words "music is music," implying also that "music is *just* music." Why not, then, equate the activities of the radio repairman with those of the theoretical physicist, on the basis of the dictum that "physics is physics"? It is not difficult to find statements like the following, from the *New York Times* of September 8, 1957: "The scientific level of the conference is so high . . . that there are in the world only 120 mathematicians specializing in the field who could contribute." Specialized music, on the other hand, far from signifying "height" of musical level, has been charged with "decadence," even as evidence of an insidious "conspiracy."

. . . And so, I dare suggest that the composer would do himself and his music an immediate and eventual service by total, resolute, and voluntary withdrawal from this public world to one of private performance and electronic media, with its very real possibility of complete elimination of the public and social aspects of musical composition. By so doing, the separation between the domains would be defined beyond any possibility of confusion of categories, and the composer would be free to pursue a private life of professional achievement, as opposed to a public life of unprofessional compromise and exhibitionism. . . .

Admittedly, if this music is not supported, the whistling repertory of the man in the street will be little affected, the concert-going activity of the conspicuous consumer of musical culture will be little disturbed. But music will cease to evolve, and, in that important sense, will cease to live.

Source: Milton Babbitt, "Who Cares If You Listen?" *High Fidelity*, vol. 8, no. 2 (1958): 38–40. Copyright Hachette Filipacchi Magazines, Inc. used by permission of Hachette Filipacchi Magazines, Inc.

idea of writing music by chance, even by a literal throw of the dice, was by no means new in the 20th century. Mozart and other composers of the Classical era were fascinated by the possibility of creating works based on modular units chosen at random from an extensive array of possibilities. The idea of aleatory music enjoyed a healthy revival in the 1950s and 1960s through such composers as John Cage, Karlheinz Stockhausen, and Pauline Oliveros.

Aleatory music can involve widely varying degrees of chance and indeterminacy. At one end of the scale are works like Terry Riley's *IN C* (Anthology, discussed later under "Minimalism"), in which a group of musicians play specific gestures in a specified sequence but are free to move on to the next gesture more or less as they please. In the middle of the chance spectrum is a composition like Cage's *Music of Changes,* a piano work from 1951, in which the performer repeatedly tosses coins and proceeds according to a carefully designed matrix of choices. At the far end of the field is Cage's *Music for Piano* (1952–1956), in which pitches are determined by tracing the imperfections that emerge from the performer's careful scrutiny of a random sheet of paper.

The most celebrated of all aleatoric compositions is *4′33″,* first performed on August 29, 1952, at the appropriately named Maverick Concert Hall in Woodstock, New York (near the site of the celebrated rock festival that would take place there 17 summers later). The work, which consists of three entirely silent movements, was inspired in part by the "white paintings" by one of Cage's friends, the artist Robert Rauschenberg. These so-called blank canvases are by their very nature never truly blank, of course. Every canvas has its own unique colors and textures, and each canvas is constantly changing because of the way it reflects the light of its surroundings. In much the same way, Cage's *4′33″* challenges the notion that there is such a thing as silence—the musical equivalent of a blank canvas—and by extension, the very idea of music itself. By listening to a supposedly silent work, we become acutely aware of the sounds around us: breathing, coughing, a room's ventilation system, a dog barking in the distance. We are listening to a work that is not silent at all and changes constantly and differs from performance to performance. These kinds of sounds, moreover, are always a part of the listening experience: if we choose to shut them out, it is because we have been conditioned to do so.

Many interpreted Cage's work as the epitome of the modernist composer's contempt for the audience. Other listeners reveled in the work's profoundly provocative absurdity. The piece is in some respects even more absurd than most people realize, for its score (and it does have a score) directs that the work "may be performed and last any length of time by any instrumentalist or combination of instrumentalists." Thus the most famous aspect of the piece—its meticulously precise duration—is optional.

Cage
4′33″

ELECTRONIC MUSIC

Electronic music was a fundamentally new phenomenon in the 20th century. In its purest form, it requires no performer: the sounds are produced by a machine, and the recorded version *is* the work. The ideal apparatus allows composers to manipulate all possible frequencies at all possible amplitudes with all possible durations. No sound—including those inaudible to the human ear—is impossible.

Electronic instruments first emerged in the 1920s. The theremin, named after its Russian-born inventor, Leon Theremin (1896–1993), was one of the first such instruments to attract widespread attention. It produced a single tone whose pitch and volume could be controlled by the motion of the player's hands around its antenna. Its eerie,

Composer Profile

John Cage
(1912–1992)

"Everything we do is music," Cage once declared, and in many respects his music was devoted to making life itself an art form. He did not see himself as a high priest of art but rather as a facilitator between listeners and sounds. Profoundly influenced by Zen Buddhism and its renunciation of striving and the will, Cage maintained his "purpose is to eliminate purpose," and many of his works from the late 1940s on seem to avoid or challenge the traditional stance of the composer as an omnipotent creator of a small musical world.

Cage's output falls into several broad categories:

◆ Works for percussion, including prepared piano. The composer's early output includes a number of works for standard and nonstandard percussion instruments. A student of Henry Cowell (see Chapter 20), Cage extended his teacher's novel approach to the piano by calling for fitting the instrument's strings with such objects as screws, rubber bands, and coins, producing a range of timbres as oddly familiar as they are strange.

◆ Aleatory works. In addition to *4'33"*, Cage wrote many works based on the element of chance. Several relate directly to the *I Ching,* also known as the *Book of Changes,* a system of interpreting the interplay of strong and weak forces based on the throw of dice. In *Music of Changes* (1951), the pianist-performer constructs the work by using charts based on the *I Ching* and by flipping three coins. Cage's *Imaginary Landscape no. 4* (1951) calls for 12 radios tuned to 12 different stations playing simultaneously. The instructions to the performers—the individuals turning the control dials on each radio—are precise, but the results are naturally unpredictable. *0'00"* (1962) consists of an amplified projection of a "disciplined action": in one of his many performances of this work, the composer sliced vegetables,

KEY DATES IN THE LIFE OF JOHN CAGE

1912 Born September 5 in Los Angeles.

1930 After visiting Europe returns to the United States and studies piano and composition with Henry Cowell.

1934 Studies harmony and counterpoint with Arnold Schoenberg at UCLA.

1938 Begins a lifelong personal and artistic association with the dancer Merce Cunningham, collaborating on a series of "happenings," performances that combine music, dance, poetry, film, and other forms of expression.

1954 Concert tour of Europe with the pianist David Tudor.

1961 Publishes *Silence,* the first of his many books on music.

1972 Sixtieth birthday is marked by concerts at The New School for Social Research and at Lincoln Center.

1988–1989 Delivers the Norton Lectures at Harvard University.

1992 Dies August 12 in New York City.

placed them in a blender, and drank the mix while standing very close to a microphone.

◆ Electronic works. Cage was part of the first generation able to explore the possibilities of electronically generated sound. *Fontana Mix* (1959) combines aleatory principles with taped music, the mix being determined by the combination of various transparencies on which are graphically notated changes in amplitude, frequency, timbre, and so on.

Cage and his music consistently polarized listeners. Most of the audience at New York's Lincoln Center walked out of his *Atlas eclipticalis* (whose score superimposes transparent staff paper on star charts to determine pitches) when it was first presented by the New York Philharmonic in 1964; even members of the orchestra hissed the composer. But Cage's provocative music and writings remained fresh over time, and toward the end of his life he was showered with honors. He delivered the prestigious Charles Eliot Norton lectures at Harvard University in 1988, continuing in the tradition of Stravinsky, Hindemith, Copland, Boulez, Bernstein, and Berio. Some saw genius in his works, others charlatanism, but all were provoked by them to rethink the nature of music and its relationship to the world around us.

John Cage. *Many of Cage's works from the 1960s and 1970s were multimedia productions created with other artists. Two of his longtime collaborators were the dancer and choreographer Merce Cunningham and the pianist and composer David Tudor (b. 1926). In this live performance of Cage's Variations V (1926–1996), Cage is seated at the far left in the foreground, manipulating electronic sound equipment along with Tudor (center) and (at the far right) the composer Gordon Mumma (b. 1935). Members of the Merce Cunningham Dance Company perform behind them, with images projected against the backdrop. In this work, Cage called for the dancers to perform within a matrix of strategically placed microphones, making the sounds of the dancers' movements an integral part of the performance.*

Source: Courtesy of Cunningham Dance Foundation, Inc.

otherworldly sound made it a favorite instrument of composers writing scores for science fiction movies, such as *The Day the Earth Stood Still* (1951) and *It Came from Outer Space* (1953), not to mention the television cartoon series *The Jetsons* (1962).

Far more significant was the development of electronic music synthesizers in the late 1940s and 1950s. These instruments made it possible for composers to create, modify, and control the entire spectrum of sound for the first time in history. The only real variants in a purely electronic composition are the quality of the sound system on which a work is reproduced and the acoustics of the space in which the work is presented. Milton Babbitt, one of the first major composers to exploit the possibilities of this new technology, praised the ability of these machines to realize complex rhythms to a degree not possible in most live performances.

Electronic music can be categorized into three major subcategories: musique concrète, synthesized electronic music, and computer music. Any and all of the three can be combined with live performers.

Musique concrète is a French term used to denote music in which the sonic material to be manipulated is a recorded sound taken from everyday life (the sounds are thus real, or "concrete"). The sounds themselves might range from that of a passing train to speaking voices, to (as in one particular work by the Greek composer Iannis Xenakis) the sound of burning charcoal. These concrete sounds are manipulated by tape splicing, mixing, and superimposing to create a larger whole.

Musique concrète was first developed in the late 1940s by the French composer Pierre Schaeffer (1910–1995) and has since been explored by a variety of others, including John Cage, Luciano Berio, and Steve Reich, whose *It's Gonna Rain* (discussed later) manipulates a single phrase of spoken text. The Canadian composer Hugh Le Caine's *Dripsody* (1955) derives entirely from an even briefer moment of sound: a single falling drop of water. By running this single recorded sound over and over again through a variable-speed tape recorder, Le Caine (1914–1977) was able to create an astonishing variety of sounds never before heard. But the work is far more than interesting sonic effects: it has a definite shape, a trajectory that projects a sense of drama and development. The ending of the work, playing on the sound of the proverbial dripping faucet, is eerily reminiscent of Haydn's String Quartet op. 33, no. 2, which leaves the unsuspecting listener uncertain just when it has ended.

Musique concrète raises provocative questions about distinctions between music and sound in general, and between music and speech. In an earlier era, music was tacitly understood to be a special type of sound, created for its own sake either with the voice or musical instruments (or both) and distinctly different from sounds that are mere by-products of daily life. But the composers who have manipulated everyday sounds have called into question this basic assumption.

Synthesized electronic music consists of sounds generated and manipulated entirely by electronic means, through an electronic oscillator or a modifying device like a synthesizer. Basic sine waves can be modified by modulators, filters, and reverberators, all of which in one way or another change the color of a tone by altering its overtones. Milton Babbitt and Karlheinz Stockhausen (b. 1928) are two of the most prominent composers associated with this kind of electronic music. As a member of the faculty at Princeton University, Babbitt had access to the RCA Synthesizer in the Columbia-Princeton Electronic Music Center in New York City in the late 1950s and early 1960s. The machine was expensive, slow, and cumbersome to operate by today's standards, but in its time was a breakthrough that allowed Babbitt to produce a new kind of music. The introduction of portable synthesizers in the mid-1960s and the rise of the personal computer in the 1980s allowed virtually anyone to pursue this kind of composition. MIDI (Musical Instrument Digital Interface) emerged in the early 1980s as the standard computer language for driving electronic synthesizers, which in turn produce sound. MIDI allows composers to control pitch, rhythm, dynamics, vibrato, and timbre in a remarkably sophisticated manner. It has eliminated the need for much (but not all) of the programming associated with electronic and computer music.

One of the earliest and still best known works of synthesized electronic music is the soundtrack to the MGM film *Forbidden Planet* (1956), composed by the husband-and-wife team of Louis Barron (1920–1989) and Bebe Barron (b. 1926). A science fiction adaptation of Shakespeare's *The Tempest*, this was the first commercially released film to feature an entirely electronic soundtrack. The eerie soundscape resonated with the story's setting on a bleak and distant planet. Audiences of the time were accustomed to

"I could specify something and hear it instantly." Milton Babbitt at the RCA Synthesizer, Columbia-Princeton Studios, New York City, late 1950s. *By today's standards, this synthesizer is limited. But in its time, it was one of the most advanced machines of its kind, and there were only a handful like it anywhere in the world. On several occasions, Babbitt praised the ability of machines like this one to realize rhythms to a degree not possible in most "live" performances. But the apparatus, containing 750 vacuum tubes, was cumbersome to control. "It had a paper drive," Babbitt recalled later, "and getting the paper through the machine and punching the holes was difficult. We were punching in binary. The machine was totally zero, nothing predetermined, and any number we punched could refer to any dimension of the machine. . . . It was basically just a complex switching device to an enormous and complicated analogue studio hooked to a tape machine. And yet for me it was so wonderful because I could specify something and hear it instantly."*

Source: Photo courtesy Milton Babbitt

lushly orchestrated scores played by a large orchestra; the stark, disembodied sounds they heard in *Forbidden Planet* had been created in a recording studio the Barrons had set up in their New York apartment, consisting of oscillators, mixers, filters, and tape recorders. By later standards, the equipment was primitive, but the sound, generated entirely by electrical sources, was distinctively new.

Computer music is music that has been generated, transformed, fully composed, or performed by a computer program. In its earliest form, computer music involved allowing a computer to determine how a work would unfold. Lejaren Hiller's *Illiac Suite* for string quartet (1957) is generally acknowledged to be the first work in which the computer actually emulated the process of composition itself. Hiller (1924–1994), working with the scientist Leonard Issacson, created the work on an Illiac computer at the University of Illinois, programming the machine to create a series of movements in specific styles, ranging from strict counterpoint to 12 tone to random. Hiller later collaborated with John Cage to produce *HPSCHD* (1969), which integrates musical quotations from Mozart, Beethoven, Schoenberg, and others, mixing them with the sounds of 56 tape recorders and 7 harpsichordists, all of it structured according to computerized models. By the 1990s, digitized computer technology had largely replaced the tape recorder, for it bypassed the physical limitations of tape and allowed for more sophisticated manipulation of sounds.

Seeking a remedy for the inherently variable and unpredictable nature of performance, composers of many different orientations welcomed electronic music as a way of achieving total control over the finished product. Viennese composer Ernst Krenek praised the "electronic medium, earlier denounced as a mechanistic degradation of music," for its ability to lend itself "to a kind of controlled compositional improvisation much more readily than the realm of live sound because the composer can mould the sound material while he is creating it."[2] Around the middle of the century, in fact, some people believed electronic music would sweep away the established instruments and performance venues of most, or even all, music in Western society. By century's end, however, it was clear that electronic music was not about to replace live performers. Instead, like serial composition, it would provide composers with another option for creating music, enriching the musical landscape with its possibilities without eliminating earlier practices.

In retrospect, electronic music achieved its greatest impact when composers began to integrate it with live performance. Karlheinz Stockhausen's *Gesang der Jünglinge* (1956, "Song of the Youths") combines the human voice with electronically generated sounds; Milton Babbitt's *Philomel* (1963) calls for a soprano soloist to perform live against a recorded tape running at the same time. By the 1980s, rock music concerts routinely combined taped (or digitally recorded) and live music; the notated music of many rock songs is in fact nothing more than an approximate transcription of an electronic original. The essential work exists not in the form of a notated score, but rather as a recording.

The recording studio also benefited from the technologies of electronic music. As early as the 1950s, technology had given artists the freedom to vary such elements as dynamics (by altering levels of amplification) and resonance (by altering reverberation). Overdubbing allowed musicians to superimpose an additional voice or voices over an existing one. Popular music, particularly rock, embraced these techniques with extraordinary enthusiasm. Electronic technology was also applied to standard instruments of the rock band in live performances, most notably the piano and the guitar. By the late 1960s, the synthesizer had become a staple of rock bands and many jazz ensembles.

ROCK MUSIC

Rock music, like jazz and country music, includes an enormous range of genres and styles. Its earliest form, known as rock and roll, grew out of a synthesis of jazz (particularly the blues), country music, and popular song in the mid-1950s. Rock and roll's characteristic sound rested on an ensemble of drums and electric guitars, often with a double bass. The persistent 4/4 rhythm of the drums typically featured a back beat (1–2–**3**–4), and most early rock and roll was written as dance music. The lyrics, mild by later standards, were often sexually suggestive; the term *rock and roll* was itself slang for sexual intercourse. Chuck Berry, Little Richard, Jerry Lee Lewis, and Elvis Presley won renown as much for their body language as for their music. Presley's pelvic gyrations during his performance of the song *Hound Dog* on *The Milton Berle Show* in 1956 generated such an uproar from critics and the (adult) public that in later television appearances—on *The Ed Sullivan Show*—he was shown in close-up only above the waist. Meanwhile, tamer performers like Buddy Holly and the Crickets, the Righteous Brothers, Ricky Nelson, and Brenda Lee gave rock and roll a more parent-friendly image.

The vocal sound of early rock and roll (and most later rock) typically rejected refinement in favor of immediacy, often involving a shoutlike singing style and pointedly using words like "ain't" and "nohow." Backup singers often reinforced the rhythm with nonsense syllables like "shu-bop shu-bop" and "doo-lang doo-lang." But the formula for a memorable rock song remained essentially the same as that for any song from any period: a good tune and resonant lyrics.

Berry
Roll Over, Beethoven

Chuck Berry's *Roll Over, Beethoven* is typical of many early rock-and-roll songs of the 1950s and early 1960s. Its melodic range is limited, its formal structure and rhythms repetitive, its essential harmonies confined to the tonic and subdominant—and for all these reasons, the work is mesmerizing. The lyrics themselves, urging the most revered of all classical composers to turn over in his grave, evoke a cultural war between so-called high and low art, contemplation and activity, old and young. The song spoke directly to a generation of teenagers, and it retains its elemental force today. Formally, *Roll Over, Beethoven* follows the 12-bar blues form. The published lead sheet provides only the barest outline of the melody, harmonies, and words; a great many aspects of the music are left to the discretion of the performer or performers.

From the 1960s onward, rock (as it had by then come to be known) began moving in many different directions. The Beatles, building on the traditions of Elvis Presley, Little Richard, and others, emerged on the American scene in 1963 and paved the way for what would be called the "British Invasion" of similar groups, including the Rolling Stones, the Animals, the Byrds, and the Who. In 1970, the Who released the first rock opera, *Tommy*. Other subgenres of rock included Motown, surf, and hard (or acid) rock. Motown flourished in Detroit with African American groups like the Temptations, Diana Ross and the Supremes, the Four Tops, and Smoky Robinson and the Miracles, and individual artists like Stevie Wonder and Marvin Gaye. The Motown sound was characterized by close vocal harmony, soaring melody, and a steady beat. Surf was in many respects the white counterpart to Motown: it, too, relied on close harmony, as is evident in the work of the Beach Boys and Dick Dale and the Deltones. Hard rock or acid rock was characterized by a louder, more aggressive sound, often involving sonic distortion. Preeminent among these groups were the Jefferson Airplane, Jimi Hendrix Experience, Janis Joplin, and Jim Morrison and the Doors.

Within a few years of their 1964 *Ed Sullivan Show* debut, the Beatles had expanded the boundaries of rock to include orchestral and non-Western instruments, more

Chuck Berry. *This image of Chuck Berry performing his signature duck walk captures two contradictory streams in the emergence of rock during the mid-1950s. What appealed to youth—and what parents found so threatening about this music—was its physical presence, its pounding rhythm, and the suggestive movements associated with it on the stage. The coat-and-tie outfit was a calculated effort to counter this. Berry was one of the first African-American rock-and-roll artists to be marketed directly to white youth, and the respectable clothing helped penetrate that market. In fact, this outfit remained standard for many rockers well into the 1960s. The Beatles, the Rolling Stones, and even the Doors made early appearances in such attire, and the male participants in Dick Clark's long-running* American Bandstand *television show were required to wear ties until the late 1960s.*

Source: MICHAEL OCHS ARCHIVES.COM

sophisticated and enigmatic texts, a broader range of harmonies and forms, and an increasingly sophisticated use of recording technology to create works that in effect could not be performed in a live setting in any recognizable fashion.

The manipulation of sound in the Beatles' *Strawberry Fields Forever* (1967), for example, is so basic to the work that it can be legitimately considered an example of electronic music. Beyond standard techniques of amplification, resonance, and overdubbing, *Strawberry Fields Forever* features electronic manipulation of the vocals that causes the pitch to drop, thereby contributing to the dreamy, other worldly quality of the sound. The technique is essentially the same as that used by Le Caine in his *Dripsody.* The cymbals and other percussion instruments were dubbed backward in places, creating a strange, unsettling effect. George Martin, the Beatles' producer at the time, deserves almost as much credit for these innovations as the Beatles themselves. *Strawberry Fields Forever* also features unusual harmonic, rhythmic, instrumental, and lyrical effects:

◆ Harmony. The opening harmonic progression, for example, moves from A to E minor to F♯ major to D and only then back to A, and at the words "nothing is real," we hear a ♭V–VI progression.

◆ Rhythm and tempo. These are irregular at many points, set in a manner that speeds up and slows down quite unpredictably, with the instruments underneath playing cross rhythms against the voice, all of which captures the essence of the words perfectly.

◆ Instrumentation. In addition to the standard guitars and drums, the work uses orchestral instruments such as flutes and cellos, as well as a non-Western instrument (the svaramandal, an Indian harp).

◆ Lyrics. These are largely unrhymed and unmetrical in structure, the words are elliptical, elusive, partly nonsensical in content (or perhaps not), but in any case markedly different from the typical lyrics of rock songs at that time.

Such techniques are even more abundant in the Beatles' landmark album, *Sergeant Pepper's Lonely Hearts Club Band,* released in 1967. This concept album, revolving around the idea of a fictional band, was one of the first to be issued with a complete set of printed lyrics. The music moved well beyond standard harmonies and forms and spawned a subgenre of its own known as progressive rock. From the late 1960s through the early 1980s, groups like Frank Zappa and the Mothers of Invention, Pink Floyd, the Moody Blues, Jethro Tull, the Who, Genesis, Emerson Lake and Palmer, and Tangerine Dream cultivated a type of rock that consistently emphasized unconventional harmonies, complex rhythms, polyphonic textures, and unusual sonorities. No resource was off limits: Gentle Giant's *On Reflection* (1975) is a four-part fugue reminiscent of a 14th-century caccia, Pink Floyd, in true musique concrète fashion, occasionally integrated into their music recorded sounds made from household objects.

Rock styles proliferated still further in the closing decades of the 20th century. Heavy metal bands from the late 1960s onward like Led Zeppelin, Kiss, and Guns 'n' Roses emphasized an unprecedented volume of sound. Disco (popular in the 1970s and 1980s) featured a relentless 4/4 beat and sweeping melody, often played by violins. Techno relied heavily on electronic and digital manipulation and made little or no effort to mimic traditional instruments in the process. Hip-hop evolved out of Jamaican roots and involved words shouted over a turntabled disk being manipulated by a disk jockey. Rap, which developed out of hip-hop, featured a vocal technique somewhat akin to *Sprechstimme,* with a decided emphasis on meter and rhyme.

FOLK MUSIC

Partly in reaction against the loud volume, insistent rhythms, and increasingly technological elements of rock and roll in the late 1950s and early 1960s, a number of musicians and their listening public gravitated toward a more natural sound, untouched (or at least only minimally touched) by electronic manipulation. A broad category of music loosely known as "folk music" rode an enormous wave of popularity at this time. The repertory was derived from or created in the spirit of the traditional songs that had been cultivated by country musicians in previous decades. The folk sound rested on acoustic (not electric) guitars, limited use of percussion instruments (or none at all), lyrical melody, and texts that harkened back to an earlier era, extolling the virtues of simplicity and the enduring themes of love and loss. From the late 1950s into the 1970s, groups like the Weavers, the Kingston Trio, Peter, Paul and Mary, and Simon and Garfunkel, and individual artists like Bob Dylan, Joan Baez, Judy Collins, Joni Mitchell, John Denver, Gordon Lightfoot, and James Taylor held their own in the charts against Elvis and, later, the Beatles.

Anonymous
Tom Dooley

The relationship of this repertory to music as cultivated in the unwritten and un-recorded tradition remains much in dispute. The song *Tom Dooley* illustrates the complexity of the ways in which much of this music was transmitted. The ballad *Tom Dooley* was a true folk ballad, a way of telling the news—in this case about the murder of one Laura Foster in 1865 in western North Carolina, allegedly at the hands of her lover, Tom Dooley. In 1938, the folklorist Frank Warner was traveling in that part of the state and took down the song as performed in unaccompanied form by a local resident named Frank Proffitt. Proffitt had learned the song from his father, who in turn had learned it from his mother, who had actually witnessed the hanging of Tom Dooley. Warner passed his transcription of the song on to his colleague Alan Lomax, who in 1947 published it in a collection called *Folk Song U.S.A.*, crediting Warner as the collector. Lomax carefully preserved the regional pronunciations ("stobbed" for "stabbed," "tuck" for "took") and commissioned Charles Seeger and his wife, Ruth Crawford Seeger (a significant composer in her own right), to add piano accompaniment. The first published version of the work thus represents a curious mixture of old (melody, text) with new (harmonizations, piano accompaniment).

Eleven years later, the Kingston Trio picked up the song from Lomax's anthology, made their own arrangement, recorded it, and scored their first hit. Warner and Lomax, realizing the immense popularity of the song, contacted Proffitt, and the three filed suit against the Kingston Trio. They began to receive small royalties on the Kingston Trio's recording after 1962, by which time the group had already sold four million copies of the song. Because of technology, what had been passed on from generation to generation orally and in a remote locale for almost eighty years had become a readily available commodity when it was first published in 1947—and an extremely valuable commodity, worth millions of dollars, when it was recorded by the Kingston Trio in 1958.

Other artists wrote entirely new works in the style of folk music. Bob Dylan's early songs draw on the traditional repertory through their uncomplicated (and often technically 'incorrect') harmonies and less-than-perfect metrical blendings of music and text. Dylan's vocal style was itself rough hewn, half sung, half declaimed, and sometimes glaringly out of tune. Like many rock artists of the day, he avoided any sense of vocal beauty in the traditional sense, preferring instead to cultivate the impression of unvarnished immediacy, no matter how many hours and studio recording takes were actually required to capture a song. Dylan was also a traditionalist in using song as a vehicle of social protest. Ballads in 18th-century England had often protested against unpopular laws or court verdicts, and Dylan extended his work to protest against racial injustice, nuclear proliferation, and governmental repression.

JAZZ

Jazz continued to develop in many directions in the second half of the 20th century. **Free jazz,** one of the more controversial strands, emerged in the late 1950s. Although improvisation had long been one of the characteristic features of jazz, free jazz extended the boundaries of the concept, eliminating such standard elements as improvisations on a given theme, fixed meters, chord progressions, and even tonality itself.

Dissatisfied with traditional forms of jazz, the saxophonist Ornette Coleman (b. 1930) assembled in 1960 a group of eight musicians—a double quartet, each consisting of a reed instrument (saxophone or bass clarinet), trumpet, bass, and drums—that included the saxophonist Eric Dolphy, trumpeters Don Cherry and Freddie Hubbard, and bassist Charlie Haden. The group began to improvise without a central theme, and the resulting "collective improvisation," as Coleman called it, runs 38 minutes without a pause. It was recorded in a single take, without splices or edits. The music blurs the line between solo and accompaniment, another important distinction in more traditional jazz. It uses no established themes, chord patterns, or chorus lengths and moves freely in and out of tonality. As if to underline the interrelationship of modernist arts, the album cover of *Free Jazz* featured an abstract painting by the American artist Jackson Pollock.

Free Jazz created a firestorm of controversy among critics and listeners, many of whom accused Coleman of creating music that was not jazz at all. Others maintained that he had overintellectualized the art. The terms of the debate are eerily reminiscent of those in the exchange between Winthrop Sargent and Duke Ellington in the 1930s (see Chapter 20).

Coleman's innovative approach opened the way for a variety of jazz styles that moved beyond traditional concepts of tonality, rhythm, and form. Foremost among the artists working along these lines were the bassist Charles Mingus (1922–1979), the pianist Cecil Taylor (b. 1933), and trumpeter Miles Davis (1926–1991), none of whom embraced free jazz to quite the extent evident in Coleman's 1960 album but all of whom were indelibly influenced by the music's blend of freedom and complexity. Taylor and Davis, in particular, were central figures from the mid-1960s onward in a type of music known as *fusion*, which blended elements of jazz and rock.

Music and Protest. *Joan Baez performs in Toronto during the early summer of 1969. The combination of music and political protest would culminate in August of that year in the Woodstock Festival, where Baez also appeared.*

Source: CORBIS BETTMANN

MINIMALISM

Minimalism, which began to emerge in the early 1960s, was another reaction against opulence and complexity, relying on multiple repetitions of small units that differ only slightly or are varied only gradually over long stretches of time. Musical minimalism was by no means a new phenomenon: it had long existed in the tradition of church bell change ringing, in which a few fixed pitches (one from each of three or more bells) are repeated at different speeds in such a way that the resulting permutations create a seemingly infinite number of combinations.

Riley
IN C

A similar strategy is at work in one of the earliest of all minimalist works, Terry Riley's *IN C* (1964). The score consists of 53 brief thematic fragments to be played in any combination of any kind of instruments, although the composer recommends a group of about 35 if possible. Each player performs these ideas in the same sequence but is free to repeat each unit as often as he or she sees fit. "There is no fixed rule as to the number of repetitions a pattern may have,"[3] the composer notes in the score, although if a performance runs between 45 and 90 minutes, then each performer would ordinarily repeat each pattern for somewhere between 45 and 90 seconds. "One of the joys of *IN C*," the composer noted in his performing directions to the score, "is the interaction of the players in polyrhythmic combinations that spontaneously arise between patterns. Some quite fantastic shapes will arise and disintegrate as the group moves through the piece when it is properly played." The one constant element of the piece is an ostinato C octave played on the high range of a piano or mallet instrument. If a performances of *IN C* runs to 90 minutes, this would mean repeating this particular figure as many as 15,000 times in succession. This might sound like a recipe for monotony, but the process of unfolding is such that the work remains constantly in motion and gradually transforms itself into whatever the performers decide it will become.

Reich
It's Gonna Rain

Another manifestation of minimalism involves what has come to be known as **phase music** or **process music,** in which we can clearly hear the process by which the elements of a work gradually transform themselves into something new and different. Steve Reich's *It's Gonna Rain* (1965) is an early example of this kind of minimalism. The work is based on a single phrase of text ("It's gonna rain"), itself part of a larger sermon about Noah and the Flood, as delivered on a New York City street corner by a preacher known as Brother Walker and recorded by Reich with a portable tape recorder in 1964. By splicing and running two copies of the same tape on machines playing at slightly different speeds, Reich is able to create a process in which the sounds gradually shift "out of phase," to use the composer's own term. The effect is remarkable: because of the extremely gradual rate of change, we can hear one sound become a completely different kind of sound. Within this process of unfolding, we begin to experience a different sense of time, and repetition that would probably be intolerable in almost any other Western idiom eventually becomes an object of fascination. The entire work runs about 17 minutes (for reasons of space, only the opening few minutes are given in the collection of recordings accompanying the present text).

POSTMODERNISM

In 1979, the distinguished American composer Charles Wuorinen (b. 1938) published a treatise on composition that opened with these words:

Most of the Western music we know from the past is representative of the tonal system. . . . But while the tonal system, in an atrophied or vestigial form, is still used today in popular and commercial music, and even occasionally in the works of backward-looking serious composers, it is no longer employed by serious composers in the mainstream.[4]

Wuorinen's thoroughly modernist pronouncement is typical of the generation of composers who came of age in the 1950s and 1960s: it rests on the assumption that a chasm exists between "high" and "low" art, between "forward-looking" and "backward-looking" composers, and that no forward-looking serious composer would write in a tonal idiom, a stylistic remnant of the past. By the last quarter of the 20th century, however, **postmodernism** had made Wuorinen's claim seem remarkably dated.

Postmodernism, like modernism itself, is an aesthetic attitude rather than a particular style. It embraces the past (including modernism) but often in an eclectic manner, synthesizing a variety of approaches in a single work. In music, tonality and atonality are both equally valid within the postmodernist approach. Postmodernist composers felt obliged neither to avoid nor to use traditional forms and genres. On an even broader scale, postmodernism abandons the pretension of art as an invariably serious enterprise.

Postmodernism emerged gradually over the last third of the 20th century and was particularly conspicuous in the field of architecture. For several decades in the mid–20th century, "serious" architects (to borrow Wuorinen's term) prided themselves on the elegant simplicity of steel-and-glass skyscrapers that conspicuously avoided anything that smacked of ornament. In the mid-1980s, Philip Johnson designed the quintessentially postmodern AT&T Building in Manhattan. It embraces the modern—most of

Postmodern architecture. *In postmodern architecture, as in postmodernism in general, modernism coexists with ornamentation, humor, and overt references to past styles. The glass-and-stone body of Philip Johnson's AT&T Building (1978) in New York City is decidedly modern in its austere functionality, but the ornamental scrolled top provides a postmodern touch. It offers a whimsical and even ironic commentary on what lies beneath; to many observers, the building as a whole resembles a Chippendale-style chest of drawers.*

Source: Richard Payne, FAIA

the building conforms to the steel-and-glass formula—but its pediment evokes a Chippendale-style chest of drawers. The very top of this modernist skyscraper is ornamental, whimsical, and draws on the idioms of the past—all hallmarks of the postmodern aesthetic, which is intensely aware of the artificiality of art and language.

By the end of the 20th century, postmodernism had become the predominant aesthetic within the concert hall. For the first time in several decades, audiences were hearing substantial quantities of new music that could no longer be described as modernist or avant-garde. Some critics called this approach "the new lyricism" or "the new Romanticism." Shock was suddenly passé. *The People United Will Never Be Defeated* (1976) by the American composer Frederick Rzewski (b. 1938), for example, uses a decidedly tonal Chilean revolutionary song as the basis of a set of 36 variations, a decidedly old-fashioned form. Rzewski thus places his work conspicuously within the tradition of Bach's *Goldberg Variations* and Beethoven's *Diabelli Variations*. He uses a variety of stylistic and technical approaches in these variations; the set as a whole constitutes a veritable history of pianistic writing—some traditional, some not, some tonal, some not. This eclectic mixture of styles is typical of postmodernism, which in many respects represents the culmination of all pluralistic trends in 20th-century music. In the postmodern outlook, the very concept of a musical mainstream becomes irrelevant.

Musgrave
Orfeo II

Like many composers of her generation, Thea Musgrave (b. 1928) cultivated but eventually moved beyond modernism, atonality, and serialism. Born in Scotland, she studied with Nadia Boulanger and eventually took a teaching position at the University of California, Santa Barbara. Her *Orfeo II* (1976), scored for solo flute and string ensemble, moves freely between tonal and atonal idioms. Long passages of its opening section ("Orfeo Laments") are centered on G and D. It would be misleading to say the music is *in* either of these keys, but it has a strong sense of a tonal center. The tonality is reinforced rhythmically by the steady, repeated pattern of eighth notes in the opening in the lower voices, almost in the fashion of a Baroque ground bass.

At figure 4, the first violin intones the opening phrase of the most famous aria from Christoph Willibald Gluck's opera *Orfeo* of 1762, *Che farò senza Euridice?* ("What shall I do without Euridice?"), Orpheus's moving lament at the loss of his beloved wife. This reminiscence from another musical world, the middle of the 18th century, has an eerie effect within the context of Musgrave's *Orfeo II*. When it appears in the first violin at figure 4, it sounds like (and is) a fleeting memory. The flute soloist, representing Orpheus, listens to the fragments of this melody and tries to imitate them (just after figure 10 through figure 14) but cannot sustain the line. Orpheus's inability to recover the tonal melody parallels his inability to recover the dead Eurydice.

León
Rituál for Piano

References to past idioms, although frequently used in postmodern music, are not essential to its aesthetic. Tania León's *Rituál for Piano* (1987) synthesizes a variety of traditions even while establishing its own unique identity. Born in Cuba in 1943, León emigrated to the United States in 1967; she became the first music director of the Dance Theater of Harlem in 1969 and has taught composition at Brooklyn College since 1985. *Rituál for Piano* begins with an introductory series of slow, unmeasured arpeggios similar in their improvisatory mood to those found in the beginning of C. P. E. Bach's Fantasia in C minor (see Chapter 11). After a brief section marked "Andante languido" (measures 1–13), the music hits its stride with the powerful rhythms of the "Avante e deciso" (beginning at measure 14). The harmonic idiom is tonal but not triadic: the emphasis on a series of repeated notes in the bass anchors the work tonally without situating it in any particular key. The driving rhythms owe as much to Afro-Cuban jazz elements and the artistry of jazz pianist Art Tatum as to the traditions of Stravinsky

FOCUS

The Business of Composing in the 20th Century

Thanks to the introduction of meaningful international copyright laws, composers and recording artists of the early 20th century could make a decent living from their art if they pursued their careers over many years. By the late 20th century, the market potential of recorded sound was so great that composers could sometimes make a fortune from one recording of a single hit song.

Not surprisingly, a great deal of 20th-century musical talent gravitated toward the recording studio. And over the course of time, that studio became increasingly accessible. For most of the century, a recording was a major milestone for any composer, musician, or musical group. The barriers to be crossed were substantial: one had to secure a contract, rent a recording studio, and pay for pressings, packaging, and distribution. By the last decade of the century, the process had become so simple that musicians could record a CD in the privacy of their own homes and distribute the music almost instantly over the Internet. Even the music itself could be created by means of machines with few (if any) actual performers. Synthesizers that had taken up the space of half a basketball court in 1960 could now fit inside a laptop computer.

Composers of the 20th century also benefited from a new source of patronage: the university. Supported by a salary based on teaching, university composers were free to write the kind of music they wished to write, without commercial pressures. The arguments for and against such an arrangement have raged endlessly. Critics maintain that this "ivory tower" setting contributes to a sense of isolation between composer and society. Aaron Copland, for one, observed that it was not "healthy" for "the whole composing community to move within university walls," on the grounds that such individuals would find themselves cut off from stimuli that would otherwise enlarge their capacities as artists.[5] Others, like Milton Babbitt, argued that the university setting allowed at least a few composers to pursue more experimental kinds of composition, in the same way that many scientists pursue knowledge for its own sake rather than for its direct commercial applications (see Primary Evidence: "Who Cares If You Listen?"). Both sides would agree, however, that the phenomenon of the university composer has added even more diversity to the 20th-century musical scene.

and Copland. Like the composer herself, who cites ancestors from China, Nigeria, France, and Spain, *Rituál for Piano* resists easy classification. It represents instead the increasing tendency of music in the late 20th century toward a synthesis of diverse styles and traditions.

Libby Larsen's *Missa gaia* (1992) is similarly difficult to pigeonhole. In its avowed genre and movement headings (Introit, Kyrie, Gloria, Credo, Agnus Dei/Sanctus, Benediction), it evokes the traditions of the Mass. But the texts of these individual movements are not liturgical; they draw instead on a variety of sources that address the relationship of human beings to the earth (*gaia* is the ancient Greek word for the earth). The text to the Introit ("Within the Circle of Our Lives") is by the American poet Wendell Berry (b. 1934), whose work often touches on issues of the environment. Larsen (b. 1950) uses the image of circles in nature as the central trope of the *Missa gaia*. Much of the work's melodic material uses ascending and descending fifths and fourths that suggest movement through the circle of fifths and whose contours outline rising and falling motions of various kinds. Like much postmodern music, the *Missa gaia* is decidedly tonal, yet not in the conventional triadic sense. The harmonies are dominated by unisons, octaves, fourths, and open fifths: melodic and harmonic thirds appear only occasionally and stand out as a result.

Larsen
Missa gaia

A native of Minnesota, Larsen represents a growing number of contemporary American composers who have developed an enthusiastic following in the concert hall. She has worked largely on commission, avoiding long-term commitments to any one institution such as a university (see Focus: "The Business of Composing in the 20th Century"). Her music has proved itself accessible to audiences yet novel at one and the same time.

CONCLUSION

The decades immediately after World War II witnessed a second wave of modernism. Combinatoriality and integral serialism manifested a widespread desire to make a fresh start and explore new systems of composition that had not been widely used before the war. Aleatory music—music of chance—fulfilled these desires in an even more radical fashion, and electronic music opened up new possiblities of timbre and form in a way that gave the composer complete or nearly complete control over the musical work. By the late 1960s, however, at least some composers were beginning to turn away from the modernist aesthetic to embrace postmodernism, a more eclectic outlook that accepted the traditions of the past, including tonality, conventional forms, and established genres, as well as modernism itself. Minimalism, based on the extended manipulation of a limited number of musical ideas, offered yet another idiom running counter to the second wave of modernism. In the meantime, other forms of music dominated in the marketplace: rock, folk music, and jazz all developed in a variety of directions over the second half of the century and contributed to a musical scene that by the year 2000 was more diverse than at any previous time in the history of Western music.

DISCUSSION QUESTIONS

1. What factors outside of music contributed to the growing diversity of musical styles in the 20th century?

2. Part of the appeal of jazz in the 1920s and 1930s lay in what was perceived to be its genuine and earthy nature, in contrast to the allegedly overrefined and decadent idioms of the concert hall and opera house. In what ways does this outlook resemble or differ from the move toward naturalness in the middle of the 18th century?

3. Tonality had long been a fundamental building block of musical form. In the absence of tonality, how did composers of the early 20th century working in the atonal idiom construct large-scale forms?

4. Does a composer adhering strictly to the principles of serial composition have more or less freedom than one not using the serial idiom?

5. How did the ideals of vocal beauty expand over the course of the 20th century?

6. Is John Cage's *4′33″* a work of music?

7. In what ways do Milton Babbitt's arguments in "Who Cares If You Listen?" (see Primary Evidence: feature in Chapter 23) resemble those put forward by Boethius in the early medieval era (Prelude to the Medieval Era) that theory is superior to practice?

8. How did the transmission of musical works change over the course of the 20th century?

9. How did the relationship of the composer to his or her public change over the course of the 20th century?

Major Composers of the 20th Century

FRANCE

Erik Satie (1866–1925) was an iconoclast and an inspiration to many later composers, most notably **Claude Debussy** (see Composer Profile, Chapter 20). Satie cultivated mostly smaller forms, and many of his works are hauntingly beautiful. Others are openly challenging. His *Three Pieces in the Form of a Pear*, for piano, was a response to critics who said he had no sense of form; he indicated that another one of his piano pieces, *Vexations*, was to be played 840 times in succession. Satie collaborated with Sergei Diaghilev to produce the ballet *Parade* in 1917. His reminiscences, published in 1912, bear the title *Memoirs of an Amnesiac*.

Best remembered for his tone poem *The Sorcerer's Apprentice* (made famous by Mickey Mouse in Walt Disney's *Fantasia* and *Fantasia 2000*), **Paul Dukas** (1865–1935) was an important figure on the French musical scene for many decades as a composer, critic, and teacher. **Maurice Ravel** (1877–1937), along with Debussy, was the most outstanding exponent of impressionism. His piano music, particularly *Gaspard de la nuit* and *Miroirs*, is of outstandingly high quality. The celebrated *Boléro* manifests Ravel's talents as an orchestrator; his orchestral version of Mussorgsky's *Pictures at an Exhibition* is in fact better known than the piano original. Ravel also wrote two operas, several ballets (most notably *Daphnis et Chloé*), two piano concertos (one for the left hand alone, written for the Austrian Paul Wittgenstein, who had lost his right arm during World War I), a string quartet, and a number of songs for voice and orchestra.

The composers **Darius Milhaud** (1892–1975), **Francis Poulenc** (1899–1963), **Georges Auric** (1899–1983), **Arthur Honegger** (1892–1955), **Germaine Tailleferre** (1892–1983), and **Louis Durey** (1888–1979) were dubbed "Les Six" ("The Six") by the journalist Henri Collet in 1920. These six composers were only loosely connected in their individual styles, but all were united in their attempts to write in a distinctively French manner, to draw on subjects from everyday life, and to integrate styles from outside the so-called classical tradition into their music. Milhaud was a prolific and wide-ranging composer whose output encompassed chamber music, piano music (see Anthology), symphony, opera, and even electronic music. His *Création du monde* and *Le Boeuf sur le toit* use jazz elements to great effect. His 18 string quartets deserve to be better known; nos. 14 and 15 can be played simultaneously as an octet. A brilliant pianist, Poulenc developed a highly idiomatic style for the instrument. His early works include a ballet for Diaghilev, *Les Biches* (1924). He later wrote a religious opera, *Dialogue of the Carmelites* (1957), that has held its own on the stage. Poulenc's *Gloria* is also frequently performed, as are many of his fine songs for voice and piano. Auric was a child prodigy: by the time he was 16 he had already written nearly three hundred songs. He wrote several ballets for Diaghilev, the best known of which is *Les Matelots* (1925). In 1946, he wrote the film score for Jean Cocteau's classic film

Beauty and the Beast. Honegger is perhaps best known for *Pacific 231,* a musical portrayal of a steam locomotive, but he also wrote many works for the stage and for chorus. The cantatas *Le Roi David* (1921) and *Jeanne d'Arc au bûcher* (1938) are widely admired, as are his five symphonies and his many sonatas for various instruments. The only woman composer of Les Six, Tailleferre studied orchestration with Ravel and wrote in a number of genres, both instrumental and vocal. Her *Concertino for Harp and Orchestra* was commissioned and premiered by the Boston Symphony Orchestra in 1927. Durey worked primarily in the area of chamber music and song but eventually used music as a means toward political ends. He was active in the French Communist Party for many years, and his *The Long March* (1949), for tenor solo, chorus, and orchestra, uses a text by Mao Tse-tung.

Edgard Varèse (see Composer Profile, Chapter 20) and **Olivier Messiaen** (1908–1992) were important figures to an entire generation of composers coming of age after World War II. Most prominent among these was **Pierre Boulez** (b. 1925), who, along with the German Karlheinz Stockhausen and the American Milton Babbitt, was one of the first composers to embrace total serialism. From 1971 to 1977, Boulez served as music director of the New York Philharmonic and introduced an unprecedented quantity of new or recent music into that orchestra's repertory. From the early 1970s until 1992, he also directed France's Institute for Research and Coordination in Acoustics/Music (IRCAM), a major government-funded center for musical research and performance.

GREAT BRITAIN

Edward Elgar (1857–1934) is best known for his *Pomp and Circumstance March no. 2* (the theme song of graduations), but his style was on the whole far more chromatic. He was widely considered the leading English composer of his day. His concertos for violin and for piano and the oratorio *The Dream of Gerontius* are mainstays of the repertory today. **Frederick Delius** (1862–1934), regarded as the finest English composer of the impressionist style, lived for a time in Florida but spent most of his life in France. His orchestrations are particularly noteworthy in such works as *Brigg Fair, Appalachia,* and *On Hearing the First Cuckoo in Spring.* His *Mass of Life* is an enormous work for soloists, chorus, and orchestra, set to texts by the German philosopher and poet Friedrich Nietzsche.

Ralph Vaughan Williams (1872–1958) was a leader in the 20th-century renaissance of English music. He was an active member of the English Folk Song Society, and many of his works incorporate folk tunes or folklike tunes. A number of his compositions evoke the modal counterpoint of another golden age of English music, the 16th century. His *Fantasia on a Theme by Tallis* for strings and his *5 Variants of "Dives and Lazarus"* are good examples of this kind of sound. Vaughan Williams's nine symphonies are significant contributions to the genre in the 20th century; he also wrote a substantial quantity of choral music that continues to be performed today, including several outstanding hymns. **Gustav Holst** (1874–1934) is best remembered for his suite *The Planets* (1916), brilliantly scored for an enormous orchestra, but his other works—for chorus and for orchestra alike—deserve wider exposure. **William Walton** (1902–1983) gained international attention with his witty music for *Façade,* a monologue with an equally witty libretto by the poet Edith Sitwell. But Walton went on to demonstrate mastery over a variety of styles and genres, from oratorio (*Belshazar's Feast*) to concerto (for violin, viola, cello) to film music.

Michael Tippett (1905–1998) composed several successful operas (including *Midsummer Marriage, King Priam,* and *The Knot Garden*), but his most widely acclaimed work is *A Child of Our Time* (1941), written in the tradition of Bach's Passions but substituting African American spirituals for Lutheran chorales. Tippett's four symphonies are also worthy of note. **Benjamin Britten** (1913–1976) is acknowledged as the greatest composer of opera in the English language since Henry Purcell. *Peter Grimes, Billy Budd,* and *The Turn of the Screw* have all become standards of the opera house. *The Young Person's Guide to the Orchestra* (1946) is a series of variations and a fugue on a theme by Purcell; each variation highlights a particular instrument or group of instruments in the orchestra. Britten wrote his *War Requiem* (1962) for the consecration of the new St. Michael's Cathedral in Coventry, England, (the original building was destroyed by German bombs in World War II). The text mixes the traditional liturgy with poems by Wilfred Owen, a British poet killed in World War I. Britten's many vocal works retain a distinctly English sound, yet their appeal extends far beyond his native land. The music of **Peter Maxwell Davies** (b. 1934) synthesizes many different styles and idioms, including some from the distant past. His *Tenebrae pro Gesualdo* deals with the chromaticism of the early-17th-century composer, and his opera *Taverner* centers on the late-16th-century English composer. But Davies's most celebrated work by far is *Eight Songs for a Mad King* (1969), which calls for the instrumentalists to sit in birdcages, a reference to King George III's bullfinches and a metaphor for his mental imprisonment.

Thea Musgrave (b. 1928), a native of Scotland, studied with both Nadia Boulanger and Aaron Copland. Her music has been enormously successful on both sides of the Atlantic. She has taught at Queens College in New York since 1987. **Andrew Lloyd Webber** (b. 1948), the most financially successful of all composers in the entire history of the stage, has demonstrated time and again the appeal of modern musical theater. A long string of hits—from *Jesus Christ Superstar* to *Evita, Cats,* and *Phantom of the Opera*—seems likely to continue unabated.

ITALY

Giaccomo Puccini (1858–1924) was widely hailed as the successor to Verdi in the tradition of Italian opera. He scored international successes with such works as *La bohème* (1896, the point of departure for the 1996 Broadway musical *Rent*), *Madama Butterfly* (1904), *Tosca* (1901), and *Turandot* (unfinished at the composer's death and premiered in 1926). Although his music is more chromatic and on the whole more polyphonic than Verdi's, Puccini was an equal master of lyricism. No subsequent Italian composer has captured the stage to the same degree.

Ottorino Respighi (1879–1936) and **Gian Francesco Malipiero** (1882–1973) are generally regarded as Neoclassicists, although this label does not do justice to the full variety of their music. Respighi's three sets of *Ancient Airs and Dances* (1916, 1923, 1931), based on chansons and dance music of the Italian Renaissance, exposed many listeners for the first time to the delights of this earlier music. Malipiero was the moving force behind the first modern edition of Monteverdi's complete works.

Luigi Dallapiccola (1901–1975) was one of the first Italian composers to embrace dodecaphonic composition. Many of his works are overtly political. The *Canti di Prigionia* (1941, "Songs of Prison"), for example, sets texts by three famous prisoners: Mary Stuart ("Queen of Scots"), Boethius, and Savonarola, a monk and Florentine leader who was martyred for his reformist beliefs. The opera *Il Prigioniero* (1948) addresses similar themes. Dallapiccola taught and traveled widely in the United States after World War II. **Luigi Nono** (1924–1990) was another composer who connected his music with politics. He embraced dodecaphonic composition and married Schoenberg's daughter Nuria. His later works incorporated aleatory and electronic techniques as well. His most significant composition is *Intolleranza* (1960, revised 1970), a setting of texts by Brecht, Sartre, and others, decrying social inequity and imperialism. **Luciano Berio** (1925–2003) is the most prominent composer of the Italian avant-garde. His music is eclectic and consistently provocative. Berio's best known work is *Sinfonia* (1968), which uses a number of collagelike techniques. Section II of the work is a tribute to the memory of Martin Luther King, Jr. In it, as the composer explains, the eight voices "exchang[e] among themselves the sounds constituting the name of the black martyr until the point when his name is clearly enunciated." Section III uses the entire third movement of Mahler's Second Symphony as an underpinning above which Berio sets a dazzling array of thematic references to the works of other composers, from Bach to Boulez.

SPAIN

Manuel da Falla (1876–1946) combined the musical idioms of his native Spain with an impressionistic style. He spent the years 1907 to 1914 in Paris and enjoyed the support of Debussy, Dukas, and Ravel, among others. He returned to Spain in 1914 but left for Argentina at the end of the Spanish Civil War in 1939. His most frequently performed works include *Nights in the Gardens of Spain*, for piano and orchestra, the ballets *The Three-Cornered Hat* and *El Amor brujo*, and several concertos.

GREECE

Iannis Xenakis (b. 1922) began his academic work in Athens as an engineering student, but he then went to Paris to study composition with Messiaen. He combined these two fields when he helped the celebrated architect Le Corbusier create the Philips pavilion for the 1958 Brussels World's Fair, for which both he and Edgard Varèse supplied electronic music. As a composer, Xenakis rejected both serialism and aleatory music, opting instead for an approach determined in large part by mathematical calculations.

GERMANY AND AUSTRIA

Composition in German-speaking countries was by no means dominated by atonalists and serialists in the first half of the 20th century. **Arnold Schoenberg, Alban Berg,** and **Anton Webern** (see Composer Profiles, Chapter 21) remain among the most celebrated composers of their era, but **Paul Hindemith** (1895–1963) achieved comparable renown as the leading German figure in the Neoclassical movement. A prolific composer in virtually every genre, he never abandoned tonality, although his works expand the concept of consonance well beyond that of earlier generations. His music was, in any event, too dissonant for the Nazi regime, which forced him to resign his teaching position at the Berlin Academy of Music. He emigrated to Switzerland and then the United Sates, becoming an American citizen in 1946. Hindemith taught composition for many years at Yale University and was an astonishingly prolific composer. His best known works include the symphonic suite derived from his opera *Mathis der Maler*; *Ludus tonalis*, a 20th-century counterpart to Bach's *Well-Tempered Clavier*; and the *Symphonic Metamorphosis on Themes by Weber*. He also wrote many sonatas and concertos for a variety of instruments. His song cycle *Das Marienleben* is a staple of the repertory.

Kurt Weill (1900–1950) was a committed Marxist whose early operas—*The Three-Penny Opera* (a thoroughly modernized version of the Gay and Pepusch classic from the 1720s) and *Rise and Fall of the City of Mahagonny* (Anthology)—were written in collaboration with the poet and playwright Bertolt Brecht (1898-1956). Both works seek to realize Brecht's idea of "epic theater," in which a sense of distance is cultivated between the viewer and the events on stage: we are repeatedly made aware of the artistry behind the artifice. With the rise of the Nazis to power in 1933, Weill emigrated to France and eventually the United States, where he wrote several Broadway musicals.

Hans Werner Henze (b. 1926) adopts an eclectic approach to music. His operas, particularly *Elegy for Young Lovers* and *The Young Lord*, have achieved some success in his native Germany. His Marxist politics have played a large role in his choice of texts to set. **Karlheinz Stockhausen** (b. 1928) was a leading figure in the German avant-garde after World War II, leading the way for a new generation of composers seeking to distance themselves from the music of the war and prewar years. He embraced serialism, total serialism, electronic music, aleatory music, and has always seemed to stay one step ahead of everyone else. He has combined his compositional energies with an immense talent for organization and showmanship in the best sense of the word.

SCANDINAVIA

Sometimes called the "Danish Mahler," **Carl Nielsen** (1865–1931) cultivated the symphony (he wrote six of them) as well as the concerto (one for flute and one for clarinet). His harmonic idiom is more dissonant than Mahler's, but his music displays a comparable sense of grandeur mixed with humor. The Finnish composer **Jan Sibelius** (1865–1957) also straddles the 19th and 20th centuries. Several of his best known works, such as *En Saga* and *Finlandia*, are overtly patriotic. After brief tours in Germany and the United States (where Yale University awarded him an honorary degree in 1914), he spent the remaining years of his life in semiseclusion and gave up composing altogether in 1929. His most important works are the seven symphonies, the last of which are written in an advanced chromatic idiom.

HUNGARY

Zoltán Kodály (1882–1967) collaborated with **Béla Bartók** (see Composer Profile, Chapter 20) in collecting folk music of eastern Europe, and his compositions reflect elements of this music as well. Kodály's best known work is the *Psalmus Hungaricus* (1923), commissioned for the festivities celebrating the 50th anniversary of the union of the cities Buda and Pest. The orchestral suite from his opera *Háry János* is also frequently performed. But Kodály is probably best remembered for having founded the Kodály Method of teaching music to young children.

György Ligeti (b. 1923) left Budapest in 1956 in the wake of the failed uprising against the Soviet Union and settled in Germany. His *Atmosphères* for orchestra (1961), used in Stanley Kubrick's film *2001: A Space Odyssey*, offers a good introduction to the work of this remarkably versatile composer.

CZECHOSLOVAKIA/CZECH REPUBLIC

Leoš Janáček (1854–1928), although born even before Mahler, did not begin to write his most important music until around 1900. It was then that he began to develop a theory of "speech melody" in which vocal lines more nearly resemble the natural contours of spoken language. His operas *Jenufa, Kátja Kabanova, The Cunning Little Vixen,* and *The Makropoulos Affair* have all held the stage in Europe. His *Slavonic Mass* is also an important work. **Alois Hába** (1893–1973) began exploring the possibilities of microtonal music around 1920, dividing all half steps into two. He also developed what he called "nonthematic music," in which all voices are melodically unrelated. His String Quartet no. 3 (1922) uses both these techniques.

POLAND

Karol Szymanowski (1882–1937) absorbed a variety of styles: German late Romanticism (Richard Strauss), Russian mysticism (Scriabin), and impressionism (Debussy). His works, although tonal, flirt with atonality at times but always sustain lyrical interest and are almost invariably virtuosic. He wrote many works for solo piano (including a number of mazurkas), for piano and orchestra, and for orchestra, including three symphonies. He was an important influence for the remarkable generation of Polish composers who followed: **Witold Lutoslawski** (1913–1994), **Krzysztof Penderecki** (b. 1933), and **Henryk Gorecki** (b. 1933). Lutoslawski's earlier works are rather in the style of Bartók, drawing on Polish folk sources; he later explored ideas of aleatory and dodecaphonic composition. Penderecki (pronounced "Pen-de-*ret*-ski") has been particularly interested in exploring new possibilities of timbre, as is evident in his most celebrated work, *Threnody for the Victims of Hiroshima* (Anthology). He has written in many genres, for instruments and voices alike. After laboring in relative obscurity for many years, Gorecki ("Go-*ret*-ski") rocketed to fame in 1994 with a work he had written in 1976, his Symphony no. 3.

RUSSIA AND THE SOVIET UNION

Alexander Scriabin (1872–1915) is noted for his many piano miniatures, ten piano sonatas, and his large-scale orchestral works, especially *Le Poème de l'extase* ("Poem of Ecstasy") and *Prometheus, or the Poem of Fire*, the latter of which includes a part for a "color organ" designed to convert specific pitches or keys into colors (C major as red, F♯ major as blue, etc.). Productions of this work during the composer's life were apparently unsuccessful from a technical point of view. Scriabin's sense of advanced chromaticism eventually merged into a kind of free atonality around 1908.

Sergei Rachmaninoff (1873–1943), by contrast, continued in the 19th-century tradition of Tchaikovsky and Rimsky-Korsakov. He was far less a modernist than his countryman and slightly younger colleague **Igor Stravinsky** (see Composer Profile, Chapter 20). Rachmaninoff's most popular works are the Piano Concertos nos. 2 and 3, the *Preludes* and *Etudes-Tableaux* for piano, and the *Rhapsody on a Theme of Paganini* for piano and orchestra. An internationally renowned pianist and conductor, he fled Russia after the Revolution in 1917 and eventually settled in Los Angeles. **Sergei Prokofiev** (1891–1953) spent much of his early career in France after the Revolution of 1917 but returned to the Soviet Union in 1932 and spent the rest of his life there working in an uneasy relationship with the regime. The communist authorities looked to

Prokofiev as a kind of prodigal son who had voluntarily returned home from the "decadent" West, and the government bestowed many honors on him. That same government would later attack Prokofiev and his colleague **Dmitri Shostakovich** (see Composer Profile, Chapter 22) for their "decadence" and "formalism."

Aram Khachaturian (1903–1978), an Armenian, is noted for his use of exotic tone colors: the frenetic "Sabre Dance" from the ballet *Gayane* is a well-known example of his ability to incorporate timbres and modes that sound vaguely Asian yet still within the Western tradition. **Alfred Schnittke** (1934–1998) was an ethnic German born in Russia. His works cover a wide range of styles and media, from electronic music to more traditional genres such as concertos, suites, and symphonies. His *Requiem* (1975) is particularly noteworthy.

LATIN AMERICA

Like his near contemporaries Bartók and Vaughan Williams, the Brazilian **Heitor Villa-Lobos** (1887–1959) traveled throughout his native land to collect folk songs. He avoided direct quotation of these materials in his compositions, preferring instead to use them as a source of inspiration for his own ideas. In the celebrated *Bachianas Brasileiras*, a series of works for a variety of different instruments, he used such themes within a polyphonic texture reminiscent of Bach. **Carlos Chavez** (1899–1978) was the preeminent Mexican composer of his era. He, too, collected and drew on native musical sources for inspiration. His single best known work is the *Sinfonia India* of 1936. The Argentinian composer **Alberto Ginastera** (1916–1983) also drew on native idioms but cultivated a variety of other styles as well. His Second Piano Concerto (1972) is based on a 12-tone row derived from the dissonant chord in the finale of Beethoven's Ninth Symphony. **Mauricio Kagel** (b. 1931), also from Argentina, has produced provocative works that are as much theater as music, even when performed in the concert hall.

UNITED STATES

Foremost among American modernists in the 20th century were **Charles Ives** (see Composer Profile, Chapter 20), Edgard Varèse (1883–1965), and three Californians: **Henry Cowell** (1897–1965), **Harry Partch** (1901–1974), and **John Cage** (see Composer Profile, Chapter 23). The Franco-Italian Varèse emigrated to the United States in 1915, where he became a leading force in the world of the avant-garde. His *Ionisation* (1931) was the first major work for percussion ensemble, and he wrote his *Poème electronique* (1958) specifically for the Philips Pavilion at the World's Fair in Brussels. Cowell, according to his student Cage, provided the "open sesame" for new music in America, experimenting with tone clusters and new timbres long before they became fashionable. Cowell was also an early champion of the music of Ives, at a time when few people knew the elder composer's work. Partch rejected almost every element of Western music and sought new models of sound in the music of ancient Greece and Asia; he also created an array of new musical instruments, including what he called a "gourd tree" and "cloud chamber bowls."

The United States produced an unparalleled abundance of outstanding song writers in the 20th century, most of whom also worked in the musical theater and film. Most prominent among many are **Irving Berlin** (1888–1989), **Cole Porter** (1891–1964), **George Gershwin** (1898 1937), **Hoagy Carmichael** (1899–1991), and **Richard Rodgers** (1902–1979). All but Carmichael achieved success on Broadway and in the movies. Berlin and Porter are remarkable for having written their own lyrics as well. Berlin came to the United States as a child from his native Russia; Porter and Carmichael were both natives of Indiana; Gershwin, born in New York City, collaborated extensively with his brother Ira as lyricist; and Rodgers, also a New Yorker, teamed with lyricists Lorenz Hart and later Oscar Hammerstein II to write an astonishing string of Broadway hits.

Often classed as "Romantics" or "Conservatives," composers like **Virgil Thomson** (1896–1989), **Roy Harris** (1898–1979), and **Samuel Barber** (1910–1981) remained within the extended tonal idiom at a time when many of their contemporaries were embracing atonality and (later) serialism. Thomson is particularly known for his operas, which include *Four Saints in Three Acts* (to a libretto by Gertrude Stein) and *The Mother of Us All* (to a libretto, also by Stein, about Susan B. Anthony and the struggle for women's suffrage). He was also one of the finest music critics of his time. Harris is remembered primarily for his symphonies, most of which reflect some aspect of the American experience (no. 4 is the *Folksong Symphony*, with chorus; no. 6 the *Gettysburg Address*). Barber's lyricism, which won great praise in his time, is evident in his *Adagio for Strings* (from his Second String Quartet), his Violin Concerto, the opera *Vanessa*, and the song cycle *Knoxville: Summer of 1915* (for soprano and orchestra, to texts by James Agee).

Gian Carlo Menotti (b. 1911) was born in Italy but spent most of his life in the United States. He is noted particularly for his operas *The Medium, The Telephone, The Consul*, and *Amahl and the Night Visitors*. His style is unpretentious but dramatically effective and generally within the technical reach of amateur opera companies. **Vincent Persichetti** (1915–1987) wrote in an idiom that was at once both modern and lyrical. His output includes nine symphonies and a number of concertos and sonatas.

A number of American composers have followed in the tradition of **Scott Joplin, Duke Ellington** (see Composer Profiles, Chapter 20), and **Aaron Copland** (see Composer Profile, Chapter 22) in mixing jazz elements into concert hall repertory. Most notable among these is **Leonard Bernstein** (1918–1990), who wrote his undergraduate thesis at Harvard on the use of jazz in classical music and went on to compose a number of works that did just that, including the musical *West Side Story* (1957). His other works include three symphonies, the *Chichester Psalms*, and *Kaddish*. In 1958, he became the first American-born permanent conductor of the New York Philharmonic Orchestra and used the position as a forum for a series of acclaimed broadcasts aimed at children. He was the first conductor to record all of Mahler's symphonies, and his recordings sold widely. His 1976 Norton Lectures were published in both book and video formats entitled *The Unanswered Question*.

Other composers developed an idiom not as immediately accessible to the wider public. **Roger Sessions** (1896–1985) wrote an opera at the age of 12 and entered Harvard University two years later; he was appointed to the faculty of Smith College at age 21. After eight years in Europe he returned to the United States to teach at Berkeley, Princeton, and Harvard. He established a reputation as a "composer's composer," one whose works were greatly admired by his colleagues yet never gained a wide following among audiences at large. His most important compositions are the eight symphonies, the Violin Concerto, the three piano sonatas, and the suite from his incidental music to the play *The Black Maskers*. **Elliott Carter** (b. 1908) is another composer whose music is enormously admired by a devoted group of followers. He won the Pulitzer Prize twice, for his Second String Quartet in 1960 and again for his Third String Quartet in 1973. His early music tends toward the Neoclassical, but he later embraced serial composition. His music tends to be highly polyphonic and metrically complex.

Milton Babbitt (b. 1916) was at the forefront of two important developments around midcentury: total serialism and electronic music. His *Three Compositions for Piano* (Anthology) was the first work by any composer to serialize pitch and nonpitch elements alike, including rhythm, timbre, and dynamics. His *All Set* (1957) is a 12-tone work for jazz ensemble. Babbitt taught composition for many years at Princeton University and exercised a profound influence on subsequent generations of American composers. **George Crumb** (b. 1929), a native of West Virginia, taught at the University of Pennsylvania. His compositions explore a remarkable variety of timbres and constructive devices. His most noted works include *Makrokosmos* for piano, *Echoes of Time and the River* (for which he won the Pulitzer Prize in 1968), *Black Angels* (for amplified string quartet), and *Ancient Voices of Children* (for soprano, boy soprano, and seven instrumentalists). In his vocal music, Crumb has frequently set texts of the poet Federico García Lorca.

Minimalists **Terry Riley** (b. 1935), **Steve Reich** (b. 1936), and **Philip Glass** (b. 1937) have all learned from John Cage and explored the musical implications of the dictum "less is more." All three of these younger composers have formed groups that perform their music in live concerts. Riley played in jazz ensembles in his early career, and his landmark work, *IN C* (Anthology), is based on the impulse toward improvisation. Reich studied composition at Mills College with Darius Milhaud and Luciano Berio before moving back to his native New York, where he has flourished as an independent composer. Glass won critical acclaim for his opera *Einstein on the Beach* in 1975, as well as the subsequent operas *Satyagraha* (1980) and *Akhnaten* (1983). His repetitive use of small units and his approach to form, rhythm, and texture have been shaped in part by his assimilation of certain Indian and African musical idioms.

A number of American women composers rose to great prominence in the second half of the century. **Pauline Oliveros** (b. 1932), born in Houston, has been a driving force behind the production and performance of new music in the San Francisco Bay Area for several decades. Some of her works involve group participation, blurring the distinction between performers and listeners. She has written for unconventional ensembles (for example, garden hoses and sprinklers) and for conventional ensembles in unconventional ways (for example, works in which the singers in a mixed chorus make all kinds of sounds with their mouths and hands). **Joan Tower** (b. 1938), a native of New York, was a founding member of the Da Capo chamber players, one of the leading ensembles of its kind, specializing in contemporary music. She has received numerous grants and awards for her compositions, which have won a wide audience. **Ellen Taaffe Zwilich** (b. 1939) was the first woman ever to receive a D.M.A. (Doctor of Musical Arts) in composition from the Juilliard School (in 1975) and received the Pulitzer Prize in Music for her Symphony no. 1 in 1983.

Tania León (b. 1943) grew up in Havana and emigrated to the United States in 1967. She served as the first music director of the Dance Theater of Harlem from 1968 until 1980 and has conducted a variety of orchestras both in the United States and abroad. Her music reflects the diversity of her ancestry in a variety of cultures, including French, Spanish, Chinese, African, and Cuban. **Libby Larsen** (b. 1950) has established herself as one of the leading composers of concert and choral music of the late 20th and early 21st centuries. Although academically trained (she earned a Ph.D. in composition from the University of Minnesota in 1978), she has remained largely independent of university positions, writing instead on commission from major orchestras and other ensembles.

Epilogue: Music at the Beginning of a New Century

The 21st century is too young to have defined itself musically, but for the moment at least, the pluralism and rapid changes of the 20th century continue. Musical genres and subgenres are still emerging and fading with remarkable speed. New styles explode into prominence, blend with other styles, fade, revive, and recombine with still newer styles.

Musical institutions continue to evolve accordingly. The recording industry, coping with declining sales for the first time after more than eight decades of uninterrupted growth, is seeking new ways to market music. Civic orchestras, which rose to prominence in the late 19th century, are adopting creative strategies to attract and retain new audiences. Concert venues accommodate increasingly diverse kinds of performances. In the 1930s and 1940s, when Benny Goodman's band and Duke Ellington's band performed at what had been a bastion of classical music—Carnegie Hall—critics hailed the events as landmarks in the history of jazz. In early 2002, by contrast, when the Roots, a Philadelphia-based hip-hop band, played in Avery Fisher Hall at Lincoln Center, the home of the New York Philharmonic Orchestra, the event created scarcely a stir.

As styles continue to proliferate, some artists are combining them in ways that break down the borders between them. So-called crossover acts, intended to appeal to the audiences for more than one genre, are now so common that the term has begun to lose meaning. The African-American jazz violinist Regina Carter exemplifies this trend. In December 2001, she was invited by the city of Genoa, Italy, to play on the violin known as The Cannon, a 250-year-old instrument once owned and used by the 19th-century virtuoso Niccolò Paganini. Carter and her group played a mixture of jazz numbers, improvisations, and arrangements of popular songs. At one point, she wove allusions to works by J. S. Bach and the Estonian-born Arvo Pärt (b. 1935) into a cadenza within her arrangement of *Don't Explain,* a song written in the mid-1940s by Billie Holiday (1915–1959).

It is, of course, impossible to predict music's future. History suggests only that it will change in ways we cannot today envision. Composers, performers, and audiences of the early 19th century could not have imagined the phonograph. Their grandchildren at the beginning of the 20th century, although familiar with recorded sound, could not have imagined the astonishing musical variety made possible by the electronic amplification and digital manipulation of sound. And so, almost certainly, our children and grandchildren a hundred years from now will be listening to music unimaginable to us today.

Whatever form it takes, however, music will surely remain one of humanity's defining characteristics. Indeed the music of Bach, Beethoven, and Chuck Berry, among others, is now on its way out of our solar system, representing humanity to the universe. In August and September 1977, the United States launched two essentially identical spacecraft to explore the outer planets and beyond. On the chance that one or both of these craft might someday fall into

Regina Carter in Genoa.   *On December 30, 2001, Regina Carter played jazz on a violin built in 1742 or 1743 by Giuseppe Bartolomeo Guarneri of Cremona (see Chapter 10), owned and used in the 19th century by Niccolò Paganini and now owned by the City of Genoa and played by invitation only.*

Source: Marco Scarpa/*The New York Times*

the hands of an extraterrestrial civilization, the National Aeronautics and Space Administration (NASA) included in the payload a series of photographs of life on earth, texts, recordings of many sounds from earth (wind, water, animals), greetings in multiple languages, and a variety of musical selections from cultures around the world.

What any nonearthbound creatures will make of this assortment is anyone's guess. But it will surely make clear to them music's central importance to the human race.

Appendix 1

A Guide to Selected Research Materials in Music History

The literature on music can sometimes seem overwhelmingly vast, but with the help of a few key sources, you can navigate it confidently.

A good place to begin is with Vincent H. Duckles and Ida Reed, *Music Reference and Research Materials: An Annotated Bibliography*, 5th ed. (New York: Schirmer Books, 1997). This resource of resources lists and describes the domain of music reference materials by category, beginning with dictionaries and proceeding through music histories, guides to musicology, bibliographies of music and works about music, journal indexes, catalogs of music libraries, and more. The rest of this appendix provides only a brief overview of what can be found in abundance in *Music Reference and Research Materials*.

DICTIONARIES AND ENCYCLOPEDIAS

The basic English-language encyclopedia of music is *The New Grove Dictionary of Music and Musicians*, 2nd ed. (New York: Grove's Dictionaries, 2000). First published in three volumes in the late 19th century, *Grove* has grown to a substantial 29 volumes and is also available online (www.grovemusic.com). It has entries for musical terms, individual composer biographies, and biographies of other important figures in music history. Every composer biography includes a list of works with essential information—such as date of composition, date of first performance, and date of publication—on all the music a composer wrote.

The most important biographical dictionary is *Baker's Biographical Dictionary of Musicians* (New York: Schirmer Books, 2001). Thoroughly revised by the late Nicolas Slonimsky, the entries in this six-volume work are more concise than the biographical entries in *The New Grove*. Still more concise biographies can be found in a one-volume reference, *The Harvard Biographical Dictionary of Music* (Cambridge, MA: Harvard University Press, 1996).

The standard one-volume reference source for musical terms is *The Harvard Dictionary of Music*, 4th ed. (Cambridge, MA: Harvard University Press, 2004).

JOURNALS

Journals (also known as periodicals) are collections of scholarly articles that appear on a regular schedule (such as monthly, three times a year, or yearly). A typical issue contains articles by several authors on a variety of subjects. Just how varied the subject matter is depends on the particular publication. The *Journal of the American Musicological Society,* for example, has a broad scope: a single issue might include an essay on the dissemination of Gregorian chant, another on the cantatas of Bach, and yet another on Wagner's early operas. A journal like *19th-Century Music*, in contrast, publishes articles only on the music of a single century, and a journal like *Beethoven Forum* focuses even more narrowly on a single composer.

Many journals also include book reviews. The purpose of these reviews is not so much to persuade people to buy (or not to buy) a particular book, but rather to move forward scholarly debate on a particular subject. If the author of a new book makes a particularly startling claim about, say, the circumstances of Mozart's death, a book reviewer has the obligation not only to summarize the argument, but also to evaluate it. In this way, book reviews constitute an important part of an ongoing dialogue among scholars.

Some of the more important journals in the field of music include the following:

Journal of the American Musicological Society

Early Music

Musical Quarterly

Journal of Musicology

Music and Letters

19th-Century Music

Journal of Music Theory

JOURNAL INDEXES

Several excellent indexes, all of them regularly updated and available in both printed and online editions, provide a guide to the abundant information available in music journals:

- The *Music Index* lists the articles in a wide range of music periodicals published since 1949 categorized by subject and author (www.harmonicparkpress.com/musicindex.htm).

- The *RILM Abstracts of Music Literature* covers books as well as journals published since 1969. (*RILM* is the acronym for *Répertoire International de Littérature Musicale,* or "International Repertory of Musical Literature.") More scholarly and international in scope than *Music Index,* it also includes abstracts—brief summaries—of every book or article it indexes (www.rilm.org).

- The *Arts & Humanities Citation Index (A&HCI),* which first appeared in 1980, indexes journal articles in a variety of fields, including music. In addition to the standard author and subject indexes, *A&HCI* also indexes every footnote appearing in each of these journal articles. This allows researchers to trace citations to a particularly central source or work. If, for example, you have identified a particular book or article as an important source for a topic you are researching, you can use *A&HCI* to find out what recent journal articles have cited that same source or work. This can often lead you to important new sources that you might not otherwise have found. For online access to *A&HCI,* consult your local library.

DISSERTATIONS

A dissertation is a book-length work written by a graduate student to earn a doctoral degree—in music either a Doctor of Philosophy (Ph.D.) or Doctor of Musical Arts (D.M.A.). Dissertations usually have a narrow focus. The standard guide to dissertations in music is Charles Adkins, *Doctoral Dissertations in Musicology,* available in printed form but more up to date in its online form (www.music.indiana.edu/ddm).

PRINTED LIBRARY CATALOGS

With the advent of computer catalogs, library card catalogs are easy to overlook, but they remain essential for the serious music scholar. A great deal of material in all disciplines issued before the 1970s has not yet found its way into any database. Some very large libraries, such as the New York Public Library and the British Library, have made the contents of their collections accessible through printed library catalogs. The New York Public Library's *Dictionary Catalog of the Music Collection* (Boston: G.K. Hall, 1964–1976), for example, consists of page after page of photographed catalog cards, most of which are still not represented in that institution's computer database. Other major collections have made their card catalogs available in a similar format; see Duckles and Reed's *Music Reference and Research Materials* for a list of the most important of these.

UNION CATALOGS

A union catalog shows the holdings of more than one library. The most important of these specifically for music-related materials is the *Répertoire international des Sources Musicales* ("International Repertoire of Musical Sources"), better known as *RISM*. This essential resource for anyone working with music written before 1800 lists the holdings of music manuscripts, prints, and books to be found in libraries throughout the world. The many volumes within this multifaceted series are indexed in Duckles and Reed's *Music Reference and Research Materials.*

Two catalogs that include music among many other disciplines are these:

◆ *OCLC* (Online Computer Library Center), the world's largest online union catalog (www.oclc.org).

◆ *National Union Catalog of Pre-1956 Imprints* (London: Mansell, 1968–1981), a printed catalog of 754 volumes covering materials published prior to 1956. This catalog shows holdings from libraries throughout North America and is particularly useful for older materials that may not appear in any online databases.

THEMATIC CATALOGS

Thematic catalogs are an invaluable resource for research in music. A thematic catalog of the works of a particular composer lists the entire output of that individual and gives details on each work, including an *incipit* (the first few notes of the work or movement in musical notation, enough to identify it unambiguously), the location of the autograph score (if it still exists), first and early editions, and a bibliography of writings about a particular work. The best source for thematic catalogs is the works lists in the composer biographies in *The New Grove*.

STYLE MANUALS

Any standard style manual—such as Kate L. Turabian's *A Manual for Writers of Term Papers, Theses, and Dissertations*, 6th ed. (Chicago: University of Chicago Press, 1996), or the Modern Language Association's *MLA Handbook for Writers of Research Papers*, 5th ed. (New York: Modern Language Association of America, 1999)—can help you prepare a research paper. But music, like any discipline, has a specialized vocabulary and specialized stylistic conventions, and three useful guides address these:

◆ Jonathan Bellman, *A Short Guide to Writing about Music* (New York: Longman, 2000).

◆ D. Kern Holoman, *Writing about Music: A Style Sheet from the Editors of 19th-Century Music* (Berkeley and Los Angeles: University of California Press, 1988).

◆ Richard J. Wingell, *Writing about Music: An Introductory Guide,* 3rd ed. (Upper Saddle River, NJ: Prentice Hall, 2002).

Appendix 2

Evaluating Musical Editions

When you study or perform a work of music, which edition should you use? If only one is available, the question is easy to answer. But often, particularly in the case of major composers, we have many editions from which to choose. If you're using the library, you might be tempted to use the first edition you find, but then you'd be relying on luck, because the quality of musical editions varies greatly.

A good edition of music conveys as closely as possible the composer's intentions. Editors sift through a variety of musical sources and other evidence to determine those intentions. In the edition they identify their sources and make clear their reasons for choosing a particular reading in cases where the correct reading is in dispute. Ideally, they also include a **critical report** that establishes the relationship among those sources and the basis for their editorial choices. Critical reports are either appended to the back of a volume or issued as a separate volume.

The original manuscript score of a work in the composer's own hand—known as the **holograph, autograph score,** or simply **autograph**—is usually the most reliable guide to a composer's intentions. The autograph score of many works, however, has not survived. And even when it is available, it is by no means infallible. Composers, after all, make mistakes. Considering how complicated and intricate a four-movement symphony is, for example, it shouldn't be surprising that the composer of one might occasionally write, say, a natural sign where a sharp sign was clearly intended. Editors would not be doing their job simply to perpetuate such mistakes. Composers also take shortcuts, such as marking the phrasing of a frequently repeated figure only the first two or three times it occurs. Editors then must decide whether or not to apply that same phrasing to all subsequent occurrences. Composers also change their minds. The autograph score and the first edition of Mozart's six string quartets dedicated to Haydn are significantly different. Mozart was almost certainly involved with the production of this first edition, and in the process of seeing it into print, he appears to have had second thoughts about certain details of tempo, articulation, and other matters. Mozart's participation in the publication process makes the first edition an authoritative source, in this case one that is arguably more important than the autograph.

Yet even an authoritative first edition is not necessarily the last word. Hector Berlioz, for instance, tinkered with matters of orchestration repeatedly after hearing his works in performance, even after a work had been published, and he wrote about these changes in some of his letters. Anton Bruckner, in turn, undertook massive revisions of many of his symphonies. Which version represents a composer's final thoughts on any given passage? Conscientious editors have to identify and evaluate carefully all relevant sources of a particular work—autograph, early copies, first editions, later editions, comments in the composer's correspondence—to make a **critical edition** of that work. What is critical about these editions is the editor's attitude toward all the sources. Editors do not merely accept, uncritically, whatever sources happen to be the earliest or most widely disseminated, but rather subject each source to careful scrutiny.

For an example of what can result from uncritical editing, consider the case of the six string quartets by Joseph Haydn now known as Opus 33. The autograph score of these quartets no longer exists. Haydn probably gave it to his Viennese publisher, Artaria, who used it to engrave the first edition in 1782. This edition consisted of a set of parts; no full score of the work was issued until the early 19th century. The publisher then probably either threw the manuscript away or reused it for packaging. (Composers' autographs were not perceived as valuable until a decade or so later, and even then publishers continued to be astonishingly cavalier with them.) Artaria's first edition, then, is the most reliable source we have for Opus 33. We know through Haydn's correspondence that he worked with Artaria in producing this edition, and for this reason we can call it an authoritative source. Surviving copies of this edition, however, are exceedingly rare, probably because few were printed and because people would have used them mostly at home the way we use sheet music today.

Another edition, published a few years later by Hummel of Amsterdam, in contrast, seems to have been widely available. This edition was the first to designate the quartets as Opus 33. It is, however, thoroughly unreliable, beginning with the opus number, which is different from the one that appears on Artaria's authoritative edition. Haydn had nothing to do with the Hummel edition; he received no payment for it and would certainly have been outraged to have his work pirated. Although it was considered unethical in Haydn's time for a publisher to print a living composer's music without any payment, the practice was nonetheless common until the emergence of effective copyright laws in the late 19th century.

What, then, was the source for Hummel's edition? We cannot know for sure, but it was clearly corrupt, both ethically and textually. One possible scenario is that these corruptions originated with one of Haydn's copyists, who in an attempt to earn some extra money made an unauthorized additional copy, which he then sold to any unscrupulous publisher, like Hummel, who was willing to pay the right price. Haydn was aware of this practice and complained about it on more than one occasion, but he could do little to stop it. Because these unauthorized copies had to be made quickly and surreptitiously, they were likely to contain errors. Another possible scenario is that the corruption came from Hummel himself or someone working for him. Troubled by the strange opening in the first movement of op. 33, no. 1 (Example A2-1), Hummel may have supposedly corrected it by filling in what he thought were missing harmonies (Example A2-2). The result is musically disastrous.

Unfortunately, bad editions have a way of perpetuating themselves. The least expensive and most widely available edition of the Opus 33 quartets today is in a volume that

Example A2-1 The opening of the first movement of Haydn's String Quartet op. 33, no. 1, as it appears in Artaria's authoritative first edition.

Example A2-2 The opening of the first movement of Haydn's String Quartet op. 33, no. 1, as it appears in Hummel's edition.

also includes Haydn's Opus 20 quartets. This volume is a reprint, an exact photographic reproduction, of an edition of these works published in the late 19th century assembled by a German scholar named Wilhelm Altmann. This is an uncritical edition: Altmann provides no indication of his sources. It is, however, clearly based on Hummel's unreliable early-19th-century edition. And because it is considerably less expensive, musicians are more likely to buy Altmann's edition than a critical edition of the quartets published as part of Haydn's complete works by the Haydn-Institut in Cologne, Germany. Thus Hummel's corrupt edition remains with us even today.

A note of caution: Many editions of music proclaim themselves as "Urtext" editions. *Urtext* is a German word that means "original text." Some of these self-proclaimed Urtext editions are in fact very carefully prepared critical editions, but others are not. The word itself has been used so indiscriminately that it is difficult to know when it really means something and when it is being used as a label to sell an item. Be critical in choosing an edition.

Appendix 3

Writing about Music

"Don't write about the music," the jazz musician Miles Davis once advised. "The music speaks for itself."[1] Anyone who has ever tried to describe a piece of music in words knows exactly what Davis meant. Yet writing about music—the most abstract and elusive of all the arts—can help us better appreciate its subtlety and magic. Our words will never replace the music, but they can help us understand it.

Writing about the emotional power of music poses particular challenges. It is not easy to put into words the passion we feel when we hear a work of music that moves us, and no two listeners respond identically to the same performance. Gushing accounts are rarely helpful. To write that a specific passage is "powerful and awesome" does not, by itself, tell us anything; we need some justification for such a statement, some explanation of what it is that makes the passage remarkable.

To avoid such difficulties, some writers avoid the subjective and emotional aspects of music and restrict themselves to objective issues like harmony and form. But if writing that focuses on the emotional aspects of music can be overblown, writing that focuses solely on its technical aspects can be dry and tedious. The playwright George Bernard Shaw (1856–1950), who supported himself as a music critic early in his career, skewered this sort of analysis in the following passage, which begins with a hypothetical description of Mozart's Symphony in G minor, K. 550:

> Here is the sort of thing: "The principal subject, hitherto only heard in the treble, is transferred to the bass (Ex. 28), the violins playing a new counterpoint to it instead of the original mere accompaniment figure of the first part. Then the parts are reversed, the violins taking the subject and the basses the counterpoint figure, and so on till we come to a close on the dominant of D minor, a nearly related key (commencement of Ex. 29), and then comes the passage by which we return to the first subject in its original form and key."
>
> How succulent this is; and how full of Mesopotamian words like "the dominant of D minor"! I will now, ladies and gentlemen, give you my celebrated "analysis" of Hamlet's soliloquy on suicide ["To be or not to be . . . "] in the same scientific style. "Shakespeare, dispensing with the customary exordium, announces his subject at once in the infinitive, in which mood it is presently repeated after a short connecting passage in which, brief as it is, we recognize the alternative and negative forms on which so much of the significance of repetition depends. Here we reach a colon; and a point pository phrase, in which the accent falls decisively on the relative pronoun, brings us to the first full stop."
>
> I break off here, because, to confess the truth, my grammar is giving out. But I want to know whether it is just that a literary critic should be forbidden to make his living in this way on pain of being interviewed by two doctors and a magistrate, and hauled off to Bedlam [an infamous mental institution in London] forthwith; whilst the more a musical critic does it, the deeper the veneration he inspires.[2]

The technical and emotional elements of music go hand in hand: no work of music is completely devoid of emotion, and every work of music is built on technical foundations of some kind (even John Cage's *4'33"*). Composers fuse the technical and emotional in their work; a writer's job is to analyze and describe how these two elements function in tandem.

Appendix 4

The Concepts of "Popular" and "Art" Music

Consciously or unconsciously, we often distinguish between music written for a serious purpose ("art" or "classical" music) and music whose function is primarily to entertain and that appeals to a broader public ("popular" music). Such distinctions have a long heritage in Western thought. Aristotle noted that certain rhythms "are noticeably vulgar in their emotional effects while others better suit freeborn persons" (see Prologue: Antiquity). And Johannes de Grocheo, writing around 1300, recommended that the motet "not be performed in the presence of common people, for they would not perceive its subtlety, nor take pleasure in its sound." He urged that motets be performed only "in the presence of learned persons and those who seek after subtleties in art" (see Chapter 2). The categories of art and popular music remain very much with us today and are fundamental to the way in which music is marketed.

Yet the distinction between popular and art music is conceptually fuzzy and impossible to define in any consistent way. To begin with, the two categories are not mutually exclusive. Just because a work of music is popular does not mean it cannot be a work of art, and just because it is a work of art does not mean it cannot be popular.

However art music is defined—as music that has survived the test of time, for example, or music with some serious purpose, or music written for an elite audience—we have no clear way to distinguish it stylistically from popular music. Works can easily shift from one category to the other over time. Take, for example, *The Beggar's Opera* (Anthology) by Pepusch and Gay in the 1730s. It was written, adapted, and readapted in many different guises over the course of the 18th century and composed in a style as different as possible from the prevailing serious opera of the upper classes. Yet it is now included in every discussion of opera from the period (as it is in Chapter 9 of this book). The same holds true for Mozart's *Magic Flute,* which premiered in 1791 in a theater that catered to a decidedly middle-brow if not low-brow public but is now performed routinely in every major opera house in the world. In the 20th century, Kurt Weill and Berthold Brecht adapted Gay's *The Beggar's Opera* into *Die Dreigroschenoper* ("Threepenny Opera"), a biting social satire. One number in particular from this work, *Mack the Knife,* became quite popular. Louis Armstrong and Frank Sinatra, for example, both recorded very different arrangements of it. Similarly the Doors, a rock group, included on one of their albums a rendition of the *Alabama Song* (Anthology) from another Weill/Brecht production, *The Rise and Fall of the City of Mahagonny.* And the Beatles, who were consistently marketed as popular musicians, produced music of enormous stylistic variety, ranging from the rock-and-roll *I Wanna Hold Your Hand* to *Revolution No. 9,* a montage of electronically manipulated sound clips that reflected trends in the world of avant-garde electronic music at the time.

Recognizing the inadequacy of the terms *art* and *popular,* some commentators have attempted to distinguish instead between "cultivated" and "vernacular" styles, but this distinction also breaks down on close inspection. Rock music, an ostensibly vernacular genre, is today produced and recorded with the most sophisticated audio equipment available; bands rehearse endlessly, and individual performers practice with as much intensity as any other kind of musician. Although vernacular music may convey an impression of spontaneity, it is often as carefully thought out—as cultivated—as any music in the ostensibly cultivated category.

But if no consistent difference exists stylistically between art and popular music, or cultivated and vernacular music, there is a difference in the attitudes composers, performers, and audiences bring to bear on music they assign (consciously or unconsciously) to one category or the other. Popular music is usually associated with a relatively relaxed approach toward the work at hand. Compare any two performances of almost any popular song and you will quickly realize they can differ enormously. Performers routinely change words, harmonies, instrumentation, even melody and form. Listeners, in turn, not only accept but welcome such changes. Ella Fitzgerald's rendition of Cole Porter's *Night and Day* differs markedly from Frank Sinatra's, and both take liberties with Porter's original. Sinatra, for example, begins one of his many recordings of the work with the chorus, ignoring the opening verse entirely. But even Porter, as a composer, expected performers to make such alterations.

Yet even here, differences in attitude cannot be assigned exclusively to one kind of music or another. Probably no one would think of 18th-century opera seria as popular music (see Chapter 9), yet composers, performers, and audiences all expected singers in this repertory to embellish da capo arias.

On the whole, however, such practices and attitudes are far less common within the repertory we tend to think of as art music or classical music, particularly in works written after the early 19th century. As we saw in Chapter 14, the respect and deference toward the composer's intentions that now characterize our attitude toward art music dates to roughly 1800, that is, to the generation of Beethoven. Mozart, a few decades earlier, had readily agreed to rewrite the music of several roles in *Don Giovanni*. He had originally composed the work for a specific cast of singers in Prague but willingly made significant changes to accommodate the strengths of the different cast that performed it in Vienna. Over the course of the 19th century, this kind of alteration became increasingly rare. Opera houses began to accommodate the composer, not the other way around.

From the 19th century onward, tradition has taught performers to approach certain repertories with a sense of veneration. Musicians go to great lengths to ascertain and execute the composer's intentions as accurately as possible, using the best edition available (see Appendix 2). Within this tradition, performers rarely change words, harmonies, form, or instrumentation. When Leonard Bernstein substituted a single word in the finale of Beethoven's Ninth Symphony at the Berlin Wall in 1989—changing *Freude* (joy) to *Freiheit* (freedom)—critics debated the alteration at great length. Some considered it appropriate to the circumstances; others found it sacrilegious, a defilement of Beethoven's original score. What is significant is that this alteration of a single word aroused so much attention.

Works that have at various times been considered both classical and popular can also tell us something about the essence of this distinction. Performers have long felt at liberty to make fundamental changes to Gilbert and Sullivan's *Pirates of Penzance* (Anthology), altering words, music, and orchestration to suit their immediate times, needs, and resources. One recent American production, for example, substituted "Coast Guard" for the original "Customs House" in order to make a particular passage more comprehensible to its audience. Joseph Papp's Broadway production of 1980 used electric guitars and synthesizers in addition to a standard orchestra. Unlike Bernstein's alteration of Beethoven's Ninth, however, these and other changes, because they are consistent with a long tradition of performance practice, elicited virtually no comment. In contrast, scholars are now preparing a critical edition of the work in an attempt to reconstruct the original version from autograph sources and the earliest editions.

Music of all kinds can be fruitfully studied and performed from both an art and popular point of view. Neither is superior to the other. Both are legitimate, and both represent valid ways of making—and listening to—music.

Glossary

Absolute music   Instrumental music without a program or any other indication of a possible extramusical content.

Accompanied recitative   Type of recitative accompanied by the orchestra.

Affect   Predominant emotion of a text or musical work.

Air de cour   Literally, "courtly air"; genre of secular song in late-16th-century and early-17th-century France that could be either polyphonic or homophonic (voice and lute).

Alberti bass   Type of accompanimental figure used in much music of the Classical era and featuring frequent repetitions of a broken triad. The device is named after Domenico Alberti (1710–ca. 1740), an otherwise obscure Italian composer who favored its use.

Aleatory music   From the Latin *alea* ("die," the singular of "dice"), music of chance, leaving one or more elements of performance to randomly determined or indeterminate circumstances such as a roll of the dice, sounds that happen to be present at given moment, or actions determined at the whim of the performer.

Ambient music   Background music, the sonic equivalent of architecture, whose primary purpose is to shape actions and attitudes rather than to be the focus of the listener's attention.

Ambitus   Range of a given melody or mode.

Antecedent and consequent   Terms borrowed from grammar to describe the relationship of units within a phrase of music. The **antecedent** phrase comes first (*ante* = "before") and in its most basic form moves from tonic to dominant. The **consequent** phrase follows, and in its most basic form moves from dominant to tonic. See also **periodic phrase structure.**

Anthem   Designation given to many motet-like works on English texts from the 16th century onward. The full anthem is for chorus throughout. The verse anthem alternates choral passages with passages for solo voice and instrumental accompaniment.

Antiphon   Type of plainchant sung before (and sometimes after) the recitation of a psalm or other type of chant.

Antiphonal   Type of performance featuring repeated alternation between two voices or groups of voices.

Antiphoner (*Antiphonale*)   The liturgical book containing the texts (and, if notated, the chants) of the Mass Propers.

Arch form   Symmetrical structure within which a unit of music progresses toward a midpoint and then more or less retraces its steps.

Ars nova   Literally, *The New Art*; the title of an early-14th-century theoretical treatise attributed to Philippe de Vitry and used, by extension, to describe French music of the period as well.

Atonality   Melodic and harmonic idiom first cultivated in the early decades of the 20th century, characterized by the absence of a tonal center.

Augmentation   Process by which the rhythmic value of a line is systematically increased.

Authentic mode   Any of the melodic modes with an ambitus running an octave above the final note.

Autograph or **Autograph score**   Score written in the composer's own hand; also known as a holograph.

Avant-garde   From the French term for military vanguard, an elite group of artists considered far in advance of all others, leading the way to the future. The term, widely used in all the arts of the 20th century, is particularly associated with the phenomenon of modernism.

Ballade   (1) One of the *formes fixes* in the music of the 14th and 15th centuries. The texts usually consist of three strophes of seven or eight lines, the last of which is a refrain. The rhyme scheme varies, but typical patterns include ababccdD, ababbcbC, ababcdE, and ababcdeF (the uppercase letter indicates the refrain, which remains constant from strophe to strophe). (2) Narrative poem, often set to music in the 19th century. (3) Instrumental work that reflects the narrative character of its poetic counterpart.

Ballad opera   Type of opera popular in England during the 18th century, featuring contemporary songs (including, but not limited to ballads) mixed with dialogue.

Ballata (plural, ballate)   Italian poetic and musical form of the 14th and early 15th centuries, formally similar to the French virelai of the same period. The form of the ballata is AbbaA, with a refrain (A) framing the internal lines of each strophe and returning unchanged in each strophe, both musically and textually.

Bar form Form associated with the repertory of the medieval minnesinger, consisting of two *Stollen* followed by an *Abgesang* (AAB).

Basse danse Type of dance popular in the 15th and early 16th centuries. The notated sources preserve only a series of long notes, around which other instruments were expected to improvise their own contrapuntal lines.

Basso continuo Literally, the "continuous bass"; the bass line of any work from the 17th or 18th century that incorporates not only the bass line itself but also the harmonies to be realized above that line. The term is also used to describe the performers playing this part: at a bare minimum, this would consist of a chordal instrument (such as organ or lute), ideally supported by one or more instruments capable of sustaining a bass line (such as viol or bassoon).

Basso ostinato Literally, "obstinate bass"; bass pattern repeated many times within the course of a movement or work.

Bel canto Italian for "beautiful singing," a term used to describe a style of Italian opera in the first half of the 19th century that emphasized lyrical melodic lines, legato phrasing, and a seemingly effortless vocal technique, even in passages of great technical difficulty. The emphasis throughout is on the voice: orchestral accompaniment in 19th-century bel canto opera is typically discreet, limited to harmonic underpinning with little or no counterpoint.

Binary form Any musical form that consists of two parts.

Bluegrass Style of country music that emerged in the 1940s, typically performed by an ensemble of banjo, acoustic guitar, fiddle, and double bass. The banjo is picked (as opposed to strummed), and vocals tend to be pitched in the upper end of the singer's register; the characteristic syncopation of the style anticipates the downbeat slightly, in contrast to jazz, in which performers often play just slightly behind the beat.

Blue note In jazz, the slightly lowered third or seventh degree in the major scale.

Blues Style of song that originated in the American South among African Americans who were slaves and the descendants of slaves. The standard **12-bar blues form** rests on a repeated harmonic pattern of 12 measures in 4/4 time, which in turn is divided into three groups of 4 measures each.

Bourrée Lively dance in duple meter with a prominent upbeat at the beginning of each section.

Branle "Line dance," sometimes in duple meter (*branle simple*), sometimes in triple (*branle gay*).

Bridge In popular song of the 20th century, the contrasting B section that connects statements of the A theme.

Cabaletta Fast closing section of an aria.

Caccia (plural, **cacce**) Poetic and musical form cultivated in 14th- and early-15th-century Italy, sometimes monophonic but more frequently for three voices, often with two canonic upper voices. The texts typically deal with hunting.

Cadence Point of musical closure indicated by pitch, harmony, rhythm, or any combination of these elements.

Cadenza Solo passage in a concerto movement or in an aria, usually toward the end, in which the soloist displays his or her virtuosic talents by embellishing themes heard earlier in the movement or aria; the orchestra remains silent throughout.

Caecilian movement Tendency among certain 19th-century composers to restore Gregorian chant and the style of 16th-century a cappella polyphony as the ideals of church music.

Canon (1) Polyphonic work written in such a way that the imitating voice or voices follow the line of the original either exactly (a strict canon) or with small modifications (a free canon). (2) Rule or direction given at the beginning of such a composition to indicate the manner in which it is to be realized (e.g., the points at which the successive voices are to enter).

Cantata In its broadest sense, a work to be sung (the Italian word *cantare* means "to sing"). More specifically, the term is used to denote a vocal work, usually sacred, for performance forces of varying size, from soloist and basso continuo to soloists, chorus, and orchestra.

Cantilena motet Type of 15th-century motet that features a florid, lyrical top voice over slower moving lower voices.

Cantus firmus (plural, **cantus firmi**) "Fixed melody" that serves as the basis of a composition. A cantus firmus can be newly composed for a work but is most often derived from an existing composition.

Canzona Instrumental work of the late Renaissance or Baroque originally based on a vocal model, such as the chanson, but later often composed independently of any vocal model.

Castrato   Castrated male singer whose voice has never broken and who therefore sings in the soprano or alto range. Castrati were common in opere serie of the 17th and 18th centuries.

Cauda   The long melisma at the end of a conductus.

Chaconne   Type of bass pattern used throughout the Baroque.

Character piece   Brief work for solo piano that seeks to portray the mood or "character" of a particular person, idea, situation, or emotion. These are sometimes specified, sometimes not. The character piece, which first appeared in the early 19th century, tends to be brief, sectional, and fairly simple in construction.

Chorale   A hymn, either in its harmonized form or as a melody alone. Chorales are associated particularly with the congregational music of the Protestant Reformation.

Chorus   In popular song of the 20th century, the principal tune or section.

Clausula (plural, **clausulae**)   Passages of measured organum that could be substituted at will into the appropriate textual section of a larger existing work of organum.

Coda   From the Italian word for "tail," a closing section of a work or movement.

Color   Melodic pattern of an isorhythmic tenor.

Combinatorial   Quality of certain 12-tone rows in which the hexachord of a row—its first six or last six notes—can be combined with one of the hexachords of an inverted, retrograde, or retrograde inverted form of the same row without producing any duplication of pitches.

Computer music   Music generated, transformed, composed, and/or performed by a computer.

Concertato madrigal   Type of madrigal that emerged in the early 17th century, using instruments (basso continuo with or without additional instruments) independently of the vocal part or parts.

Concertino   Small group of soloists within a concerto grosso, often consisting of two violins and basso continuo.

Concerto   Term used in the 17th century to indicate broadly any work consisting of multiple forces, such as voices and instruments. From the 18th century onward, the term was reserved primarily for works featuring a soloist or soloists contrasted against a larger ensemble.

Concerto grosso   Type of Baroque concerto typically featuring soloists (the concertino) and a larger ensemble (the ripieno). The term also encompasses the ripieno concerto, a work for large ensemble with no soloists.

Concert overture   Single-movement work for orchestra associated with a programmatic idea of some kind. The genre grew out of the 18th-century tradition of performing opera overtures in the concert hall; the concert overture is, in effect, an overture without an opera.

Concitato   See *genere concitato.*

Conductus (plural, **conductus** or **conducti**)   Genre of vocal monophony or polyphony cultivated in the 12th and 13th centuries. Conductus of one, two, three, or occasionally four voices were not based on borrowed musical material of any kind; their texts consist of freely composed poetry written in metered verse that lend themselves to syllabic and strongly metrical musical settings. In the polyphonic conductus, all voices move in roughly the same rhythm.

Conjunct motion   Melodic motion exclusively or predominantly by half or whole steps.

Contenance angloise   Literally, "the English guise"; term used by the French poet Martin le Franc in 1442 to describe the music of Dunstable, Binchois, and Du Fay. This "new way of composing with lively consonances" probably refers to the triadic sonorities and panconsonance of their music.

Contratenor   Literally "against the tenor"; name first given in the 14th century to a voice line moving in the same range as the tenor.

Countersubject   Contrapuntal theme played against the subject of a fugue.

Couplet   In a rondo, a contrasting theme (B, C, D, etc.) within the pattern ABACADA. Also called an *episode.*

Critical edition   Edition prepared by an editor who critically evaluates the relative merits of all sources for a work, such as the composer's autograph score, authorized copies, first and early editions, and later revisions by the composer. A critical edition is usually issued with a critical report.

Critical report   Editor's report on all significant discrepancies between the critical edition and the various sources (autograph score, first edition, etc.) used to create that edition.

Cross-relation   Simultaneous or nearly simultaneous sounding of two pitches a half step apart.

Cyclical coherence Manner in which the various movements of a multi-movement cycle (sonata, quartet, symphony, etc.) are related to one another, through thematic ideas, distinctive textures, or other musical elements.

Cyclic Mass Cycle of all movements of the Mass Ordinary integrated by a common cantus firmus or other musical device.

Da capo aria Type of aria consisting of three sections: an opening A section, a contrasting B section, and a return of the A section. In performance, singers were expected to embellish and elaborate the notated music, particularly in the return of A.

Development In sonata form, the section following the exposition and preceding the recapitulation, so called because it develops the ideas originally presented in the exposition. The typical development manipulates themes, moves through a variety of keys, and avoids the tonic.

Diastematic neumes Neumes that indicate the relative relationship of notes (higher, lower, same) according to their vertical placement on the page. In early plainchant notation, diastematic neumes (also known as heightened neumes) were written without staff lines of any kind.

Diminution Speeding up of note values within a theme that has already been presented.

Divine Office (or **Office**) Series of eight services held daily in monastic communities from dawn through the middle of the night, consisting musically of the chanting of psalms and hymns.

Doctrine of ethos In ancient Greece, the belief that music had the power to elevate or debase the soul, to enlighten or degrade the mind, and to arouse in listeners certain kinds of emotions and behaviors.

Dodecaphony From the Greek *dodeca,* meaning "12." A method of serial composition based on a series or row of 12 pitches drawn from the chromatic octave (C, C♯, D, D♯, etc., up through B).

Double-exposition concerto form Type of sonata form found in many concertos of the late 18th and 19th centuries, in which the opening tutti exposition remains in the tonic and the subsequent solo exposition modulates from the tonic to a secondary key area.

Double leading-tone cadence Type of cadence favored in the 14th and early 15th centuries that featured two leading tones a fifth apart resolving upward to the octave and fifth.

Duplum From the Latin word for "second," the added second voice in organum and polyphony of the 12th and 13th centuries.

Empfindsamkeit The German word for "sensibility," used by some music historians to identify an aesthetic attitude prevalent in the mid-18th century and reflected in much music of that time as well. The style of *Empfindsamkeit* is associated with music that focuses on detail and avoids thick textures and grandiose gestures.

Episode (1) Nonimitative section within a fugue. (2) In a rondo, an extended passage that appears between entrances of the main theme (the refrain); also known as a *couplet.*

Equal temperament System of tuning that came into widespread use over the course of the 18th century, based on a division of the octave into 12 absolutely equal semitones.

Exit convention Convention of opera seria in which the singer who has just finished an aria leaves the stage.

Exposition (1) In a fugue, the opening section that introduces the subject in all voices. (2) In a sonata-form movement, the opening section that presents the principal themes of the movement over the course of a harmonic plan that typically moves from tonic to dominant or (in minor-mode works) from tonic to relative major.

Expressionism Broad artistic movement of the early 20th century that sought to give voice to the unconscious, to make manifest humanity's deepest and often darkest emotions. In Freudian terms, expressionist art bypasses the ego and aims straight for the id, the unconscious repository of primal urges.

Faburden Style of three-voice writing found in some English music of the 15th and 16th centuries, featuring one notated and two unnotated lines. The uppermost voice moves parallel to the notated voice at the interval of a fourth above; the lowermost voice moves in thirds and fifths below the notated line.

Fantasia Type of work that follows no structures of large-scale convention but follows instead (or at least gives the impression of following) the composer's free flight of fantasy.

Fauxbourdon Style of three-voice writing popular in the 15th century in which two voices are notated and a third, unnotated voice (the fauxbourdon), runs parallel to the uppermost notated line at the interval of a fourth below.

Figured bass   Notational convention of the basso continuo in the 17th and 18th centuries using numbers ("figures") to indicate the desired intervals—and thus the harmonies—to be played above a given bass line.

Finalis   Characteristic final note of a given mode.

Florentine Camerata   Group of artists and noblemen who met in Florence between roughly 1573 and 1587 to discuss, among other things, the possible means of recreating the music of ancient Greece.

Folia   Type of bass pattern used throughout the Baroque.

Formes fixes   Literally, "fixed forms"; the poetic and musical structural patterns in French music of the 14th and 15th centuries. The most important of the *formes fixes* were the ballade, virelai, and rondeau.

Franconian notation   Earliest system of mensural notation, used in the second half of the 13th century and ascribed to Franco of Cologne. Franconian notation assigned specific durational values for the first time to specific note forms.

Free jazz   Subgenre of jazz that emerged in the early 1960s, characterized by extreme improvisation, often without a central theme, fixed meters, chord progressions, or even tonality itself.

French overture   Type of overture that begins with a slow introduction featuring dotted rhythms and moves to a fast imitative section. Commonly used in French operas and opere serie of the 17th and 18th centuries.

Frottola (plural **frottole**)   Secular Italian vocal genre of the late 15th and early 16th centuries. The texture tends to be chordal and the texts are often lighthearted, comic, or ironic.

Fugue   Type of composition that incorporates a series of imitative entries, usually on a single theme but capable of accommodating multiple themes as well.

Galant   Term used by some historians to describe the musical style of the mid–18th century, emphasizing the music's lightness and grace.

Galliarde   Type of dance, similar to the saltarello but even more vigorous, with larger leaps by the dancers.

Gamut   In medieval theory, the entire range of available pitches, conceived of as a series of seven interlocking hexachords beginning on C, F, or G (see Example 1-4).

Genere concitato   Literally, the "agitated" or "warlike" manner; a style of writing, developed by Monteverdi, for evoking a mood of agitation or anger, often through the use of rapid repeated notes and fanfarelike figures.

Gesamtkunstwerk   German for "integrated art work"; Richard Wagner's ideal of the highest form of art, synthesizing music, drama, and gesture.

Gradual (*Graduale*)   (1) The liturgical book containing the texts (and, if notated, the chants) of the Mass Ordinary. (2) The second element of the Mass Propers.

Gregorian chant   Name often given to plainchant in honor of Pope Gregory I (later Saint Gregory), long believed to have been the originator of the repertory.

Ground bass   Short bass pattern that, repeated many times over the course of a movement or work, provides the structural basis for the voice or voices above it.

Guidonian hand   Mnemonic device attributed to the medieval theorist Guido d'Arezzo, used to teach solmization syllables.

Half cadence   Cadence on the dominant.

Harmonic rhythm   Rate of harmonic change within a given passage of music. A passage is said to have a slow harmonic rhythm if it maintains the same harmony over a relatively long span of time, such as a full measure or half a measure, depending on meter and tempo.

Harmonics   Effect created by a technique of string playing in which the performer touches the bowed string lightly at a designated point. The resulting sound is a harmonic overtone two octaves higher than the notated pitch, and the sound is light and ethereal.

Head motif   Thematic idea that occurs at the beginning of a movement or work and returns prominently throughout the course of the music that follows.

Heightened neume   See **diastematic neume.**

Hemiola   Brief passage of duple-meter rhythms within an otherwise triple-meter context.

Hexachord   Any grouping of six pitches. Through the Baroque era, a hexachord was conceived of as a series of six ascending notes, all separated by whole steps except the third and fourth notes, which are separated by a half step. In 20th-century dodecaphony (12-tone serial music), a hexachord is half of a 12-tone row.

Historicism   Approach to artistic creation that openly embraces the forms and styles of earlier generations even while presenting them in original ways.

Hocket Passage featuring rapid-fire voice exchange, a favorite device of 14th- and early-15th-century composers.

Holograph Score written in the composer's own hand; also known as an autograph score or simply as an autograph.

Homophony Type of texture in which a principal melodic line is accompanied by a clearly subordinate voice or voices.

Hymn Setting of a sacred but nonliturgical text, usually strophic and predominantly syllabic.

Idealism System of thought based on the premise that objects in the physical world are a reflection of ideas in the mind. The rise of Idealism in the late 18th and early 19th centuries played a key role in the rising status of instrumental music.

Impressionism Musical style that flourished in the period 1890 to 1920, associated chiefly with the French composer Claude Debussy and characterized by a blurring of distinct harmonies, rhythms, timbres, and forms.

Intabulation Arrangement for keyboard or for a plucked stringed instrument—lute, guitar, vihuela, cittern, pandora—of a work originally written for voices.

Integral serialism System of serial composition in which elements beyond pitch, such as rhythm and dynamics, are also subjected to serial treatment. Also known as **total serialism.**

Intermedio (plural, **intermedi**) Dramatic work, often with music, performed between the acts of a larger theatrical presentation such as a play or opera.

Intermezzo Sung dramatic work staged between the acts of a larger opera, usually an opera seria.

Inversion Mirror image of a melodic line. The inversion of a line that moves up a major third and then down a minor second would be a line that moves down a major third and then up a minor second.

Isorhythm Term coined in the 20th century to describe the rhythmic and melodic structure of certain tenor lines in polyphony of the 14th and 15th centuries. An isorhythmic tenor features a rhythmic pattern (the *talea*) and a melodic pattern (the *color*), each of which is repeated at least once. The *talea* and *color* may be of equal duration, but more often they are not.

Italian overture Type of overture found in many operas and oratorios of the 18th century consisting of three movements in the sequence fast-slow-fast.

Jazz Musical style that emerged in the early decades of the 20th century in the American South, covering a wide range of substyles connected by an approach toward music that embraces improvisation and rhythmic and intonational freedom, along with a general acceptance that the musical work exists in performance rather than in the form of a written score.

Jubilus In plainchant settings of the Alleluia within the Propers of the Mass, the long melisma on the final syllable of the word *Alleluia.*

Klezmer Type of instrumental music originally cultivated in the 19th century by the *klezmorim,* the professional Jewish musicians of eastern Europe, and characterized by a steady bass and rhythmically free winds above, often with chromatic passages in thirds, exaggerated accents, and repeated half steps back and forth.

Leitmotiv German for "leading motif," a brief musical idea connected to some person, event, or idea in a music drama. The leitmotiv distinguishes itself from the earlier device of the musical reminiscence by virtue of its malleability and its context within a network of related musical ideas. It was first pioneered in the music dramas of Richard Wagner.

Liber usualis Literally, "Book of Use"; anthology of many different kinds of plainchant for both the Mass and the Office.

Lied (pronounced "leet"; the plural, **Lieder,** is pronounced like the English word "leader") German term for the genre of song.

Ligatures Notational signs used in plainchant and polyphony through the Renaissance to represent two or more pitches within a single unit. In mensural notation, ligatures were often used to indicate rhythmic values.

Lute song Type of strophic secular song cultivated in England during the early 17th century for lute and voices (usually four). The lute could substitute for or double as many as three of the four voices.

Madrigal Poetic and musical form first used in 14th-century Italy and then taken up later again in the 16th century. (1) The texts of 14th-century Italian madrigals usually consist of two or three strophes, each with three lines, plus a two-line ritornello (refrain) at the very end. (2) The 16th-century Italian madrigal is a poem of a single strophe using a free rhyme scheme and meter, such as an alternation of 7- and 11-syllable lines.

Madrigal comedy Series of polyphonic madrigals loosely connected through plot and characters. The genre enjoyed its heyday in the closing decades of the 16th century.

Mannerism   Term used to describe an artistic style prevalent in the works of certain artists of the 16th and early 17th centuries—both in painting and in music—that emphasized unusual degrees of distortion, exaggeration, and unsettling juxtaposition for dramatic effect. In music, these devices could include extreme dissonance, unusual harmonic progressions, and exaggerated word-painting.

March   Genre of music originally intended to keep soldiers in formation during movement, characterized by duple meter and a steady tempo.

Masque   Theatrical genre of 17th-century England featuring a mixture of declaimed poetry, songs, scenery, dance, and instrumental music.

Mass   The central service of the traditional Christian liturgy, a ritualistic celebration of Christ's Last Supper with his disciples. The liturgy of the Mass consists of the Ordinary (fixed texts said or sung at every Mass) and the Propers (texts that vary according to the date within the liturgical year, such as a particular feast day or season).

Mean-tone tuning   System of tuning used widely in the Renaissance and Baroque eras in which perfect fifths were altered in such a way to make major and minor thirds more pleasing to the ear.

Melisma   Passage featuring many notes per syllable.

Melismatic organum   Type of organum in which multiple notes in the added voice(s) run against the individual notes of an original chant.

Mélodie   French for "melody," also used for the genre of song in France from the 19th century onward.

Mensural notation   System of musical notation that first emerged in the mid-13th century, in which rhythmic durations were indicated by distinct note shapes as opposed to ligatures. In its broadest sense, mensural notation is still in use today, but the term is generally understood to refer to the various forms of mensural notation used between approximately 1250 and 1600.

Mensuration signs   Notational devices used at the beginning of a work to indicate the mensural relationship of note values, such as the number of semibreves per breve or the number of minims to a semibreve.

Middle entries   Those sections within a fugue that present a point of imitation, in contrast to episodes, which feature little or no imitation.

Minimalism   Artistic movement that emerged in the early 1960s, relying on multiple repetitions of small units that differ only slightly or are varied only gradually over long stretches of time.

Minnesinger   Medieval German poet-composer-performer who sang songs of love.

Minstrel song   Type of song typically performed in the 19th and early 20th centuries by white performers in blackface. The songs themselves purportedly represent the perspectives of African-American slaves or their descendants.

Minuet   Dance form that became a common feature in instrumental cycles of the Baroque and Classical eras. The typical minuet consists of two binary forms, the first known as the *minuet proper,* the second as the *trio.* The minuet proper is repeated at the end of the trio.

Minuet proper   In a minuet, the opening and closing section (A) within a basic ABA form.

Mode   (1) Melodic mode—a scale type characterized by a specific pattern of whole steps and half steps. Melodies in any of the eight so-called church modes of the medieval era end on a characteristic pitch (the *finalis,* or final) and move up and down within a particular range (ambitus). (2) Rhythmic mode—in the medieval era, one of six consistent patterns of repeated units of long and short durations. (3) Since the early 18th century, one of the two principal forms—major and minor—of the diatonic scale.

Modernism   Artistic movement of the early 20th century that emphasized novelty at almost any cost, based on the conviction that the New must be as different as possible from the Old. Modernism in music frequently involved a rejection of tonality, conventional forms, and established genres.

Modified strophic form   Type of strophic form in which the music varies to some degree from strophe to strophe—through melodic embellishment, for example, or alteration of texture or harmony—but remains otherwise recognizably the same.

Monody   Any work of the 17th century consisting of a solo voice supported by basso continuo.

Monophony   Musical texture of a single voice or line, without accompaniment of any kind.

Moresca   "Moorish" dance, supposedly influenced by the Arabic cultures of northern Africa and Spain.

Motet   Polyphonic vocal work, usually sacred.

Motetus   In the 13th-century motet, the voice added above the tenor. Its counterpart in organum was known as the *duplum,* but with an underlaid text of its own in motets, this part became known as the motetus.

Musica ficta   Convention of the late medieval and Renaissance eras in which certain notes were sharped or flattened in performance according to various conventions, such as creating cadential leading tones or avoiding cross-relations between voices.

Musica reservata   Term used in the 16th and early 17th centuries to describe certain kinds of music "reserved" for connoisseurs and not intended for wide-scale distribution. These works were demanding for performers and listeners alike and often included unconventional elements of notation, chromaticism, or the use of ancient Greek genera.

Music drama (*Musikdrama*)   Term coined by Richard Wagner to distinguish traditional opera from what he felt to be his fundamentally new approach to sung drama. The music drama is characterized by the ideal of the *Gesamtkunstwerk,* in which music, words, and gesture are all inextricably linked yet at the same time self-sufficient.

Musique concrète   French term for "concrete music," used to denote music in which the sonic material to be manipulated is a recorded sound taken from everyday life. The sounds are thus real, or "concrete."

Neoclassicism   Style that emerged in the 1910s and 1920s, characterized by a return to the tonal idiom, conventional genres and forms, the ideal of absolute music, conciseness of expression, and a general tendency toward transparent textures, lighter orchestration, and small ensembles.

Neumatic   Musical setting of several notes per syllable of text. The term is used primarily in connection with plainchant.

Neume   Sign used in early chant notation to indicate pitch.

Nonretrogradable rhythm   Olivier Messiaen's term for a palindromic rhythmic unit—that is, one that is the same forward as backward and whose retrograde form is therefore identical to its original form.

Obbligato accompaniment   Style of homophony associated particularly with music of the later decades of the 18th century in which the accompanying voices contribute material essential to a work's musical fabric.

Octatonic scale   Scale that alternates between half and whole steps and contains within itself all possible intervals, from the minor second to the major seventh.

Opera   In the narrowest sense, a drama sung entirely from beginning to end. In a looser sense, any drama consisting primarily of singing, as opposed to speaking.

Opera buffa   Literally "comic opera," a subgenre of opera that emerged in Italy out of the tradition of the intermezzo, based on humorous subjects and featuring everyday characters rather than the heroes, rulers, and gods typically found in opera seria.

Opéra comique   Type of opera in 19th-century France that incorporated spoken dialogue as well as music. In spite of its name, the subject matter of the genre was not always comic.

Opera seria   Literally, "serious opera." Type of opera cultivated in the period ca. 1680 to 1810, particularly in Italy. Its characteristic features were a strict division between recitative and aria, an emphasis on virtuoso singing, particularly in da capo arias, and the use of castrati. The librettos were typically drawn from ancient history or mythology.

Operetta   Lighter type of opera that emerged in the mid–19th century out of the traditions of the singspiel and the opéra comique. Operettas mix spoken dialogue with sung numbers and deal invariably with humorous and lighthearted subjects.

Oratorio   Genre of vocal music similar to opera in its musical elements (recitatives, arias, choruses, etc.) but performed without staging or costumes. Most oratorios revolve around religious subjects, but some are written on secular themes.

Organum (plural, organa)   Polyphonic work of the 9th to 12th centuries consisting of an original plainchant melody in one voice along with at least one additional voice above or below. In **parallel organum,** the added voice or voices run parallel to an established plainchant melody at a constant interval. In **free organum** (also known as **unmeasured organum**), the added voice(s) move rapidly against the slower moving notes of the original chant. In **measured organum,** all the voices move at about the same speed.

Ostinato   Figure presented repeatedly in succession.

Panconsonance   Style of writing associated with Dunstable and Du Fay in the early 15th century that makes ample use of triads and restricts the use of dissonance considerably, compared to the idioms of the 14th century.

Paraphrase   Free variation of an existing melodic line or polyphonic network.

Paratactic form Any structure that consists of a series of more or less discrete units unrelated to one another musically. Paratactic form can be represented schematically as A, B, C, D, E, and so on.

Parisian chanson Term coined by 20th-century scholars to describe a type of song that emerged in the French capital during the 1520s, featuring predominantly chordal textures.

Parlor song So called because of its preferred place of performance in the 19th-century home, a type of song whose texts are invariably strophic and sentimental, and whose music is melodically and harmonically straightforward.

Passacaglia Type of bass pattern used throughout the Baroque.

Passamezzo (1) Type of bass pattern used throughout the Baroque. (2) Dance similar to the pavane, but with a lighter step.

Pasticcio Work whose individual units are written by several different composers.

Pavane Slow, courtly dance in duple meter.

Pentatonic scale Any scale based on five notes.

Pervading imitation Compositional technique in which a series of musical ideas are stated imitatively in all voices across the course of an entire work or section of a work. The technique first began to be cultivated in a widespread manner in the second half of the 15th century.

Petronian notation System of mensural notation used in the late 13th and early 14th centuries, ascribed to Petrus de Cruce and based on the principles of Franconian notation, but including the shorter note values of the minim and semiminim and allowing for as many as nine semibreves within the duration of a single breve.

Phase music or **process music** Subgenre of minimalism in which the listener can clearly hear the process by which the elements of a work gradually transform themselves into something new and different.

Pitch class Any set of notes associated with a particular note regardless of register: any A, any B, any C, and so on.

Plagal mode Any of the melodic modes with an ambitus running roughly a fifth above and a fourth below the final note.

Plainchant Monophonic music of the medieval Christian church.

Point of imitation Unit of music in which all the voices of a polyphonic composition take up more or less the same musical idea in succession. Points of imitation are a by-product of pervading imitation.

Polyglot motet Any motet with multiple texts in different languages performed simultaneously. The polyglot motet was cultivated most intensely in the 13th century.

Polyphony Musical texture of two or more voices essentially equal in importance.

Polytextual motet Any motet with multiple texts performed simultaneously. The polytextual motet was cultivated most intensely in the 13th century.

Polytonality Simultaneous juxtaposition of contrasting triads or keys.

Postmodernism Aesthetic attitude that emerged in the last third of the 20th century, embracing the past (including modernism) but often in an eclectic manner, synthesizing a variety of approaches in a single work. Postmodernist composers felt obliged neither to avoid nor use tonality or atonality, conventional forms, and established genres.

Prima prattica Term coined in the early 17th century to describe an older attitude toward text setting in which the projection of a sung text was subordinated to the established conventions of good counterpoint. The *prima prattica* is closely associated (but not synonymous) with polyphony. Literally, the "first practice," so called because it existed before the emergence of the *seconda prattica*, the "second" (or newer) practice.

Primitivism Aesthetic movement of all the arts in the early 20th century that consciously avoided the cultivated traditions of Western art. In music, primitivism gave special importance to rhythm, the most basic of all musical elements, and abandoned or substantially altered such arbitrary (so-called civilized) concepts as voice leading, triadic harmony, and the major and minor forms of the diatonic scale.

Program music Any instrumental work that in one way or another—through a title or accompanying poetry or prose—is connected with a story or idea that lies outside the music itself.

Prosula (plural, *prosulae*) Type of trope in which words were added to an existing chant.

Psalm tone Plainchant formula used to recite the psalms.

Quadruplum From the Latin word for "fourth," the added fourth voice in organum and polyphony of the 12th and 13th centuries.

Quartal harmonies Chords built on the interval of a fourth rather than a third.

Quattrocento   Italian term for the 15th century (literally, "the 1400s").

Ragtime   Style that grew out of traditions of African American dance and flourished at the end of the 19th century and in the early decades of the 20th. Ragtime music is usually in duple meter and based on units of 8 or 16 measures. Syncopation is prevalent throughout, thrown into relief by the steadiness of the bass line.

Recapitulation   In sonata form, the section following the development. In its simplest form, the recapitulation begins with a return of the opening idea of the movement in the tonic key; it continues by restating the entire exposition in the tonic, without modulation. In practice, recapitulations are not nearly so regular and often incorporate substantial changes in relation to the exposition.

Recitation tone   In plainchant, and particularly in psalm tones, a central pitch used repeatedly in immediate succession to declaim large quantities of text.

Recitative   Style of singing characterized by syllabic declamation, with greater emphasis on the projection of the text at hand than on melody, more nearly approximating the inflections of speech even while adhering to the basic musical elements of pitch and rhythm.

Refrain   (1) In the broadest sense, any theme and/or text that returns repeatedly over the course of a work after contrasting material. (2) In a rondo, the recurring theme (A) within the pattern ABACADA.

Reprise   Unit of music to be repeated in performance immediately after it has been first presented. A binary form often consists of two reprises.

Respond   Refrain portion of a responsorial chant, sung before the verse.

Responsorial chant   Any of the plainchants, such as the Gradual, Alleluia, and Tract, in which the chorus and soloist alternate.

Retrograde   Melodic line presented backward, that is, from its end to its beginning.

Rhythmic mode   See **mode.**

Ricercar   In the early 16th century, a freely composed work that is improvisatory and preludial in character, often for lute or keyboard. By the mid–16th century, the term had become identified with polyphonic works for keyboard or for instrumental ensembles. By the 18th century, the term was associated with fugues that used a large number or variety of contrapuntal devices.

Ripieno   Literally, "full"; designation used in the Baroque era for the large ensemble within a concerto grosso.

Ripieno concerto   Type of concerto for large ensemble, without soloists.

Ritornello   Literally, a "small return"; musical idea that returns at several points over the course of a work, usually after contrasting material of some kind. The **ritornello principle** is the structural basis by which composers construct large-scale forms around successive returns of an opening idea. This principle is especially important in the genre of the concerto.

Rococo   Term borrowed from art history and used by some music historians to describe the musical style of the mid-18th century, emphasizing qualities of lightness and grace.

Romanticism   Mode of thought that emerged in the late 18th and early 19th centuries and placed unprecedented importance on imagination and subjectivity over reason and objectivity.

Rondeau (plural, **rondeaux**)   One of the *formes fixes* used in music of the 14th and 15th centuries. Each strophe consists of eight lines of text set to music following the rhyme scheme ABaAabAB (uppercase letters indicate refrains, which remain constant from strophe to strophe).

Rondellus   Type of polyphonic composition cultivated in the medieval era, in which the voices exchange extended phrases repeatedly (e.g., A over B, followed by B over A, followed by A over B, etc.).

Rondo   Dance form (a "round dance") that became a common feature in instrumental cycles of the late 18th and 19th centuries, especially as a finale. The basic pattern of the rondo in its simplest form is ABACA, with the recurring theme (A) constituting the *refrain* and the contrasting themes (B, C, etc.), constituting the *episodes* or *couplets*.

Root position triad   Triad whose root or fundamental pitch appears in the lowest sounding voice.

Row   In serial composition, another name for the series of 12 different pitch classes.

Saltarello   Lively dance that often follows a slower one.

Scat singing   Technique of singing in which the voice mimics an instrument, singing syncopated nonsense syllables against the steady beat of the bass.

Scherzo   From the Italian word for "joke," a movement type that emerged in the early 19th century and eventually supplanted the minuet within such multi-movement cycles as symphonies, quartets, and sonatas. Like the minuet, the scherzo is in ABA form; in contrast to the minuet, the scherzo is typically faster and at times humorous or even grotesque in its gestures.

Secco recitative   Literally, "dry recitative," accompanied by basso continuo alone; also known as *recitativo semplice* ("simple recitative").

Seconda prattica   Term coined in the early 17th century to describe a new attitude toward text setting in which all musical means were subordinated to the effective delivery of the text being sung. The *seconda prattica* is closely associated (but not synonymous) with the emerging practice of monody. Literally, the "second practice," so called because it appeared after the *prima prattica*, the "first" (or older) practice.

Semi-opera   Type of theatrical entertainment that flourished in England during the second half of the 17th century. These were essentially plays with a large proportion of musical numbers, both vocal and instrumental.

Sequence   (1) Element of the Mass Propers, authorized for special feast days, appearing after the Alleluia. (2) Any musical ed on successively different pitches.

Serial composition   Method of composition based on the repeated manipulation of an established row (series) of pitches and/or rhythms and/or dynamics. Transpositions and permutations of the series (inversion, retrograde, retrograde inversion) provide variety. Dodecaphony is the most common form of serial composition, based on a row of 12 different pitch classes.

Series   In serial composition, another name for the row of 12 different pitch classes.

Singspiel   Literally, "song-play"; German-language spoken drama with interpolated musical numbers (arias, duets, trios, etc.). The singspiel of the 18th century was an important forerunner of the later operetta and musical.

Socialist realism   Aesthetic doctrine espoused by Soviet bloc authorities in the 20th century to encourage artists to produce works in a readily accessible style. In music, works written under the influence of socialist realism typically incorporate folk or folklike elements and project an overwhelmingly optimistic tone.

Solmization syllables   Syllables associated with the pitches of a hexachord, in ascending order: *ut, re, mi, fa, sol, la.*

Solo concerto   Type of concerto featuring a soloist and a larger ensemble, as opposed to a ripieno concerto.

Sonata   Literally, "that which is sounded" (i.e., played on instruments). Term used in the Renaissance and Baroque in the broadest sense to indicate a work for an instrument or instruments of any combination. From the 18th century onward, the term was used to indicate a work for one or more solo instruments, usually in three or four movements.

Sonata da camera   Literally, "sonata of the chamber"; type of sonata featuring a series of dance-related movements, popular in the Baroque era.

Sonata da chiesa   Literally, "sonata of the church"; type of sonata featuring a slow first movement and at least one additional imitative movement, popular in the Baroque era.

Sonata form   Structural convention frequently found in first movements, slow movements, and finales of instrumental works, particularly from the second half of the 18th century and all of the 19th century. A movement in sonata form incorporates an *exposition*, a *development*, and a *recapitulation*. An introduction and coda are sometimes added but are not essential elements of the form.

Sonata form with varied reprise   Type of sonata form in which the exposition is not repeated note for note but instead written out and changed in subtle ways.

Sonata-rondo form   Type of rondo (ABACABA) in which B corresponds to the secondary key area of a sonata-form movement; that is, it is presented first in a contrasting key and then (toward the end) in the tonic, as in a sonata-form recapitulation.

Song cycle   Collection of songs ordered in such a way as to convey at least the outline of a story or idea.

Song form   A form frequently used in popular song of the 20th century, featuring four units of eight measures each, following the thematic pattern AABA.

Sprechstimme   Literally, "speech-voice," with "voice" understood here in the sense of "singing." A style of vocal declamation that lies midway between speech and song, cultivated particularly in the early 19th century by such composers as Arnold Schoenberg and Alban Berg.

Stop   On an organ, a lever that controls the flow of air through sets or combinations of sets of pipes, thereby altering the timbre of the instrument's sound.

Strophic   (1) In poetry, any text made up of stanzas (strophes), each of which has the same number of lines and follows the same rhyme scheme and meter. (2) In music, any setting of a strophic text in which each strophe is sung to the same music.

Sturm und Drang   Literally, "Storm and Stress"; designation, given by 20th-century scholars, to a style of writing that appears in certain works by Haydn, Mozart, Gluck, and others in the late 1760s and early 1770s. The characteristics of *Sturm und Drang* music include a predilection for the minor mode and such extreme gestures as large melodic leaps, jagged syncopations, and sudden dynamic contrasts.

Style brisé   Literally, "broken style"; style of writing for the keyboard that imitates the broken (arpeggiated) chords often played on a lute or guitar.

Subject   Theme of a fugue.

Syllabic   Musical setting of one note per syllable of text.

Symphonic poem   Term coined by Franz Liszt in 1854 to replace the generic name of what had previously been called the *concert overture,* a one-movement work for orchestra with some kind of programmatic association.

Symphony   (1) In the 17th and early 18th centuries, a work or movement for large instrumental ensemble. (2) In the 18th century, an overture to an opera or stage play. (3) From about 1720 onward, a multi-movement work for instrumental ensemble.

Syntactic form   Any formal structure that maintains one or more thematic ideas consistently across the course of an entire movement or work. Syntactic form involves an interrelationship of musical units in the same way that syntax relates to the functional relationship of a sentence's verbal units (nouns, verbs, etc.). Syntactic form is the opposite of paratactic form, in which the units of a movement are thematically unrelated.

Synthesized electronic music   Music consisting of sounds generated and manipulated entirely by electronic means, through an electronic oscillator or a modifying device like a synthesizer.

Tactus   From the Latin word for "touch," the basic unit of temporal measurement used in Renaissance music. One theorist of the late 15th century claimed the rate of the *tactus* was equivalent to the heartbeat of an adult man breathing at a normal speed—that is, roughly 60 to 70 times per minute.

Talea   Rhythmic pattern of an isorhythmic tenor.

Temperament   Manner of adjusting ("tempering") the intervals of a scale.

Tempo rubato   Literally, "robbed time"; practice of performing with subtle accelerations and decelerations of tempo not otherwise indicated in a score.

Tenor   (1) The high voice range of the adult male, running roughly from the G above middle C to the B slightly more than an octave below middle C. (2) In medieval and Renaissance music, the vocal part that "holds" (Latin, *tenere*) the chant melody.

Tenorlied   Type of secular song cultivated in Germany in the 16th century in which the principal melody appears in the tenor voice, with three contrapuntal voices surrounding it.

Tetrachord   Any grouping of four pitches.

Through-composed   Term used to describe song settings that are not strophic—that is, settings that provide new music for each section of the text.

Tierce de picardie   Literally, "Picardy third"; major third at the end of a work otherwise in minor mode. The raised third was not always notated but instead left to the discretion of the performer.

Toccata   Type of work for keyboard that is freely constructed, based on no preexistent material, and typically features rapid passagework.

Total serialism   See **integral serialism.**

Trecento   Italian term for the 14th century (literally, "the 1300s").

Triad   Chord of three notes whose adjacent pitches are separated by intervals of a major or minor third.

Trio   (1) Any work for three voices or instruments. (2) In a minuet or scherzo, the contrasting middle section (B) within a basic ABA form.

Trio sonata   Type of sonata for two instruments of a high range (violins, flutes, oboes, etc.) and basso continuo, popular throughout the 18th century.

Triplum   From the Latin word for "third," the added third voice in organum and polyphony of the 12th and 13th centuries.

Trope   Musical or textual addition to an existing plainchant. Tropes could be added to the beginning or end of a chant, or they could be interpolated into the chant itself.

Troping   Process of creating a trope.

Troubadours and trouvères   The mostly wandering minstrels—often composer, poet, and performer in the same person—who entertained the courts of the nobility in southern (troubadour) and northern (trouvère) France in the 12th and 13th centuries.

Tutti   Literally, "all"; term used to indicate the large ensemble within a concerto grosso. Also used to designate the sections of the work played by this ensemble.

Vamp   In popular song of the 20th century, a short progression of chords that can be repeatedly indefinitely before the entrance of the voice.

Variation suite   Set of contrasting dance-related movements based on one basic thematic idea.

Verse   In popular song of the 20th century, the opening section that leads into the song's chorus or principal melody.

Villancico   Principal genre of Spanish song in the Renaissance. The term was first used in the late 15th century to identify a poetic form equivalent to the French virelai (AbbaA).

Villanella   General term used to describe a variety of Italian song types of the 16th and early 17th centuries. These songs were often to bawdy texts and featured predominantly chordal textures.

Virelai   One of the *formes fixes* in the music of the 14th and 15th centuries. Each strophe consists of a variable number of lines but always begins and ends with the refrain, an unchanging unit of text and music. The general pattern of rhyme is AbbaA (the uppercase letter indicates the refrain).

Vocalize   To sing a melodic line to a vowel sound, without a text.

Voice leading   Manner in which two or more voices move in relationship to one another.

Volta   Vigorous "turning" dance (*voltare* means "to turn" in Italian), often in compound duple meter.

Whole-tone scale   Scale of six notes, each a whole tone apart.

Word-painting   Use of musical elements to imitate the meaning of a specific passage of the text being sung at that moment, such as a falling melodic line to indicate descent, a leap to indicate jumping, and so on.

Source Notes

Prologue

1. E. M. Forster, trans., "Problems 19.20 (919a)," in *The Works of Aristotle*, vol. 7 of *Problemata*, ed. W. D. Ross (Oxford: Clarendon Press, 1927).

2. Warren D. Anderson, *Ethos and Education in Greek Music* (Cambridge, MA: Harvard University Press, 1966), p. 127.

3. Plato, *Republic*, Book 4, 424b–c, in *The Collected Dialogues of Plato*, ed. Edith Hamilton and Huntington Cairns (New York: Pantheon Books, 1961).

Chapter 1

1. Quotation from Saint Basil, *Homily on Psalm 1,* trans. James McKinnon, in *Music in Early Christian Literature,* ed. James McKinnon (Cambridge: Cambridge University Press, 1987), p. 65. Reprinted with the permission of Cambridge University Press.

2. Quotation from Hildegard von Bingen, "Epistle 47: To the Prelates of Mainz," in Oliver Strunk, *Source Readings in Music History*, 2nd ed. (New York: Norton, 1998), pp. 183–6. Copyright 1998 W. W. Norton & Company, Inc. Used by permission.

Chapter 2

1. Quotation from John. In *Hucbald, Guido, and John on Music; Three Medieval Treatises*, trans. Warren Babb, ed. Claude Palisca (New Haven: Yale University Press, 1978), p. 160. Copyright Yale University Press, 1978. Used by permission of the publisher.

Chapter 4

1. Quotation from Bartolomé Ramos de Pareja, from Edward Lowinsky, "Music of the Renaissance as Viewed by Renaissance Musicians," in his *Music in the Culture of the Renaissance and Other Essays,* vol. 1, edited and with an introd. by Bonnie J. Blackburn; with forewords by Howard Mayer Brown and Ellen T. Harris; 2 vols. (Chicago: University of Chicago Press, 1989), I, 97. Copyright The University of Chicago, 1989. Reprinted with permission of the University of Chicago Press.

2. Quotation from Guide of Arezzo, Lowinsky, "Music of the Renaissance," p. 91. Reprinted with permission of The University of Chicago Press.

3. Quotation from Tinctoris, Lowinsky, "Music of the Renaissance," p. 92. Reprinted with permission of The University of Chicago Press.

4. Bartolomé Ramos de Pareja, *Musica Practica*, ed. and trans. Clement Miller (Neuhausen-Stuttgart: American Institute of Musicology/Hännsler-Verlag, 1993), p. 55.

5. Vincenzo Galilei, *Dialogo dell musica antica e della moderna* (1581), ed. Fabio Fano (Milan: Alessandro Minuziano, 1947), p. 55.

6. Quotation from Martin Luther writing about Josquin, in *The New Grove Dictionary of Music and Musicians*, ed. Stanley Sadie (London: Macmillan, 2000). Used by permission of Oxford University Press.

7. Quotation from a courtier of Duke Ercole d'Este of Ferrara. Trans. in Lewis Lockwood "Josquin at Ferrara: New Documents and Letters", in Edward E. Lowinsky, ed., *Josquin Des Prez* (New York and Oxford: Oxford University Press, 1976), pp. 132–3. Reprinted by permission of Oxford University Press.

8. Quotation from Pietro Aron, *Toscanello in musica* (1520 ed.), Book II, ch. 16. Trans. in Blackburn, "On Compositional Process in the Fifteenth Century," *Journal of the American Musicological Society* 40 (1987): 215. Copyright 1987 The American Musicological Society, Inc. Reprinted by permission of the University of Chicago Press.

9. Quotation from Giovanni Spataro, 1529. Trans. in Blackburn, "On Compositional Process in the Fifteenth Century," *Journal of the American Musicological Society* 40 (1987): 224. Copyright 1987 The American Musicological Society, Inc. Reprinted by permission of The University of Chicago Press.

Chapter 6

1. Jane Bowers, "The Emergence of Women Composers in Italy, 1566–1700," in *Women Making Music: The Western Art Tradition, 1150–1950*, ed. Jane Bowers and Judith Tick (Urbana and Chicago: University of Illinois Press, 1985), p. 140.

2. Thomas Morley, *A Plain and Easy Introduction to Practical Music* (1597), ed. R. Alec Harman (London: Dent, 1952), p. 293.

3. Johannes Riedel, *The Lutheran Chorale and Its Basic Traditions* (Minneapolis: Augsburg, 1967), p. 47.

4. Walter E. Buszin, "Luther on Music," *Musical Quarterly* 32 (1946): 88.

5. Council of Trent, "Canon on Music to Be Used at Mass," September 1562, quoted in Gustave Reese, *Music in the Renaissance*, 2nd ed. (New York: Norton, 1959), p. 449.

6. Nicola Vicentino, *L'Antica musica,* quoted in Henry Kaufman, *The Life and Works of Nicola Vicentino* (Rome: American Institute of Musicology, 1966), pp. 38–9.

7. Thomas Morely, *A Plain and Easy Introduction to Practical Music* (1597), ed. R. Alec Harman (New York: Norton, 1952), p. 296.

8. Peter Bergquist, "The Poems of Orlando di Lasso's *Prophetiae Sibyllarum* and Their Sources," *Journal of the American Musicological Society* 32 (1979): 533.

Chapter 7

1. Nicola Vicentino, *Ancient Music Adapted to Modern Practice* (1555) trans. Maria Rika Maniates, ed. Claude Palisca (New Haven: Yale University Press, 1996), p. 150.

2. Vincenzo Galilei, *Dialogo della music antica e della moderna* (1581), ed. Fabio Feno (Milan: Alessandro Minuziano, 1947), p. 127. Trans. MEB.

3. Piero Weiss and Richard Taruskin, eds., *Music in the Western World: A History in Documents* (New York: Schirmer, 1984), p. 176.

Chapter 8

1. Claudio Monteverdi, *The Letters of Monteverdi*, ed. & trans. Denis Stevens, rev. ed. (Oxford: Clarendon Press, 1995), pp. 190–1. Used by permission of Denis Stevens.

2. Tim Carter, "The Seventeenth Century," in Roger Parker, ed., *The Oxford Illustrated History of Opera* (Oxford and New York: Oxford University Press, 1994), p. 7.

3. Heinrich Schütz, preface to *Geistliche Chormusik* (1648), trans. David Bryant, in Lorenzo Bianconi, *Music in the Seventeenth Century* (Cambridge: Cambridge University Press, 1987), pp. 297–8. (Modifications to translation by MEB)

Chapter 9

1. Quotation from A. Félibien, *Rélation de la feste de Versailles du 18e juillet 1668* (Paris, 1668), trans. in *The Early Baroque Era*, ed. Curtis Price (Upper Saddle River, N.J.: Prentice Hall, 1994), p. 243. ©Reprinted by permission of Pearson Education, Inc. Upper Saddle River, NJ.

2. Charles Burney, *Memoirs*, ed. Fanny Burney, 3 vols. (London: Moxon, 1832), II, 135–6.

3. External evidence suggests that the poet John Dryden was the actual author of this letter; still, Purcell signed it and presumably endorsed its contents even if he did not write it himself.

4. Howard Smither, *A History of the Oratorio*, vol. 1 (Chapel Hill: University of North Carolina Press, 1977), p. 266.

5. Athanasius Kircher, *Musurgia universalis*, 2 vols. (Rome, 1650), I, 603; translation from Claude Palisca, *Baroque Music*, 3rd ed. (Englewood Cliffs, N.J.: Prentice Hall, 1991), p. 125.

6. Charles Burney, *An Account of the Musical Performances in Westminster Abbey . . . in Commemoration of Handel* (London, 1785).

7. Quotation from J. S. Bach letter, in Jacques Barzun, *Pleasures of Music* (Chicago: University of Chicago Press, 1977), pp. 283–4. Reprinted with the permission of Jacques Barzun.

Chapter 10

1. Quotation from Michael Talbot, "Arcangelo Corelli," *The New Grove Dictionary of Music and Musicians*, ed. Stanley Sadie (London: Macmillan, 2000), vol. 6, p. 459. Used by permission of Oxford University Press.

2. *The New Bach Reader: A Life of Johann Sebastian Bach in Letters and Documents*, edited by Hans T. David and Arthur Mendel; revised and enlarged by Christoph Wolff (Norton, 1998), p. 46. Copyright 1998 Christoph Wolff. Used by permission of W. W. Norton & Company, Inc.

Chapter 11

1. Quotation from Johann Mattheson parody of BWV 21 text, trans. in *The New Bach Reader: A Life of Johann Sebastian Bach in Letters and Documents*, edited by Hans T. David and Arthur Mendel; revised and enlarged by Christoph Wolff (New York: Norton, 1998), p. 325. Copyright 1998 Christoph Wolff. Used by permission of W. W. Norton & Company, Inc.

2. Georg August Griesinger, *Biographische Notizen über Joseph Haydn*, ed. Karl-Heinz Köhler (Leipzig: Reclam, 1975; 1st edition 1810), p. 78. Transl. MEB

Chapter 12

1. Jean Jacques Rousseau, *Dictionnaire de musique* (Paris: Veuve Duchesne, 1768), article "Sonate." Transl. MEB

2. Cramer's *Magazin der Musik*, 23 April 1787, Transl. MEB

3. Leopold Mozart, letter of 16 February 1785 to Maria Anna Mozart. Transl. MEB

4. Johann Abraham Peter Schulz, "Sinfonie," in Johann Georg Sulzer's *Allgemeine Theorie der schönen Künste* (Leipzig, 1771–1774). Transl. MEB

5. Karl Geiringer, *Haydn: A Creative Life in Music*, 3rd ed. (Berkeley and Los Angeles: University of California Press, 1982), pp. 65–67.

Chapter 13

1. Letter of 28 December 1782.
2. Mozart, letter of 26 September 1781. Transl. MEB

Chapter 14

1. Arthur Schopenhauer, *The World as Will and Idea*, vol. 1, trans. R. B. Haldane and J. Kemp (London: Kegan Paul, Trench, Trubner & Co., 1896), I, 338.
2. Max Kalbeck, *Johannes Brahms: Leben und Werk*, 4 vols. (Vienna, Leipzig, and Berlin, 1904–1914), IV, 109.
3. Walter Pater, "The School of Giorgione," in his *Studies in the History of the Renaissance* (1873).
4. James Gibbons Huneker, *Mezzotints in Music* (New York: G. Scribner's Sons, 1899), p. 122.
5. Robert Schumann, *Gesammelte Schriften über Musik und Musiker*, 5th ed., 2 vols. (Leipzig: Breitkopf & Härtel, 1913), I, 167 (1837).
6. Hector Berlioz, *Symphonie fantastique* (New York: Kalmus, n.d.). Transl. MEB

Chapter 15

1. Cosima Wagner, *Die Tagebücher*, vol. 2, ed. Martin Gregor-Dellin and Dietrich Mack (Munich: Piper, 1976), p. 1103 (entry for January 30, 1883). Transl. MEB
2. Robert Schumann, "A Symphony by Berlioz" (1835), trans. Edward T. Cone, in Hector Berlioz, *Fantastic Symphony*, ed. Edward T. Cone (New York: Norton, 1971), pp. 227–8.
3. Richard Wagner, *Das Kunstwerk der Zukunft* ("The Art-Work of the Future") (1850).
4. From the Diaries of Carl Friedrich Baron Kübeck von Kubau (1797), cited in H. C. Robbins Landon, *Beethoven: A Documentary Study* (New York: Macmillan, 1970), p. 71.
5. Alexander Wheelock Thayer, *Thayer's Life of Beethoven*, rev. and ed. Elliot Forbes (Princeton: Princeton University Press, 1967), pp. 304–6.
6. Thayer, *Thayer's Life of Beethoven*, p. 115.
7. Robert Schumann, "A Symphony by Berlioz" (1835), trans. Edward T. Cone, in Hector Berlioz, *Fantastic Symphony*, ed. Edward T. Cone (New York: Norton, 1971), pp. 227–8.
8. Mendelssohn, *Briefe an deutsche Verleger* (Berlin: de Gruyter, 1968), pp. 25–6, letter of 15 February 1833. Transl. MEB

Chapter 16

1. Quotation from letter to Gerard Souchay, 15 October 1842, trans. in Oliver Strunk, *Source Readings in Music History*, rev. ed., ed. Leo Treitler (New York: Norton, 1998), pp. 120–1. Copyright 1998 W. W. Norton & Company, Inc. Used by permission.

2.   Jean-Jacques Eigeldinger, *Chopin: Pianist and Teacher as Seen by his Pupils*, trans. Krysia Osostowicz and Naomi Shohet, ed. Roy Howat (Cambridge: Cambridge University Press, 1987), p. 276, quoting in turn Carl Mikuli, Preface to *Chopin's Pianoforte-Werke*, ed. Mikuli (Leipzig: Kistner, 1880).

3.   Quotation from letter from Frederic Chopin ca. 1838–39, in *Chopin's Letters*, ed. Henryk Opienski, trans. E. L. Voynich (New York: [no publisher]: 1931; reprinted NY: Vienna House 1971; and 1988: Dover Publications), p. 186. Used by permission of Dover Publications.

4.   Adrian Williams, *Portrait of Liszt: By Himself and His Contemporaries* (Oxford: Clarendon Press, 1990), pp. 55, 58.

5.   Alan Walker, *Franz Liszt,* vol. 1 (New York: Knopf, 1983), p. 371.

6.   Goethe, "Ballade," in Johann Wolfgang Goethe, *Sämtliche Werke*, XIII/1 (Munich: Hanser, 1985), p. 505.

Prelude to Part VI

1.   http://www.fordemocracy.net/electoral.shtml.

2.   John Cage, "History of Experimental Music in the United States" (1959), in Cage, *Silence* (Boston: M. I. T. University Press, 1966), p. 73.

3.   Leonard Bernstein, *The Infinite Variety of Music* (New York: Simon & Schuster, 1966), p. 10.

Chapter 19

1.   http://www.sonyclassical.com/artists/gould/bio.html.

2.   http://www.oneworld.org/tvandradio/live_aid.html.

3.   Nikita Khrushchev, speech delivered March 8, 1963. Quoted in Glen Watkins, *Soundings: Music in the Twentieth Century* (New York: Schirmer, 1995), p. 550.

4.   Brian Eno, liner notes to *Music for Airports/Ambient 1*, PVC 7908 (AMB 001), 1978.

Chapter 20

1.   Harold C. Schonberg, *The Great Pianists*, rev. ed. (New York: Simon & Schuster, 1987), p. 477.

2.   William W. Austin, *Music in the 20th Century* (New York: Norton, 1966), p. 25.

3.   Letter to Maurice Emmanuel, August 4, 1920, published in *La Revue musicale*, 1947. Transl. MEB

4.   Quotation from Charles Ives, Foreword to the score of *The Unanswered Question* (New York: Southern Music Publishing, 1953), p. 2. Published by Southern Music for Peer International. Used by permission.

5.   Quoted in Jan Swafford, *Charles Ives: A Life with Music* (New York: Norton, 1996), p. 143.

6.   Igor Stravinsky, *Stravinsky: An Autobiography* (New York: Simon & Schuster, 1936), pp. 72–3.

7.   Leo Oehmler, "Ragtime: A Pernicious Evil and Enemy of True Art," *Musical Observer* (September 1914), p. 15.

8.   *The Duke Ellington Reader*, ed. Mark Tucker (New York: Oxford University Press, 1993), p. 326.

9.   John Edward Hasse, *Beyond Category: The Life and Genius of Duke Ellington* (New York: Simon & Schuster, 1993), p. 380.

10.   Quotation from lyrics, Edward Kennedy "Duke" Ellington, "It Don't Mean a Thing (if it ain't got that swing)." Published by Warner Bros. Used with the permission of Warner/Chappell Music, Inc.

11.   http://www.southernmusic.net/grandoleopry.htm.

12.   Interview with Cowell recorded on *Henry Cowell: Piano Music* (Washington, DC: Smithsonian Folkways, CD SF40801).

13.   Review of the Pan-American Association of Composers Concert, March 6, 1933, Carnegie Hall, *Musical Courier*, vol. 106, no. 11 (1933): 12.

Chapter 21

1.   Arnold Schoenberg, "My Evolution (1949)," in *Style and Idea*, ed. Leonard Stein, trans. Leo Black (Berkeley and Los Angeles: University of California Press, 1984), p. 91.

2.   Arnold Schoenberg, *Harmonielehre*, 3rd ed. (Vienna: Universal Edition, 1922), pp. 487–8.

3.   Hermann Bahr, quoted in *Art in Theory, 1900–1990: An Anthology of Changing Ideas*, ed. Charles Harrison and Paul Wood (Oxford: Blackwell, 1993), p. 119.

Chapter 22

1.   Paul Hindemith, *The Craft of Musical Composition* (1937), trans. Arthur Mendel (New York: Associated Music Publishers, 1941), p. 4.

2.   Bryan Simms, ed., *Composers on Modern Musical Culture* (New York: Schirmer, 1999), p. 85.

3.   Quotation from lyrics by Bertolt Brecht, "Alabama Song" from Kurt Weill & Bertolt Brecht, *Aufstieg und Fall der Stadt Mahagonny*, 1927. © 1927 by European Music Corporation, © renewed. All Rights Reserved. Used by permission of European American Music Distributors LLC, sole US and Canadian agent for European American Music Corporation.

4.   www.sony.classical.com/music/60593/main.html.

5.   Quotation from lyrics, Cole Porter, "Night and Day." Published by Warner Bros.

6.   Quotation from lyrics, Duke Ellington, "Sophisticated Lady." Published by Warner Bros. Used with the permission of Warner/Chappell Music, Inc.

7.   Quotation from lyrics, "Tonight" from West Side Story. Music by Leonard Bernstein, lyrics by Stephen Sondheim. © Copyright 1956, 1957, 1958, 1959 by Amberson Holdings LLC and Stephen Sondheim. Copyright Renewed. Leonard Bernstein Music Publishing Company LLC, Publisher Boosey & Hawkes, Inc., Sole Agent. Reprinted by permission.

Chapter 23

1.   Quotation from Pierre Boulez to an unidentified New York journalist, 1963, quoted in Robert Jacobson, *Reverberations: Interviews with the World's Leading Musicians* (New York: Wm. Morrow, 1974), pp. 25–6. Copyright © 1974 by Robert Jacobson. Reprinted by permission of HarperCollins Publishers Inc.

2.   Ernst Krenek, *Horizons Circled* (Berkeley and Los Angeles: University of California Press, 1974), p. 151.

3.   Performance instructions in score of *In C* by Terry Riley. © 1964 Composed by Terry Riley. Published by Ancient Word Music, Administered by Celestial Harmonies.

4.   Charles Wuorinen, *Simple Composition* (New York: Longman, 1979), p. 3.

5.   Howard Pollack, *Aaron Copland* (New York: Henry Holt, 1999), p. 286.

Appendix 3

1.   Gary Carner, ed., *The Miles Davis Companion: Four Decades of Commentary* (New York: Schirmer, 1996), p. 85.

2.   George Bernard Shaw, *Music in London,* 3 vols. (London: Constable, 1932), II, 321. Originally published May 31, 1893.

Index